American Jewish Landmarks

a travel guide and history

FOREWORD BY

Jacob R. Marcus
Director
American Jewish Archives

American Jewish Landmarks

a travel guide and history
by
Bernard Postal and Lionel Koppman
volume I

fleet press corporation/new york

Published by Fleet Press Corporation, 160 Fifth Avenue,
    New York, N. Y. 10010
Library of Congress Catalogue Card No.: 76-27401
ISBN: Hardcover: 0-8303-0151-8
    Paperback: 0-8303-0152-6
Manufactured in the United States of America

Research for this work was supported in part by a grant
from the Memorial Foundation for Jewish Culture.

Foreword

In this period of the American Bicentennial Celebration I am delighted to welcome the appearance of *American Jewish Landmarks,* by the team of Bernard Postal and Lionel Koppman. The book contains valuable historical data on all 50 states, Washington, D.C., Puerto Rico, and the Virgin Islands. For people interested in the Jewish landmarks of the United States and her territorial possessions, this work is invaluable; it is the only guidebook of its kind; there is nothing else like it.

It is worth bearing in mind that this book is more than a manual for the tourist; it is an important book for students of American Jewish history. America's present-day Jewish community is the largest the world has yet known. Jewish Palestine at her zenith could probably never have boasted more than two million or three million Jews; today America shelters a Jewish population of nearly six million. This is a Jewry of some 5,000 to 10,000 Jewish clubs, societies, synagogues, and organizations, a community which has sprung up in the memory of men and women still living, for in 1880 there were only some 250,000 Jews in the United States.

This is not only the largest Jewry in the Diaspora, it is the most affluent, the most generous, the most cultured, the most advanced in the arts and sciences. It is obvious, therefore, why historians, both Jews and Gentiles, will want to know more about a community which has made such a great career for itself in the last two generations. *American Jewish Landmarks* supplies the information people seek. Because it is a ready reference book, adequately indexed, replete with an infinity of important detail, the student will keep it on his desk next to his Jewish encyclopedias.

When I pick up my telephone in my study to answer a call and think of Emile Berliner who invented the first practical telephone microphone, I know that the authors have described the work and personality of Berliner. And when I need data about Frederic William Wile, the author of a large-scale biography of Berliner, the assurance is mine that this book will tell me something about Wile and even inform me that his father, Jacob Wile, was the lay rabbi of LaPorte, Indiana, where the latter's achievements are memorialized in the name of Wile Street.

In a way this volume by Bernard Postal and Lionel Koppman is the only complete history of the American Jew, for it deals not only with the great and the mighty; it deals as well with the men and women of the towns and villages. Here are the annals of Jews whose communities reach from Portland, Maine, to San Diego, California—and on into the northernmost reaches of North America and into the Pacific and the Caribbean.

This is real history, grass roots history, the chronicle of an old people in a new world. It is also a delightful book, carefully researched, and well written. We are truly grateful for *American Jewish Landmarks: A Travel Guide and History*.

Jacob R. Marcus

Director
American Jewish Archives
Cincinnati, Ohio

Introduction

This book is part of a three-volume work that is a guide to and description of American Jewish landmarks and other places of Jewish interest or association in the United States, Puerto Rico, and the Virgin Islands.

It is the only book of its kind in this country. Its purpose is to identify, locate, and describe the thousands of landmarks, sites, shrines, memorials, public buildings, institutions, and other places whose collective story constitutes the chronicle of over three centuries of Jewish life in America.

Alphabetically arranged by states, cities, and towns within the states, and by places within the cities and towns, the three volumes are divided into 54 chapters, one for each state, the District of Columbia, Puerto Rico, the Virgin Islands, and one for New York City and environs.

Each chapter has two parts: an introductory essay devoted entirely to the highlights of Jewish history in the state or area covered, and a travel section listing and describing specific places.

Thirty-six categories of places have been included: shrines of Jewish history; monuments and memorials to Jews and portraits or bas-reliefs of Jews in public places; geographical places named for, founded by, or discovered by Jews; sites of early Jewish agricultural colonies; historic residences and other historic sites or buildings erected by, owned by, or named for Jews;

monuments and statuary having some Jewish connection; places of general historic importance having some Jewish association; monuments and memorials to non-Jews who were philo-Semites; interfaith shrines; historic places and buildings preserved by or donated to the public by Jews; graves of Jewish personalities celebrated in American or Jewish history; works of art depicting Jewish themes or characters on display in public places; Jewish religious objects in non-Jewish places; public collections of Judaica; Jewish museums; general museums housing Jewish artifacts; major Jewish libraries; housing complexes for aged Jews; public buildings or institutions donated by, named for, or dedicated to Jews; Jewish art collections; major libraries and art collections established by Jews for public use; major public works designed, built, or named for Jews; Holocaust memorials; institutions of Jewish higher learning; Hillel Foundations; Chabad Lubavitcher Student Centers; Jewish book and gift shops; major local Jewish institutions and agencies such as Jewish Community Centers, Homes for the Aged, Bureaus of Jewish Education, Jewish Federations and Welfare Funds, Jewish hospitals, and Jewish Vocational Services; synagogues; kosher eating facilities; selection of Jewish communally-sponsored camps; streets, avenues, and boulevards named for Jews; historic Jewish cemeteries; educational institutions named for, or founded by Jews; Israeli consulates; and Jewish community newspapers.

We have produced what we hope is a book that will be readable as well as useful. Our objective was a work that would provide pleasurable reading to armchair tourists, add to the enjoyment of the convention, business, or pleasure-bound traveler, answer the questions of all who seek hard-to-find information about Jewish beginnings, growth, and contemporary status in every state, and serve as supplementary reading in classes on American Jewish history and civics.

Each historical section is a fusion of information culled from countless sources—scholarly and popular, published and unpublished, familiar and newly-tapped.

The biographies that dot each travel section of each chapter lift from obscurity countless forgotten figures in American Jewish history, place in new settings numerous, well-remembered figures of yesterday, and describe the beginnings of many Jewish institutions, local and national.

We had a wonderfully exciting time making this armchair journey through the past and present of the American Jewish community, now well into its fourth century. En route we corresponded with several thousand people in nearly 1,000 different towns and cities. On the way, we read or consulted some 850 books, directories, city and state guides, histories, diaries, memoirs, biographies, almanacs and other reference works, and a vast collection of newspaper and magazine articles. Scattered through the three volumes are thumbnail biographies of more than 500 men and women, details about some 2,000 sites and landmarks, facts about over 800 national and local Jewish institutions, and information about nearly 2,000 synagogues.

American Jewish Landmarks is the successor to *A Jewish Tourist's Guide to the U.S.*, which was published in 1954.

The traveler who makes all or any part of the journey mapped out in the three volumes of *American Jewish Landmarks* is sure to stub his toe on American Jewish history wherever he goes. The reader who dips into these pages will find answers to his increasing curiosity about the Jewish past in America and its tenacious connection with the Jewish present.

Bernard Postal
Lionel Koppman

We tip our hats

Years of independent research went into this book, but much of the material in the landmark sections was distilled from correspondence with thousands of people. Since we do not pretend to have visited all the places we describe, we saw large numbers of them through the eyes of good friends and correspondents in every state and Washington, D.C.

A torrent of material came from the staffs of Federal, state, and municipal agencies, Jewish and non-Jewish organizations, museums, libraries, synagogues, historical societies, universities, scholars, researchers, rabbinical seminaries, Jewish Community Centers, B'nai B'rith Hillel Foundations, Jewish Welfare Federations and Jewish Community Councils, Boards of Jewish Education, Jewish schools, and editors of American Jewish newspapers. The editors were a particularly fertile source both for historic data and contemporary information.

To this small army of men and women who cheerfully furnished information, patiently checked data, helpfully undertook local research, resourcefully unearthed new facts, and graciously answered our incessant inquiries, we tip our hats and record their names.

Among the nearly 2,000 individuals with whom we were in contact, a number made unusually distinctive contributions to this book:

Harold E. Katz, Birmingham, who checked out the data for Alabama; Bernice Bloomfield, Anchorage, who helped avoid errors of omission and commission for

Alaska; Pearl Newmark, Phoenix, whose information was of great help for Arizona; Rabbi Ira Sanders, Little Rock, answered all questions about Arkansas.

Julius Bisno, Los Angeles, the unfailingly helpful source of data on Los Angeles; Dr. Robert Levinson, San Jose, who contributed an immense volume of facts about Northern California and mobilized the help of Stephen D. Kinsey, Suzanne Nemiroff, and Ruth Rafael of the Judah L. Magnes Memorial Museum in Berkeley, California, whose help was priceless; Seymour Fromer, of the Judah L. Magnes Memorial Museum, who put his staff's know-how at our disposal; Dr. Norton B. Stern, Santa Monica, who provided a large volume of data on Southern California; and Henry Schwartz, our valuable source on San Diego.

Mrs. Sam Uchill, Denver, who added much to the accuracy of the facts about Colorado; Mrs. Morris N. Cohen, West Hartford, who checked out everything for the Hartford area of Connecticut; Rabbi Arthur A. Chiel, Woodbridge, who did the same for the New Haven area; Rabbi David Geffen, Wilmington, who added greatly to the data on Delaware; Lillian Barsky and Robert Shosteck, whose expertise on Washington, D.C., was put at our disposal; Richard Rosichan and Vivian Becker, Miami, who updated the data on the Greater Miami area and other fast-growing parts of Florida.

Vida Goldgar and Adolph Rosenberg, Atlanta, who were unfailingly cooperative on Georgia; Mrs. Rachel Heimovics, Evanston, whose knowledge and resourcefulness were an invaluable asset in preparing the Chicago segment and the rest of Illinois; Joseph Levine, Fort Wayne, who had all the answers for Indiana; David Berman, Lexington, who checked out the data on Kentucky; Rabbi David Lefkowitz, Jr., Shreveport, who responded to our queries on Louisiana.

Dr. Moses Aberbach, Baltimore, who provided much information about Baltimore and the rest of Maryland; Bernard Wax, Boston, executive director, American Jewish Historical Society, and Robert Brauner, of "Jewish Boston," who checked out the entire Massachusetts chapter and provided much new data; Irving Katz, Detroit, who contributed much information about all of Michigan; Leo Frisch, Minneapolis, who checked out all of Minnesota; Rabbi Leo E. Turitz, Meridian, who added considerable data on Mississippi; Frank J. Adler, Kansas City, who checked out the Greater Kansas City area in the Missouri chapter; and Dan Makovsky, who checked out the St. Louis area and added much new material.

Carol Gendler, Omaha, who provided data on Nebraska; Saul Schwartz and William Pages, South Orange, who checked all data for Essex County, New Jersey; Rabbi M. Reuben Kesner, Whiteville, and Dr. Abram Kanof, who added much data on North Carolina; Sarah Grossman, Cincinnati, who checked out all the data for Cincinnati; Judah Rubinstein, Cleveland, who checked out all data for Greater Cleveland; Nathan Loshak and Julius Livingston, Tulsa, who provided much Oklahoma material; Rabbi Joshua Stampfer, who added greatly to the data on Oregon; Maurie H. Orodenker, Philadelphia, who checked out all data on Greater Philadelphia and added much new information; Mrs. Ida Cohen Selavan, Pittsburgh, who checked out all data on Pittsburgh and Western Pennsylvania and added much new material; Mrs. Seebert J. Goldowsky, Providence, who checked out all Rhode Island data and provided new information.

Stanford M. Adelstein, Rapid City, who reviewed all South Dakota data and added considerable new information; Jack Lieberman, Memphis, who checked out all of Tennessee data; Mrs. Perry Kallison, San Antonio, who reviewed the entire Texas chapter, adding much new data and helping to avoid errors of omission and commission; Seymour Siegel, Houston, who checked out the Texas data; and Edward B. Eisen, Salt Lake City, who reviewed the Utah data.

Fred W. Windmueller, who checked out all the Richmond, Virginia, data; Mrs. Jeanette B. Schrieber, Aberdeen, who checked out all the Washington material; Jocelyn Cooper, Wheeling, who added much to the West Virginia chapter; Rabbi Manfred E. Swarsensky, Madison, who checked out all the Wisconsin material.

To all of the following, we also tip our hats in thanks:

ALABAMA
Board of Education, Birmingham
Friedman Library, Tuscaloosa
Rabbi Harrold A. Friedman, Mobile
* Rabbi J. S. Gallinger, Birmingham
Mendel P. Goldstein, Mobile
Ralph G. Holberg, Jr., Mobile
John A. Newfield, New York City
University of Alabama, Birmingham
ALASKA
Anchorage Public Library
E. L. Bartlett, Nome
Chaplain Israel Haber, Anchorage
Dr. Isaac Knoll, Sitka
Chaplain Theodore H. Staiman, Anchorage
State Department of Community and
    Regional Affairs, Nome
U.S. Department of Interior, Anchorage
ARIZONA
Dr. Merrill M. Abeshaus, Flagstaff
Arizona Highway Department, Phoenix
D.A. Gershaw, Yuma
Rabbi David B. Kaplan, Yuma
Rev. Francis J. O'Reilly, Chandler
Hyman B. Parks, Sun City
Rabbi Albert Plotkin, Phoenix
Tucson Public Schools
Stewart L. Udall, Tucson
Henry F. Unger, Phoenix
ARKANSAS
Alan Altheimer, Chicago
Lewis T. Apple, Little Rock
Sam Levitt, Jonesboro
Hugh Park, Van Buren
* Rabbi Samson A. Shain, Lancaster, Pa.
CALIFORNIA
Hal Altman, Sacramento
Brandeis Camp Institute
Calavaras Publishing Co., Angels Camp
City of Hope, Duarte
Cottage of Israel, San Diego
Sidney Eisenshtat, Los Angeles
Geoffrey Fisher, San Francisco,
    San Francisco Jewish Bulletin
Rabbi Joseph Gitin, San Jose
Rabbi David L. Greenberg, Fresno
Herbert Luft, Beverly Hills
Judas L. Magnes Memorial Library
Dr. A.P. Nasatir, San Diego
Rabbi Bernard D. Rosenberg, Stockton
Santa Barbara Museum of Natural History
Santa Barbara Public Library
Santa Rosa-Sonoma County Free Public
    Library, Santa Rosa
Save-the-Redwoods League, San Francisco
Skirball Museum, Los Angeles
Ephraim Spivak, Sacramento
Stanford University, Stanford
Tom Tugend, Los Angeles
University of California, Berkley
University of California at Los Angeles
University of Southern California,
    Los Angeles

Rabbi Isaiah Zeldin, Los Angeles
COLORADO
Robert Gamzey, Denver,
    Intermountain Jewish News
Mrs. Miriam Goldberg, Denver,
    Intermountain Jewish News
Mrs. Harry Hoffman, Denver
Ida Hurwitz, Denver
National Jewish Hospital, Denver
Oscar Sladek, Denver
University of Colorado, Boulder
University of Denver

CONNECTICUT
Rabbi Abraham N. AvRutick, Hartford
Connecticut College, New London
Berthold Gaster, Hartford,
    Connecticut Jewish Ledger
Rabbi Melvin Jay Glatt, Stratford
Rabbi Theodore Gluck, Derby
Jewish Historical Society of Greater
    Hartford
Rabbi Samuel M. Silver, Stamford
Submarine Library, Groton
University of Bridgeport
University of Hartford
David P. Ward, Hartford
Yale University, New Haven

DELAWARE
Mrs. Nina Roffman, Wilmington
Winterthur Museum, Winterthur

DISTRICT OF COLUMBIA
A.F. of L.—C.I.O.
American University
Architect of The Capitol
Armed Forces Institute of Pathology
Meyer Brissman
Seymour S. Cohen
Department of State
Julian Feldman
Albert Friedman, *Jewish Week*
Saul Goldberg
Rabbi Joshua O. Haberman
Moe Hoffman
Samuel Holland
Jewish Historical Society of
    Greater Washington
Jewish War Veterans of the U.S.A.
Library of Congress
Military Chaplains Association of U.S.A.
National Historical Wax Museum
National Park Service
Rabbi Stanley Rabinowitz
Bernard Simon
Smithsonian Institution
Supreme Court of the U.S.
United States Board of Geographic Names
U.S. Department of Commerce
U.S. Postal Service
Veterans of Foreign Wars of U.S.
Harry S. Wender

FLORIDA

I. Edward Adler, West Palm Beach
Rabbi Herbert Baumgard, Coral Gables
Harold H. Benowitz, Maitland
Myron A. Berezin, Miami
Myron J. Brodie, Miami
Department of Parks and Recreation,
    Miami Beach
Rabbi David Max Eichhorn,
    Satellite Beach
Mrs. Norman Elson, Coral Gables
Florida Department of Transportation,
    Tallahassee
Florida State Chamber of Commerce,
    Jacksonville
International Swimming Hall of Fame,
    Fort Lauderdale
Rabbi Sidney M. Lefkowitz, Jacksonville
H. Irwin Levy, West Palm Beach
Seymour B. Liebman, Miami
Isadore Moskowitz, Jacksonville
Leonard Neuman, Hollywood
Palm Beach Atlantic College, Palm Beach
Palm Beach Times, West Palm Beach
Fred K. Shochet, Miami, *Jewish Floridian*
Nathan Skolnick, Miami
Rabbi David J. Susskind, St. Petersburg
University of Florida, Gainesville
University of Miami, Coral Gables
University of Tampa
Samuel W. Wolfson High School,
    Jacksonville

GEORGIA

D.A. Byck, Savannah
Irwin B. Giffen, Savannah
Rabbi Alfred L. Goodman, Columbus
Paul Kulick, Savannah
Rabbi Abraham I. Rosenberg, Savannah

HAWAII

Jacob Adler, Honolulu
Morris N. Freedman, Honolulu
Bernard H. Levinson, Honolulu
Rabbi Roy A. Rosenberg, Honolulu
Rabbi Alexander Segel, Honolulu
Chaplain Samuel Sobel, Fort Belvoir, Va.
Kenneth C. Zwerin, Honolulu

IDAHO

Boise Public Library
Secretary of State, Boise
Sun Valley Travels, Sun Valley
Temple Emanuel, Pocatello

ILLINOIS

Board of Education, Waukegan
Chicago Board of Rabbis
Hebrew Theological College, Chicago
Illinois Institute of Technology, Chicago
Illinois State Historical Society,
    Springfield
International Museum of Surgical
    Science, Chicago
Julian Jablin, Skokie
La Salle Public Library
Howard B. Lazar, Northfield
McCormick Place, Chicago
Maywood Public Library
Northwestern University, Evanston
Hyman Ruffman, East St. Louis
Walter H. Sobel, Chicago
University of Chicago
University of Illinois at Medical Center,
    Chicago
Village of Skokie

INDIANA

Alexandrian Free Public Library,
    Mt. Vernon
Hammond Public Library
Indiana Harbor Public Library
Frank H. Newman, Indianapolis
Terre Haute Public Library
Valparaiso Public Library
Whiting Public Library

IOWA

Burlington Public Library
Cedar Rapids Public Library
Gerald S. Ferman, Des Moines
Fort Dodge Public Library
Rabbi Jay B. Goldburg, Des Moines
Herbert Hoover Library, West Branch
Oscar Littlefield, Sioux City
Mason City Public Library
Musser Public Library, Muscatine
Temple B'nai Jeshurun, Des Moines

KANSAS

Baker University, Baldwin
Boot Hill Museum, Dodge City
Dodge City Chamber of Commerce
Humboldt Public Library
Kansas State University, Manhattan
Pittsburgh Public Library
Salina Public Library
Rabbi Elbert S. Sapinsley, Topeka
Frank B. Stiefel, Salina
University of Kansas, Lawrence

KENTUCKY

Ashland Public Library
Moses Bohn, Hopkinsville
Herman Landau, Louisville
William W. Orbach, Louisville
Owensboro Public Library
Paducah Public Library
St. Joseph's Church, Bardstown
Southern Baptist Theological Seminary,
    Louisville
University of Louisville

LOUISIANA

Rabbi Murray Blackman, New Orleans
B'nai Israel Synagogue, Alexandria
Daily Iberian, New Iberia
Morton J. Gaba, New Orleans
Jewish Welfare Federation, Baton Rouge
New Orleans Public Library
Orleans Parish School Board, New Orleans
Rabbi Marvin M. Reznikoff, Baton Rouge

MAINE
Rabbi David Berent, Lewiston
Colby College, Waterville
Barnett I. Shur, Portland

MARYLAND
Dept. of Economic Development of
State of Maryland, Annapolis
Johns Hopkins University, Baltimore
Samuel Lichtenstein, Silver Spring
Maryland Institute College of Art,
Baltimore
Maryland Jewish Historical Society,
Baltimore
Enoch Pratt Free Library, Baltimore
Secretary of State, Annapolis
Mrs. Abraham D. Spinak, Pocomoke City
Samuel S. Strouse, Baltimore
Lowell E. Sunderland, Columbia
Dr. Daniel Thursz, Baltimore
United States Naval Academy, Annapolis
University of Maryland, College Park
Joseph Weinstein, Baltimore
Wheaton Public Library

MASSACHUSETTS
American Jewish Historical Society,
Waltham
Ashland Public Schools
Boston Public Library
Boston Symphony Orchestra
Boston University
Brandeis University, Waltham
Isaac Fein, Boston
Genesis 2, Cambridge
Eli Grad, Brookline
Harvard University, Cambridge
"Jewish Boston," Boston
Jewish Community Council of Greater
Boston
Gerald A. Kleinman, North Dartmouth
Naismith Basketball Hall of Fame,
Springfield
Mrs. David Rappaport, Oak Bluffs
Dr. Samuel Rosenfeld, Burlington
Rabbi H. David Rutman, Milford
Robert E. Segal, Boston
Rabbi Herman E. Snyder, Springfield
State Library of Commonwealth of
Massachusetts, Boston

MICHIGAN
William Avrunin, Detroit
Stanley J. Elias, Trenton
Mrs. J.M. Fivenson, Traverse City
Rabbi Richard C. Hertz, Detroit
John Henry Richter, Ann Arbor
Irwin Shaw, Detroit
Philip Slomowitz, *Jewish News*, Detroit

MINNESOTA
Rabbi Allen Bennett, Rochester
Norman Gold, *American Jewish World*,
Minneapolis
Rabbi Arnold M. Goldman, Minneapolis
St. Paul Public Library
State of Minnesota Dept. of Business
Development, St. Paul

MISSISSIPPI
Cong. Beth Israel, Biloxi
Hebrew Union Congregation, Greenville
Rabbi Benjamin Schultz, Clarksdale
Society of the Divine Word, Bay Saint
Louis
Temple B'nai Israel, Natchez
Karl Weil, Port Gibson

MISSOURI
Rabbi Stephen A. Arnold, St. Joseph
Cape Girardeau Public Library
Robert Cohn, *Jewish Light*, St. Louis
Culver-Stockton College, Canton
Division of Parks and Recreation of the
City of St. Louis
Milton Firestone, *Jewish Chronicle*,
Kansas City
Rabbi Morris B. Margolies, Kansas City
Dr. Mitchell J. Rosenblatt, Columbia
Rabbi Alvan D. Rubin, St. Louis
Rabbi Jeffrey Stiffman, St. Louis
Washington University, St. Louis

MONTANA
Rabbi Samuel Horowitz, Butte

NEBRASKA
Rabbi Kenneth Bromberg, Omaha
Mrs. Morton Greenberg, Tustin, Calif.

NEVADA
Rabbi Erwin L. Herman, Los Angeles
Rabbi Harry Sherer, Las Vegas
Jack Tell, *Las Vegas Israelite*, Las Vegas

NEW HAMPSHIRE
Dartmouth College, Hanover
Rabbi Bela Fisher, Nashua
Rabbi Oscar Fleishaker, Portsmouth
Kevin Lowther, Keene
Manchester City Library
Portsmouth Public Library

NEW JERSEY
Rabbi Aaron Chomsky, West New York
Fairleigh Dickinson University,
Rutherford
Dr. Harold Gabel, Oakhurst
Arthur A. Goldberg, Jersey City
Sam Hatow, Paterson
Zev Hymowitz, West Orange
Howard A. Kieval, Highland Park
Dr. Harry B. Lasker, North Brunswick
Rabbi Pesach Z. Levovitz, Lakewood
Rabbi Ely E. Pilchik, Short Hills
Mrs. Adolf Robinson, Teaneck
Rutgers University, New Brunswick
Rabbi Sidney Schulman, Asbury Park
Israel Silver, Perth Amboy
Rabbi Abraham Simon, Bridgeton
Rabbi Howard A. Simon, Margate
Rabbi Sheldon J. Weltman, Morristown

NEW MEXICO
Mrs. Melwin J. Klein, Las Cruces
Rabbi Abraham I. Shinedling,
Albuquerque
Rabbi David D. Shor, Albuquerque
Judge Lewis Sutin, Santa Fe

NEW YORK CITY

Samuel H. Abramson
American Jewish Committee
American Veterans of Israel
Board of Jewish Education
Brooklyn Museum
Sam Brown
Central Conference of American Rabbis
City College
Columbia University
Rabbi Wayne D. Dosick
Encyclopedia Judaica
Federation Employment and Guidance
    Service
Federation of Jewish Philanthropies
Dr. Louis Finkelstein
Rabbi Joseph Gelberman
Leonard Gold
Rabbi Harold H. Gordon
Leslie Gottlieb
Sam Hartstein
* Harry Herbert
Jewish Association for Services for the
    Aged
Jewish Theological Seminary of America
Mae Koppman
Rabbi Yehuda Krinsky
Brenda Leibowitz
Sesil Lissberger
Metropolitan New York Coordinating
    Council of Jewish Poverty
National Council of Young Israel
New York University
New York Board of Rabbis
Susan Nueckel
Pace University
Rabbinical Assembly
Rabbinical Council of America
Ramah Camps
George Salomon
Morris U. Schappes
Abner Sideman
Belle Sideman
Henry B. Stern
Rabbi Malcolm Stern
Union of American Hebrew
    Congregations
Union of Orthodox Jewish Congregations
United Jewish Council of the East Side
United Synagogue of America
Professor Gerard R. Wolfe
Workmen's Circle
Marjorie Wyler

NEW YORK STATE

Albany Medical Center
Amsterdam Public Library
Beth El Synagogue, New Rochelle
B'nai Israel Congregation, Olean
Buffalo and Erie County Public Library
Sam Clevenson, *Jewish World,* Albany
Cornell University, Ithaca
Rabbi Herman Eisner, Ellenville
Ellenville Journal

Finkelstein Memorial Library,
    Spring Valley
Rabbi Samuel Z. Glaser, Elmont
Gloversville Chamber of Commerce
William Grossman, Amherst
Harrison School District
Jewish Community Federation of
    Rochester
Marian Kramer, Rockville Centre
Samuel Kurzon, Albany
Long Island State Park & Recreation
    Commission, Babylon
Merchants Association of Sag Harbor
Nassau County Museum, Syosset
National Baseball Hall of Fame,
    Cooperstown
National Museum of Racing, Saratoga
    Springs
New York State Court of Appeals,
    Albany
Greater Newburgh Chamber of Commerce
New York State Dept. of Law, Albany
New York State Office of General
    Services, Albany
Orange County Historian, Goshen
Norman Pallay, North Bellmore
C.W. Post Center of Long Island
    University, Greenvale
Pound Ridge Public Library
Mrs. Arthur H. Printz, Hampton Bays
Rochester Public Library
Franklin D. Roosevelt Library, Hyde Park
Sagamore Hill National Historic Site,
    Oyster Bay
St. Bonaventure University,
    St. Bonaventure
Saranac Lake Free Library
Schenectady Museum
Mrs. Morris Shimansky, Amityville
State Education Dept., Albany
State University of New York
    at Purchase
Ella Stuzin, Monticello
Suffolk County Historical Society,
    Riverhead
Sullivan County Historian, Hurleyville
Sullivan County Publicity and Tourist
    Dept., Monticello
Syracuse University
Town of Bedford, Bedford Hills
Town of Huntington
Town of Monroe
Town of Wawarsing, Ellenville
Union College, Schenectady
U.S. Military Academy, West Point
University of Rochester
Donald Wolin, *Jewish Ledger,* Rochester
Yonkers Dept. of Parks and Recreation

NORTH CAROLINA

I.D. Blumenthal, Charlotte
Irving S. Cheroff, Fayetteville
Rabbi Martin M. Weitz, San Diego,
    California

NORTH DAKOTA
Rabbi Jeffrey Bearman, Fargo
Toba Geller, Fargo
OHIO
Antioch College, Yellow Springs
Rabbi Morton M. Applebaum, Akron
Aviation Hall of Fame, Dayton
Stanley Chyet, Los Angeles, Calif.
Cleveland Public Library
Rabbi Gordon L. Geller, Elyria
Mrs. Anne Hammerman, *Jewish Chronicle*,
Dayton
Ben Mandelkorn, Columbus
Dr. Jacob R. Marcus, Cincinnati
Ohio Historical Society, Columbus
Ohio State University, Columbus
Sidney J. Silvian, Cincinnati
Rabbi Gerald Turk, Kent
Julius Weil, Shaker Heights
OKLAHOMA
Fort Sill Information Office, Fort Sill
Melvin Moran, Seminole
Muskogee Public Library
Walter Neustadt, Jr., Ardmore
Oklahoma Hall of Fame, Oklahoma City
Oklahoma State University, Stillwater
Meyer Sobol, Oklahoma City
Tulsa City-County Library System, Tulsa
OREGON
Sylvan F. Durkheimer, Portland
Rabbi Louis Neimand, Eugene
Oregon Museum of Science & Industry,
Portland
Oregon State University, Corvallis
Portland Art Museum
Arthur C. Spence, Portland
PENNSYLVANIA
Albert W. Bloom, Pittsburgh,
Pittsburgh Jewish Chronicle
Leon Brown, *Jewish Times*, Philadelphia
Bucks County Dept. of Parks &
Recreation, Doylestown
Cambria County Library System,
Johnstown
Rabbi Robert Chernoff, Chambersburg
Commissioner of Fairmount Park,
Philadelphia
Drexel University, Philadelphia
Dropsie University, Philadelphia
Federation of Jewish Agencies,
Philadelphia
Mrs. Lillian Mermin Feinsilver, Easton
Franklin Mint, Franklin Center
Freedoms Foundation, Valley Forge
Hebrew Sunday School Society,
Philadelphia
Thomas Jefferson University,
Philadelphia
Juniata College, Huntingdon
Dr. Bertram W. Korn, Philadelphia
Lions Club, Glassport
Mikveh Israel Cong., Philadelphia
Leon J. Obermayer, Philadelphia

Pennsylvania Historical and Museum
Commission, Harrisburg
Pennsylvania State University,
Middletown
Philadelphia Jewish Archives
Philadelphia Museum of Art
Philadelphia '76 Inc.
Philadelphia Union of Jewish Students
Pittsburgh Baseball Club
Sayre Public Library
Rabbi Elihu Schagrin, Coatesville
School District of Philadelphia
A. Singer, Middletown
Temple University, Philadelphia
University of Pennsylvania, Philadelphia
University of Pittsburgh
Rabbi David H. Wice, Philadelphia
Rabbi Leonard Winograd, McKeesport
Wolfsohn Memorial Library, King of
Prussia
Rabbi Gerald I. Wolpe, Philadelphia
Frank F. Wundohl, Philadelphia,
Philadelphia Jewish Exponent
York School District
RHODE ISLAND
Brown University, Providence
Jewish Community Relations Council of
Rhode Island, Providence
Rhode Island Jewish Historical
Association, Providence
Jesse M. Smith Memorial Library,
Harrisville
SOUTH CAROLINA
City of Rock Hill
College of Charleston
Cong. Beth Elohim, Charleston
Mrs. Herbert A. Rosefield, Sumter
South Carolina Confederate Relic Room,
Columbia
University of South Carolina, Columbia
SOUTH DAKOTA
Manny Feinstein, South Aberdeen
University of South Dakota, Vermillion
TENNESSEE
Churchmen's Sports Hall of Fame,
Tullahoma
Harriet Cohn Guidance Center, Clarksville
Memphis Eye, Ear, Nose and Throat
Hospital, Memphis
Oak Ridge Institute of Nuclear Studies,
Oak Ridge
Siskin Memorial Foundation, Chattanooga
TEXAS
Seymour Cohen, Houston
El Paso Public Library
Rabbi Harold A. Friedman, Waco
Rabbi Newton J. Friedman, Beaumont
Mrs. I.B. Goodman, El Paso
Philip Hewitt, San Antonio
Harry R. Rosen, Dallas
David M. Seligman, Edna
Southern Methodist University, Dallas
Shimshon Zeevi, San Antonio

UTAH
Rabbi Abner L. Bergman, Salt Lake City
VERMONT
Rabbi Max B. Wall, Burlington
VIRGINIA
Mrs. Ruth Sinberg Baker, Alexandria
Leroy S. Bendheim, Alexandria
Department of Defense, Arlington
Fort Monroe Casemate Museum,
    Fort Monroe
Thomas Jefferson Institute for Study
    of Religious Freedom, Fredericksburg
Mrs. Murray Loring, Williamsburg
Mariners Museum, Newport News
Rabbi Philip Pincus, Virginia Beach
Chaplain Samuel Sobel, Fort Belvoir
Saul Viener, Richmond
Virginia Military Institute, New Market
Virginia Museum of Fine Arts, Richmond
WASHINGTON
Seattle Chamber of Commerce
Murray Shiff, Seattle
State Capitol Museum, Olympia
University of Washington Libraries,
    Seattle

WEST VIRGINIA
Rabbi Philip M. Aronson, Huntington
Rabbi Samuel Cooper, Charleston
Edward I. Eiland, Logan
Kanawha County Public Library,
    Charleston
WISCONSIN
Edwarde Perlson, Milwaukee
Mrs. Norton Stoler, Madison
University of Wisconsin-Milwaukee,
Waukesha Chamber of Commerce
Jack Wiener, Milwaukee
Wisconsin Society for Jewish Learning,
    Milwaukee
Melvin Zaret, Milwaukee
WYOMING
Mrs. Martin Bernstein, Cheyenne
Mrs. Joseph Feldman, Cheyenne
Laramie County Library, Cheyenne
Laramie County School District No. 1,
    Cheyenne
Steve Weinstein, Laramie
University of Wyoming, Laramie
Wyoming State Archives and Historical
    Department, Cheyenne

* *Deceased*

Contents

Jewish Landmarks Series

About the authors

BERNARD POSTAL, editor, journalist, and author, is associate editor of *The Jewish Week,* editor of *The Jewish Digest,* and co-author of 10 other books on travel, Jewish history, and Israel. He was the director of public relations of the National Jewish Welfare Board for 25 years. Prior to that he was national public relations director of B'nai B'rith for eight years. He is a member of the executive council of the American Jewish Historical Society and the Jewish Historical Committee of B'nai B'rith. In 1954 he received the National Jewish Book Award (together with Lionel Koppman) for his contributions to American Jewish history. He was similarly honored by the American Jewish Historical Society.

LIONEL KOPPMAN, editor, writer, and publicist, is director of public information and publications for the National Jewish Welfare Board. He is a former newspaperman in Texas; medical editor for the United States government; and winner of the National Jewish Book Award in 1954 (together with Bernard Postal) for his contributions to American Jewish history. He was also the recipient of the Outstanding Filmstrip of the Year Award for his filmstrip on Sholom Aleichem in 1970. He is the author of a number of manuals and plays on various aspects of American Jewish life.

note

A new national program to provide Orthodox Jewish travelers with local information centers for their unique needs while traveling has been instituted by Agudath Israel of America. Information encompassing many areas of the United States, Canada, and Mexico, regarding kosher food, synagogues, and other pertinent information can be obtained by writing: Agudath Israel of America, 5 Beekman Street, New York, N. Y. 10025.

Information on special tours of Jewish sites and landmarks in New York City can be obtained from the following:
1. Sam Brown, 281 Avenue C, Apt. 7C, New York, N. Y. 10009.
2. Professor Gerard R. Wolfe, New York University, School of Continuing Education, 3 Washington Square North, New York, N. Y. 10003.
3. *Tours of Jewish New York*, American Jewish Congress, 180 East 79th Street, New York, N. Y. 10021.

American Jewish Landmarks

a travel guide and history

CONNECTICUT

Although Connecticut was the strictest of all the New England colonies in curbing religious dissenters, individual Jews found their way to the Nutmeg State six years before the Hartford and New Haven settlements were united to form the province of Connecticut in 1665.

Connecticut's charter of 1662 (which remained in force until 1818), proclaimed that "the Christian faith is the only and principal end of this plantation." (The portrait of Charles II which decorated this charter was the work of the celebrated Restoration miniaturist, Samuel Cooper, whose brother, Alexander, embraced Judaism.) On the other hand, Connecticut made the Mosaic Code the law of the colony in 1650. The first assembly of New Haven colonists in 1639 unanimously voted that the word of God as recorded in the Hebrew Bible was to be the only rule observed "in executing the duties of government in this plantation." In 1642, John Davenport, one of the Puritan founders of New Haven, introduced Hebrew in the town's first public school.

Because the first Jews in Connecticut came from New Amsterdam, they were caught in the middle of the Anglo-Dutch struggle for control of the Connecticut River Valley. The Dutch, who had established the first white settlement at Hartford in 1633, were later ousted by the English who came west from Massachusetts two years later. Jewish merchants from a Dutch colony were, therefore, doubly unwelcome at Hartford. As aliens, the Jews could count on little hospitality in a colony whose law required that all newcomers be "accepted by a major part of the town" before being permitted to take up residence. Lumped with heretics, Quakers, and Adamites, to whom it was illegal to give food or lodging under the codes of New Haven and Hartford, the Jews found little welcome.

These harsh regulations were not enforced too rigorously, for the Jews who came were permitted to stay and their trading was tolerated. Hammond Trumbull, in his memorial history of Hartford, claims Jews were in Connecticut as early as 1650. The first recorded reference to a Jew in the colony was in November, 1659, when "David the Jew" was fined 20 shillings by the Hartford general court for illegal trading.

Evidence that the presence of Jews had some kind of legal sanction is preserved in the Hartford town records of February 11, 1660, where it is noted "that there remains in John Allyns hands 10 shillings for the Jews." This entry indicates that the town fathers may have made some kind of grant for the Jewish strangers in their midst. On September 2, 1661, the Hartford authorities ruled: "The same day ye Jews which at present live in John Marsh his home have liberty to sojourn in ye town for 7 months." A majority of the residents apparently had approved permitting the Jews to stay. John Marsh, in whose home the Jews lived, was one of the original proprietors of Hartford.

Some of these Jews must have stayed beyond the permitted seven months, or others had arrived later, for in a "List of Families in Hartford with Quantity of Grain in Possession of Each," dated March 9, 1669, the names of two Jews are included: David a Jew and Jacob a Jew. David was probably the man who had been fined in 1659. Jacob has been identified as Jacob Lucena who had settled in New Amsterdam in 1656, and engaged in trade in the various Dutch colonies. The Hartford records for 1667 list him as having transported three horses to New Amsterdam.

Three years later Lucena became the center of a legal cause célèbre. Tried and found guilty of immoral behavior, he was sentenced by the Hartford authorities in 1670 to pay a fine of 20 pounds—a huge sum for those days—or be flogged. When Lucena appealed the verdict, the General Court rendered a remarkable decision: "The court see cause, considered he is a Jew, to shew him what favore they may, abate him tenn pownds of his fine." Still not satisfied, Lucena appealed again, and this time the judges reduced the penalty to five pounds, "as a token of their respect to the sayd Mr. Assur Levy." The latter was Asser Levy, the eminent New Amsterdam burgher and merchant, whose influence reached into Connecticut and enabled him to intercede for Lucena.

In 1685, a Dutch sea captain named John Carsen, who was probably bound for Newport, Rhode Island, attempted to land goods at New London where it was impounded for being non-English and its owner, Carsen, a Jew, and thus an alien not entitled to trade in English colonies. Carsen appealed to the governor, claiming that although he was a Dutch Jew, his cargo was British and bound for a British port. He was eventually released on his promise to leave New London. No permanent Jewish settler is known to have settled in New London until Jacob Schwartz and family turned up in 1860.

By the early 1700s, Jewish traders and merchants from New York and Rhode Island were doing business in Connecticut from Woodstock on the west to Stamford on the east. Those who preferred to remain Jews did not stay long, returning to Newport and New York. Those who stayed disappeared as Jews, victims of what Dr. Jacob R. Marcus, director of the American Jewish Archives, calls "conversion through default." In the absence of a Jewish community, even those who tried to resist the impact of a totally Christian environment were lost to Judaism within a generation or two through intermarriage.

Historians have pieced together the story of some of these Jewish pioneers from court records, letters, and family papers. Anshil Troib, a German or Polish Jew, who settled in Fairfield in 1722 and who was a member of New York's Shearith Israel Congregation in 1729, was one of the signers of a petition submitted by Fairfield County merchants in 1749 to the Colonial Assembly in protest against an import tax. His name appears twice, once in Hebrew characters as Anshil Troib, and again in Latin script as Andris Trube. When he died in 1758, he was buried as Anshil Truby, or Trubee, and his children were both Christians. Their names were Samuel Cohen Trube and Gitla Trube. When Troib died he was no longer a member of Shearith Israel. Among his descendants were F. Trubee Davidson, father of the United States Naval Reserve, and Herbert Trube of Norwalk, a member of the 1908 Unites States Olympic track team. In Bridgeport, there is still a stock brokerage firm by the name of Andris Trube.

There were also Jews named Boghragh in Salisbury and Solomon in Middletown in the mid-1770s. One who tried to resist assimilation was Michael Judah. He had settled at Norwalk in 1736, establishing a business on the 5 pounds he had borrowed from Shearith Israel Congregation. He, too, married a Christian, Martha Raymond, but when his son David was born in 1756, the boy was circumcised. David Judah, who was raised as a Christian, was the grandfather of Theodore Judah (see California), the pioneer railroad builder on the Pacific coast.

The most influential Jewish family in Colonial and Revolutionary days were the Pintos. Abraham Pinto, who had been the *shohet* of the New York Jewish community, turned up in Stratford in 1725. Jacob Pinto made his way to New Haven about 1740, where he joined the Congregationalist Church and married a woman whose Christian name was Thankful. There was an Isaac Pinto in Stratford in 1748 and a Solomon Pinto in New Haven in 1758. When 102 New Haven citizens petitioned the governor of Connecticut in 1776 for the removal of suspected Tories to other parts of the country, and for stronger measures to put an end to their disloyalty, Abraham and Jacob Pinto were among the signatories.

Jacob Pinto's three sons by his second wife—Abraham, Solomon, and William—were among New Haven's leading citizens in the closing years of the Revolution and for many years thereafter. All three attended Yale. Solomon and William, who graduated in 1777, were the first persons of Jewish origin to receive a Yale degree. The Pinto brothers and David Judah served with distinction in the Revolution. Two were wounded and the third was captured. Solomon became one of the founders of the Society of the Cincinnati in Connecticut—the exclusive organization of Revolutionary officers.

Ezra Stiles, president of Yale from 1778-1795, did not regard the Pintos or David Judah as Jews. In 1760, when he was minister of a church in Newport, Rhode Island, he noted in his famous diary that "on inquiry it seems there are no Jews in Connecticut." Two years later he wrote, "I learn in conversation with Capt. Jno. Nichols that there are no Jews in New Haven or Bristol." In 1763, Stiles observed that "Dr. Hubbard of New Haven (his father-in-law), writes me that five Papists but no Jews live there."

Stiles was much concerned with Jews whose customs and ceremonies he had learned through his friendship with Hazzan Isaac Touro and with Rabbi Haim Carigal in Newport. He studied Hebrew with them and interested himself in a search for the "Ten Lost Tribes" of Israel. When he was inducted as president of Yale, Stiles delivered an oration in Hebrew. Later he made Hebrew compulsory for Yale freshmen. It was Stiles who reported the first known formal Jewish worship in Connecticut. His diary contains the following entry for September 13, 1772:

> "The summer past a family of Jews settled here, the first real Jews (except two Jew brothers Pinto who renounced Judaism and all religion) that settled in New Haven. They came from Venice, sat down some time at Eustatia in West Indies, and lately removed there. They are three brothers (adults) with an aged mother, and a widow and her children, being in all about 10 or 8 souls, Jews, with 6 or 8 Negroes. Last Saturday they kept holy; Dr. Hubbard was sent for, then, to see one of them sick. He told me the family were worshipping by themselves in a room in which were lights and a suspended lamp. This is the first Jewish worship in New Haven. These Jews indeed worship in the Jewish manner; but they are not enough

to constitute and become a synagogue for which there must be twelve (sic) men at least. So that if there should thereafter be a synagogue in New Haven, it must not be dated from this. Besides here is a few (Jews) in Town that belong to none of these meetings but are separate and associate with others scattered in the neighboring parishes."

The Revolutionary War brought the first large influx of professing Jews to Connecticut. In 1776 when Hazzan Gershom Mendes Seixas closed the doors of Shearith Israel synagogue in New York rather than continue worship under the British occupation, he led some of his congregants to Norwalk and Stratford across the state line. Other Jews came from Rhode Island, where the British were also in control. Since Seixas brought the Torah Scrolls with him, it is likely that public Jewish worship services were held at Norwalk or Stratford. But no synagogue or permanent community was established because the war refugees had come only for the duration.

The Connecticut exile turned out to be dangerous when the Tory General Tryon raided the Long Island coast towns in 1779. The Jewish refugees who had established business firms at Stamford, Wilton, Danbury, Norwalk, and Stratford suffered heavy losses. Eight Jews from Norwalk received state compensation for damages incurred during the British attack on Norwalk in 1779. One of these was the noted New York silversmith, Myer Myers, who had been recommended to Connecticut when the need for bullets made the authorities eager for skilled help in refining the ore from the Middletown lead deposits.

Even though they planned to return to New York and Newport after the war, the Jewish exiles joined with their Connecticut neighbors in defending the state against the British and in warring on the Tories. Jews were among those who petitioned the governor to set up an armed patrol on Long Island Sound. Among the refugees were two with distinguished descendants: Solomon Simson, whose son Samson, the first Jewish graduate of Columbia University and the chief founder of Mt. Sinai Hospital, was born at Danbury during the war; and old Aaron Isaacs of East Hampton, Long Island, who supported Shearith Israel Congregation but married a Christian and became the grandfather of John Howard Payne (see East Hampton, New York), composer of *Home Sweet Home.*

At the beginning of the 19th century, there were no known practicing Jews in Connecticut. A Mr. Edwards, a delegate to the 1818 state constitutional convention, was quoted in the *Hartford Courant* as saying he was "willing that the legislature should tolerate Jews and Mohammedans; at the same time there had never been any in the state and probably never would be."

A permanent community took root in the early 1840s with the arrival of German Jews in New Haven (1840), Waterbury (1840), and Hartford (1843). The first congregation was formed in New Haven in 1840, when a number of families from Bavaria established what is now Congregation Mishkan Israel. Until 1843 no Jewish congregation could be organized with a legal corporate entity. In that year an amendment to the statutes provided that "Jews who may desire to unite and form religious societies shall have the same rights, powers, and privileges as are given Christians of every denomination by the laws of the state." Under this authority Temple Beth Israel was chartered in Hartford in 1843. Bridgeport's earliest congregation (Congregation Beth Israel—the Park Avenue Temple), dates from 1850. Bequests from Judah Touro (see Louisiana), enabled Mishkan Israel and Beth Israel to acquire their first synagogue buildings in 1856. The first structure built as a synagogue was dedicated by Beth Israel in Hartford in 1876.

The Civil War found the Jewish community well established. Sigmund Waterman, who taught German at Yale from 1844-1847, became the first professing Jew to win a Yale degree when he received his M.D. in 1848. His brother, Leopold, was among the New Haven citizens who greeted the Hungarian patriot Louis Kossuth when he visited the city. Isaac Mayer, who came to Hartford as Beth Israel's first rabbi in 1856, was the father of one of Connecticut's Civil War heroes, Dr. Nathan Mayer. Named assistant surgeon of the 11th Regiment of Connecticut Volunteers when he was on 23, Mayer served for three years through the bloodiest battles. He was captured in 1864 and, after being paroled, returned to duty. Mayer wrote the official poem read at the dedication of the Connecticut Civil War monument on the Antietam battlefield.

Among the early German arrivals were Gershon Fox and Morris Ullman. Fox established a one-room fancy goods shop in Hartford in 1847 which became the city's leading department store and a New England landmark. His granddaughter, the late Mrs. Beatrice Fox Auerbach, who died in 1968, headed the G. Fox Department Store for nearly 30 years during which time it became "the center of Connecticut living." Ullman, who came to New Haven in 1847 and established a corset manufacturing business with Isaac Strouse and Max Adler, who arrived in 1843, was the father of the eminent Jacob Ullman. The latter was president of Mishkan Israel, president of the first New Haven community chest, and a leader of the state's Republican party for many years. In 1905 he was named judge of the Common Pleas Court—probably the first Jewish judge in the state.

Meier Zunder, who settled in New Haven in 1852, was a printer and importer of fine wines and whiskies, who served on the school board from 1867-1887. Until the middle 1950s there was a public school named for him on George St. Zunder organized the B'nai B'rith lodge in New Haven in 1856. Lewis Osterweis, who had owned a cigar factory in Fort Madison, Iowa, in 1856, moved his business to New Haven in 1858. His grandson, Rollin G. Osterweis, was professor of history at Yale. Bernard Shoninger founded the Shoninger Organ Co. in New Haven in 1858. Rabbi Samuel Willner, who came to New Haven's Congregation B'nai Sholom in 1877, was the father of Rabbi Wolf Willner, the first Yale alumnus to enter the rabbinate.

By 1877 there were 1,492 Jews in Connecticut. At the turn of the century the state had a Jewish population of 8,500 spread out over 18 towns and cities where there were 18 synagogues and 13 other Jewish institutions, and 11 places where Jews lived but still had no synagogue. The coming of the Russian Jewish immigrants in the 1880s (the first to arrive in New Haven in 1882 was a family of nine), greatly enlarged the Jewish population and led to the establishment of a large number of new synagogues and a network of Jewish communal organizations.

In the 1890s, some of the Russian Jews settled on farms in Colchester where a Jewish cigarmaker and several Jewish storekeepers—Shenyan, Nahinsky and Luntz—had preceded them. In 1899, on the 200th anniversary of the founding of Colchester, it had fewer than 2,000 inhabitants but the Jewish influx checked a total decline. The Jewish farmers who bought land around Colchester with the aid of loans from the Baron de Hirsch Fund later took in boarders in their farmhouses, and then expanded into small hotels. Colchester was once known as the Catskills of Connecticut because thousands of Jewish summer visitors from Connecticut and New York came to stay at hotels, rooming houses, and on farms. The greatest Jewish settlement occurred between 1910-1925 when Jews accounted for more than half the population. In the 1920s there were seven major Jewish hotels and all the town's markets carried only kosher meat. In 1893 the Jewish farmers organized the Love of Brotherhood Cemetery Association, and founded Congregation Ahavath Achim in 1898. For a time Colchester was the center of a state federation of Jewish farm associations, drawing members from Chesterfield, Oakdale, Montville, and other towns. Inexperience in farming and misguided in land purchases, most of the Jewish farmers did not remain on the land although other Jewish colonies were established at Moodus, Marion, Norwich, Deep River, Ellington, Lebanon, Chestnut Hill, Columbia, Hebron, and Danielson.

Some Jewish farmers gave up tilling the soil and shifted to dairy farming, tobacco growing, and egg farming. Others opened factories where they manufactured leather goods, clothing, and some established summer camps. As recently as 1966, the Jewish Agricultural Society reported that there were 30 Jewish dairy farmers in the state and about a dozen Jewish tobacco and potato growers. Of the state's 5,000,000 egg-laying chickens, 3 million were raised by Jewish farmers. The Jewish community in Danielson is an outgrowth of a settlement of displaced persons from Europe who were settled on farms there between 1947-1950. In Lebanon, Harold Liebman, a Jewish farmer, served on the town council and was elected to the state legislature. Harry Zack and his son operated a famous nursery and greenhouse at Deep River. Some of the farming communities established their own synagogues, a few of which still exist, but most of the Jewish farmers belonged to congregations in New Haven, Hartford, Bridgeport, Waterbury, Meriden, Middletown, New London, Norwich, and Willimantic.

Senator Abraham Ribicoff, who had also served as governor and as a member of the House of Representatives, is the son of one of the Russian Jewish immigrants. By 1906 there were Jewish residents in 19 towns and cities where they had established 80 Jewish organizations from synagogues to YMHAs, as they laid the groundwork for the present Jewish communities that dot the state.

The Jewish population rose swiftly from 22,000 in 1907 to 36,860 in 1910; 57,750 in 1912; 66,882 in 1917; 91,538 in 1927; 94,080 in 1937; and 105,000 in 1969. By the 1970s the Jewish population had reached 110,000 with the heaviest concentrations around Hartford, New Haven, and Bridgeport. There were 12 other places with 1,000 or more Jews, including Westport and Greenwich, where well-to-do residents live and commute to New York for their livelihoods.

In January 1974, the *Hartford Courant* published an article calling attention to a marked drop in the Jewish population of Hartford. The paper, however, failed to note that while the Jewish population within the corporate city limits had greatly declined and few Jewish institutions were left in the city, there had been an immense increase in the Jewish population of the nearby suburbs of West Hartford, Bloomfield, Farmington, East Hartford, Windsor, and East Windsor. The same trend developed in New Haven as Jews moved to suburban Woodbridge, Hamden, Orange, Derby, and Shelton, and in Bridgeport, where many residents resettled in Fairfield, Westport, and Stratford. In 1975 there were 52 towns and cities with one or more congregations.

Nevertheless, until 1965, owing to a long forgotten clause in the state constitution, Jews did not have a legal constitutional right to live in Connecticut. The late Rabbi Morris Silverman of Hartford discovered that the 1818 state constitution had adopted an article which gave rights of residence only to members of "every society or denomination of Christianity." Rabbi Silverman made his discovery while serving as a chaplain of the 1965 constitutional convention and was instrumental in having an amendment passed that changed the wording of Article 7 to members of "every religious society or denomination." Rabbi Silverman signed the new constitution and thus may have been the only rabbi with the distinction of having been a signer of a state constitution.

Article 7 of the 1818 constitution had never been used to deny Jews the right to hold public office. Jacob Klein was mayor of Bridgeport from 1886-1889. Jacob Ullman of New Haven served as judge of the Common Pleas Court in 1905, and Isaac Wolfe was a probate court judge in 1907. Bloomfield, New London, New Haven, Stamford, and West Hartford have had Jewish mayors. New London has had two Jewish mayors. Samuel Campner at the age of 27 became mayor of New Haven in 1917.

On the statewide basis Jews have held some of the highest offices from senator and governor down. Mildred Pomerants Allen and Gloria Schaffer were both elected secretary of state. Robert I. Berdon was state treasurer; David Goldstein was president pro tem of the state senate and acting governor; Louis I. Gladstone was the Democratic majority leader in the state senate; and Louis Shapiro, Samuel Mellitz, and Abraham S. Borden were judges of the State Supreme Court. In addition to Ribicoff, Herman Kopplemann and William Citron were members of the House of Representatives. Jon O. Newman, George Cohen, and Simon S. Cohen served as United States district attorneys for Connecticut. Newman and Joseph Blumenfeld were judges of the United States District Court.

Yale University, which once barred Jews from representing it in intercollegiate sports, has since had many distinguished Jewish academicians on its faculty, including deans of the law and medical schools. William Horowitz, the first and only Jew elected to Yale's board of trustees, also served as chairman of the Connecticut State Board of Education. Jon Newman was for a number of years chairman of the board of regents of the University of Hartford. In 1974, 23-year old Edward A. Zelinsky, a former national president of Aleph Zadick Aleph, (the boys component of the B'nai B'rith Youth Organization), became the first enrolled Yale student elected to public office in New Haven. A student in the Yale Law School, he was elected to the New Haven Board of Aldermen.

* * * * *

AMSTON

United Brethren Synagogue.

ANSONIA
(see Derby)

AVON
Wenograd Memorial, at the Talcott Mountain Science Center, a bronze plaque mounted on a rock platform on Talcott Mountain, honors the late Dr. Joseph Wenograd, associate dean for science at the College of Arts and Sciences of the University of Hartford. Wenograd, who died in 1972, was largely instrumental in setting up the program where university students take Talcott courses in such earth science areas as astronomy, geology, and meteorology.

BLOOMFIELD
Beth Hillel Synagogue, 160 Wintonbury Ave., has a sanctuary roof shaped like a Magen David, with the six points going downward interlocked with the "outstretched fingers" of the congregation going upward. The Ark doors have small openings to let out "light of Torah."

Cong. Teferes Israel, 27 Brown St., has a sculptured Burning Bush on its outside wall facing the street. It is a 14 foot high hammered copper piece.

Cong. Tikvoh Chodosh, 180 Still Rd.

Hebrew Academy of Greater Hartford, 53 Gabb Rd.

Interfaith Housing, Mountain Rd., sponsored by Beth Hillel Synagogue and a number of churches.

BRIDGEPORT
Arnold Bernhard Arts and Humanities Center of the University of Bridgeport, 380 University Ave., houses the university's music, theatre, and art departments. A theatre, art gallery, and an exposition hall in a seven-story building was named for a Jewish investment counselor from New York, who is the university's greatest benefactor.

Carlson Library of the University of Bridgeport, 303 Park Pl., is named for William and Philip Carlson, in whose honor there is a bronze plaque on the outer foyer that bears a bas relief likeness of the Jewish brothers. The inscription reads: "Through their generosity this library was erected. Appreciation for the opportunities America provides prompted them to leave a tangible memorial enhancing the cultural environment of Bridgeport and inspiring all who study here to greater service to their fellow men." Oil portraits of the Carlsons hang in the library's third floor periodical room.

Cong. Adath Israel, 540 E. Washington Ave.

Cong. Adath Yeshurun, 100 Butler Ave.

Cong. Beth Israel, 2710 Park Ave., third oldest congregation in the state, has on the front of the edifice an artistic representation of the Ten Commandments.

Cong. Bikur Cholim, 1541 Iranistan Ave.

Cong. Rodeph Sholom, Park and Capitol Aves.

Cong. Shaare Torah, 3050 Main St.

Geduldig Ave., running east off Park Ave. to Madison Ave., is named for Abe S. Geduldig, a former city prosecutor of Bridgeport, who gave the city a large tract of land in 1934 near 90 Acres Park.

Hebrew Sheltering Home, 699 W. Jackson Ave.

Hillel Foundation at University of Bridgeport, 276 Park Ave.

Jewish Community Center, 4200 Park Ave.

Jewish Family Service, 144 Golden Hill St.

Klein Memorial, 910 Fairfield Ave., the city's largest auditorium, was erected in 1932 through a bequest of $500,000 from Jacob B. Klein, who was mayor of the city from 1886-1889.

Schine Hall, a University of Bridgeport ten-story student dormitory, is a memorial to Isaac E. Schine, one of the founding trustees of the university.

United Jewish Council of Greater Bridgeport (see Fairfield).

BRISTOL

Cong. Beth Israel, 339 West St.

CHESHIRE

Temple Beth David, South Main and Spring Sts., occupies a landmark building that was once the historic United Methodist Church, built in 1834.

COLCHESTER

Beth Jacob Synagogue, 49 Church St.

Cong. Ahavath Achim, Lebanon Ave., was founded by Jewish farmers who settled in this area in the late 1890s with the help of the Baron de Hirsch Fund.

Jewish Aid Congregation, Mill St.

COLUMBIA

Cong. Agudath Achim.

DANBURY

Cong. B'nai Israel, 347 Main St.

Jewish Federation, 8 West St.

Stanley Lasker Richter Memorial Park, Aunt Hack Rd., was a gift from Mrs. Irene Untermyer Richter in memory of her husband. Mrs. Richter was the daughter of Samuel Untermyer, eminent lawyer and Jewish communal leader.

United Jewish Center, 141 Deer Hill Ave.

DANIELSON
Temple Beth Israel, Killingly Dr.

DEEP RIVER
Jewish Community Center of Lower Middlesex County, 93 Union St., is a synagogue and communal headquarters that serves the scattered Jewish residents of Chester, Higganiun, Killingworth, Ivorytown, Old Saybrook, Lyme, Centerbrook, Westbrook, Clinton, and Deep River.

DERBY
Beth Israel Synagogue Center, 300 Elizabeth St., represents a merger of Cong. Sons of Israel in Derby, the Jewish Community Center of Associated Towns in Ansonia, and Cong. Beth El. The Center serves the Jews of Derby, Ansonia, Shelton, Seymour, and Oxford.

EAST HARTFORD
Temple Beth Tefilah, 465 Oak St.

ELLINGTON
Cong. Sons of Israel, Pinney St., was founded by Jewish farmers.

ELMWOOD
Feldman Walkway in this Hartford suburb is named for Dr. Abraham J. Feldman, rabbi emeritus of Temple Beth Israel, West Hartford. A stone and bronze plaque marks the beginning of Feldman Walk, which runs from Manchester Circle to Beachland Park.

FAIRFIELD
Ahavas Achim Synagogue, 1571 Stratfield Rd.
Cong. Beth El, 1200 Fairfield Woods Rd.
Hillel Academy, 1571 Stratfield Rd.
Jewish Home for Elderly of Fairfield County, Jefferson St.

GILMAN
Nathan Gilman, Jewish industrialist and philanthropist, who settled in this New London County village in 1899, is memorialized by the town name which was changed from Bozrahville in 1929. The Gilman Bros.' textile plant, founded by Nathan Gilman, was converted to plastics by his sons, Charles and Lawrence. A third generation Gilman, Marty, was postmaster of the village for a number of years.

GREENWICH

Pryor Doll Library, founded in a converted barn by Samuel Pryor, includes a number of dolls from Israel.

Temple Isaac, 25 Storey Wilde Lane.

Temple Shalom,300 East Putnam Ave., is moving to Waterford.

GROTON

Submarine Library, Thames St., at the north entrance to the shipyard of the Electric Boat Divsion of General Dynamics Corp., has a collection of material about Admiral Hyman Rickover, father of the atomic submarine, and about Commander Edward Ellsberg, an expert in the raising of sunken submarines.

Temple Emanuel, 16 Fort St.

HAMDEN

Jewish Center, 27 Laconia St.

Temple Beth Sholom, 1809 Whitney Ave.

Temple Mishkan Israel, 785 Ridge Rd., is the oldest congregation in the state, founded in 1840 in New Haven, but was moved to Hamden, a New Haven suburb. The synagogue was organized three years before any Jewish congregation could be organized in Connecticut with a corporate legal entity.

HARTFORD

Auerbach Art Library, in the Wadsworth Atheneum, 600 Main St., was a gift of the late Mrs. Beatrice Fox Auerbach, whose grandfather, Gershon Fox, founded the city's famed G. Fox & Co., department store, in 1847, in honor of her daughters, Mrs. Richard Koopman and Mrs. Bernard Schiro. The library has a fine collection of silver by Myer Myers, the Colonial Jewish silversmith. Auerbach-Schiro-Koopman House, 1040 Prospect Ave., is the University of Hartford's guest house and is named for Mrs. Auerbach and her daughters.

Cong. Ados Israel, 215 Pearl St., has the original bima and Ark from the congregation's old Market St. synagogue.

Cong. Chevra Lomday Mishnayes, 191 Westbourne Pkwy.

Connecticut Historical Society, 1 Elizabeth, has the Rabbi Morris Silverman collection on Jewish history.

Federal Building, 450 Main St., has in its north courtroom a portrait of Judge M. Joseph Blumenfeld, who served as a U.S. District Court judge from 1961-1975.

Aaron Fien Sq., Ridgefield and Greenfield Sts., is named for an engineer who worked for the city from 1913-1950.

Annie Fisher Elementary School, 280 Plainfield St., is named for a Jewish principal in Hartford.

Miriam Stern Fox Interfaith Chapel at Hartford Hospital, 80 Seymour St., memorializes the mother of Lewis Fox.

Fox Middle School, 305 Greenfield St., is named for a one-time chairman of the Board of Education.

Hebrew Book Store, 262 S. Whitney St.

Hebrew Home, 615 Tower Ave., is connected by a 500-foot bridge to Mount Sinai Hospital to provide direct and rapid access for residents of the home.

Hillel Foundation at Trinity College, 30 Crescent St.

Mount Sinai Hospital, 500 Blue Hills Ave.

Nahum Dr., in a northwest housing project, is named for former Alderman Milton Nahum.

Abraham A. Ribicoff Portrait, in Memorial Hall of the State Library and Supreme Court Building, Capitol Ave., honors the most distinguished Connecticut Jew, who was a two-term governor of the state, and the first Jew elected chief executive of a New England state, U.S. Secretary of Health, Education and Welfare under President John F. Kennedy, and a U.S. senator. Ribicoff declined an offer from George McGovern in 1972 to be his running mate as the Democratic candidate for vice-president.

LEBANON

Jewish Congregation of Lebanon, Goshen Rd., also serves Jews of Hebron.

MADISON

Shoreline Jewish Community Organization.

Temple Beth Tikvah, serves the eastern shoreline Jewish communities of Branford, Guilford, Madison, Clinton, and Old Lyme.

MANCHESTER

Temple Beth Sholom, 400 East Middle Tpke.

MERIDEN

Temple B'nai Abraham, 127 East Main St.

MIDDLETOWN

Cong. Adath Israel, Church and Broad Sts.

MILFORD

Temple B'nai Shalom, 76 Noble Ave.

MOODUS

Cong. Rodfe Zedek, N. Moodus Rd.

NAUGATUCK

Cong. Beth Israel, 148 Fairview Ave.

NEW BRITAIN

Cong. Tiphereth Israel, 76 Winter St.

Jewish Federation, 272 Main St.

Abraham A. Ribicoff Apartments, a federally-built low income housing development for the elderly, named for Senator Abraham Ribicoff, 67 Hartford Ave., is located near the place where Ribicoff was born in 1910.

Temple B'nai Israel, 265 W. Main St.

NEW HAVEN

Biblical Garden, 400 Canner St., around the residence of the dean of Yale Divinity School, includes plantings of many flowers and shrubs mentioned in the Bible.

B'nai B'rith Hillel Foundation at Yale University, 206 Elm St.

Bureau of Jewish Education, 1184 Chapel St.

Cong. Beth El-Keser, 85 Harrison St.

Cong. Beth Israel, 232 Orchard St.

Cong. Bikur Cholim Shevet Achim, 278 Winthrop Ave.

Cong. B'nai Jacob (see Woodbridge).

Cong. Mishkan Israel (see Hamden).

Jewish Community Center, 1156 Chapel St., displays in its chapel an oil painting, *The Synagogue,* which depicts two figures in a synagogue. In the older adult lounge is an oil painting, *Body of the Torah,* and another entitled, *Psalm 133.*

Jewish Community Council, 1184 Chapel St.

Jewish Family Service, 1184 Chapel St.

Jewish Home for the Aged, 169 Davenport Ave.

Temple Emanuel, P.O. Box 398.

Westville Synagogue, 74 W. Prospect Pl.

Yale University

Emblazoned on the walls of the famous 221-foot Harkness Tower in the Harkness Quadrangle is the Hebrew coat-of-arms of the nation's third oldest college. The Hebrew words on the seal, *Urim* and *Thummin,* are superimposed on an open Bible. Translated as "light and truth," *(lux et veritas)* also appear on the seal. ●The Beinecke Library, High and Wall Sts., houses one of the great collections of Hebraica and Judaica. Dating from the beginning of the university, when an edition of the works of Flavius Josephus was among the 40 volumes contributed by the clergymen who founded the Collegiate College of America (Yale's original name), the collection was greatly enlarged during the presidency of Ezra Stiles. Among his contributions were Hazzan Isaac Touro's copy of the Book of Numbers, in Hebrew, and a Yiddish work printed in Zurich in 1546. The great Josephus Collection was added to by Selah Merrill, U.S. consul in Jerusalem at the turn of the 20th century. The heart of the Judaica Collection is the Alexander Kohut Collection of several thousand volumes presented by his son, George Alexander Kohut, who also bequeathed to Yale a portion of his own library, including some Heinrich Heine manuscripts. The Asch-Rabinowitz Collection, a gift of Louis Rabinowitz, New York philanthropist, contains many manuscripts of Sholom Asch and his contemporaries. Altogether, the special Hebraica and Judaica collections include some 12,000 volumes, 29 incunabula, and several hundred manuscripts. •Schulman Portrait, in the Yale Law School, memorializes the late Harry Schulman, dean of the school. •Steinert Collection of early keyboard and stringed musical instruments of the 17th and 18th centuries, on the 3rd floor of Memorial Hall in the Hewitt Triangle, is a gift of Morris Steinert of New Haven. Among the items is a piano that belonged to Beethoven.☐

Young Israel House at Yale, 35 High St.

Young Israel of New Haven, 232 Orchard St.

NEWINGTON

Cong. B'nai Sholom, 26 Church St.

Temple Sinai, 41 West Hartford Rd., has a Sabbath Menorah and the Tablets of the Law built into the rear exterior wall.

Isidore Wise Pavilion, at the Newington Hospital for Crippled Children and Adults, is named for a prominent Hartford merchant who was president of Temple Beth Israel of West Hartford.

NEW LONDON

Cong. Ahavath Chesed, 203 Montauk Ave.

Cong. Beth El, 660 Ocean Ave.

Cong. Ohave Sholom, 109 Blinman St.

Joanne and Nathan Cummings Arts Center at Connecticut College, is named for Mr. and Mrs. Nathan Cummings, Canadian and American philanthropists and art patrons. •The Greer Music Library in the center was the gift of Mr. and Mrs. Jesse Greer of Willimantic. •The Castle Sculpture Court was given to the college by Mr. and Mrs. Irving Castle. •The Rosenthal Cube on the center's west terrace, was the gift of Mrs. Isadore Levin of Palm Beach, Fla. •The S. Ralph Lazrus House, a cooperative dormitory, is a gift from Mrs. Lazrus, in memory of her husband, New York Jewish communal leader and president of Benrus Watch Co.

Jewish Community Council, 86 State St.

Jewish Leader, 86 State St.

NEW MILFORD

Temple Shalom, Route 7.

NEWTON

Cong. Adath Israel, Newingtown Rd.

NORWALK

Beth Israel Synagogue, King St.

Burndy Library, alongside the Connecticut Turnpike, west of Norwalk and housed in a special building next to the Burndy Corporation's electronics plant, is a unique private library devoted entirely to the history of science. It was established by Bern Dibner, a Russianborn Jewish electrical engineer. The library is open to the public and is widely used by high school science classes. Many of the choicest items in the library are now facsimiles, the originals having been given by Dibner to the Smithsonian Institution in Washington, D.C.

Jewish Community Center, Shorehaven Rd. (East Norwalk).

Jewish Community Council, Shorehaven Rd. (East Norwalk).

Temple Beth El, 109 East Ave., has frescoes representing Law, Prophetic Idealism, Learning, and the Ideals of Zion.

Temple Shalom, Richards Ave.

NORWICH

Beth Jacob Community Synagogue, 63 Church St.

Norwich Hebrew Institute (Cong. Brothers of Joseph), 2 Broad St.

OLD LYME

Cong. Beth El, Groton Ave., in Old Colony Beach area.

OLD SAYBROOK

Jewish Community Center of Lower Middlesex County.

ORANGE

New Haven Hebrew Day School, 261 Derby Ave.

Orange Synagogue-Center, 205 Old Grassy Hill Rd.

Temple Emanuel, 150 Derby Ave.

PUTNAM

Sons of Zion Synagogue, Church St., has a large Magen David at the peak of its colonial roof. Cement from Israel was used in rebuilding the synagogue's foundation, following severe damage to the building from Hurricane Diane in 1955. Israel's Histadrut contributed 1,000 bags of cement to the American Red Cross, and from this, 100 bags were allotted to the synagogue.

RIDGEFIELD
Temple Shearith Israel, 14 Peaceable St.

ROCKVILLE
Cong. B'nai Israel, 54 Talcott Ave.

SIMSBURY
Farmington Valley Jewish Congregation, Bushy Hill Dr.

SOUTH WINDSOR
Temple Beth Hill, Miller Rd. and Foster St. Extension (in Wappinger).

STAMFORD
Cong. Agudath Sholom, 301 Strawberry Hill Ave.

Rose Hartman Memorial Park, Brownhouse Rd. and Greenwich town line, is named for the mother of Jesse Hartman, local building contractor. He also gave the city a 12-acre tract on Woodway Rd., near the New Canaan town line, which has been developed into a park and center for the performing arts.

Jewish Community Center, 132 Prospect St.

Temple Beth El, 144 Prospect St.

Temple Sinai, Lakeside Dr., whose sanctuary exterior suggests the ancient tabernacle in the wilderness, has a huge pipe organ donated by the Norton Presbyterian Church of nearby Darien.

Tresser Blvd., formerly Willow St., between West Main and Atlantic Sts., was named in 1974 for Samuel Tresser, the second Stamford man to die in World War I.

STORRS
B'nai B'rith Hillel Foundation at University of Connecticut, N. Eagleville Rd.

STRATFORD
Shakespeare Festival, which performs for 27 weeks a year, was founded in 1955 by the late Lawrence Langner, Theatre Guild producer, partly with his own funds. The biggest tourist attraction in the state aside from Mystic Seaport, the festival and the theatre housing it were directed in the 1970s by Michael Kahn.

Temple Beth Sholom, 275 Huntington Rd.

TORRINGTON

Cohn Brook, one of the streams that overran its banks during the 1955 Hurricane Diane and created widespread havoc in this town, is named for Capt. Merrill Cohn of the U.S. Army Engineers, whose efforts helped rehabilitate the flood stricken area.

Cong. Beth-El, 124 Litchfield St.

TRUMBULL

Cong. B'nai Torah, 5700 Main St.

WALLINGFORD

Cong. Beth Israel, 22 N. Orchard St.

Interfaith Flora Hewitt Chapel at the Masonic Home, has a piece of stone from the Western Wall in Jerusalem donated by Rabbi Abraham J. Feldman of Temple Beth Israel, West Hartford. The chapel has three panels behind the tabernacle with symbols representing the major denominations. Two can be concealed while services are being conducted by the third. The panel representing Judaism shows the Tablets of the Ten Commandments in front of a Torah,

WATERBURY

Beth El Synagogue, 359 Cooke St.

Cong. B'nai Sholom, 135 Roseland Ave., has a sanctuary-in-the-round, and a substantial membership of Sephardim. The congregation merged in 1969 with Sharis Israel Congregation, a Sephardic synagogue founded in 1909.

"Holy Land U.S.A.," atop Pine Hill, is a 17-acre religious theme park built out of cement, stone, and bits of junk by John Greco, a local attorney and a devout Catholic. The park includes Mount Zion, the Western Wall, and the Garden of Eden.

Jewish Federation, 1020 Country Club Rd.

Temple Israel, 100 Williamson Dr.

Western Connecticut Jewish Community Center, 1020 Country Club Rd. Half of the center is located in Middlebury and the other in Waterbury, and serves communities within a 30-mile radius.

WATERFORD

Ben Kornzweig Memorial, a bronze plaque in the Eugene O'Neill Memorial Theatre Center, honors the late Ben Kornzweig, prominent theatrical press agent, who was the center's press representative for many years.

WEST HARTFORD

Agudas Achim Synagogue, 1244 N. Main St.

Beth David Synagogue, 20 Dover Rd., has an Oren Kodesh built in the shape of an open Torah Scroll, with the arms of the Scroll supporting the center beams of the sanctuary.

Beth El Temple, 2626 Albany Ave., has a roof with symbols of the 12 Tribes of Israel, and a skylight in the form of a Magen David.

Connecticut Jewish Ledger, 2475 Albany Ave.

Emanuel Synagogue, 160 Mohegan Dr., has a memorial to the 6,000,000 victims of the Holocaust in the lobby. The exterior sanctuary wall fronting on Mohegan Dr., is faced with black on which a Menorah the height of the building has been carved.

Hartford Jewish Community High School, 2626 Albany Ave.

Hebrew Funeral Home (a nonprofit communal burial society), 906 Farmington Ave.

Interfaith Housing, Starkel Rd., is sponsored by Beth David Synagogue, Beth El Temple, and Temple Beth Israel.

Jewish Community Center, 335 Bloomfield Ave., which is built campus-style, has 52 panels cast in concrete that gird the eight elevations of the center complex and depict the story of Creation. Each panel is four feet high and four feet wide. Several acres of the land on which the center stands were donated by the Roman Catholic Archbishop of Hartford, Father Henry J. O'Brien. In the lobby is a metal sculpture called *Chanukah Symbols.* The center has a permanent collection of Jewish art.

Jewish Family Service, 333 Bloomfield Ave.

Jewish Federation, 333 Bloomfield Ave.

Jewish Historical Society of Greater Hartford, 335 Bloomfield Ave., has a large collection of pictures of Jewish life in old Hartford and a growing collection of taped interviews with prominent Jews.

Solomon Schechter Day School, 160 Mohegan Dr.

Temple Beth Israel, 701 Farmington Rd., is the oldest congregation in the state sanctioned by law, having been founded in 1843 after an amendment to the statutes gave Jews equal rights with Christians in creating religious societies. The 12-sided building of Byzantine design has a dome which is said to be a replica of the St. Sofia dome in Istanbul. Each side represents one of the 12 Tribes of Israel. There are 12 pairs of stained glass windows, six of them representing the symbols of the 12 Tribes and six portraying heroes of the Bible. The pulpit desk has enshrined in it a stone from the never-completed Third Wall of Jerusalem. In the center of each of the synagogue's nine arches are symbols of the major occasions in the Hebrew calendar. One stained glass window was installed by the Christian community in honor of Rabbi Emeritus Abraham Feldman. In commemoration of the fellowship that enabled the First Church of Christ to use the synagogue lobby and a similar one in the church's meeting house. In the synagogue lobby there is a plaque honoring Judah Touro, (see

Louisiana), the famous philanthropist, whose bequest enabled the congregation to acquire its first synagogue in 1856. There are also a library of Judaica and a Jewish Museum.

United Synagogues of Greater Hartford, 840 N. Main St., is designed in the shape of a Magen David. At the entrance to the synagogue is a ten x eight foot monument to the 6,000,000 martyrs of the Nazi Holocaust, designed as six interlocked Stars of David.

University of Hartford

University of Hartford, 200 Bloomfield Ave., is dotted with evidences of Jewish generosity: Mildred P. Allen Memorial Library, in Paranov Hall, is a memorial to a woman who was a musician and secretary of state in Connecticut from 1925-1929. ●Auerbach Hall, 200 Bloomfield Ave., which houses the university's School of Business Administration, and Auerbach Auditorium, in University Hall, are named for the late Mrs. Beatrice Fox Auerbach, who for almost three decades headed G. Fox & Co., Hartford's leading department store. ●Berkman Recital Hall, in Paranov Hall of the Hartt College of Music, is named for Samuel Berkman, dean emeritus of the College of Music. ●The Jewish Student Union is in the Campus Ministry Office, located in Gengras Center. ●The Joseloff Exhibition Gallery in the Art School, was donated by Morris and Lillian Joseloff. ●Paranov Hall, in the Alfred C. Fuller Memorial Center of the university's Bloomfield Avenue Campus, is named for Dr. Moshe Paranov, president emeritus and co-founder in 1920 of the School of Music. His career began as a pianist in 1911, and he later conducted more than 500 opera productions. ●Samuel I. Ward Technical College, one of eight colleges of the University of Hartford, was originally the CRL School of Communications, owned by Ward's Crystal Research Laboratories. In 1952, Ward donated the CRL School of Electronics to Hillyer College which then changed its name to honor Ward. In 1971 Ward College became part of the University of Hartford. ●WWUH, the Louis K. Roth Memorial Station, the University's FM-stereo radio station, honors a former university trustee. □

Young Israel of Hartford, 1137 Trout Brook Dr.

Young Israel of West Hartford, 2240 Albany Ave.

WEST HAVEN

Cong. Sinai, 426 Washington Ave.

WESTPORT

Cong. for Humanistic Judaism, 133 Hillandale Rd.

Temple Israel, 14 Coleytown Rd.

WETHERSFIELD
Temple Beth Torah, 130 Main St.

WILLIMANTIC
Temple B'nai Israel, 327 Jackson St.

WILTON
Adath Israel Synagogue

WINDSOR
Cong. Beth Am, 362 Palisade Ave.

WINSTED
Temple Beth Israel, 74 Park Pl., replaced an older structure destroyed during the August 1955 flood. Contributions for the new building came from all parts of the country as well as Canada, and from a Synagogue Restoration Fund sponsored by the *Connecticut Jewish Ledger*.

WOODBRIDGE
Cong. B'nai Jacob, 75 Rimmon Rd., has a monumental stained glass window affixed to the facade of the sanctuary and an equally large semi-circular modernistic bronze Menorah which can be seen at a great distance. A circular chapel features stained glass windows with holiday themes.

DELAWARE

Delaware was the second of the 13 original American colonies to which Jews were legally admitted—New York having been the first. Except for a couple of Jews who strayed into Maryland and New England in the late 1640s, the only known Jews found in the area in the 1650s were the handful who had been grudgingly permitted to settle in New Amsterdam in 1654 and a much smaller number who found their way to Delaware a year later.

When the Swedish colony established the first permanent white settlement on Delaware soil, in what is now Wilmington, in 1638 (later annexed by the Dutch in 1655), the Jews of New Amsterdam petitioned for the right to engage in the fur trade with the Indians on the Delaware River. Governor Peter Stuyvesant and his council, reluctantly tolerating the first Jews in New Amsterdam, denied the request. Since Jewish traders had already dispatched a stock of goods to Delaware for barter with the Indians, the Dutch authorities conceded that outright and immediate exclusion would cause serious loss to the Jews. The Jewish businessmen were, therefore, allowed to send two agents to Delaware to dispose of their merchandise.

The designated emissaries were Isaac Cardoso and Isaac Israel. In December, 1655, one month after the petition to Stuyvesant, these men went to Fort Casimir (now New Castle), for a pow-wow between local traders and neighboring Indians. That pair were the first known Jews in Delaware. The Dutch and Swedish residents had agreed to give the Indians a bonus in order to keep the peace, but the Jewish traders refused to be a party to the agreement. As Rabbi Abram Vossen Goodman points out in *American Overture,* they saw no reason for keeping the good will of the Indians with whom they were forbidden to do business and whom they would never see again.

Later events proved they were mistaken. On specific instructions from the directors of the Dutch West Indies Company in Holland, Stuyvesant lifted the curb on Jewish fur trading in Delaware. In a communication dated June 14, 1655, the directors rebuked Stuyvesant for having ignored previous instructions and ordered him to "execute punctually and with more respect" their orders to allow the Jews to do business at Fort Orange (Albany, N.Y.) and in Delaware.

By March, 1656, Joseph d'Acosta was sending goods to the Delaware River. In April, Isaac Israel was back in Delaware, trading baubles for pelts. Some writers have speculated that notwithstanding the Dutch ban on Jewish officeholders, Israel, or a man by the same name, may have become a member of the High Council governing trade in Delaware. A document in 1663, reporting that "the Honorable Councillor Israel" directed the trading at Passajongh, is cited in *American Overture* in connection with this intriguing possibility.

Jewish merchants from New Amsterdam, who were operating along the Hudson River, followed d'Acosta and Israel to Delaware. David de Ferera and Isaac Mesa were doing business there in 1657 and 1658 as traders and importers of tobacco leaf from Virginia. Mesa's name is mentioned in several pieces of litigation involving the quality and delivery of tobacco. Others whose names have not been recorded were probably in Delaware at various times in the closing decades of the 17th century. There is no evidence, however, that any of these businessmen ever settled in Delaware. Had these Jews wished to settle there, they would not have been welcome. A Mennonite colony, founded in 1662 at what is now Lewes, specifically barred not only Catholics and "all intractable people" but also "usurious Jews."

Even in the 18th century Delaware had few if any Jews, as Dr. Jacob R. Marcus points out in *Early American Jewry.* Those who did live there were linked spiritually and commercially to the Jewish community of Philadelphia. There were no religious restrictions that barred Jews from pre-Revolutionary and post-Revolutionary Delaware. As part of William Penn's lands, Delaware enjoyed religious freedom and its people were not obliged to contribute to the support of any established church. As the first state to ratify the Federal Constitution, Delaware removed all religious tests from its constitution in 1792. The previous requirement that officeholders avow a belief in the divine inspiration of the New Testament, was aimed as much at deists and atheists as at Jews.

The first Jew to live in Wilmington, according to Rabbi David

Geffen, was Abraham Judah who registered ships there in 1751 and that same year bought Thomas Canby's property on Kennett Pike, a transaction recorded by a deed in the archives of the Delaware Historical Society. Judah was involved in a lawsuit in 1758, and was awarded damages by another Wilmingtonian. By 1761 Judah had moved to Philadelphia, but he still owned property in Wilmington which he advertised for sale in the *Pennsylvania Gazette.*

Two factors probably accounted for the absence of more than a handful of Jews in Delaware until a generation after the Civil War. One was the remoteness of the greater part of the state from the main northern and southern travel routes. The other was the proximity of Wilmington, the only large city, to Philadelphia. Because Delaware and Pennsylvania were reckoned as virtually a single state until after the Revolution, there were undoubtedly Pennsylvania Jews who had commercial interests in Delaware, but few of them lived there.

Judge Moses Levy, who was already a Christian when he became one of the leading figures of the Philadelphia bar in the late 18th and early 19th centuries, was equally prominent in Delaware legal circles. Mathias Bush, prominent 18th century Philadelphia merchant, who was a brother-in-law of Barnard Gratz and a partner of David Franks, built at least one ship in Delaware, the 130-ton merchantman *Priscilla,* launched at Sussex in 1770.

Records of Jews in Delaware in the early 19th century are equally scanty. In 1817 there were two well-known Jews in Delaware—Jacob and Daniel de Solis. Hyman B. Grinstein points out in *The Rise of the Jewish Community of New York,* that when New York's Congregation Shearith Israel was rebuilding its Mill Street Synagogue in 1817, it sent a circular letter asking for contributions "to congregations or individuals" in all American cities where a Jewish community existed or even a few Jews lived. Wilmington was among the cities included, and the letter was sent to Jacob de Solis, as indicated in the Shearith Israel archives. The Solis brothers opened a store in Wilmington at 22 and 24 Third St., between Market and King Sts., in 1814. Members of a prominent Sephardic family in Philadelphia, the Solis brothers regularly advertised their dry goods merchandise in the *Delaware Gazette* and the *Peninsula Advertiser,* offering merchandise at "Philadelphia prices." The Solis brothers were wholesalers. All of their ads carried the line, "N.B. No business transacted on the 7th day." Besides dry goods, they also manufactured quill pens, used in transcribing deeds, mortgages, wills, and the like. The partnership was dissolved in 1816 and Jacob went into business alone, opening a dry goods establishment at 3 East 3rd St., in Wilmington. He remained in business in Wilmington until 1821. Jacob Solis' three children, and David Solis' daughter, were probably the first Jewish children born in Delaware. Jacob Solis' children were Esther Etting, 1815; Judith Simiah, 1817; and Solomon, 1819. David's daughter was Benevenida Valentina, born in 1815.

No other Jew is known to have lived in Delaware until the 1840s when Henry B. Nones, son of Benjamin Nones, the Revolutionary War patriot of Philadelphia, took up residence there in 1843. The younger Nones was a Revenue Naval officer who commanded a cutter based in Wilmington for many years. His commissions were signed by Presidents Andrew Jackson, Martin Van Buren, and Abraham Lincoln. Nones, who was cited for bravery during the Mexican War, also served in the Civil War. When he married he probably converted to Christianity since he, his wife, and their four children are buried in the Christian Wilmington and Brandywine Cemetery beneath a tombstone on which there is a cross.

In 1855 Mose Stern was in business in Milford and Henry Lieberman in Dover. Lewis Richenberger opened a clothing store in Wilmington in 1859, and Nathan Lieberman did the same in 1862. The latter, together with Jacob deWolf and Henry Buxbaum, two other clothing dealers, appear to have been the prime movers in the first attempt to found a synagogue in Wilmington in 1872. Its founders planned to call it "Roudof Shalom," and its chief function, apart from conducting worship services, was to acquire ground for a Jewish cemetery. Although this synagogue never came into being, Jewish worship services in Wilmington were held for the first time on the High Holy Days in 1873. During the 1870s there were worship services for the High Holy Days in makeshift quarters in the Morrow Building, 215 Market St., the Lieberman Building, 5th and Market Sts., and on Shipley St., between 3rd and 4th Streets. In 1875 a Rabbi Herzberg was brought from Philadelphia to officiate. In that year a Wilmington newspaper reported that there are "in this city twenty families of Jewish persuasion aggregating about 100 persons."

In 1879 a reporter for the *Wilmington Every Evening* described the Yom Kippur service in the Morrow Building. He said there were 30 persons present, including four or five women and a dozen children. "All the men kept their hats on," the reporter wrote, "most of them wearing neatly brushed and glossy head-coverings of the stovepipe variety. Reverend Julius Weil of Philadelphia officiated." The service was conducted in German and Hebrew.

The day after this service, September 28, 1879, the Moses Montefiore Beneficial Society was founded in Nathan Lieberman's home. Incorporated in 1883, this first Jewish organization in Delaware is still in existence. It was established "to succor needy brethren, to accumulate a fund for the payment of sick benefits, and to aid indigent and unfortunate brethren who may be cast ashore, so to speak, in this city." The organizer was Bernard Rosenblatt, a hairdresser, about whom little else is known.

Some months later, on March 19, 1880, a synagogue was dedicated on the third floor of the Lieberman Building. A Rabbi S. Rosenberg, who doubled as *shochet,* conducted the service for this first congregation in Delaware, which was named Ohabe Shalom. The rabbi's sermon, delivered in German, was summarized the next day in a front page story in the *Wilmington Every Evening.* The reporter described the service fully, noting that 40 persons were present, "the number being restricted to those to whom cards of invitation had been issued. Isaac Isaacs, the oldest Wilmington Israelite, carried the Thara (sic!) containing the sacred five books of Moses." The reporter concluded by saying that "an uncircumcised newspaperman then turned off the gas jets and the congregation dispersed."

George Jacobs was the first president of this congregation, which was listed in the Wilmington City Directory until 1883, with Rabbi Morris Faber mentioned as spiritual leader.

Cong. Adas Kodesch, the first enduring congregation, was founded in 1885, and its synagogue was dedicated by the celebrated Rabbi Sabato Morais of Philadelphia. In 1898, the Wilmington Lodge of B'nai B'rith was organized by Moses Weil, a Civil War veteran from Ohio who was elected Delaware state commander of the Grand Army of the Republic, an organization of Union Civil War veterans. Nathan Levy, also a Civil War veteran, from Michigan, arrived in Wilmington about the same time as Weil. Though they were German Jews, the bulk of the newcomers to Wilmington at the turn of the century were East European Jews. In 1900, Delaware's Jewish population was 1,200.

Before the end of the 19th century, a Reform congregation, called Oheb Shalom, was established in Wilmington in 1895, but endured only until 1898, the year Cong. Adas Kodesch acquired the old Zion Lutheran Church and converted it to the first synagogue building in the state. The Reform group, however, maintained a tie with Rabbi Joseph Krauskopf of Philadelphia's Reform Congregation Keneseth Israel by having him officiate at their children's weddings. Cong. Beth Emeth, the first permanent Reform congregation, was organized in 1906.

Rabbi David Geffen has pointed out that while most of Delaware's Jews are located in Wilmington, Dover's Jewish history goes back more than 110 years. Boyd's Delaware Directory of 1865-66 lists Henry Levy, general merchant, and Henry Lieberman, owner of a general store. The latter's brother, Nathan, appears to have joined him in Wilmington during the Civil War when the Liebermans became highly successful. When Henry Lieberman died in 1878, his widow continued to operate the store. She was so highly regarded in the capital city that she and her sons were often guests at the Governor's balls. Other Jews in Dover after the Civil War were Henry Kirschbaum, M. Goldwater, Emanuel Newman, and Joseph Levy.

Between 1910 and 1920 East European Jewish immigrants who received grants from the Baron de Hirsch Fund were settled on farms near Dover by the Jewish Agricultural Society. In that ten-year period 25 Jewish families became farmers around Dover and there are still some there. Worship services were first held in Dover in the 1920s but no congregation was established until 1936 when Erwin Snellenberg, son of David Snellenberg, prominent Wilmingtonian, came down to help organize a congregation. An increase of Jewish population during World War II led to the establishment of the Beth Sholom Community Center in 1949. The present building was occupied in 1963 and dedicated in 1965.

In 1901, Moses Weil was appointed a magistrate in Wilmington, the first Jew known to have held public office anywhere in the state. Barnett Gluckman was named to the same post in 1909, and was reappointed six times by the governor. A second congregation, Chesed Shel Emeth, came into being in 1901 as the result of a disagreement over the burial policies of Adas Kodesch. The document in which Chesed Shel Emeth announced its formation and recorded on December, 24, 1901, says that "for the purpose of becoming incorporated, a meeting of a congregation of Christians consisting of more than fifteen persons was held." This language was employed, according to Rabbi David Geffen, historian of Delaware Jewry, because of an existing law which provided for the incorporation of Christian church groups but made no reference to Jewish organizations, and was intended to be ironic. In the 1950s Adas Kodesch and Chesed Shel Emeth merged and became Adas Kodesch-Shel Emeth Synagogue. Cong. Beth Shalom was established in 1922 and the Jewish Community Center had its origin in a Jewish social club formed in 1901. The B'nai Zion, a fraternal Zionist order, was founded in 1897.

On the eve of America's entry into World War I, the state's Jewish population was reported to be 3,806, fewer than those in all but ten other states. By 1937 this figure had nearly doubled to 6,587. Of this number, 6,200 resided in Wilmington, the state's only major city. The rest were scattered as follows: Dover (92), Georgetown (15), Harrington (12), Hartly (17), Middletown (43), Milford (39), Newark (47), and Seaford (19). None of these places had any congregation or other Jewish organization at that time.

The leading Jews in the state during the 1920s and 1930s were Magistrate Barnett Gluckman, Dr. Albert Robin (see below), Louis and

William Topkis, Magistrate Aaron Finger, Milton Kutz, David Snellenburg, Morris Levy, and I.B. Finkelstein.

Aware that there was no well-equipped hospital in Wilmington where Jewish physicians were permitted to practice, Robin is credited with having influenced Mrs. Irenee duPont to establish the Wilmington General Hospital. The Topkis brothers were generous supporters of local Jewish philanthropies and were the first Wilmingtonians to earn national Jewish leadership positions. Snellenburg, who was a citywide communal figure, was the chief organizer of the General Jewish Committee in 1917, the forerunner of the Jewish Federation of Delaware. In 1910 he was president of the Delaware Air Club, which developed the two-winged Delaplane, one of the earliest planes of its type. Snellenburg encouraged Samuel Saretsky, executive director of the YMHA, to enter a contest to select a motto for Wilmington. Saretsky's winning slogan, "Wilmington, the First City in the First State," is still in use. I.B. Finkelstein, son of an immigrant and a prominent businessman who helped found the Jewish Federation of Delaware, was also the founder of the annual Delaware Arts Festival at Arden, and later organized the Brandywine Festival of the Arts. Although not a social worker, he was chairman of the Delaware Conference on Social Work, encouraged prison reform, and was elected president of the Delaware Chamber of Commerce three times. One of the early suffragette leaders was the late Mrs. James N. Ginns, a member of the Topkis family, who picketed the White House in support of women's suffrage during the Wilson Administration.

It was Snellenburg who was responsible for getting Pierre S. duPont, head of the immense duPont Company, to attend a Jewish War Relief campaign dinner in Wilmington in 1918. Wilmington was then being made the testing ground in the first organized effort to get non-Jews to contribute to a Jewish relief fund. At the dinner, duPont created a sensation when he announced dramatically that "I have a special reason for being here. I have one-eighth Jewish blood in me—my grandfather (sic!) having been a Jew." Whereupon duPont underwrote the entire Wilmington quota of $75,000. With this unlooked-for inspiration, Wilmington raised $148,000 within a week.

DuPont was right about having a Jewish ancestor, but it was not his grandfather on either side of his family but his great-great-grandfather. A couple of sources erroneously stated that duPont's Jewish ancestor was Augustus Belin, the duPonts' first employee, whose granddaughter, Mary Belin, married Lammot duPont in 1865. It is true that Mary Belin, who was three generations removed from a Jewish ancestor, married Lammot duPont in 1865 and was at first shunned by his family, although her father, Henry Hedrick Belin, was a trustee of Christ Church. Pierre duPont's Jewish ancestor was Moses

Homberg, a German Jew who came to the United States from Holland. In 1786 he wrote a letter to "His Excellency, the President and the Honourable Vice-President of the State of Pennsylvania," in which he described himself as a Philadelphia merchant, and asked permission to ship to Baltimore a consignment of goods which had arrived for his firm in New York. Homberg died in 1793 during the yellow fever epidemic that struck Philadelphia. A fleeting reference to him and his wife, Anna, in a manuscript record of Mickveh Israel Congregation's Spruce Street Cemetery in Philadelphia may indicate that Moses was buried there, but no trace has survived. A year before his death Homberg applied for membership in Mickveh Israel which was in financial difficulties because many of its members had moved away during the Revolutionary War. It may be, as Dr. Malcolm Stern, genealogist of the American Jewish Archives, points out, that even those Jews like Homberg, who is mentioned by Dr. David Nassy of Philadelphia, as "one of the inter-married families in which the husband attends synagogue and the wife church, yet mix in the best society," were welcomed into Mickveh Israel. Homberg must have been in New York for a while because his name appears among those who owed the charity fund of Cong. Shearith Israel eight shillings, which he paid in 1787.

That was the year Homberg married Elizabeth Ax, daughter of a non-Jewish German named Jacob Naglee, and widow of Danish-born Adolphus William Hedrick, who had served in the 11th Pennsylvania Regiment during the Revolution. When Hedrick died he left one daughter, Mary Aletta, who later married Augustus Belin. Homberg's wife had inherited from her first husband the Franklin Tavern, on Race Street, near 2nd Street, in Philadelphia. That was the address at which Moses Homberg was listed in the United States census of 1790. Isabella Homberg, one of Moses' two daughters, married her first cousin, Henry Hedrick Belin, son of Augustus Belin, and his wife, Mary Aletta Hedrick. Isabella and Henry Belin were the parents of Mary Belin who on October 3, 1865 married Lammot duPont, Pierre Samuel duPont's great-great-grandfather.

Apart from Wilmington, the only other organized Jewish communities are in Dover, the capital, where Jews have resided since the middle of the 19th century, and Newark. High Holy Day services were held in Dover early in the 20th century for Jewish farmers in southern Delaware and residents of Dover and neighboring towns. David Snellenburg helped the Dover Jews organize Temple Beth Sholom in 1946. One of its members, Ernst Dannemann, has served on a number of state commissions. The space suits worn by America's first astronauts and moon explorers were made by the ILC Industries of Dover, of which Dr. Nisson Finkelstein was president.

In Newark, where there have been Jewish residents since the early years of the 20th century, Temple Beth El was founded in 1954 as the Newark Jewish Community when there were less than 100 Jewish families in the Greater Newark area. The present building is also the home of the Hillel Foundation at the University of Delaware. Norma Handler, a member of the temple, served several terms as mayor of Newark, and was an important leader of the state Democratic party. There are small Jewish settlements in Middletown and Odessa, both of which once had Hebrew benevolent societies; New Castle; Christiana; Glasgow; and Milford. At the end of 1974 the Jewish population of Delaware was 9,000, 96 percent of it in Wilmington. Only 17 states had fewer Jews.

The highest statewide elective political office held by a Jew was the attorney-generalship, to which Albert Young was elected in 1950 and reelected in 1952. He had previously served as president of the State Bar Association. James Rosbrow was Secretary of Labor and Daniel Weiss was Speaker of the State House of Representatives. Alexander Greenfield was appointed United States Attorney for Delaware in 1961, and Ralph V. Keil was named to the same post in 1973. Among the lower court Jewish judges were Aaron Finger (1916-20); Henry R. Isaacs (1940); Robert H. Wahl (1968); Bernard Balick; Carl Goldstein; Herbert Cobin; Roxanna Arsht; and Albert Stiftel. Daniel L. Hermann, a former president of the Jewish Federation of Delaware, has been chief justice of the Delaware Supreme Court since 1973. William Penn Frank, a columnist on the *Wilmington Morning News* for many years, was a Wilmington newspaperman for more than half a century. In 1973, too, the duPont Co. chose Irving S. Shapiro, a long-time attorney for the firm, as its president and chief executive. Henry Topel served as chairman of the Democratic State Committee from 1972 to 1974. The late Dr. Louis Gluckman, son of Barnett Gluckman, the late Dr. Harry Kurfirst, and Dr. Leon Levy all served on the State Board of Dental Examiners.

* * * * *

DELAWARE CITY

Fort Delaware, on Pea Patch Island, a granite pentagon encircled by a moat, was a Union prison for Confederates where 12,000 prisoners, among them at least three Jews, were confined under horrible conditions. The three Jews, who wrote to Rabbi Isaac Mayer Wise in Cincinnati in 1864 for assistance, were Louis Meyersburg, Mobile, Ala., Max Neugas, Darlington, N.C., and Aaron Waterman, Hawkinsville, Ga., all of whom survived.

DOVER

Delaware State Museum, 316 S. Governor's Ave., has a unique collection of fire-fighting memorabilia of Delaware Volunteer fire companies from 1780 to the present, assembled and presented to the museum by Fred S. Brown of Wilmington, a Jewish fire buff, who was known as "Mr. Volunteer Fire Department."

State Highway Administration Building, has in its lobby the Delaware Highway Hall of Fame, and one of those honored there with a plaque outlining his contributions to the state highway system is the late Samuel Knopf of Wilmington. Starting with the Coleman duPont Co. that built the state's first modern highway in 1912, Knopf served with the Highway Department until his death in 1944 during which he was involved in the planning and building of the state highway system.

Temple Beth Sholom, Queen and Clara Sts.

NEWARK

Hillel Foundation, University of Delaware, 70 Amstel Ave.

Temple Beth El, 70 Amstel Ave., also houses the Hillel Foundation and the same rabbi serves both.

WILMINGTON

Adas Kodesch-Shel Emeth Synagogue, Washington Blvd. and Torah Dr., is the oldest existing congregation in Delaware, having been founded in 1885. When it moved into its present building in 1965, the street in the Brandywine Hills section where the synagogue was located had its name changed from Tyndale Rd. to Torah Rd. City officials explained that the change in name was not intended as an affront to the memory of Rev. William Tyndale, the Protestant Reformation leader who translated the Bible from Greek into English. The synagogue's former site, at 6th and French Sts., was one of the most historic spots in Delaware for it was once occupied by Delaware's first Lutheran church, the first public school in Wilmington, and also the city's first post office.

B'nai B'rith Building, 2809 Baynard Blvd.

Cong. Beth Emeth, 300 Lea Blvd.

Cong. Beth Shalom, 18th St. and Baynard Blvd., has a uniquely sculptured Ark door, Ner Tamid, and Menorot in bronze by Luise Kaish.

Delaware Art Museum, 2301 Kentmere Pkwy., has a portrait of Rebecca Gratz, the celebrated Philadelphia Jewish philanthropist and educator by Thomas Sully (see Philadelphia).

Delaware Historical Society, 505 Market St., has a treasure trove of documentary material about American Jews in its archives which are being researched by Rabbi David Geffen, founder of the Delaware Jewish Historical Society. Among the documents in the archives are: the deed to the first piece of property bought by a Jew—Abraham Judah—in Wilmington in 1751; a commission to Isaac Franks in 1789 signed by Thomas Mifflin, mayor of Philadelphia, appointing Franks a justice of the peace; a Book of Genealogy by Mary Levy Milligan, tracing the genealogy of the Samson Levy family; a letter from Louis D. Brandeis to Senator Thomas Bayard in 1885; the commission of Nathan Levy of Maryland as U.S. consul to the island of St. Thomas, dated in 1826 and signed by President John Quincy Adams and Secretary of State Henry Clay; and the naval commissions of Henry B. Nones, who commanded a cutter for more than 30 years and was decorated for bravery by Commodore Matthew Perry during the Mexican War in 1846. Nones was the son of Benjamin Nones, a French-born Jew who settled in Philadelphia and served heroically during the siege of Savannah and the Battle of Camden, S.C. In 1800 he wrote a now famous letter to the printer of the *Gazette of the United States & Daily Advertiser* defending himself against an attack in an anti-Semitic article as a Jew, as a democrat, and as a poor man. His son, Henry, who also served in the Civil War, had his commissions signed by Presidents Andrew Jackson, Martin Van Buren, and Abraham Lincoln. He is buried with his wife and four children in the Wilmington and Brandywine Cemetery, 701 Delaware Ave. There is a cross on his tombstone, which may indicate that he converted to Christianity.

Albert Einstein Academy, 300 Lea Blvd.

Eleutherian Mills Historical Foundation, Greenville, preserves letters from the Gratz Brothers of Philadelphia early in the 19th century to the duPont Co.; letters to Admiral Samuel duPont from Henry B. Nones and his children; letters and responses to Pierre S. duPont from such Jewish leaders as Herbert H. Lehman, Julius Rosenwald, and Nathan Straus; and a newspaper article in Yiddish about Pierre S. duPont's gift to the 1918 Jewish War Relief Drive and his assertion of Jewish ancestry.

Jewish Community Center, 101 Garden of Eden Rd., has in its lobby a portrait of Louis Topkis, the first Delaware Jew to become a national figure in Jewish affairs. He was one of the founders of the American Jewish Joint Distribution and treasurer of the Zionist Organization of America. Together with his brother William he led the early campaigns to build a YMHA building in Wilmington.

Jewish Family Service of Delaware, 3617 Silverside Rd., on the second floor of the Talleyville Shopping Center.

Jewish Federation of Delaware, 701 Shipley St.

Jewish Voice, 701 Shipley St.

Milton and Hattie Kutz Home, 704 River Rd., has portraits of the donors of the Home For The Aged, who also established the Kutz Chair of American Jewish History at Hebrew Union College-Jewish Institute of Religion in Cincinnati which was occupied for many years by Dr. Jacob R. Marcus. Kutz owned a small Tennessee chemical factory which was acquired by the duPont Co. and the Kutzes moved to Wilmington. Kutz became a vice-president of duPont and one of the principal leaders of the Jewish community. For a number of years he was president of the Jewish Federation of Delaware.

Machzekei HaDat Cong., worships in the B'nai B'rith Building, 2809 Baynard Blvd.

Robin Hall, in the Nurses Home of the Wilmington General Hospital, Chestnut and Broom Sts., memorializes Dr. Albert Robin, the first Jewish physician to practice in Delaware as a member of the Delaware Medical Association. He came to Delaware in 1899 as the bacteriologist of the Delaware State Board of Health. In 1904 he helped establish the Delaware Anti-Tuberculosis Society. When the little shack housing eight TB patients was on the verge of closing in 1907, Robin enlisted the aid of Miss Emily Bissell, a local civic leader, in devising some novel way of raising funds. Recalling Jacob Riis' story about a Christmas stamp originated in Denmark in 1904 by a postal clerk and was sold in post offices not as postage but to raise funds for a sanitarium for tubercular children, Miss Bissell came up with the idea of a Christmas stamp to educate people about TB. Encouraged by Robin and his associates, she printed up 50,000 stamps and put them on sale in the Wilmington Post Office on December 7, 1907. The sale netted $3,000 and gradually grew into the annual Christmas stamp sale of the National Tuberculosis Society. Robin, whose portrait hangs in Robin Hall, was secretary of the Delaware General Jewish Community, president of the Wilmington YMHA, and through the local B'nai B'rith lodge, established the Mt. Sinai Dispensary, the state's first free nonsectarian medical and dental clinic which was maintained by B'nai B'rith until 1919 when the state took it over. Robin persuaded the Irenee duPonts to purchase the site of the Wilmington General Hospital which he did not live to see completed. Mrs. duPont commissioned the portrait of Robin.

Town Hall Museum, 512 Market St., displays a silver salver made for Gunning Bradford (one of the Delaware signers of the Declaration of Independence), in 1770 by Myer Myers, the famous Colonial Jewish silversmith.

Wilmington and Brandywine Cemetery, an old Christian cemetery at 701 Delaware Ave., has its main entrance guarded by a magnificent cedar of Lebanon brought from Palestine in 1950.

Wilmington-Gratz Hebrew High School, 101 Garden of Eden Rd.

Wilmington Public Building, 1000 King St., which houses the city and county offices, has a carving of a figure of justice above the entrance at 11th and King Sts. In the hands of the figure are the Ten Commandments in Hebrew. The Hebrew words at the beginning of the first two Commandments and of the fourth and fifth Commandments are clearly visible.

WINTERTHUR

Henry Francis duPont Winterthur Museum has on display in Morattico Hall an oil painting of Dr. John de Sequeyra, an 18th century Italian-born Jewish physician who practiced in and around Williamsburg, Va., where his house still stands (see Virginia). Dr. Sequeyra was also known as Dr. Secarri. Also in the museum are the following items of Jewish interest: A high chest in the Port Royal Parlor, 4th floor, that once belonged to the Gratz family of Philadelphia, as is a dressing table near by. ●In the Bertram Room, 3rd floor, are a silver coffee pot, silver cream pitcher, and silver sugar bowl, made by Myer Myers, 18th century Jewish silversmith. ●In the Ineson-Bissell Collection are four silver tablespoons made by Myer Myers. ●In the dining room porch on the 5th floor is an iron chandelier that once hung in the Colonial era synagogue in Bridgetown, Bahamas.

DISTRICT of COLUMBIA

The Congress of the United States was the godfather of the Jewish community of Washington, D.C. It is a community whose past and present have been greatly shaped and influenced by Jews in government service. It was in 1857 that the 34th Congress enacted the legislation which gave the city's first Jewish congregation full equality with the Christian churches.

That was 62 years after the first Jews had settled in Washington. In 1795, Isaac Polock, a merchant and resident of Savannah, Georgia, took up residence in Washington. That was five years before Congress transferred the seat of the Federal government to the banks of the Potomac in 1800. Polock was well-known in the city's business and social life. On a large land parcel on Pennsylvania Avenue he built six large brick houses, one of which still stands. The first Secretary of the Navy established his office in one of the buildings. Another was occupied by the State Department. A third became the residence of James and Dolly Madison while Madison was Secretary of State. Polock's name appears often in early Washington real estate records, in the proceedings of the Board of Commissioners, and in newspaper advertisements beginning in 1795. As an important builder he was asked to submit bids for two executive office buildings to be erected in 1798 and 1799. Polock's home was often the stopping off place for friends and neighbors visiting between Georgetown and Washington, and many social events were held there.

Polock, who was a grandson of one of the founders of the Touro Synagogue in Newport, Rhode Island, engaged as tutor to his children one Raphael Jones, who was conversant in Hebrew and also served as a *shohet*. Jones had served in the militia during the War of 1812 and later became a dry goods merchant.

The city directory of 1834 was the first to list identifiable Jewish names: E.A. Cohen, whose only claim to fame is that he published the directory, and Capt. Alfred Mordecai, an Army officer. Mordecai's daughter, Rosa, told three generations of Jewish Washingtonians that she was the first Jewish child born in the city. One of Mordecai's six children, she was 97 years old when she died in 1939. Miss Mordecai said that when her infant brother, Frank, died in 1841, there were not enough identifiable Jews to hold a *minyan* for the funeral service.

Captain Mordecai, scion of a prominent Jewish family with important educational, mercantile, and military connections in New York, Philadelphia, Richmond, and Warrenton, North Carolina, was a West Point graduate. Top man in the class of 1823, he was barely 30 when he was assigned to the Army's Ordnance Board in Washington in 1828. He gained new fame as a military engineer in the Mexican War, and after the war he became widely known in his field. His wife was a niece of the celebrated Rebecca Gratz (see Philadelphia).

By the time Mordecai returned from the Mexican War in 1847 there were some 25 Jewish residents in Washington. Most of them were recent arrivals from Germany and Hungary, and had to make the long trip to Baltimore for the nearest synagogue. They had come to Washington from Baltimore where they had relatives or *landsmen*.

Mordecai also found two Jews in Congress: David Levy Yulee (see Florida), who had been elected one of Florida's first two senators in 1845, after serving in the House of Representatives since 1841 as Florida's first territorial delegate; and Congressman Charles Lewis Levin, temperance advocate and a leader of the anti-alien American Party, who had been elected from a Philadelphia district.

Neither Yulee nor Levin identified themselves with the other Jews, most of whom were peddlers or storekeepers. Twenty of these Jews—among them the ancestors of the Hamburgers, Hechts, Kanns, Hochschilds, and Kohns who founded important mercantile establishments in Washington—met in the home of Herman Listberger in 1852 and organized the Washington Hebrew Congregation. Its first synagogue was a room in the Concordia Lutheran Church, located today, as it was then, at 20th and G Streets. Among those who probably worshipped with the pioneer congregation, though not among its founders, was Emanuel Hart. He had come to Washington in 1851 as a Tammany Congressman from New York where he was a member of Congregation Shearith Israel. For several years after the congregation was established, Dr. Henry Hochheimer, the rabbi of Baltimore's Eden

Street Synagogue, came to Washington every three months to examine the children at the Hebrew day school sponsored by the Washington congregation.

The first real leader of the Jewish community was Navy Captain Jonas Phillips Levy, whose Philadelphia family had pre-Revolutionary roots in America. Younger brother of the celebrated Commodore Uriah P. Levy (see Virginia), Captain Levy had distinguished himself in the Mexican War as commander of the gunboat *America* and captain of the port of Vera Cruz after its surrender by the Mexicans. He was the author of a bizarre plan to build a road between New York and San Francisco by way of Mexico, for which the Mexican Congress had granted him an exclusive franchise in 1850. He also organized the Peruvian navy at the invitation of that government.

Levy came to Washington in 1852 and under his guidance the new congregation became permanently organized. Acting in the belief that existing laws discriminated against Jewish religious worship, Levy framed a petition to Congress requesting a charter for the synagogue. In response to this plea, the 34th Congress gave legal sanction in 1857 to the Jewish community by proclaiming "that all rights, privileges and immunities heretofore granted by law to the Christian churches in the City of Washington, be, and the same hereby are, extended to the Hebrew Congregation of the said city." Under this charter Levy became the first president of the Washington Hebrew Congregation.

Previously (in 1854) Levy had taken a leading part in setting in motion the formal Jewish protests against a proposed commercial treaty with Switzerland which discriminated against Jews doing business in that country. In the very year that Congress chartered the synagogue, the first official Jewish delegation to call on the White House laid before President James Buchanan a formal protest against the treaty. Two years later Levy sought, but failed, to get permission of Mayor Richard Wallach, who was not a Jew, for Jewish merchants to keep their stores open on Sundays because they were closed on Saturdays.

In the Senate that debated the Swiss treaty sat Judah P. Benjamin (see Louisiana), and David Levy Yulee. While Secretary of State Lewis Cass and the White House denounced the treaty, Benjamin virtually ignored it, as did Yulee, referring only to the receipt of a petition from Jewish citizens opposed to it. Yulee, who was the first Jew elected to Congress, and Benjamin differed greatly in their attitude to the local Jewish community from most of the Jews who later served in Congress. There is a story that Benjamin was given the honor of holding the new Torah Scrolls dedicated by the Washington Hebrew Congregation in 1856, but this is pure fiction. When he was invited to participate in a benefit party to raise funds to buy the Torah, he acknowledged the invitation with a perfunctory note of regret. Philip Phillips, who was practicing law in Washington after having served in Congress as a representative from Alabama from 1853-1855, also declined to attend, but sent a contribution of ten dollars.

Two early Jewish settlers who had a major impact on the history of the city as well as on the life of the Jewish community were Adolphus S. Solomons and Simon Wolf. Solomons, who came from New York where he had been one of the founders of Mt. Sinai Hospital, opened a printing business in Washington in 1859. When he settled in Washington, he had just returned from Berlin as Daniel Webster's bearer of dispatches. Solomons' firm, Philips and Solomons, was one of the city's leading business establishments. As booksellers, printers, and publishers, the firm did much business with the government and supplied stationery to Congress. Washington artists often exhibited in Solomons' gallery. Later, Solomons became one of the founders of the American Red Cross. Wolf, who had come from Cleveland in an unsuccessful attempt to enlist in the Union Army, stayed on and began a law practice in 1862. For more than half a century thereafter he was the unofficial Jewish ambassador in the capital. Wolf was appointed a municipal judge of Washington in 1880 by President Rutherford B. Hayes—the first Jew to hold local public office in the city. By appointment of President Ulysses Grant, Wolf became recorder of deeds in Washington in 1869. He also served as president of the Washington Hebrew Congregation.

Other prominent Jews who resided in Washington shortly before or during the Civil War were Michael Heilprin, editor, scholar, and militant foe of slavery; Max Conheim, a popular playwright and producer for the German theatre in New York, who established a German-language weekly, *Columbia,* in Washington in 1863, while working for the Treasury Department; Max Weyl, the noted painter; Dr. Jonathan P. Hurwitz, a medical officer in the Bureau of Medicine and surgeon in the United States Navy from 1859-1865; Edward Rosewater, who worked in the Army telegraph office and later became a well-known newspaper editor in Omaha (see Nebraska); Abraham Hart, lawyer; Gritzer and Cohen, patent agents; Julius Lowenthal, claims attorney; Dr. Leonard Baum; and the family of Bernhard Behrend, who had settled on a farm at Narrowsburg, New York, in 1856 but moved to Washington in 1861. Behrend fathered one of the best known Jewish families in Washington. His sons were among the founders of Washington Hebrew Congregation. Benjamin Behrend married the daughter of Captain Levy, the first president of the congregation. Bendiza Behrend was one of the founders of Adas Israel Synagogue, in 1869, the city's second congregation. Adijah Behrend was one of the first Jewish doctors to practice in the city. Rudolph Behrend, Bernhard's grandson, was a prominent lawyer who served as master of ceremonies when President Calvin Coolidge laid the cornerstone of the new Jewish Community Center building in 1925.

On the eve of the Civil War there were some 200 Jews in the city of a total population of 75,000. The 1860 census showed that there were 52 Jewish families. During the Civil War many Jews from Baltimore and Philadelphia came to Washington seeking government employment or to engage in business. By 1862, the *Jewish Messenger* reported that there were 2,000 Jews in the city, but the 1863 wartime income tax records listed only 114 Jews. Some 120 Southern Jews who left the South to escape conscription in the Confederate Army or to join relatives in the North, were among the 16,000 people arrested in Washington during the war on charges ranging from spying and smuggling to secessionist sympathies. All of those arrested spent time in Old Capitol Prison. When they were released, some remained in Washington. Demobilized Union soldiers also stayed on in Washington while some Southern Jews who had been bankrupted by the war, came to post-bellum Washington to make a new start.

Among the war veterans who became Washingtonians were Leopold Karpeles, the first known Jew to win the Congressional Medal of Honor, and Benjamin Nordlinger, who had served in the Confederate Army. Karpeles, who received the nation's highest military award for heroism at the Battle of the Wilderness in May, 1864, was a color bearer who rallied the remnants of his regiment under a hail of fire. While convalescing in Providence Hospital, he met the daughter of Rabbi Simon Mundheim of the Washington Hebrew Congregation, one of the many local Jewish women who served as hospital volunteers. She became Karpeles' wife, and when she died he married her sister. Karpeles worked in the Treasury Department from 1875-1909. Nordlinger, who was wounded at the 2nd Battle of Bull Run, also convalesced in a Washington hospital. He was said to have served as a civilian chaplain in a Georgia regiment during the war. After the war he settled in Georgetown (then a separate city), where he opened a shoe store. In 1875 he was one of the founders of Georgetown's Mt. Sinai Congregation.

In 1861, the Washington Hebrew Congregation sought the aid of the Jews of Philadelphia and New York in carrying the burden of providing aid to the large number of Jewish soldiers on duty around Washington. Captain Levy personally appealed for help. Simon Wolf tried to establish a Jewish military hospital, while the ladies of the congregation served as volunteer nurses at Army hospitals. The tiny Washington Jewish community had 33 of its men in the Union Army.

Wartime growth made it necessary to seek a larger synagogue

and an appeal for funds was issued to other sects, with the endorsement of Mayor Wallach. In 1863, the congregation purchased the South Methodist Church, on 8th St., between H and I Streets. Financing this modest little frame structure was not easy, as evidenced by the congregation's request for funds to other Jewish communities. When the famed Rabbi Isaac Leeser of Philadelphia visited Washington to officiate at the Jewish community's memorial for President Abraham Lincoln, he criticized the inadequate attendance at the synagogue.

In 1862, Bernhard Behrend had written to the President asking that Jewish soldiers be freed from unnecessary work on Saturday as Christians were on Sunday, by Lincoln's order of that year. Nathan Grossmayer, another Washington resident, proposed in a letter to President Lincoln the establishment of a veterans' home, and offered $500 as an initial contribution. This gesture eventually led to the founding in 1866 of the National Military and Naval Asylum. The first proposal of a memorial to President Lincoln came from Lansburgh Brothers' store, together with an offer to give $500 toward the erection of a statue. By 1868 the money had been raised so that the statue, the first public monument to the martyred President, could be dedicated on the third anniversary of his death.

Not long after the Civil War, the Washington Hebrew Congregation erected a brick house of worship on the site of the former church it had acquired in 1863. Before the war other Jewish organizations had come into being. The Hebrew Literary Association was established in 1856, and a year later a lodge of the Free Sons of Israel was chartered. There was also the Literary and Dramatic Society, all of whose members were Jewish, that maintained its own library and sponsored lectures by Jewish and non-Jewish notables. The Elijah Lodge of B'nai B'rith was founded in 1864.

The city's second congregation, Adas Israel Synagogue, dedicated its first house of worship at 6th and G Streets, N.W., in 1878, in the presence of President Ulysses Grant and members of his cabinet. In 1897, Washington Hebrew Congregation built an imposing Moorish-style synagogue. President William McKinley and his cabinet participated in the cornerstone-laying. The attendance of Presidents Grant and McKinley at synagogue exercises set a precedent followed by other presidents. President Theodore Roosevelt addressed a meeting of the B'nai B'rith executive committee in 1903, in connection with protests over the Kishinev pogrom. President William Taft attended a joint meeting of the American Jewish Committee and B'nai B'rith leaders in the White House in 1911 to consider the Russian passport question. Taft made three speeches to B'nai B'rith audiences in Washington in 1910, 1911, and 1913. President Calvin Coolidge spoke at the dedication of the Jewish Community Center in 1925. President Harry Truman addressed a Jewish National Fund rally in the White House garden in 1952 and laid the cornerstone of the new Washington Hebrew Congregation sanctuary the same year. President Dwight Eisenhower spoke at the dedication of the synagogue in 1955. Presidents John Kennedy and Lyndon Johnson addressed B'nai B'rith Anti-Defamation League events in Washington. Richard Nixon, during his vice-presidency, participated at the dedication of the B'nai B'rith Building in 1957. Every president from Theodore Roosevelt to Gerald Ford received one or more Jewish delegations at the White House in connection with national and international Jewish problems.

Since the Civil War, Washington Jewry has had to cope with wars, crises, celebrations, conventions, demonstrations, and protest meetings in connection with almost all the epochal events of a century of Jewish history. But in 1861 the handful of Jews had neither the organization nor the resources to cope with the critical needs of the families of Jewish men who had enlisted in the Union Army, leaving behind penniless wives and hungry children who turned to their coreligionists for help. Nor was the community in any position to do very much in the way of welfare work for the large numbers of wounded Jewish soldiers from all parts of the country who were in Washington military hospitals. Food and clothing packages shipped from New York, Baltimore, Philadelphia, and the west were distributed, and some spiritual and morale services were provided, but the community could not do more. One thing, however, American Jewry was grateful for—their brethren in Washington faithfully provided traditional burials for all Jewish soldiers who died in Washington military hospitals.

The Civil War boom attracted Jewish business and professional men from all parts of the country and gave the community its first large growth in numbers. In 1875 there were 1,375 Jews in the city, many of the heads of families being employed in the government. At the turn of the century this figure had nearly doubled.

Shortly after President James Garfield was shot in a railroad station a few blocks from the Washington Hebrew Congregation and the Adas Israel Synagogue in 1881, the first prayers for his recovery were recited in both synagogues. Because there was no hospital in Washington to which the wounded President could be taken, he was removed to a hospital in New Jersey where he died. At a special prayer service for the President at Adas Israel Synagogue, Adolphus Solomons proposed that the city establish a hospital to be named for Garfield. The city adopted the idea and the first contributions toward the opening of Garfield Memorial Hospital came from the sisterhoods of the two Jewish congregations.

Until the 1880s the Jews of Washington were almost entirely of

German and Hungarian origin. The first trickle of East European Jews reached Washington in 1882. One of the first arrivals was Isaac Stearman, who later owned several stores at Forest Glen and Four Corners. Another was a *shohet* and *mohel* by the name of Yoelson, whose son became famous as Al Jolson, the well-known entertainer. Most of the Russian Jews who settled in Washington in the late 1880s and 1890s came via Baltimore where some had been employed in Jewish-owned clothing factories. The social, economic, and cultural needs of the growing number of East European immigrants gave rise to new Jewish organizations—synagogues, Hebrew schools, loan societies, Americanization agencies, and the United Hebrew Congregation Temple—a forerunner of the United Hebrew Relief Society. The latter was founded in 1890 and its direct descendant is the Jewish Social Service Agency. By 1907 the Jewish population stood at 5,100.

Rapid expansion of the city during and after World War I was paralleled by a major growth of the Jewish population. In 1917 it was 8,000, and in 1921 it had reached 13,782. In the 1920s and 1930s many Jews went into the real estate field, and later became important developers of suburban housing complexes and high-rise office and residential buildings that changed the city's skyline.

The New Deal and its many new agencies brought a large influx of young Jewish lawyers, social workers, scientists, and economists who became an important part of the government bureaucracy. World War II swelled the Jewish population further as the number of government workers expanded rapidly. Many of the Jewish employees who originally came to Washington on a temporary basis stayed on after the war and made careers in government or related fields. At the end of World War II, there were 25,500 Jews in the Greater Washington area and the spillover into the Maryland and Virginia suburbs had already begun, owing to housing shortages in the city. By 1948 the Jewish population had increased to 30,000. It continued to climb year after year. The 1950 figure was 45,000 and in 1956 it reached 80,000. In the 1950s many young Jewish male government employees found a shortage of young Jewish girls. One estimate was that these young men of marriageable age outnumbered Jewish young women of that age four to one. The situation had been different during World War I when the arrival of large numbers of single Jewish girls as government clerks created an immense oversupply of girls of marriageable age. A 1957 study by the Jewish Community Council of Greater Washington found that there were 89,000 Jews in the city and suburbs, representing 4.7 percent of the total population. About a third of the Jews were government employees and another third were professionals, many of them engaged in occupations that involved them with government.

Twenty years later an entirely new picture became evident. As the city expanded, mainly northward toward Rockville and Baltimore, the Jewish population moved in the same direction. In 1946, the suburban Jewish population was said to number 3,377 (1,450 households), with 400 families in Silver Spring, Maryland, 150 in Chevy Chase and Bethesda, Maryland, 700 in Arlington, Virginia, and 200 in Alexandria, Virginia. A 1973 report by the Institute for Jewish Policy Planning and Research of the Synagogue Council of America said that three-fourths of the Jews in the Greater Washington area had moved there since World War II, mostly as professionals in the government or in related organizations. Most of the Jewish families who filled up one suburban area after another had moved to Metropolitan Washington suburbs without ever residing in the city itself.

As the black population of the District of Columbia rose from 35 percent in 1950 to 71 percent in 1970, and the public schools became 90 percent black, Jews emulated other white families with school age children and poured into the Maryland and Virginia suburbs. The move to the suburbs was also influenced by the location of major government agencies employing large numbers of Jews in the Maryland suburbs. As the Greater Washington Jewish community expanded from the prewar level of about 20,000 to 120,000 in 1973, many synagogues dating from the prewar years relocated in the suburbs. The two oldest congregations, Washington Hebrew Congregation and Adas Israel Synagogue, retained many suburban members because of the congregations' prestige and wealth. Older, less affluent Orthodox and Conservative synagogues moved further uptown closer to the Maryland state line. At the same time, 15 new congregations were established in the inner and outer suburbs between 1962 and 1974. Some of the larger city congregations opened suburban branches of their religious schools. It was reported that 80 percent of the children confirmed at Washington Hebrew Congregation in the 1970s had Maryland suburban addresses.

The move to the suburbs also involved the community's major Jewish agencies. The United Jewish Appeal of Greater Washington, which is the community's federation, now has its offices in Chevy Chase, Maryland. The Jewish Community Center of Greater Washington, the Hebrew Home for the Aged, and the Jewish Social Service Agency occupy an $8 million complex in Rockville, Maryland. These agencies did not abandon the core city but moved in order to be of more service to the large majority who no longer lived in the city. The majority of Jews living in those areas of the city that are still predominantly white are older families whose children have grown up, singles, the divorced, and widowers and widows. The statistics show what happened: in 1956 half of the Jews in Greater Washington lived in the city proper. By 1966 only 20 percent lived there while more than half of the Jews, some 50,000, lived in the adjacent Maryland counties of Montgomery and Prince George. By the mid-1970s barely 15 percent of the Jews resided within the city, while 68 percent were located in the Maryland suburbs, and 17 percent in the Virginia suburbs.

Some city synagogues have made a determined effort to maintain a Jewish presence in the city in the face of the steady exodus to suburbia. The Jewish Community Council of Greater Washington has remained in the city. The B'nai B'rith, which was the first national Jewish organization to move its national headquarters to Washington in 1937, has added a new wing to its building. The headquarters of the Jewish War Veterans of the United States has enlarged its facilities. Reform Judaism's social action program is operated from Washington. The American Israel Public Affairs Committee and the Institute for Jewish Policy Planning and Research of the Synagogue Council of America have their offices in the city. Many of the major national Jewish organizations also have permanent offices fully staffed in the city in order to maintain contact with Congress, government agencies, and foreign diplomats.

Of the 48 synagogues in the Greater Washington area, only one has been organized in the city itself in recent years—Temple Micah, which shares facilities with a Protestant church in the rebuilt southwest section. Once the oldest area of Jewish settlement and later a slum, the whole section changed under the impact of massive urban development projects in the 1960s which brought new Jewish residents into the area.

Throughout its history, the Jewish community of Washington, D.C. has taken a special pride in the eminent Jewish figures who came to be part of the Washington scene by virtue of the offices they held in the Federal government. The imprint of these Jewish personalities—justices of the Supreme Court, cabinet members, members of both Houses of Congress, heads of major government commissions, consultants to government inquiries, and a second level among the unsung deputies, assistants, and administrative aides of government VIPs, as well as the contributions of Jewish engineers, architects, artists, and theatrical producers to the growth and beauty of the city, have left their mark on the city and the Jewish community.

Before Congress changed the status of the District of Columbia, which had long been voteless and unrepresented in Congress and was not even allowed to choose its own mayor, Walter N. Tobriner, a native of Washington and a former president of its Board of Education, served as chairman of the Board of Commissioners for the District of Columbia by appointment of President John Kennedy. This office was unofficially recognized as tantamount to mayor.

Other Washingtonians who held high local public office were:

U.S. Court of Appeals Judge Harold Leventhal; Federal District Court Judge Alexander Holtzoff and Harold H. Greene, Chief Judge of the District Superior Court; Milton Kronheim, Judge of the Court of Special Sessions; Nathan Cayton, Chief Judge of the Municipal Court of Appeals; Municipal Court Judge Nathan Margold; Municipal Court Judge Milton Strassburger; Otto Praeger, postmaster of the District in 1914; Isaac Gans, an original member of the A.B.C. Board; Gregory Hankin, chairman of the District Public Utilities Commission; David G. Bress, United States Attorney for the District of Columbia; David L. Bazelon, Chief Justice of the United States Court of Appeals for the District of Columbia; Joseph Singer, chief doorkeeper of the United States Senate; and Earl J. Silbert, first prosecutor of the original Watergate case and United States Attorney for the District of Columbia.

* * * * *

Adas Israel Synagogue, 2850 Quebec St., N.W., the city's second oldest congregation, occupied its present premises in 1951, after having worshipped for 43 years in a building at 6th and I Sts., N.W. Monumental in character, in keeping with the architecture of the Federal buildings, the synagogue's main facade has in its center a huge Menorah. A youth building on Porter St., adjoining the synagogue, is known as the Joseph A. Wilner Memorial Bldg., in tribute to a former president of the congregation. In the synagogue's Hall of Memories there hangs a collection of paintings and watercolors by the late Mykola Shramchenko, a Ukrainian Christian who lived in the household of a Jewish family and was arrested by the Nazis who considered him a Jew. He used his artistic talents to forge credentials for Ukrainian Jews attempting to escape from the Nazis. His paintings are a vivid representation of what he saw in Nazi concentration camps.

Adas Israel Synagogue Landmark, 3rd and G Sts., N.W., a national historical landmark by designation of the Department of Interior's National Register of Historical Places, is Washington's oldest synagogue building. A two-story red brick structure, it was dedicated in 1876 at services attended by President Grant. In 1908, the property at 5th and G Sts., N.W., was sold. Adas Israel moved into a new edifice at 6th and I Sts., N.W., where it worshipped until it occupied the Quebec St. site. The old building was successively occupied by the Greek Orthodox St. Sophia Church, an evangelistic church, a succession of other tenants, and finally by a fast-food barbecue shop which displayed over the former synagogue's door a neon sign outlined in the shape of a pig. When the entire block on which the old synagogue stood was acquired by the Washington Metropolitan Transit Authority for use as part of the new subway system, the Jewish Historical Society of Greater Washington began a series of moves to save the building from destruction.

The first step was to have the structure designated as a national historical site. An Act of Congress enabled the District of Columbia to acquire the building from the Transit Authority and lease it to the Jewish Historical Society. Once a new site was located, the Department of Housing and Urban Development gave the Jewish Historical Society a $100,000 matching grant for the renovation and restoration of the building on the new site to which it was moved on Dec. 18, 1969. The building has been completely restored to its original design. The restored sanctuary with its original Ark, woodwork, women's balcony, floors, doors, and at least one of its pews, is on the second floor. On the ground floor is the Albert and Lillian Small Jewish Museum of Washington, housing the library, archives, and artifacts of the Jewish Historical Society. The museum is named for Albert Small and his wife, whose substantial gift made possible the completion of the restoration work. Small is the son of the man who had helped build the 6th and I Sts. synagogue of Adas Israel.☐

Agudath Achim Cong. 6343 13th St., N.W.

American Israel Public Affairs Committee, 1341 G St., N.W.

Armed Forces Medical Museum, 6825 16th St., N.W., has an extensive collection of material relating to the contributions of many Jewish physicians to various branches of medicine. Among those represented in the museum are Dr. Simon Flexner, Dr. Jonas Friedenwald, Dr. Max Einhorn, Dr. Selman Waksman, Dr. J.F. Schamberg, and Dr. Joseph B. DeLee.

Bernard M. Baruch Bench, in Lafayette Park opposite the White House, is the park bench on which Bernard M. Baruch, advisor to presidents, often sat while working in his role of unofficial counselor (see South Carolina). The bronze plaque embedded in a granite monument beside the bench was sponsored by the Boy Scouts of America.

Behrend Park, 4200 Benning Rd., at Blaine St., N.W., memorializes Suevia and Rudolph B. Behrend, members of an old Jewish family, who were closely associated with the District of Columbia Youth Gardens, whose members are the principal users of the park. Behrend, long identified with the Jewish Community Center of Greater Washington, was master of ceremonies when President Coolidge laid the cornerstone of the center's original building on 16th and Q Sts. in 1925.

B'nai B'rith Building, 1640 Rhode Island Ave., N.W., international headquarters of the oldest and largest Jewish service organization in the world, houses in addition to offices, the Klutznick Exhibit Hall and the B'nai B'rith Library. The latter is a research library on human rights and Jewish history. The Klutznick Exhibit Hall, named for Philip M. Klutznick, a former president and one-time U.S. Ambassador to the United Nations Economic and Social Council, is Washington's first Jewish museum. The exhibit hall seeks to tell the story of Jewish contributions to American life and to portray the development of the American Jewish community since 1654. Among the notable items on permanent exhibit is the famous letter George Washington wrote to the Hebrew congregation at Newport, R.I., a collection of letters from American presidents to B'nai B'rith, and the Joseph Horwitz and Abram Kanof collections of Jewish ceremonial objects, both modern and traditional 17th to 19th century pieces. The hall's art gallery offers monthly shows of the works of leading Jewish artists, as well as a wide variety of historical exhibits. The gift shop has the largest selection of books, prints, ceremonial objects, coins, jewelry, china, and glassware of Jewish interest in the Washington area. When Richard M. Nixon was vice-president, he was the principal speaker at the dedication of the building in 1957. Also on exhibit is Phillip Ratner's *Four Covenants Triptych*. The triptych, three large paintings portraying the history of the Jewish people, was a gift from Harry S. Wender and his wife on B'nai B'rith's 120th anniversary. The glass sculptures entitled *Sholom* and *Commodore Uriah P. Levy*, by Herman Perlman, are on permanent dispaly, and were also gifts of the Wenders who own one of the city's notable private collections of Jewish art.

Bureau of Printing & Engraving, 14th and C Sts., S.W., the world's greatest paper money manufacturing installation. There can be seen, among other things, the original plate of the one-dollar bill on the back of which appears the Great Seal of the U.S., showing the 13 stars grouped in the form of a perfect Star of David.

Morris Cafritz Memorial Hospital, 1310 Southern Ave., S.E., is named for the late Jewish civic leader and philanthropist, whose wife Gwen was one of the city's leading hostesses for many years.

Cardozo High School, 13th and Clifton Sts., N.W., is named for the late Benjamin Cardozo, Justice of the Supreme Court of the U.S. The neighborhood around the school is known as the Cardozo Area.

Emanuel Celler Portrait, in the Judiciary committee room of the House of Representatives, honors the Brooklyn Congressman who headed the committee for nearly 25 years and served in the House for 50 years (less a few months)—a record only surpassed by one other Congressman.

Center for Religious Action, 2027 Massachusetts Ave., N.W., also known as the Emily and Kivie Kaplan Center, is the Washington headquarters of Reform Judaism, and the base from which the Union of American Hebrew Congregations carries on its social action and social justice activities. Kaplan, a Boston businessman and a leading supporter of civil rights organizations, was for several years the president of the National Association for the Advancement of Colored People (NAACP).

Combined Congregations, 6405 16th St., N.W.

Cong. Beth Sholom, 13th St. and Eastern Ave., N.W., has an interior lobby and Ark made entirely of stone quarried in Israel. The 200-year old Eternal Light was made by Jewish craftsmen in Venice, Italy.

Cong. Ezras Israel, 7101 7th St., N.W.

Cong. Kesher Israel, 1134 25th St., N.W.

Cong. Ohev Sholom, 1600 Jonquil St., N.W., is housed in a gleaming white building that is entered through a 24-foot high archway.

Cong. Tifereth Israel, 7701 16th St., N.W.

Department of Justice Building, Pennsylvania Ave., between 9th and 10th Sts., N.W., has on the walls of its two-story library, Maurice Sterne's painting, *The Judgement of Solomon* as part of a giant mural on the general theme of the "Search for Truth."

Farbrengen, 2027 Massachusetts Ave., N.W., a Jewish counterculture movement that seeks a Judaism divorced from establishment synagogues and community, and appeals to young people who are alienated by organized congregations. It meets in the Kivie Kaplan Center.

Folger Shakespeare Library, 201 East Capitol St., has on its white marble exterior facade, bas relief sculptures of characters from nine of Shakespeare's plays, among them *The Merchant of Venice.* From this play, the bas relief shows Shylock, ready with his knife.

Ford Theatre Museum, 511 10th St., N.W., has among its extensive Lincolnia collection a portfolio of facsimiles of documents on *Lincoln and the Jews,* produced by the B'nai B'rith Jewish Historical Committee.

Foundry Methodist Church, 1500 16th St., N.W., has two stained glass windows incorporating the Star of David and a Menorah.

Freer Gallery of Art, 12th St. and Independence Ave., S.W., has among its collections a painting of Noah's Ark.

Georgetown University Law Center houses part of the Harry Wender collection of paintings on the theme of justice. One painting by Phillip Ratner is a heroic work showing Justice with scales surmounted by a jury of unidentified members with vignette portraits of the Warren Supreme Court, including Justice Arthur Goldberg. Another Ratner painting, the *Supreme Court,* includes oil portraits of the Warren Court sitting with Justice Felix Frankfurter. A Ratner bas relief, *Judicial Tryptich* depicting blind Justice with scales, a judge in robes, and a Moses with the Tablets of the Law, is also on display.

Samuel Gompers House, 2122 First St., N.W., home of the late labor leader, is a registered historic place.

Gompers Memorial, 10th St. and Massachusetts Ave., in Samuel Gompers Memorial Park, was erected by the American Federation of Labor through contributions from its members, and dedicated by President Franklin D. Roosevelt on Oct. 7, 1933. Of bronze and marble, the monument shows Gompers, the English-born Jew who was one of the founders and for nearly 40 years the president of the AFL, seated in front of three allegorical figures representing unionism, fraternalism, and brotherhood. In the main lobby of the AFL-CIO Building, 815 16th St., N.W., there is a circular wood carving of Gompers. His portrait hangs on the 8th floor of the building.

Gompers, born in 1850, became a cigarmaker and emigrated to this country in 1863. Joining the Cigarmakers Union and the National Labor Union in 1870, he won his trade union spurs in these early labor organizations. He was among the early exponents of craft unionism and helped organize the Cigarmakers International Union and the Federation of Organized Trades and Labor Unions. When the AFL was formed in 1886, he was chosen its first president. It was Gompers who led and helped win the battle against sweatshops and starvation wages. He succeeded in outlawing the company union and labor injunctions and defeated the first Communist attempt to control the American labor movement. During World War I, he served on the Council of National Defense, winning status for the unions by his patriotic mobilization of labor behind the war effort. When he died in 1924, the AFL had grown to a membership of 5,000,000. Gompers won his place in history as one of the leaders who had helped set American labor free.□

Health, Education, and Welfare Dept. Building, 330 Independence Ave., N.E., displays in the foyer leading to the Secretary's office, portraits of the two Jews who served as Secretary of Health, Education, and Welfare, Abraham Ribicoff and Dr. Wilbur J. Cohen. Ribicoff, a former governor of Connecticut and a one-time member of the House of Representatives, was named to the Cabinet by President Kennedy, and served from 1961-1962, when he was elected to the U.S. Senate. Cohen, who held the office under Presidents Kennedy and Johnson, is credited with having drafted part of the original Social Security legislation when he began his government service in 1935. After serving as assistant to the commissioner of Social Security and director of the Social Security Statistics Division, Cohen became professor of public welfare at the University of Michigan. President Kennedy appointed him chairman of the task force on health which submitted a report which ultimately led to Medicare. When President

Johnson signed the Medicare Act, he presented the pen he used to Cohen.

Hebrew Home for Aged, (see Rockville, Md.)

Joseph Hirshhorn Museum and Sculpture Garden, 7th St. and Independence Ave., to 9th St. and Madison Dr., an integral part of the Smithsonian Institution, is a huge, four-level, doughnut-shaped structure that houses more than 8,000 sculptures and paintings representing significant examples of many of the major artists of the last 100 years. The collection was amassed by Joseph Hirshhorn, an immigrant from Russia who made his fortune in uranium mines in Canada. He donated the collection to the people of the U.S. Valued at anywhere from $50 to $100 million, the gift was accepted by President Lyndon Johnson on May 17, 1966, after which Congress set aside a site and appropriated more than $15 million for construction of a building to house this collection. Hirshhorn also contributed a million dollars to the building fund. The museum is a striking building of white marble, 231 feet in diameter (larger than a city block), with an adjoining sunken garden bisecting the mall. The museum rests on a podium 300 feet long and 400 feet wide. The outdoor sculpture garden, located in a plaza sunk seven feet below grade level to preserve the vista from the steps of the Capitol to the Washington Monument and Lincoln Memorial, displays most of the larger sculptures in the collection. The garden, the first of its kind, was suggested by Mrs. Lyndon B. Johnson. President Johnson and Chief Justice Earl Warren officiated at the groundbreaking and President Ford did the same at the dedication in 1974. On the museum grounds there is a 200-foot aluminum structure entitled *Needle Tower,* by J. Snelson, which features concentric Stars of David.

House of Representatives Prayer and Meditation Room, a tiny nonsectarian chapel just off the Capitol rotunda, halfway between the House and Senate chambers, was opened in 1955 by House Concurrent Resolution No. 60, authored by Representative Brooks Hays of Arkansas, and adopted in May, 1954. Once a cloakroom, the 17-foot square chapel was carefully designed and equipped to reflect the American concept of separation of church and state and respect for religion. There is no sign on the entrance door. Inside the room intended for prayer and meditation by members of Congress, is a stained glass window. The center panel depicts the kneeling figure of George Washington, representing the people of the U.S. in prayer. The upper and lower panels show the reverse and obverse sides of the Great Seal of the U.S., the latter showing the 13 stars within the halo above the eagle's head grouped in the form of a perfect Magen David. Immediately below the upper panel is the inscription, "This Nation Under God." In the two corners of the oval window are shown a candle and a book, representing the Bible. Between them is a quotation from the 119th Psalm, "Thy word is a lamp unto my feet and a light unto my path." A white oak altar contains an open Bible and two vases of freshly cut flowers. Shielded wall lights and two seven-armed candelabra illuminate the room.

Opening the Prayer and Meditation Room was delayed for some months in order to change the design of the stained glass window to eliminate a scroll prominently shown in the original design, along with a candle and open Bible. The scroll was criticized on the ground that it might have been regarded as depicting the Torah, thus conflicting with the desire to maintain a wholly nondenominational decor in the chapel which would not offend any religious group. Ten years after the room was opened, it was the scene of the first, and to date, the only Rosh Hashanah services ever held in the Capitol. It was on Sept. 28, 1965 that ten Jewish members of the House, led by Rep. Herbert Tenzer of Lawrence, N.Y., participated in private first day Rosh Hashanah services. The service in the House chapel became necessary because the first day of Rosh Hashanah coincided with the beginning of debate on a bill that the White House said was a "must." Speaker John McCormack agreed that the Jewish members of Congress could use the chapel since there was no synagogue within walking distance of the Capitol. Rabbi Hyman Shapiro of Long Beach, N.Y., officiated, and Cantor Aryeh Maidenbaum of Tenzer's own synagogue, Cong. Beth Sholom of Lawrence, N.Y., was the cantor. Orthodox, Conservative, and Reform prayer books were available. When the service was over at 11:15 A.M., the Jewish members of the House went to the House chamber to vote, and since voting in the House is by voice, no writing was required. □

I.F.A. Gallery, 2623 Connecticut Ave., N.W., displays and sells original prints by Israeli artists.

Israel Embassy, 1621 22nd St., N.W., houses the mission of Israel to the U.S. When the U.S. granted *de jure* recognition to Israel on May 14, 1948, this mission became the first foreign embassy of the Israel Government. Apart from offices, the embassy has a large hall for receptions and a permanent display of Israeli handicrafts, newspapers, and magazines. The embassy's walls are decorated with Israeli pictures and paintings, among them the famous *Jacob's Dream* by Ardon Bronstein.

Jaffa Gate, 5512 Connecticut Ave., N.W., exhibits and sells original prints and sculptures by Israeli artists.

Thomas Jefferson Memorial, south bank of Washington Tidal Basin, has a striking sculptural panel depicting the father of religious liberty in America reading the first draft of the Declaration of Independence to a committee of the Continental Congress. On the four panels within the Memorial Room are inscribed inspirational quotations from Jefferson's writings, expressing his philosophy of liberty, including religious liberty. The quotation on religious liberty reads:

Almighty God hath created the mind free. All attempts to influence it by temporal punishments or burthens. . .are a departure from the plan of the Holy Author of our religion. . .No man shall be compelled to frequent or support any religious worship or ministry or shall otherwise suffer on account of his religious opinions or belief, but all men shall be free to profess and by argument to maintain their opinions in matters of religion. I know but one code of morality for men, whether acting singly or collectively.

Jewish Chapel Downtown, Room 621, 1404 New York Ave., N.W., holds midday worship services and provides a place to say Kaddish in the business district.

Jewish Community Center of Greater Washington, (see Rockville, Md.).

Jewish Community Council of Greater Washington, 1330 Massachusetts Ave., N.W.

Jewish Social Service Agency, (see Rockville, Md.).

Jewish Week, 744 National Press Building.

Justice Department Bldg., Pennsylvania Ave., bet. 9th and 10th Sts., N.W., has on the walls of its two-story library, Maurice Sterne's huge mural on the general theme of "The Search for Truth," a panel, *The Judgment of Solomon.* In the Attorney General's office a place is reserved on the walls for a portrait of Dr. Edward H. Levi, former president of the University of Chicago, and great-grandson, grandson, and son of rabbis, who was appointed Attorney General by President Gerald Ford in 1975, the first Jew to hold this office.

A.S. Kay Spiritual Life Center, at American University, Massachusetts and Nebraska Aves., houses the headquarters of all student religious associations on the campus, including the Hillel Foundation at American and Georgetown Universities. The center is named for Abe Kay, one of the city's leading philanthropists and builders, who helped change the city's skyline.

John F. Kennedy Center for the Performing Arts, a memorial to President Kennedy, overlooking the Potomac River on Rock Creek Parkway, houses a unique gift of Israeli art in the concert hall lounge, which is used by the President of the U.S. and other dignitaries. The art covers the walls and ceiling of the lounge adjacent to the concert hall, on the balcony level. The room's interior, valued at more than $500,000, was designed by Ralph Blumenfeld, one of Israel's leading architects. The art displays three different media, all following the theme of music in Biblical stories. The north wall is covered by panels of carved walnut, two feet thick, created by Nehemiah Azaz. The huge wood sculpture, 20 feet long and 20 feet wide and carved to a depth of nine inches, depicts some 43 of the musical instruments mentioned in the Bible. The other three walls carry mural panels of heavy cream-colored silk done in sepia ink by Ezekiel Kinche, and depicting scenes of life in modern Israel. A ceiling mural by Shraga Weil describes Biblical scenes remembered for the part music played in them, such as the trumpets at Jericho and King David's lyre. The Israeli flag flies in the center's Hall of Nations, which is decorated with the national emblems of every country recognized by the U.S. Leonard Bernstein's *Mass,* composed at the request of Mrs. John F. Kennedy, had its world premiere the night the Kennedy Center opened, Sept. 8, 1971. The concert hall was opened by the National Symphony Orchestra under the baton of Antal Dorati, Hungarian-born Jewish conductor, with Isaac Stern as soloist. Julius Rudel, the Austrian-born music director of the concert hall, conducted the world premiere of Albert Ginastera's *Beatrice Cenci,* while wearing in his jacket lapel the gold leaf symbol of Palmach, which he received for directing the Israel Symphony Orchestra in the Negev.

Labor Department's Hall of Fame, in the lobby near the office of the Secretary of Labor, on the 3rd floor of the Department of Labor Building, 14th and Constitution Ave., N.W., has a series of plaques commemorating memorable achievements in labor-management relations. One plaque is a tribute to the Amalgamated Clothing Workers Union, founded and for many years led by Sidney Hillman, and then by his successor, Jacob Potofsky, and another to the Jewish-founded and owned Hart, Schaffner & Marx clothing manufacturing company of Chicago, for "fifty-years of constructive contribution to the private democracy of labor-management relations." Nearby is a portrait of Arthur J. Goldberg, Secretary of Labor from 1961-1962.

Library of Congress Annex, east of the Main Bldg., on 2nd St., S.E., houses on the first floor the Hebraic Section, the greatest collection of Hebrew books, manuscripts, documents, and pamphlets under government auspices. Although the library was collecting works in Semitic languages from its very inception in 1800, it was not until 1914 that a separate Hebraic section was established by an Act of Congress. The Hebraic section originated with the gift of 19,936 volumes and pamphlets brought together over a period of many years by the world traveler and bibliophile, Ephraim Deinard, and presented to the library in 1912 by Jacob H. Schiff (see New York). In 1914 Schiff enlarged this collection with an additional gift of 4,200 volumes. Two more collections totaling 5,500 volumes were acquired in 1917 and 1921. Today the Hebraic section numbers nearly 100,000 items in

Hebrew, Yiddish, Ladino, Aramaic, Syriac, Ethiopic, and other languages, plus 250,000 volumes in Western languages that deal with Hebrew, Semitic, Biblical history, literature, civilization, Israel, Jewry throughout the world, Judaism as a religion, and Zionism. The Hebraic section includes virtually every edition of the Bible and Talmud published in most languages since the 16th century; an extensive collection of Responsa, prayer books, over 600 Haggadahs from all parts of the world, some dating back almost five centuries; literature of the golden age of Jewish letters under Arab rule in the Middle Ages; Hebrew poetry; rare pamphlets and incunabula; the most complete collection outside of Israel of official printed matter relating to Israel; Biblical manuscripts; items on modern Hebrew literature; and several thousand Yiddish monographs, brochures, newspapers, and periodicals from many countries.

Library of Congress Main Building, 1st St., bet. E. Capitol and B Sts., N.E., has many individual items and collections of great Jewish interest. On the first floor, in the visitor's gallery, there is a statue of Moses by Charles H. Niehaus. ●The dome of the main reading room has, among other symbolic figures, one that represents Judea, shown as a woman lifting her bonds in ecstatic prayer to Jehovah. The overgarment she wears falls partly away and reveals the ephod, a vestment worn by the High Priest in the Temple in Jerusalem, ornamented with a jeweled breast-plate on which are engraved the names of the 12 Tribes of Israel. On the face of a stone pillar set beside her is inscribed in Hebrew the injunction from Leviticus 19:18: "Thou shalt love they neighbor as thyself." ●Among recent collections acquired by the library are: 75,000 papers of the late Dr. J. Robert Oppenheimer, who headed the group of scientists working on the first atomic bomb project (see New Mexico); 300 volumes of the papers of Samuel Gompers, the great labor leader; the manuscripts of Dr. Alfred Adler, one of the founders of modern psychiatry; the personal papers of Edward L. Bernays, numbering 250,000 items, which trace the rise of public relations; the personal papers and correspondence of Groucho Marx; the papers of the late Supreme Court Justice Felix Frankfurter; a collection of rare books worth more than $1 million, presented by Lessing J. Rosenwald, the library's greatest benefactor; and the Lenore and Charles E. Feinberg Walt Whitman Collection. ●Thanks to the late Barney Balaban, film industry leader, the library possesses one of the original 14 copies of the Bill of Rights. The library never owned an original copy. The originals were given to the 13 states and the National Archives. Because the copy owned by the latter had deteriorated badly and only Virginia and Connecticut still owned their original copies, Balaban's gift (purchased at an auction sale), on Feb. 21, 1945, was an historic acquisition by the Library. The Balaban copy of this cherished document of American liberties is on permanent display in a special shrine near the exhibit of originals of the Declaration of Independence and the Constitution until their removal to a permanent resting place in the National Archives. •Among the Library's hundreds of Bibles is the 500-year-old, illustrated manuscript Bible known as the Great Bible of Mainz, hand-lettered and illuminated at the exact time and in the same place as Gutenberg printed his Bible. The Great Bible of Mainz was given to the Library in 1952 by Lessing Rosenwald, son of Julius Rosenwald (see Chicago). •In the Library's manuscript collection is a receipt dated Dec. 24, 1781, signed by Daniel Boone, showing that he received "six pounds specie" from Jacob J. Cohen and Isaiah Isaacs of Richmond, for staking out a 10,000 acre tract these Jews owned in Kentucky (see Richmond, Va.). The Library has a collection of George Gershwin's most valuable original manuscripts, presented in accordance with the will of his mother. Included in the collection are the original penciled score of *Rhapsody in Blue;* full ink score of *Porgy and Bess;* and the pencil draft of the *Concerto in F.* •The Library also houses and administers the Serge Koussevitzky Music Foundation, established by Serge Koussevitzky, the eminent Jewish conductor and his wife, to stimulate the creation and study of 20th century contemporary music. •In the Library's art collection are Enrico Glicenstein's six dry-points of Old Testament figures. •Also in the Library are 95 miles of audio tape containing the entire proceedings of the four-month trial of Adolph Eichmann in Israel.

Eugene Meyer Elementary School, 11th and Clifton Sts., N.W., on the site of the old Garfield Hospital, is named for the late publisher of the *Washington Post* who headed the War Industries Board under Presidents Coolidge and Hoover.

Military Chaplains Association of U.S.A., 7758 Wisconsin Ave., N.W., has in its national headquarters a large plaque honoring the memory of more than 300 chaplains in the U.S. Armed Forces who were killed in action or died while on active duty from the Revolutionary War through the Korean War. The Jewish chaplains listed are: Alexander D. Goode, one of the famed four heroic chaplains of World War II, April 17, 1943; Irving Tepper, August 13, 1944; Nachman S. Arnoff, May 9, 1946; Frank Goldenberg, May 22, 1946; Henry Goody, Oct. 19, 1943; Samuel D. Hurwitz, Dec. 9, 1943; and Louis Werfel, Dec. 24, 1943.

National Archives, Pennsylvania and Constitution Aves., bet. 7th and 9th Sts., N.W., has among its historic letters one from Prof. Albert Einstein to President Roosevelt first alerting him to the work on a uranium nuclear chain reaction by which "vast amounts of power and large quantities of new radium-like elements would be generated"—a phenomenon which led to the construction of atomic bombs. ●Under the dome of this building in a specially constructed shrine, is the permanent home of the Bill of Rights, the first ten Amendments to the Constitution, including the one establishing religious liberty, and of the original drafts of the Declaration of Independence and the Constitution. ●Also on display here is the text of the surrender of Nazi Germany in May, 1945, and the Emancipation Proclamation, which was first made public in a telegraphic message tapped out from the War Department's telegraph office by Edward Rosewater (see Nebraska). ●Permanently on file among the Federal government's valuable documentary records are many of great Jewish interest, including Presidential, State Department, and diplomatic statements on Jewish rights abroad.

National Gallery of Art, Constitution Ave., bet. 4th and 7th Sts., N.W., an internationally famous treasure house of art, displays the priceless Lessing J. Rosenwald Collection containing more than 20,000 examples of graphic art. It includes more than 30 important early illuminations from manuscripts, a number of famous early drawings, an exceptionally fine collection of early German woodcuts, many rare 15th century engravings, as well as superb impressions of all the great masters of graphic art, i.e., Durer, Schongauer, Cranach, Rembrandt, Goya, Daumier, etc. ●Among the paintings to be seen in the National Gallery are: Savaldo's *Elijah Fed by the Raven;* Piazetta's *Elijah Taken Up in a Chariot of Fire;* Bacchiacca's *Finding of Moses;* Mantegna's *Judith and Holofernes;* Durer's *Lot and His Daughters;* Rubens' *Meeting of Abraham and Melchizedek;* Veronese's *Rebecca At the Well;* and two sculptures of David by Delliano and Verrochio.

National Historical Wax Museum, 4th and E Sts., S.W. includes among its historical tableaux one that shows the four heroic chaplains of World War II, including Rabbi Alexander D. Goode, surrendering their lifebelts to GIs, and going down with their torpedoed military transport. In the Hall of Americans, Albert Einstein and Henry Kissinger are represented.

National Jewish Welfare Board, 1012 14th St., N.W.

National League of Women Voters, 1026 17th St., N.W., displays on a framed parchment in its national headquarters, the names of 72 of the most distinguished American pioneers in woman suffrage, among them Ernestine Rose (see New York), a Polish-born daughter of a rabbi who from 1840 until her death in 1892, was in the vanguard of the struggle for women's emancipation.

National Portrait Gallery, F and G Sts., from 7th to 9th Sts., N.W., housed in the old Patent Office, was created by Congress in 1962 for "the exhibition and study of portraiture and statuary depicting men and women who have made significant contributions to the history, development, and culture of the people of the United States and of the artists who created such portraiture and statuary." Included are statues of Dr. Isaac Mayer Wise, founder of the major institutions of American Reform Judaism, Dr. Albert Einstein, and a portrait of Mrs. Golda Meir, former prime minister of Israel. ●Also on exhibit: a sculpture by William Zorach, eminent sculptor and painter, of his 13-year old daughter; a bronze of Raphael Soyer, sculptor, by his brother Eugene, and another of William Zorach; a sculpture of William and Marguerite Zorach by Rhode Sherbel; a self-portrait of the painter Alfred Maurer; a majestic sculpture of King Saul by William Wetmore Story; a painting *Moses Viewing the Promised Land* by Robert W. Weird; a sculpture of the late Ben Shahn, sculptor and painter, by his son, Jonathan; Ben Shahn's underpainting of a mural for a housing development in Roosevelt, N.J., that includes Albert Einstein, the Triangle Shirt Waist Fire (see New York), and labor leaders; a sculpture of Albert Einstein by Joseph Scharl; and Jo Davidson's sculptured heads of Samuel Gompers and of Otto Kahn, banker and art patron.

National Press Club, 14th and F Sts., N.W., displays in one of its corridors an autographed photograph of Mrs. Golda Meir, presented to the club the day the then Prime Minister of Israel spoke there by Harry Wender, Washington attorney and art collector. In the library of the club, which is a rendezvous of the capital's editors and correspondents, is a woodcut of the prophet Jeremiah, by the Israeli artist, Jacob Steinhardt, presented by an Israeli and an American Jewish journalist as a symbol of American-Israeli friendship. Among the reproductions of historic front pages from American newspapers on display in the club's foyer is one from the *Jewish Daily Forwrd.*

National Shrine to Jewish War Dead, 1712 New Hampshire Ave., N.W., houses memorabilia, souvenirs, and records of military achievements by American Jews from Colonial days to the present. In the Hall of Heroes are portraits of Jewish fighting heroes from various wars, some of the decorations they were awarded, and a small chapel with a portable Ark. The shrine was dedicated in 1955 by the then Vice-President Richard M. Nixon. In the same building is the national headquarters of the Jewish War Veterans of the U.S., and its ladies auxiliary. The JWV is the oldest existing veterans organization in the U.S.

Navy Memorial Museum, Washington Navy Yard, Main Gate at 9th and M Sts., S.E., has an exhibit of the achievements of Dr. Albert A. Michelson, U.S. Naval Academy graduate, who won the Nobel Prize in Physics in 1907 for first measuring the speed of light. Also on display are models of nuclear submarines designed by Admiral Hyman Rickover, father of the nuclear submarine; a navy belt buckle worn by Commodore Uriah P. Levy; and a two-man Nazi submarine with a swastika still visible.

New York Presbyterian Church, 1313 New York Ave., N.W., displays in a specially fabricated case in the Lincoln Parlor of the church which Abraham Lincoln attended, the original manuscript of Lincoln's first proposal leading to the Emancipation Proclamation. The handwritten document was presented to the church by Barney Balaban, film executive, on Dec. 20, 1951 and was dedicated by President Eisenhower on Feb. 13, 1953.

Oak Hill Cemetery, 30th and R Sts., is the last resting place of John Howard Payne, composer of *Home Sweet Home,* and grandson of Aaron Isaacs, an early Jewish settler on Long Island (see Long Island, N.Y.).

Organization of American States, N.W. cor. 17th St. and Constitution Ave., N.W., home of the Inter-American agency once known as the Pan-American Union, has two busts of the late Dr. Leo S. Rowe, life-time exponent of Pan-American friendship, who was director-general of the Union from 1920 until his death in 1946. This Iowa-born Jew had much to do with overcoming anti-American feeling in Latin America. From the time President McKinley named him head of a commission to revise and codify the laws of Puerto Rico in 1899, Rowe was identified with every major effort to achieve Pan-American unity. He served as delegate to scores of Pan-American congresses, was Assistant Secretary of the Treasury for two years, and chief of the State Department's Latin-American Affairs Division. One bust of Dr. Rowe, with the inscription of "a citizen of the world," stands in the Hall of the Americas. The other is in the director-general's office.

Polock House, 2109 Pennsylvania Ave., N.W., was one of a group of buildings erected in 1796 by Isaac Polock, the earliest known Jewish resident in the nation's capital. In 1800, when the government established itself in the District of Columbia, contemporary reports said that the most prominent landmarks between "the President's House" and Georgetown was the group of buildings known as "the six buildings." The structure at 2109 Pennsylvania Ave., which was once part of "the six buildings," is now occupied by Billy's III, a bar and restaurant.

Post Office Department Building, S.W. cor. Pennsylvania Ave. and 12th St., N.W., has in the stamp exhibit room the original designs of almost every stamp issued by the U.S. since 1847, including seven that honor Jews. The first was the 3¢ Joseph Pulitzer Commemorative, issued in 1947 on the 100th birthday of the great editor and publisher. Pulitzer, born in Hungary of a Jewish father and a Catholic mother, came to the U.S. during the Civil War, and served as a private in the Union Army. After the war, he settled in St. Louis where he became a reporter on a German language daily and then editor and publisher of the *Post-Dispatch.* In 1883 Pulitzer moved to New York, after purchasing the *New York World,* which he built into one of the country's great newspapers. He was elected to Congress in 1885 but resigned halfway through his term because of illness which culminated in blindness. Pulitzer never considered himself a Jew; nor did the Jews regard him as one of them, but his enemies assailed him as a Jew and he is identified as of Jewish origin in all reference works. ●The second stamp containing reference to a Jew was the 3¢ Four Chaplains Commemorative, issued in 1948 in honor of Chaplains George J. Fox, Clark V. Poling, John P. Washington, and Alexander D. Goode (see Pennsylvania). Across the top of this stamp are the words: "These Immortal Chaplains. . .Interfaith in Action." ●The third stamp, issued in 1950, was the 3¢ Samuel Gompers Commemorative, honoring the great labor leader on the centennial of his birth. ●The fourth stamp, an 8¢ issue, bore the likeness of Albert Einstein. ●The fifth was an 8¢ commemorative bearing a large profile of George Gershwin, one of the immortals of American music, and a montage of characters from his folk opera, *Porgy and Bess.* ●The sixth stamp of Jewish subject matter is one of Haym Salomon, the Polish-Jewish patriot of the American Revolution who was included in a four-stamp set honoring unheralded persons who played important roles in the American Revolution. It was issued in March, 1975. ●The seventh is a 13¢ commemorative honoring Adolph S. Ochs, publisher of *The New York Times* from 1895 until his death in 1935. Issued in September, 1976, it has a likeness of Ochs. ●A 6¢ stamp honoring the astronauts who landed on the moon has the first words from the Hebrew Bible, "In the beginning. . ."

Raphael House, 1305 Fern St., N.W., is the first and so far as is known the only orthodox superivsed home for the emotionally disturbed.

Red Cross World War I Memorial, 1730 E St., N.W., a memorial to the heroic women of World War I, was made possible by a Congressional appropriation and contributions from noted Americans, among them Mortimer Schiff. Among the historic objects housed in the Red Cross Museum, 17th St., bet. D and E Sts., N.W., are many mementoes of Adolphus S. Solomons. It was in his Washington home that the first meeting to organize the American Red Cross was held. In 1881, President Arthur named Solomons and Clara Barton as the American representatives to the first International Red Cross Congress in Geneva. In the museum may be seen Solomons' passport and calling card, the State Department commission of appointment, a letter from Clara Barton, and a dinner invitation from the President of Switzerland. Solomons headed the publishing house of Philips and Solomons in Washington, which did much of the government printing until the Government Printing Office was established. It was in Solomon's establishment that the last known photo of Abraham Lincoln was taken, sharpening a pencil for his son. A prominent figure in the city's life for nearly 40 years, Solomons served in the District of Columbia House of

Representatives when the city first had its own government. He declined President Grant's offer of an appointment as governor of the District of Columbia. In 1891 Solomons became the general agent of the Baron de Hirsch Fund in the U.S. He was also active in the organization of the Jewish Theological Seminary of America. •In the Red Cross World War I Memorial, large individual contributors are memorialized, among them: Mortimer Schiff (see New Jersey); Eugene Meyer; Otto Kahn, banker and art patron; Adolph S. Ochs, publisher of *The New York Times* (see Tennessee); Felix M. Warburg, communal leader and philanthropist (see New York); Simon Guggenheim, mining tycoon (see Colorado); George Blumenthal, New York civil leader; Julius Garfinckel, Washington merchant; Haskell Levy; Jacob Epstein, Baltimore art patron (see Maryland); and Simon Stein, clothing manufacturer. One of the 12 white marble columns in the war memorial building—all memorials to American womanhood—bears the inscription: "To the Women of the Jewish Welfare Board." This column is on the east side of the building.

SMITHSONIAN INSTITUTION
National Museum of History and Technology,
Constitution Ave., between 12th and 14th Sts., N.W.

•Dibner Library of the History of Science and Technology, a gift in 1975 of Bern Dibner, Russian-born Jewish electrical engineer and manufacturer, was at that time one of the most extensive and important private collections of instruments, manuscripts, and books documenting the history of science and technology. The gift was estimated to be worth many millions of dollars. In the collection of more than 25,000 rare books, letters, and experimental devices, are 200 publications which were epochal in the history of the physical and biological sciences. Among the items are several manuscripts of Sir Isaac Newton; 10 surviving manuscript pages from Darwin's *Origin of the Species;* Einstein's corrected proof summary of his general theory of relativity; and a copy of Pliny's *Historia Naturalis,* published in Venice in 1461, and considered the first published book on science.
•World of the Newspaper Cartoon section: there are representative drawings by Al Capp, creator of L'il Abner; Rube Goldberg; and Herblock, whose political cartoons are world famous.
•American Masters area: there are five prints by Aaron Siskind, five by Lee Friedlander, and a silver print portrait by Henry Leach Robinson of Samuel Adam Salomon (1811-81). On the wall is a long shot of the crowd entering Warner Bros. Theatre in Hollywood. Over the marquee is a large billboard picture of Al Jolson in *The Jazz Singer,* the first successful feature film with sound.
•In the Newsroom there is a lighted sign with the heading

"OCHS SAVES FAILING N.Y. TIMES." On the International News Wall there is a photo of Adolph S. Ochs telephoning, with the caption, "the first regular transatlantic phone call was made by Adolph Ochs, publisher of *The New York Times,* to Geoffrey Davis, editor of the *London Times.*" On the photogravure wall is a picture of Sarah Bernhardt, the great French actress. In the printing area is an offset lithograph machine described as the first practical offset press invented about 1904 by Ira W. Rubel of Nutley, N.J., and Alex Sherwood of Chicago. Rubel also pioneered offset printing on paper, building his first press in 1903-04. Rubel's offset press of 1905 is on exhibit.

•Graphic Arts section, Print Reference Room: the half-tone screens invented by Max and Louis Levy of Philadelphia can be seen. The Levys, who invented the levytype photoengraving process and perfected the manufacture of the half-tone screen, are credited with making possible the wide use of half-tone screens.

•Hall of Medical Sciences preserves a number of items relating to Dr. Selman Waksman, discoverer of streptomycin and 1952 Nobel Prize winner in medicine. Among them: the innoculating needle he used to isolate and transfer the first strains of streptomyces griseus which produced streptomycin; a sample of actinomycin, the first antibiotic produced by an actinomyces; notebook pages (replica copies by Dr. Waksman from his original notes), which describe four crucial experiments establishing the nature and effectiveness of streptomycin; and samples of streptomycin. •In the U.S. Drug Store Segment there are old furnishings provided by Sydney N. Blumberg and Mischel H. Wagman. •In the Bacteriological Research Laboratory there is a portrait of Dr. Simon Flexner, noted medical educator, and the microscope, laboratory table, cabinet, and chair used by him at Rockefeller University, of which he was the first president. •In the same section there are portraits of Paul Ehrlich, best known for his discovery of salvarsan, a specific against syphilis, and Robert Koch, who proved that the anthrax bacillus causes specific disease.

•Triumph Over Disability Area: there is a pencil drawing by disabled Kathy Kahn. There is also an acrylic and watercolor by her of Dr. Jonas E. Salk administering vaccine from deactivated polio virus to the first child. Nearby, is a picture of Dr. Albert B. Sabin, who also developed a polio vaccine from weakened live virus that could be taken orally.

•In the Hall of Rehabilitative Medicine there is a heart pacemaker donated and used by Dr. Adrian Kantrowitz, one of the pioneers in heart transplants.

•Hall of Petroleum has a 57-foot mural depicting the history of the petroleum industry, that includes a portrait of the late Jacob Blaustein, who, with his father, built American Oil Co. (AMOCO) from a one-horse and wagon operation in Baltimore to an industrial giant. He later became president of the American Jewish Committee.

●Hall of American Merchant Shipping has a ⅛-scale model of the SS *President Warfield,* a one-time Chesapeake Bay passenger boat which was renamed the *Exodus* and became one of the fleet of Haganah ships which brought illegal immigrants to Palestine. The plaque, attached to the model, presented by the American Veterans of Israel, describes the role of the *Exodus* in the epic of the Jewish underground railway during the years just preceding the birth of Israel in 1948.

●Division of Engineering has in its reference collection many of the inventions of Emil Berliner. Among these is a reproduction of the original microphone he invented in 1877. It was this Jewish, German-born physicist whose development of the loose contact transmitter made Bell's telephone a practical instrument. A decade after Edison invented the phonograph in 1877, it was still largely a toy until Berliner's invention of the disk record, much like those in use today, made the talking machine a reality. Berliner's patent was incorporated in the Victor talking machine. He was also the inventor of the present method of duplicating disk records, and of the acoustic tile for soundproofing. A pioneer in dealing with public health problems, he was one of Washington's most beloved citizens for three decades.

●Hall of Electricity has the original laser developed by Theodor Maiman, and a ¼-scale model of Heinrich Hertz performing an experiment.

●In the Reference Collection are early selenium cells invented by Samuel Wein for use in translating voices photographically recorded back into sound; some of the more than 600 electrical devices invented by William Dubiler; the first reading machine, invented by Jacob Rabinow; and a 1910 model of "an adding and subtracting machine," invented by Rabbi Judah L. Levin of Detroit.

●Hall of Nuclear Energy displays a bronze sculpture of Albert Einstein's head and exhibits items related to his theoretical work. ●Also on exhibit here is the cyclotron used by Leo Szilard and Walter Zinn, Jewish physicists, in the experiment on March 3, 1939 which demonstrated for the first time that large-scale nuclear energy was practicable. This test was crucial in persuading the Federal government to subsidize further atomic research that led to the building of the atomic bomb. The atomic beam apparatus, which involved the measurement of the spin of atomic nuclei, developed by Dr. Isador I. Rabi, a Columbia University Nobel Prize winner in physics in 1944, and Dr. Victor W. Cohen, physicist at the Brookhaven National Laboratory, is also on view here.

●Postal History Museum has on display a number of items relating to Capt. Benjamin Lipsner, pioneer aviator who was the first to suggest Federal airmail service to be operated by the Army Air Corps.

He was the pilot of the first plane to carry mail. Also here are the first pieces of automated sorting equipment invented by Jacob Rabinow to be used by the Post Office.

●Division of Numismatics displays many examples of modern Israeli coinage.

●Division of Political History displays 12 of Max Kalish's bronze statuettes of notable American leaders of World War II, including Bernard M. Baruch. A statuette of Henry Morgenthau, Jr., is part of 36 other Kalish statuettes that are in the reference collection.

●Nation of Nations Exhibit displays among hundreds of items depicting the growth of the United States, the upright piano on which Irving Berlin composed the songs *White Christmas* and *Easter Parade,* and a pair of old levis developed by Levi Straus, one of the California gold rushers.

(A number of Jewish religious objects and artifacts identified with Jews, normally on exhibit in the various museums that make up the Smithsonian Institution, are included in the "The Nation of Nations" exhibit on display at the National Museum of History and Technology from June 1976 to June 1981. Among the more than 6,000 items on display are a Decalogue used in 19th century Philadelphia; silver Torah bells made by Myer Myers, Colonial Jewish silversmith; Irving Berlin's piano; Eddie Cantor's makeup kit; and neon signs from kosher restaurants.)

National Museum of Natural History,
Constitution Ave. at 10th St.

●Hall of Gems and Minerals has on display the 44½ carat Hope diamond, donated by Harry Winston, noted jeweler. Winston also gave the museum an 875-carat uncut emerald, said to be the finest in the world.

●Department of Anthropology, Reference Section, has the famous *Bat Creek Stone,* excavated in Loudon County, Tenn., in 1885, which has strange writings on it which some anthropologists claim is proof of the early arrival in North America of Semitic people.

●Judaism Ceremonial Objects from the Near East and North Africa, in Hall 7, Peoples of Asia and Africa, consists of several cases of ceremonial objects of the Kanof Collection, a gift of Dr. and Mrs. Abram Kanof.

Air and Space Museum,
10th St. and Independence Ave., S.W.,

On display is the first successful monoplane, *Walden II,* invented by Dr. Henry Walden, a Jewish dentist who was an aviation pioneer. The first light monoplane made its maiden flight in Mineola, N.Y., in 1909. The museum also owns models of Dr. Walden's first radio-controlled guided missile. Walden held patents for more than 100 inventions, among them a coffee-packing machine and animated electric signs, including the one that flashed news bulletins on the former Times Tower in Times Square, New York City. ●Also on display are a number of photos of Arthur L. Welsh of Washington, D.C., who was one of the first students of the Wright Brothers Flying School at Montgomery, Ala. In 1911, Welsh became a flying instructor and helped train the late Henry A. Arnold, later famous as "Hap" Arnold, first chief of the U.S. Army Air Corps. The pictures show Welsh with some of his tropies and in early model planes. He met his death on June 11, 1912 while testing a new military biplane. ●The Charles A. Lindbergh plane, *The Spirit of St. Louis,* which he used for the first solo flight across the Atlantic, is on display here. It was powered by an engine designed in part and built by the late Herman B. Ring, assistant to the president of the Wright Aeronautical Corp.

●Other items of Jewish interest in this museum are: The B-29 bombers that dropped the first atomic bombs on Hiroshima and Nagasaki in August, 1945. The radar officer on the bomber *Enola Gay* which exploded the first atomic bomb over Hiroshima was Lt. Jacob Beser, a one-time rabbinical student from Baltimore. The bombardier in the second plane over Nagasaki was Lt. Charles Levy of Philadelphia; Emil Berliner's helicopter, a 1924 invention that was a landmark in vertical flying machines; the model of the *Delgado Flash,* a small airship named for Isaac Delgado, a New Orleans philanthropist (see Louisiana), which broke the world's record for planes of its size and class; and a model of the celebrated airship invented by Otto Lilienthal, a German-Jewish scientist, whose 1894 craft is universally recognized as one of the pioneer lighter-than-air ships.

●The 250-seat theatre or Spacearium, a gift to the U.S. on its Bicentennial from the Federal Republic of Germany, is named the Albert Einstein Spacearium at the specific suggestion of the West German Government which said that the famous physicist and Nobel Prize winner was "the most significant person of German extraction to contribute to the study of the cosmos." Einstein, who renounced his German citizenship after Hitler's rise to power, also held Swiss citizenship which he acquired in 1910. After he settled in the U.S. in the 1930s Einstein became an American citizen.☐

Spingarn High School, 24th St. and Benning Rd., N.E., a public high school once open only to black students, is named for Joel Elias Spingarn, poet, critic, book publisher, educator, and army officer, who was one of the small group of Jews that helped found the National Association for the Advancement of Colored People in 1909. One-time head of the Department of Comparative Literature at Columbia University, Spingarn was president of the NAACP from 1930 until his death in 1939. The Spingarn Medal, awarded annually to an American Negro for outstanding achievement, is named for him.

State Department Building, 21st St. and Virginia Ave., N.W., has at the west end of the Diplomatic Lobby a large memorial plaque honoring the more than 80 American foreign service officers who lost their lives "under heroic and tragic circumstances." The following Jews are among those memorialized: Alfred M. Gottschalk, 1918; Robert K. Franzblau, 1967; Frederick J. Abramson, 1968; and Thomas M. Gompertz, 1968. ●In the reception hall outside the Secretary's office, space has been set aside for the portrait of Secretary of State Henry Kissinger. ●In the Department's Division of Protocol is the seal of the U.S., the obverse face of which shows the 13 stars within the halo above the eagle's head, grouped in the form of a perfect Magen David. This seal is the national arm and emblem of authority and it appears on all official documents, medals, currency (the one dollar bill), official stationery, above the entrance to U.S. embassies, legations, and consulates, and on army service caps and uniform buttons. Until 1882, each star in the seal was also a six-pointed Star of David. Many efforts have been made to explain the meaning of the Magen David on the seal, but there is no authoritative interpretation of this feature beyond the Act of Congress of June 20, 1782, fixing the design of "the Great Seal for the United States." When the Continental Congress in 1776 appointed Benjamin Franklin, Thomas Jefferson, and John Adams as a committee to prepare a design for the Great Seal, they submitted a sketch depicting the exodus of Israelites from Egypt and their passage through the Red Sea under the leadership of Moses, with the Egyptians in pursuit. This theme reflected the parallel which the founding fathers of the Republic saw between the American Revolution and the redemption of Israel from Egyptian slavery. The design was not acted upon by Congress, nor did they act upon another design prepared by Jefferson. The second design showed the children of Israel being led through the wilderness by Moses. The final design adopted in 1782 provided for the 13 stars above the escutcheon, without indicating how the stars should be arranged.

Oscar S. Straus Memorial, on the Great Plaza in front of the Commerce Department Building, 14th St., bet. Pennsylvania and Constitution Aves., N.W., honors the first Jew to serve in a President's Cabinet. A circular fountain flanked by two pedestals supporting allegorical figures, the memorial was dedicated Oct. 26, 1947, with President Truman accepting it on behalf of the nation. Oscar S. Straus, younger brother of Nathan and Isidor Straus (see New York), was the son of Lazarus Straus of Otterburg, Germany, who first settled in Talbottom, Ga., before the Civil War. Impoverished by the war, he moved his family to New York where he launched the business that ultimately led to the Straus family ownership of R.H. Macy.

Oscar Straus was a lawyer by profession, a merchant by family tradition, and a civic leader and historian by inclination. He was one of the founders of New York's 92nd St. YM-YWHA in 1874, and of the American Jewish Historical Society in 1892, of which he was president for a number of years. Appointed U.S. Minister to Turkey in 1887 by President Cleveland, Straus held the same post under Presidents McKinley and Taft. From 1902 until his death in 1926 at the age of 76, Straus was one of the American members of the Permanent Court of Arbitration at The Hague. In 1906, President Theodore Roosevelt named him Secretary of Commerce and Labor. When Roosevelt ran for president in 1912 on the Bull Moose ticket, Straus was the Bull Moose candidate for governor of New York. In a central position on the terrace around the memorial's fountain is a bronze plaque on which is inscribed a resumé of the public positions held by Straus. □

Supreme Court Building, E. Capitol and 1st Sts., N.E., displays portraits of three of the five Jews who have served on the Supreme Court bench. A bust of Louis D. Brandeis is in the West Conference Room, and an oil portrait hangs in the ground floor exhibit hall. There is a bronze bas-relief of Benjamin N. Cardozo in the east end of the Lawyers Library, and an oil portrait in the ground floor exhibit area. Felix Frankfurter's portrait also hangs there. The Court does not yet have portraits of Justices Arthur J. Goldberg and Abe Fortas, but provision has been made to display them. •Brandeis (see Kentucky), was the first Jew named to the Supreme Court, serving from 1916 when President Wilson appointed him, until his retirement in 1939. •Cardozo was appointed to the Court by President Hoover in 1932, to fill the vacancy left by the retirement of Oliver Wendell Holmes. Ranked with John Marshall, Joseph Story, and Holmes among the ten greatest judges in American history, Cardozo came to the Supreme Court with a towering reputation. He had been a judge of the New York State Supreme Court for only a few weeks in 1913 when he was elevated to the Court of Appeals, which he served on until his designation to the Supreme Court. From 1927-1932 Cardozo was Chief Justice of the Court of Appeals, New York's highest court. His decisions on the state and federal benches made legal history and his opinions have been acclaimed as models of English writing. A loyal Jew, Cardozo numbered among his forebears Gershom Mendes Seixas, the patriot minister of the Revolution, and a certain captain in the Revolutionary Army. Cardozo was a member of New York's Shearith Israel Congregation and the second Jew to serve as a trustee of Columbia Univer-

sity. His ancestor, Hazzan Seixas, was the first. Cardozo died in 1938.
●Frankfurter, who was appointed to the Court in 1939 by President Franklin Roosevelt to fill the seat formerly held by Brandeis, had no previous judicial record. His influence on law and government, however, had been far-reaching through the many students he taught at Harvard Law School and who subsequently filled key posts in the government. Born in Austria in 1882, Frankfurter was 12 when he came to the U.S. He served as an assistant U.S. Attorney in New York, was on the staff of the War Department's Bureau of Insular Affairs, and acted as chairman of the War Labor Policies Board during World War I. Before and after his elevation to the Supreme Court, Frankfurter was regarded as an intimate advisor of President Roosevelt and an important figure in what was known as the New Deal "Brain Trust." Government officials whose appointments were said to have been influenced by Frankfurter were dubbed "New Deal hot dogs." Like Justice Brandeis, with whom he was associated in Zionist leadership and with whom he was allied in the historic events that led to the issuance of the Balfour Declaration in 1917, Frankfurter took an active part in Jewish affairs until he sat on the bench. He died in 1965. ●Arthur Goldberg, who was Secretary of Labor from 1961-1962 under President Kennedy, succeeded to Frankfurter's seat on the Court when the latter resigned in 1962. Goldberg left the Supreme Court at the insistence of President Johnson who appointed him senior U.S. delegate and ambassador to the United Nations in 1965. He resigned after two years and served a year as president of the American Jewish Committee. In 1970 Goldberg ran on the Democratic ticket for governor of New York, but was defeated by the incumbent, Nelson Rockefeller. ●Abe Fortas was appointed to the Supreme Court in 1965 and later named Chief Justice by President Johnson. However, before he could be confirmed by the Senate, he was forced to resign because he had accepted lecture fees while on the bench. One of Johnson's closest friends, Fortas wrote a number of historic decisions while on the Supreme Court. ●Moses, together with Solon and Confucius, lawgivers of the past, are the central figures of the pediment on the east front of the nation's supreme temple of justice. The two medallions on the west side facing the Capitol are presumed likenesses of Moses and Hammurabi. In the elaborate courtroom, the south wall is decorated with a procession of historical lawgivers, including Moses and Solomon.

Temple House (or House of the Temple), 16th and S Sts., N.W., a huge building that is the world headquarters of the Supreme Council of the Ancient and Accepted Scottish Rite of Freemasonry, Southern Jurisdiction, has in the center of the square temple room a great altar of black and gold marble on the front side of which are inscribed the

Hebrew words "God said, Let there be light, and there was light." The temple was erected in 1911 on the 110th anniversary of the founding of the Supreme Council in Charleston, S.C., under the leadership of Emanuel de la Motta, whose portrait hangs in one of the temple corridors. De la Motta was an active member of Congregation Beth Elohim in Charleston. Born in what is now the Virgin Islands in 1761, De la Motta was one of four Jews of the original nine founders of the Supreme Council. He was its first treasurer-general. Abraham Alexander served as secretary-general, and Israel Delieben and Moses C. Levy were inspectors-general. De la Motta is buried in Charleston's Coming Street Cemetery, one of the oldest Jewish burial grounds in America. •In the Temple library is the Simon Wolf Collection of Hebraica and Judaica, bequeathed by Simon Wolf. On terms of personal friendship with every president from Lincoln to Harding, Wolf was for two generations a key figure in virtually every effort involving diplomatic intervention to protect Jewish rights abroad and in legislation and hearings affecting immigration to the U.S. For many years he acted as the Washington representative of and spokesman for the Union of American Hebrew Congregations, B'nai B'rith, and the American Jewish Committee. He was the channel through which official and unofficial representations were made to Washington. President Grant appointed him recorder of deeds of the District of Columbia, and President Arthur named him consul general to Egypt. Wolf's library originally consisted of some 1,000 volumes on Jewish history, but the Supreme Council added to it over the years. Also in the Temple library is a collection of Hebrew manuscripts assembled by Albert Pike, a non-Jew, who was grand master of the Council from 1859-1891, and a respected Hebrew scholar.

Temple Micah, 6th and M Sts., S.W., in Washington's reconstructed southwest section, shares the facilities of St. Augustine's Episcopal Church on a joint partnership basis. The permanent arrangement was entered into in 1972 after five years of a tenant-landlord relationship. The rabbi occupies an office adjoining that of the church's vicar. The two congregations have alternate use of meeting rooms for religious school and other functions, as well as the worship hall. Temple Micah paid for the structural modifications and shares in the annual cost of the chapel's overall maintenance. Except for a unique four-section Ark for the Torahs, the sanctuary has no permanent religious symbols of either faith. The large bronze Maltese cross that forms the base of St. Augustine's free-standing altar is covered by a frontal during Jewish services. The only other permanent symbols are twin redwood signs on the lawn, the *mezuzahs* on the doorpost, and a centuries-old baptismal font in the forum. In the early days of the reconstruction of southwest Washington, it was generally believed that

Jews would not be attracted to the new neighborhood. When the redevelopment authorities sought to reserve a site for synagogue use, the offer was not accepted by the Jewish community agencies. But once it became apparent that Jews were settling as tenants and homeowners, Temple Micah was organized in 1963 as the Southwest Hebrew Congregation. Outside there is a Menorah five feet by eight over the front door and a simple Latin cross tops the open-sided steeple.

Temple Sinai, 3100 Military Rd., N.W.

Treasury Department Building, 15th St. and Pennsylvania Ave., N.W., has in the office of the Secretary of the Treasury a portrait of Henry Morgenthau, Jr., who served in this post longer than any man in history with the exception of Albert Gallatin. The second Jew to be a member of the Cabinet, Morgenthau was appointed by President Franklin Roosevelt and served all through the New Deal, World War II, and for four months under President Truman. Morgenthau had been a lifelong friend of Roosevelt. He was conservation director when Roosevelt was governor of New York. Morgenthau came to Washington in 1933 as chairman of the Federal Farm Board, later moving up to the governorship of the Farm Credit Administration, and Under Secretary of the Treasury. As Secretary of the Treasury he raised nearly $37 billions. Son of Henry Morgenthau, Woodrow Wilson's ambassador to Turkey, Morgenthau, Jr. became national chairman of the United Jewish Appeal after the war, and later headed the Israel Bond drive. He was also chairman of the Franklin D. Roosevelt Memorial Foundation.

United Jewish Appeal Federation of Greater Washington (see Chevy Chase, Md.)

Veterans of Foreign Wars National Memorial Building, at intersection of Maryland and Constitution Aves., and 2nd St., N.E., has in its assembly room a gallery of past national commanders-in-chief, including Paul C. Wolman of Baltimore, who held the office from 1930-1931, and Max Singer of Boston, who held it from 1941-1942.

War College, 4th, Main and P Sts., S.W., has in the library a bust of Bernard M. Baruch (see South Carolina), erected in honor of his services as chairman of the War Industries Board during World War I.

Washington Hebrew Congregation, Massachusetts Ave. and Macomb St., N.W., the oldest Jewish congregation in the city, worships in a modernistic synagogue dedicated on May 6, 1955 at ceremonies addressed by President Dwight D. Eisenhower. President Truman was the speaker on Nov. 16, 1952 when the congregation marked its centennial by laying the cornerstone of the new building. A stone used 2,000 years ago in the Wall of Agrippa, one of the defensive walls surrounding ancient Jerusalem, was among the items placed in the cornerstone. In the lobby is the treasured original charter of the congregation issued by Congress in 1857 and signed by President Franklin Pierce. President McKinley participated in the cornerstone laying ceremony of the congregation's former temple at 8th and I Sts. N.W., in 1897. The main sanctuary is noted for the large white marble Ten Commandments which serve as the doors to the Ark, and for its massive 500-pipe organ. Adjacent to the sanctuary is an art gallery which includes Elbert Weinberg's heroic statues, *The Processional,* Van Leon's *The Judge,* Alcalay's *The Burning Bush,* and Jim Dine's *Creation.* In Ring Hall is the Hyman J. Cohen Judaica Collection.

Washington Monument has at least one stone that was paid for by funds raised among American Jews in a campaign sponsored in 1871 by the New York *Jewish Messenger.* Although the cornerstone of the great shaft was laid in 1848, lack of funds prevented the completion of the monument until 1885. In the interim, many fundraising devices were employed, including an effort to get individuals, organizations, and states to buy stones. It was during one of those periodic drives that the *Jewish Messenger* undertook to solicit American Jewry. Somewhere in the monument is a copy of the *American Advertiser* containing the text of Washington's Farewell Address. It was owned by Naphtali Phillips, a Jewish reporter for the *Advertiser,* a New York daily, who stood near the press as the issue was being printed, and kept the first copy for himself. Fifty years later, when New York City proposed its own monument to Washington, Phillips offered his prize memento and it was placed in the cornerstone. This memorial, however, was never erected. When Congress authorized the monument in Washington, New York presented its cornerstone and the Phillips gift as a permanent part of the Washington Monument.

Washington National Cathedral, 1728 Massachusetts Ave., near Wisconsin Ave., N.W., has at the rear of the south nave, over the tomb of President Woodrow Wilson, a huge stained glass window dedicated to Samuel Gompers, a founder and first president of the American Federation of Labor. Donated by the AFL-CIO in memory of three labor giants of different faiths, (Gompers, a Jew; William Green, a Baptist; and Philip Murray, a Catholic), the window is known as *The Artisans and Craftsmen Window.* Among the eight scenes in the window are Noah building the Ark and the building of King Solomon's Temple. The *Law Window,* a tribute to the legal profession, shows Moses the Lawgiver as the central panel. The high altar of the cathedral, a Protestant shrine, is known as the Jerusalem Altar because it is built of 12 stones from King Solomon's quarry in Jerusalem. Also in the cathedral is an ancient manna pot from the synagogue of the Chinese Jews of Kaifeng; oak choir stalls depict the Ark of Noah, the discovery of the infant Moses in the bulrushes, David and Goliath, a statue of King David and his lyre, and Ruth with a sheaf of wheat.

George Washington University, Lisner Hall, 2033 G St., N.W., is a six-story structure housing the university library. It was a gift of Abraham Lisner, a Washington merchant who served on the university's board of trustees for 27 years. ●The Charles B. Smith Center for Physical Education and Athletics, named for Charles B. Smith, a university trustee, real estate developer, and Jewish Communal leader. In the lobby there is a profile of Smith in relief and a plaque citing him as a humanitarian and civic leader.

The White House has a number of Jewish artifacts. In the library is an old siddur belonging to the late Rabbi David de Sola Pool of New York's Shearith Israel Congregation, the oldest existing congregation in the Western Hemisphere. ●On display in the China Room is a set of seven plates depicting the seal and the several buildings of the Touro Synagogue in Newport, R.I., the oldest existing synagogue building in the U.S. The handmade sketches on the plates are the work of Mrs. Esther Oppenheim of Kings Point, L.I., who presented the plates to President Eisenhower in 1954 on behalf of the Shearith Israel Congregation. The artist was the 12th generation to worship in that historic synagogue. The presentation was made in connection with American Jewish Tercentenary. ●Somewhere in the White House there is an antique Chanukah Menorah rescued from Nazi Germany and presented to the White House during President Kennedy's administration by the National Council of Young Israel. ●A famous portrait of Benjamin Franklin, done in 1767 by David Martin, and valued at $200,000, was given to the White House by Walter Annenberg, then publisher of the *Philadelphia Inquirer* and U.S. Ambassador to Great Britain during the Nixon administration. ●A sculptured head of President Franklin D. Roosevelt, a gift of Max Band, an internationally known Jewish artist, was accepted for the White House in 1961 by President Kennedy. ●In what was then the office of the secretary to the Cabinet, but is now used for other purposes, there hangs a portrait of Maxwell Rabb, who, under President Eisenhower, served as the nation's first secretary of the Cabinet. ●A handmade Menorah, a gift of Israel's Knesset, is also in the White House.

Wholly Bagel Coffeehouse, a project of the Tzedek, Tzedek Collective, which meets at Quaker House, 2121 Decatur Pl., N.W., is a popular gathering place for Jewish young people.

MAINE

A marine from Maine is one of the heroes of whom the United States Marine Corps sing as they recall their exploits "from the Halls of Montezuma to the shores of Tripoli." He was Joseph Israel. In 1804 he gave his life in an almost forgotten daring act of bravery on the shores of Tripoli. During America's naval war with the Barbary States of Algeria, Tunis, Morocco, and Tripoli, Commodore Edward H. Preble and Captain Stephen Decatur planned to destroy the Tripolitan fleet by exploding a small boat loaded with explosives in Tripoli's harbor. When the call went out for volunteers to man the fittingly named vessel, the *Intrepid*, 6 men stepped forward. One of these was Israel, a young marine from Portland, Maine.

Loaded to the gunwales, the *Intrepid* sailed on its fateful mission under cover of darkness. The tiny ship reached the harbor of Tripoli safely and the fuses were lit, but before the crew could get away, a premature explosion carried all six marines to their deaths. Israel's role in this mission is recorded in a letter from Commodore Preble.

When Lieutenant Israel (whose Jewishness has not been definitely established), lived in Maine it was still a district of Massachusetts. Admitted to the Union in 1820, Maine barred any religious test as a qualification for public office in its first constitution. Although 82 years elapsed before a Jew was elected to office, Jews were no strangers in Maine.

Families with remotely Jewish antecedents, such as the Moses, Abrams, Campanals, and Decosters, have been prominent in Maine for nearly two centuries, and lone Jewish traders from Massachusetts undoubtedly traveled through the Maine towns in the early 1800s and later. The first known Jewish resident on record was Susman Abrams, a native of Hamburg, Germany, who settled at Waldborough during the Revolutionary War. He also lived at Thomaston and Union at various times. While there is no documentary proof that he embraced Christianity, Abrams did marry a Christian and, until his death in 1830 at the age of 87, was a faithful attendant at church.

A history of Maine published in 1832 does not mention Jews among the state's religious sects, however, by the early 1840s there was already a Jewish community of considerable size in Bangor. These Jewish settlers were engaged in various retail businesses catering to the workers in the lumber industry centered around Bangor: When the prime timbering areas had been cut and the industry moved west, almost all of the Jews departed, too. They were there long enough, however, to organize the state's first Jewish congregation, Ahabat Achim, in the 1850s. The earliest modern Jewish settler was Haiman Philip Spitz, who had been one of the founders of the Boston Jewish community.

Spitz came to Bangor in 1848 when the lumber industry was at its peak, and opened a clothing store that catered to the lumberjacks. He was followed by five other Jewish families whose living came from clothing and dry goods stores, and peddling. Moses Silber was the first president of Ahabat Achim and Spitz was vice-president. When the lumber industry declined during the panic of 1856-57, the congregation and the pioneer Jewish community disintegrated. Captain A. Goldman, of Bangor, who served with Maine's 17th Regiment during the Civil War, was probably a member of one of the Bangor families.

Immigrants from Eastern Europe who settled in Portland and in the factory towns of Lewiston, Auburn, Bangor, and Waterville founded the present Jewish community in the early 1880s. The Jewish population must have been considerable by 1884 since in that year the State Legislature liberalized the Sunday closing law to permit Jews who kept their places of business closed on Saturdays to work at their regular trades and vocations on Sundays.

There is no agreement as to which community established Maine's oldest existing synagogue. When the Union of American Hebrew Congregations took a census of the country's Jewish population in 1877, it listed a synagogue in Portland, but the government's religious census of 1890 reported no Jewish congregations anywhere in Maine. The Portland Hebrew School was founded in 1884. The *American Jewish Year Book* for 1901 reported seven towns in Maine with one or more Jewish institutions and with synagogues in Biddeford, Rockland, Portland, Lewiston, Bangor, and Auburn. Bangor's Congregation Beth

Israel erected the state's first synagogue in 1890. Biddeford had a congregation in 1892, and Auburn in 1897.

By 1912, Maine had over 5,000 Jews, nearly half in Portland. In 1917 there were 7,387 Jews in the state. Portland had 3,650; Lewiston, 1,100; Auburn, 825; Bangor, 1,650; Biddeford, 250; Bath, 180; Rumford Falls, 176; Waterville, 215; Rockland, 90; and Gardiner, 80. There were also 25 other towns with ten or more Jews. Twenty years later, the Jewish population had risen to 9,000. The 1954 population figures showed little change. In the early 1970s there were 8,190 Jews in the state, with Portland accounting for 3,500.

In 1975 there were one or more synagogues in Auburn, Bangor, Bath, Aroostock, Biddeford, Lewiston, Old Orchard, Old Town, Portland, Rockland, and Waterville. There were Jewish federations in Portland, Lewiston-Auburn, and Bangor; Jewish Community Centers in Portland and Lewiston-Auburn; and Hillel Foundations at the University of Maine and Bates College.

The Grossman family of Quincy, Massachusetts, have revitalized industrially declining towns in Maine such as Limerick, Passamaquoddy, and Sanford. They have bought and sold industrial properties in Maine and used the profits to revitalize whole communities. They have restored over 2,500 square feet of abandoned industrial areas and put it to constructive use at a cost of over a million dollars. Louis Bernstein of Portland, son of one of the 1880s immigrants, served as president of the board of overseers of Bowdoin College, the state's oldest university, in the early 1970s. He also served as president of the Higher Education Assistance Foundation of Maine. Bernstein was the first president of the Portland Jewish Community Center. The Lipman brothers of Augusta were among the leading poultry raisers in that part of the state, and Israel and Maurice Stein operated the Maine Egg Farms at Auburn.

The first Jew elected to public office in the state was Harry Taylor, who served on the Portland Board of Aldermen, 1902-04, and in the State Legislature, 1904-06. Louis Kaplan was elected tax assessor of Portland in 1910. Max L. Pinansky of Portland, who was a municipal court judge (1927-31) and a member of the State Senate (1934-36), served as a member of the Maine Public Utilities Commission. Albert Abramson, who had been a professor of economics at Bowdoin College, was the state's WPA director from 1936-1940. Edward Glaser was a judge of the Bangor City Court 1926-30; Louis Bernstein was a member of the Portland Civil Service Commission and judge of the Municipal Court; Barnett Shur served as Portland city attorney. Simon Spill and David Berman held a similar office in Biddeford and Lewiston, respectively. Ben L. Berman was state's attorney for Androscoggin County and his brother, Jacob Harrison, was state's attorney for Cumberland County and United States Commissioner for Maine. Herman S. Gerrish was chairman of the Old Orchard Board of Selectmen. The late Abraham M. Rudman of Bangor, the first Jew to serve on Maine's Superior Court, 1955-1965, was also the first Jew on the State Supreme Court, 1965-1970. William S. Cohen, who was elected to Congress from Maine's 2nd District in 1970 and 1972, and formerly served as mayor of Bangor, is a half-Jew raised by his Christian mother as a Unitarian. Cohen, who reads and writes Hebrew and quotes from Jewish sources, learned Hebrew from his Jewish father—a baker in Bangor. In the 1970s, Bennett D. Katz of Augusta was in the State Senate. Alan S. Grossman of Rockland served as first chief justice of the Maine Probate Court, 1970-75.

AUBURN
Cong. Beth Abraham, Laurel Ave. and Main St.
Jewish Community Council (see Lewiston).

BANGOR
Community Chapel, Center St., between Cumberland and Garland, is one of the three community-sponsored Jewish funeral chapels (the others are in San Francisco and Passaic, N.J.) in the United States. The chapel stands on almost the exact spot where Bangor's first synagogue was erected in 1890.
Cong. Beth Abraham, 145 York St.
Cong. Beth Israel, 144 York St.
Cong. Toldos Itzhock, 37 Essex St.
Hebrew Academy of Bangor, 28 Somerset St.
Jewish Community Council, 28 Somerset St.

BATH
Cong. Beth Israel, 862 Washington St.

BIDDEFORD
Cong. Etz Chaim, Bacon St.

CARIBOU
Aroostock Hebrew Cong., 1 Sumner St.
"Blotner Radar Ballistics Site" are the words on a sign on U.S. Highway 1, halfway between Caribou and Van Buren. The site was donated to the U.S. Air Force by Samuel Blotner, a dealer in government surplus property. In 1962 he acquired from the General Services Administration the surplus Nike-Ajax missile site. A year later, when the Air Force wanted to buy back the control section of the base for a

radar ballistics installation, Blotner asked $30,000 and the government offered $5,000. Blotner then offered it for one dollar if the Air Force would name the site for his father and erect a sign to that effect. The exchange also provided that if the Air Force again decided to leave the site, the property would revert to Blotner.

CUSHING

Olson House Museum, overlooking the mouth of the St. George River, where Christina and Alvaro Olson died, was bought and restored at a cost of $300,000 by Joseph Levine, film producer and art collector. It was converted into a museum for the paintings of Andrew Wyeth, who immortalized Christina Olson in his best known painting, *Christina's World*. Levine also contributed 20 Wyeth paintings from his own collection.

HANCOCK

Pierre Monteux Memorial Foundation is named for the late French-born Jew who was for many years conductor of the San Francisco Symphony. He made his home in this seaside town for many years. The foundation annually offers young instrumentalists the opportunity to learn and to play under the direction of established conductors.

LEWISTON

Cong. Beth Jacob, Sabbatus and Shawmut Sts.
Hillel Foundation at Bates College, 7 Field Ave.
Jewish Federation, 134 College St.
Lewiston-Auburn Jewish Community Center, 134 College St.
Isaac L. Rice collection of French literature and music in the Coram Library of Bates College, is named for the famed inventor, industrialist, chess master, and editor. Assembled by Rice while he was studying in Paris and later as a music historian and teacher, the collection was presented to Bates College in 1916 by Mrs. Rice. The college had conferred an honorary LL.D. in 1902 to Mr. Rice.

LIMERICK

The late Louis Grossman, industrialist and philanthropist from Quincy, Mass., bought this little factory town soon after World War II when most of the factories had closed, and guaranteed its inhabitants security and prosperity. The town's 52 houses were sold to their occupants at a low cost and easy terms, and those unoccupied were offered to World War II veterans. The profits from the town's woolen mills were used for charitable purposes only.

OLD ORCHARD

Cong. Beth Israel, East Grand Ave., is known as the "international synagogue" because its membership is composed of Americans and Canadians.

OLD TOWN

Temple Israel, Center St., is open only during the summer and for the High Holy Days.

ORONO

Hillel Foundation at University of Maine, The Maples.

PORTLAND

Cong. Etz Chaim, 296 Congress St.

Cong. Shaarey Tphillah, 76 Noyes St.

Jacob Cousins Memorial, a plaque on the Eastern Promenade, memorializes the first Jewish servicemen from Maine killed in World War I.

Hillel Academy, 76 Noyes St.

Jewish Community Center, 341 Cumberland Ave.

Jewish Family Service, 341 Cumberland Ave.

Jewish Federation-Community Council of Southern Maine, 341 Cumberland Ave.

Jewish Home for the Aged, 158 North St.

ROCKLAND

Rockland Hebrew Cong., 34 Fulton St.

ROCKPORT

Lands End Cultural Center was converted from the Straitsmouth Coast Guard Station, which the U.S. government gave up in 1964, through a community campaign headed by Dr. Louis Schwartz, a former professor of medicine and sociology, and one-time commander of the U.S. Naval Hospital at Great Lakes, Ill., and of the hospital ship, *Refuge,* in the South Pacific during World War II. Schwartz was the first president of the center.

SOUTH PORTLAND

Jewish Cemetery, Smith St., in this suburb of Portland, is the oldest Jewish burial ground in southern Maine and is maintained by the Jewish Federation-Community Council of Southern Maine.

WATERVILLE

Harold Alfond Hockey Rink in the Colby College physical

education-athletics compound, was a gift of Harold Alfond and was dedicated as an ice hockey rink in 1967. In Colby College's science building there is a plaque recording the fact that the initial gift of $120,000 toward the cost of the structure came from Mr. and Mrs. Allan Goldfine of New York.

Cong. Beth Israel, 291 Main St.

MARYLAND

Of all the original 13 colonies, Maryland was the last one to have permanent Jewish residents. Prior to the American Revolution full citizenship rights were accorded only to those who professed a belief in Christianity.

The royal charter, in 1632, gave Maryland to George Calvert, the first Lord Baltimore, warning him that nobody was to be admitted to the colony "by which God's holy and truly Christian religion may in any thing suffer any prejudice or diminution." Calvert's son, Cecelius, however, wanted to make Maryland a refuge for persecuted British Catholics, but also sent Protestants to his colony. The latter quickly became a majority. To placate the Catholics, Calvert issued the Toleration Act of 1649 which declared that "no person or persons professing to believe in Jesus Christ shall henceforth be in any ways troubled or discountenanced for or in respect of his or her religion." It also provided the death penalty for anyone who "denied Jesus Christ to be the sonne of God" or "the holy Trinity." Blasphemy under that Act was also a violation and liable to the death penalty.

These edicts were not directed specifically at Jews since there were no Jews in Maryland or in any of the other colonies at that time. The 1649 statute was amended in 1723 by the elimination of the death penalty for first and second offenders who were to be fined and branded, but for third offenders the penalty was burning at the stake. In 1718 the Church of England was made Maryland's established church and every resident had to contribute, in the form of tobacco, to the local minister. That same year the Colonial Assembly barred

Catholics from voting. On the eve of the Revolution the Catholics were more discriminated against in Maryland than in any other colony.

The only recorded trial under the 1649 act involved the curious case of Jacob Lumbrozo, the "Jew doctor," who came to Maryland in 1656, and is the first known Jew in Maryland. He was also the first Jewish doctor to practice in what is now the United States. Lumbrozo was also an innkeeper, an Indian trader, a farmer, and a plaintiff or defendant in many legal actions. In 1658 Lumbrozo went on trial for blasphemy, a charge based on testimony of witnesses that in a conversation with a Quaker missionary the doctor had denied the divinity of Jesus and had uttered words of blasphemy against him. In court, the Jewish doctor asserted that he had been prodded into expressing his opinions on Jesus, and testified that he was forced *"to declare his Opinion, & being by profession a Jew he answered to some particular demands then urged & as to that of miracles done by Art magick, he declared what remains written concerning Moses & the Magicians of Egipt; But sayd not any thing scoffingly or in derogation by him Christians acknowledge for their Messias."*

Lumbrozo was found guilty and placed in the sheriff's custody until the next court session, but ten days later the doctor was released as part of a general amnesty proclaimed in honor of Richard Cromwell's becoming Lord Protector of England. In 1663, Lumbrozo was granted letters of denization, which gave him many of the rights of a native-born or naturalized subject, but only after he had taken the oath of fealty "on the faith of a Christian" and after marrying a Christian. Two years later he received a tract of land along Nangemy Creek, Charles County, which was recorded as "Lumbrozo's Discovery." While he is accepted as having been the first Jew in Maryland, Father J. Elliot Ross, writing in the Catholic weekly *Commonweal,* in 1934, referred to the "established fact" that a Jew named Mathias de Sousa was among the settlers who arrived in Maryland in 1634 to establish Lord Baltimore's colony.

The first permanent Jewish settler is believed to have been Benjamin Levy, who came to Baltimore in 1773 from Philadelphia where he had been a prominent merchant, and one of the signers of the Non-Importation Resolutions of 1765. He opened a general store in Baltimore. When Philadelphia was on the verge of being captured by the British in 1776, Levy invited Robert Morris, the financier of the Revolution, to come to Baltimore and stay with him. Levy's father-in-law, Nathan Levy, had bought the first Jewish cemetery in Philadelphia in 1733, but Benjamin Levy and his wife were buried in a non-Jewish cemetery in Baltimore.

Old court records cited by Paul and Rita Gordon in their book *The Jews Beneath the Clustered Spires,* indicate that Benjamin Levy had been in business in Frederick for 20 years before he settled in Baltimore. These and other records examined by the Gordons appear to demonstrate the presence in Frederick of persons named Henry Lazarus, Isaac Etting, Levi Cohen, Solomon Bush, Moses Mordecai (all of whom were probably Jews), twenty years before the Revolution.

Benjamin Levy was not the only Jew in Baltimore at the time of the Revolution. Abraham Peters and Wolf Samuel were in the city in 1775 as escaped indentured servants who had sold themselves to masters for seven years in exchange for their passage from Europe. Peters was described in a newspaper advertisement by his master as a "bearded Jew" and a cripple. Samuel's return was also sought by his master in a newspaper advertisement. A fleeting mention of one Isaac Abrahams tells of his reporting a Sabbath violation by a fellow Philadelphian visiting in Baltimore. A Sampson Levy won a judgment in a Baltimore court in 1775. The "Jew tailor" Henry Hart of Arundel County, was convicted in 1752 of having fathered an illegitimate child and sentenced to six months of servitude to the man who had employed the wronged woman. A different sort of Hart, Jacob Hart, was the father-in-law of Haym Salomon's son, Mordecai M. Salomon, who headed the list of subscribers to a patriotic loan after General Lafayette had told the citizens of Baltimore of the urgent needs of George Washington's troops. Nathaniel Levy, also of Baltimore, served under Lafayette in a Baltimore cavalry regiment. Benjamin Levy was so highly regarded by Robert Morris that he was authorized to sign bills of credit on behalf of the Continental Congress. Elias Pollock, who for some reason went by the name of Joseph Smith, enlisted as a private in the 3rd Maryland Regiment in 1778 and saw active service in New Jersey, Pennsylvania, and New York, and then went with his regiment to Charleston, South Carolina in 1780. He was wounded in the Battle of Camden and taken prisoner and detained at St. Augustine, Florida, until the end of the war. In 1818, when he applied for a veteran's pension, the customary oath "was administered to him on the Five Books of Moses, he being a Jew." He signed himself "Elias Pollock," in Hebrew letters. Reuben Etting of Baltimore was also captured in South Carolina.

When Maryland adopted its first constitution in 1776, the Jews were given religious freedom in a clause that recognized the duty of every man to worship God "in such manner as he thinks most acceptable to Him." This was, however, limited by a qualification that "all persons professing the Christian religion are equally entitled to protection in their religious liberty." More serious, however, was the inclusion in the constitution of a test oath which provided that only Christians could hold public office, even though Jews were allowed to vote. Some scholars believed that this limitation on Jewish rights might not have been included in the constitution if there had been any number of Jews in Maryland in 1776 to protest, or at least so phrased as not to discriminate against them.

Members of Baltimore's first prominent Jewish families, the Ettings and the Cohens, began a 30-year struggle to end the constitutional bar against Jewish officeholders. In 1790, Shina Etting, widow of Elijah Etting, an Indian trader from York, Pennsylvania, moved to Baltimore with her five daughters and opened a "gentlemen's" boarding house. Her sons, Solomon and Reuben, joined her in 1792. Solomon, who was the first America-born *shohet,* was the son-in-law and partner of the famed Lancaster Jewish merchant, Joseph Simon. His second wife was Rachel, the daughter of Barnard Gratz, Simon's partner. The younger son, Reuben, had served in the Revolution.

One of the first Jewish merchants in Baltimore, Solomon was an important business and civic leader. He was a founder of the German-American Society and one of its vice-presidents for two decades. During the War of 1812 he served on the citywide committee of vigilance and safety. He was also a bank director, one of the founders of the city's first water system, and a director of the first hospital in Maryland. Etting was also active in the Republican (Democratic) party. Reuben, the older brother, less successful than Solomon, was a partner in a millinery shop. In 1798, when war with France loomed, Reuben joined a volunteer outfit called the Marion Corps of which he was elected captain. But when it was pointed out that under the state's constitution no Jew could be a commissioned officer, practice law, or hold public office, the military unit decided against choosing a new captain until Jews were given equal rights. In 1801, President Thomas Jefferson appointed Reuben Etting United States marshal for Maryland. Isaac M. Fein, in his book *The History of Baltimore Jewry from 1773 to 1920,* calls this appointment a major breakthrough for the Jews of Maryland.

The Cohen family was even more important in Baltimore than the Ettings. Judith Cohen, whose husband Israel had died in Richmond in 1803, settled in Baltimore with her children soon after she was widowed. Her sons ran a lottery in Baltimore (then a legal enterprise), from which they branched into banking. The firm of Jacob I. Cohen, Jr. and Brothers, was one of the few banks to weather the panic of 1837. Jacob Cohen was one of the founders of the Baltimore & Ohio Railroad, president of a convention to promote the city's commercial interests, and secretary of the board of education. His brother, Mendes, also a banker, was a famous world traveler. He was the first person to carry the American flag to the cataracts of the Nile River. Joshua L. Cohen, the youngest brother, was a prominent physician. Benjamin Cohen was one of the founders of the Baltimore Stock Exchange.

Cohens and Ettings were among the eight Jews who helped defend Fort McHenry during the War of 1812. They were Mendes, Philip, and Samuel Cohen, Jr., Samuel Etting, Israel Davidson, Jacob Moses, Solomon Myers, and Samuel Solomon. Reuben Etting fought in the defense of Baltimore in 1814. Simon Levy, one of two Jewish members of the first class graduated from the United States Military Academy in 1802, was the son of Levy Andrew Levy, who had been a member of the Board of Health in Hagerstown in 1793 before settling in Baltimore in 1796. He was a nephew of the Lancaster merchant, Joseph Simon.

Like the aristocratic Christian families of New England and Virginia, who looked down on later arrivals, the Ettings and Cohens held themselves aloof from other Jews in Baltimore. Both families maintained private *minyanim* in their homes, and each acquired its own cemetery. Neither Ettings nor Cohens were involved in the founding of the first synagogue in 1830, but one of the Cohens participated in an abortive attempt to found a Sephardic congregation in the 1850s. The Ettings retained their membership in Philadelphia's Mikveh Israel Congregation. When Shearith Israel Congregation of New York asked Solomon Etting to contribute to its building fund in the 1820s, he sent $150 but cautioned that little could be expected of Baltimore since there were only three other Jewish families in the city. Actually, by then there were over 100 Jewish families in town and they had their own *mohel* and *shochet*.

In 1797, Solomon Etting began the long struggle—nearly 30 years—to achieve full civil equality for the Jews of Maryland. In a petition to the Maryland Assembly, "Solomon Etting and others," declared that they were "a sect of people called Jews and thereby are deprived of invaluable rights of citizenship and praying to be placed on the same footing as other good citizens." The legislature failed to act that year and similar petitions for the next seven years were also pigeonholed. Following 1804 there were no further petitions offered for 14 years. In 1818 the struggle was renewed under the leadership of Thomas Kennedy, a non-Jewish member of the State Assembly from Washington County. At Kennedy's request, the Assembly appointed a committee "to consider the justice and expediency of placing the Jewish inhabitants on equal footing with the Christians." Kennedy, chairman of the committee, received a report from Jacob Cohen on the plight of the Jews of Maryland. The three-man committee recommended that "Jews and Christians be placed on equal footing in regard to their civil rights."

The bill- introduced after the report, declared that "no religious test, declaration, or subscription of opinion as to religion, shall be required from any person or sect called Jews, as a qualification to hold or exercise any office or employment of trust in this state. . .and. . .that every oath to be administered to any persons of the sect of people called Jews, shall be administered on the five books of Moses, agreeable to the religious education of that people, and not otherwise." In supporting the measure, which was called Kennedy's Jew Baby and the Jew Bill, Kennedy pointed out that without such an amendment Jews were barred from practicing law and from serving on juries, in addition to being denied the right to hold any local or state public office. In 1819 the legislature defeated the bill after prolonged debate.

In 1822, Kennedy sponsored a universal version of the bill which would have extended to all citizens of Maryland the same civil and religious rights, and privileges enjoyed under the Constitution of the United States. The bill passed the Lower House by a vote of 40-33 and by 8 to 7 in the Senate. As an amendment to the Constitution, passage by two successive legislative sessions was required. In 1824 a petition was presented to the Legislature signed by Jacob Cohen, Solomon Etting, and his uncle, Levi Solomon, pointing out they were not seeking any special privileges but only equality with all other citizens. In supporting a new bill, Colonel W.G.D. Worthington submitted a document based on Etting's answers to Worthington's questions. In this document Etting estimated the Jewish population of Maryland as "at least 150," with a wealth of $10,500,000. On the last day of the 1824 session, February 26, 1825, the Jew Bill finally passed, and was confirmed on January 5, 1826. The act repealed the test oath under which Jews could not hold office. However, it still required a belief in a future state of rewards and punishments, thus excluding from public office atheists, deists, and nonconforming Jews. Kennedy, who had spearheaded the long fight for the bill, had never met a Jew until he first became involved in the Jew Bill struggle.

Within a few months after the Jew Bill became law, Solomon Etting and Jacob Cohen were both elected to the Baltimore City Council. Three years later the first *minyan* which is documented, met in the home of Zalma Rehine, a nephew of the eminent Rabbi Isaac Leeser of Philadelphia. Rehine had first come to Baltimore in 1789 but moved to Richmond, Virginia, where he became a successful merchant and communal leader. He was 72 years old when the first official services were held in his house in 1829. Isaac Fein, however, believes that there were too many Jews in the city prior to 1820 for the service in Rehine's house to have been the first. In December 1829, some of the members of that first *minyan*—including Rehine, Moses Millem, Lewis Silver, John M. Dyer, Levi Benjamin, Joseph Ancker, Levy Collmus, Joseph Osterman, Tobias Myers, and Jacob Aaron—asked a member of the Legislature to offer a bill chartering a synagogue to be known as the Baltimore Hebrew Congregation. It passed on first reading but when it came up for a second vote, the bill was defeated. On reconsid-

eration it was approved and the first Jewish organization in Maryland, whose Hebrew name was Nidche Israel (Dispersed of Israel), came into being.

In 1826 there were 150 Jews in Baltimore and a handful in other cities. By 1840 there were 200 families or about 1,000 individuals. Nidche Israel's first meeting place was a rented room over a grocery on the corner of Fleet and Bond Streets. In 1837, the congregation moved into a brick building at the corner of Etna Lane and Harrison Street. By then the congregation had over 60 members as immigration from Germany rapidly increased during the 1830s and 1840s. Most of the Jewish immigrants started as peddlers. In two generations they were part of the city's leading mercantile and industrial enterprises. The early immigrants lived primarily in East Baltimore, around Lloyd and Lombard Streets. It was on Lloyd Street that the Baltimore Hebrew Congregation erected Maryland's first synagogue in 1845. That building, now a Jewish museum, was used by the pioneer congregation for 44 years.

Nidche Israel's first president, John M. Dyer, was a butcher who came to America in 1812 and lived in New England before coming to Baltimore in 1820. His son, Leon Dyer, who was president from 1840-1847, was Baltimore's acting mayor during the bread riots caused by an economic crisis in 1834. He later went to Texas to join the fight for freedom from Mexico. When President James Polk called for volunteers in 1846 for the war with Mexico, Baltimore Jews organized the First Hebrew Guards regiment. The surgeon of this outfit was Dr. Phineas J. Horwitz. His father, Dr. Jonathan Horwitz, also an army surgeon, was a Dutch-born Jew who came to the United States in 1812 with a trunk full of Hebrew type and a plan to publish the first Hebrew grammar and Hebrew Bible in the United States. Another printer, however, accomplished this before him. The elder Horwitz received a medical degree from the University of Pennsylvania and later was assistant director of the United States Army's Bureau of Medicine and Surgery.

Splinter groups that broke away from the Baltimore Hebrew Congregation created Baltimore's other early synagogues: Fell's Point Hebrew Friendship Congregation (1832), which disbanded in 1904; Har Sinai (1842); Shearith Israel (1851); Oheb Shalom (1853); and Chizuk Amuno (1870). By 1855 Baltimore had 4,000 Jews and four congregations. The city's first rabbi was Abraham Rice. He was the first rabbi to be ordained in the United States and occupied the pulpit of the Baltimore Hebrew Congregation from 1840-1849. Har Sinai was the first Baltimore congregation established as a Reform group. As a result of the introduction of women into its choir, Jonas Friedenwald led a secession that produced Chizuk Amuno. Four generations of

Friedenwalds were among the city's chief Jewish communal leaders. Aaron, Jonas' younger son, was a physician specializing in eye diseases who taught at the University of Maryland Medical School. He was also an early Zionist, and one of the founders of the American Jewish Historical Society and the Jewish Publication Society of America. Aaron's son, Harry, was also an ophthalmologist of national repute. From 1904-1918 he was president of the Federation of American Zionists, and in 1919 was acting chairman of the Zionist Commission to Palestine. All of the Friedenwalds held office in Chizuk Amuno.

Benjamin Szold, father of Henrietta Szold, was Oheb Shalom's rabbi for nearly 40 years. At the turn of the century Baltimore Hebrew Congregation's rabbi was Adolph Guttmacher, father of Dr. Alan F. Guttmacher, the pioneer leader of the Planned Parenthood Organization. The influx of impoverished Jews from Germany in the 1830s, 1840s, and 1850s led to the formation of a network of social welfare agencies: United Hebrew Assistance Society (1846), later reorganized as the Hebrew Benevolent Society, and the direct ancestor of the Jewish Family and Children's Service; the Society for Educating Poor and Orphan Children (1852), which became the Hebrew Education Society and the ancestor of the city's celebrated Jewish education system; the Young Men's Hebrew Literary Society which, in 1854, became the first organization to call itself YMHA; and the Hebrew Hospital and Sinai, which became Sinai Hospital and Medical Center.

On the eve of the Civil War there were some 7,000 Jews in Baltimore. Maryland had many secessionist sympathizers, among them some Jews. Rabbi Bernard Illoway of Baltimore Hebrew Congregation defended and justified slavery and endorsed secession. Most members of the Friedenwald family were Southern sympathizers. Ike Friedenwald joined the Confederate army. Aaron Friedenwald, who was strongly for the Union, was nevertheless arrested by Union forces as a smuggler. Dr. Friedenwald and Dr. Abraham B. Arnold attended wounded soldiers in military hospitals around Baltimore. Moses Wiesenfeld, Friedenwald's son-in-law, and a pioneer in ready-to-wear clothing, was sent to a Union prison for two years after being framed by one of his employees who planted Confederate military buttons in his factory. Mendes Cohen belonged to the Peace Party, one of many pro-secessionist groups. Baltimore Jews served in both armies. Brig. General Leopold Blumenberg, who came to Baltimore from Germany in 1854, joined the state militia in 1862 and won fame at the Battle of Antietam, where he was severely wounded. In 1863 President Lincoln appointed him provost marshal of the 3rd Maryland District.

Blumenberg was a disciple of Rabbi David Einhorn, the great exponent of Reform Judaism. He was called to Har Sinai in 1856 from

Budapest after the Hungarian government had closed his synagogue because of his sermons in defense of liberty. From the pulpit of Har Sinai and in the pages of his newspaper, *Sinai,* he denounced slavery as the cancer of the country and attacked other rabbis who defended it. Week after week he thundered against slavery and when war broke out he urged his congregants to enlist. In a city with strong Southern sympathies, Einhorn's position troubled many of his congregants who called a protest meeting to make clear to the general public that he spoke only for himself and not the Jewish community. On April 19, 1861, Union troops passing through Baltimore en route to Washington were attacked by a proslavery mob and among those arrested was Joseph Friedenwald. Twenty-four hours later, a mob smashed the print shop where Einhorn's paper was printed and he himself was threatened with violence. His congregation persuaded him to leave the city for his own safety and he spent the war years in Philadelphia as rabbi of Congregation Keneseth Israel. At Oheb Shalom, on the other hand, Rabbi Szold advocated a position of neutrality on slavery and secession. He was a strong advocate of peace and reconciliation.

The first Jewish immigrants from Eastern Europe arrived in the 1860s and 1870s. In 1865 they formed Bikur Cholim, and by 1875 there were enough Jews from Poland and Lithuania to establish the Ohel Yaakov Bialystoker Shul. Twenty-five years later there were 20 East European congregations. When Chizuk Amuno moved uptown in 1895 its original building was acquired by Bikur Cholim. Bikur Cholim suffered a split in 1873 which gave birth to B'nai Israel.

The Yiddish-speaking East European Jews began pouring into Baltimore in the 1880s and 1890s. The community of only 10,000 Jews in 1880 absorbed 24,095 newcomers between 1881 and 1890, and 17,367 more from 1891 to 1898. By 1907 Maryland had 41,000 Jews, of whom 40,000 lived in Baltimore and the rest were located in Annapolis, Brunswick, Cumberland, Frederick, Hagerstown, Frostburg, and in the agricultural towns of the eastern shore. The immigrants settled in east Baltimore in houses vacated by the well-established German Jews who came to the aid of their coreligionists with a network of new agencies. The German Jews, though helpful, did not associate with the East European Jews who created many social welfare, cultural, and religious institutions of their own. By the turn of the century, Baltimore had two well established parallel Jewish communities—the uptown Jews and the downtown Jews. The former integrated their organizations into the Federated Jewish Charities in 1906, and the latter followed a year later with the United Hebrew Charities.

The uptown Jews tried to reduce the number of Russian refugees settling in Baltimore by three abortive attempts at agricultural colonies. Two were launched in 1882. One was in Middlesex County, Virginia, on land owned by Joseph Friedenwald and David Wiesenfeld, but after six years the colony disintegrated. Another settlement called Pisgah was established in Charles County, Maryland, but that too failed. The third and last attempt to make farmers out of the refugees from the *shtetl* was made at Halofield, just outside Ellicott City, Maryland in 1902. Despite their attitudes toward the Russian Jews, the German community did help them extensively. On one occasion after a shipload of Russian Jews was refused admission at Baltimore harbor for fear they would become public charges, the German Jews obtained their admission by pledging as security the community's hospital and orphan asylum buildings. The Baltimore Evening Night School, the first of its kind in the country, was organized by Henrietta Szold in 1889 for the benefit of the Russian Jews. The Yiddish-speaking newcomers, many of whom worked in clothing factories owned by the German Jews such as L. Greif, Henry Sonneborn, and Henry Strauss, helped organize labor unions and were active in strikes against sweatshop conditions and low wages.

Meanwhile, the German Jews helped establish the scholarly reputation of Johns Hopkins University. One of its first faculty members was the distinguished Jewish mathematician, Dr. J.J. Sylvester, who was brought from England. Other early faculty notables were Maurice Bloomfield, later professor of Sanskrit and philology, who also taught Hebrew, and Paul Haupt, professor of Semitics. One of Haupt's early students was the young Cyrus Adler, who married Racie Friedenwald, a daughter of Moses Friedenwald. Adler collaborated with Henrietta Szold in editing the first books issued under the imprint of the Jewish Publication Society by the Friedenwald Press, later known as the Lord Baltimore Press. Fabian Franklin was a member of the first graduating class at Johns Hopkins in 1876 and later was a professor of mathematics and associate editor of the *Baltimore News*. Jacob Hollander, the noted economist, David S. Blondheim, authority on the Romance languages, and Florence E. Bamberger, the first woman professor at Johns Hopkins, were other Baltimore luminaries associated with the institution.

It was Louis Levin, a brother-in-law of Henrietta Szold, who brought the German and Russian communities together. Lawyer, editor, short story writer, social worker, Levin was a bookkeeper for the Straus brothers. Levin wrote for *The Jewish Exponent* of Philadelphia, and later edited *The Jewish Comment of Baltimore*. As the first full-time executive director of the Federated Jewish Charities, he had the ear of the leading German Jews. In 1920 he succeeded in bringing the two federations together into the Associated Jewish Charities, of which he was also the first executive director. During World War I he headed the American Jewish medical mission to Palestine. The formation of the Associated Jewish Charities integrated the philanthropies and interests of the once mutually antagonistic and separate uptown and downtown communities, and paved the way for the future growth of the Jewish community.

Twenty years after the Associated Jewish Charities was formed, 73,000 of Maryland's 76,000 Jews lived in Baltimore. The rest were scattered in 29 cities, each with 10 or more Jews, and 41 places with ten or less Jews. In the latter group were Silver Spring, Bethesda, and Rockville—all in Montgomery County, which borders on Washington, D.C. Until the early 1940s there was no organized Jewish life in Montgomery County. A scattering of Jews had lived in the larger towns such as Bethesda, Rockville, Kensington, and Silver Spring but they were never numerous enough to create any Jewish institutions. Their Jewish identification, if any, was with the synagogues in Washington, D.C. In the years just preceding World War II when the New Deal of the Roosevelt administration attracted thousands of new employees for the newly-created agencies, a substantial number of them were young Jewish economists, lawyers, and administrators who decided to settle in the Washington, D.C. area. They found housing in Washington, D.C. unavailable or too expensive, and began moving across the District line into northern Virginia and Maryland's Montgomery and Prince George Counties. Silver Spring, Bethesda, and Chevy Chase, Maryland, became the area of major Jewish settlement. In the 1960s and early 1970s the second generation of Washington, D.C. area Jews pushed further north and west into new Maryland suburbs. By 1974 it was estimated that there were some 65,000 Jews in Montgomery County compared with 94,000 in the city of Baltimore and Baltimore County. Another 15,000 Jews resided in Prince George County. There were 30,000 Jews in Silver Spring, 20,000 in the Bethesda-Chevy Chase area, and 5,000 in and around Rockville. The Jewish Community Center of Greater Washington moved to Rockville in the late 1960s where it is the hub of a Jewish communal complex that includes the Hebrew Home for the Aged and the Jewish Social Service Agency. The United Jewish Appeal—the Greater Washington area's Jewish federation—has its headquarters in Chevy Chase. There are now so many Jewish children in the Montgomery County public schools that they are closed on Rosh Hashanah and Yom Kippur. The county has 23 synagogues of all denominations and many other Jewish organizations.

In the early 1970s there were nearly 100,000 Jews in Baltimore and its suburbs, out of a total of 226,610 in the whole state. The center of Jewish life in Baltimore moved successively from Lloyd Street to Eutaw Place to Park Circle and Garrison Boulevard to upper Park

Heights Avenue and Liberty Road and then beyond the city into the Baltimore County suburbs of Pikesville, Reisterstown, Randallstown, and Owings Mills. Northwest Baltimore is now the heart of the Jewish community. Almost all of the major Jewish institutions have been transplanted from downtown to the northwest section. At the beginning of the 1970s there were 30 synagogues in Baltimore city and 20 more in the suburbs.

Besides Baltimore County, Montgomery County, and Prince George County communities, there were also Jewish communities in Bowie, Laurel, Aberdeen, Cumberland, Frederick, Hagerstown, Columbia City, Salisbury, Greenbelt, Hyattsville, Lexington Park, Olney, Randallstown, and Reisterstown. Between Baltimore and Washington, D.C. there is almost a solid line of Jewish settlement and organization.

Maryland has elected five Jews to the House of Representatives and one to the Senate. Maryland is also one of the few states to have had a Jewish senator, a Jewish governor, and a Jewish mayor of its biggest city. Isidor Rayner, who served in Congress from 1887-1889 and again from 1891-1895, was elected to the United States Senate in 1905 and served until 1912. Philip B. Perlman was secretary of state 1920-23. Marvin Mandel was in his second full term as governor in 1976. Louis Goldstein was elected state controller five times. Philip H. Goodman served two terms as mayor of Baltimore in the 1960s. Besides Rayner, Maryland elected to Congress Harry B. Wolf (1907-09); Samuel Friedel (1953-71); Daniel Ellison (1943-45); and Mrs. Gladys N. Spellman (1974-   ). The late Simon E. Sobeloff, who was a justice of the Fourth U.S. Circuit Court of Appeals, had previously served as United States Solicitor General, United States Attorney for Maryland, and chief judge of the Maryland Court of Appeals. Philip Perlman also served as United States Solicitor General and secretary of state of Maryland. Isidor Rayner and Isaac Strauss were attorneys-general of Maryland. In 1975 Walter Orlinsky was president of the Baltimore City Council. Irving A. Levine was a judge of the State Court of Appeals in 1975. In 1935 Emanuel Gorfine was speaker of the State Assembly. The first Jew elected to public office from Baltimore County (outside the city of Baltimore) was Suzanne Mensh, elected a judge of the Orphans Court in 1962 and its chief judge since 1966.

* * * * *

ABERDEEN
Hartford Jewish Center, Md. Route 155 and Earlton Rd.

ANNAPOLIS
Knesseth Israel Congregation, Hilltop Lane and Spa Rd., the

only synagogue in the capital city of Maryland, is also the official chapel for Jewish midshipmen at the U.S. Naval Academy. The congregation's rabbi is designated as the Jewish chaplain for Jewish personnel at the Academy by the JWB Commission on Jewish Chaplaincy.

State Capitol has a spot reserved in the Governor's office for a portrait of Marvin Mandel who was serving as speaker of the State House of Delegates when Governor Spiro Agnew became vice-president in 1968. Mandel was elected governor by the House of Delegates and filled out the remaining two years and 18 days of Agnew's term. He was elected on his own in 1970 and reelected in 1974. The first professing Jew elected chief executive of a southern state, he had been a member of the House of Delegates for 16 years before his election as speaker. Born in Baltimore in 1930, Mandel is the son of East European immigrants. His father was a cutter in a men's clothing factory.

State Governor's Mansion displays among its portraits, a painting of Mrs. Barbara Mandel, who was married to Governor Marvin Mandel until their divorce in 1973. This portrait hangs on the wall of the mansion's winding staircase.

U. S. Naval Academy

Jewish Prayer Chapel is located in a corner of the rotunda of Bancroft Hall. ●Memorial Hall of the U.S. Naval Academy's Bancroft Hall displays a full length portrait of Commodore Uriah P. Levy, who worked for many years for the abolition of flogging as punishment in the Navy (see Virginia).

●An exhibit case containing the names of all Academy graduates who died in action, includes a large number of Jews. ●The Herbert Schiff Trophy is named for Lt. Herbert Schiff, a Naval reserve officer killed in 1924. The trophy was presented to the Navy Department by Col. William Schiff, in memory of his brother. For many years the Schiff Trophy was awarded annually by the President to naval aviators for outstanding flying safety. ●Michelson Hall, a science building at the Academy, is named for Dr. Albert A. Michelson, an 1873 graduate, a member of its science faculty from 1875-1879, and the first American scientist to win a Nobel Prize. He was awarded the Nobel Prize in physics in 1907 for his measurements of the velocity of light. Michelson, who was born in Poland, grew up in Virginia City, Nev., when it was a boom town where his father ran a drygoods store. On examination for Congressional appointment to the Academy, he tied with another boy and was named alternate appointee. After he had given up hope of a vacancy at the Academy, he received word from its commandant that President Grant had given him an "appointment at large." Since this was Grant's 11th such appointment—the President had informed Michelson that he had already exhausted his 10 appointments at large—Michelson used to joke that his career was launched by an illegal act. After four years on the Academy's faculty, he taught at Case School of Applied Science in Cleveland, Clark University, and for 37 years at the University of Chicago. His improvements in methods of measuring the velocity of light catapulted him into the international scientific limelight at the age of 26. He invented the interferometer, which was used to test the relative velocity of the earth and the ether, and was also applied to the measurement of the diameter of the stars. In its day the Michelson interferometer was considered the most useful instrument available to this branch of science. Michelson also developed the echelon spectroscope and designed the most powerful instruments of diffraction yet developed. Dr. Michelson's brother Charles, a long-time Washington correspondent for the *New York World*, was also public relations director of the Democratic National Committee. ●Naval Academy Library includes the Harry S. Guggenheim Collection of many first editions and rare volumes, and all the works of Dr. Robert Goddard, the American scientist whose pioneer experiments in rocketry paved the way for space science, and who was supported for many years by Guggenheim, a patron of aeronautical science. ●Naval Academy Museum houses the Michelson Museum which contains an array of instruments, data records, publications, awards, photographs, and other memorabilia relating to Michelson's personal life and career, as well as an exact replica of his laboratory. ●Tripoli Monument, located between the Officers Club and Sampson Hall, has inscribed on its base the names of the six young officers who lost their lives in naval action at Tripoli during the war against the Barbary pirates in 1804. One of the names is that of Lt. Joseph Israel of Portland, Me., who is believed to have been Jewish (see Maine).

ARNOLD

Temple Beth Sholom, Old Annapolis Rd., east of Gov. Ritchie Hwy.

BALTIMORE

Abraham Street, which runs for one block south of Monument St. from Hartford Ave. east to Ajax Alley, is named for one of the early Jewish families in Baltimore.

Associated Jewish Charities, 5750 Park Heights Ave.

Associated Placement and Guidance Service, 5750 Park Heights Ave.

Attorney General's Office, 1 South Calvert St., has on permanent display photographs and portraits of Maryland's attorneys-general. Likenesses of Isidor Rayner, who held the post in 1904, and of Isaac L. Strauss, who held it in 1907, are included.

Bais Yaakov School for Girls, 4901 Greenspring Ave., is housed in the Robert G. Cohn Memorial Building.

Baltimore Hebrew College, 5800 Park Heights Ave., is both an institution for Jewish higher learning and a school for training qualified teachers for Jewish religious schools. The college also includes a high school department, a college of Jewish studies, and a women's institute of Jewish studies. The Joseph Meyerhoff Library, which serves as a primary source of Jewish information to scholars and students in the Baltimore area, also houses important archival material, including the papers of the Szold and Friedenwald families. The college also houses the administrative offices of the Board of Jewish Education and the Jewish Historical Society of Maryland. The Baltimore Hebrew College is a monument to Dr. Louis L. Kaplan, who headed it for 40 years while also serving as director of the Board of Jewish Education. In 1970 he was named chairman of the Maryland Board of Regents on which he had served for 18 years.

Baltimore Hebrew Congregation, 7401 Park Heights Ave., the oldest congregation in Maryland, chartered in 1830, has in its Hoffberger Chapel 16 unique stained glass windows, each 16 feet high and two feet wide, depicting Judaism from the Creation to the birth of the State of Israel. Unlike most stained glass windows in synagogues that are usually abstract in nature, these depict well-known figures, among them Abraham sacrificing Isaac, Moses, King David, Judah the Maccabee, and the Wandering Jew. Nissan Engel, an Israeli artist, designed the windows. A mural in the lobby depicts Moses and the Burning Bush.

Baltimore Museum of Art, Wyman Park, has a Cone Wing that houses the Cone Collection, one of the most comprehensive collections of modern art in the world, bequeathed by Claribel and Etta Cone, daughters of Herman and Helen Guggenheim Cone. Claribel was the first woman to receive a medical degree from Johns Hopkins University. •The museum's 17th century room, displaying stained glass from the 13th and 14th centuries, and a children's wing—the Saidie A. May Young People's Art Center—were contributed by Mrs. Saidie A. May. •In addition, there are the Julius Levy Collection of Oriental Art, and the Jacob Epstein Collection, the latter contributed by Jacob Epstein, a noted Baltimore art patron. This collection has a bronze of Epstein by the renowned Jewish sculptor, Sir Jacob Epstein.

Harry Bard Library of Community College of Baltimore, 2901 Liberty Heights Ave., is named for Dr. Harry Bard, president of the college since 1959, and a prominent member of the Jewish community.

Blaustein Building, 1 N. Charles St., is named for the late Jacob S. Blaustein and his father, who founded the Amoco Oil Co. in 1910 with one small tank wagon and a horse. Jacob Blaustein served as president of the American Jewish Committee and as a U.S. Delegate to the United Nations.

Block Street, formerly called Queen St., is named for Judah

Block, an early resident of Baltimore, whose daughter married Benjamin F. Jonas, U.S. Senator from Louisiana.

Board of Jewish Education, 5800 Park Heights Ave.

Cohen Section of Baltimore Hebrew Congregation Cemetery, Belair Rd., is the old Cohen Cemetery once located on Saratoga St. near Carey St. In 1837 Jacob I. Cohen, Jr. deeded the property to Mendes J. and Jonas I. Cohen as trustees for use as a cemetery. There are 44 graves of members of the Cohen family buried there between 1834 and 1952. The relocation of the historic cemetery was completed in 1974 with court approval.

Cong. Beth Abraham Anshe Sfard, 6210 Wallis Ave.

Cong. Beth Am, Eutaw Pl. and Chauncey, a new traditional congregation, occupies the old building of Cong. Chizuk Amuno which is now located in Stevenson (see Stevenson).

Cong. Beth El, 8101 Park Heights Ave., has over the main entrance to the sanctuary three large plaques, executed in brass and ceramics by Raymond A. Katz, representing the three ways in which the Divine Power enters the life of man—Creation, Revelation, and Redemption.

Cong. Beth Isaac Adath Israel, 4901 Greenspring Ave.

Cong. Beth Jacob, 5713 Park Hts. Ave., has an open courtyard with two archways symbolizing the two Tablets of the Law.

Cong. Beth Jacob Wisheer, 1016 Hillen St.

Cong. Beth Tfiloh, 3300 Old Court Rd.

Cong. B'nai Israel, 3701 Southern Ave.

Cong. B'nai Jacob, 6605 Liberty Rd.

Cong. Chizuk Amuno, Eutaw Pl. and Chauncey, is an in-town synagogue for those members who have not moved into the suburbs. The congregation's suburban synagogue is located in Stevenson, (see Stevenson).

Cong. Chofetz Chaim Adath Bnei Israel, 3702 West Rogers Ave.

Cong. Darchei Tzedek, 3615 Seven Mile Lane.

Cong. Mogen Abraham, 3114-C Parkington Ave.

Cong. Ohr Knesseth Israel Anshe Sphard, 3910 W. Rogers Ave.

Cong. Shaarei Tfiloh, Auchentroly Terr. and Liberty Height Ave., is a landmark because of its uniquely domed synagogue.

Cong. Tzemach Tzedek V'Shomrie Hadas, 7037 Surrey Dr.

Council House, 7241 Park Heights Ave., is the headquarters of the Baltimore section of the National Council of Jewish Women.

Darnal Young People's Museum of Maryland History, 201 W. Monument St., exhibits, among other things, a photograph of the Lloyd Street Synagogue (see below), the oldest existing synagogue building in the state and the third oldest in the entire country; a portrait of Rabbi Abraham Rice, the first spiritual leader of Baltimore Hebrew

Congregation and the first ordained rabbi to officiate anywhere in the U.S.; a handwritten draft of Thomas Kennedy's *Jew Bill,* which gave Jews in Maryland full civil and political rights in 1826. ●Other material about Jews is also included in the display on "Early Religious Groups in Maryland."

Downtown Hebrew Cong., YMCA Building, Franklin St. and Park Ave.

Downtown Minyan, 4th floor, Title Building, 106 St. Paul St., conducts daily afternoon Orthodox services at 1 p.m., from Monday through Thursday for downtown businessmen who have to say Kaddish or who are observing *yahrzeit.*

Etting Street, a narrow thoroughfare which stretches for many blocks north from Hoffman St., almost to Druid Hill Park, is named for Solomon Etting, one of the first Jews in Baltimore to hold a public office. He was a prime mover in seeking legislation to enable Jews to enjoy civil liberties. He fought for the passage of the Jew Bill in the State Legislature. In 1794 he was a member of a committee which protested to President George Washington the terms of John Jay's treaty with Great Britain. Soon after the passage of the Jew Bill in 1826, Etting was elected to the City Council of Baltimore, of which he was later president. He was also one of the founders of the Baltimore & Ohio Railroad.

Fort McHenry National Monument, on the site of bombardment by a British fleet on Sept. 13, 1814 during the War of 1812, is the place where the still-flying flag inspired Francis Scott Key to write *The Star Spangled Banner.* Eight Jews, including members of the Cohen and Etting families, were among the defenders of Fort McHenry.

Harry Greenstein Social Service Building of Associated Jewish Charities and Welfare Fund, 5750 Park Heights Ave., is named for the late eminent social worker, educator, and communal leader who directed the Associated Jewish Charities from 1928 until his retirement in 1965. Greenstein, who died in 1972, was the agency's head when the building was planned and opened. During the 1940s he served as director of welfare for the United Nations Relief and Rehabilitation Administration, and advisor on Jewish affairs to the U.S. Army in Occupied Germany and Austria. Greenstein's portrait hangs in the building's lobby. In addition to the Associated Jewish Charities, the building is occupied by the Jewish Family and Children's Service Agency, the Hebrew Free Loan Association, the Jewish Big Brothers League, the Associated Placement and Guidance Service, and HIAS. The building is flanked on either side by the Jewish Community Center and the Baltimore Hebrew College, both of which were erected during Greenstein's administration of the AJC.

Har-Brook Hebrew Cong., 4303 Gov. Ritchie Hwy.

Har Sinai Congregation, 6300 Park Heights Ave., second oldest congregation in Baltimore, and said to be America's oldest continuous Reform congregation, was founded in 1842. Its aluminum dome has made it a city landmark. Tablets of the Law in the sanctuary measuring 18 by 8 feet and using the style of Hebrew letters in use in Israel, in a design by Ludwig Wolpert, dominate the altar. Har Sinai was the pulpit from which Rabbi David Einhorn vigorously denounced slavery at the risk of his life.

Har Zion Tifereth Israel Cong., 6221 Greenspring Ave.

Hendler Memorial, in the headquarters of the Baltimore chapter of the American Red Cross, 23rd and St. Paul Sts., is a plaque citing L. Manuel Hendler's more than 30 years of service to this organization.

Hoffberger School of Painting, an endowed graduate division of the Maryland Institute-College of Art, 1300 Mount Royal Ave., is named for the prominent Hoffberger family active in Jewish philanthropies and civic and communal affairs.

Hollander House, a division of the Johns Hopkins University Alumni Memorial Dormitory, is named for Jacob Hollander, for many years professor of economics at the university. In 1897 he was named to the U.S. Bimetalic Commission and sent to Europe to negotiate monetary agreements with several countries. After the Spanish American War, when the U.S. acquired Puerto Rico, Hollander was named a special commissioner by the Secretary of War and assigned to revise the taxation laws of the island. Later he was named the first treasurer of Puerto Rico. In the central lobby of the university's Gilman Hall there is an oil portrait of Hollander in academic robes.

Jew Alley, in the western section of the city near the location of the old Cohen Cemetery, runs from Lexington St., one block east.

Jewish Community Center, 5700 Park Heights Ave., is the descendant of the Baltimore YMHA, founded in 1854 as the first agency with that name. A mammoth tile mural, which flows from the outside lobby to the inside lobby, emphasizes the center's role in bringing together all Jewish groups. The theme of the mural, 25 feet at its highest point, is embodied in the quotation, partially inscribed in Hebrew on the center panel: "Behold how good and pleasant it is when brethren dwell together in unity." The mural was presented to the Center in honor of the late Harry Greenstein, who was president of one of the center's predecessor agencies. A strictly kosher cafeteria in the center serves lunch and dinner, from Sunday to Thursday.

Jewish Convalescent Home, 5601 Pall Mall Rd.

Jewish Family Service, 5750 Park Heights Ave.

Jewish Historical Society of Maryland, 5800 Park Heights Ave., an affiliate of the Baltimore Hebrew College, collects and preserves material about Maryland Jewish history, encourages research in that field, and prepares taped interviews with prominent members of the Jewish community. It also acquires the papers of important Baltimore Jewish families, including the Benjamin and Henrietta Szold papers and the Harry Friedenwald papers. The society also owns and administers the historic Lloyd Street Synagogue and its museum.

Jewish Times, 2104 North Charles St.

Johns Hopkins University

Johns Hopkins University Kosher Dining Hall, in the main dormitory dining hall, is sponsored by the Council of Orthodox Jewish Congregations of Baltimore. ●Shriver Hall has in its lobby a 640 square foot mural made up of panels depicting early faculty members, the city's famous ladies, and prominent philanthropists. Among those identified in the panel are Dr. James J. Sylvester, the renowned mathematician, and Dr. Simon Flexner, eminent bacteriologist and the first head of Rockefeller University. ●The University Library has the Strouse Rabbinical Library, the Loewenberg Collection of Modern German Drama, and the Cohen Collection of Egyptian Antiquities. The latter is comprised of some 600 items collected by Mendes I. Cohen in Egypt, which illustrate the history of minor arts. ●In Gilman Hall there are more than 3,000 volumes of Judaica. ☐

Levindale Hebrew Geriatric Center and Hospital, Belvedere and Greenspring Aves., is a part of the Sinai-Jewish Medical Center. It is named for Louis H. Levin, editor, communal leader, and social worker, who was a brother-in-law of Henrietta Szold, founder of Hadassah.

Levindale Road is named for the above center.

Lloyd Street Synagogue, Lloyd and Watson Sts., a national shrine owned by the Jewish Historical Society of Maryland, is the third oldest synagogue building in the country (only Touro Synagogue in Newport, R.I., which dates from 1763, and Cong. Beth Elohim, Charleston, S.C., dedicated in 1843, predate the Lloyd Street Synagogue, which was dedicated in 1845). The first Jewish house of worship in Maryland built as a synagogue, was erected in 1845 by the Nidche Israel Congregation (The Dispersed of Israel), the original Hebrew name of the Baltimore Hebrew Congregation, under the direction of Rabbi Abraham Rice, the first American-ordained rabbi to officiate in an American synagogue. In 1888, the building was sold to the Church of St. John the Baptist, a Lithuanian Roman Catholic church. In 1905, the building reverted back to a synagogue when it was acquired by Congregation Shomrei Mishmeres, an Orthodox congregation of Russian immigrants. Its rabbi was Abraham N. Schwartz, a noted Talmudic scholar who founded the Talmudical Academy of Baltimore in 1917, the first Hebrew day school established outside of New York City. He was the father of the late Dr. Joseph Schwartz, European director of the Joint Distribution Committee, and later executive vice-president of the United Jewish Appeal and the Israel Bond Organization. By 1958, most of the members of Shomrei Mishmeres had moved to new sections of the city, and the few elderly people left in the old downtown neighborhood could not maintain the synagogue. It was on the verge of being torn down to make room for a parking lot, when Wilbur J. Hunter, director of the Peale Museum of Maryland, brought to the attention of the National Park Service and the Baltimore Jewish community the historic and architectural significance of the building. Hunter's writing and lectures about the synagogue led to the establishment of a committee which persuaded the officers of Shomrei Mishmeres to sell the building to the community in order to preserve it.

While the synagogue's fate was being considered, the same community group, headed by Dr. Isaac Fein, was preparing to organize the Jewish Historical Society of Maryland. It was logical, therefore, for the Lloyd Street Synagogue to be acquired in 1962 by the Jewish Historical Society. Two years later the historic edifice was rededicated as a museum and historic shrine. The *mezuzah* at the museum's entrance was affixed by James Fensterwald, then 15 years old, who was a lineal descendant of Rabbi Abraham Rice who had dedicated the building on Sept. 26, 1845. Both the interior and exterior of the Greek Revival style building have been restored to their original style, except for a 30-foot extension at the eastern end of the structure, which was added in 1860. Most of the pews on the main floor and the balcony date from 1845. At the east end of the ground floor are two *mikvas*, one dating back to 1845. In the basement is a matzoth-baking oven. All the brass studs on the doors are the original, as are most of the locks and hardware and the iron foot-scrapers on the portico. The large round stained glass window over the Ark, which has been restored so skillfully that it is difficult to detect the new portions from the original, has as a major motif the Star of David, which is believed to be its first use in a synagogue stained glass window. The Orthodox congregation that sold the building laid down as one condition of the sale that no religious services of any kind be held in the building. This condition was motivated by concern that Reform or Conservative services might be held in the building. ☐

Lubavitcher Chabad House, 5721 Park Heights Ave.

Manhattan Park Apartments, 5715 Park Heights Ave., is a senior citizens apartment house of nine stories, jointly sponsored by Baltimore's Nathan Hackerman B'nai B'rith Lodge, the Associated

Jewish Charities, and Beth Jacob Congregation. The residents have access to the programs and facilities of the Jewish Community Center and Jewish Family Service, both located directly opposite the apartment building which adjoins Beth Jacob Congregation.

Maryland Historical Society, 201 W. Monument St., houses the Eleanor S. Cohen Collection which contains paintings and miniatures of the Cohen family—Mrs. Benjamin I. Cohen (Kitty Etting), Benjamin I. Cohen, et al.—silverware, and period furniture. The collection is located in the Cohen Room. Eleanor Cohen, daughter of Israel Cohen, was one of the principal benefactors of the society of which her cousin, Mendes Cohen, was president from 1904-1913. The society also has portraits of members of the Etting family. Among the more recent acquisitions is the Levy Collection of 200 pieces of sheet music and music books pertaining to *The Star Spangled Banner,* a gift of Lester S. Levy.

Morris Mechanic Theatre, on one side of Charles Center, which is connected physically to the Civic Center by an elevated promenade, one of the city's architectural showplaces, was built by and memorializes the prominent theatrical impressario.

Memorial to the Six Million, a bronze plaque 3½ feet high by 4½ feet long, and weighing 278 pounds, is in the reception room of the HIAS offices in the Harry Greenstein Social Service Building of the Associated Charities, 5750 Park Heights Ave. Paid for by the New Americans Club, the memorial design is a Star of David at the apex of an inverted triangle and a grill-enclosed memorial candle. Light beams radiate to scrolls on either side, one bearing the inscription in English, "In memory of the 6,000,000 of our people who perished under the Nazis," the other engraved with quotations in Hebrew from Lamentations: "Behold and see if there be any pain like unto my pain. . . The youth and the old man. . . My virgins and my young men are fallen by the sword."

Ner Israel Rabbinical College, 400 Mt. Wilson Lane, is believed to be the first American institution of Jewish higher learning to be accorded the right to grant graduate degrees in Talmudic Law by the Maryland State Board of Education in 1953.

Ner Tamid Greenspring Valley Synagogue and Center, 6214 Pimlico Rd.

Oheb Shalom Temple, 7310 Park Heights Ave., founded in 1853, was the synagogue whose pulpit was occupied from 1859-1902 by Rabbi Benjamin Szold, the father of Henrietta Szold.

Ohel Yaakov Cong., 3200 Glen Ave., founded in 1875, was facetiously known as *Die Franzaizische Shul* because so many of its members from East Europe came to synagogue dressed in formal clothes. Baltimoreans unacquainted with this amusing facetious reference were, for many years, under the impression that the congregation was made up of Jews from France.

Park Heights Ave. is itself a noteworthy point of Jewish interest because within a few blocks of this avenue there are four prominent synagogues, The Jewish Community Center, the Baltimore Hebrew College, the Associated Jewish Charities, the Board of Jewish Education, HIAS, the Council of Jewish Women, the Lubavitcher Chabad House, the Jewish Historical Society of Maryland, the Jewish Family Service, and the Associated Placement and Guidance Service.

Pickwick Jewish Center, 6221 Greenspring Ave.

Pimlico Race Track has in its Jockeys Hall of Fame a portrait of Walter Miller, the Brooklyn-born Jewish jockey who was recognized as the greatest rider of the early 20th century.

Rayner Avenue, which runs from 1801 Kirby Lane West one block north parallel to Harlem Ave., is named for William Solomon Rayner, industrialist, financier, and a founder of Har Sinai Congregation. By the mid-1850s, Rayner was one of the city's leading industrialists. He was also president of a gas company and had mining interests in Pennsylvania and North Carolina. After the Civil War, Rayner led the way in developing Locust Point as an industrial center.

His son, Isidor Rayner, was U.S. Senator from Maryland. He began his political career as a member of the General Assembly in 1878. In 1885 he was elected to the State Senate. He resigned to run for Congress to which he was elected in 1888 and reelected in 1890 and 1892. In the House of Representatives he was a staunch supporter of President Grover Cleveland, a leader in the fight for the repeal of the Sherman Silver Act, and an early advocate of the popular election of U.S. senators. From 1899-1902 he was attorney-general of Maryland. In 1905 Rayner was elected by the General Assembly to the U.S. Senate where he served until 1912. In and out of the Senate he led the fight against a move to disenfranchise Maryland's black citizens. He was also a strong supporter of the move to abrogate the Russo-American Commercial treaty because of Czarist discrimination against American Jews holding U.S. passports. At the 1912 Democratic National Convention at which Woodrow Wilson was nominated for president, William Jennings Bryan proposed that Rayner be nominated for vice-president. ☐

Shaar Zion Cong., 660 Park Heights Ave.

Sinai Hospital and Medical Center, Belvedere and Greenspring Aves., a $20,000,000 8-building complex opened in 1959, is the successor to the Hebrew Hospital and Asylum, founded in the 1860s. In the lobby of the main building there is a plaque memorializing Thomas Kennedy, sponsor of the Jew Bill. It pays tribute to Kennedy as "a Christian gentleman and an earnest advocate of civil and religious liberty" who "during his struggle for what he conceived to be right," said, "pray God, I may die before I cease to be the friend of civil and religious liberty, and a supporter of the rights of the people."

Star Spangled Banner Flag House, 844 E. Pratt St., a museum devoted to artifacts relating to the American flag, was saved from permanent closure in the 1930s by the late Aaron Straus, philanthropist and businessman.

Suburban Orthodox Synagogue, 7504 Seven Mile Lane.

Szold Drive, in the northwest section of Baltimore, is named for Henrietta Szold, founder of Hadassah, who was born in Baltimore. A plaque on the first home built on Szold Dr. (cor. of Szold Dr. and Bonnie Pl.) bears the seal of Hadassah and Miss Szold's name. Although she was prominent in a variety of activities, Henrietta Szold is best remembered as the founder of Hadassah. In her first visit to Palestine in 1909, she saw the appalling prevalance of trachoma (an eye disease which leads to blindness), and other maladies. While there, (Miss Szold was nearly 50 years old with a long career in Americanization work among Jewish immigrants in this country, having founded Baltimore's first evening high school), she conceived the idea of district nursing in the Holy Land.

This was the inspiration for Hadassah, founded in New York in 1912. Before Hadassah developed into the women's Zionist organization and a major influence on health and medicine in Palestine, it was the sponsor of the American Zionist medical unit that went to Palestine during World War I. Miss Szold was a Zionist before she had ever heard of Theodor Herzl. Her first Zionist address was made in 1895 before the Baltimore section of the National Council of Jewish Women, of which she was an active member. There she stressed the importance of Zionism to Jewish immigration problems and to the cultural and spiritual development of Judaism. Born Dec. 21, 1860, she was the daughter of Rabbi Benjamin Szold. After study in Baltimore schools, she became a teacher. In 1892 she was appointed editorial secretary of the Jewish Publication Society, a post she held for nearly 25 years. From 1904-1908 she edited the JPS's *American Jewish Year Book.* She translated into English Louis Ginzberg's *Legends of the Jews,* Moritz Lazarus' *Ethics of Judaism,* and Nahum Slouschz's *Hebrew Renaissance.* In 1935, recognizing the urgency of rescuing German-Jewish children from Nazi persecution, Miss Szold, then 75, became the director of the Youth Aliyah movement which brought the youngsters to Palestine. She died in 1945 at the age of 84. There are a number of memorials to her, among them the School of Nursing in Jerusalem, and Kfar Szold, a colony in southern Israel. □

Talmudical Academy of Baltimore, 445 Old Court Rd., is the oldest Hebrew day school in the U.S. outside of New York City. The study hall is named for the late Theodore R. McKeldin, former mayor of Baltimore and governor of Maryland, in appreciation of his many manifestations on friendship to the Jewish community.

Temple B'nai Sholom 4303 Ritchie Hwy.

Temple Emanuel, 3301 Milford Mill Rd.

United Orthodox Services, 3700 Labryinth Rd.

University of Maryland School of Social Work and Community Planning, 525 W. Redwood St., displays in its main building a portrait of the late Harry Greenstein, in recognition of the role he played in its founding. There is also on display a portrait of Henrietta Szold, who pioneered in many social activities. The Szold family lived on Lombard St., just a block from the present site of the University of Maryland's downtown campus.

Woodmore Hebrew Cong., 3607 Milford Mill Rd.

BETHESDA

Bethesda Jewish Cong., 6601 Bradley Blvd.

Cong. Beth El of Montgomery County, 8215 Old Georgetown Rd., has among its Torah Scrolls one that was a gift of the Jewish community of the West German state of Wuertemberg in memory of Dr. Otto Hirsch of Stuttgart. He was president of the Central Organization of German Jews until his deportation to the Mauthausen concentration camp, where he died in 1941. After World War II, the revived Jewish community of Stuttgart dedicated the Torah to Dr. Hirsch and stipulated that his son and two daughters should select the congregation in the U.S. to receive the Torah. Hans George Hirsch is a member of Beth El.

BOWIE

Temple Nevey Shalom, 12218 Torah Lane, originally known as the Jewish Congregation of Belair, occupies a site given it by Levitt Brothers, builders of the huge Belair community. When the congregation first acquired the site, the street was known as Trinity Lane but it was changed on a petition from the congregation. One of the principal contributors to the building fund was Paul Himmelfarb, Washington synagogue leader and philanthropist.

Temple Solel, 2901 Mitchelvale Rd.

BRUNSWICK

Beth Israel Synagogue, "A" St., stands empty and unused, a remnant of a Jewish community that no longer exists. The sign that reads "Kaplon's" can still be seen at the corner of Maryland Ave. and Potomac St., although the company started by Victor Kaplon is gone, as is the Jewish community he started in 1885.

CHEVY CHASE

National Institute of Health has in its administration building portraits of Dr. Milton J. Rosenau and Dr. Joseph Goldberger. Rosenau's portrait hangs in Wilson Hall, an auditorium on the 3rd floor, and the portrait of Goldberger is in the director's office on the first floor. While on the staff of the U.S. Public Health and Marine Hospital Service, Rosenau mastered the problem of anaphylaxis, or sensitivity to proteins. He standardized the diphtheria antitoxin and worked with Goldberger and others on the conquest of yellow fever. Later, he was professor of preventive medicine at the Harvard Medical School (see Cambridge, Mass.). Goldberger was also associated with the U.S. Public Health Service. He is best known for his research and discoveries in pellagra, and is credited with having proved that pellagra is related to an unbalanced diet.

Ohr Kodesh Congregation, 8402 Freyman Dr., occupies the first Jewish building of any kind erected anywhere in Montgomery County during its more than 300 years of existence. Founded in 1942 under the leadership of the Montgomery Lodge of B'nai B'rith, the congregation was first known as the Montgomery County Jewish Community when it was more of a community center than a synagogue. Freyman Drive is named for that organization's first president, Myer Freyman. One of the first stained glass Arks in a synagogue is in the congregation's sanctuary. The design and work of Philip Ratner, the Ark is a unit with six stained glass windows. The Hebrew letter *aleph* forms the central part of each window and is carried through to the Ark. In the front lobby of the synagogue is a memorial to the 6,000,000 victims of the Nazi Holocaust on which are inscribed the names of the relatives of congregational members lost during this tragic period. The memorial was given in the memory of the parents of Mr. and Mrs. Charles Liff. There is also a memorial plaque honoring by name the 11 Israel athletes murdered by Arab terrorists at the Olympic Games in Munich, Germany, Sept. 5, 1972. In the lobby there is a larger-than-life stone bust of Golda Meir by Bernice Marker.

Temple Shalom, 8401 Grubb Rd., has as part of its landscaping, a dwarf apple tree beautifully pruned into a seven-branched Menorah.

United Jewish Appeal Federation of Greater Washington, 4701 Williard Ave.

CHILLUM

Shaare Tefila Cong., 11120 Lockwood Dr.

COLLEGE PARK

Hillel Foundation at University of Maryland, 7505 Yale Ave., is said to have the largest kosher campus dining facility. *Breirah,* (Hebrew for "choice" or "alternative"), is the name of Hillel's outreach facility at 7712 Mowatt Lane.

Lefrak School of Architecture at University of Maryland is named for Samuel Lefrak, New York housing builder who is an alumnus of the university and was a varsity two-miler as an undergraduate.

M'Karev House, 7505 Dartmouth Ave., is the residence and headquarters of the Chassid on campus. (*M'Karev* means "to bring near"· in Hebrew.)

COLUMBIA

Interfaith Center, adjacent to Wilde Lake Village Green in this new city in Howard County, between Baltimore and Washington, D.C., is the home of all the religious groups in the village of Wilde Lake, one of seven villages which will form the city when it is completed in 1980. The Interfaith Center was erected by the Columbia Religious Facilities Corp. (CRFC), in which the Jewish Council of Howard County represents the Jews. Its partners are the Roman Catholics, the United Methodist-Presbyterians, the Lutherans (Missouri Synod), and the American Baptists. As the Jewish member of CRFC, the Council serves as the umbrella organization for the four congregations that use the center and also for the growing number of secular Jewish groups. The oldest Jewish congregation is Beth Shalom (Conservative); the others are Temple Isaiah (Reform); the nondenominational Columbia Jewish Congregation, which engages in what it describes as "innovative Judaism," and Cong. Ner Torah (Conservative). Under the Council's auspices, the four congregations co-sponsor a Sunday school and a weekday Hebrew school. Occasionally the Jewish congregations hold joint services and they co-sponsor community seders, cooperative Chanukah and Purim programs, and adult Jewish study activities. There is also an alternative Jewish Family School not affiliated with any congregation. The Interfaith Center is designed not as a house of worship in the traditional sense, but with a view to creating an environment conducive to new patterns of worship and community life. Under a single roof, tiered to give dimensions to the rooms, there are separate Catholic, Protestant, and Jewish worship areas which lead into a common foyer. The close proximity of the three areas allows one group to utilize another's space when needed. No group is permitted to have permanent religious appurtenances or symbols in its room. Everything is movable except the *mezuzah* on the door of the Jewish space. Banners and posters are used to decorate the rooms when they are being used for worship. Each of Columbia's six other villages will have its own interfaith center. The Jewish Community Council is involved in planning the interfaith center in the village of Oakland

Mills. The Jewish community of Baltimore is aiding the Council in meeting its share of construction costs. At the beginning of 1975 there were some 400 Jewish families in the city but this is expected to grow to about 600 by 1980.

CUMBERLAND
Cong. Beth Jacob, 11 Columbia St.
Jewish Welfare Fund, 72 LaValle Ct.
Temple B'er Chayim, 107 Union St.

EASTON
Temple B'nai Israel, Adkins Ave.

ELLICOTT CITY
Yaazor, a Jewish agricultural colony, was founded in 1902 by the Hebrew Colonial Society of Maryland, on 351 acres on Johnnycake Rd., between Rolling Rd. and the Patapsco River, northeast of Ellicott City. The original 25 settlers did not stay long but moved to Baltimore. Joseph Tobesman, a retired Air Force officer, remains on the plot his father owned, and operates a tree nursery.

ESSEX
Cong. B'nai Sholom, 401 Eastern Blvd.

FOREST HEIGHTS
Beth Chayim Cong.

FREDERICK
Cong. Beth Sholom, 20 W. 2nd St. Jews settled here in the 1740s.

GAITHERSBURG
Gaithersburg Hebrew Cong., P. O. Box 35.
Henry Diamond Ordnance Laboratory of the National Bureau of Standards, memorializes one of the nation's foremost scientists and inventors whose contribution to navigational landing aids saved countless American airmen during World War II. Diamond, who died at the age of 48 in 1948, pioneered in the development for American and Allied use of "blind landing" aids, the radiosonde for forecasting weather from the upper atmosphere, and the radio proximity fuse that explodes through electronic contact with its target. The fuse is widely used in bombs, rockets, and mortar shells.

GREENBELT
Mishkan Torah Cong., Ridge and Westway Rds.

HAGERSTOWN

Cong. B'nai Abraham, 55 E. Baltimore St.

Thomas Kennedy Monument is a tall graveside shaft over the grave of Thomas Kennedy, sponsor of the Maryland Jew Bill in the State Legislature. The plaque on the monument reads: "One who loved his fellow man." This monument was erected in 1918 by Brith Sholom in recognition of services rendered by Thomas Kennedy in the Legislature in 1818.

HAVRE DE GRACE

Adas Shalom Temple, Route 155 at Earltown.

HYATTSVILLE

Beth Torah Cong., 6700 Adelphi Rd.

KENSINGTON

Albert Einstein High School, 11135 Newport Mill Rd., is named for the famed scientist and Nobel Prize winner.

Temple Emanuel, 10101 Connecticut Ave.

LAUREL

Cong. Oseh Shalom, Briarwood Dr. off Route 197.

Jachman Drill Field, at the Army's Fort George Meade, memorializes Staff Sgt. Isadore S. Jachman, an alumnus of the Baltimore Talmudical Academy, who received the Congressional Medal of Honor posthumously for conspicuous gallantry at Flamierge, Belgium, on Jan. 4, 1945, during World War II. A member of Company B, 513th Parachute Infantry Regiment, Jachman was one of two Jewish soldiers to receive the Congressional Medal of Honor for heroism in World War II. President Harry Truman presented the medal to his parents at a White House ceremony.

LEXINGTON PARK

Beth Israel Cong.

LIBERTY LAKE

Holniker's Farm, a few minutes drive past the bridge over Liberty Lake, where there is a sign extending a welcome to Carroll County, and past the intersection of the Old Liberty Rd. and Rte. 97, there is a wrought iron gate marking the farm's entrance, and the site of Jewish worship services on the last Friday night of the month. Serving the 25-30 Jewish families who have moved into Carroll County in recent years, the services are hosted by Ken and Peggy Holniker, whose son, Scott David, was the first bar mitzvah in the County. Plans are in the making to establish Carroll County's first synagogue.

MT. RAINIER
Northeast Hebrew Cong., 4601 Eastern Ave.

NEWCOMB
Temple B'nai Israel, P.O. Box 12.

OCEAN CITY
Popular summer resort, and an increasingly year-round community on the eastern shore, has a growing number of Jewish residents and businessmen. There are, however, no synagogues or Jewish organizations, and those wishing to attend religious services can go to Salisbury, 23 miles away.

OLNEY
B'nai Sholom Congregation, Box 493, an Orthodox Shabbat *minyan* serving Olney and Rockville, has no synagogue as of 1976. There are, however, plans for two small synagogues, one in Rockville and one in Olney.

OWINGS MILLS
Jewish Museum, in the Enchanted Hills Apartments, cor. of Reisterstown Rd. and Enchanted Hills Rd., a Baltimore suburb, exhibits art works with Jewish themes, works by Jewish artists regardless of theme, and art belonging to Jewish collectors.

Youth Service Building, Baltimore Jewish Community Center, s.w. corner Garrison Forest Rd. and Gwynnbrook Ave.

PIKESVILLE
Central Hebrew Book Store, 228 Reisterstown Rd.

Sabra Room, a *glatt* kosher restaurant in this Baltimore suburb, is located just up the road from the Baltimore Yeshiva and down the road from Exit 20 of the Baltimore Beltway.

POCOMOKE CITY
Congregation of Israel, 3rd St., serves the dwindling Jews of this farm town on the eastern shore of Chesapeake Bay as well as those from Berlin, Snow Hill, Crisfield, and Princess Anne, in Maryland, and a few towns from nearby Virginia.

POTOMAC
Beth Ami Congregation, 8213 Lakenheath Rd.
Beth Sholom Cong., 11825 Seven Locks Rd.

Cong. Har Shalom, 11510 Falls Rd., occupies a building named for Ilene and Joel Kline, benefactors of the congregation. The sanctuary is named for Rabbi Morris Gordon, the congregation's first rabbi.

Washington Hebrew Cong., Falls Rd. at intersection of Tuckerman Rd., is the suburban branch of the oldest congregation in Washington, D.C.

RANDALLSTOWN

Ahavas Sholom Randallstown Synagogue Center, 8729 Church Lane.

Cong. Anshe Emunah-Aitz Chaim Liberty Jewish Center, 8615 Church Lane.

Cong. Beth Israel, 9411 Liberty Rd.

Memorial to Holocaust Victims, a nine-foot marble shaft on which is inscribed the Eleventh Commandment in Hebrew, *Thou Shalt Not Forget,* was erected in 1964 in the Randallstown Cemetery by Holiday Services of Baltimore, a group founded in 1939 by German-Jewish refugees. The group's burial society arranged for the placement of the memorial. The shaft is topped by a Star of David and the Hebrew inscription. Below this are the words: *In memory of the six million victims of tyranny in Europe and to those who fell in the defense of human dignity and freedom 1938-1945.*

Winands Road Synagogue Center, 8701 Winands Rd.

REISTERSTOWN

Reisterstown Jewish Center, 109 Cherry Valley Rd., serves some 400 Jews in this Baltimore suburb and a smaller number in Owings Mills, another suburb.

ROCKVILLE

Bethesda-Chevy Chase Jewish Community Group, 6125 Montrose Rd.

Beth Tikva Synagogue-Rockville Wheaton Synagogue, 2200 Baltimore Rd.

B'nai Israel Cong., 6301 Montrose Rd.

Lake Bernard Frank, off State Hwy. 28 (Norbeck Rd.) near Bauer Dr., was named by Maryland-National Capital Park and Planning Commission in honor of the late Bernard Frank, a prominent forester, land economist, and conservationist, who played an important role in helping to preserve the beauty of the Potomac Valley.

Jewish Community Center of Greater Washington, 6125 Montrose Rd., houses the first Jewish museum in the Washington suburban area. It stages changing exhibits but also has a permanent collection of Judaica and archeological artifacts, as well as the Kass Judaica Library. *Mitzvah Dance,* a sculpture by Wilton Hebald, is in the Center lobby. The drive fronting the center is known as Kochubiyevsky Drive, named for one of the first Soviet Jews imprisoned for seeking permission to emigrate to Israel.

Jewish Day School of Greater Washington, Montrose Rd. and Jefferson.

Jewish Social Services Agency of Washington, 6123 Montrose Rd., is part of the community complex that includes the center and the Hebrew Home of Greater Washington, 6121 Montrose Rd.

Silver Spring Hebrew Day Institute, Montrose Rd.

Temple Beth Ami, 6 Purdue Court.

ST. MARY'S CITY

Center for the Study of Major World Religions is being developed here by the Temple of Understanding, Inc., which seeks to promote better understanding of Buddhism, Christianity, Confucianism, Hinduism, Islam, Judaism, and others. It was at St. Mary's City in 1649 that the so-called first Act of Religious Tolerance was signed in the New World. This act extended its benefits only to those who believed in Jesus Christ.

SALISBURY

Cong. Beth Israel, 600 Camden Ave.

SILVER SPRING

Agudas Achim Academy Cong., 2107 Briggs Rd.

Cong. B'nai Israel, 1050 Georgia Ave.

Cong. Har Tzeon, 1840 University Blvd., W.

Cong. Ohavei Zekek, 8055-13th St.

Cong. Shaarei Tefila, 11120 Lockwood Dr.

Ezras Israel Cong., 8055-13th St.

Goodman Hebrew Books & Gifts, 2305 University Blvd.

Greater Washington Board of Jewish Education, 7961 Eastern Ave.

Hebrew Academy of Greater Washington, Seminary Rd. and Georgia Ave.

Kosher Kitchen of Greater Washington, bottom floor of the Eldorado Apts., 11200 Lockwood Dr., is a community-sponsored, nonprofit strictly kosher restaurant supervised by the Vaad HaKashruth of the Orthodox Council of Rabbis.

ORT Road, a street named for the local chapter of the American Women's ORT, is the approach to Parking Facility No. 7 between

Fenwick Lane and First Ave., near the Georgia Ave. and Colesville
Rd. intersection.
    Silver Spring Jewish Center, 1401 Arcola Ave.
    Southeast Hebrew Cong., 1090 Lockwood Dr.
    Summit Hill Cong., 8512 16th St.
    Temple Israel, 420 University Blvd., E., has a unique outdoor
memorial to the victims of the Nazi Holocaust in the form of an elaborate garden-patio and two massive sculptured tablets symbolic of the
Ten Commandments. Each Commandment is represented by its first
Hebrew letter. There are seven *lameds,* each of a different design. On
the first tablet there are *aleph, lamed, lamed, zayin,* and *kaf.* The second tablet has five *lameds,* for each of the last five Commandments
which begin with the word *lo,* which means "thou shalt not."
    Weizmann Yiddish Hebrew School, 11724 Auth Lane.
    Yeshiva High School of Greater Washington, 815 University
Blvd.
    Yom Tov Sephardic Society of Washington, 2410 Spencer Rd.
    Young Israel Shomrei Emunah, 1132 Arcola Ave.

SOLOMONS
    Isaac Solomon is memorialized in both this Calvert County vil-
lage of 183 people, and the nearby Solomons Island. Both places were
named for him in 1867. The village was originally part of the plantation of Alexander Somerville whose daughter married Solomon.

STEVENSON
    Cong. Chizuk Amunah, 8100 Stevenson Rd., located on a 72-
acre tract, the structure is built around three gardens, the largest of
which is known as the Garden of Hebrew Culture. All of the buildings
are of glass and fieldstone and the several gardens can be seen from
all of the buildings. The front wall of the synagogue, 60 feet high, has
sculptured windows reaching from floor to ceiling and in front of them
is an indoor garden.

TEMPLE HILLS
    Cong. Shaare Tikvah, 5404 Temple Hills, serves families drawn
mainly from workers employed at nearby Bolling Field and Andrews
Air Force Base. Two years after its dedication, it was virtually demolished by an unsolved bomb explosion. It was entirely rebuilt in
1969.

TOWSON
    Hoffberger Science Hall at Goucher College, dedicated in 1954,

was a gift of the Hoffberger Foundation, a philanthropic fund established by the well-known Baltimore Jewish family of industrialists and communal leaders.

WHEATON

Washington Jewish Book Store, 11250 Georgia Ave.

WOODLAWN

Afternoon *minyan* is conducted Mon. thru Thurs. at 12:30 p.m. in the main building of the Social Security complex.

MASSACHUSETTS

The *Mayflower* which carried the Pilgrim Fathers across the Atlantic to Plymouth Rock in 1620 brought no Jews, but it did carry men and women deeply imbued with ancient Hebrew traditions. The founders of Plymouth Colony and Massachusetts Bay Colony were, as James Truslow Adams, the England historian, said, "in spirit. . .Jews not Christians."

While living Jews were virtually unknown to the Puritans, Adams pointed out, their God was the God of the Jews, their laws the laws of the Hebrew Bible, and their guides the heroes and prophets of Israel. Nourished on the ancient Jewish moral and juridical traditions, the early New Englanders likened their intolerable status in England to the fate of the Jews of old. The Puritans saw England as a modern Egypt. King James I was hated as another Pharoah. Their hazardous crossing of the Atlantic was compared to Israel's crossing of the Red Sea. The barren shores of New England were cherished as the Promised Land. The Indians were identified with the "lost ten tribes" of Israel. Their wars with the Indians, on the other hand, recalled the struggles of the Israelites with the Philistines and Amalekites.

The "Christian Israelites," as some of the Puritans called themselves, sought methodically to recreate in a new land the theocracy developed by the Jews in Canaan, even to the extent of patterning their legal codes on Hebrew models. In 1642, Governor Bradford of Plymouth Colony wrote to Governor Bellingham of Massachusetts that "ye judicials of Moses are immutable and perpetual" for the guidance of the colony. When the famous Mayflower Compact was revised in 1658, it was prefaced by the statement that:

> *"it was the great priviledge of Israel of old, and soe was ac-*
> *knowledged by them. . .that God gave them right judgements*
> *and true lawes. . .and accordingly wee. . .can safely say. . .that*
> *wee have had an eye primarily and principally unto the*
> *aforesaid Platforms."*

Because they shaped their lives by the Hebrew Bible, the Puritans set great store on Hebrew learning. Daily prayers in Hebrew
were part of the early curriculum at Harvard, whose founder gave the
college its first Hebrew books. John Dunster, Harvard's first president,
consistently encouraged Hebrew scholarship. Three of the six orations
given at Harvard's first commencement, in 1642, dealt with Hebrew
themes. All of the leading Puritan divines knew Hebrew and did everything possible to further study of the language. One of the 1675
commencement addresses at Harvard referred to the college as "a beth
hamidresh," (a house of study), and quoted from Maimonides and from
speeches of John Harvard to compare the college's founder to the Jews
because he, like they, considered a school of greater importance than a
synagogue, and accordingly left his entire fortune for the endowment
of a college rather than to a church.

The ability to read the Hebrew Bible in the original was much
prized among the Puritans. The *Bay Psalm Book,* the first book published in America, appeared in 1640 with several words in the Hebrew
alphabet. An original translation of the Psalms from Hebrew, this
book was the most widely used prayer book in Colonial New England.
Even after the Pilgrim Fathers were gone, the Hebraic tradition remained potent in Massachusetts. In the absence of newspapers or
other means of communication, the pulpit was almost the only force
for molding character and ideals. Drawing freely on Old Testament
lore, the New England pastors ingrained in their people hatred of
monarchy and a passion for free government. From the lives and deeds
of Moses, Joshua, David, Gideon, and Samuel the preachers distilled
the spiritual influences that helped develop in the New Englanders
the old Hebraic characteristics of rugged individualism and resistance
to tyranny.

Biblical arsenals were among the chief source of weapons during
the pre-Revolutionary years of struggle between the colonies and England. By citing the doctrines and history of Israel, the clergy nourished
the rebellious spirit of the people. Sermons comparing King George III
to Pharoah and predicting that the same God who had saved Israel
from Egyptian bondage would free the colonies from British domination, were common in the decades before the Revolution. William E.H.
Lecky, the British historian, asserted that "in the great majority of instances the early Protestant defenders of civil liberty derived their
political principles from the Old Testament and the defenders of de-

spotism from the New." Other writers have said that "Hebraic mortar cemented the foundations of American democracy."

Although they patterned their lives on that of the ancient Hebrews, the Puritans admitted no kinship with living Jews, who were no more welcome in Colonial Massachusetts than pagans, Catholics, Turks, and Protestant dissenters. The atmosphere of Puritan America was hostile to all strangers, whatever their religion. A society which rigorously curbed differences and dissents, established bigotry as a way of life, and made control of conscience the law, had no room for living Jews. The Puritans were unaware of the glaring inconsistency of holding up the Jews of Biblical days as models to be emulated while simultaneously regarding their contemporary descendants as persons to be shunned. Yet, while Jews were rarities in the early days of Massachusetts, they were neither outlawed, like Catholics, Turks, and heathens, nor persecuted like Quakers and other Protestant dissenters. There was no official recognition of the Jews' right to live in Massachusetts, but stray Jews came and went with comparative freedom and a few even settled in Massachusetts Bay Colony within two decades after Boston was founded in 1630.

There is a slight possibility, as yet unproved, that Massachusetts' first Jew arrived only a few months after the Pilgrims landed on the *Mayflower*. In a letter to the *Philadelphia Public Ledger* of November 15, 1920, the Reverend Paul Sturtevant Howe of the Church of the Advent, Cape May, New Jersey, a genealogist, suggested that Moses Simonson, a passenger on the *Fortune* that arrived in Plymouth early in 1621, might have been a Jew from Amsterdam, Holland. Simonson's daughter Rebecca married John Soule, whose father, George, was a *Mayflower* passenger. Rebecca's son, Benjamin Soule, married Sarah Standish, granddaughter of Miles Standish.

That there may have been Jews in Massachusetts as early as 1644 is hinted at in a letter of 1645 from Plymouth's Governor Winslow to Governor John Winthrop of Massachusetts, reporting the failure of an effort in the Plymouth Legislature to enact a law that would have permitted religious toleration for all, including Jews. Historically, the first would-be Jewish resident, Solomon Franco, arrived in 1649, although one Isaac Abrahams is recorded as having sold a ship in Boston in 1648 and appeared before a notary. Franco had come from Holland with a cargo of goods for the colony's major general and found himself penniless when the fee to which he was entitled was refused. Alarmed lest he remain in Boston, the authorities supported him with an allowance for ten weeks until he could book passage back to Holland. Another 20 years elapsed before a Jewish resident was found in Massachusetts.

It was in 1668 that "Sollomon, ye Malata Jue," was arrested

and fined for violating the strict Sunday observance law. Probably an early peddler hawking his wares from a wagon, he had been apprehended traveling towards New Hampshire. On Boston's first published tax list, issued in 1674, appeared the name of Rowland Gideon, "ye Jew," who was taxed at 18 shillings. Another Jew, Joseph Bueno, who settled in Boston in 1680, was permitted to stay only after he had put up a bond guaranteeing that he would not become a public charge. The city's official list of residents for 1695 contained the names of two Jews, Raephaell Abandana and Samuell the Jew.

By 1697, the Frazon brothers, Joseph, Samuel, and Moses, were numbered among Boston's leading merchants. They maintained a large warehouse in Charlestown and owned ships plying between Boston and the West Indies. One of the Franzons successfully warded off the Reverend Cotton Mather's determined efforts to convert him. Another Frazon was probably the Jew to whom the Earl of Bellemont, a royal governor of Massachusetts, referred in 1699 when he investigated the reported circumcision and conversion to Islam of a captured English pirate. "I had him searched by a surgeon and a Jew in this town," the governor wrote: "they both declared on oath that he is circumcised." When Joseph Frazon died in 1703, the event was noted in the diary of the Reverend Samuel Sewall, pastor of the Second Church of Boston. Sewall recorded that Frazon "is carried in Simons's coach to Bristow, from thence by water to Newport (Rhode Island) where there is a Jew burying-place." This referred to the only Jewish cemetery in New England.

A number of Jewish merchants and shipowners were in and out of Boston on business by the early 1700s, as that city became the hub of Colonial commerce and the busiest port in the Americas. Among these were Michael Asher and his partner, Isaac Solomon, Isaac Lopez of London, Solomon and Joshua Isaacs, Joseph Brandon, Isaac Bar Judah, Judah Levy, Simon Barzelay, David Franks of the eminent Colonial family, and Jacob Judah. The latter got to Boston as a released prisoner of war in 1747.

By 1728, it appeared that a good-sized community was in the making when Asher and Solomon bought a lot on what is now Chambers Street and set it aside as a burial ground for "the Jewish nation." After 1750, all trace was lost of this cemetery. No permanent Jewish community materialized and the handful of Jews turned to Newport and New York for religious services and burial. Levy and Barzelay were among the Boston contributors in 1729 and 1730 to the building fund of New York's Congregation Shearith Israel.

The best known Jew in Colonial Massachusetts was Judah Monis, Italian-born, who came to Boston as a merchant with a little rabbinical training. In 1723 he received from Harvard the first degree granted a Jew by any college in America. Named instructor of Hebrew at Harvard after he had been publicly converted to Christianity, Monis wrote a Hebrew grammar for his pupils, which, when published by Harvard in 1735, was the first Hebrew book issued in North America. The first Jew to be elected to an office in Massachusetts was Isaac Lopez who was elected to the onerous post of constable in 1720, but he chose to pay a fine rather than serve.

The first Jew to be naturalized in Massachusetts was Aaron Lopez (no kin of Isaac), Newport merchant prince and shipowner, whose fleet of merchant ships became part of the American naval forces during the Revolution. Denied citizenship in Rhode Island because he was not a Christian, Lopez was naturalized at Taunton, October 15, 1762. In his application he said he had lived for a number of years both in Newport and Swansea. This same Lopez in 1777 created the first Jewish settlement in Massachusetts outside of Boston when he moved his family, and business from Newport to Leicester after the British occupied Newport.

During the Revolution there were still only a handful of Jews in Boston, among them the celebrated Moses Michael Hays, uncle of Abraham and Judah Touro, who were raised in Hays' home. Another was Isaac Moses, probably the same man who had been "warned out" of the city in 1762 because he was a penniless stranger. Later celebrated as a Revolutionary patriot who bolstered the credit of the Continental Congress, Moses helped relieve hunger in Boston during the British siege of 1775 by handling the bill of exchange for a cargo of corn consigned from Virginia to John Hancock and John Adams.

Two Jews are known to have served with Massachusetts regiments during the Revolution. Isaac Franks (see Philadelphia), was commissioned in the 7th Massachusetts Regiment. Abraham Solomon of Marblehead fought in the Battle of Bunker Hill and witnessed George Washington taking command of the Continental Army. When Solomon received a new uniform, he signed the muster roll in Hebrew letters characteristic of a Sephardic hand. He served with Colonel Grover's 21st Regiment of Marbleheaders which had the distinction of carrying Washington's troops across the Delaware on Christmas eve, 1776, to surprise the British at Trenton and Princeton.

After the Revolution, when there were still only a few Jewish residents in Massachusetts, mostly in Boston, and no organized Jewish community anywhere in the state, Boston counted among its leading citizens, Moses Michael Hays, his son Judah, his nephews, Abraham and Judah Touro, and their widowed mother. Judah Hays was one of the founders of the Boston Athenaeum, the first library association in the United States. In 1806 he was elected fire warden. Abraham Touro, who held the same post in 1809, provided some of the land for the Middlesex Canal. Hays and Touro were also shareholders in Boston's first theatre.

There were undoubtedly other Jews in Boston and perhaps elsewhere in the state, too, between 1800 and 1840, but seemingly never enough for a congregation. In 1815 a farmer in Pittsfield turned up one phyalactery while ploughing and set off much excitement over this "link" between the Indians and the "ten lost tribes" of Israel. The phylactery had probably been lost by some Jewish peddler who had bedded down in a farmer's field.

Massachusetts' permanent Jewish settlement probably dates from the 1830s when a group of Sephardic Jews from Algeria is said to have settled in Boston. In 1837 there arrived in Boston Isaac Wolf, a peddler. He was followed in 1841 by Peter Spitz, a cloth cap manufacturer; in 1842 by William Goldsmith, a hotel keeper; Bernard Fox; Charles Heineman, a peddler; Jacob Borton, a furrier; and Abraham Block, a soapmaker; in 1843 by Moses Ehrlich, drygoods dealer, and Bernard Wurmser, storekeeper. There were others too, whose names were not recorded, mostly peddlers who moved north and west of Boston with their merchandise and returned to Boston for the weekend and religious worship.

Most of the newcomers were from southern Germany or German Poland. They began holding worship services in Peter Spitz's home on Fort Hill, in 1842, with Wurmser acting as lay rabbi. On February 26, 1843, 18 families organized Massachusetts' first congregation, Congregation Ohabei Shalom, with Moses Ehrlich as the first president and Abraham Saling as rabbi. Later, services were held in Saling's home. Until 1844, when deaths occurred, these early Boston Jews had to take the bodies to Newport or New York for burial. A petition to the city government on April 29, 1844, asking permission to establish a Jewish cemetery on the outskirts of east Boston aroused such a storm of protest, much of it anti-Semitic, that it was rejected. On July 25th of the same year, the town council reversed itself and authorized the consecration of Massachusetts' first Jewish cemetery. There were 40 members in the congregation when it was chartered in 1845. They worshipped in private homes until 1852 when the first synagogue was erected—a wooden structure on Warren St. (the present Warrenton Street)—in Boston. In 1855 most of the German members of Ohabei Shalom seceded and formed Adath Israel, the ancestor of the present Temple Israel. Another split in 1858 gave birth to what is now Mishkan Tefilah.

The founders of the Jewish community settled first in Boston's South End but gradually moved to the North End where they did not have to compete with the Irish and Italians. Only one Jew had been known to live in the North End, then the city's commercial hub, until the 1850s, when some Jews opened men's and boy's clothing stores, the largest of these being owned by Leopold Morse. He was followed to the North End by Simon Vorenberg, Nathan Waxman, Asher Ratshesky, Simon Barnard, Wolfs, Isaacsons, Hermansons, Raphaels, and Wingerskys. Then came the second hand clothing dealers who lived in the back of their stores. By the end of the 1860s some Jewish peddlers from the South End also moved to the North End. Before long several *minyanim* were established in the North End. The Civil War industrial boom in the New England cotton and woolen mills and shoe factories attracted new Jewish immigrants, a few as factory workers but most as tradesmen and peddlers. By 1870 there were 2,500 Jews in Boston.

In 1864 the community had so many needy Jews that a Jewish relief agency was needed. This led to the establishment of the United Hebrew Benevolent Association, ancestor of the Combined Jewish Philanthropies, founded at a meeting of 27 of the more well-to-do Jewish businessmen. The Hebrew Women's Sewing Society was organized in 1878 to implement the work of the Benevolent Association. In 1888 Leopold Morse founded the state's first Jewish institutional agency, the Leopold Morse Home for Aged and Infirm Hebrews and an orphanage in Mattapan. Morse was then Boston's leading Jew. In 1876 he was a delegate to the Democratic National Convention. The following year he was elected to Congress. He served four consecutive terms and then was reelected in 1887, each time as a Democrat. No other Jew has ever been elected to Congress from Massachusetts. Morse's younger brother, Godfrey, was elected president of the Boston Common Council in 1883.

Many of the East European Jews who began arriving in the late 1870s and early 1880s had relatives in Boston's North End and they settled there. The newcomers were mechanics, carpenters, tailors, jewelers, shoemakers, and traders but some went to work in the textile mills and shoe factories. By 1894 Boston Jewry had grown to 20,000, almost three-quarters of them being recent immigrants. Some of the latter began finding their way to the booming mill towns where they first arrived as peddlers and then went into business or opened shoe repair shops and tailoring establishments. In 1882, Boston's Jews had raised $4,000 to bring over victims of Czarist pogroms but the community was not organized to handle them when they arrived. Some landed in the poorhouse. In 1895 Rabbi Solomon Schindler and Abraham Spitz proposed a unification of all Jewish charitable agencies in the city and the Federation of Jewish Charities was born, the first Jewish federation in the United States. The first president was Jacob Hecht whose wife had founded Hecht Neighborhood House in 1889 as a Hebrew industrial school to teach immigrant girls cooking, sewing, and other domestic arts.

New waves of immigration after the turn of the century raised

Boston's Jewish population to 60,000 in 1905 and to 85,000 ten years later. By the turn of the century the North End was becoming less and less Jewish as the West End became the heart of the Boston Jewish community and New England's counterpart of New York's Lower East Side. By 1920, however, Jews had almost entirely gone from the West End and settled down in the Dorchester-Roxbury-Mattapan area, which became Boston's equivalent of New York's Bronx and Harlem in the 1920s and 1930s. The rich Jewish life of Boston's Jews has been preserved in Charles Angoff's literary saga of the Polonsky family. At the end of World War I there was also considerable Jewish migration to Chelsea, Malden, Revere, and Everett. On the eve of World War II, the Jewish population of the state had grown to 190,000. Of this number, 118,000 were in Boston; 12,000 in Brookline; 5,000 in Newton; 18,000 in Chelsea; 12,000 in Malden; 6,000 in Revere; 4,000 in Cambridge; 1,900 in Everett; and 3,900 in Brockton.

The exodus from Boston began in the early 1950s when World War II veterans began leaving Roxbury, Dorchester, and Mattapan where most of them had grown up. In the late 1930s two out of every three Jews in Greater Boston lived in the Roxbury-Dorchester-Mattapan area. The more well-to-do settled down in the Brookline-Newton area, but much of the postwar Jewish settlement took place in the suburbs south of Boston—Canton, Holbrook, Sharon, Stoughton, and Randolph—where large medium priced housing developments attracted thousands of young Jewish families and gave birth to instant Jewish communities. Sharon quickly became half-Jewish; Randolph counted 6,000 Jews out of a total population of 30,000. Brookline is 30 percent Jewish and Newton 40 percent. Further dispersion created new Jewish communities in Natick, Lexington, Framingham, Weston, Belmont, Wellsley, and in many towns along Massachusetts Bay.

By 1960, the state's Jewish population had grown to an estimated 226,000, with Greater Boston accounting for 150,000. There was no significant change in the state's total number of Jews in the 1970s. Greater Boston's Jewish population rose to 180,000 but the newer settlements showed much greater increases as the exodus from Dorchester-Roxbury-Mattapan accelerated. A 1965 study by the Combined Jewish Philanthropies of Greater Boston reported that 176,000 Jews lived in its areas of service and 32,000 more in adjacent towns of Metropolitan Boston. Three-fourths of Greater Boston Jewry resided in the suburbs to the north, west, and south, while Boston itself, including Roxbury-Mattapan-Brighton-Dorchester, had only 40,000 Jews. Only 14,000 remained in the Dorchester-Mattapan-Roxbury section while in the Chelsea-Malden-Revere area, which was 40 percent Jewish in 1940, the number was declining steadily. By 1975, these historic Jewish neighborhoods were either dead or dying. Street after street had former Jewish stores boarded up, and many synagogues stood empty, or were converted into churches or schools by blacks. The handful of poor and elderly Jews who remained in the once thriving Jewish neighborhoods were being cared for through special programs of the Combined Jewish Philanthropies and its affiliated agencies. The shift from the older neighborhoods in and around Boston to the suburbs were reflected in the establishment of new synagogues in dozens of new communities within an hour's ride of Boston. Beyond Boston there were 35 cities and towns with 100 or more Jewish residents, all with one or more synagogues, many with a panoply of Jewish communal services and organizations. The largest of these were Lynn-Peabody (19,000); Brockton (5,200); Framingham (16,000); Springfield (11,000); Worcester (10,000); Haverhill (2,275); Holyoke (1,150); Lawrence (2,550); Lowell (2,000); New Bedford (3,100); Pittsfield (2,400); Fall River (3,300), and Leominster (1,500). There are communities with synagogues in Plymouth and Salem, where the Pilgrims first settled, as well as on Cape Cod (Hyannis) and Martha's Vineyard, popular seashore resorts.

Massachusetts is the home of two major national Jewish institutions, Brandeis University, founded in 1948, in Waltham, and the American Jewish Historical Society, whose headquarters is on the Brandeis campus. Harvard University, in Cambridge, has a long history of Jewish association even though it had earlier limited Jewish students by a quota system. The roster of Harvard alumni and eminent faculty reads like a who's who of American Jewry. Among them were Louis D. Brandeis and Felix Frankfurter, both justices of the Supreme Court; Judge Charles E. Wyzanski of the U.S. Court of Appeals, a former head of the Harvard Board of Overseers, whose grandfather founded the state's first Hebrew school in 1852; Paul Freund, the eminent authority on constitutional law; the late Dr. Harry Wolfson, Jewish philosopher; Oscar Handlin, historian and Nobel Prize winner; and Dr. Paul J. Sachs, who headed the Fogg Museum of Art for 25 years. The Menorah Society, now displaced by the Hillel Foundations, was founded at Harvard in 1906 as the first Jewish intercollegiate movement. The prestigious Massachusetts Institute of Technology had a Jewish president in the 1970s, Dr. Jerome Wiesner, former science advisor to the White House, and three Jewish Nobel Prize winners, Kenneth Arrow, Simon Kuznets, and Paul Samuelson. The Jewish student protest against the Jewish establishment's priorities began in Boston in 1969 and the first Jewish student publication, *Response,* appeared in Waltham. The Combined Jewish Philanthropies, which in 1920 succeeded the Federation of Jewish Charities, was the first federation to give financial support to Jewish education locally.

It is widely known that Secretary of State Henry Kissinger was once a professor at Harvard, but few know that in the 1970s the world's greatest authority on linguistics was Dr. Noam Chomsky of the Massachusetts Institute of Technology, that Dr. Henry Rosovsky was dean of the faculty of arts and sciences at Harvard, that Albert Sachs was dean of the Harvard Law School, a post once held by Felix Frankfurter, that Joel Trachtenberg was dean of the Boston University College of Liberal Arts, and that so many Jewish students attend the Catholic-sponsored Boston College that it has removed the crucifixes from its classrooms and closes on Yom Kippur.

Despite their prominence in the State's business, civic, cultural, professional, and philanthropic life, Massachusetts Jewry, the sixth largest in the country, has not been too well represented in public office. There have been many Jews elected to municipal and state legislative bodies and many Jews have served and are now serving as judges in the lower county and state courts. But only one Jew has been elected to a state-wide office. The late George Fingold, who was elected attorney general of Massachusetts in 1952, and twice reelected, was the Republican nominee for governor when he died suddenly in 1958 at the age of 49. Three Jews were Federal judges—Frank H. Freedman of Springfield on the United States District Court; Herbert N. Maletz of Boston on the United States Customs Court; and Charles Wyzanski of Federal Circuit Court of Appeals. Two Jews served on the State Supreme Court, Jacob J. Spiegel of Boston, who was appointed in 1961, and Benjamin Kaplan in 1969. Judge Franklin Faschner was named chief justice of the District Court system in 1970. Holyoke, Springfield, Worcester, Pittsfield, Chelsea, Salem, and Revere have had Jewish mayors. Boston had a Jewish acting-mayor (William Berwin) in 1905.

* * * * *

ACTON
Cong. Beth Elohim, 82 High St.

ALLSTON
Charlesview, a 212-unit housing complex opposite Harvard Stadium, North Harvard St. and Western Ave., was the first housing development in the state to be jointly sponsored by Catholics, Jews, and Protestants. Cong. Kadimah-Toras Moshe is one of the owners. About one-fourth of the residents are Jewish.

ALTON
Hillel Foundation at Nichols College, 18 Strawberry Hill Rd. (Dudley).

AMHERST

Hillel Foundation at Amherst College, Chaplain's Office, Chapin Hall.

Hillel Foundation at University of Massachusetts, 215 Student Union Bldg.

Lubavitcher Chabad House, 30 N. Hadley Rd.

ASHLAND

David Mindess Middle School, 90 Concord St., is named for the town's school superintendent who died in 1972. A bronze plaque with his likeness is in the lobby.

ATHOL

Temple Israel, 107 Walnut St.

ATTLEBORO

Cong. Agudas Achim, N. Main St.

BELMONT

Beth El Temple Center, 2 Concord Ave.

BEVERLY

Cong. Ohav Sholom, 3 Beckford St.

Temple B'nai Abraham, 200 E. Lothrop St.

BOSTON

Associated Jewish Community Centers of Greater Boston, 72 Franklin St.

Associated Synagogues of Greater Boston,   177 Tremont St., a six-story building, has a daily *minyan* in downtown Boston. It houses the Massachusetts Board of Rabbis, the Massachusetts Rabbinical Court of Justice (Beth Din), the Vaad Harabonim, and a reading room with many Jewish periodicals.

Beth Israel Hospital, 330 Brookline Hospital, is a world-famous medical center which is one of the major teaching hospitals of the Harvard Medical School.

Boston Evening Clinic, 314 Commonwealth Ave., has treated millions of patients since it was founded in 1927 by Dr. Morris A. Cohen.

Boston University

Mugar Memorial Library, 771 Commonwealth Ave., houses the Rabbi Joseph S. Shubow Collection of books and manuscripts dealing with the Nazi era, and a wide selection of Judaica literature, bequeathed by the late rabbi of Cong. B'nai Moshe, Brighton. ●The Samuel Weisberg Collection of Jewish Ritual Silver, including several superb examples of Menorahs, Torah ornaments, seder plates, spice boxes, and other religious objects in silver ●In the chapel of the University School of Theology, 775 Commonwealth Ave., are two stained glass windows of special Jewish interest; one depicts the entrance to King Solomon's Temple in Jerusalem, and a balcony window frames a medallion picture of the Four Chaplains of World War II, from left to right, George Fox, Boston U. alumnus; Clark V. Poling, a Baptist; John P. Washington, a Catholic priest; and Alexander A. Goode, a rabbi. ●Center for Applied Social Science, 270 Bay State Rd., has the Joseph G. Brin Library, named for the editor of the *Boston Jewish Advocate,* and his portrait. ●The Paul Simons Memorial Room, named for the first chairman of the center's board. ●The Lipsky Reading Room, named for Mr. and Mrs. Benjamin Lipsky of Brookline. ●Dewey D. and Harry K. Stone Science Building, 675 Commonwealth Ave., was a gift of two Brockton businessmen and noted Zionist leaders. ●Alfred L. Morse Auditorium, 602 Commonwealth Ave., once the home of Temple Adath Israel, is named for the shoe magnate whose gifts made possible the acquisition of the building and its complete renovation. ●Sherman Student Union Bldg., 775 Commonwealth Ave., is named for George Sherman, university trustee and Jewish philanthropist. ●Portrait bust in marble of Dr. Samuel M. Waxman, a professor of Romance languages at the University, is in Room 17 of the Department of Foreign Languages, 675 Commonwealth Ave. ●Housman Research Center, Harrison Ave. and E. Concord St., was a gift from David Housman, pioneer manufacture of automobile radios. ●Dr. Abraham Krasker Memorial Film Library, in the School of Education Building, 765 Commonwealth Ave., memorializes the late Abraham Krasker, a member of the university faculty for more than 30 years and founder of the film library, one of the first in the country, in 1930. ●Ziskind Lounge in the Sherman Student Union Bldg., is named for Jacob Ziskind, a Fall River manufacturer and philanthropist. ●Hillel Foundation, 233 Bay State Rd., has a metal sculpture, *Triumph of the Torah,* on an inside wall. ●School of Medicine, 80 E. Concord St., has in the lobby of its instructional building, the Bernard Appel Hall of Medicine, named for Dr. Bernard Appel, professor emeritus of dermatology at Tufts University School of Medicine. The Appel Hall consists of 12 massive stone plaques, each 8 feet high, depicting in bold relief the great figures in the history of medicine. The work was conceived and executed by medical historian and sculptor Doris Appel, the wife of Dr. Bernard Appel, for the Medical Musuem of the Armed Forces Institute of Pathology in Washington D.C. in 1940, and donated in 1976 by two of Dr. Appel's daughters and their husbands, Dr. and Mrs. George M. Sanger and Dr. and Mrs. G. Robert Baler. □

Boys Clubs of Boston, Evan D. Jordan Gym, in Charleston, displays a portrait of the late Nate Cohasset, for more than two decades physical education director of the Bunker Hill unit of the Boys' Clubs.

Peter Bent Brigham Hospital, 721 Huntington Ave., has a cardiac research laboratory named for the late Dr. Samuel A. Levine, world-renowned cardiologist.

Bunker Hill Monument, famous shrine across the Charleston Bridge from downtown Boston, near the Navy Yard, would never have been completed but for the generosity of Judah Touro (see New Orleans). In memory of the Battle of Bunker Hill, a group of citizens planned a monument after the Revolution. Early support for the memorial soon petered out and from the time General Lafayette laid the cornerstone in 1825 until 1840 there was great difficulty in raising funds. For many years the monument remained unfinished, a taunt to civic pride. Finally, a Boston merchant, Amos Lawrence, agreed to give $10,000 if another citizen would be found to match his offer. Half a continent away, Judah Touro, of New Orleans, remembering his happy days in Boston, in the home of his uncle, Moses Hays, wrote a check for $10,000 and thus made possible the completion of the monument. At its dedication on June 17, 1843, President John Tyler, Daniel Webster, and Oliver Wendell Holmes paid tribute to Touro. Webster, Joseph Story, Edward Everett, and ex-President John Quincy Adams were commissioned to prepare an inscription for a plaque on the monument, as a permanent tribute to Touro and Lawrence. But to this day there is nothing on the monument to link Touro and Lawrence with the shrine whose completion they made possible. A verse read at the Faneuil Hall banquet marking the dedication is part of the American epic:

Amos and Judah–venerated names,
Patriarch and Prophet, press their equal claims.
Like generous coursers, running neck and neck,
Each aids the work by giving it a check.
Christian and Jew, they carry out one plan,
For though of different faiths, each in heart is a man.

Bureau of Jewish Education, 72 Franklin St.

Charles River Park Synagogue, 55 Martha Rd., was the first congregation to return to the inner city and locate in the renovated West End after its old North Russell St. synagogue (Cong. Beth Hamedresh Hagodol Beth Jacob) was torn down to make way for urban renewal. In a new modern building, and under its new name, the synagogue continues the Orthodox tradition but now seeks to serve the young Jewish professionals who have repopulated the area.

Charles Street Playhouse, Warrenton St., is the oldest building still standing in Boston that was once a synagogue. Temple Ohabei Shalom acquired the building in 1863 and used it as a synagogue until 1887.

Combined Jewish Philanthropies, 72 Franklin St., serves all of Greater Boston. In its entrance foyer there is a 16-foot bas-relief depicting the theme of zedekah, based on a quotation from the Ethics of the Fathers. The Gerald Wohlberg Middle East Research Library is located in the CJP building.

Consulate General of Israel, 450 Park Square Bldg., 31 St. James Ave.

Emerson College Hillel Foundation, c/o Michael Markman, 323 Newberry St.

Sidney Farber Cancer Center, 35 Binney St., part of the Harvard Medical School, is named for the late Dr. Sidney Farber, renowned pathologist whose work with chemotherapy in treating leukemia and other childhood cancers brought him world-wide recognition.

Arthur Fiedler Bridge, a walkway crossing Storrow Dr. and connecting Beacon St. with the park along the Charles River where the Hatch Memorial Hall is located, is named for the popular conductor of the free outdoor summer Boston Pop Concerts which he started in 1930.

Edward A Filene Memorial, a plaque at the corner of Boylston St. and Carver, near the entrance to Boston Common, honors the famous merchant as one of the founders of the credit union movement in the U.S. The tablet was erected by the National Credit Union Association.

Lee Max Friedman Hall, the concourse level of the Central Library's general library building, on the west side of Copley Sq., is named for the late attorney, historian, and president of the American Jewish Historical Society. He was one of the four benefactors from whom the library received funds used toward the construction of its addition. Friedman Hall includes a lecture hall and several conference rooms. Friedman's name is inscribed to the left of the entrance to the audio-visual area.

Genesis 2, 233 Bay State Rd., is the Jewish student paper for the Boston Metropolitan area.

Greek Orthodox Church, Union Park St., originally built as a church, was the synagogue of Temple Ohabei Shalom from 1887 until its present structure in Brookline was occupied.

Greenbaum St., formerly Macallen St., is named for Joseph

Greenbaum, head of the Court Square Press and a former president of Temple Emanuel in Newton.

Harvard Club, 374 Commonwealth Ave., honors 83 of Harvard's most distinguished alumni, including Supreme Court Justices Louis D. Brandeis and Felix Frankfurter, with the display of their portraits.

Harvard School of Public Health, 55 Shattuck St., displays in its lobby a portrait of Dr. Milton J. Rosenau, a founder of the school and one of the great pioneers in the field of preventive medicine and public health. It was at Harvard, in 1909, that Dr. Rosenau organized the first department of preventive medicine. He was also one of the founders of the first postgraduate school of public health in the country, jointly operated by Harvard and M.I.T. A plaque honoring the founders, including Dr. Rosenau, is affixed to one of the lobby walls.

Jewish Advocate, 251 Causeway St.

Jewish Community Council of Metropolitan Boston, 72 Franklin St.

Jewish Crafts Center, 233 Bay State Rd.

Jewish Family and Children's Service, 31 New Chardon St.

Jewish Vocational Service, 20 Boylston St.

Jewish War Veterans Drive, in heart of Franklin Park section, is named for the country's oldest existing veterans organization by act of the State Legislature.

Kivie Kaplan Building of Boston's branch of National Association for Advancement of Colored People, is named for the late philanthropist and civil rights champion, who was national president of NAACP from 1966 until his death in 1975.

John F. Kennedy Presidential Library and Museum is to be built at the University of Massachusetts' Columbia Point campus in the Dorchester section of Boston. It will have among its thousands of documents and memorabilia, a number of items of Jewish interest. One is a Torah Scroll which belonged to Rabbi Isaac Mayer Wise and was presented to President Kennedy in 1961 by the Union of American Hebrew Congregations. ●A silver menorah given to the President at the same time will also be in the library. ●Among the papers will be those of James P. Warburg, a member of President Franklin D. Roosevelt's first "Brain Trust," and during World War II deputy director of the overseas branch of the Office of War Information. ●Drafts, manuscripts, and proofs of Theodore H. White's books on presidential campaigns. ●A large number of microfilms of speeches, photographs, and clippings dealing with Secretary of Labor Arthur J. Goldberg. ●A Nieman Fellow's plaque that lists David Halberstam, co-winner of the 1964 Pulitzer Prize for his newspaper coverage of the Vietnam War. Pending the completion of the library, all of its contents are stored in the Federal Records Center in Waltham.

Kirstein Memorial Library, branch of the Boston Public Library,

20 City Hall Ave., was erected in 1930 and given to the city by the late Louis E. Kirstein as a memorial to his parents. The library contains one of the finest collections of books on business, trade, commerce, and industry. A plaque outside the front door records Kirstein's gift. Inside is a photograph of Kirstein and an inscription noting that he was a trustee of the public library from 1919-1942. There is also a large framed scroll presented to Kirstein by the city. Born in Rochester, N.Y., in 1867, Kirstein once owned the Rochester Baseball Club of the International League. Settling in Boston in 1894, Kirstein became one of the city's leading merchants as head of the Filene Store. A pioneer in labor-management relations, he devoted himself to the civic welfare of his adopted city for a generation. Kirstein helped found Harvard's School of Business Administration and served on the National Labor Relations Board in the early days of the New Deal. Equally active in Jewish affairs, he was the first president of the Associated Jewish Philanthropies, chairman of the executive committee of the American Jewish Committee, president of the Graduate School for Jewish Social Work, and honorary national chairman of the United Jewish Appeal. He died in 1942.

The Madonna, a 30-foot statue atop a six-foot sphere in front of the Don Orione Home for Aged Italian-Americans, was designed by Arrigo Minerbi, a prominent Italian-Jewish sculptor. He was saved from the Nazis when he was in his 60s by the Don Orione fathers who hid him in their home in Rome. In appreciation, Minerbi promised to repay the debt one day, and when he heard there was to be a Don Orione home in America, he offered to create an appropriate religious monument.

Masonic Temple, Boylston and Tremont Sts., a shrine of New England Masonry, displays a portrait of Moses Michael Hays, a copy of an original by Gilbert Stuart, alongside the portrait of Paul Revere. Son of a New York merchant, Hays moved to Newport, R.I., sometime before the Revolution. In reply to a challenge to his loyalty to the American cause he published a notable petition to the Rhode Island General Assembly in 1776 in which he refused to sign a loyalty oath on the ground that it was unconstitutional and discriminatory. Hays settled in Boston after the Revolution began where his home attracted the city's mercantile and social leaders. Hays was prominently identified with the introduction into the U.S. of the Ancient and Accepted Scottish Rite of Masonry. He was named in 1768 deputy inspector-general of Masonry for North America and authorized to establish the Scottish Rite in America. From 1788-1792 he was grand master of the Grand Lodge of Massachusetts, and Paul Revere was his deputy grand master. One of the country's leading marine insurance brokers, Hays was a founder of Boston's first bank, which through reorganizations, is now the First National Bank. He died in 1805 and is buried in the famous Touro Cemetery at Newport, R.I.

Massachusetts General Hospital, displays in the corridor leading to the trustees room of this pioneer hospital on Fruit St., a Gilbert Stuart portrait of Abraham Touro, brother of Judah, who was one of Boston's leading businessmen in the early 19th century. He bequeathed $10,000 to the hospital and $15,000 to the Newport Synagogue in whose cemetery he is buried. He also left large sums to other Boston charities. Judah Touro also bequeathed $10,000 to the hospital in 1854.

Museum of Fine Arts, 465 Huntington Ave., displays many works by Jewish masters, but the best known painting of Jewish interest is Jacob Binder's *The Talmudist*. This painting is said to have been commissioned as a protest against John Singer Sargent's painting, *The Synagogue,* in the Boston Public Library. Binder denied this, even though his work was completed in the same year as the controversial Sargent mural. Binder was Sargent's protégé and studied with him. ●Also in the museum is the M. and M. Karolik Collection of 18th century American arts, a gift of the Karoliks in 1941. They spent six years assembling the 350 objects (paintings, furniture, textiles, silver, glass, and porcelains), all representing Colonial and early Federal America. ●There is also the Lee M. Friedman Collection of prints and impressionistic art.

Museum of Science, Science Park, near Lechmere Sq., has the Cahners Theatre, named for Norman Cahners, magazine publisher, and Mrs. Cahners. The museum's elegant conference room is also named for Cahners.

New Courthouse, Pemberton Sq., has portraits of the late Justice Jennie Loitman Barron, first woman justice of the Massachusetts Superior Court, and the late Judge Lewis Goldberg. In 1950 Justice Barron was named the "national American mother" of the U.S. A local school is named in her honor.

Northeastern University Law School, Huntington Ave., is housed in Gryzmish Hall, named for industrialist-philantrophist Reuben Gryzmish. ●In the Law School library is the Sara R. Ehrmann Collection of books, pamphlets, studies, and documents on capital punishment amassed by Sara R. Ehrmann, a lifelone crusader against capital punishment. Her husband, Herbert Ehrmann, an eminent Boston lawyer, was a member of the team of attorneys that vainly sought to save the lives of Sacco and Vanzetti in the 1920s. ●The library itself is named for Abram Berkowitz, who earned his law degree at Northeastern in 1915. ●The lobby of the university's Carl S. Ell Student Center, 360 Huntington Ave., is known as the Clara and Joseph F. Ford Lobby in honor of a couple whose philanthropies are widely known. Portraits of the Fords hang in the lobby. ●The university's Hillel Foundation is in the student center. ●The Riesman Lecture Hall in the Graduate Center Bldg. is named for an electrical manufacturer from Brookline who, in 1914, received a scholarship from the university. ●The Lovinger Conference Room in Hayden Hall is a memorial to Merrill Lovinger, a young lawyer from Newton who was murdered in his home by gunmen in 1957.

Old Vilna Shul, 16 Phillips St., a traditional Orthodox congregation, is the last synagogue on Beacon Hill.

Posner Hall, on Harrison Ave., the residence hall for medical students of Tufts College and for interns and residents of the New England Center Hospital, is named for Mr. and Mrs. Harry Posner of Medford. In 1953 they gave Tufts $1 million in stock in a company the Posners owned. Russian-born immigrants who came to America in 1900, the Posners made the gift "as part payment of the debt we owe this land of freedom and opportunity." The Posners also gave the Tufts School of Dentistry the Daniel E. Ziskin Research Laboratory in memory of Posner's brother-in-law, a pioneer in oral pathology at Columbia University.

Public Library, on the west end of Copley Sq., has in the John Singer Sargent Gallery, the artist's famous wall painting, *The Synagogue,* one of a series of mural paintings on Judaism and Christianity. In the 1920s, when *The Synagogue* was first installed in the library, it created a great stir in Jewish circles where it was regarded as a slur on Judaism. Petitions were submitted to the mayor of Boston and to the library trustees demanding the removal of the picture. Jewish objections to the painting grew out of the fact that Sargent depicts the synagogue as a grim, ugly old woman, with blinded eyes and bent head from which a crown is falling. In her hands is a broken sceptre and she clutches to her breast what are supposed to be the Tablets of the Law. All about her is in chaos and ruin. The protest was based on the fact that the painting suggests that the synagogue represents what is broken and passed away. Jewish criticism was heightened by the fact that an adjoining panel, also by Sargent, depicted the Christian church as a bright young maiden, alert, proud, and dignified. Today the controversy is all but forgotten and visitors hardly notice the once talked-about murals. More attention is paid to Sargent's *Frieze of the Prophets,* a painting depicting Moses holding the Tablets of the Law, with the prophets of the Bible lined up beside him. ●The library's Fanny Goldstein Judaica Collection was built up over 30 years by the late Fanny Goldstein, branch librarian of the West End branch. It is now in the Central Library where it serves as the nucleus for a larger collection of books, some of which are now on open shelves in the General Library Building.

Pucker-Safrai Gallery, 171 Newbury St., is devoted to the exhibition of the art of Israel, as well as to "modern Judaica."

State House, on Beacon St., facing the north east section of Boston Common, has a bronze bust of Justice Louis D. Brandeis commissioned by the Commonwealth of Massachusetts on the 3rd floor near the chamber of the House of Representatives. It was the first such memorial in honor of a judge in Massachusetts' history. ●The State House Library, known as the George Fingold Memorial Library, was named in honor of Fingold in 1960. A Republican nominee for governor, he had served as attorney-general of the Commonwealth from 1953 until his death in 1958. There is a memorial plaque in the library with a bas-relief of Fingold. ●In the Archives Museum of the State House is the manuscript history of Plymouth Plantation by Gov. William Bradford, Plymouth Colony's second governor. What gives this celebrated document Jewish pertinence is the fact that it contains a Hebrew preface occupying eight and a half pages. On the first two pages the Hebrew words are written in English characters. The other pages are in Hebrew characters. ●Also in the museum is a Civil War battle flag carried by Sgt. Leopold Karpeles, a Union Army regimental color bearer, who was the first Jew to win the Congressional Medal of Honor. ●In the archives, beneath the State House, is displayed the Massachusetts State Convention of 1770, written largely by John Adams. His bill of rights antedates the Federal Bill of Rights, including the religious freedom clause. ●In the Old State House, on Devonshire St., is a naval museum which displays advertisements for packet boats between Liverpool and Boston, one of which is called *The Wandering Jew.* ●In the State House's Hall of Fame is the Chaplain's Memorial, a piece of sculpture that represents a Protestant and a Catholic chaplain ministering to a wounded Jewish soldier.

Temple Israel, 260 Riverway, Plymouth St. and Longwood Ave., has a Louise Nevelson 20-foot high steel sculpture entitled *Covenant,* completely covering the exterior concrete wall to the left of the Riverway entrance of the new temple dedicated in 1973. The sculpture is the first public work in or near Boston by Nevelson, who is regarded as one of the greatest sculptors of her day. The windowless walls of the temple's main sanctuary retain contact with the outside through a transparent ceiling and walls of the clerestory embracing the pulpit and skylight roofing the main foyer. The Ark is designed with sloping sides to symbolize Mount Sinai. There is an outdoor memorial garden containing Biblical flowers and plants. The Meeting House segment of the temple, an older unit, is named for the late Rabbi Joshua Loth Liebman. The auditorium in the complex is named for Rabbi Harry Levi, Liebman's predecessor.

Zion African Methodist Episcopal Church, Columbus Ave. and

Northampton St., occupies the first building erected in 1885 by Temple Israel.

Zionist House, 17 Commonwealth Ave., headquarters of local Zionist organizations, is used for meetings, conferences, and rallies. It serves as an information center, houses a library, and makes its facilities available to community groups.

BRAINTREE

Temple B'nai Sholom, 41 Storrs Ave.

BRIDGEWATER

Horace Mann Auditorium of the Southeast Massachusetts State University, founded in 1840 by the great educator, Horace Mann, has a panel of five murals depicting the progress of education through the ages in which the fifth mural is called *The Lord Thy God Is One Lord*. This panel is a monument to early synagogue schools and depicts the High Priest, Joshua ben Gamla, instructing children in the Torah. Behind the High Priest is an open Ark and a seven-branched Menorah.

BRIGHTON (Section of Boston)

Bluestone Square, cor. Chiswick Rd. and Commonwealth Ave., is named for Sgt. Edward Bluestone, who was killed in France on D-Day (June 6, 1944).

Brookline-Brighton-Newton Jewish Community Center, 50 Sutherland Rd.

Cong. Beth David, 64 Corey Rd.

Cong. Chai Odom, 77 Englewood Ave.

Cong. Kadimah-Toras Moshe, 113 Washington St.

Lt. Kalish Sq., Commonwealth and Chestnut Aves., honors Sumner J. Kalish, killed in 1944.

Kaplan Square, Washington St. at Commonwealth Ave., is named for Stanley N. Kaplan, who was killed in World War II.

Leventhal House, 40 Wallingford Rd., a Jewish community housing complex for the elderly, is sponsored by the Jewish Community Housing for the Elderly, a project of the Combined Jewish Philanthropies of Greater Boston.

Rabbi Joseph S. Shubow Memorial Park, a small green area in front of Temple B'nai Moshe, memorializes the Temple's late rabbi, who, during his many years of service in the Jewish and general community, had sought to preserve the park now named for him.

Temple B'nai Moshe, 1835 Commonwealth Ave.

Ulin House, 30 Wallingford Rd., is a housing project for the elderly sponsored by the Jewish Community Housing for the Elderly.

BROCKTON

Combined Jewish Philanthropies of Greater Boston, 71 Legion Pkwy.

Cong. Agudas Achim, 144 Belmont Ave.

Jewish Family Service, 71 Legion Pkwy.

South Areas Jewish Community Center of Associated Jewish Community Centers of Metropolitan Boston, 71 Legion Pkwy.

Temple Beth Emunah, Torrey and Pearl Sts.

Temple Israel, 184 W. Elm St.

BROOKLINE

Allerton Hospital, Chestnut St.

Cong. Beth David, 64 Corey Rd., the congregation of the Talner Rebbe (the late Meshulem Z. Twersky), is now led by his son, Prof. Yitzhak Twersky, who occupies the Littauer Chair of Hebrew and Jewish Philosophy at Harvard University.

Cong. Kehillath Israel, 384 Harvard St.

The Hebrew College, 43 Hawes St. (formerly the Hebrew Teachers College), was founded in 1921. It trains Hebrew teachers for Jewish schools, and grants B.A. and M.A. degrees in Hebrew, Jewish education, and Hebrew literature. The college has exchange programs with secular colleges in the Boston area. The college has a growing library of Judaica and occupies a building named for Abraham and Yetta Goodman. The college owns the famed Oscar Feinsilver Collection of Ancient Judaic and Related Coins, a gift of Dr. Feinsilver, a member of the class of 1924, who died in 1974.

Israel Book Shop, 410 Harvard St., is said to be New England's largest supplier of Judaica, as well as Jewish ritual and art objects.

Jewish Times, 118 Cypress St.

Maimonides School, Philbruck Rd., oldest and largest Hebrew day school in New England, is where Rabbi Joseph Soloveitchik, the eminent Talmudist and authority on Halachah, lectures twice a week.

New England Chassidic Center, 1710 Beacon St., also houses the Machseke Torah Institute (Cong. Beth Pinchas, home of Bostoner Rebbe) and the Lionel Goldman Seminary, a women's seminary in Judaic ethics.

New England Hebrew Academy (Lubavitz Yeshiva), 9 Prescott St.

I.L. Peretz School of Workmen's Circle, 1762 Beacon St.

Senior Centre of Brookline-Brighton-Newton Jewish Community Center, 82 Centre St.

Temple Beth Zion, 1556 Beacon St.

Temple Emeth, 194 Grove St., has a stained glass window dedicated to the memory of President John F. Kennedy. The artist's theme for the design is based on the first verse of the 127th Psalm: "except the Lord keep the city, the watchman waketh in vain"—Kennedy's last words in his undelivered Dallas speech.

Temple Ohabie Shalom, 1187 Beacon St., oldest existing congregation in the state, founded in 1842.

Temple Sinai, 50 Sewall St.

Young Israel, 62 Green St.

CAMBRIDGE

Harvard University

Harvard University, mother of American colleges, is a treasure trove of Jewish culture. One of the world's great collections of Hebrew books and manuscripts is housed in the Andover-Harvard Theological Library (Dean St.) and the Houghton and Widener Libraries (Harvard St.). Harvard's Hebrew Collection dates from the beginning of the college in 1636, when its founder, John Harvard, had among his 39 volumes several commentaries on the Old Testament, four Hebrew grammars, a Talmudic Aramaic lexicon and *The Calling of the Jews,* by Sir Henry Finch, the earliest Zionist book in English, published in 1621. All but two of the books were destroyed by fire in 1764. Among Harvard's most prized possessions is a Hebrew Bible owned by John Dunster, the college's first president, which bears his signature in Hebrew. Also in the college library is Judah Monis' Hebrew grammar, published by Harvard in 1735, and original commencement addresses in Hebrew dating back to the college's early days. ●The college's Semitics library, now distributed through various collections, was established in the 1880s through the generosity of Jacob H. Schiff. It contains among its cherished items a set of the Babylonian Talmud printed in 1774 which once belonged to the Rev. Calvin Ellis Stowe, whose wife wrote *Uncle Tom's Cabin.* In 1920 an alumnus gave the college 2,000 Hebrew volumes. The Morris Alberts Collection was added in 1926. In 1929 the great collection of Amos Deinard, consisting of 12,000 items and representing Hebrew lore from almost every period and every center of Hebrew printing, was presented to the college by Lucius N. Littauer. That year, Julius Rosenwald gave the college 3,000 volumes of rabbinic literature, modern Hebrew literature, fiction, essays, and many rare periodicals, in honor of Judge Julian W. Mack. Among Harvard's 3,000 Hebrew manuscripts is one of Maimonides' *Mishneh Torah,* which was given to the college in 1951 by a committee headed by Lee M. Friedman. In 1968 Harvard University Press published a remarkable six-volume *Catalogue of Hebrew Books,* a photographic reproduction in book form of the 75,000 cards in the university's Hebrew card catalogue, representing the 40,000 volumes in the Hebrew collection. It is the leading research collection of Hebraica in an American university. The late Dr. Harry Wolfson, for nearly 40 years the Littauer Professor of Hebrew and Jewish Philosophy, who was the founder of the Hebrew collection, was its honorary curator for many years. With some additional 60,000 volumes of Judaica in English, French, German, Russian, and Yiddish, Harvard's collection of Hebraica and Judaica is one of the world's major bibliographic sources in the field of Jewish studies. The Hebrew and Yiddish collections include thousands of rare works and manuscripts.●Semitics Museum, Divinity Ave., was founded in 1889 by Jacob H. Schiff. In the building, erected in 1902, hangs an oil portrait of Schiff. The museum was created to aid in the regular instruction given in the Semitics Department and to furnish the means of research and illustrations of the civilization and history of the Near East in ancient and modern times. The museum contains collections on the history and arts of the Hebrews, Arabs, Assyrians, Babylonians, and Hittites. Among the exhibits are scale-size models of the Hill of Zion, Herod's Temple, the Temple of Solomon, and the Hebrew Tabernacle. ●Houghton Library, Massachusetts Ave., preserves a copy of a little known broadside issued by George Washington to the Continental Army some time in 1777 while it was encamped at Peekskill, N.Y. Washington calls on his soldiers to live up to the standards of cleanliness maintained by "a great army" of the "Children of Israel. . .that continued forty years in their different Camps under the Guidance and Regulations of the wisest General that ever lived." Washington was specific in the Mosaic practices he wanted emulated, quoting chapter and verse from Numbers and Deuteronomy. ●Littauer Center, intersection of Kirkland St. and Massachusetts Ave., which now houses the John F. Kennedy School of Government, was originally erected as the Graduate School of Public Administration, established through an endowment of $2 million by Lucius N. Littauer. A portrait of the donor, a member of Harvard's class of 1878, hangs in the center's library. Littauer (see Gloversville, N.Y.), was the coach of Harvard's first football team and rowed on the college's varsity crew. ●Straus Hall, on the western side of the Harvard Yard, is a student dormitory erected in 1926 through a gift of Jesse, Percy, and Herbert Straus, all Harvard alumni, in memory of their parents, Ida and Isidor Straus, who were lost in the sinking of the *Titanic.* A portrait of Isidor Straus hangs in the office of the assistant to the college president. Carved into the stone facade of the fireplace is an inscription recording the tragic death of the

Strauses. •Lehman Hall, in the southwest corner of the Yard, the university's business administration office, was a gift of Arthur Lehman, brother of the late Senator Herbert H. Lehman. •Harvard's Music Bldg., off Kirkland St., was erected in 1914 through the generosity of James Loeb. •Harvard-Radcliffe Theatre in the Loeb Drama Centre, 64 Brattle St., was made possible through a gift of $1 million from John L. Loeb. •Frances Loeb Library in the Harvard Graduate School of Design, Gund Hall, Quincy St., is named for Mrs. John L. Loeb. •Spalding Room in the Music Bldg., was endowed by Walter W. Naumburg. •David and Arnold Hoffman Laboratory of Experimental Geology, 24 Oxford St., was endowed by Robert Hoffman in memory of his younger brothers, one of whom went down with the USS *Tampa* in 1918 when torpedoed by a German U-boat. •Harvard Law School Library, 3rd floor, Langdell Hall, has a bust of Supreme Court Justice Felix Frankfurter and a portrait of Justice Louis D. Brandeis. Among the library's treasures is an original broadside listing Biblical authority for 15 offenses punishable by death in Colonial New England. The document, dated 1643, is entitled *The Capitall Lawes of New England,* and represents the Puritans' efforts to derive laws directly from the Bible without reference to English statutory or common law. •Gutman Library, Appian Way and Brattle St., part of the university's Graduate School of Education and Library Research Center, is named for the late Monroe C. Gutman, class of 1905, and a member of the banking firm of Lehman Brothers. •Paul J. Sachs Gallery of Fogg Museum of Art, Quincy St., of which the late Dr. Paul J. Sachs was director from 1923 to 1948, houses his famous collection of prints and drawings which he contributed to Harvard. •Daniel and Florence Guggenheim Center for Aerospace Health and Safety. •Hillel Foundation at Harvard University, and Radcliffe, and Lesley Colleges, 1 Bryant St. □

Daniel Guggenheim Aeronautical Research Building, on the campus of the Massachusetts Institute of Technology. •Hillel Foundation at M.I.T., Religious Counselors Bldg., 312 Memorial Dr.

Jewish Community Center, 298 Harvard St., also houses Tzavta, an Israeli coffeehouse for students. Also here is headquarters of Project Kehillah of *Genesis 2,* the newspaper of Boston's Jewish student and young adult community. Project Kehillah seeks to establish continuing links between the Jewish college community and the remnant of the non-college community, mostly elderly people isolated by the departure of familiar institutions. On the grounds of the center is a memorial to Cambridge Jews who died in World War II.

Temple Shalom, 8 Tremont St., is the last synagogue in the city. What used to be the building of Cong. Beth Israel Anshe Sfard at 238 Columbia St., is still recognizable as a former synagogue by the Stars of David in its windows.

CANTON
Temple Beth Abraham, 1301 Washington St.
Temple Beth David, 250 Randolph St.
Young Israel, 6 Ridgehill Rd.

CHATHAM
Brandeis House, Neck Lane, off Cedar St., 8 miles SW of State Harbor Rd., is the gray-shingled summer house of the late Supreme Court Justice Louis D. Brandeis, preserved as an historic house, but privately owned.

CHELMSFORD
Cong. Shalom, 3 Waco Circle.

CHELSEA
Chelsea Hebrew Academy, 48 Washington St.
Cong. Agudas Sholom, 145 Walnut St.
Cong. Ahavas Achim Anshe Sfard, 15 Elm St., is a merger of three of the old Orthodox synagogues. Urban renewal and the shift of the Jewish population to the outer suburbs have greatly shrunk the Jewish community.
Cong. Shaari Zion, 75 Orange St.
Cong. Shomrei Linas Hazedek, 140 S. Shurtleff St.
Sampson Square, on Revere Beach Pkwy., adjacent to Union St., is named for James Sampson, a municipal engineer.
Temple Emanuel, 16 Cary St.
YM and YWHA Jewish Community Center, 19 Crescent Ave.
Young Israel, 23 Heard St., absorbed Congs. Toras Chaim and Shaari Israel.

CLINTON
Cong. Shaarei Zedek, Water St.

DEDHAM
Norfolk County Superior Courthouse has on display a portrait of the late Judge Abraham E. Pinanski, who served on the Superior Court for 19 years.

DORCHESTER (section of Boston)
Bloom Square, cor. Woodrow Ave. and Lucerne St., is named for Pfc. Frederick J. Bloom, who was killed in action in Korea.
Epstein Square, cor. of Fairmount and Morton Sts., memorializes Seaman First Class Jack Epstein, who was killed in 1943 during World War II.

Franklin Field Housing Project, is a residence of the fast dwindling elderly Jews who are the last remnant of the once vibrant Dorchester Jewish community. The Combined Jewish Philanthropies of Greater Boston serves hot lunches to the old folks. Students from Brandeis University visit them to conduct worship services and to provide a link with the Jewish community since the last operating synagogue, Cong. Agudath Israel, was sold in 1972.

Rabinowitz Memorial Square, at intersection of Maxwell St. and Milton Ave., honors Marine Col. Jack Rabinowitz, who was killed in action in Korea.

EVERETT

Cong. Tifereth Israel and Community Center, 34 Malden St.

FALL RIVER

Cong. Adas Israel, 1647 Robeson St.
Jewish Community Council, 56 N. Main St.
Jewish Home for the Aged, 199 Hanover St.
Temple Beth El, 385 High St.

FITCHBURG

Cong. Agudath Achim, 40 Boutelle St.
Fitchburg-Leominster Jewish Community Center, 40 Boutelle St.
Jewish Federation, 40 Boutelle St.

FORT DEVENS

Col. Martin R. Beck Memorial, a life-size statue of a Green Beret soldier, which honors members of the 10th Special Forces Group (ABN) who gave their lives in Vietnam. It is named for Lt. Col. Martin R. Beck, the former deputy commander of the group, who was killed in Vietnam in 1969. He was a native of Baltimore.

FRAMINGHAM

Jewish Community Center, 1000 Worcester Rd.
Jewish Federation, 1000 Worcester Rd.
Jewish Reporter, 1000 Worcester Rd.
Shachna Galleries, 605 Worcester Rd., on Rte. 9, specializes in Israeli giftware, art, jewelry, and religious objects.
Temple Beth Am, 7 Travis Dr.
Temple Beth Shalom, Pamela Rd. (Saxonville)

GARDNER

Cong. Ohave Sholom, 152 Pleasant St.

GLOUCESTER

Bible Museum, 62 Middle St., which exhibits some 500 Bibles from around the world, has a Hebrew Alcove containing a 500-year old Torah Scroll, a 1667 edition of the Hebrew Bible printed in Amsterdam, several *mezuzahs*, a number of sets of phylacteries, a prayer shawl, yarmulkes, siddurim, and Menorahs. The walls of the museum are covered with a large colored map of the Holy Land (pre-1948), with notes and markings setting forth the events of the Old Testament.

Temple Ahavath Achim, 86 Middle St.

GREAT BARRINGTON

Cong. Love of Peace, 29 North St.

Eisner Camp Institute of Union of American Hebrew Congregations.

GREENFIELD

Greenfield Hebrew Cong., 256 Federal St.

HAVERHILL

Temple Emanuel-Jewish Center, 514 Main St.

United Jewish Appeal, 514 Main St.

HINGHAM

Jewish Community Center of South Shore.

Temple Beth Am, 349 Lincoln St.

HOLBROOK

Jewish Community Center, 27 Marion St.

HOLYOKE

Cong. Rodphey Sholom, 1800 Northampton St.

Cong. Sons of Zion, 378 Maple St.

HULL

Temple Beth Sholom, 600 Nantasket Ave.

HYANNIS

Cape Cod Synagogue, 145 Winter St.

John F. Kennedy Memorial has at its entrance the seal of the United States with the stars laid out in the familiar design of a Star of David.

HYDE PARK

Temple Adas Israel, 28 Arlington St.

JAMAICA PLAIN
New England Sinai Hospital, 215 Forest Hills St.

LAWRENCE
Cong. Anshei Shalom, 411 Hampshire St.
Cong. Tifereth Anshai Sfard, 492 Lowell St.
Jewish Community Center, 580 Haverhill St.
Jewish Community Council, 580 Haverhill St.
Temple Emanuel, 483 Lowell St.

LEICESTER
Leicester Academy, in the southwest part of what is now Leicester Common, is one of the oldest schools in the country. Its main building was originally erected as the double house which Aaron Lopez, America's leading merchant and shipowner up to the Revolution, built in 1777 when he fled from Newport, R.I., with his family, ahead of the British who had captured Newport. Taking with him some 60 people, Lopez established here what was the first Jewish settlement in the state outside of Boston. At that time he owned some 30 ships that sailed the seven seas. In Leicester, Lopez opened what was virtually a department store to which customers came from as far away as Hartford. Lopez kept his business shut on Saturday, and together with his large family, observed all the Jewish holidays during the six years the community remained in Leicester. After the Revolution the community dwindled away.

LENOX
Berkshire Music Centre at Tanglewood was founded by Serge Koussevitzky while he was conductor of the Boston Symphony Orchestra. The Berkshire Music Festival has been underwritten for many years by the Fromm Foundation of Chicago, headed by Paul Fromm.

LEOMINSTER
Cong. Agudas Achim, 268 Washington St.
Jewish Community Council, 30 Grove Ave.

LEXINGTON
Hastings Park, Massachusetts Ave. and Worthen Rd., has a cypress tree from Israel, planted in 1963 on the 250th anniversary of the founding of Lexington and the 15th anniversary of Israel.
Minuteman Monument, erected in 1949 on the Green in this historic Revolutionary town, was the result of a single-handed seven-year campaign by the late Julius Seltzer, an immigrant tailor from

Russia. Seltzer was president of the Lexington Minutemen, an organization that seeks to preserve Colonial landmarks, of which he was a founder. He was also vice-president of the Lexington Historical Society.

Temple Emunah, 9 Piper Rd.
Temple Isaiah, 55 Lincoln St.

LONGMEADOW (see also Springfield)

Beth Israel Synagogue, 137 Wolf Swamp Rd., has bronze motifs of the revelation of the Decalogue and the seven-branched Menorah exhibited on two separate design panels, the former at the extreme forefront of the building and the latter over the hooded main entrance.

Cong. B'nai Jacob, 2 Eunice Dr.
Jewish Nursing Home of Western Massachusetts, 770 Converse St.

Kamberg Collection of Prints, owned by and housed in the home of Abraham Kamberg, 102 Meadowbrook St., contains some 850 items in the graphic medium, but also included are oils, watercolors, and sculpture. The collection began as an exhibit of works by Jewish artists and about 180 of the items are by 60 artists of Jewish descent. On the front door of the Kamberg home the word "Shalom" is spelled out in large brass letters.

LOWELL

Cong. Montefiore, 460 Westford St.
Temple Beth-El, 105 Princeton Blvd.
Temple Emanuel, 101 W. Forest St.

LYNN

Cong. Ahavat Shalom, 151 Ocean St.
Cong. Anshe Sfard, 150 S. Common St.
Cong. Chevra Tehillim, 12 Breed St.
Jewish Home for Aged, 31 Exchange Pl.
Jewish Social Service Agency, 45 Market St.

MALDEN

Cong. Agudas Achim, 160 Howard St.
Cong. Beth Israel, 10 Dexter St. (Beth Israel West)
Cong. Beth Israel, 78 Faulkner St. (Beth Israel East)
Salem Towers, near Beth Israel West, was the first middle-income apartment house built by a synagogue with a Federal grant. The elderly Jewish residents in the apartment house are served by Beth Israel West.

Tartikoff Square, at the junction of Willow, Suffolk, and Cross

Sts., memorializes Pvt. David Tartikoff, who was killed in Belleau Woods, France, during World War I.

Temple Ezrath Israel, 245 Bryant St.
Temple Tifereth Israel, 539 Salem St.
Young Israel, 45 Holyoke St.

MANOMET

Landers Park, a memorial to the daughter of Mrs. Pearl Landers of Brookline, was established on one of the lots Mrs. Landers donated for home sites to the first five repatriated Korean War veterans from Massachusetts who were prisoners of war. Mrs. Landers was known to two generations of servicemen and hospitalized veterans as "Ma Landers" because of her long years of service on their behalf.

MARBLEHEAD

Jewish Federation of the North Shore, 4 Community Rd.
North Shore Jewish Community Center, 4 Community Rd.
Temple Emanuel, 393 Atlantic Ave.
Temple Sinai, 1 Community Rd.

MARLBORO

Temple Emanuel, 130 Berlin Rd.

MARTHA'S VINEYARD (see Vineyard Haven)

MATTAPAN (section of Boston)

Mattapan-Dorchester Combined Jewish Philanthropies of Greater Boston Centre, 1421 Blue Hill Ave,, is the focal point for many services being provided to the tiny remnant of the once proud and vigorous Jewish community of 65,000 in this area, where the Jews used to constitute 90 percent of the total population. Until 1958 this was the largest Jewish community in the Greater Boston area, with some 50 synagogues. The area now is almost "Judenrein," after most of the Jewish residents moved to the suburbs. In 1974 it was estimated that about 2,400 Jews remained in Mattapan, almost half of whom were in their middle 60s. With synagogues closed, kosher butchers gone out of business, Jewish establishments shut down, the Mattapan-Dorchester CJP Center was established to provide a visible Jewish presence for those Jews still living there. Through the Center and other CJP agencies, the Jewish residents are assisted with hot and cold lunch programs, security guards for worship services, transportation to shopping areas, and community activities. Many of the former Jewish institutional buildings are occupied by black organizations.

Myers Square, at junction of River and Mattakeeset Sts., memorializes Marine Corps Corp. Jeffrey P. Myers, who was killed in action in Vietnam.

Ohel Torah Cong., 149 Greenfield St.

MEDFORD

Edward E. Cohen Auditorium and Arts Center at Tufts College is the gift of Dr. Edward E. Cohen, Boston industrialist and philanthropist. In the medical library of the Tufts Medical College is an oil painting of Dr. Benjamin Spector, for more than 30 years professor of anatomy and the history of medicine.

Hillel Foundation at Tufts College (see Somerville)

Temple Shalom, 475 Winthrop St.

Touro Avenue in this northern suburb of Boston is named for Abraham Touro, brother of Judah Touro, who was a great philanthropist and merchant in his own right. In addition to his business interests in Boston, Touro owned a shipyard at Medford, and his summer home here was the town's showplace. He died in 1822 at the age of 48 as the result of an accident.

MEDWAY

Cong. Agudath Achim, 73 Village St.

MELROSE

Old Sephardic Cemetery here recalls a long vanished Sephardic Jewish community.

Temple Beth Shalom, 21 Foster St.

MILFORD

Cong. Beth Chaverim, 19 Whip-O'Will Lane (c/o Alan Wolpin), worships at St. Mary's Elementary School, Winter St.

Cong. Beth Shalom, 30 Pine St.

MILLIS

Cong. House of Jacob, 343 Village St.

MILTON

Cong. B'nai Jacob, 100 Blue Hills Pkwy.

Drapkin Student Center at Curry College is named for Mr. and Mrs. Joseph Drapkin of West Newton who gave generous support to the college.

Temple Shalom, 180 Blue Hill Ave.

NANTASKET BEACH

Cong. Beth Israel, Sunet Dr., open only during the summer.

NATICK
Temple Israel, 145 Hartford St.

NEEDHAM
Temple Aliyah, 1664 Central Ave.
Temple Beth Shalom, 670 Highland Ave.

NEW BEDFORD
Cong. Ahavath Achim, 385 County St.
Cong. Tifereth Israel, 145 Brownell Ave.
Jewish Community Center, 467 Hawthorn St. (North Dartmouth)
Jewish War Memorial, cor. Rockdale Ave. and Hawthorn St., erected in 1962 by the Jewish War Veterans of this city, is a monument of six 14-foot granite pillars dedicated to the New Bedford Jews who died in the wars of the U.S. Each of the inside four pillars is inscribed with one of the Four Freedoms.
Jewish Welfare Federation, 467 Hawthorn St. (New Darthmouth).
Joseph Irving Segall Square, at east end of Hawthorn St. on County St., is named for Ensign Joseph Irving Segall, the first Jew from the city to die in World War II.
Stones of Old Sephardic Cemetery date from mid-19th century when Sephardic Jews settled here.
Temple Sinai, 169 William St.

NEWBURYPORT
Cong. Ahavas Achim, Olive and Washington Sts.

NEWTON
Cong. Beth El-Atereth Israel, 561 Ward St.
Cong. Chevra Shas, 35 Moreseland Ave.
Cong. Kehilath Jacob, 858 Walnut St.
Temple Mishkan Tefila, 300 Hammond Pond Pkwy., which was founded in 1858, has a very large collection of Jewish ceremonial objects and material on Boston Jewish history in its Herman and Mignon Rubenovitz Museum, named for a former rabbi and his wife.
Temple Reyim, 1860 Washington St., uses a Menorah as a large exterior identifying symbol integrated into the structure of the outer wall.

NEWTON CENTRE (section of Newton)
Temple Beth Avodah, 45 Puddingstone Lane.
Temple Emanuel, 385 Ward St.

NORTH ADAMS
Cong. Beth Israel, 265 Church St.

NORTHAMPTON
Cong. B'nai Israel, 253 Prospect St.

Hillel Foundation at Smith College, Helen Mills Chapel, Elm St. and Round Hill Rd.

Ziskind Hall at Smith College is named for the late Jacob Ziskind of Fall River who bequeathed $500,000 to the college.

NORTHBOROUGH
Judah Monis grave, behind the old Congregational Church on a triangular green in an old cemetery, is the last resting place of the man who taught Hebrew at Harvard for 40 years. He was probably born in Italy, having studied in the Jewish schools in Leghorn and Amsterdam. He came to America in 1715 and was admitted as a freeman in New York. By profession he was described as a merchant. Monis turned up in Boston in 1720 with a plan for a Hebrew grammar which, as he explained in a letter to Harvard, would "facilitate the instruction of youth in the Hebrew language." Impressed with his learning, Harvard gave Monis the honorary degree of Master of Arts at its commencement in 1723, the first Jew to receive a college degree in America. A year earlier he had been publicly baptized and was received into the Congregational Church at ceremonies held before a capacity audience in the college hall. Not long after, he was engaged as instructor in Hebrew at Harvard. The Hebrew grammar he had proposed in 1720 was published in 1735—the first Hebrew book produced in North America. To eke out a living, Monis also sold hardware and tobacco and acted as an interpreter. The royal governor of Massachusetts appointed him a justice of the peace for Middlesex County in 1740. When his wife died in 1760, Monis, then 77, retired to Northborough where he died in 1764. On his grave he is identified as a rabbi. Monis' modest estate was bequeathed as a permanent fund for the relief of clergymen's widows. The American Unitarian Association administers this trust.

NORTH RANDOLPH (section of Randolph)
Davidson's Hebrew Book Store, 1100 N. Main St.

NORWOOD
Temple Shaare Tefila, 556 Nichols St.

ONSET
Cong. Beth Israel, Onset Ave., cor. Locust St., is the only Or-

thodox synagogue on Cape Cod, holding services from June to Sept. only, and on the High Holy Days. For information on services and reciting Kaddish, call 295-5016.

PALMER

Camp Ramah in New England.

PAXTON

All-Faith Chapel at Treasure Island Boy Scout Camp, was contributed by the Probus Club of Worcester, a Jewish service organization.

PEABODY

Cong. Sons of Israel, Spring St.
Temple Beth Shalom, 489 Lowell St.
Temple Ner Tamid, 368 Lowell St.

PINEHURST

Shalom Emeth Temple-Shawsheen Valley Community Center.

PITTSFIELD

Cong. Ahavath Sholem, 177 Robbins Ave.
Cong. Knesseth Israel, 16 Colt Rd., has a building designed in the shape of a Star of David.
Jewish Community Center, 235 East St.
Jewish Community Council, 235 East St.
Temple Anshe Amunim, 26 Broad St.

PLYMOUTH

Burying Hill, the oldest cemetery in the country, having been established by the Pilgrims shortly after their arrival in 1620, is the last resting place of Gov. William Bradford, the colony's second governor. On the tombstone, the oldest in the cemetery, are three Hebrew words. Only the first and third words can still be read but from the faint vestiges of letters in the second word, scholars believe the words read: "The Lord is the light of my life," which does not differ from the words in the first verse of the 27th Psalm, "The Lord is the strength of my life."

Temple Beth Jacob, 8 Pleasant St., is believed to be the oldest synagogue building in Massachusetts still in use as a synogogue. It was dedicated in 1913.

QUINCY

Beth Israel Synagogue, 33 Grafton St.

Reuben A. and Lizzie Grossman Park and Nature Trail, Quincy Shore Dr. and Fenno St., are on land given to the people of Quincy by the children of Reuben and Lizzie Grossman in 1972. Reuben Grossman was the oldest son of Louis Grossman, founder of a noted family of industrialists, civic leaders, and philanthropists who have specialized in revivifying dying New England communities. Louis Grossman began the business in 1890 when he arrived from Russia and became a pack-peddler. The plaque at the entrance to the park reads: "This land and its natural resources made available to the people of the City of Quincy by the children of Reuben A. and Lizzie Grossman in memory of their parents who will always be remembered for their humility, humanity, kindliness, and Godliness." The Beechwood Knoll Elementary School, stands on a site donated by the Grossmans in memory of "Louis Grossman, 1862-1948— Humanitarian—Industrialist." The site of Reuben Grossman's home is also marked by an inscription near the city's municipal park lot which he first proposed and then developed.

South Area Jewish Community Center, 10 Merrymount Rd.

Temple Adas Shalom, 435 Adams St.

Temple Beth El, 1001 Hancock St.

RANDOLPH

Holocaust Memorial Courtyard, at Temple Beth Am, 871 N. Main St., is an atrium on the 2nd floor consisting of an 18-foot by 5-foot mosaic depicting plight of Jews during the Nazi era, and an eight ton Star of David with an eternal flame. There is also a small museum housing memorabilia of the Holocaust.

Jewish Family and Children's Service of Greater Boston, 44 Highland Ave.

I.L. Peretz Yiddish School, 51 N. Main St.

Temple Beth Am, 871 N. Main St.

Young Israel, 374 Main St.

REVERE

Cong. Ahavas Achim, 89 Walnut St.

Cong. Tifereth Israel, Shirley Ave. and Nahant Ave.

Housing Complex for Elderly, Revere Beach Blvd., is sponsored by the Hebrew Rehabilitation Center for the Aged Housing for the Elderly Inc.

Jacobs Recreation Area and Park, Hastings St., memorializes Eli and Anna Jacobs, parents of William M. Jacobs, Boston investment banker and philanthropist.

Temple B'nai Israel, 1 Wave Ave.

ROSLINDALE (section of Boston)
Hebrew Rehabilitation Center for the Aged, 1200 Centre St. The newest wing is named for Milton Berger, a prominent worker for the center.

ROXBURY
There are virtually no Jewish residents left in this area where there once was a large and lively Jewish community. In 1974 the Combined Jewish Philanthropies of Greater Boston reported that there were no more than 25 elderly Jewish households left in Roxbury. The religious school of Temple Mishkan Tefila is now the Elma Lewis School of Fine Arts, a black institution. The old synagogue building of Mishkan Tefila, later occupied by the Lubavitz Yeshiva, is also part of the Lewis School. Both buildings, appraised at $1,200,000, were contributed by the CJP in 1968 to the black community.

Ulin Skating Rink, an outdoor recreation area sponsored by the state, is named for State Senator Max Ulin who was a member of the Metropolitan District Commission.

SALEM
Peabody Museum, 161 Essex St., has among its great collection of old sailing vessel prints one of the ship *Touro,* which was owned by the eminent Jewish philanthropist and merchant, Judah Touro.

Temple Shalom, 287 Lafayette St.

SAUGUS
Cong. Ahavas Shalom, 343 Central St.

SHARON
Cong. Adath Sharon, Harding St.
Temple Israel, 125 Pond St.
Temple Sinai, 100 Ames.
Young Israel, 12 Oakland St.

SOMERVILLE
Cong. B'nai B'rith, 201 Central St.

Havurot Shalom Community Seminary, 113 College Ave., founded in 1968, is a group of students, professors, and rabbis, all dissatisfied with existing synagogue practices, who banded together to explore the possibilities of Jewish study within the context of intensive communal life. All members of the havurat live within walking distance of the seminary.

Hillel Foundation at Tufts College, 108 Bromfield Rd.

SPRINGFIELD

Basketball Hall of Fame, Springfield College, Alden St., where the sport was first developed, included eleven Jewish players, coaches, and managers among the 94 immortals of the game who are enshrined in ceiling-to-floor hand painted stained glass window plaques. The ten are: Barney Sedran and Nat Holman, who played with the "Original Celtics"; Adolph Schayes, who starred at New York University and later with the Syracuse Nationals in the National Basketball Association; "Red" Auerbach, long-time coach and general manager of the Boston Celtics; Abe Saperstein, who founded and managed the Harlem Globetrotters; Abe Radel, manager of the SPHAS basketball team in the old Eastern and American Basketball Leagues; Maurice Podoloff, who was one of the founders and first president of the National Basketball Association; Harry Litwack, former Temple University coach; and Edward Gottlieb; Marty Friedman; and Leonard Sachs.

Beth Israel Synagogue, 148 Ft. Pleasant Ave.

B'nai Jacob Synagogue, 2 Eunice Dr. (Longmeadow).

Cong. Kesser Israel, 17 Oakland St.

Cong. Kodimoh, 124 Sumner Ave.

Cong. Sons of Israel, 1321 Dwight St.

Alfred M. Glickman School, Ashland Ave., is named for the late Dr. Alfred M. Glickman, surgeon, school board member, and civic leader, who died in 1954. A portrait of Glickman hangs in the lobby.

Hebrew Academy, 89 Randolph St.

Heritage Academy Beth Morasha, 302 Maple St.

Hillel Foundation at Springfield College, 14 Henshaw Ave.

Jewish Community Center, 1160 Dickinson St.

Jewish Family Service, 184 Mill St.

Jewish Federation, 1160 Dickinson St.

Jewish Home for the Aged, 44 Copley Terrace.

Jewish Nursing Home of Western Massachusetts, 770 Converse St. (Longmeadow).

Jewish Weekly News, 99 E. Mill St.

Lubavitcher Yeshiva, 29 Oakland St.

Newhouse Rehabilitation Center, adjacent to the Springfield Hospital Medical Center, is named for the late Donald R. Newhouse, general manager of the Springfield Newspapers, who died in 1963. Newhouse had served on the board of the hospital and had been a vigorous champion of state funding for the mental health center named for him.

John I. Robinson Gardens, Berkshire and Bay Aves., a public housing development named for the former chairmen of the National Association of Housing Officials, vice-chairman of the Massachusetts State Board of Housing, and a leader in Sinai Temple.

Sinai Temple, 1100 Dickinson St.

Temple Beth El, 979 Dickinson St., has an exterior 19-foot bronze sculpture, *Pillar of Fire,* that rises from the low foundation to a point even with the tip of the synagogue roof, recalling the Burning Bush. Inside there is an 8-foot tapestry depicting the symbols of 12 Jewish holidays. There is also a *yahrzeit* wall, with memorial candleholders on the ledge below the inscription of the opening words of the Kaddish in Aramaic, not Hebrew. One of Beth El's Torahs was a gift from the then Bishop Robert M. Hatch of the Roman Catholic Diocese of Western Massachusetts, presented in 1965, when the synagogue burned down.

STONEHAM
Temple Judea-Jewish Community Center, 188 Franklin St.

STOUGHTON
Cong. Ahabath Torah, 1179 Central St.
New England Sinai Hospital, 50 York St.

SUDBURY
Temple Beth El, Hudson Rd.

SWAMPSCOTT
Jewish Rehabilitation Center for Aged of North Shore, 330 Paradise Rd.
Temple Beth El, 55 Atlantic Ave.
Temple Israel, 837 Humphrey St., has an exterior copper relief depicting the heavens.

TAUNTON
Cong. Agudath Achim, 133 High St.

VINEYARD HAVEN
Hebrew Center, on Center St., in this principal town of the resort island of Martha's Vineyard, has about two dozen year-round Jewish residents. The first Jewish settlers were Sam Cronig and his family, who arrived in 1905, and were followed in 1911 by Yudel Brickman. The synagogue was established in 1940 as an Orthodox congregation. It switched to Conservative and then Reform, depending on the views of the latest rabbi to vacation there. During the summer the Jewish population increases by four or five-fold.

WAKEFIELD
Temple Emanuel, 120 Chestnut St., has an auditorium named for Dr. Chaim Weizmann, the first president of Israel. On the outside

wall above the entrance to the temple is a large granite tablet on which the Ten Commandments are engraved. On the ground beneath the Tablet is another tablet in the shape of a pulpit with an open book on which are recorded the names of the four heroic chaplains of World War II—two ministers, a priest, and a rabbi.

WALTHAM

American Jewish Historical Society, 2 Thornton Rd., on the campus of Brandeis University, is open to visitors as well as scholars and researchers the year round. It is closed on major Jewish holidays, Saturdays, some legal holidays, and Sundays from June to September. Founded in 1892, the AJHS collects, catalogs, displays, and publishes material relating to the Jewish experience in America. It maintains a library of over 50,000 books, 4 million pages of manuscripts, and thousands of issues of newspapers and periodicals. The society sponsors exhibits, lectures, and meetings at which research papers are presented. The archival material is in English as well as Hebrew, Yiddish, German, French, Russian, and Ladino. A large collection of American Yiddish theatre posters and sheet music is maintained as are microfilms and photographs. The Society owns a unique collection of American newspapers containing items of Jewish interest and a group of over 40 oil portraits, some dating back to 1740, of Jewish notables. There is also a collection of daguerreotypes that provide views of a number of mid-19th century individuals and families. Special collections include the records of early B'nai B'rith lodges, Board of Delegates of American Israelites, Hebrew Orphan Asylum of New York, Synagogue Council of America, American Association for Jewish Education, American Jewish Congress, and Phi Epsilon Pi. Papers of noted Jewish personalities preserved at AJHS include those of the poetess Emma Lazarus, Dr. Cyrus Adler, actress Molly Picon, Nobel Prize winner Dr. Selman Waksman, Adolphus Solomons, Isaac Leeser, Haym Salomon, Rebecca Gratz, and Dr. Stephen S. Wise. The society sponsors exhibitions throughout the year in its two galleries where its own historic possessions and items on temporary loan are placed on display.

Brandeis University

Brandeis University, established in 1948, was the first nonsectarian institution of higher learning in the Western hemisphere to be founded by Jews. It was established in an effort to make a corporate Jewish contribution to American higher education in the tradition of the great universities which had their origin in denominational generosity. Named for Justice Louis D. Brandeis, the first Jew appointed to the Supreme Court of the U.S., the university occupies a 300-acre campus overlooking the Charles River. A nine-foot high bronze statue of Brandeis stands on a knoll facing the university's administration building and the Sherman Student Center. The statue was unveiled in 1966 on the centennial of Brandeis' birth by Chief Justice Earl Warren. By 1975, the major buildings on the campus were: Rosenstiel Basic Medical Sciences Research Center; Florence Heller Graduate School for Advanced Studies in Social Welfare; Spingold Theatre; Rabb Graduate Center; Rose Art Museum; Usdan Swig Student Center; Goldfarb Library; Usdan Castle; Shapiro Athletic Center; and the Ullman Amphitheatre. All told there are 75 major structures on the campus. ●The world-famous Three Chapels area at Brandeis consists of separate Jewish, Catholic, and Protestant houses of worship, grouped in a cluster around a heart-shaped pool. The Jewish chapel, which houses the Hillel Foundation, is known as the Mendel and Leah Berlin Chapel, in memory of the parents of Dr. David Berlin, a Boston surgeon. The Newman Club and the Student Christian Association sponsor the Catholic and Protestant chapels, respectively. Although Jewish-sponsored, some of the student body is non-Jewish. ●Holocaust Monument, next to the Berlin Chapel on the Brandeis campus, is a statue of Job cast in bronze from the original which stands at Yad Vashem in Jerusalem. Both statues are the work of sculptor Nathan Rapaport. Six feet high, the statue was commissioned and sponsored by the New Americans of Boston, a group of Holocaust survivors. Ashes from the Treblinka Concentration Camp are interred at the base of the statue.□

Temple Beth Israel, 25 Harvard St., also serves as a Jewish community center.

WARE
Temple Beth Israel, 89 Main St.

WELLESLEY
Temple Beth Elohim, 10 Bethel Rd.

WESTBORO
Westboro Jewish Association, P.O. Box 136.

WESTFIELD
Westfield Jewish Community Association, c/o Martin Kaufman, 666 Western Ave., or Judy Brown, 7 South St.

WEST ROXBURY
Hebrew Rehabilitation Center for Aged, 1200 Center St., includes a synagogue specially designed for the convenience of infirm,

convalescent, and aged persons. The synagogue can accommodate wheel chairs and has permanent pews for ambulatory patients. The bimah is situated so that ambulatory patients may pray at the ark.

WESTWOOD
Temple Beth David, 40 Pond St.

WILLIAMSTOWN
Bronfman Science Center, at Williams College, was a gift of the late Samuel Bronfman, Candian philanthropist and liquor manufacturer, whose children contributed $1,250,000 toward the center.

Lehman Hall, the freshman dormitory at Williams College, was a gift of the late Senator (and Governor) Herbert H. Lehman (see New York), who was an alumnus of the college.

WILMINGTON
Temple Sholom, 68 Salem St.

WINTHROP
Cong. Tifereth Abraham, 283 Shirley St.
Temple Tifereth Israel, 93 Veterans Rd.

WOBURN
Temple Shalom Emeth, 14 Green St.

WORCESTER
American Antiquarian Society, 185 Salisbury St., has in its collection material shedding light on the history of Jews in the 17th, 18th, and 19th centuries in America. This is primarily a research library and casual visiting is discouraged.

Cong. Beth Israel, Kinnicutt Rd., has an outdoor worship area.
Cong. Beth Judah, 889 Pleasant St.
Cong. Magen David, 1029 Pleasant St.
Cong. Shaarai Torah Sons of Abraham, East, 32 Providence St.
Cong. Shaarai Torah, West, 835 Pleasant St.
Cong. Sons of Jacob, 14 Woodford St.
Cong. Tifereth Israel, 22 Newton Ave.

Green Hill, famous old estate which was deeded to the city for park purposes more than 75 years ago, figures in an interesting, but unsubstantiated incident in American Jewish history. On this estate once stood "Lopez trees," two giant sycamores planted by Aaron Lopez, patriot merchant of Newport, R.I., who fled inland with his family when the British captured Newport during the American Revolution. When Lopez and his family reached Worcester, no one was willing to give them refuge except John Green, who offered the Jews the hospitality of his home. After spending two nights with Green, the Lopez family moved on to Leicester. When the war was over, Lopez, returning to Newport (he drowned en route), stopped again at Green Hill and in memory of his host's kindness planted two trees in front of the house. One of the trees was cut down many years ago when in old age it threatened the main house. The other was blown down in the hurricane of 1938. Members of the Green family, including Andrew H. Green, legislative architect of New York City and father of Central Park, the Museum of Natural History, and the Metroplitan Museum of Art, and the late U.S. Senator Theodore Green of Rhode Island, delighted in telling this story of their ancestor's close friendship with Jews. Although a non-Jew, Andrew Green was a good friend of New York's Congregation Shearith Israel and an active member of the American Jewish Historical Society. He was guest of honor at the dedication of two synagogue buildings of Shearith Israel.

Hillel Foundation at Clark University, 18 Strawberry Rd.

Hirshberg Square, cor. Hadwen Rd. and Chandler St., memorializes Lt. Jack Hirshberg who was killed in action in Dec., 1944 while piloting a bomber over Germany.

Jewish Civic Leader, 11 Norwich St.

Jewish Community Center, 633 Salisbury St.

Jewish Family Service Center for Older Adults, 270 Park Ave.

Jewish Federation, 633 Salisbury St.

Jewish Home for Aged, 629 Salisbury St.

Katz Square, at junction of Lodge and Waverly Sts., is a memorial to Private Maxwell B. Katz who was killed in World War I.

Silver Square, at intersection of Harrison and Coral Sts., is named for Private Jack B. Silver who was killed in World War II.

Starr Square, at junction of Grantic, Jones, and Loxwood Sts., is named for Private Samuel J. Starr, who was killed in World War I.

Temple Emanuel, 280 May St.

Temple Sinai, 661 Salisbury St.

NEW HAMPSHIRE

Entombed where earthborn troubles cease
A son of faithful Abraham sleeps.

These are the first two lines of the epitaph on a tombstone in Portsmouth's North Burying Ground. Beneath that stone "sleeps in peace" Abraham Isaac, the "Jew of Portsmouth," the first known Jewish resident of New Hampshire, who settled there some time after the Revolutionary War. His epitaph was written by J.M. Sewall, the celebrated Revolutionary poet, whose ballad, *Vain Britons Boast No Longer,* was sung at every Continental campfire. In the fading inscription of Sewall's epitaph there is this moving characterization of Isaac:

In life's first bloom he left his native air
A sojourner as all his fathers were.
Through various toils his active spirit ran,
A faithful steward and an honest man.
His soul we trust, now freed from mortal woes,
Finds in the Patriarch's bosom sweet repose.

An old history of Portsmouth records that Isaac and his wife were natives of Prussia "and Jews of the strictest sect." Described as "the first descendants of the venerable Patriarch that ever pitched their tent in Portsmouth," the Isaacs "during their lives were the only Jews among us."

Isaac was obviously a man of some status, for "he acquired a good property and built a house on State Street." This lone Jew in New Hampshire was an observant son of the Covenant for the historian notes that "their shop was always closed on Saturday." He was also a leading Mason, participating in the work of the State Grand Lodge as early as 1798. Isaac died Feb. 15, 1803. He left one son who, like so many other Jews who lived alone in the early days of America, was absorbed in the general population and lost to Judaism.

Stray peddlers and traders from Massachusetts, so-called "Christian Jews" and baptized descendants of the early Jewish settlers at Newport, Rhode Island, preceded Isaac to New Hampshire in the middle of the 17th century. "Sollomon ye Malata Jue" was tried and convicted at Ipswich, Massachusetts, in 1668 for traveling toward New Hampshire on a Sunday by horse and wagon. An early history of the town of Sanbarton lists the Abrams and Moses families as "Jewish descendants." One Aaron Moses lived at New Castle in 1693. The Abrams family, kin to Daniel Webster, was started by William, a ship's carpenter, and his brother, John, "Christian Jews who came from Palestine to New England at an unknown date."

William Campanal, whose great-grandfather, Mordecai, settled in Rhode Island in the 1650's and was one of the two Jews who bought the land on which the Newport Jewish cemetery was established in 1677, founded a family whose descendants are widespread in New Hampshire and Maine. William Campanal, who fought in the Revolutionary War, was the grandson of David Campanal, "a Jew from Rhode Island," who settled down at Ipswich, Massachusetts, as a weaver and farmer, after having been ordered out of Boston in 1726 as a penniless stranger. The town records of Ipswich, in whose village churchyard David Campanal is buried, contain a special notation that he was a Jew. His son, also named David, is buried there. This David Campanal's granddaughter, Hannah, who married Richard Taylor, moved to New Hampshire after the Revolution and settled at Effingham.

Old New Hampshire land records contain the name of Joseph Levy who was granted a home site near Ossipee in 1777. In that same year William Levy of Somersworth is listed as a private in the 2nd New Hampshire Continental Regiment. Had there been more professing Jews in New Hampshire after the Revolution they would have wondered at the strange language in the state's constitution. The ninth and deciding state to ratify the Federal Constitution, New Hampshire, in its own bill of rights, granted freedom of worship to all; but in another section of the state constitution, which is still the law of the state, there appear these two sentences:

And every denomination of Christians, demeaning themselves quietly and as good subjects of the state, shall be equally under the protection of the law. And no subordination of any one sect or denomination to another, shall ever be established by law.

New Hampshire, the first of the 13 colonies to declare its independence from Great Britain, was the last of the original states to grant complete political equality to Jews. Until 1877, Jews and Catholics were excluded by law from some political offices, but by 1894 two Jews had served in the State Legislature: Abraham Stahl of Berlin (1891), and Louis Goldschmidt of Dover (1894). The state also had a quasi-religious establishment until 1817, with everyone except members of recognized dissenting churches required to pay a tax for the support of the established Congregational Church.

Until the end of the 19th century, the history of Jews in New Hampshire was confined to scattered individuals. Leopold Morse, a native of Bavaria, settled at Tamworth about 1850, but soon moved to Massachusetts where he was elected to Congress from a Boston district in 1877. Abraham Cohn, who had fought with the 68th New York Regiment in the early days of the Civil War and was then honorably discharged because he was not physically fit for active duty, reenlisted in the 6th New Hampshire Infantry. As Sgt. Major Cohn, he won the Congressional Medal of Honor for bravery at the Battle of the Wilderness in 1864.

While there was a small Jewish settlement in Portsmouth in 1877, the first permanent Jewish community was established by immigrants from Russia and Poland who arrived about 1885. Largely peddlers and storekeepers who came into the state via Boston, the newcomers struck roots in Manchester, Portsmouth, Concord, Nashua, Dover, Berlin, Keene, and Laconia. The state's first Jewish organization, the Hebrew Ladies Aid Society, was founded in Manchester in 1896, followed the next year by Congregation Anshe Sphard, the oldest in the state. By 1905, there were 1,000 Jews scattered through the state, more than 650 of them in Manchester which had a second congregation, while Berlin, Concord, and Nashua each had single congregations.

In 1905, at the height of the anti-Jewish persecutions in Russia, from which the founders of the New Hampshire Jewish community had but recently fled, New Hampshire became the scene of a dramatic event in Jewish history which must have deeply stirred the refugees from the land of the Czar. In the midst of the negotiations to settle the Russo-Japanese War, which President Theodore Roosevelt initiated with a meeting in Portsmouth, the emissaries of the Czar sat down in New Hampshire with spokesmen for American Jewry. Attending this notable meeting—at which a futile attempt was made to convince Russia to halt its anti-Jewish program—were Jacob H. Schiff, Adolph Lewisohn, Oscar S. Straus, Isaac N. Seligman, Count Witte, the Russian prime minister, Baron Rosen (a non-Jew), the Russian ambassador to the United States, and Gregory Wilensky, a Russian Jew who was financial attache to the Russian embassy in Washington.

On the eve of World War I, there were 3,257 Jews in the state. Manchester was already the largest Jewish community, with 600 Jews, followed by Portsmouth (550), Nashua (350), Concord (158), and Derry (42). Dispersed in 58 small towns were a total of 2,149 Jews. In 1937 the state's Jewish population showed no growth over what it had been two decades before. By 1960 the Jewish population had increased to 5,200, with just about half living in Manchester. The other major communities were Portsmouth, Nashua, Concord, Claremont, Laconia, and Dover. In 1975 there was a falling off in the Jewish population to 4,220, attributed to a decline of more than 1,000 in Manchester's Jewish population.

In 1976, the rabbi of Manchester's Temple Israel, which claimed to have the only regular daily *minyan* in the whole state, warned that it might fade away.

William Loeb, the right wing publisher of the *Manchester Union-Leader,* the state's most influential newspaper, takes delight in such headlines as "Kissinger the Kike." In private conversation Loeb makes it a point to note when a person he is talking about happens to be a Jew. Loeb, who is an Episcopalian, and has a baptismal certificate to prove it, is the son of the late William Loeb, Sr., a Jew who was private secretary to President Theodore Roosevelt from 1901-1909. In 1947, Loeb took in as a partner in the Manchester paper, the late Leonard Finder, who had been assistant national director of the Anti-Defamation League from 1937-1947. When Loeb and Finder quarreled, Finder started a new daily in Dover which lasted only a short time. While Finder was associated with the *Union-Leader* he scored one of the great journalistic scoops of the day when in response to an inquiry, General Dwight D. Eisenhower told him he would be interested in a presidential nomination.

Eight Jews have served in the State Legislature since 1891. The late Samuel Green, who was a member of the House of Representatives from 1957-1961, was elected to the State Senate in 1961 and named its president in 1962. Leo Liberson, one-time city attorney of Portsmouth, was a delegate to the New Hampshire Constitutional Convention in 1938. Kennard E. Goldsmith was only 23 when he was elected mayor of Portsmouth in 1936. Milton Shapiro of Concord was chairman of the State Department of Resources and Economic Development from 1963-1968. Abraham Stahl of Berlin, the first Jew elected to the State Legislature (1891), later served as president of the New Hampshire Bankers Association.

* * * * *

BERLIN
Cong. Beth Israel, Exchange St.

BETHLEHEM
Bethlehem Hebrew Cong., Strawberry Hill.

CLAREMONT
Gellis Street was named in 1953 for the late Morris A. Gellis, one of the founders of the Claremont Jewish community and the first Jew to be elected to public office here.

Temple Meyer-David, 19 High St., is named for David Blumberg and Meyer Satzow, New Hampshire boys who were killed in World War II.

CONCORD
Temple Beth Jacob, 67 Broadway.

DOVER
Temple Israel, 45 Fourth St.

DURHAM
Hillel Foundation at University of New Hampshire, 200 State St., Temple Beth Israel, Portsmouth.

EXETER
Philips Exeter Academy, one of the country's leading private secondary schools, has The Jewish Congregation, a synagogue founded by Jewish students which meets on the school grounds.

HANOVER

Dartmouth College

Dartmouth College's seal includes two Hebrew words: *El Shaddai*, God Almighty. The words are contained in a triangle at the top of the seal, a large replica of which is on the front of the Baker Library on Dartmouth Green. ●Filene Auditorium in Gerry Hall, a classroom and faculty office building housing the psychology department, is named for the late Lincoln Filene, Boston department store owner and philanthropist. ●Charles Gilman Life Science Laboratory, housing the department of biological sciences, is named for the late paper manufacturer. ●Hillel Foundation, Box 5051, Hinman Hall. ●Jaffe-Friede Gallery in the Hopkins Center was a gift of William B. Jaffe, New York attorney and a board member of the Jewish Museum, and his wife, Evelyn Annenberg Friede Jaffe. The gallery is used for art exhibitions. ●Jacob H. Strauss Memorial Gallery in Hopkins Center, was a gift of Mrs. Strauss of Swampscott in memory of her husband, a Dartmouth alumnus, class of 1922. ▢

KEENE

Community Synagogue of Cong. Ahavas Achim, Hastings Ave., is a tent-like structure resembling the sanctuary in the desert of the ancient Israelites. It was dedicated in 1974, although services were first held here in 1900. The city's Christian churches held fundraising events for the synagogue and hundreds of non-Jews sent in unsolicited donations. The religious appurtenances were built mostly by non-Jews. The community's first synagogue had been the old Red Cross building on Court Street.

LACONIA

Temple B'nai Israel, 208 Court St.

MANCHESTER

Bronstein Park, bounded by Amherst, Beech, Hanover, and Union Sts., is named for the late Lt. (J.G.) Richard Bronstein, the first commissioned officer from New Hampshire killed in World War II. Bronstein was the medical officer on the destroyer USS *Jacob Jones* when it was torpedoed and sunk by a German submarine in February, 1942. In December, 1943, the Navy commissioned a destroyer-escort, USS *Bronstein*. When that ship was transferred to Uruguay in 1952, a second ship, USS *Bronstein,* was christened in 1962.

Jewish Community Center, 698 Beech St.

Temple Adath Yeshurun, 152 Prospect St.

Temple Israel, 678 Pine St.

NASHUA

Temple Beth Abraham, 4 Raymond St.

PORTSMOUTH

Hymanson USO Center, 53 Market St., was rededicated in 1968 in memory of Harry Hymanson, who had been director of the club for many years, former executive director of the USO Council of New England, and a member of the staff of the National Jewish Welfare Board.

Temple Israel, 200 State St.

Warner House, Chapel and Daniel Sts., a town landmark since 1716, has some unusual murals on both sides of the stairwell, including one showing Abraham preparing to offer his son Isaac as a sacrifice. It is the work of an unknown artist.

RINDGE

Cathedral of the Pines, a unique outdoor sanctuary where religious services of all faiths are held during the summer, was created in

1946 by Mr. and Mrs. Douglas Sloane in memory of their son, Lt. Sanders Sloane, who was killed in Germany in 1944. The Altar of Nations was dedicated as a shrine to all American war dead. It has incorporated in it soil from all World War II battlefields and stones from all parts of the world, including one from the Normandy beachhead contributed by President Dwight Eisenhower, and stones from the old city of Jerusalem and Buchenwald concentration camp. Nestling atop a knoll facing Mt. Monadnock, near the Massachusetts line, the cathedral has become internationally famous for its services conducted by a different denomination each week. The Jewish service is usually held the first Sunday in August. The first Jewish service was conducted on August 1, 1947, with Rabbi David Max Eichhorn, World War II chaplain and then director of field operations of the National Jewish Welfare Board's Commission on Jewish Chaplaincy, officiating at the dedication of the Magen David. The Aron Kodesh and Torah Scroll, gifts of Charles Gottesman of White Plains, N.Y., were dedicated at a service conducted by Rabbi Lawrence W. Schwartz of the White Plains Jewish Center. The Aron Kodesh and Torah memorializing the heroic Four Chaplains of World War II, were consecrated by Rabbi Roland B. Gittelsohn of Temple Israel, Boston, a former Marine Corps chaplain. In inclement weather the service is held in Hilltop House and broadcast over the public address system to parked cars. At the entrance to the cathedral are two large boulders containing inscriptions in English and Hebrew. The two stones are reminders that the Ten Commandments were received by Moses on two stone tablets. The inscription reads: "Thou shalt Love the Lord Thy God," and "Thou shalt Love Thy Neighbor as Thy Self."

Franklin Pierce College has the Kermit Bloomgarden Theater, named for the prominent Broadway producer.

NEW JERSEY

Benjamin Levy, of London, England, never set foot in New Jersey—or anywhere else in America—but he was 28th on the list of the 32 proprietors who owned West Jersey before it was united with East Jersey in 1702 to form the royal colony of New Jersey. West Jersey included all of the territory west of a diagonal line from Little Egg Harbor, near Atlantic City, to a point on the Delaware River just north of the Delaware Water Gap.

Levy's ownership of a slice of New Jersey came about through a complicated series of deals. Until 1664 New Jersey was an unnamed section of New Netherland. When the British took New Netherland, the Duke of York, (later King James II), who had received all of the Dutch domain from his brother, Charles II, created New Jersey by the stroke of a pen and made a present of the whole area to Lord Berkeley and Sir George Carteret. Berkeley disposed of his share to British Quakers in 1674 from whom William Penn and others ultimately acquired it. Levy, an elder of London's first synagogue and a prominent late 17th and early 18th century broker and merchant, became one of the proprietors of West Jersey through the forfeit of security on a loan he had made to one of the Quaker shareholders of the territory.

Levy owned three shares in the West Jersey Society in 1691 but he never claimed his shares and they appear on a list of 31¼ unclaimed shares. When the proprietors of the two Jerseys surrendered their civil rights in the colony to the British crown, Levy, as a shareholder, was entitled to sign a petition to Queen Anne, (1702), asking that Andrew

188

Hamilton be reappointed governor and another document agreeing to the cession of stockholders' rights to the crown.

Under the rule of the proprietors, the province of West Jersey declared that "liberty of conscience in matters of faith and worship towards God shall be granted to all people within the province aforesaid who shall live peaceably and quietly therein, and that none of the free people of the said province shall be rendered uncapable of office in respect of their faith and worship." In her instructions to Governor Hamilton in 1702, Queen Anne declared that "you are to permit a liberty of conscience to all persons (except Papists) so that they may be contented with a quiet and peaceable enjoyment of the same, not giving offense or scandal to the government."

The site of William Penn's first refuge for persecuted Quakers, and one of the four original colonies in which no established church of any denomination existed on a statewide basis, New Jersey was known for its religious tolerance from its earliest days. To supplement the first regulations governing New Jersey issued in 1665 by Berkeley and Carteret, which permitted each inhabitant to "have and enjoy his and their judgments of conscience in matters of religion," the proprietors, freeholders, and inhabitants of West Jersey adopted in 1676 "concessions and agreements" which proclaimed "that no men, nor number of men upon earth, hath power or authority to rule over men's consciences in religious matters." This document also guaranteed that no one was to be interfered with "for the sake of his opinion, judgment, faith or worship towards God." William Penn, who is believed to have been the author of this document, visited the Quaker colony in West Jersey in 1681 and described the Indians there as closely resembling Jews. Penn's report that the Indians were descended from the "Ten Lost Tribes" of Israel became the basis later for a book on this subject by Elias Boudinot, the New Jersey silversmith and Revolutionary patriot. He served as a president of the Continental Congress and became an avid supporter of efforts to convert Jews to Christianity.

While the West Jersey Quakers banned any religious test for public office in 1681, East Jersey, also owned by Quakers, instituted a religious test in 1683, and West Jersey followed suit a decade later. Full freedom of worship was granted to all by the constitution adopted by the New Jersey Provincial Congress on June 10, 1776, but only Protestants were permitted to hold office. This curb remained in effect until 1844, when a new state constitution finally established complete religious and civil equality for all.

Although Benjamin Levy, the proprietor, never visited West Jersey, other Levys were among the handful of Jews who lived or did business in New Jersey all through the 18th century, and perhaps even earlier. Among the enterprising New Amsterdam Jewish traders who dickered with the Indians along the Delaware River as early as 1660 or 1670, there were some who probably visited what is now New Jersey. Another Benjamin Levy, who is identified as a Jew in the New Jersey archives, lived near what is now Camden in 1702. Moses Levy (see New York), the eminent New York merchant and shipowner, whose son, Nathan, was the founding father of the Philadelphia Jewish community, had extensive business interests in New Jersey in the first decades of the 18th century and may even have owned an estate there. When 12 inhabitants of and traders in New Jersey petitioned King George I, in 1718, to override the governor who had permitted the Quakers to hold office by making a solemn affirmation instead of taking an oath, Moses Levy's name appeared as one of those who claimed that the concession damaged their interests. This is one of the rare instances of a Jew in Colonial America taking a position against religious freedom. This same Moses Levy, however, was one of the New York Jews who contributed to the fund for the erection of Trinity Church's steeple.

Isaac Emanuel, Joseph Isaac, and Solomon Isaac were all in business at Freehold in 1720. Emanuel was involved in considerable litigation in Monmouth County Court from 1720-1724. Daniel Nunez of Piscataway Township in Middlesex County, served as town clerk and justice of the peace in Quarter Sessions Court at New Brunswick in 1722, while running his store. He was also town treasurer and tax collector, and one of the first Jews in America to hold public office. The Louzada family, active members of New York's Congregation Shearith Israel, was identified with Bound Brook from 1698 until midway through the Revolutionary War.

Aaron Louzada, who settled at Bound Brook in 1698, after retiring from business in New York, built Bound Brook's third house, "the Jew House." He later acquired the Codrington homestead on which much of Bound Brook now stands. Aaron's daughter, a widow, was the last Louzada to live in "the Jew House." A Tory sympathizer in the Revolution, she invited Lord Cornwallis and his staff to make "the Jew House" their headquarters in 1777 when the British occupied Bound Brook. Dr. David de Sola Pool in *Portraits Etched in Stone*, records that "when the British left Bound Brook, one of the officers who had arrived as a bachelor went away as a married man, taking his hostess, the widow, with him as one of the prizes of war." The Americans later seized the house and sold it, as they did with the property of Jacob Louzada, who had to leave Bound Brook hurriedly because of his Loyalist sympathies. Another Aaron Louzada, who was a generous supporter of the New York synagogue, and his brother, Moses, also lived at Bound Brook. During the second quarter of the 18th century they were large landowners and leading citizens. They operated a grist mill, owned a general store, and helped their neighbors erect a Lutheran church. A letter from Hannah Louzada, Moses' widow, is in the archives of the American Jewish Historical Society.

Contemporaries of the Louzadas were Rodrigo Pacheco, who was in business around New Brunswick in 1742, and David Hays, kinsman of the New York Hays and Seixas families, who owned a plantation in Griggstown in Somerset County in 1742. Pacheco was a New York merchant who had helped build that city's first synagogue and also contributed toward the construction of Trinity Church's steeple.

A pair of rascals named Levy completes the list of Jews known to have lived in New Jersey prior to the Revolution. One was Myers Levy, of Spotswood, a black-bearded trader who disappeared with a large assortment of unpaid goods, taking along his wife and five children, but leaving behind enraged creditors. Among these were the Gratzes and Franks (see Pennsylvania), of Philadelphia, as well as some non-Jewish merchants in Pennsylvania, who inserted an advertisement in the *New York Mercury* in 1760 offering a reward for information about Levy's whereabouts. Nathan Levy, of Phillipsburg, was the subject of another advertisement, this one in the *Pennsylvania Journal* in 1765. The advertiser was John Farnsworth, Levy's neighbor, whose wife had run away with the Jewish shopkeeper. Besides proclaiming that he was no longer responsible for the debts of his wife, Deborah, Farnsworth told the world that "she likes said Levy better than me, and intends to live with him, as he will maintain her as a gentlewoman; I have waited on Levy respecting the affair, from whom I have received no other satisfaction than insolent language. . ."

A Levy of a different stripe was Asser Levy, who was probably the only Jew to serve with Jersey troops in the Revolution. An ensign in the 1st New Jersey Regiment, Levy may have been a grandson as well as the namesake of the celebrated Asser Levy of New Amsterdam (see New York). There was a Moses Levy of Philadelphia in Washington's army of 2,500 picked men who, on Christmas eve, 1776, crossed the ice-choked Delaware to defeat the surprised British and their Hessian mercenaries at the Battle of Trenton. But this Levy was already a Christian. One of Philadelphia's ablest lawyers, he is said to have been considered by Thomas Jefferson in 1804 as attorney general of the United States.

With the 21st Regiment of Marbleheaders from Massachusetts, which had the distinction of carrying Washington's troops across the Delaware, was Abraham Solomon (see Massachusetts). Among the Hessians who survived the Battle of Trenton was Alexander Zuntz, a Westphalian Jew who had come to America with the British forces. He later served as a commissary and adjutant to the British general staff in New York. When Zuntz reached New York in 1779, he became the leader of a handful of Jews who had remained in the city after the British captured it. He was president of Congregation Shearith Israel until the end of the war. Immediately thereafter, following the return of the congregation's patriot leaders, Zuntz resigned, but he was elected to the synagogue's governing board. He remained active the rest of his life, and when he died in 1819, was buried in the historic Bowery Cemetery (see New York). David Franks (see Pennsylvania), the Philadelphia merchant, was an involuntary resident of New Jersey in 1779. Suspected of Loyalist sentiments, he was prevented from returning to Pennsylvania and thus found himself in Elizabeth and Camden, while he vainly sought to obtain payment for the funds he had advanced to free British prisoners of war held by the Americans.

Although individual Jews continued to find their way to New Jersey all through the 18th century, no Jewish community developed in the state until the fourth decade of the 19th century because of the state's geographical position between two metropolises. From the very first days of Jewish association with New Jersey, the Jews who lived there were in a kind of hinterland of the New York and Philadelphia Jewish communities. Those who resided or did business in West Jersey maintained community ties with Philadelphia, while those whose interests lay in East Jersey were bound to New York. This was as true after the Revolution as before. The Jewish merchants from Philadelphia who moved their families and businesses to Trenton in 1793 while yellow fever raged in the City of Brotherly Love, went back to Philadelphia when the plague abated. Isaac Moses (see New York), whose company was probably the largest Jewish mercantile firm in America during the Revolution, and who helped bolster American credit at a crucial point in the War of Independence, had large business interests around Montclair and Passaic after the Revolution, and may even have lived in Montclair for a time. But he considered himself a New Yorker. Harmon Hendricks and his partner and brother-in-law, Solomon Isaacs, opened America's first copper rolling mill in America in 1812 at Belleville. As agents in New York of the Boston firm of Paul Revere & Sons, the Hendricks-Isaacs mill supplied the Reveres with much of its metal needs, including some copper used to build the famed warship, *Constitution,* and Robert Fulton's first steamboat, the *Clermont.* Hendricks and Isaacs were members of leading New York Jewish families.

The earliest Jewish communities were established in Paterson, Newark, Trenton, and New Brunswick between 1840-1850 by immigrants from Germany, Hungary, and Bohemia. The pioneer silk factories of Paterson must have attracted Jewish settlers in the 1840s, since the first Jewish congregation in the state, B'nai Jeshurun, was formed there in 1847. The Ashmans, who arrived in 1844, and the Harrises, who came in 1848, are regarded as the founders of the Paterson Jewish community.

Newark, where a government patterned on the Mosaic Code was set up in 1666 by New England Puritans, had no known Jewish residents until the 1840s. (The name Newark is believed by scholars to be the Biblical New Ark, or the commonplace New Work, meaning a new project.) The first arrivals, Louis and Aaron Trier, settled there in 1844. Trier, who founded a tannery, was the father of Abraham Trier, born in 1845, said to be the first Jewish child born in Newark. Emanuel and Isaac Newman came in 1845. Isaac opened a boarding house and later was in the wholesale meat business. Abraham Newman, who came in 1847, was a peddler, Bernard Hauser, who arrived in 1848, sold cigars, ran a grocery store, and owned a boarding house that served as a social center for Jewish peddlers. Isaac Cohen, who located in Newark in 1847, is credited with being the chief organizer of the first *minyan,* which met in his home in 1847. This was the beginning of Temple B'nai Jeshurun, organized in 1848, New Jersey's second congregation. The first, also named B'nai Jeshurun, was organized a year earlier in Paterson. Newark's second congregation was B'nai Abraham, the product of a split in B'nai Jeshurun. The third congregation, Oheb Shalem, was a split off from B'nai Abraham, which was named for Abraham Newman, one of the founders of B'nai Jeshurun. By 1855 there were 200 Jewish families in Newark. Ten years later all of the leading drygoods stores in the city were owned by Jews. Louis Bamberger established the store that would grow into the state's largest department store. The Ullman & Isaacs drygoods store had a young clerk by the name of Benjamin Altman who later founded New York's B. Altman & Co. Newark's first philanthropic organization was the Young Men's Benevolent Society, founded in 1861, the ancestor of the present Jewish Community Federation of Metropolitan New Jersey.

Dr. Daniel Levy Maduro Peixotto, who edited the *Emporium and True American* while practicing medicine in Trenton, lived there in the late 1830s, but the first permanent Jewish settlers did not arrive until a decade later. They were Simon, Emanuel, and Leon Kahnweiler, who came from Germany. Simon was one of the sponsors of a protest meeting at city hall in 1848 when German-Americans demonstrated against autocratic rule in their native land. Samuel Kahnweiler, a son of Leon, was one of the early steamboat pilots on the Delaware and Raritan Rivers. Although Temple Har Sinai was not organized until 1860, some kind of Jewish community seems to have existed as early as 1856 when the *Trenton Gazette* reported that the Jews were observing Passover. Rosh Hashanah services were held in Trenton for the first time in 1858.

One of the city's leading citizens in those years was David Naar, the state's most prominent Jew in the 1850s and 1860s. Naar, a Sephardic Jew who was related to Peixotto, was born in St. Thomas, Danish West Indies, in 1800. Educated in New York, he returned to St. Thomas where he went into business and simultaneously served as military commander. In 1834 he settled in New York and a year later a fire wiped out his business and he moved to a farm at Wheatsheaf, near Elizabeth, which was then part of Essex County. He became active in the community, and in 1843 the State Legislature appointed him mayor of Elizabeth and lay judge of the Court of Common Pleas. In 1844 Naar stumped the state for James K. Polk, the Democratic presidential nominee,who later appointed him United States Consul at St. Thomas where he served from 1845-1848.

As a member of the state constitutional convention in 1844, Naar was a member of the committee that added a bill of rights to the constitution, and he fought for a motion that provided that minutes of the proceedings be kept. The bill of rights outlawed a religious test for public office. Naar also advocated universal suffrage. In the 1850s he moved to Trenton where he bought the *True American* which through mergers incorporated the paper previously edited by Peixotto. One of the founders of what is now Trenton State University, Naar was a strong supporter of the South. Before and after Lincoln's election to the presidency, he spoke and wrote in support of the South. In 1861 his pronounced Southern sympathies led to his being threatened by a mob. Denounced by another Trenton daily as "a treasonable editor" and assailed as the author of "treasonable babblings of a West India Jew," Naar lost circulation because he remained a Confederate sympathizer. Nevertheless, in 1865 he was elected state treasurer. Naar had little to do with the Jewish community but he was the principal speaker when Temple Har Sinai dedicated its first synagogue in 1866.

While Daniel Nunez and the Louzadas of Bound Brook were identified with New Brunswick in the 1700s, the first Jewish organization in the latter city dates from 1852. Congregation Anshe Emeth was incorporated in 1859 by German, Bohemian, and Polish peddlers and storekeepers but its existence was mentioned a year earlier by the *Jewish Messenger*. For its first Torah, however, the congregation looked not to its coreligionists in New York or Philadelphia but to the Prague *kehillah* to which it wrote asking if the historic Alteneu Synagogue could provide a scroll. When the first large numbers of Jews from Eastern Europe came to New Jersey in the 1880s they found established Jewish communities in Hoboken (1855), Jersey City

(1864), Elizabeth (1864), Perth Amboy (1870), Montclair (1875), East Orange (1873), and Bayonne (1880). Before 1900 there were also Jewish settlements in Passaic (1899), Atlantic City (1890), Camden (1894), and Englewood (1896).

Hoboken was first settled by German Jews in 1855 and beginning in the 1860s worship services were held in private homes. The first permanent congregation, Adas Emuno, founded in 1871, moved into its own building in 1872, and in 1883 built its first temple on land donated by the Stevens family who founded Stevens Institute of Technology.

Isaac Moses was alone when he did business around Montclair and Passaic during and after the Revolution, but about 1800 there were reports of Jewish peddlers around Cranetown, Speertown, and West Bloomfield, which later became part of Montclair. Hirsh Salov was an early settler around Lodi, and Louis and Jacob Harris opened a drygoods store in Montclair in 1875. They were among the founders of Shaarey Tefila in East Orange, the first suburban synagogue in the state. Felix Marx was probably one of the earliest New Jersey commuters because he lived in Plainfield in the early 1870s and journeyed daily to New York where he owned a restaurant. Jewish services were first held in Elizabeth in the 1850s; Louis Strauss, Samuel Eichberg, and Mayer Sontheimer were the earliest Jewish settlers.

Bergen County's earliest Jewish residents were shopkeepers and a few farmers who settled in and around Englewood in the 1880s. Jersey City's first Jewish settler was Joseph Mayer, a tobacconist, who arrived in 1858. The city's first congregation known as Isaac Ephraim Congregation, now known as Temple Beth El, dates from 1868. Israel Goldstein opened a store in Kearny in 1879. Bayonne's first Jewish resident, Louis Lazarus, arrived in 1880. His son, Hyman, a successful lawyer, acquired the *Bayonne Times* in 1901. It remained in the Lazarus family until 1971 when it was sold to Samuel Newhouse, who had begun his career as a clerk in Lazarus' office. When Lazarus became a judge in 1922, he sent for Newhouse and engaged him as the paper's business manager, marking the start of Newhouse's newspaper career. In North Hudson the first Jews arrived in the 1880s. A Mr. Bloom owned some land in New Durham, now called North Bergen. Joseph Backenroth was a tinsmith in West New York where a Mr. Brody did much to build the town's commerce. Max Smith operated a milk route and cattle business in Union Hill. William Lieberman was a butcher in West Hoboken in 1888, a Mr. Moose dealt in cattle, and Isaac Smith owned a milk route. Many of the first residents were peddlers. Hudson County's oldest Orthodox synagogue, Congregation Sons of Israel in Jersey City, dates from 1880.

Among the newcomers to New Jersey from Eastern Europe were

the pioneers who established the South Jersey farm colonies, the cradle of the Jewish agricultural movement in the United States. Of all the agricultural colonies founded in the 1880s, 1890s, and early 1900s for and by the immigrants who poured in from Russia, only the settlements in New Jersey survived. Drought, floods, poor land, inexperience, inadequate funding, lack of water, absence of transportation, and poor marketing facilities contributed to the failure of the agricultural experiments in the Dakotas, Kansas, Colorado, Nebraska, Michigan, Louisiana, Maryland, Virginia, and Washington, but the South Jersey colonies weathered all these difficulties.

The first South Jersey colony, Alliance, was founded in May, 1882, by members of the Am Olam movement, established in Odessa in 1881 by Sidney Bailey, Michael Bakal, and Moses Herder. In the triangle formed by the cities of Vineland, Millville, and Bridgeton, 35 miles south of Philadelphia, 67 families from Odessa, Kiev, and Elizabetgrad were settled on a 1,100-acre tract. The land was fertile but uncleared. Later in the same year a second colony was established nearby in Rosenhayn in Salem County, and a third at Carmel. Between them and around them there grew up the Jewish farm villages of Six Points, Brotmanville, Norma, and Garton Road. Alliance was named for the Alliance Israelite Universelle, the Paris-based organization that aided Jews around the world. At first the colonists did not know whether potatoes grew above or under ground, but their lack of experience was compensated for by a series of fortunate circumstances. They had the advantage of nearby markets for their products. The factories of Vineland, Millville, and Bridgeton, and the industries of Philadelphia provided essential sources of supplementary income. Most important of all was their proximity to New York and Philadelphia which kept them in the Jewish public eye and heart, and thus enabled them to get the support needed to tide them over the rough years. While the fate of the first colonies was still in doubt, the newly created Baron de Hirsch Fund established the Woodbine Colony in Cape May County, the first all-Jewish town in modern times. The Baron de Hirsch Fund's grant to the Jewish Agricultural Society, founded in 1900, enabled the latter to guide and counsel the Jewish farmers and to lend them money when they needed credit.

The sons of the pioneer Jewish farmers included many notable people. Among them were Benjamin Golder, a member of Congress from Philadelphia; Israel Lubin, theatre builder; Theodore Rosen, a judge; Raymond and Jacob Lipman, noted agricultural scientists and educators; Charles Lipman, dean of the graduate school at the University of California; Joseph Perskie, a judge of the New Jersey Supreme Court; and Arthur D. Goldhaft, the first veterinarian to specialize in poultry diseases, who established a plant for making vaccines for chickens—an enterprise now conducted by his son, Dr. Tevis Goldhaft, and son-in-law, Dr. M.L. Werhicoff.

In the 1970s, the old Jewish farm settlements had 2,450 Jews, most of them in the poultry and egg business. In the 1920s the Jewish Agricultural Society settled Jewish families on poultry and truck-gardening farms in Toms River and Farmingdale. By the 1950s there were 2,500 Jewish poultry and egg-raising farmers in the state who owned 7,500,000 egg-laying chickens. In the 1930s, the Jewish Agricultural Society placed some German-Jewish refugees in the poultry-raising area, and after World War II a number of concentration camp survivors also found their way to the South Jersey poultry-raising towns. The postwar settlers created a Jewish Poultry Farmers Association and were active in forming farm cooperatives. From 1906-1936 the number of Jews in Monmouth County climbed from 205 to 7,000. During the same span the Jewish population in Ocean County increased from 25 to 1,760.

From the farm communities came many of the first Jewish settlers in the resort cities of Atlantic City, Lakewood, Bradley Beach, Belmar, and Asbury Park. Lakewood, the most famous winter resort in the east from the 1880s-1930, had few hotels that admitted Jews until the turn of the century. In 1891, however, Nathan Straus, the philanthropist, who had himself been turned away from the Laurel House, built the Lakewood Hotel. Thereafter, Lakewood became a popular resort for middle-class Jews from New York, Newark, and Philadelphia. Elberon, Deal, and Long Branch were summer resorts for wealthy Jews from the 1880s to the 1920s, when the whole area was known as "the Jewish Newport." Atlantic City's first Jewish settlers arrived from Philadelphia in the 1880s. That city's well-to-do Jews had long summered in Atlantic City where the Bacharach family, which produced a mayor and a member of Congress, owned a hotel. Belmar's earliest Jewish settler was Solomon Weinstein, who arrived in 1886, but the present community dates from about 1920. In the adjoining town of Bradley Beach there were Jewish hotel and boarding-house owners before World War I. There are also Sephardic communities in Bradley Beach and Deal.

From less than 6,000 Jews in 1877, New Jersey has seen its Jewish population grow to 25,000 in 1900; 40,000 in 1905; 149,476 in 1917; 267,790 in 1937; 326,300 in 1960; and 418,000 in 1974. In that year New Jersey had more Jews than any other state except New York, California, and Pennsylvania. Only in New York (11.8) was the Jewish percentage of the total population greater than in New Jersey (5.7).

The bulk of the Jewish population lived in the northeastern part of the state, from Bergen County in the north to Middlesex County on the south, with substantial numbers in Camden County across the river from Philadelphia, in and around Trenton, in the two major shore areas—Atlantic City and environs—and the Long Branch, Asbury Park, Deal, Bradley Beach, Belmar, and Elberon axis.

Major demographic changes, however, began in 1948. Of the 86,300 Jews in Essex County, 56,800 lived in Newark, the state's largest city. Two decades later, there were only 8,000 Jews in Newark, largely older people over 65 years of age, mostly foreign-born, and largely Orthodox. The move to the suburbs which had been gaining headway through the 1950s reached runaway proportions in the late 1960s after the Newark race riot of 1967. Of the 100,000 Jews in Essex County in 1974, about 5,000 still resided in Newark. The rest live in the many suburban communities west of the Garden State Parkway, in such places as Maplewood, the Oranges, Millburn, Livingston, Short Hills, Parsippany, and Springfield. A growing number of Jews in the older Essex County suburban communities such as Irvington, Summit, and Montclair, where there have been major changes in neighborhoods, have moved to newer communities. The move from Newark to the suburbs was underscored by the changed location of the city's three oldest congregations: Oheb Shalom moved to South Orange in 1959; B'nai Jeshurun occupied a new site in Short Hills in 1968; and a year later B'nai Abraham established itself in Livingston. The Essex County Jewish Community Council, renamed the Jewish Community Federation of Metropolitan New Jersey, left Newark for East Orange, which is also the headquarters of other county-wide Jewish agencies. Vast stretches of Newark which once housed flourishing Irish and Jewish communities are now solidly black. Where once a dozen synagogues flourished, only one or two survive. Weequahic, once Newark's well-known neighborhood of substantial Jewish middle-class families living in private homes on tree-lined streets made famous by the fiction of Philip Roth, is now part of a black area.

Similar changes have occurred in other parts of the state. Up to 1937 about one-third of all the Jews in the state lived in Newark. By the late 1960s the bulk of them resided not only in the suburban areas of Essex County but in new Jewish areas of residence in suburban Bergen, Passaic, Union, Middlesex, and Camden Counties. The example of the federation in Essex County taking a name reflecting its broader scope was similar to name changes that occurred in other parts of the state.

Bergen County had barely 5,000 Jews until 1930. The completion of the George Washington Bridge in 1931 opened the door to a large migration from New York. By 1950 the Jewish population had quadrupled to 20,000 and in the next decade it quintupled, with major communities in Englewood, Teaneck, Fair Lawn, Palisades Park, and Leonia. In 1963 Bergen County's Jewish population was estimated at 68,000, 70 percent of whom had moved to the county since 1950. In 1973 the Jewish population topped 100,000.

In Hudson County, just south of Bergen County, there has been a sharp decline in Jewish population since the late 1950s. Hoboken, which once counted 4,000 Jews, was down to 50 families. The oldest congregation, Temple Adas Emuno, moved to Bergen County. Before World War II there were more than 45,000 Jews in Hudson County. In the early 1970s it had fallen to less than 20,000. Jersey City is down to 10,000 from its high of 21,000. Union City, Weehawken, and West New York now have very few Jewish residents but a good number of Jewish businessmen in an area that has become heavily Cuban and Puerto Rican. In Bayonne the Jewish population dropped from nearly 10,000 in 1950 to 8,500 in 1973.

Paterson, once the state's second largest Jewish community, has lost population to the newer suburbs of Midland Park, Saddle Brook, Glen Rock, Waldwick, Wayne, Wyckoff, Allendale, East Paterson, Rochelle Park, Franklin Lakes, and Pompton Lakes. A 1972 study found 20,000 Jews in the area served by the Jewish Federation of North Jersey. In 1960 Paterson accounted for 16,000 Jews, but by 1970 it had only 7,800 Jews, while Fair Lawn had 13,100, Wayne, 5,100, Rochelle Park, 17,000, and other towns in the area had a total of 2,200.

Atlantic City's Jewish population has dropped from 12,000 to 9,500 in 20 years, while the city's total population fell from 60,000 in 1960 to 45,000 in the 1970s. Blacks and Puerto Ricans now constitute half the city's population. The Jews in the city are mostly elderly and retirees. The whites, including the Jews, have moved to the nearby residential communities of Ventnor, Margate, Brigantine, Hammonton, Longport, and Pleasantville. A similar shift occurred in Camden County and Union County. Of the 50,000 Jews in Union County, only a small proportion reside in Elizabeth itself. New Brunswick, which had 5,000 Jews in 1950, had less than 900 in the 1970s, as the Jewish population moved into the Middlesex County suburbs—Highland Park, Bound Brook, Sayreville, and East Brunswick. In Lakewood and the neighboring shore communities the Jewish population has remained stable and even increased owing to the building of tract houses, condominiums, and the mushrooming growth of retirement communities in Ocean and Monmouth Counties.

Joseph Weintraub, who was chief justice of the New Jersey Supreme Court for 16 years, held the highest office of any Jew in the State's history. Other Jews who served on the State Supreme Court were Justices Samuel Kalisch, Harold Kolovsky, William A. Wachenfeld, Nathan L. Jacobs, Sidney M. Schreiber, Sydney Goldman, James Rosen, Nathan L. Jacobs, Joseph Perskie, and Morris Pashman. David Wilentz and Arthur J. Sills served as state attorney-generals. Nelson G. Gross, who was state Republican chairman, was the Republican nominee for the United States Senate in 1971. Leon Leonard, who once was acting governor, was speaker and majority leader of the State Assembly. Other Jews who served as speaker were Paul M. Salsburg, Joseph Altman, Joseph A. Greenberg, and Edward Schoen.

Only two Jews have been elected to Congress from New Jersey, Isaac Bacharach of Atlantic City, 1915-1937, and Charles Joelson, Paterson, 1961-1969. Stanley S. Brotman of Vineland, president of the New Jersey Bar Association, who was appointed a United States Federal Court judge in 1975 by President Gerald Ford, was the sixth Jew to hold such a post in New Jersey. The others were Philip Forman, Mendon Morrill, Mitchell H. Cohen, Herbert Stern, and James J. Rosen. Rosen and Forman also served on the United States Circuit Court of Appeals. Jews who have served as United States Attorneys in New Jersey were Jonathan J. Goldstein, Herbert J. Stern, Donald Horowitz, David M. Satz, Jr., Philip Forman, and Isaac Gross.

The following have served as mayors of New Jersey cities: David Naar, Elizabeth (1850-52); Moses Wolf, Bordentown (1850s); Samuel Barnert, Paterson (1883-85, 1889-91); Isaac Taussig, Jersey City (1881-83); Isaac Schoenthal, Orange (1904-08); Harry Bacharach, Atlantic City (1911-1935); Hirsch L. Sabsovich, Woodbine; Joseph Rabinowitz, Woodbine (1912-14); Joseph Mayer, Belmar (1931-33); Samuel Greenstein, Woodbine (1930); Henry Hershfield, Pompton Lakes (1910-18); Joseph Levenson, Woodbine (1936-38); Aaron J. Bach, Deal (1922-24); Meyer G. Ellenstein, Newark (1933-35); Abram Blum, Nutley; Mrs. Katherine Elkus White, Red Bank (1950-58); Burt Ross, Fort Lee (1973-75); Abraham Rosenberg, Bogota (1961-65); Sol Needles, Jr., Cape May (1954); Albert Moskin, Englewood (1956-60); Joseph Altman, Atlantic City (1944-52); Charles Kiva Krieger, Jersey City (1971); Ned Feldman, Englewood (1950-54); Milton Conford, Cranford (1952); Matthew Feldman, Teaneck (1961-65); Burton S. Goodman, Cranford (1975); and Joseph Lazarow, Atlantic City (1976).

* * * * *

ADELPHIA
Talmudical High School of Central New Jersey, Adelphia Rd.

ALLIANCE
Shearith Israel Cong., Gershel Ave., serves the farmers of the oldest surviving Jewish agricultural colony in the U.S., where there

are still some 50 Jewish families. The congregation, the second in Alliance, was founded in 1890. The colony's first synagogue was erected in 1888. Alliance is named for the Alliance Israelite Universelle which was founded in Paris in 1860, under the leadership of Adolph Cremieux, to unite Jews of different lands for the defense of Jewish rights wherever threatened. For more than 50 years the Alliance was the principal international Jewish organization whose political, educational, and colonizing efforts did much to ameliorate the lot of Jews in the Balkans, Mideast, and North Africa. After the Russian pogroms of 1881, when 20,000 Jews fled to Galicia, in Austria-Hungary, the Alliance was largely responsible for enabling some to come to America. The town was named in honor of this international organization.

ALPINE

Nathan Ohrbach Scout Arena at Alpine Boy Scout Camp is a circular social center and dining hall accommodating 1,000 persons that was donated by and named for Nathan Ohrbach, New York merchant and philanthropist.

ASBURY PARK

Cong. Sons of Israel, 412 Asbury Ave., built its first synagogue on land donated by James A. Bradley, founder of the city. Part of the synagogue's recreation and education building is dedicated to Bradley, a devout Roman Catholic.

ATLANTIC CITY

Atlantic City Boardwalk, the famous promenade of this resort city, was the joint idea of Alexander Boardman, a Jewish train conductor on the old Camden and Atlantic City Railroad, and Jacob Keim, a non-Jewish hotel man. Boardman conceived of a plank walk from the beach when he tired of having passengers spilling sand on the seats and floor of his train. Simultaneously, Keim had the same idea, hoping that a wooden walk would prevent people from tracking sand into his hotel. When the first boardwalk was built (the present structure is the fifth) in 1870, it was eight feet wide and was removed after the tourist season.

Atlantic County Jewish Community Center, (see Margate).

Bacharach Boulevard, from North Carolina Ave., to Pennrose Blvd., is named for Harry Bacharach, three-time mayor of the city. The Bacharach family settled in Atlantic City in the 1880s and gave the city three of its most distinguished citizens. Harry was president of the City Council in 1900, postmaster from 1901-1909, and became mayor for the first time in 1911. He remained mayor until 1916, when he was appointed to the State Public Utility Commission. In 1930 he was again elected mayor, serving until 1935. With his brothers, Benjamin and Isaac, Bacharach headed the campaign to build the local Jewish Community Center, now moved to the suburbs. Isaac was a Republican member of Congress from 1915-1937.

Best of Life Park, S. Virginia Ave., is a senior citizens' housing development, sponsored by the Community Synagogue.

Chelsea Hebrew Cong., 4001 Atlantic Avenue.

Community Haven, Virginia and Pacific Aves., a 15-story highrise senior citizen housing development is sponsored by the Community Synagogue.

Community Synagogue, 906 Pacific Ave. The Senior Citizens Service Center, housed in the synagogue, is sponsored by the Federation of Jewish Agencies of Atlantic County.

Cong. Beth Israel, 901 Pacific Ave., is the oldest congregation in the city, having been founded in 1893. It has another location in Margate.

Cong. Beth Jacob Amunath Israel, 506 Pacific Ave.

Cong. Rodef Sholom, 2016 Pacific Ave.

Cong. Sharreth Zion Sephardic, 212 Pacific Ave.

Hebrew Old Age Center, 3850 Atlantic Ave.

Jewish Record, 1537 Atlantic Ave.

AVENEL
Cong. Sons of Jacob, Lord St.

BAYONNE
Bayonne Bridge, the longest steel arch span bridge in the world, linking New York City with New Jersey via Staten Island. It was designed by the late Leon Moisseiff, one of the world's foremost bridge builders. The 1,675-foot single span structure is a monument to the Latvian-born Jew who was the consulting engineer or designer on bridges connecting New York City's five boroughs, as well as other major spans in the U.S. Moisseiff, who fled Russia because of his political activities as a leader of the Jewish Bund, arrived in America penniless in 1892 when he was 20. In his younger days he was active in Jewish radical circles in New York, edited the Yiddish language magazine, *Freie Gesellschaft,* through which he introduced Walt Whitman, Ibsen, and other noted writers to the Yiddish masses. One of the founders of the New York Kehillah, he was for many years on the editorial board of the Jewish Publication Society of America and the board of directors of the Yiddish daily *The Day.* Moisseiff, who died in 1943 at the age of 70, was for a time chairman of the scientific committee of the American Friends of the Hebrew University.

Cong. Beth Abraham, 42 N. 21st St.

Cong. Ohab Sholom, 1016-22 Avenue C.

Cong. Ohave Sholom Anshe Sfard, 190 Avenue B.

Cong. Talmud Torah, 489 Kennedy Blvd.

Harry D. Dembe portrait hangs in the District Courthouse where Judge Dembe served for many years.

Jewish Community Center, 1050 Kennedy Blvd., has on its outside wall a bronze sculpture entitled *The Family*.

Jewish Community Council, 1050 Kennedy Blvd.

Temple Beth Am, 111 Avenue B.

Temple Emanu-El, 735 Kennedy Blvd.

BELLEVILLE

Belleville Rolling Mill, the first copper rolling mill in the United States, built in 1812 by Harmon Hendricks, member of an old New York Jewish family, was still in use as late as 1939, when the Hendricks family sold its plant to the Andrew Jergens Co. as the site for a new factory. A stone wall and brick building near the Jergens plant are the last vestiges of this pioneer industrial enterprise.

Cong. Ahavath Achim, 125 Academy St.

BELMAR

Cong. Sons of Israel, 503 11th Ave.

BERGENFIELD

Bergenfield-Dumont Jewish Center, 169 North Washington Ave.

Cong. Beth Abraham, South Prospect Ave.

Workmen's Circle Center, 52 East Johnson Ave.

BLOOMFIELD

Cong. B'nai Zion, 430 Franklin St.

Temple Menorah, 934 Broad St.

BOONTON

Hebrew Academy of Morris County, 219 Hill St.

Temple Beth Shalom, Harrison St.

BORDENTOWN

Cong. B'nai Abraham, 55 Crosswick St.

BOUND BROOK

Cong. Knesseth Israel, 229 Mountain Ave., was once known as the Jacob H. Schiff Congregation after the famed philanthropist whose gift helped Jewish farmers establish the congregation.

BRADLEY BEACH
Cong. Agudath Achim, 301 McCabe Ave.
Magen David Congregation, 101 5th Ave.

BRICKTOWN
Cong. Beth Or, Van Zile Rd. and Highway 70.

BRIDGETON
Cong. Beth Abraham, Fayette St. and Belmont Ave., has among its membership survivors of the old Jewish farm colony at Rosenhayn.

Dix Public Hunting and Fishing Area, a few miles southeast of Bridgeton, on the Delaware River, memorializes Henry A. Dix, a Russian Jew who arrived a penniless immigrant in 1890, and became a millionaire making and selling Army and Red Cross uniforms. He became the leading citizen of the Bridgeton-Millville area.

BRIGANTINE
Jewish Center, Brigantine Blvd.

BROWNS MILLS
Deborah Heart and Lung Center, Trenton Rd., is an independent gift-supported center for the medical and surgical treatment and care of patients with heart and lung diseases, originally founded as a free tuberculosis sanitarium by Mrs. Dora M. Shapiro.

BURLINGTON
Cong. B'nai Israel, 212 High St.

West New Jersey Proprietors' Office, Broad St., bet. High and Wood Sts., a tiny, one-room brick building, is the headquarters of the 200-year old corporation known as the Proprietors of West New Jersey. Still in business under a charter granted by Charles II in 1676, this strange organization meets annually to carry out its privilege of disposing of any new land created in West Jersey. Benjamin Levy of London, England, was once one of the proprietors. In the tiny building, which is not open to the public, are housed historic documents, including William Penn's charter of religious liberty for the first colonists.

CALDWELL
Cong. Agudath Israel, 20 Academy Rd.

CAMDEN
Cong. Beth Israel, 331 Grand Ave.

CARMEL
Site of an agricultural colony for immigrant Jews established in 1883.

CARTERET
Jewish Community Center, 42 Noe St.

CEDAR GROVE
Temple Sholom of West Essex, 760 Pompton Ave.

CHERRY HILL
Bureau of Jewish Education, 2395 W. Marlton Pike
Camden Jewish Community Center, 2295 W. Marlton Pike, has an eternal light as a permanent reminder of the plight of Soviet Jewry.
Cong. Beth El, 2901 W. Chapel Ave., has a memorial room dedicated to the 6,000,000 Jewish martyrs of the Holocaust.
Cong. Sons of Israel, 220 Cooper Landing Rd.
Jewish Family Service, 2397 W. Marlton Pike.
Jewish Federation of Camden County, 2393 W. Marlton Pike.
Jewish Geriatric Home, 3025 W. Chapel Ave., adjoins a residential housing complex for the aged.
Jewish Voice, 2393 W. Marlton Pike.
Harry B. Kellman Hebrew Academy, 2901 W. Chapel Ave.
Temple Emanuel, Cooper River Pkwy.

CINNAMINSON
Temple Sinai, New Albany Rd. and Route 130.

CLARK
Temple Beth Or, 111 Valley Rd.

CLAYTON
Cong. Sons of Israel, East Center St.

CLIFFSIDE PARK
Temple Israel Community Center, 207 Edgewater Rd.

CLIFTON
Beth Sholom Reform Temple, 733 Passaic Ave.
Clifton Jewish Center, 18 Delaware St.
Daughters of Miriam Center for the Aged, 155 Hazel St.
Memorial to the Six Million, King Solomon Memorial Park, Dwas Line Rd. and Alwood Rd.

CLOSTER

Temple Beth El, 221 Schraalenburd Rd., has 28 stained glass windows representing the books of the Bible and Jewish historical events.

COLONIA

Temple Beth Am, 220 Temple Way.

CRANFORD

Temple Beth El, 338 Walnut Ave.

DEAL

Synagogue of Deal, 128 Norwood Ave., is a Sephardic congregation composed largely of Syrian Jews whose original seashore community is at Bradley Beach.

DEAL PARK

Jewish Federation of Monmouth County, 100 Grant Ave.
Jewish Voice, 100 Grant Ave.
Monmouth County Jewish Community Center, 100 Grant Ave.

DOVER

Adath Israel-Dover Jewish Center, 18 Thompson St.

EAST BRUNSWICK

East Brunswick Jewish Center, 511 Ryders Lane.
Reform Temple of East Brunswick, Old Stage Rd.
Young Israel of East Brunswick (this group meets in homes and schools until a permanent home is established).

EAST ORANGE

Cong. Emunath Israel, 175 Breakwood.
First Lutheran Church, 156 Glenwood Ave., has four stained glass windows portraying the history of the ancient Israelites.
Jewish Community Federation of Metropolitan New Jersey, 60 Glenwood Ave.
Jewish News, 60 Glenwood Ave.
Jewish Vocational Service of Metropolitan New Jersey 454 William St.
Temple Sharey Tefilo, 57 Prospect St., has the Rabbi Marius Ranson Brotherhood Chapel in honor of the rabbi's efforts to achieve racial and religious amity.

EAST PATERSON

Jewish Center of East Paterson, 100 Gilbert Ave.

EDISON
Edison Jewish Center, 91 Jefferson Blvd.
Moriah Yeshiva Academy, 2 Harrison St.
Temple Emanu-El, 100 James St.

EGG HARBOR CITY
Mordecai and Sheftall Sheftall (see Georgia), used Egg Harbor as a port for their privateering ventures during the American Revolution.

ELBERON
St. James Chapel, a turreted structure on Shore Dr., where seven presidents of the U.S. worshipped, was saved from destruction in the 1950s by neighboring residents, most of them Jewish, who provided the funds to prevent foreclosure of the mortgage on the building, and then gave it to the Long Branch Historical Museum Association.

Temple Beth Miriam, Lincoln Ave., has in its Haupt Memorial Chapel a Torah Ark that rests on an urn-shaped mahogany base bearing a carved representation of Moses, the Lawgiver. Frescoes on either side of the Ark depict the "shema" and a memorial prayer.

ELIZABETH
Bruria High School for Girls (Jewish Educational Center Branch), 35 North Ave.
Cong. Adath Jeshurun, 200 Murray St.
Cong. Bais Yitzchok Chevra Thilim, Bellevue and Jersey Aves.
Cong. B'nai Israel, 1005 E. Jersey St.
Elmora Hebrew Center, 420 West End Ave.
Elmwood Park Jewish Center, 100 Gilbert Ave.
Jewish Educational Center, 330 Elmora Ave.
Mesifta High School of Jewish Educational Center, 607 Park Ave.
Temple Beth El, 1374 North Ave.
Whitken Library of the Theodore Roosevelt School, 650 Bayway, is named for Donald Whitken, who was principal of the school for 25 years and served on the board of library trustees of Elizabeth and as president of the Jewish Federation of Central New Jersey.
Workmen's Circle Center, 225 W. Jersey St.
Workmen's Circle Home for the Aged, 225 W. Jersey St.

ELWOOD
Adat Beyt Mosheh Hebrew Community, a congregation of black Jews, Moss Mill Rd. (Route 561).

EMERSON
Emerson Jewish Center, 53 Palisade Ave.

ENGLEWOOD
Cong. Ahabath Torah, 240 Broad St.
Jewish Community Center, 153 Tenafly Rd.
Moriah School, 53 S. Woodland St.
Research Center for Kabbalah, 22 Lane Dr., is a spiritual center for alienated Jewish youth and those attracted by Eastern religions.
Temple Emanu-El, 147 Tenafly Rd., is an elliptically-shaped structure enclosed in a garden compound, reminiscent of the setting of synagogues in the Middle Ages. The tent effect of the walls and the roof of the synagogue, with colonnades rising above the ellipse, expresses the traditional use of the *chupah* (canopy) which has its roots in the simple tent of Biblical days. Above the Ark is a stained glass window 19 feet high by 6 feet wide that spans the pulpit. Designed by Chaim Gross, the window is entitled *Rebirth,* and incorporates many aspects of Jewish holidays and rituals.
United Jewish Fund, 153 Tenafly Rd.

ENGLISHTOWN
Cong. Sons of Israel, 4 Park Ave.
Temple Shaari Emeth, Craig Rd.

FAIR LAWN
Cong. B'nai Israel, 30th St. and Pine Ave.
De Lucena Drive, Fair Lawn Ave. to Lindell Dr., between Prospect Ave. and Lindell Dr., is named for Abraham de Lucena, one of the first Jewish settlers in New Amsterdam, who arrived in 1655, bringing with him the settlement's first Torah Scroll.
Fair Lawn Jewish Center, 10-10 Norman Ave.
Fair Lawn Orthodox Cong., 19-09 Morot Ave.
Jewish War Veterans Memorial Home, Plaza Rd.
Temple Avoda, 10-10 Plaza Rd.
Temple Beth Sholom, 40-25 Fair Lawn Ave.

FARMINGDALE
Jewish Community Center, Peskin's Lane, is on a street named for the first Jewish farmer in the area where there still is a community of Jewish poultry farmers.

FLANDERS
Mount Olive Jewish Center, Box 52.

FLEMINGTON
Jewish Center, East Main St.

FORDS
Gross' Corner in this Middlesex County town is named for William Gross, who developed the area.

FORT LEE
Fort Lee Jewish Community Center, 1449 Anderson Ave.

FRANKLIN
Cong. Sons of Israel, Oak St.

FREEHOLD
Jewish Community Center (Cong. Agudath Achim), Broad and Stokes Sts.

GARFIELD
Jewish Community Center, 1 Gaston Ave.

GARTON ROADS
Washington Hall, a recreation center built by the Jewish Agricultural Society for Jewish farmers in the vicinity of this hamlet, which was one of the early Jewish farm colonies in South Jersey.

GLASSBORO
Cong. Sons of Israel, 6 Green Ave.

GLEN RIDGE
Temple Shomrei Emunah, 959 Bloomfield Ave.

GLEN ROCK
Glen Rock Jewish Center, 682 Harristown Rd.

GLOUCESTER CITY
Cong. Beth-El, 1221 Lengham Ave.

HACKENSACK
Family Service of Jewish Welfare Council, 170 State St.
Jewish Welfare Council of Bergen County, 170 State St.
Moses returning from Mt. Sinai with the Ten Commandments is depicted in an interior mural in the Bergen County Courthouse, opposite the Green.

Temple Beth El, 280 Summit Ave., absorbed the Hasbrouck Heights Jewish Center in 1974.

YM & YWHA of Bergen County, 211 Essex St.

HADDON HEIGHTS
Temple Beth Sholom, White House Pike at Green St.

HAMMONTON
Temple Beth El, Bellevue Ave.

HIGHLAND PARK
Cong. Etz Chaim, 230 Dennison St.

Highland Park Conservative Temple, 201 S. 3rd Ave.

Jewish Family Service, 2 S. Adelaide Ave.

Jewish Federation of Raritan Valley, 2 S. Adelaide Ave.

Jewish Journal, 2 S. Adelaide Ave.

Moriah Yeshiva Academy, 201 S. 3rd Ave.

Workmen's Circle School, 73 Woodbridge Ave.

YM & YWHA of Raritan Valley, 2 S. Adelaide Ave.

HIGHTSTOWN
Walter H. Annenberg Library at Peddie School, is named for the Philadelphia newspaper publisher and one-time U.S. Ambassador to Great Britain, who donated the three-story building.

Cong. Beth El, 237 Franklin St.

Hechalutz Farm Shomria, training farm for young American Jews planning to settle in Israel, is maintained by Hashomer Hatzair, 40 miles west of Exit 8 on the New Jersey Turnpike. In addition to training future *olim,* the farm is the scene of frequent Jewish youth conferences.

Temple Beth Chaim, P.O. Box 128.

HILLSIDE
Cong. Sinai-Torah Chaim, 1531 Maple Ave.

Hillside Jewish Center, 1548 Summit Ave.

Temple Shomrei Torah, 910 Salem Ave.

HOBOKEN
United Synagogue of Hoboken, 830 Hudson St.

HOWELL
Solomon Schechter Academy, Kent Rd.

IRVINGTON
Cong. Agudath Israel, 1125 Stuyvesant Ave.
Cong. Ahavath Achim Bikur Cholim, 644 Chancellor Ave.
Cong. Anshe Lubowitz, 74 Mill Rd.
Cong. B'nai Israel, 706 Nye Ave., has a Holocaust memorial.
Cong. Chevrah Thilim Tifereth Israel, 745 Chancellor Ave.
Jewish Reconstructionist Group, 1040 Springfield Ave.

ISELIN
Cong. Beth Shalom, 90 Cooper Ave.

JACKSON
Jewish Center, in Whitesville section.

JAMESBURG
Cong. Sons & Daughters of Israel, Sedgwick St.
Rossmoor Congregation in the Rossmoor retirement village.

JERSEY CITY
Bayview Cemetery, Chapel Ave., holds the remains of oldest Jewish settlers.
Bergen Hebrew Institute, 2 Oxford Ave.
Chavurah, 83 Montgomery St., occupies an old bank building converted into a 13-apartment condominium occupied by 13 families who share Jewish experiences together in a Jewish atmosphere. They are all affiliated with the New Synagogue (see below).
Cong. Agudath Sholom, 472 Bergen Ave.
Cong. B'nai Jacob, 176 West Side Ave.
Cong. Emanu-El, 633 Bergen Ave.
Cong. Mount Sinai, 128 Sherman Ave.
Cong. Mount Zion, 233 Webster Ave.
Cong. Ohal Sholom-Hebrew Institute, 126 Rutgers Ave.
Cong. Sons of Israel, 35 Cottage St., and 294 Grove St.
Cong. Tifereth Israel, 247 5th St.
Grover Park, Kennedy Blvd. and Broadman Pkwy., is a memorial to Lt. Robert P. Grover, first Jewish serviceman from Jersey City to be killed in World War II.
Jewish Community Center, 604 Bergen Ave., has on its front lawn a stone memorial to Jewish veterans of all wars of the U.S.
Jewish Hospital and Rehabilitation Center of New Jersey, 2520 Kennedy Blvd.
Jewish Standard, 924 Bergen Ave.
Journal Square Menorah, a permanent Menorah installed by

the city at one of its main crossroads, Journal Square and Kennedy Blvd.

B. Manischewitz Matzoth Factory, 143 Bay St.

New Synagogue, 100 Sherman St., is an innovative congregation, which is related to the Chavurah (see above).

Pollak Hospital for Chest Diseases, 100 Clifton Pl., is a public institution named for the late Dr. Berthold S. Pollak, a pioneer in the treatment of tuberculosis and related diseases. The hospital's clinic is named for Dr. Abraham Jaffin.

Rabbi Eliezer Regosin Yeshiva High School, 25 Cottage St.

Temple Beth-El, 2419 Kennedy Blvd.

Tikva (Hope) Towers, Washington and Montgomery Sts., a moderate income housing project of 200 units, located in the urban renewal area, is sponsored by Cong. Sons of Israel, the oldest Orthodox congregation in the city and in Hudson County.

JEWSTOWN

Jewstown was listed on Revolutionary War maps of New Jersey on the present site of the town of Jobstown. Some historians claim that Jewstown and Jobstown were interchangeable names.

KEARNY

Henrietta Bernsted Senior Citizens Building, Columbia Ave. and Chestnut St., has a flagpole dedicated by the United Veterans Organizations to the memory of Aaron Kahn, a prominent leader in local veterans affairs. The local Sanford L. Kahn Post of the Jewish War Veterans is named for his son, who was killed in France during World War II.

Cong. B'nai Israel of Kearny and North Arlington, 780 Kearny Ave.

KENDALL PARK

Herbert J. Kendall, builder and developer, is honored in the name of this town.

Temple Beth Sholom, 9 Stanworth Rd.

LAKE HIAWATHA

Hebrew Academy of Morris County, 20 Lincoln Ave.

Jewish Center, 140 Lincoln Ave.

LAKE HOPATCONG

Lake Hopatcong Jewish Community Center, 15 Durban Rd., near River Styx. A pair of stained glass windows by Sol Nodel, known as *The Song of Song Windows* are on either side of the Ark overlooking Lake Hopatcong.

LAKEWOOD

Bazelel Hebrew Day School, 419 Fifth St.

Cong. Ahabat Sholom, Forest Ave. and 11th St.

Cong. Sons of Israel, Madison Ave. and 6th St., oldest congregation in this resort community, most of whose hotels cater to Jewish guests, has an octagonal synagogue topped by a multi-faced dome similar in structure to an old East European synagogue. The all-copper dome appears from a distance as two hands clasped and raised in prayer.

Rabbi Aaron Kotler Institute for Advanced Jewish Learning, 6th St. and Private Way, originally known as the Beth Hamedrash Govoha, is named for its founder, the late Rabbi Kotler, a famed Talmudic scholar.

Temple Beth Am, Carey St. and Madison Ave.

LEDGEWOOD

Morris-Sussex Jewish News, 500 Route 10.

United Jewish Federation of Morris-Sussex, 500 Route 10.

LEONIA

Cong. Adas Emuno, 148 High St., moved into this Bergen County community in 1966 after having been located in Hoboken for 95 years.

Cong. Sons of Israel, 150 Grand Ave.

LINDEN

Cong. Anshe Chesed, St. George Ave. and Orchard Terr.

Temple Mekor Chayim, Academy Terr. and Deerfield Rd.

LIVINGSTON

Cong. Beth Shalom, 193 E. Mt. Pleasant Ave.

Suburban Torah Center, 85 West Mt. Pleasant Ave.

Temple B'nai Abraham, 300 East Northfield Rd., the third oldest congregation in the state, is named for its chief founder, Abraham Newman, and for the patriarch Abraham. The architectural design of the synagogue creates a union of Ark, bima, sanctuary, and landscape.

Temple Emanu-El, 264 W. Northfield Rd.

LONG BRANCH

Cong. B'nai Sholom, 622 Ocean Ave.

Cong. Brothers of Israel, 85 Second Ave.
Hillel Foundation at Monmouth College, 166 Morris Ave.
Home for Chronic Sick, 81 Washington St.

LONGPORT
Betty Bacharach Home for Children was founded by Benjamin, Harry, and Isaac Bacharach of Atlantic City, in 1924 in memory of their mother.

LYNDHURST
Lyndhurst Jewish Hebrew Center, 333 Valley Brook Ave.

McKEE
Jewish Farmers Cong., English Creek Rd.

MADISON
Friendship Library on Madison campus of Fairleigh Dickinson University, is a gift from Samuel Silberman, New York philanthropist, who named the library "Friendship" in honor of his friend, Fairleigh Dickinson, Jr. This friendship began at sea three days before the attack on Pearl Harbor when both were serving in the U.S. Navy. The Samuel Silberman College of Business Administration at Fairleigh Dickinson's Madison campus is named for the New York philanthropist.

MANAHAWKIN
Stafford Township Memorial Building, a mile east of the center of Manahawkin, on Route 72, is a memorial to M.L. Shapiro, home builder. His sons, Herbert L. and Jerome Shapiro, gave the building to the township in 1959.

MANALAPAN
Temple Shaari Emeth, Craig Rd.

MAPLEWOOD
Cong. Ahavath Zion, 421 Boyden Ave.
Cong. Beth Ephraim, 520 Prospect St.
Sky Book Associates, 1923 Springfield Ave.

MARGATE
Atlantic County Jewish Community Center, 5321 Atlantic Ave.
Cong. Beth Israel, 8401 Ventnor Ave.
Cong. Or Chodesh, 39 N. Exeter Ave.

Hebrew Academy of Atlantic City, 501 N. Jerome Ave.
Temple Beth El, 500 N. Jerome Ave.
Temple Emeth Sholom, 8501 Ventnor Ave.

MARLBORO

Cong. Ohav Sholom, P.O. Box 98.

MATAWAN

Cong. Beth Tefilah, meets in South Matawan First Aid Squad, Church St., near Lloyd Rd.
Temple Beth Am, 550 Lloyd Ave.
Temple Shalom, 5 Ayrmont Ave.

MAYS LANDING

Lauderdale Jewish Center, Hickory St. and Route 50, is the religious and cultural center of a community of poultry farmers, many of them survivors of the Holocaust.

MAYWOOD

Temple Beth Israel, 34 W. Magnolia Ave.

MENDHAM

Mortimer L. Schiff Scout Reservation, the national training center for Boy Scout leaders, is named for Mortimer L. Schiff, son of Jacob H. Schiff (see New York), who at the time of his death in 1931 was president of the Boy Scouts of America. The 480-acre tract was given to the Boy Scouts by Mrs. Jacob H. Schiff. An 1,800 foot lake on the reservation is called Lake Therese in honor of Mrs. Schiff. Only son of Jacob H. Schiff, Mortimer Schiff devoted most of his life to social service. He was one of the founders of the Boy Scout movement in the U.S. to which he gave large sums of money. He was also one of the leaders of the National Jewish Welfare Board during World War I, serving as its overseas commissioner. Mortimer Schiff was the prime mover in the creation of the Jewish Committee on Scouting. His son, John, followed in his footsteps in JWB leadership, and as president of the Boy Scouts of America.

MERCHANTVILLE

Cong. Beth Jacob, 109 East Maple Ave.

METUCHEN

Jewish Federation of Northern Middlesex County, 210 Durham Ave.
Temple Neve Sholom, 250 Grove Ave., has an exterior

sculptural panel whose design depicts the Tree of Life with the Ten Commandments.

MILLBURN

Cong. B'nai Israel, 162 Millburn Ave., has on its outside wall a sculpture by Herbert Ferber based on the quotation from Exodus 3.2, "And the bush was not consumed." A 12-foot section of metal, no part of it actually touches the wall on which it hangs. In the synagogue foyer is a large mural depicting the symbols of Judaism.

Jewish Counseling and Service Agency of Metropolitan New Jersey, 161 Millburn Ave.

National Council of Jewish Women, Essex Section, 321 Millburn Ave.

MILLVILLE

Beth Hillel Temple, Oak and 3rd Sts.

MONMOUTH JUNCTION

Cong. Shaari Sholom, Georges Rd.

MONTCLAIR

Charles Bierman Home for the Aged, 10 Madison Ave.
Temple Shomrei Emunah, 67 Park Ave.

MORRISTOWN

Chabad House of Lubavitcher Movement, 226 Sussex Ave.
Morristown Jewish Community Center, 177 Speedwell Ave.
Rabbinical College of New Jersey, 226 Sussex Ave.

Seeing Eye, the widely known institution for training dogs to guide the blind, and for teaching the blind to use dogs, was founded here in 1929 by Morris Franks, the first blind man in the U.S. to use a dog for this purpose. He was the director of the Seeing Eye from 1929 until his retirement in 1957.

Temple B'nai Or, Overlook Rd.

MOUNT FREEDOM

Mount Freedom Jewish Community Center, Sussex Tpke.

MOUNT HOLLY

Cong. Har Zion, Ridgway and High Sts.

NEWARK

Beth Israel Medical Center, 201 Lyons Ave.
Club for the Elderly, 24 Lyons Ave.

Cong. Ahavas Sholom, 145 Broadway.

Cong. Beth David Jewish Center, 821 Sanford Ave.

Cong. B'nai Moshe, 19-29 Ross St.

Cong. B'nai Zion, 215 Chancellor Ave.

Cong. Knesseth Israel, 882 Bergen St.

Cong. Mount Sinai, 250 Mt. Vernon Pl.

Dreyfus Planetarium, housed in the Newark Museum, 49 Washington St., was a gift of Mr. and Mrs. Leonard Dreyfus of Essex Falls. Its 24-foot aluminum dome has become a city landmark.

Friendly Fuld Neighborhood Centers, headquarters at 71 Boyd St., in the Rev. William P. Hayes Homes, is the product of a 1971 merger of the Friendly Neighborhood House, a nonsectarian settlement house founded in 1926, and the Fuld Neighborhood House, founded in 1906 as the Jewish Sisterhood Day Nursery to aid working mothers of children and immigrants. Named for Mrs. Felix Fuld, sister of Louis Bamberger, Fuld House's program gradually changed as its neighborhood changed, and it turned to serving people in the central ward. The combined agency operates the Fuld quarters as well as three other centers that were branches of the Friendly Neighborhood House.

Jewish Student Services, serving Rutgers State University-Newark, and Newark College of Engineering, 61 Washington St.

B. Manischewitz Co., matzoth factory, 9 Clinton Ave.

Newark Museum, 49 Washington St., which houses one of America's great collections of art and science, was a gift of the late Louis Bamberger, merchant prince who, when he died in 1944 at the age of 88, was acclaimed "Newark's first citizen." The museum building, opened in 1926, was made possible by Bamberger's gift of $750,000. A memorial plaque in the lobby "records the gratitude of the people of Newark to Louis Bamberger who in the year 1925 gave them this building." Bamberger also gave the museum its collection of paintings of American artists, a unique array of 150 working models of industrial devices, and the museum's permanent exhibition of masterpieces of art. A modest millionaire who converted a bankrupt drygoods store into one of the nation's leading department stores, Bamberger was born in Baltimore in 1855 and settled in Newark in 1892. For half a century he was identified with the commercial, cultural, and civic growth of the state's largest city. With his brother-in-law, Felix Fuld, he contributed generously toward the building funds of virtually every Jewish Community Center erected in New Jersey in the 1920s. Bamberger made large gifts to Jewish hospitals and overseas Jewish philanthropies, as well as to Newark charities. When he retired from business in 1929, he gave more than $1 million in cash to 236 employees. A valuable collection of books and records on Jewish life from the 13th to the 18th centuries was given by Bamberger to the Jewish Theological Seminary of America.

St. Mary's Catholic Church, 528 High St., has a Star of David under its roof.

Louis Schleifer Memorial Park, Elizabeth Ave. and West Runyon St., is named for one of Newark's World War II heroes.

Weequahic High School, 279 Chancellor Ave., has a portrait of the late Judge William M. Unterman in its lobby. The school's athletic field and part of its library are named for Unterman.

Zion Towers, a 28-story housing development for the elderly, is sponsored by Cong. B'nai Zion.

NEW BRUNSWICK

Anshe Emeth Memorial Temple, 222 Livingston Ave.

Cong. Ahavas Achim, Morris St.

Cong. Ohav Emeth, 35 Richmond St.

Jelin Street, which runs for one block from 85 Paterson St. to cor. of Church and French Sts., in the downtown business district, is named for Abraham Jelin, who settled in New Brunswick in 1889. President of the local Jewish Welfare Federation, Jelin was State Road Commissioner and held several offices in the city government.

Moriah Yeshiva Academy, 35 Richmond St.

Poile Zedek Cong., 145 Neilson St.

Rutgers University

Hillel Foundation at Rutgers State University, Clifton Ave. and Ryder's Lane, on the campus of Douglass College. ●Institute of Microbiology, Hoes Lane and University Heights, built at a cost of $4,500,000, is a monument to the late Dr. Selman A. Waksman, discoverer of streptomycin, whose medical discoveries contributed enormously to the virtual elimination of tuberculosis as a major health problem. A Russian immigrant, the famous microbiologist won the 1952 Nobel Prize in medicine. Dr. Waksman donated 82 percent of all royalties from his discoveries to Rutgers State University's Research and Endowment Foundation which used the money to build the institute. Dr. Waksman was the Institute's first director. In the Institute's building there is a bust of Waksman and also a memorial plaque presented by the students and faculty in 1954. ●In the administration building of the former New Jersey State College of Agriculture, now Cook College, there is a plaque noting that Waksman's laboratories were once located here. His portrait hangs in the University Art Gallery, in Voorhees Hall. ●Jacob Goodale Lipman Hall, on the Cook College Campus, is a memorial to the internationally known agricultural chemist and pioneer in soil conservation. Born in Latvia in 1875, Lipman first became interested in agriculture when his father settled in the farming community at Woodbine, N.J. in 1891 (see Woodbine). He was among the first graduates of the Baron de Hirsch Agricultural School at Woodbine and was called to Rutgers in 1902 to organize the first department of soil chemistry and bacteriology in the country. From 1915 until his death in 1939, Lipman was dean of the New Jersey College of Agriculture, now known as Cook College, and director of the State Agricultural Experiment Station. His research led to many major discoveries in soil chemistry and to important achievements in agriculture. Lipman trained many of the nation's leading soil chemists, among them Dr. Selman A. Waksman. Lipman had a large role in encouraging cooperative enterprises among New Jersey truck farmers, particularly Jewish farmers. □

NEW MILFORD
Temple Beth Tikvah, 435 River Rd.

NEW SHREWSBURY
Monmouth Reform Temple, 322 Hance Ave.

NEWTON
Jewish Center of Sussex County, 13 Washington St.

NORMA
Norma Congregation Brotherhood, Almond Rd., serves the Jewish farm families in this old Jewish agricultural colony.

NORTH BERGEN
J. George Fredman Memorial Park, 75th St. and Boulevard East, honors the late national commander of the Jewish War Veterans of the U.S.

Temple Beth Abraham, 8410 Fourth Ave.

Temple Beth-El, 7501 Hudson Ave., has in its main entrance a memorial plaque to the 6,000,000 victims of the Holocaust in the form of a tablet and an eternal light.

NORTH BRUNSWICK
National Scouting Museum has a number of items on exhibit of special Jewish interest: A Hebrew edition of *Scouting for Boys*, by Robert Baden-Powell, founder of the Boy Scouts; an olive wood plaque presented by the Israel Scout Federation to the Boy Scouts of America; scout patches of the Boy Scouts of Israel; a bronze plaque presented to the Boy Scouts of America by District 1 of B'nai B'rith; and a collec-

tion of postage stamps from all over the world commemorating scouting events, including Israeli and Israeli Scout Anniversary stamp.

NUTLEY
Temple B'nai Israel, 192 Centre St.

OAKHURST
Temple Beth El, 301 Monmouth Rd.

OAKLAND
Jewish Center of Oakland, 192 Ramapo Valley Rd.

OCEAN
Temple Beth Torah, 1200 Roseld Ave.

OLD BRIDGE
Cong. Beth Ohr, 300 Matawan Rd.

ORANGE
Cong. Beth Torah, 270 Reynolds Terr., has nine stained glass windows each 14½ feet high, whose theme is based on the three paragraphs of the Shema.
Young Israel of the Oranges, 42 High St.

PALISADES PARK
Cong. Sons of Israel, Broad and Edsall Aves.

PARAMUS
Cong. Beth Tefillah, 241 E. Midland Ave.
Frisch School, Frisch Court, Route 4 and Forrest Ave., a Jewish day school.
Jewish Center, Spring Valley Rd. and Midland Ave.

PARK RIDGE
Temple Beth Sholom, 32 Park Ave.

PARSIPPANY
Temple Beth Am, 879 South Beverwyck Rd.

PASSAIC
Beth Israel Hospital, 70 Parker Ave.
Cong. Adas Israel Synagogue Center, 565 Broadway.
Cong. Bikur Cholim, 22 Market St.
Cong. Chevra Thilim, 132 Spring St.
Cong. Hungarian Hebrew Men, 71 Dayton Ave.

Cong. Tifereth Israel, 180 Passaic Ave.

Hillel Academy, 65 Broadway.

Jewish Community Council, 178 Washington Pl.

Jewish Family Service, 184 Washington Pl.

Jewish Memorial Chapel, 66 Howe Ave., is a non-profit chapel sponsored by the United Hebrew Burial Association.

Passaic-Clifton YM & YWHA, 178 Washington Pl.

Temple Emanuel, 181 Lafayette Ave., has an unusual accordion-shaped facade containing 24 stained glass windows representing the 12 Tribes of Israel and the 12 Jewish holidays.

Workmen's Circle Center, 50 Howe Ave.

Young Israel, 220 Brook Ave.

PATERSON

Barnert Memorial Hospital, 680 Broadway, is one of the many institutions established for the Jewish community by Nathan Barnert, one of the city's early industrial leaders.

Barnert Statue, in City Hall Sq., is a life-size monument to Nathan Barnert, one of the city's leading benefactors. It was erected in 1925 by public subscription while the 87-year-old philanthropist was still alive. The statue stands near those of Alexander Hamilton, a founder of Paterson, and Garret Hobart, a vice-president of the U.S. in the McKinley administration. Born in Germany in 1838, Barnert was only eleven when he began working in his father's tailor shop on New York's Lower East Side. In 1851 he crossed the country alone to seek his fortune in California. Though he did not find gold, he made enough to return east in style, opening a clothing factory in New York in 1856. Two years later he moved his plant to Paterson where he branched out into silk manufacturing. Barnert erected many of the city's large silk factories. During his lifetime he gave over $1,000,000 to various philanthropies. He was elected mayor in 1883 and served two four-year terms.

Community Synagogue, 660 14th Ave.

Cong. Anshai Lubavitz, 427 11th Ave.

Cong. Beth Hamedrash Hagodol, 115 Vreeland Ave.

Cong. B'nai Israel, 561 Park Ave.

Cong. B'nai Jeshurun, 152 Derrom Ave., the oldest congregation in the state, was founded in 1847. It is also known as the Barnert Memorial Temple because its former sanctuary at Broadway and Straight Sts., stood on land donated by Nathan Barnert, who also provided much of the money to build the temple.

East Side Hebrew Center, 440 East 36th St.

Federation Apartments, 510 E. 27th St., independent housing for older citizens, is sponsored by the Jewish Federation of North Jersey. The lobby is dedicated to the late Herman Yucht, president of the

Federation when the housing project was launched.

Hebrew Free School, 660 14th Ave.

Jewish Federation of North Jersey, 140 Market St., will be moving to the new community complex at Ratzer Rd. and Hinchman Ave., in Wayne, N.J.

Kushner Field in East Side Park is a softball diamond named for the late Jacob Kushner, a recreation and sports figure.

Lipschulz Village, Building No. 4 in Permanent Veterans Housing, a veterans housing project at McLean Blvd., memorializes Pfc. Kenneth D. Lipschulz, the first paratrooper from Paterson to die in World War II. A plaque outside the building notes that the memorial was erected June 24, 1952.

Plaza of Memories and Plaza of the Gay Nineties, East Side Park, is an unusual collection of statues and monuments presented to the city by the late Harry B. Haines, publisher of the *Paterson Evening News.*

Schneider Branch of YM & YWHA, 26 East 39th St.

United Brotherhood Linath Hasedek, 611 E. 26th St.

Workmen's Circle Center, 463 12th Ave.

Yavneh Academy, 413 12th Ave.

YM & YWHA of North Jersey, 152 Van Houten St., has plans for an ultimate move to a Jewish community complex in suburban Wayne.

PAULSBORO

Jewish Community Club, 411 Cook Ave.

PENNS GROVE

Cong. Shaari Tzedek, North Broad St.

PERRINEVILLE

Jewish Center, Perrineville Rd.

PERTH AMBOY

Cong. Beth Israel, 166 Jefferson St.

Cong. Beth Mordecai, 224 High St., is named for Mordecai Wolff, whose father, Henry, was one of the founders of the congregation. A Yad Vashem memorial light perpetuates the memory of the victims of the Holocaust.

Cong. Shaarey Tefiloh, Water and Market Sts.

Hillel Academy, 100 First St.

Jewish Federation of Northern Middlesex County (see Metuchen).

YM & YWHA of Raritan Bay Area, 316 Madison Ave.

PINE BROOK
Pine Brook Jewish Center, Change Bridge Rd.

PLAINFIELD
Hebrew Day School, 532 W. 7th St.
Jewish Community Center, 403 W. 7th St.
Jewish Community Council, 403 W. 7th St.
Temple Beth El, 225 E. 7th St.
Temple Sholom, 815 W. 7th St.
United Orthodox Synagogues, 75 Somerset St.

PLEASANTVILLE
Cong. B'nai Israel, West Jersey Ave. and Franklin Blvd.

Holocaust Memorial, in Rodef Sholom Cemetery, is a large three-paneled stone bearing the names of immediate relatives of Holocaust survivors who live in Atlantic City and belong to the Club of New Americans, which erected the memorial.

PRINCETON

Princeton University

Elmer Adler Graphic Arts Collection, in the Princeton University Library, consisting of 4,000 prints and books, is named for the late Elmer Adler, a noted book designer and authority on typography, and expert on fine printing. ●Corwin Hall at Princeton University is named for the late Dr. Edward S. Corwin, first chairman of the department of political science, and a faculty member for 41 years. ●Daniel and Florence Guggenheim Laboratories for Aerospace Propulsion Science and the Guggenheim Jet Propulsion Center, both at Princeton University, were established by the Daniel and Florence Guggenheim Foundation. ●Hillel Foundation at Princeton University, Murray-Dodge Hall. □

Institute for Advanced Study, 20 Nassau St., which is both a university and a research center devoted to the encouragement, support, and patronage of higher learning, is a world famous center of scholarship established in 1930 through a $5 million endowment by the late Louis Bamberger, Newark department store magnate, and his sister, Mrs. Felix Fuld. Fuld Hall is the home of the Institute's School of Mathematics of which the late Dr. Albert Einstein was the first director. The room where Einstein worked at the Institute has been maintained in its original state and the last problem on which he worked is still chalked on the blackboard. Einstein Dr., between Olden Lane and Springfield Rd., near the Institute, memorializes the Nobel

Prize laureate and father of the theory of relativity who worked at the Institute for Advanced Study from 1933 until his death in 1955. The former Einstein Cottage at 112 Mercer St., still stands. Dr. Abraham Flexner (see Kentucky), was the first director of the Institute. He was succeeded in 1954 by the late Dr. J. Robert Oppenheimer (see New Mexico), who had been director of the Los Alamos Laboratory of the Atomic Energy Commission, where the first atomic bomb was assembled. Oppenheimer retired in 1965. The Institute's library is partly dedicated to the late Senator Herbert H. Lehman (see New York). The papers of the late Bernard M. Baruch (see South Carolina), adviser to presidents, and of David E. Lilienthal (see Tennessee), first administrator of the Tennessee Valley Authority and later chairman of the Atomic Energy Commission, are in the Institute Library.

Jewish Center, 435 Nassau St.

Princeton Theological Seminary, Mercer St., bet. Library Pl. and Alexander St., has a large stained glass window depicting five great characters from the Hebrew Bible—Abel, Noah, Abraham, Melchizedek, and Job.

David Sarnoff Research Center, Trenton Rd. and New Brunswick Tpke., the focal point of the major research laboratories of the Radio Corporation of America, was dedicated in 1951 and named for the man who was then chairman of the board. A commemorative plaque affixed to the center building declared that "David Sarnoff's work, leadership and genius comprise radio's preeminent record of the past, television's brilliant performance of the present, and a rich legacy in communications of the future."

Yavneh House at Princeton University, 21 Olden St., headquarters for Orthodox students, provides kosher meals.

RAHWAY

Rahway Hebrew Cong., 1389 Bryant St.

RAMSAY

Temple Beth Sholom, Plaza Lane and Maple St.

RED BANK

Cong. Beth Shalom, 186 Maple Ave.

Eisner Public Library was presented to the city in 1937 by the heirs of Sigmund Eisner, a clothing manufacturer.

RIDGEFIELD PARK

Temple Emanuel, 120 Park St.

RIDGEWOOD

Temple Israel, 475 Grove St.

RINGOES
Site of one of the first South Jersey Jewish agricultural colonies. The Ringoes Synagogue no longer exists.

RIVER EDGE
Temple Sholom, 385 Howland Ave.

RIVERSIDE

Kenesseth Israel Temple, 45 Hancock St.

RIVER VALE

Jewish Hospital & Rehabilitation Center, 685 Westwood Ave.

ROCHELLE PARK
Cong. Ohav Shalom, 385 W. Passaic St.

ROCKAWAY
White Meadow Temple, 153 White Meadow Lake Rd.

ROOSEVELT
Originally known as Jersey Homesteads, this town was built in 1935 by the Rural Resettlement Administration of the U.S. Department of Agriculture as a cooperative agricultural-industrial community for unemployed Jewish garment workers from Philadelphia and New York. Prime mover in the creation of the town was the late Benjamin Brown, a pioneer in farm cooperatives, (once the "turkey king" of New York), who persuaded the New Deal administration to settle some 200 Jewish needle trades workers on the land under a plan that would enable them simultaneously to work at their trade. The experiment never succeeded and today the town is no longer predominantly Jewish. The name of the town was changed in 1945 following the death of President Roosevelt. One of the first settlers in the area was the late Ben Shahn, the artist, whose bright lobby murals in the community building depict Jews escaping from Old World oppression and their rise to better conditions in the New World. On the wall of the Roosevelt School is Shahn's *Roosevelt Mural,* a fresco 55 feet long and 11 feet high, that is a panorama of the United States in the early 20th century. It shows the reception room of Ellis Island, and Albert Einstein and Charles Steinmetz arriving as immigrants. Also there is Sidney Hillman, the labor leader, who was involved in planning the community. Over grim-faced Nazi storm troopers are signs that read: "Germans protect yourself. Do not buy from Jews," and "Jew, you cannot enter." The FDR Memorial Park and Amphitheatre was Ben

Shahn's idea. The massive bronze head of Roosevelt in the park is the work of Shahn's son, Jonathan.

ROSELLE
Cong. Emanuel, Brooklawn and Schafer Ave.
Temple Beth Torah, 11101 Frank St.

ROSENHAYN
Synagogue of Cong. Kadish Anshe Ashkenaz, built by the Jewish families that founded an agricultural colony here in 1882 under the auspices of the Hebrew Emigrant Aid Society, now stands empty and unused. Its Torah Scrolls and records are stored in Cong. Beth Abraham, Bridgeton. Rosenhayn was the second Jewish farm settlement established in south Jersey. Franklin Hall, a building adjoining the synagogue, and which was used as a Hebrew school and social center, collapsed some years ago.

RUMSON
Cong. B'nai Israel of Greater Red Bank, Hance and Ridge Rds., has a covered folded wooden roof pinpointed on four masonry piers that suggest the tent of the ancient Israelites.

RUTHERFORD
Ann Robison House on the Rutherford Campus of Fairleigh Dickinson University, 223 Montrose Ave., is named for Mrs. Adolf Robison of Teaneck, prominent civic and Jewish communal leader.
Temple Beth El, 185 Montrose Ave.

SALEM
Oheb Sholom Synagogue, 240 Grant St.

SALEM COUNTY
Salem County is the only county in the U.S. whose name is of Hebrew origin, Salem being an anglicized form of the Hebrew "Shalom," and an abbreviation of "Jerusalem."

SAYREVILLE
Jewish Center, Bordentown Ave., south of Ernston Rd.

SCOTCH PLAINS
Temple Israel, 1920 Cliffwood Ave.

SHORT HILLS
Temple B'nai Jeshurun, 1025 South Orange Ave., is the second

oldest congregation in the state, having been founded in 1848. Situated on a 21-acre wooded hillside, the building is approached via a landscaped entrance and a brick-paved courtyard in which there are dense plantings and a decorative fountain, surrounded by a ring of benches and small shade trees. The building won a 1969 prize for architectural design. The sanctuary, in the form of a diamond, has walls of unadorned brick and a roof made entirely of exposed wood beams and planks, hovering free of the brick walls. At the apex of the diamond, the walls spread to clasp a stained window which rises in ten six-foot panels, each containing an abstract of one letter of the Ten Commandments. The Ark is 30-feet high and the pews are continuous seats rather than theatre type seats, to increase the sense of community participation. In the lobby are two heroic-sized murals created by women of the congregation. One is an 11-foot mural-in-stitchery that depicts in visual imagery the lines from Psalm 24. The mural is executed in linen, silk, leather, and man-made fabrics through surface stitchery, applique, and needle weaving. The second mural, an assemblage of three dimensional embroidery, translates into contemporary fabrics the shape and spirit of the ancient musical instruments referred to in the Bible.

SIX POINTS
Site of an early Jewish agricultural settlement linked to the Salem and Norma colonies.

SOMERSET
Central New Jersey Jewish Home for the Aged, 380 De Mott Lane, is sponsored by the Jewish federations of Eastern Union County, Plainfield, Somerset, Perth Amboy, Raritan Valley, and Somerville.
Temple Beth El, 1495 Amwell Rd.

SOMERVILLE
Cong. Beth Israel, 16 Union St.
Jewish Center of Somerset County, 11 Park Ave.
Jewish Federation of Somerset County, 11 Park Ave.
Temple Beth El, 1495 Amwell Rd.
Temple Sholom, Upper N. Bridge St.

SOUTH BRUNSWICK
Cong. Sharri Sholom, Georges Rd.

SOUTH ORANGE
Cong. Beth El, 222 Irvington Ave., has a series of front court panels representing the seven days of Creation. In the lobby there is a

7 by 4 foot tapestry whose design reflects the symbols and letters of the Hebrew alphabet.

    Cong. Oheb Shalom, 170-180 Scotland Rd.

    Hebrew Youth Academy, 457 Centre St.

    Temple Israel of Oranges and Maplewood, 432 Scotland Rd.

    Young Israel, 457 Centre St.

SOUTH PLAINFIELD

Schindler Drive was named by three former Nazi concentration camp prisoners, all Jews and all builders, for the late Oskar Schindler, a Roman Catholic, who saved 1,400 Jewish men and women from the Nazi gas chambers while he was operating munitions factories for the Nazis in Poland.

SOUTH RIVER

    Cong. Anshe Emeth, 88 Main St.

SPRINGFIELD

    Cong. Israel Springfield, 339 Mountain Ave.

    Temple Beth Am, 60 Baltusrol Way.

    Temple Shaarey Shalom, 75 Springfield Ave.

SUCCASSUNA

    Temple Shalom, 215 South Hillside Ave.

SUMMIT

    Jewish Center of Summit, 67 Kent Pl. Blvd.

    Temple Sinai, 208 Summit Ave.

TEANECK

    Cong. Beth Aaron, 950 Queen Anne Rd.

    Cong. Beth Abraham, Queen Anne Rd.

    Cong. Beth Am, 510 Claremont Ave.

    Cong. Beth Sholom, Rutland Ave. and Rugby Rd.

    Hillel Foundation at Fairleigh Dickinson University, 1000 River Rd.

    Jewish Community Center of Teaneck, 70 Sterling Pl., has on its front lawn an abstract memorializing Israeli soldiers who died in the Yom Kippur War of 1973.

    Judaica Shop, 1345 Queen Anne Rd.

    Robison Hall of Science at Fairleigh Dickinson University, is named for Mr. and Mrs. Adolf Robison of Teaneck.

    Temple Emeth, 1660 Windsor Pl.

Weiner Library at Fairleigh Dickinson University, 1000 River Rd., is named for the late Mr. and Mrs. Martin Weiner. Weiner, a former trustee of the university, and a prominent textile manufacturer, helped raise funds for the university. The library's periodical room is named for their daughter, the late Iris Weiner Bluestein.

TENAFLY
Temple Sinai of Bergen County, 1 Engle St.

TOMS RIVER
Cong. B'nai Israel, Old Freehold Rd., serves Jewish poultry and egg farmers in this south Jersey poultry center.

TRENTON
Cong. Adath Israel, 715 Bellevue Ave., has a memorial to the victims of the Holocaust in the Bellevue Ave. wall of the Lewis Auditorium. The memorial is an aluminum sculpture affixed to a bronze plaque on which there is a couplet in Hebrew and English from one of Abraham Shlonsky's poems.
Cong. Ahavath Israel, 1130 Lower Ferry Rd.
Cong. Brothers of Israel, 499 Greenwood Ave.
Cong. People of Truth, 1201 W. State St.
Helene Fuld Medical Center, 750 Brunswick Ave., is named for the mother of the late Dr. Leonhard Felix Fuld, an eccentric self-made millionaire, who spent his last years giving more than 20 hospitals around the country substantial gifts for nurses' residences, nurses' training, and scholarships. In the main lobby there is a memorial to and a portrait of Fuld and his mother and a small display case containing Fuld memorabilia. He died in 1965 at the age of 82.
Fuld Street memorializes Dr. Leonhard Felix Fuld.
Greenhouse Home for Jewish Aged, 547 Greenwood Ave.
Har Sinai Temple, 491 Bellevue Ave.
Jewish Community Center, 999 Lower Ferry Rd.
Jewish Family Service, 225 S. Hanover St.
Jewish Federation of Trenton, 999 Lower Ferry Rd.
David Naar portrait, in the second floor rotunda of the State House, New Jersey's capitol, 121 W. State St., honors the eminent public figure and newspaper publisher (see above).
State Capitol Annex, West State St., opposite Taylor Pl., has a display in Part 2 Court Room an oil painting of Justice Samuel Kalisch, the first Jew to serve on the New Jersey Supreme Court. Son of Rabbi Isidor Kalisch, one of the pioneers of Reform Judaism, Judge Kalisch was one of Newark's leading lawyers when Gov. Woodrow

Wilson appointed him to the bench in 1911 for a seven-year term. He was reappointed by two other governors and was serving his third term when he died in 1930 at the age of 79. There are also portraits there of former Chief Justice Joseph Weintraub, Justices Harold Kolovsky, William A. Wachenfeld, Sydney Goldman, James Rosen, Joseph Perskie, Nathan L. Jacobs, and room is left for portraits of Justices Morris Pashman and Sidney M. Schreiber.

State Museum, on West St., one of the four buildings that make up the state's Cultural Center complex, exhibits the brilliant Ben Shahn mosaic that was once a mural on the S.S. *Shalom,* Israel's onetime luxury liner. Shahn is also represented in the museum by a 30-foot mural on the periodic tables of the elements, and by a mural of similar size entitled *The Tree of Life.*

UNION

Cong. Beth Shalom, Vauxhall Rd. and Plane St.
Jewish Community News, Green Lane.
Jewish Family Service of Union County, Green Lane.
Harry Lebau Jewish Center of Eastern Union County YM & YWHA, Green Lane, memorializes the late Harry Lebau who was associated with the Y for 50 years and who served as JWB field worker in World War I. This is the first Y to be named for a professional center worker.
Solomon Schechter Day School, Vauxhall Rd. and Cedar St.
Temple Israel, 2373 Morris Ave.

UNION CITY

Cong. Beth Jacob, 325 Fourth St.
Temple Israel Emanuel, 33rd St. and New York Ave.
Yeshiva of Hudson County, 2501 New York Ave., occupies the building abandoned in the 1960s by the North Hudson Jewish Community Center when it went out of existence. Also known as the Mesifta Sanz Yeshiva, the school was moved from Brooklyn by Grand Rabbi Solomon Leib Halberstamm, who heads the Klausenberg sect of Chasidim. The building converted into a school for 150 students, with a dormitory on the top floor, was once occupied by a Jewish Masonic lodge. Some 60 married couples, all adherents of the Klausenberger Rebbe, live in the area between 30th and 34th Sts., and Kennedy Blvd. and Park Ave.

VENTNOR

Cong. Beth Judah, 6725 Ventnor Ave.

Federation of Jewish Agencies of Atlantic County, 5321 Atlantic Ave.

Jewish Family Service, 31 S. Surrey Ave.

VERONA
Jewish Community Center, 56 Grove Ave.

VINELAND
Cong. Ahavas Achim, 618 Plum St.

Cong. Beth Israel, 1015 E. Park Ave., has a sculpture 18 feet long and six feet wide commemorating the Holocaust and the Jewish resistance to the Nazi terror. The work of Vermont artist Dennis Sparling, it was commissioned by Mr. and Mrs. Miles Lerman, who are survivors of the Holocaust.

Cong. Sons of Jacob, 321 Grape, like the other two synagogues in this town, serves the descendants of the Jewish immigrants who established an agricultural colony here in the early 1880s. Some of the colonists' descendants still live here and are engaged in truck farming as well as agricultural chemistry.

Jewish Community Council, 629 Wood St.

WALDWYCK
Jewish Reform Temple of Northwest Bergen County, 1 Franklin Turnpike.

WAYNE
Temple Beth Tikvah, 950 Preakness Ave.

Temple Emanuel, 12 Stockler Ave.

YM & YWHA of North Jersey, Ratzer Rd. and Hinchman Ave., also houses the Jewish Federation of North Jersey, the Jewish Family Service, and the Board of Jewish Education.

WEST ENGLEWOOD
Cong. B'nai Jeshurun, 641 W. Englewood Ave.

Temple Beth Emeth, 1666 Windsor Rd.

WESTFIELD
Temple Emanu-El, 657 E. Broad St., has in its social hall a huge needlepoint mural shaped as a Star of David within a Star of David. In the center, representing the rock of Judaism, is the Torah. Surrounding six points of the inner star represent the major holidays. Beyond these points are representations of ceremonies important in Jewish life. The outermost points represent the history of Judaism. Each piece of canvas is separately mounted on a block of wood and the

whole is covered with sheer muslin to resemble a stained glass window. The canvas took three years to make by 32 members of the sisterhood.

WEST LONG BRANCH

Murry and Leonie Guggenheim Library at Monmouth College, Cedar and Norwood Aves., occupies the former Guggenheim estate, donated by the Guggenheim Foundation. A bronze plaque in the foyer opposite the main entrance acknowledges the Guggenheim gift, and just inside the entrance to the main building are plaques recording the contributions to Monmouth College of Milton Erlanger, Florence Kridel, and Maurice Pollak.

Hillel Foundation at Monmouth College, 166 Morris Ave.

WEST NEW YORK

Cong. Shaare Zedek (Talmud Torah of West New York and Guttenberg), 5308 Palisade Ave.

WEST ORANGE

Cong. Ahavas Achim B'nai Jacob and David, 700 Pleasant Valley Way.

Cong. Tifereth Zion, 700 Pleasant Valley Way.

Daughters of Israel Pleasant Valley Home, 1155 Pleasant Valley Way.

Theresa Grotta Center for Restorative Services, 20 Summit St.

Jewish Center of West Orange, 300 Pleasant Valley Way.

Kessler Institute for Rehabilitation, Pleasant Valley Way, founded by Dr. Henry I. Kessler in 1940, is a voluntary nonprofit institution for rehabilitating handicapped adults.

YM & YWHA of Metropolitan New Jersey, 760 Northfield Ave., has on its mezzanine level, a *Wall of History* depicting the growth of the Y since 1925. The wall features pictures etched on brass plaques highlighting activities and events in the growth of the Y. Next door to the Y is a 134-unit senior citizens housing complex sponsored by the Jewish Community Federation of Metroplitan New Jersey.

Young Israel, 567 Pleasant Valley Way.

WESTWOOD

Temple Beth Or, 56 Ridgewood Rd.

Temple Emanuel, 111 Washington St., is named for Charles Emanuel, one of the early settlers here.

WILDWOOD

Temple Beth Judah, Pacific and Spencer Aves., has a large

stained glass window donated by Edwin Zaberer, a former member of the Cape May County Board of Freeholders and a prominent Catholic layman, in memory of his mother.

WILLINGBORO
Cong. Beth Torah, Rancocas Rd. and Beverly.
Temple Emanu-El, John F. Kennedy Way.

The town was once known as Levittown, in honor of the Levitt brothers, builders. In 1959 the voters of the then-271 year old borough approved a change from Willingboro. In 1963 the voters restored the old name of Willingboro as a result of a campaign led by Stanley Goldstein, editor-publisher of the local weekly.

WOODBINE
Brotherhood Synagogue, 614 Washington Ave., is the only synagogue in this first all-Jewish town of modern times (Tel Aviv was not established until 1909). It was founded in 1891 by the Baron de Hirsch Fund. The first 60 Jewish families, all from Russia, arrived in 1892 and began clearing part of the 5,300 acres of land that had been acquired in Cape May County, 30 miles southwest of Atlantic City. Simultaneously, the Baron de Hirsch Fund arranged for the opening of small factories to enable the settlers to supplement their income. In 1895, Professor Hirsch I. Sabsavage, the colony's superintendent, opened the now famous Woodbine Agricultural School, America's first high school for agriculture. From this school came a host of teachers, scientists, research workers, soil chemists, and agronomists who pioneered many far-reaching developments. When the school was closed in 1917, its building and farms were deeded free to the State of New Jersey for an institution for retarded girls.

The red-letter day in Woodbine's history was April 14, 1903, when it became an independent community, with its own municipal government. Jews filled all public offices and manned the police and fire departments. The principal buildings were the synagogue and Talmud Torah. Jews and non-Jews came to see this unique experiment launched, among them Ab Cahan, editor of the *Jewish Daily Forward;* General William Booth of the Salvation Army; and Booker T. Washington, the great black leader. Woodbine is still a largely Jewish but no longer an all-Jewish town whose residents engage in farming and poultry-raising, and work in or own a number of small factories.

De Hirsch Avenue is named for Baron Maurice de Hirsch, who established the de Hirsch Fund in 1891. Grandson of a Bavarian court banker, de Hirsch, who was born in Munich in 1831, became one of the wealthiest men of the 19th century through his gigantic railroad and industrial enterprises in Turkey, Russia, Romania, France, and

Switzerland. Until the beginning of the Russian pogroms in the early 1880s, de Hirsch had made extensive but not lavish contributions for Jewish education, philanthropy, and the work of the Alliance Israelite Universelle in the Balkans and Middle East. After the Russian May Laws of 1881, he offered the Czar 50,000,000 francs for agricultural and industrial training provided Russia would agree to spend the money without regard to race or creed. When the Russian government refused to accept this condition, de Hirsch marshalled all his resources for the task of mass emigration of Jews from the Czar's empire. Because of his abiding faith that the Jews of Russia could rebuild their lives as farmers, de Hirsch created the Jewish Colonization Association (ICA), which settled thousands of Jews in Latin America and Canada, and the Baron de Hirsch Fund, which helped establish large numbers of Jews who arrived in the United States after 1891. Through trade schools, settlement houses, loan societies, model homes, and public bathhouses, the de Hirsch Fund had a major part in the orientation of the first generation of Jewish immigrants. It was this fund that initiated the plan to remove Jews from the crowded eastern seaboard cities to the south and west. This work was taken over in 1900 by the Industrial Removal Office which received substantial financial support from the de Hirsch Fund.

The fund's agricultural activities were turned over to the Jewish Agricultural Society, which in some 70 years of effort helped create a substantial Jewish farming population not only in New Jersey but in many other states as well. De Hirsch was one of the great philanthropists of modern times. When his only son died in 1887, he replied to a message of condolence on the loss of his heir by saying: "My son I have lost, but not my heir; humanity is my heir." He proved this by giving with equal generosity to all regardless of race and creed. Even his race horses ran for charity, for he gave all his winnings to philanthropies in France and England. During his lifetime, and in his will, he gave away nearly $100 million, a colossal sum in the 19th century. The original capital of the Baron de Hirsch Fund of $2,400,000 was increased to $4 million by the will of Baroness de Hirsch. The successful Jewish farmers in New Jersey would have pleased de Hirsch whose money enabled the Jewish Agricultural Society to aid Jewish farmers all over the U.S. ☐

Heilprin Avenue, is named for Michael Heilprin, one of the leading spirits in the organization of the early South Jersey colonies. Scholar, journalist, encyclopedist, and colonizer, Heilprin was born in Poland in 1823. He emigrated to Hungary in 1843 and became active in the 1848 revolution. His role as secretary of the department of interior's literary bureau in the short-lived Kossuth government compelled him to flee. He came to America in 1856 and settled in Philadelphia and later in New York. A passionate and outspoken foe of slavery, Heilprin's amazing memory and scholarship and his mastery of 12 languages won him a position as an editor of Appleton's *New American Encyclopedia*. Later he became an editor of *The Nation*. He translated Dr. David Einhorn's prayerbook into English and wrote *The Historical Poetry of the Ancient Hebrews*. Heilprin was perhaps the most distinguished non-rabbinical Jewish scholar in America from 1860-1890. When the exodus of Jews from Russia began, Heilprin threw himself into the work of agricultural colonization. The detached scholar became a feverish organizer, and one of the prime movers in the establishment of the Russian Emigrants Relief Committee. Out of this body came the Hebrew Emigrant Aid Society, the first unified organization of all Jewish elements in New York and the agency which sponsored the first Jewish agricultural colonies in the west. Heilprin founded the Carmel colony in New Jersey and also helped establish colonies in Kansas, Oregon, and the Dakotas. He died in 1892. His son, Angelo, was an eminent explorer and geologist who led the Peary Relief Expedition to Greenland in 1892.

WOODBRIDGE

Bible Gardens of Israel, in Beth Israel Memorial Park, is a park in the cemetery where all the plants, flowers, trees, and shrubs mentioned in the Bible are being raised. At each plant is a sign bearing a Biblical quotation mentioning the plant in question. The cemetery also has a monument known as the Archway to Israel on which there is an enormous bronze bas-relief map of ancient Palestine depicting many major Biblical events. Each of the 12 arches in the monument is dedicated to one of the 12 Tribes of Israel, and is adorned with the appropriate tribal symbol. Also in the cemetery is a simple memorial to the victims of the Holocaust in the form of two large stone replicas of the Ten Commandments, with lions at either end.

Cong. Adath Israel, 424 Amboy Ave.

WOODBURY

Cong. Beth Israel, Warner and High Sts.

NEW YORK

Excluding New York City, Westchester, Nassau, and Suffolk Counties—see separate sections on these areas.

Jewish history in New York State north of Westchester County began soon after the first Jews reached New Amsterdam in 1654. Within a year, they were attempting to trade at Fort Orange, the first permanent settlement at what is now Albany.

On February 15, 1655, the directors of the Dutch West India Company upheld a request to permit the Jews of New Amsterdam to "travel and trade to and in New Netherland and live and remain there." Since Fort Orange was part of New Netherland, the Jews had won the right to do business up the Hudson. When Governor Peter Stuyvesant sought to circumvent the company's orders, the directors, on June 14, 1656, ordered him to allow the Jews to trade and buy real estate throughout New Netherland.

Probably the first trader to take advantage of this right was Asser Levy. In *Collections on the History of Albany*, there is a record of a Dutch merchant mortgaging his house and lot in Beverwyck (another early Albany settlement) as security for beaver skins bought from Levy in 1660. The same source indicates that in 1661, Levy bought a house and lot in Beverwyck, agreeing to pay for them in beaver skins over a three-year period. A year later Levy disposed of this property.

Another early Jewish trader along the Hudson was Jacob Lucena, who quickly learned to deal with the Indians. By 1670, Lucena was in business for himself, sending goods to Esopus (Kingston) and Albany, and east to Connecticut. In 1678, the British authorities in New York barred him from shipping merchandise to Esopus and Albany without the special permission of the royal governor. Lacking such a permit (it had not been required of him before), Lucena petitioned the governor, and ultimately was allowed to send his goods north.

Some time between 1717 and 1720, Lewis Gomez and his son, Daniel, built a stone trading post and blockhouse at the junction of Hudson River Indian trails. This structure, still standing, is the oldest one erected and occupied by Colonial Jews.

As the chief fur trading center of the English colonies in the late 17th and early 18th centuries, Albany and the country north of it attracted Jews engaged in a flourishing business with the Indians and in furnishing supplies to British troops during the wars with the Indians and the French.

Jonas Phillips (see Pennsylvania) was living in Albany in 1759, trading groceries, liquor, and drygoods for furs, and outfitting British forces bound for Canada. In 1761, he advertised his intention of leaving the city, and asked for a settlement of accounts. Levy Solomons, later of Montreal, was manufacturing chocolate and snuff in Albany in 1763. Some of his descendants are said to have lived in the city until the 1840s.

During the French and Indian War, Hayman Levy was one of the active fur traders around Fort Edward, north of Albany, and in the Lake Champlain area. Among suppliers to the British forces were two Jews, a man called Lyon at Fort William Henry, and Manuel Josephson at Fort Edward. Both men were agents of Levy, who is said to have been the first employer of John Jacob Astor. Lyon was one of the survivors at the time the French and their Indian allies captured Fort William Henry in 1757.

Samuel Jacobs, a leading Montreal merchant, tried to establish a branch of his business at Crown Point in 1759 after the British occupied that fort. In 1761, Jacobs was selling supplies to the British at Crown Point and trading with the nearby Indians. Hyam Myers, who journeyed regularly between Montreal and New York on business missions in the 1760s, traveled via the Lake Champlain route to Albany and then down the Hudson. En route, he stopped at Crown Point where he, Gershom Levy, and Jacobs had commercial interests.

Chapman Abraham, who was caught by Indians on the Detroit River in 1763 during Pontiac's War (see Michigan), may have been a prisoner of the Indians once before in upper New York. In 1759, a man named Abraham was captured with the scouting party sent by General Amherst from Crown Point to Canada to establish communications with General Wolfe, who was closing in on Quebec.

In the 1780s, Harry Hart was living at Kingsburg, 55 miles north of Albany, on the portage between the Hudson and Lake George. Hart was a brother and business associate of Aaron Hart, then the wealthiest Jew in Canada.

Concerned only with trade and bound by family and community ties either in New York City or Montreal, these 17th and 18th century entrepreneurs never regarded themselves as anything but temporary residents of upstate New York. They never intended to create Jewish communities since they had no need of them.

Not until the first permanent Jewish settlers arrived in the towns along the Erie Canal and on both sides of the Hudson River, in the 1830s and 1840s, did Jewish communities begin to take root upstate. When Mordecai M. Noah selected Grand Island, a wooded area in the Niagara River opposite Buffalo, as the site of his proposed Jewish city of refuge, in 1825, there was not a single Jewish community anywhere in the state outside of New York City.

Individual Jews probably lived in upstate towns prior to 1830. One Hessel Rosenbach is said to have arrived in Syracuse in 1824 via stagecoach. In 1830 the State Legislature amended the laws to permit Jews to solemnize marriages according to their own regulations. An old statute of 1684 had allowed only ministers of religion and justices of the peace to perform wedding ceremonies, and the Jews of New York City had altered their practices to conform to this law. The 1830 change, which gave any adult Jew the right to officiate at a wedding, may possibly have been due to a request from upstate Jewish residents who lacked rabbis and other Jewish functionaries and could not easily come to New York City whenever rabbinical services were required.

The first Jewish community north of New York City came into being in 1837 at Wawarsing, in what is now the center of the Ulster County resort country. Twelve Jewish families from New York City, who had acquired farm land at Wawarsing, established a short-lived colony known as Sholom, which had its own congregation, synagogue, and cemetery. The oldest existing Jewish community north of New York City is in Albany, where Congregation Beth El, now part of Temple Beth Emeth, was founded in 1838. This congregation opened what is believed to have been the first synagogue in the state outside of New York City (the exact date of the synagogue at Wawarsing is not known), in 1839, in a building at 166 Bassett Street. Albany's second congregation, Beth El Jacob, was organized in 1841.

Jewish businessmen from Albany and New York City who had traveled through the towns along the Hudson-Erie waterway were indirectly responsible for the establishment of the Jewish community in Syracuse. Early in 1839, a group of Jews met in the home of H. Weiksheimer in New York City and decided to make their homes in Syracuse. They had been impressed by the favorable reports of the city's commercial future brought by coreligionists who had been in Syracuse on business and obtained goods and news from the store of Bernheimer and Block. Their establishment was a peddlers' exchange where they gathered for merchandise and companionship. The New York City group came to Syracuse together in 1839 and with goods obtained on credit from Bernheimer and Block, they began peddling through central New York. On the Sabbath they returned for worship in the Bernheimer and Block store. A few Jews had preceded the settlers from New York. In addition to Bernheimer and Block, the Rosenbach, Garson, and Sloss families were in Syracuse before 1839. The formal existence of the Syracuse Jewish community dates from 1839 when the members of the Sabbath *minyan* meeting in the Bernheimer and Block store organized Keneseth Sholom—the Society of Concord—which in 1841 became a congregation and the ancestor of the present Temple of the Society of Concord. In 1846 the city's first synagogue was dedicated.

Among the second wave of Jewish settlers in Syracuse was Jacob Marshall, father of Louis Marshall, who arrived in New York from Europe with less than a dollar. He worked his way north with an Erie Railroad construction gang and later with a track-laying outfit of the Central Railroad. Later he worked on the Erie Canal and as a porter in a warehouse. He reached Syracuse in the 1850s.

The Jewish community of Syracuse was one of two in the north (Chicago the other), that recruited and equipped a Jewish company during the Civil War. Members of the Temple of the Society of Concord volunteered to outfit and equip what became Company A of the 149th Regiment of Volunteers. Three members of the congregation became officers in the company. The campaign to raise the company began with a war rally in the synagogue, and continued for a full week. In the daytime the synagogue served as a recruiting office and at night it was the scene of patriotic rallies. When the campaign ended, over $3,000 in cash had been raised and the company was ready to march. One Syracuse Jew, Daniel Doppelmayer, who settled in Texas in 1857, saw service in the Confederate army.

In 1854, there were 184 Jewish families in Syracuse. A second congregation, Beth Israel, had been founded in 1844 by Polish Jews who for a time used Mayer's saloon as a temporary synagogue until they erected one in 1856. Rabbi Isaac Leeser reported in an 1851 issue of *The Occident and American Jewish Advocate*, after a visit to upstate New York, that he had found a congregation in Utica with a poorly kept place of worship, one congregation with a minister but not a synagogue in Rochester, and three benevolent societies and one synagogue in Syracuse.

The 1840s saw the birth of Jewish communities in Rochester, Buffalo, Utica, Oswego, Poughkeepsie, and Plattsburgh, as well as the arrival of individual Jews at Watertown, Gloversville, and Watervliet. Jesse and Henry Seligman, later members of the banking house of J. and W. Seligman, were in the drygoods business in Watertown in 1848 where they became friendly with Ulysses S. Grant (see Missouri), then a lieutenant stationed at Sackett's Harbor. About the same time, Nathan Littauer began peddling at Gloversville where he later established the glove business which his son, Lucius, built into a great industry. Jewish merchants were in business in Watervliet as early as 1843. Some Jews also settled in Oswego in the 1840s, but until Congregation Berith Sholom was founded in 1848, the Oswego Jews worshipped in Syracuse.

Jews who had settled in the Erie Canal towns of Brockport and Lockport in the 1830s moved on to Rochester about 1844. Meyer Greentree was the first peddler in the Rochester area and he was joined by Joseph and Gabriel Wile and Hirsh Britenstone. The day after a Yom Kippur service in the home of Henry Levi in 1848, twelve young men organized the Society of

Berith Kodesh, now Temple B'rith Kodesh. It dedicated its first synagogue in 1856 in a remodeled church on St. Paul Street. Mordecai Tuska, the congregation's first minister, who came to the congregation in 1849 when it had only 18 members, was admitted to the University of Rochester in 1847. A number of the early Jewish settlers were tailors who founded the city's ready-to-wear men's clothing industry in the 1850s. During the Civil War, they made uniforms for the Union Army.

Buffalo's first recorded Jewish resident was L. H. Flerscheim, a teacher of German, who arrived in 1835. The first Jew in the area was Captain Mordecai Myers, a native of Virginia, who was stationed at the Williamsville cantonment during the War of 1812 and who distinguished himself at the Battle of Sackett's Harbor. He later settled in Schenectady, where he served as mayor 1851-54. Individual Jews were undoubtedly in and out of Buffalo in the 1820s and 1830s, among them Mordecai M. Noah. But there were not enough Jews for religious worship until 1847. Following a Passover service that year in the Western Hotel, the 26 participants formed Congregation Beth El under the presidency of Mark Moritz. One of the founders, it is claimed, was Michael W. Noah, a distant relative of Mordecai M. Noah. The former was one of the city's wealthiest Jews when he died in 1853, having owned the city's first large retail clothing store. Soon after the congregation was organized, another group of young Jews organized the Jacobson Society as a mutual benefit organization. In 1850, Beth El dedicated the city's first synagogue in a converted schoolhouse on downtown Pearl Street near Eagle Street. At that time 25 of the city's 30 Jewish families were members of the congregation. In 1850, a split in Beth El gave birth to Congregation Beth Zion which later merged with a Reform congregation of the same name, organized in 1864.

Utica's Congregation House of Jacob dates from 1848, although Jews are believed to have settled there earlier. The *Utica Sentinel and Gazette* published news about Mordecai M. Noah's Hebrew city at Ararat and printed a digest of his dedicatory address. One Utican, Erasmus H. Simon, was so impressed with Noah's scheme that he offered his services to Noah. The famous Philadelphian, Rebecca Gratz, was in Utica in 1837 on her way to Trenton Falls, a popular vacation spot in those days, 17 miles from Utica. The first Jew to settle in Utica was Abraham Cohen, a peddler, who opened an account in the Savings Bank of Utica on October 15, 1847. The bank's records from 1847-1855 carried the names of 40 other Jews, all from Poland and all peddlers. They formed their first *minyan* in 1847 in the home of Max Levy. On October 1, 1848, they organized Congregation Beth Israel. A new congregation called Adas Jeshurun was established in 1850 with 50 members, and in 1858 a new Beth El came into being. In 1863 the second Beth El (the first one had gone out of existence), was absorbed by Adas Jeshurun.

The Jewish settlement in Poughkeepsie also began in the 1840s. Vassar Temple, the city's oldest congregation, was founded in 1848 as Congregation Brethren of Israel. The oldest Jewish community in the

Adirondacks had its origin in the 1840s when peddlers from northern New York and western Vermont began making their headquarters in Plattsburgh, site of a military reservation and the commercial center for the north Lake Champlain region. Long before Congregation Beth Israel was organized in 1862, Jews from as far west as Ogdensburg, from Whitehall on the south, and from Vermont on the east, met regularly for Rosh Hashanah and periodic Sabbath services in Plattsburgh. After the High Holy Days, the roads leading out of Plattsburgh were clogged with peddlers' wagons heading for the Green Mountains, the Adirondack villages, and the towns and farms in the Champlain Valley.

In the 1850s, Jewish communities came into being in Troy (1856), Schenectady (1856), Elmira (1850), Kingston, and Newburgh. By the end of the Civil War, Jews had also established themselves permanently at Hudson, Ogdensburg, Amsterdam, and Niagara Falls. Louis and Lottie Gross, who arrived in Troy in the 1850s, were among the founders of the city's first congregation, Temple Berith Sholom, in 1856. They were the parents of Charles Gross, born in Troy in 1857, who was probably the first unconverted Jew named to the faculty of Harvard University. He became an instructor of history in 1888 and a full professor in 1901. By 1877 there were well over 5,000 Jews in the upstate towns and cities north of Westchester County, and they maintained some 35 congregations. Albany, with 2,000 Jews, was then the largest Jewish community, followed by Buffalo with 1,500, Syracuse and Rochester, each with 1,200, 500 in Troy, 150 in Newburgh, and 300 in Elmira.

The migrations from Eastern Europe after 1880 enlarged all of the existing upstate communities and gave impetus to new settlements. Many of the East European Jews who arrived in New York City did not stay there long but headed north to such smaller cities as Ithaca, Hudson, Suffern, Haverstraw, Auburn, Massena, Lake Placid, Spring Valley, Binghamton, Glens Falls, Olean, Saratoga Springs, Cohoes, and Saranac Lake.

Among the East European Jewish settlers upstate were the founders of Jewish farming communities in Sullivan and Ulster Counties who began settling there after 1900 with the aid of the Baron de Hirsch Fund and the Jewish Agricultural Society. One of the earliest Jewish settlers in the Catskills was Bernhard Behrend, founder of a prominent Jewish family in Washington, D.C. In 1832, while a resident of Rodenberg, Germany, he had proposed the establishment of a Jewish colony somewhere in the United States and submitted a plan for it to Baron Rothschild and later to Gabriel Riesser, champion of civil rights for German Jews. In 1845, Behrend called on his fellow German Jews to buy shares in a company that would create the colony he envisaged. In 1849 Behrend emigrated to the United States, with his wife and 13 children, and bought a farm in Narrowsburgh, Sullivan County. He supplemented his income by operating a candy store in the village of Narrowsburgh where he remained until 1864.

Lewis Meinhold, Nathan Leopold, and David Woolf settled in

Ellenville in 1858 and were among the incorporators of the village in 1875. Meinhold was a distiller, Nathan owned a store, and Woolf was the town's first butcher. A. Flatow, a jeweler, arrived in 1869, and A. Yesky, a tailor, opened a shop in 1872. Moses Wolf settled at Kerhonksen in the 1890s and moved to Ellenville before 1900, serving as a member of the town's board of trustees. Hyman Levine peddled between Kingston and Ellenville during the 1880s and 1890s before settling in Ellenville in 1895. The area's first Jewish services are said to have been held at his farm on Cape Avenue.

Among the first Jewish farmers in the 1900s in the Catskill region were the Goldsteins of Mountaindale, the Levinsons and Kanfers of Greenfield, the Meyersons, Lefkowitzes, and Kriegers at Spring Glen, the Simrins at Dairyland, the Bergers and Cohens at Kerhonksen, and the Slutzkys in Ellenville. Charles Slutzky, the first of his family to settle in the Catskills, acquired a farm in 1901 and ran it with the help of his son Joseph while his other children worked in New York to supplement the family income. His brother, Morris, bought a farm in 1904. The Slutzkys named their Nevele Country Club for the 11 children of the original Slutzky family, Nevele being eleven spelled backwards. By 1907, when the Ellenville Hebrew Aid Society was organized, there were over 1,200 Jews on farms in the Ellenville area. In 1909 the society dedicated a synagogue, which together with Anshei Hashara in Tannersville, are believed to have been the first Jewish congregations in the Catskills in this century. Many of these Jewish farmers operated small summer boarding houses for Jews from New York, and out of these tiny enterprises there developed the now famous Jewish hotels in and around Woodridge, Ellenville, Kiamesha, Monticello, Liberty, South Fallsburgh, Hurleyville, and Mountaindale.

Until the 1950s, most of the Catskill resorts catering to Jews closed after Labor Day and did not reopen until Passover. However, with the increased popularity of skiing, many of these establishments winterized their facilities, opened ski runs, and now cater to tourists all year. There are still some Jewish dairy, vegetable, and egg-producing farmers in the Catskills where a year-round Jewish population of some 12,000 reside. Since the 1960s, the area has become popular with Orthodox Jewish groups that have established yeshivas, schools, camps, and residential communities in many of the towns.

Flourishing Orthodox communities have also grown up in Spring Valley, Monsey, and Nyack, in Rockland County. New Square, also in Rockland County, is an all-Jewish village established by a Chasidic sect. Rockland County, just north of Westchester County, became the fastest-growing Jewish area in the state during the 1970s as families from Brooklyn, Queens, and The Bronx settled in many of the new housing developments, raising the Jewish population of the county to 30,000. The great expansion of the State University of New York, with enlarged campuses and student bodies in small towns and cities that once could only boast of teachers' training colleges, brought Jewish faculty people and businessmen into these areas for the first time. Changing neighborhoods in Syracuse, Rochester, and Buffalo brought synagogues and growing Jewish communities into suburban towns where few, if any, Jews had ever lived before. The Buffalo and Rochester Jewish Community Centers both opened main buildings in suburbs, as did some of the larger synagogues in Buffalo, Rochester, Albany, and Syracuse.

In the 1970s there were about 100,000 Jews living north of the Westchester line. Buffalo had the largest Jewish community, with 23,500. Rochester was second, with 21,500, followed by Albany, with 13,500 and Syracuse, with 11,000. Other large Jewish communities upstate were Poughkeepsie (6,000); Schenectady (4,500); Newburgh (4,600); Binghamton (3,960); Monticello (2,400); Kingston (2,300); Elmira (1,400); Gloversville (1,400); Liberty (2,100); Niagara Falls (1,000); Troy (1,300); Ithaca (960); Middletown (1,920); South Fallsburgh (1,100); Saratoga Springs (525); and Port Jervis (560). All told there were 64 places in upstate New York each with 100 or more Jews.

Of the 51 Jews elected to Congress from New York State, only four came from upstate districts: Lucius N. Littauer, Gloversville, 1897-1907; Meyer Jacobstein, Rochester, 1923-1929; Joseph Y. Resnick, Ellenville, 1965-1969; and Benjamin A. Gilman, Middletown, 1972-. None of the two Jewish United States Senators (Herbert Lehman and Jacob Javits), the one Jewish governor (Herbert Lehman), the four Jewish chief justices of the State Court of Appeals (Benjamin Cardozo, Irving Lehman, Stanley Fuld, and Charles Breitel), the one Jewish State Controller (Arthur Levitt), the five Jewish State Attorneys General (Simon Rosendale, Carl Sherman, Albert Ottinger, Jacob Javits, and Louis Lefkowitz), were upstaters. But in 1972, Richard M. Rosenbaum, a native of Oswego, resigned a seat on the State Supreme Court to become chairman of the State Republican Committee. Upstate cities that have had Jewish mayors are: Rochester, Samuel Dicker (1940-56); Oswego, Ralph Shapiro (1959-67); Auburn, Maurice Schwartz (1959-67); White Plains, Richard Maass (1975-); Schenectady, Mordecai Myers (1851-54); and Kingston, Morris Block (1906-10, 1924-26).

*****

ALBANY

Albany Medical College of Union University, 47 New Scotland Ave., has the Neil Hellman Medical Research Center, named for the movie theatre owner and breeder of race horses, who gave $2 million to the center in 1975. Hellman's father, Harry, built Albany's first movie theatre. The Medical College also has the Schaffer Library of Health Sciences, named for Mr. and Mrs. Henry Schaffer. A large plaque in raised metal letters adorns the entrance to the building to record the Schaffers' gift.

Bet Shraga Hebrew Academy of the Capital District, 3489 Carman Rd., is named for the late Shraga (Philip) Arian, the school's first principal.

B'nai B'rith Parkview Apts., 400 Hudson Ave., a 12-story residence for elderly citizens, is sponsored by Gideon Lodge of B'nai B'rith.

Cong. Beth Abraham Jacob, 66 Hackett St., is the third oldest congregation in the state outside of New York City, having been founded in 1841. It is a merger between Congs. Beth El and United Brethren, and a merger of these with Cong. Sons of Abraham, founded in 1882.

Cong. Beth Emeth, 100 Academy Rd., is the oldest existing congregation in the state outside of New York City, having been founded in 1838 as Cong. Beth El. One of its rabbis, Isaac Mayer Wise (see Ohio), came to its pulpit in 1846. His reforms led to a schism and the formation of Cong. Anshe Emeth, which Rabbi Wise led until he was called to Cincinnati. Beth El and Anshe Emeth merged in 1865 to create Beth Emeth.

Cong. Ohav Sholom, New Krumkill Rd. Adjoining the synagogue is the Ohav Sholom Senior Citizens Housing Project, a 12-story building with 212 apartments.

Daughters of Sarah Jewish Home, Washington Ave. Ext. and Rapp Rd.

Empire State Plaza, the massive complex of New York State office buildings, has on its dedication tablet the names of State Comptroller Arthur Levitt, Attorney General Louis Lefkowitz, and Joseph Zaretzki, who was Democratic minority leader of the State Senate when the complex was authorized.

Hillel Foundation at Russell Sage College, Chaplain's Office.

Hillel Foundation at State University of New York at Albany, 1400 Washington Ave.

Jewish Community Center, 340 Whitehall Rd., has a memorial to the 6,000,000 victims of the Holocaust. The sculptured memorial is based on the episode of the Burning Bush. At the front entrance there is an impressionistic sculpture by Nathan Rapoport. He is also the sculptor of the Memorial to the 6,000,000 in Philadelphia, the memorial to the Warsaw Ghetto Revolt in Warsaw, and the B'nai B'rith Holocaust monument in Israel. The Albany sculpture, a memorial to the late Anita L. Winter, who bequeathed $80,000 to the center, suggests dancers circling in the hora around a tree trunk whose branches suggest the Menorah and the Tree of Life.

Jewish Community Council, 567 New Scotland Ave.

Jewish Family Service, 291 State St.

Kosher Pizza House of Lubavitcher Movement, 483 Washington Ave.

Lubavitcher Chabad Center (Shabbas House), 67 Fuller Rd.

New York State Capitol, atop Capitol Hill in Capitol Park, has in its Hall of Governors an oil portrait of the late Herbert H. Lehman, the first and only Jew elected governor of the state. In the Capitol's cornerstone is a memorial from the Jewish citizens of Albany, a brief history of the Jewish community and a *mezuzah*. First elected governor in 1932, Lehman was reelected three times and became the first chief executive to win a four-year term in Albany. When he was elected to the U.S. Senate in 1949, he became the first Jewish member of that body elected by the people. All Jews who had previously been in the Senate served prior to 1916 when senators were still elected by state legislatures. Lehman was born in New York City in 1878. His father, Mayer Lehman, was an immigrant who settled in Alabama in 1848, and moved to New York after the Civil War. The governor's father and uncle, Emanuel Lehman, established the Lehman Brothers banking house and were among the founders of the New York Cotton Exchange. Herbert Lehman's lifelong interest in public welfare began when he became a volunteer worker at the Henry Street Settlement on the Lower East Side. A partner in Lehman Brothers when World War I began, Lehman was one of the organizers of the Joint Distribution Committee in 1914. He was its treasurer and later served as vice-chairman. When the U.S. entered the war, Lehman was ten years beyond draft age but he volunteered for duty. He served first as an aide to Franklin D. Roosevelt, then Assistant Secretary of the Navy, and later as a captain on the General Staff. His services in procuring, shipping, storing, and distributing supplies for the American Expeditionary Force won him the Distinguished Service Medal and a colonelcy. After the war, Lehman helped rebuild Jewish life in Eastern and Central Europe as chairman of the JDC's Reconstruction Committee.

Lehman made his political debut in 1926 as manager of Alfred E. Smith's campaign for governor. When Franklin D. Roosevelt accepted the nomination for governor to strengthen Smith's bid for the presidency in 1928, Lehman was prevailed upon to run for lieutenant governor. Smith failed to carry the state, but Roosevelt and Lehman won by a slim margin. This marked the beginning of a political and personal friendship between the two men that endured until Roosevelt's death. As Roosevelt's lieutenant governor, Lehman was given more responsibilities than any previous occupant of that office. On many occasions he was acting-governor and became widely known as an administrator and leader. In 1932, Lehman backed Roosevelt for president against Smith, and that same year succeeded Roosevelt as governor. Lehman was reelected by ever larger majorities in 1934 and 1936. He wanted to retire in 1938, but was prevailed upon to run again by Roosevelt who called him "my good right arm."

In his ten years as governor, Lehman fought successfully for Social Security legislation; legal protection for women, children, and labor; banking, insurance, and prison reforms; and a host of statutes that made New York the leader in progressive state government. During his record-breaking fourth term, he prepared the state for war and organized a civilian defense organization. A few weeks before the expiration of his term in 1942, Lehman resigned to accept President Roosevelt's appointment as director of the Office of Foreign Relief and Rehabilitation. In this post he organized vast shipments of food, clothing, and shelter to the people of North Africa, Sicily, and the liberated areas of Italy until the establishment of the United Nations Relief and Rehabilitation Agency (UNRRA). The 44 nations participating in UNRRA unanimously elected him the first director-general of the first organization of the United Nations. He served from 1943-1946. In

1946 Lehman ran unsuccessfully for the U.S. Senate. In 1949 he was elected to fill a one-year Senate vacancy, and in 1950 he won a full six-year term. In or out of public office, Lehman remained identified with the Jewish community. As governor and senator he never hesitated to speak out in behalf of Jewish causes and to take an active role in Jewish life. In the Senate he was an uncompromising champion of liberal immigration laws and a militant advocate of civil rights. For some years he was a vice-chairman of the Palestine Economic Corporation. □

Moses Smiting the Rock at Kadesh, is the central feature of the King Fountain in Washington Park.

New York State Court of Appeals, Eagle and Pine Sts., has in its courtroom behind the judges' seats, a portrait gallery of those who have served as Chief Justices, among them Benjamin N. Cardozo, Irving H. Lehman, and Stanley H. Fuld. Charles Breitel was elected Fuld's successor in 1973. Cardozo was Chief Justice from 1927-1932 when he was appointed to the Supreme Court of the U.S. Irving Lehman, brother of Governor Lehman, served as Chief Justice from 1939 until his death in 1945. Elected to the State Supreme Court in 1908 when he was only 32, he was reelected in 1922 as the candidate of both major parties. Justice Lehman was elected to the Court of Appeals in 1923. From 1939-1942 New York had two brothers at the head of its executive and judicial departments. Justice Lehman twice swore in his brother as governor. Justice Lehman was widely known for his scholarship and liberal interpretation of law. A number of his decisions in cases involving social and economic questions made legal history. An opinion he wrote in 1928, nearly a decade before the right of collective bargaining achieved general statutory recognition, won wide attention when it voided an injunction obtained by a transit company in a dispute with its employees. He was also the author of a famous opinion upholding the right of a member of Jehovah's Witnesses not to salute the American flag, on the ground that such action violated their religious scruples. When New York City tendered a public reception to Gen. Dwight D. Eisenhower as the hero of World War II, Justice Lehman was chosen to deliver the address of welcome. He served as president of New York's Temple Emanu-El, president of the National Jewish Welfare Board, of which he was a founder, and as a member of the board of the Jewish Theological Seminary of America.

Fuld, who was a member of Thomas E. Dewey's "gang busting" staff in the 1930s, was appointed to the Court of Appeals by Governor Dewey in 1946. A judge whose dissenting and majority decisions had an immense influence on the law, he was elected Chief Justice in 1966 and served until his retirement at the end of 1973. Fuld was chairman of the board of governors of the Jewish Theological Seminary from 1966-1974.

Chief Justice Charles Breitel, son of immigrants, grew up on the Lower East Side. He served as Supreme Court justice from 1950 until his election to the Court of Appeals in 1968. □

New York State Justice Building, in the Empire State Plaza, has in the second floor lobby leading to the Attorney General's office, portraits of four of the five Jews who have served as State Attorney General: Simon Rosendale of Albany (1892-94); Carl Sherman, New York City (1923-25); Albert Ottinger, New York City (1924-28); and Jacob K. Javits, New York City (1954-56). Louis Lefkowitz, New York City, who was first elected Attorney General in 1956, was elected to his fifth term in 1974. His portrait will be hung when his term is completed.

New York State Legislative Building, in the Empire State Plaza, has in its Legislative Library a large photo of Governor Herbert H. Lehman. In the Speaker's office there is a portrait of Irwin Steingut of Brooklyn, who was speaker of the State Assembly in 1935. His son, Stanley, was elected Speaker in 1975 and his picture, too, will hang in this office.

New York State Museum, State Education Bldg., Washington Ave., owns a set of seven commemorative plates depicting the various buildings of Congregation Shearith Israel of New York City during its more than 300 years of history. Each plate is 10⅝ inches in diameter. There are also five coin-quality silver spoons which belonged to the founders of the Albany Jewish community, (these items are not always on display).

Perlman Yards of the Penn-Central Railroad, opened in 1970, is named for Alfred Perlman, president and chief administrative officer of the railroad in the 1970s. Perlman had been president of the New York Central Railroad before it merged with the Pennsylvania Railroad.

State University of New York at Albany, has an outstanding collection of Judaica of over 6,000 volumes and manuscripts. The collection was assembled by the late Mordechai Kosover, a scholar in Hebrew and Oriental linguistics. It was bought from his heirs through a public subscription sponsored by the Jewish Community Council.

Temple Israel, 600 New Scotland Ave.

ALFRED

Hillel Foundation at Alfred University, Box 761.

AMENIA

Cong. Beth David, Main St.

AMHERST

Amherst Synagogue, 115 Millbrook.

Halpern Memorial, a bronze plaque at the State University of New York at Buffalo Law School, in John Lord O'Brien Hall, Millersport Hwy., honors the late Supreme Court Justice Philip Halpern. He served for a number of years as the U.S. Representative on the United Nations Human Rights Commission's Subcommission on the Prevention of Discrimination and Protection of Minorities, and was one of the leading members of the New York State Constitutional Convention in 1938. The plaque reads: *In memory of Philip Halpern, dean and professor of this Law School, public servant and judge, warm friend who devoted a brilliant command of the law to the service of the highest aspirations for human brotherhood.*

Jewish Center, 2600 N. Forest Rd., the suburban building of the Jewish Center of Greater Buffalo, situated adjacent to the New York State University's new campus complex, also houses a Hillel Foundation. In the center's courtyard is a memorial to the victims of the Holocaust. The abstract sculpture, which rests on a 16-foot high center post, is designed in the form of a book with movable pages inscribed with quotations and thoughts of the survivors.

Lubavitcher Movement Chabad Center, 30 N. Hadley Rd.

Temple Beth Am, Sheridan Rd. and Indian Trail Rd.

Temple Shaarey Zedek, 621 Getzvulle Rd.

Temple Sinai Reconstructionist, 50 Alberta Dr., has a garden court as part of the temple, which is open to the sky.

AMSTERDAM

Cong. Sons of Israel, 355 Guy Park Ave.

Temple of Israel, 8 Mohawk St.

Wasserman Memorial Laboratory, Amsterdam Memorial Hospital, Upper Market St., was donated by David Wasserman in memory of his father, Julius Wasserman, one of the founders of the city's carpet and broom industries. The elder Wasserman, who settled here in 1865, was postmaster in 1886. David Wasserman, who died in 1953, was born here in 1867. He also established a similar laboratory in memory of his father at St. Mary's Hospital, 427 Guy Park Ave. Wasserman was president of Temple of Israel.

AUBURN

Cong. B'nai Israel, 18 Seminary Ave.

BATAVIA

Temple Beth El, 124 Bank St.

BEACON

Beacon Hebrew Alliance, 55 Fishkill Ave.

BINGHAMTON

Beth David Synagogue, 39 Riverside Dr.

Jewish Community Center, 500 Clubhouse Rd., has a large permanent outdoor Menorah.

Jewish Family Service, 96 Hawley St.

Jewish Federation of Broome County, 500 Clubhouse Rd.

Margolis Holocaust Collection of books, documents, and other materials pertaining to the death of the 6,000,000, is housed at the State University of New York, Binghamton. The collection is named for the late Mrs. Belle Margolis, who lost 32 close relatives in the Holocaust.

Reinhardt Library at the State University of New York at Binghamton houses the most complete collection of material relating to the life and work of Max Reinhardt, the eminent Austrian-born Jewish theatrical producer and director. The Library includes Reinhardt's 10,000-volume personal library, copies of 150 production books used in stage productions, and microfilm copies of all the Reinhardt material in the Salzburg Institute for Max Reinhardt Studies and the University of Vienna's Institute of Theatre Research.

The Reporter (Jewish weekly), 500 Clubhouse Rd.

Temple Beth El, (see Endicott).

Temple Concord, 9 Riverside Dr.

Temple Israel, Deerfield Pl.

BREWSTER

Temple Beth Elohim, Route 22.

BRIGHTON

Cong. Beth Haknesses Hachodosh, 19 St. Regis Dr.

Jewish Community Center of Greater Rochester, 1200 Edgewood Ave., is said to be the largest center in the country. The open-air chapel of the center's day camp, Markus Park, 183 Quaker Meeting House Rd., is known as the Ma'alot Chapel in memory of the children massacred by Arab terrorists in Ma'alot, Israel, in May, 1974.

Temple B'rith Kodesh, 2956 Elmwood Ave., is the oldest congregation in the Rochester area, having been founded in 1848. It has a unique Ark in the form of a monumental bronze sculpture comprising 18 panels which give visual and symbolic form to the words of the ancient Hebrew patriarchs and prophets in an unremitting dialogue with God, Rising high above the sanctuary is a 12-sided, 65-foot high dome of wood and glass. Each of the 12 panels of the dome represents one of the 12 tribes of Israel. In the atrium that links the sanctuary to the school wing are a number of ancient Israelite artifacts, the cornerstone from the temple's old Gibbs' St. synagogue which it occupied from 1909-1962, and three huge stones resembling those of the Western Wall in Jerusalem, brought from Israel. In the temple auditorium is a bronze relief of Rabbi Philip S. Bernstein, spiritual leader of the congregation from 1926-1973.

Temple Sinai, 363 Penfield Rd., has in its sanctuary two majestic pylons, symbolizing the Ten Commandments, and a glass wall behind the bimah that draws the world around into the sanctuary.

BROCKPORT

Hillel Foundation at State College at Brockport, Havurah Office.

Interfaith Chapel, University of Rochester, River Campus Station.

BUFFALO

Ahavas Achim Lubavitz Synagogue, 345 Tacoma Ave.

Buffalo Jewish Review, 110 Pearl St.

Bureau of Jewish Education, 787 Delaware Ave.

Chabad House of Lubavitcher Movement, 3292 Main St.

Chasen's Hebrew Gift Shop, 998 Kenmore Ave.

Chavurah Cong., 11 Huxley Dr.

Cong. Beth Abraham, 1073 Elmwood Ave.

Cong. Brith Israel-Anshe Emes, 1237 Hertel Ave.

Cong. Brith Sholom, 1052 Hertel Ave.

Rosa Coplon Jewish Home and Infirmary, 10 Symphony Circle.

Delaware Park, Humboldt Pkwy., has a bronze copy of Michelangelo's statue of David, one of the only three made from the original marble statue in Florence, Italy.

Hebrew Academy of Buffalo, 85 Saranac Ave.

Hillel Foundation at State University at Buffalo, 40 Capen Blvd., memorializes Arthur Goldberg, one-time Washington correspondent of *The Buffalo Evening News*, and the first chairman of the Hillel Advisory Board. There is another Hillel unit at 1209 Elmwood Ave.

Jewish Center of Greater Buffalo, 787 Delaware Ave., has in its entrance lobby a 22 by 11 foot mural, specially lighted and visible from the street. The mural depicts life in the center, a central motif being a folk dance—the hora. A young tree growing out of a cutdown stump symbolizes the center's role in revitalizing Jewish life. The theme is amplified in a group of children and a teacher. On the right side of the mural some of the solemn aspects of Jewish life are represented. In the center's adult lounge is an art gallery with a permanent collection of Jewish art, including an original Chagall lithograph entitled, *The Exodus*. (See also Amherst above.)

Jewish Family Service, 775 Main St. There is also a branch in the Jewish Center's building in Amherst.

Jewish War Veterans Headquarters, 1460 Hertel Ave.

Kadry's Kosher Restaurant and Delicatessen, Hertel Ave.

Monument to Holocaust Victims, in Pine Hill Cemetery, is the final resting place of several bars of soap made from the remains of Jews cremated in the Nazi death camps.

Saranac Synagogue, 85 Saranac Ave.

Temple Beth El, 2368 Eggert Rd.

Temple Beth Zion, 805 Delaware Ave., has in its sanctuary giant Tablets of the Law flanked by stained glass windows by Ben Shahn, depicting the Creation as described in the Book of Job. The Ark in the chapel is held up by poles, recalling the time when the ancient Israelites carried the Ark with them. In a wall of the Ark in the main sanctuary is the cornerstone from the old building, destroyed by fire in 1961, indicating that the congregation was founded in 1850.

Temple Shaarey Zedek, 500 Starin Ave.

United Jewish Federation, 775 Main St.

CANANDAIGUA
Canandaigua Veterans Administration Hospital has its own Jewish chapel. The interior is decorated with 12 large wooden shields, each depicting one of the 12 tribes of Israel.

CATSKILL
Temple Israel, 438 Main St.

CHAUTAUQUA
George Gershwin's Shack, is the practice hut where Gershwin composed his *Concerto in F* in 1925. It was dedicated to the composer in 1952 as one of 32 memorial shacks on the grounds of the famous adult education center.

CLIFTON PARK
Cong. Beth Sholom, Clifton Park Center Rd.

COHOES
America, a 3-verse poem written by the late Rabbi Abba Hillel Silver of Cleveland during World War I, is inscribed on a bronze plaque affixed to the Mohawk St. entrance of the Cohoes City Hall. The poem was written in 1917 and were the closing words of a Victory Loan speech Dr. Silver gave in Cleveland.

COLD SPRING
Surprise Lake Camp, the oldest Jewish summer camp for Jewish children established by community organizations, was founded in 1901 by the New York Educational Alliance and the 92nd St. YM-YWHA. Opening of this camp marked the beginning of organization-sponsored camping for Jewish children.

COLONIE
Colonie Jewish Community Association.

COOPERSTOWN
National Baseball Hall of Fame, Main St., bet. Fair and Pioneer Sts., has two Jews immortalized. The first to be so honored in 1956 was Henry "Hank" Greenberg, first baseman and outfielder for the Detroit Tigers from 1933-1941, and from 1945-1946 (with time out for service in World War II). The Bronx-born Greenberg won the American League's Most Valuable Player award twice. Greenberg created national discussion in 1934 over whether he would play in the World Series on Rosh Hashanah and Yom Kippur. He played on Rosh Hashanah and helped his team win, but remained in synagogue on Yom Kippur while his team lost. The second Jewish player elected to the Hall of Fame is Bronx-born Sanford "Sandy" Koufax who set

many records as a pitcher for the Brooklyn and Los Angeles Dodgers from 1955-1966. He holds the all-time record for no-hitters in four years, the earned-run title for five consecutive years, 25 or more wins in a season three successive years, strikeout leader four times, most valuable player in 1963, and Cy Young award winner in 1963, 1965, and 1966 as the best pitcher of the year. Koufax was elected to the Hall in 1971 at 36, the youngest player ever so honored. Also in the Hall of Fame are the cap of Bo Belinsky, who pitched a no-hit game, and the bat of Ronnie Blomberg, who as a player with the N.Y. Yankees got the first hit under a new rule providing for a designated hitter in the American League.

CORTLAND
Temple Brith Sholem, 117 Madison St.

DELMAR
B'nai Sholom New Reform Cong., 48 Hunterfield Rd.

DEWITT
Cong. Beth Sholom, 5205 Jamesville Rd.

Temple Beth El, 3528 East Genesse St., represents a 1963 merger of two Rochester congregations, Poiley Zedek and Beth Israel. The latter was founded in 1854 and was the second oldest congregation in Rochester.

DUNKIRK
Temple Beth El, 507 Washington Ave.

ELLENVILLE
Cong. Ezrath Israel, 31 Center St., the only synagogue in this Ulster County resort town, was the first synagogue in the Catskill Mountains area, having been founded in 1907 as the Hebrew Aid Society Synagogue. The Hebrew Aid Society Cemetery, also the first in the region, was established in 1908.

The oldest Jewish gravestone in the Catskills, however, is dated 1851. It is a solitary monument enclosed in a wall in a wooded area now owned by the Rockland Light & Power Co., in southern Lumberland Township, Sullivan County, near the Mongaup River. The stone marks the grave of Nathan Friesleben, an immigrant from Bohemia, who died at the age of 59, having been murdered while traveling his peddler's route. The inscription on the stone says "he was an honest man. A quarter of an acre of the ground where his remains lie has not been sold nor shall it be."

Friesleben and members of his family arrived in the area in 1843 when there is a record of their having bought some farm land. The Frieslebens, who were isolated Jewish pioneers in this rural farming area, left in 1855. Other early Jewish settlers in Ellenville, which was established in 1823, were Lewis Meinhold, Nathan Leopold, and David Woolf, who arrived in 1848.

Meinhold, who had originally been one of the Jewish colonists at Sholom (see below), was a distiller whose cider mill on the Shawangunk Trail was well-known. Leopold was one of the town's first merchants, while Woolf was its first butcher. All three signed the petition for the incorporation of Ellenville in 1855. A fourth Jewish family, that of A. Flatow, a jeweler, arrived in 1869.

In the Ezrath Israel Synagogue, the Town of Wawarsing hung a memorial plaque in 1972 to the Sholom Colony, the first Jewish agricultural settlement in the United States, established in 1838 on a site that is now 11 miles away from Ellenville. The inscription on the plaque, dedicated in 1972, reads: *Some eleven miles North is the site of the first Jewish farm settlement in the United States. In 1837 a small group of New York City Jews purchased about 500 acres from Edmund Bruyn. Sight unseen, they named their colony Sholom, peace. They found barren land, but no peace. Unable to farm, they tried manufacturing caps and quill pens and peddling. Starvation faced them. Mortgages were foreclosed. Most returned to the city by 1842. In tribute to their brave experiment, the Town of Wawarsing has erected this memorial.*□

Cong. Knesset Israel of Ulster Heights.

Joseph Slutsky Center, 34½ Center St., was established by and is named for the late Joseph Slutsky, who, with his brother Charles, and later with their sons, began small-scale farming around Ellenville in 1903, and later opened summer boarding houses for New York City's lower middle-class and working class Jews. Out of these boarding houses grew some of the best known summer, and now year round hotels, among them Slutsky's Nevele. Joseph Slutsky was one of the founders of the Hebrew Aid Society Synagogue and its president for many years. In the lobby area of the circular Tower Building of The Nevele is a bronze plaque commemorating the day President and Mrs. Lyndon B. Johnson stayed at the hotel in the summer of 1966, during their visit to the Catskills. The Johnsons dined in privacy but ate The Nevele's customary strictly kosher food. They were accompanied on their visit by the late Congressman Joseph Resnick, the first Democrat elected to Congress from the Ellenville area. He had become a millionaire through the establishment of the locally based Channel Master Corp.—the world's largest manufacturer of television antennas and related accessories. The Nevele's golf course was once the site of a Hebrew school founded in 1913 to serve the children of Jewish farmers in the Leurenkill district who lived too far away to attend the Hebrew school in Ellenville.

Temple Rodeph Sholom, Webster Ave.

ENDICOTT
Temple Beth El-Jewish Center, 117 Jefferson Ave.

ELMIRA

Cong. Shomray Hadath, Cobbles Park.

Jewish Community Center, 115 East Church St.

Jewish Welfare Fund, 115 East Church St.

Temple B'nai Israel, 900 West Water St.

Woodlawn National Cemetery, adjacent to Woodlawn Cemetery, at the north end of David St., contains the graves of 24 Jews who died in the Elmira prison during the Civil War when thousands of Confederate prisoners of war were housed in hastily built and unsanitary pens. The Jewish graves are among 2,963 Confederate war dead. Woodlawn Cemetery is the last resting place of Ossip Gabrilowitsch, Jewish-born pianist and composer, who married Clara Clemens, daughter of Samuel L. Clemens, better known as Mark Twain. Gabrilowitsch is buried in the same plot as Twain and the gravestone bears twin relief heads of Twain and his son-in-law.

ELMORA

Satellite Reform Jewish Community of Southern Saratoga County, sponsored by Temple Beth Emeth in Albany and Temple Gates of Prayer in Schenectady, for their members living in Southern Saratoga County, holds Friday evening services at 50 Oakwood Blvd., once a month, and also has a midweek Hebrew school.

FAIRPORT

Memorial to Murdered Israeli Athletes is a grove of pine trees in the town of Perinton, Beechwoods Area, Squirrels Heath Rd., in this Rochester suburb. The grove was dedicated in 1973 by the Perinton Recreation and Parks Commission in memory of the 11 Israeli athletes who were killed by Arab terrorists at the 1972 Olympic Games in Munich, Germany.

FERNDALE

Ferndale Synagogue, 72 Academy St.

P'Nimia Bais Yaacov Residence High School for Girls.

FLEISCHMANNS

Cong. B'nai Israel, Vagner Ave.

This Delaware County resort village is named for the Fleischmann family of Cincinnati, whose founder, Charles, invented the compressed yeast cakes that bear his name. The Fleischmanns used to summer here in the 1880s when the place was called Griffin Corners. Julius Fleischmann, who was mayor of Cincinnati from 1900-1904, and his brother, Louis, both built summer homes here. When the village was incorporated in 1913, it was renamed Fleischmanns. Members of the Fleischmann family beautified the whole area with fish ponds, bathing pools, flower gardens, deer parks, and mountain drives. The hill above the railroad station, where Louis Fleisch-

mann built the first of the Fleischmann homes, is called Fleischmann Hill.
The local baseball park is known as Fleischmann Field—a gift from the
Fleischmanns. In the village's Skene Memorial Library hangs a portrait of
Charles Fleischmann, founder of the family.

FLORIDA
>Temple Beth Shalom, Roosevelt Ave.

FONDA
>Littauer Recreation Center was a gift of Lucius N. Littauer of nearby
Gloversville (see below).

FREDONIA
>Hillel Foundation at State College at Fredonia, 437 Dove St.

GARDINER
>Tuthilltown Grist Mill is where nearly all the flour used in the baking
of *shmurah* matzoh for the eastern part of the U.S. is produced. There is
constant and careful rabbinic supervision from the time the wheat is
harvested until it is finally baked. Before the grinding of the wheat begins, an
Orthodox rabbi takes the machinery apart and spends three days cleaning it
thoroughly. During the grinding period, a rabbi sleeps at the mill to protect
the *shmurah* flour.

GENESEO
>Hillel Foundation at State College at Geneseo, University of Roches-
ter Interfaith Chapel, River Campus Station, Rochester.

GENEVA
>Temple Beth El, 755 S. Main St.

GLENS FALLS
>Cong. Shaaray Tefila, 68 Bay St.
>Jewish Welfare Fund, 90 Broad St.
>Temple Beth El, 3 Marion Ave.

GLEN WILD
>Glen Wild Synagogue.

GLOVERSVILLE
>Jewish Community Center, 30 East Fulton St., is known as the
Lucius N. Littauer Building. It was erected in 1930 by Lucius N. Littauer,
leader of the glove industry, who was born and raised in Gloversville where
half the public buildings are monuments to his generosity.
>Knesseth Israel Synagogue, 34 East Fulton St.

Eugene Littauer Laboratory of Fulton County, 99 East State St., is Lucius Littauer's memorial to his brother.

Harriet Littauer Nurses Home, Littauer Pl., is Littauer's memorial to his sister.

Lucius N. Littauer Monument, on the grounds of Gloversville High School, Lincoln St. Extension, was erected by public subscription in 1929, on the 70th birthday of Littauer, whose benefactions to the city included a hospital and many recreational facilities.

Littauer's father, Nathan, was a peddler who settled in Gloversville in the 1840s and later opened a glove factory. Born here in 1859, Lucius played football for Harvard in 1875 and 1877, rowed on its freshman crew, and later became Harvard's first football coach, thus going down in sports history as the first Jew to coach a college team in any sport. The glove business he inherited from his father expanded so greatly that gloves and Littauer became almost interchangeable words. In 1897 he was elected (as a Republican), to Congress from New York's 21st District. Reelected four times, he fought for liberal immigration legislation and helped bring to Secretary of State John Hay's attention the plight of Romanian Jews. In 1925, Littauer made Jewish academic history by establishing at Harvard the Nathan Littauer Professorship in Jewish Literature and Philosophy in honor of his father. This was the first chair in Judaica at an American university, and its only occupant, for nearly 50 years, was Dr. Harry Wolfson. In 1929 Littauer again created an academic stir when he gave Harvard over 12,000 volumes of rare Hebrew books and manuscripts. Eight years later he contributed $2,000,000 to Harvard for the establishment of a Graduate School of Business Administration. Hundreds of Jewish scholars, researchers, authors, libraries, and Jewish cultural enterprises are indebted to Littauer because of the unique and continuing grants for Jewish scholarship by the Littauer Foundation which he founded with an endowment of $4,000,000.

The Littauer monument at Gloversville High School does not mention the fact that he was a Jew, but it is implied in the words inscribed on one side of the statue: "Adherent to duty, high ideals, and simple piety . . . a lover of mankind." ☐

Nathan Littauer Hospital, 99 East State St., was erected in 1894 as a memorial to Littauer's father. It was then the only hospital in Fulton County.

Littauer Outdoor Swimming Pool and Skating Rink, West St. Extended, was built by Littauer and deeded to the Gloversville Board of Education.

GRAND ISLAND

City Hall of this island town in the Niagara River, opposite Buffalo, has in its new building what was to have been the cornerstone of a proposed Jewish city-state on Grand Island. The slab of Ohio sandstone is inscribed with the Hebrew words, *Shema Yisroel Adonai Elohenu Adonai Echod*, and the following legend: *Ararat, A City of Refuge for the Jews Founded by Mordecai Manuel Noah in the month of Tizri Sept. 1825 & in the Fiftieth Year of American independence*. Until 1968 the stone was owned by the Buffalo and Erie County Historical Society in whose building it had rested since 1866. In 1968 the society turned it over to the Grand Island Historical Society for use by the Grand Island City Hall. This stone is the only visible reminder of Mordecai Manuel Noah's quixotic colonization scheme which created a stir among American and European Jews when it was made public in 1825. Noah attempted to buy Grand Island in 1820 from the State of New York as the future site of a Jewish colony. Five years later he prevailed upon a number of his non-Jewish friends to organize a syndicate which bought 2,500 acres on Grand Island and secured an option on more. The investors hoped to sell the land to the prospective settlers envisaged in Noah's plan. There is no evidence that Noah owned any of the land or even set foot on Grand Island, which he picked as the site of Ararat in a "Proclamation to the Jews," dated September 15, 1825, the day after Rosh Hashanah. The manifesto reaffirmed Noah's faith in the restoration of Zion, but in the meantime invited all the Jews of the world to come to Ararat as a way station on the road to Zion where they could reacquire skill in agriculture in preparation for a new life in Palestine. Included in his invitation were the American Indians, since Noah shared the strange belief that they were the descendants of the Ten Lost Tribes.

Dubbing himself "governor and judge of Israel," Noah said, "In the name of God, I revive, renew and reestablish the government of the Jewish nation under the auspices and protection of the Constitution and the laws of the United States of America." He commanded that a census be taken of Jews throughout the world, forbade polygamy among Jews, ordered prayers to be said in Hebrew, levied a tax of three shekels in silver upon every Jew in the world to finance Ararat, and asked that a judge of Israel be elected every four years by the Paris Consistoire. The fantastic document concluded with the appointment of European rabbis and laymen as commissioners charged with organizing the mass migration to Grand Island, and with a prayer for universal peace. Noah scheduled September 15 as the date of the proclamation and just a month before the opening of the Erie Canal, as the day for the dedication of Ararat's cornerstone. The exercises were held in Buffalo's St. Paul's Episcopal Church, a frame structure that occupied the site where St. Paul's Episcopal Cathedral now stands in Shelton Square, West, because not enough boats were available to Grand Island for the throngs anxious to see the ceremony. A booming cannon and a magnificent procession through the streets of Buffalo preceded the dedication rites. City officials, army officers, Masonic dignitaries, clergymen, Knights Templar, and stewards carrying wine, oil, and corn paraded toward the church, while the city's populace of 2,500 (not a Jew among them) and thousands of visitors gaped. At the head of the procession strode Noah, garbed in his own conception of the robes of a judge in Israel. The cornerstone rested on the church's communion table, while the Reverend Addison Searle conducted the Episcopal service. Noah's dedicatory address in which he repeated the bizarre proclamation was the climax. The service was both the beginning and the end of Ararat. Noah's scheme earned him almost universal condemnation and ridicule in Jewish circles, and he soon forgot Ararat and its cornerstone. For a number of years the stone lay exposed behind the church. Later, it rested on the lawn of Gen. Peter B. Porter's house in Buffalo. Lewis F. Allen, who deposited it with the Buffalo Historical Society in 1866, acquired the stone from Porter in 1834, and moved it to a Grand Island settlement. There it was set in a niche in a specially constructed brick monument, 14 feet high and six feet square. Tourists to Buffalo and Niagara Falls regularly visited it, artists sketched it, and an old guide book to Niagara Falls contained an engraving of the monument.

Before and after the abortive Ararat project, which gave its sponsor a permanent niche in Jewish history, Noah expressed views which have led some writers to describe him as the first political Zionist. Early in the 19th century and again in the 1840s, Noah advocated Jewish restoration in Zion by Jewish self-effort, demanded the support of the Christian world for Jewish resettlement in Palestine, and suggested that the land be acquired through purchase. He also predicted the settlement of Palestine by *halutzim* from Eastern Europe, foresaw a Balfour-like Declaration, the granting of the Palestine Mandate to England, and prophesied some Jewish opposition to a Jewish state.

Born in 1785 in Philadelphia, where he was raised by his grandfather, Jonas Phillips, Revolutionary patriot (see Pennsylvania), Noah was the great-great-grandson of Dr. Samuel Nunez, a Marrano who settled in Savannah in 1733 (see Georgia). Noah's father served in the American Revolution, and there is a legend that George Washington attended the wedding of Noah's parents. Successively an apprentice guilder and carver, clerk in the U.S. Treasury, and reporter of the sessions of the Pennsylvania Legislature, Noah wrote his first play, *The Fortress of Sorrento*, in 1808. Soon thereafter he moved to Charleston, S.C., where he became editor of the *City Gazette*. Author of a series of anonymous letters on political issues, he fought several duels as a result of political disputes and received and declined an appointment as U.S. Consul at Riga. In 1813, President James Madison named Noah consul to Tunis, with instructions to ransom a group of Americans held captive by the Barbary pirates. He succeeded in this mission, but in the process found that the State Department had rejected his expenditures as unauthorized. In addition, Noah was dismissed from his post by Secretary of State James Monroe on the ground that at the time of his appointment "it was not known that the religion which you profess would form any obstacle to the exercise of your consular functions." Ultimately, Noah was vindicated and, in 1818, Madison conceded that Noah's Judaism was no secret at the time of his appointment. On his return to the U.S., Noah settled in New York City where he became a well-known politician, playwright, journalist, and leader in the Jewish community. A power in Tammany Hall (he once served as Grand Sachem), Noah was appointed sheriff of New York in 1822. When some of his opponents protested that a Jewish sheriff might have to hang Christians, Noah countered: "Pretty Christians to require hanging." He also served as surveyor of the Port of New York, by appointment of President Andrew Jackson, and was a judge in the Court of General Sessions. Among the newspapers Noah edited or published were the *National Advocate*, the *New York Enquirer* (which through mergers became the *New York World*), the *Commercial Advertiser*, *The Messenger*, *The Union*, and *The Times* (not the same as the present *New York Times*). In the 1830's Noah was one of the founders of a pioneer news-gathering service which operated fast boats to bring foreign dispatches from incoming steamers in New York harbor, and established a pony express to rush news from Washington. Noah's wife, Rebecca Jackson, was a sister of Solomon Jackson, who edited *The Jew*, the first Jewish journal published in the U.S. In 1818 Noah was the principal speaker at the dedication of the new synagogue of Congregation Shearith Israel, the oldest in America. His address was passionate expression of faith in the restoration of Israel to Zion.

For a quarter of a century after the Ararat fiasco, Noah was actively concerned with many Jewish and communal causes. He was a founder of Congregation B'nai Jeshurun, second oldest in New York City, and of New York University. He delivered important addresses on major Jewish occasions, advocated minor reforms in religious practices, proposed the establishment of a Jewish college, and urged the creation of a Jewish hospital. Noah died in 1851 and his funeral is said to have been one of the most elaborate in the history of the city. One of the last Jews to be buried within the limits of the old City of New York, his last resting place is the Shearith Israel burying ground on West 21st St. □

GRANIT

Granit Synagogue.

GRANVILLE

Granville Elementary School has a large Star of David on the exterior of its west wall. Tourists noticing this on their way north have wondered why a public school building has this Jewish symbol on its wall. It was put there by the Jewish building contractor.

Jewish Center, 31 East Main St.

GREENWOOD LAKE

Jewish Community Center, Old Monroe Rd.

GROSSINGER'S (LIBERTY)

Grossinger's Hotel is a self-contained 1,300-acre site, larger than the principality of Monaco, and the most famous in the Catskill Mountains. The mammoth hotel can handle 1,500 guests a week and feed over 3,000 at one sitting in its dining room. It had its beginnings in 1914 when Selig Grossinger, an Austrian immigrant, found the N.Y.C. climate bad for his health, and bought a 50-acre farm near Ferndale. But the best crops turned out to be rocks, and soon the Grossingers—papa Selig, mama Malka, daughter Jennie, and son Harry—began taking boarders at $9 a week. Grossinger's first gained attention in 1934 when Barney Ross, a *kashrut*-observing boxer, established his training camp here. The first big booster for Grossinger's was Eddie Cantor, who chanced on the place while hiking in the Catskills one summer. Dusty and unshaven, he stopped for a drink of water, and Jennie Grossinger, thinking him a tramp, insisted on giving him a free meal. Cantor was delighted with the people and the place and mentioned it often on his shows. Grossinger's became the showcase for many entertainers. Jennie Grossinger, as the house mother and hostess of the resort, became a noted personality in her own right, greeting the great and near great—King Baudoin of Belgium; Governor Nelson Rockefeller; Senator Robert Kennedy; Nobel Prize winners Ralph Bunche, Selman Waksman, Arthur Kornberg; Dr. Jonas Salk, and Cardinal Francis Spellman. Grossinger's has its own post office, synagogue, printing plant, rabbi, and a full-time *shochet* and *mashgiach*. Although about one-third of the guests are now non-Jews, the policy of strict *kashrut*, no smoking on the Sabbath in public rooms, and the removal of stationery from writing desks on Saturday remains in force. The long passageway connecting Grossinger's main building to its theatre is divided into two units. One is called George Jessel Way and displays photos, clippings, plaques, and mementos of Jessel. The other unit is named Tin Pan Alley and is decorated with sheet music, song manuscripts, and photos of the great show people who have been to Grossinger's as guests or entertainers.

HAMBURG

Temple Beth Shalom serves Buffalo's southern suburbs.

HARRIS

Jewish Center and Synagogue.

HAVERSTRAW

Cong. Sons of Jacob, 37 Clove Ave.

HENRIETTA

Temple Beth Am, 3249 E. Henrietta Rd., is a tent-like structure resembling an old world synagogue.

HERKIMER

Hannah Basloe Field, Gilbert St., the city's municipal recreation field, was donated by Frank Basloe in memory of his mother.

Temple Beth Joseph, 327 N. Prospect St., is named for Joseph Basloe, father of Frank Basloe, one of the early Jewish settlers here.

HIGHLAND FALLS

Jewish Community Center, Mountain Ave.

HILLBURN

McKosker-Hershfield Cardiac Home is named in part for the late Harry Hershfield, cartoonist, humorist, and raconteur, who was one of the home's founders.

HORNELL

Temple Beth El, 12 Church St.

HUDSON

Cong. Anshe Emeth, Joslen Blvd.
Jewish Welfare Fund, Joslen Blvd.

HUNTER

Cong. Anshe Kol Israel, Main St.

HURLEYVILLE

Cong. Anshe Hurleyville.

HYDE PARK

Franklin D. Roosevelt Library, which houses documents and other materials dealing with the President's career, has among its collections several specifically Jewish items. Among the collection of miniature books is a miniature Torah Scroll. ●In the library is a full size Torah rescued from a burning synagogue in Czechoslovakia after the Nazis took over that country in 1939, and a map of Israel in the form of a gold plaque mounted on a board. ●There is also a portrait of FDR in stone that simulates marble. It is the work of the Israeli artist Shmuel Toker, and a gift of the Farband Labor Zionist Order. ●Among the several American flags displayed in the library is one banner six by ten feet square, with five-inch stars, hand sewn by Mrs. Fannie Freedman of Seattle for FDR's third inauguration. ●Among FDR's papers, which are open to researchers, are many letters, documents, and other items written to FDR by some of his Jewish associates—Henry Morgenthau, Jr., Felix Frankfurter, Stephen S. Wise, Benjamin V. Cohen, Lawrence Steinhardt, etc.—and also letters on specific Jewish questions written to or by FDR. ●In the Eleanor Roosevelt wing of the building there are Mrs. Roosevelt's papers and many items related to her life. Among the latter is a framed testimonial from the American Red Magen David. ●An original of a letter from David Ben-Gurion dated July 2, 1957. ●A framed award of merit for 1957 from the Decalogue Society of Lawyers in Chicago. ●The academic doctorate hoods she wore when she received honorary degrees from the Jewish Theological Seminary, Yeshiva University, and the Hebrew Union College. ●The Anti-Defamation League award of 1948. ●Among the unusual items is an olive drab woolen sweater Mrs. Roosevelt knitted for her young Jewish protégé, Joseph P. Lash, when he was in the Army during World War II. Lash won the Pulitzer Prize for his two-volume biography, *Eleanor and Franklin*, published in 1972. ●In Mrs. Roosevelt's papers there is a large volume of correspondence with people in Israel, which she visited several times. Her correspondence with the United Jewish Appeal, Hadassah, B'nai B'rith, and other Jewish organizations with whom she was identified and on whose behalf she spoke many times can also be seen. ☐

IRONDEQUOIT

Temple Beth David, 2939 St. Paul Blvd., has a 36-foot dome supported by 12 arches symbolizing the 12 original tribes of Israel.

Temple Emanu-El, 2956 St. Paul Blvd.

ITHACA

Cornell University

Cornell University Library, S.W. cor. of the main quadrangle, contains the Eisenlohr collection of works on Egyptology, a gift of Abraham Abraham, Brooklyn merchant. ●A Spinoza collection bought in Europe by Dr. Andrew D. White, the university's first president. ●The Kaplan Collection of early civil service records—a gift of H. Eliot Kaplan, for many years executive secretary of the National Civil Service Reform League. ●B'nai B'rith Hillel Foundation at Cornell is housed in Annabel Taylor Hall, the home of all student religious activities. There is an interfaith chapel in the hall. In the apse, arranged in triangular fashion on a turntable, are Christian, Jewish, and non-denominational altar settings. ●The Hillel unit at Ithaca College is also located here. ●Uris Hall, a social sciences building, is named for Harold D. Uris and his brother, Percy, founders of the Uris Buildings Corp. ●The Uris Undergraduate Library is also a gift of the Uris brothers. ●Morrill Hall, the University's oldest building, which has been declared a national monument, was rehabilitated through a $1 million grant from Jerome K. Ohrbach of Los Angeles. His portrait hangs in the hall. ●In the John M. Olin Library there is the Satinsky Collection of Lincolnia, assembed by Sol Satinsky, Philadelphia philanthropist. ●A collection of the brains of famous people, located in Stimson Hall, includes that of Rosika Schwimmer, Hungarian-born feminist, pacifist, and linguist, who died in 1948. □

Temple Beth El, Tioga and Court Sts.

Young Israel, 106 West Ave.

JAMESTOWN

Temple Hesed Abraham, 215 Hall Ave.

KAUNEONGA LAKE

Temple Beth El.

KERHONKSEN

Cong. Tifereth Yehuda Ve Yisroel, Minnewaska Trail.

Jewish Center, Minnewaska Trail.

KIAMESHA LAKE

Hebrew Day School of Sullivan and Ulster Counties.

KINGSTON

Block Park, in the heart of the city, is named for Morris Block, mayor of Kingston from 1922-1926.

Civil War cannons, facing the City Hall, were donated to the city by Sol Appel in 1897.

Cong. Agudas Achim, 254 Lucas Ave.

Cong. Ahavath Israel, 100 Lucas St.

Jewish Community Center and Council, 96 Maiden Lane.

Temple Emanuel, 243 Albany Ave.

LAKE PEEKSKILL

Temple Israel, Lake Dr.

LAKE PLACID

Lake Placid Synagogue, 30 Saranac Ave., serves the handful of year-round Jewish residents and the larger number of Jewish vacationers who spend their summers here. The synagogue, built largely with the help of a substantial gift from Adolph Leon and his estate, is near the Lake Placid Club, once one of the most notorious anti-Semitic establishments in the country.

LIBERTY

Cong. Ahavath Israel, 39 Chestnut St., serves the year-round Jewish community in this Sullivan County city in the heart of the hotel and resort area.

Liberty Maimonides Hospital and Grossinger Clinic are nonsectarian institutions built by and managed by Jews.

LIVINGSTON MANOR
Cong. Agudas Achim, Rock Ave.

LOCKPORT
Temple Beth David, 115 Genesee St.

MAHOPAC
Jewish Center of the Mahopacs, Route 6.
Temple Beth Shalom, Croton Falls Rd.

MASSENA
Adath Israel Cong., P.O. Box 196. The first, and probably only, appearance in the U.S. of the ancient myth that Jews use Christian blood for ritual purposes surfaced in this St. Lawrence County town on September 22, 1928, two days before Yom Kippur. Following the disappearance of a four-year old Christian girl, a state trooper, acting on the authority of the mayor, questioned the local rabbi and another Jewish resident as to whether Jews had a custom of offering human sacrifices. During the questioning in the local police station a mob gathered outside. The day before Yom Kippur, the child was found alive and well in the woods where she had wandered. After nationwide protests by Jewish organizations and many non-Jewish groups, Governor Alfred E. Smith ordered an investigation. The outcome was a public apology by the mayor and a reprimand to the trooper.

Robert Moses Powerdam, the huge dam on the U.S. side of the St. Lawrence River power project, is named for Robert Moses, chairman of the New York State Power Authority when the dam was completed in 1959 as part of the St. Lawrence River power development.

MIDDLETOWN
Kleiner Mental Health Center, on the grounds of the Middletown State Hospital, is named for the late Dr. Solomon Kleiner, who was for many years the hospital's clinical director of psychiatry.

Middletown Hebrew Association, 13 Linden Ave.
Temple Beth Am, P.O. Box 113.
Temple Sinai, 75 Highland Ave.
United Jewish Appeal, 24 Robertson Dr.

MONROE
Monfield, Forest Rd., is a housing development of 80 garden apartments and 25 single-family homes. It is entirely occupied by members of the ultra-Orthodox Satmar sect of Chasidim who relocated here from the Williamsburg section of Brooklyn in 1974. The Satmar are militantly opposed to the State of Israel in the belief that no Jewish State can be born until the Messianic era arrives.

Monroe-Woodbury Jewish Community Center, 251 Spring St.
Temple Beth El, 314 N. Main St.

MONSEY

Beth Jacob High School, 114 College Ave.

Beth Midrosh Elyon, 73 Main St.

Beth Rochel School for Girls, 210 Maple Ave.

Community Synagogue, 1½ Cloverdale Lane, is one of a number of Orthodox congregations serving this fast-growing Rockland County community which has become a center of Orthodox Jewish life.

Cong. Beth Israel, 92 Main St.

Cong. Beth Torah, 221 Viola Rd.

Cong. Beth Yitzhock, 184 Maple Ave.

Cong. B'nai Jeshurun, Park Lane.

Cong. Tifereth Efraim, 229 Maple Ave.

Hebrew Institute of Rockland County, 70 Highview Rd.

Mesivta Beth Shraga, Saddle River Rd.

Monsey Jewish Center, 100 Route 306.

Yeshiva Ahavas Yisroel, Phyllis Terrace.

Yeshiva Beth David, 20 W. Maple Ave.

Yeshiva of Spring Valley, 229 Maple Ave.

MONTICELLO

Cong. Tifereth Israel, 18 Landfield Ave.

Jewish Community Center, Park Ave.

Remembrance Shrine of the Holocaust, situated in a small two-room building behind the residence of Mr. and Mrs. Joseph Merfeld, 12 Osborne St., was entirely built by the Merfelds who donated it to the Monticello chapter of Hadassah. The Merfelds, who lost a score of relatives in the Nazi gas chambers, survived the Holocaust and settled in the U.S. in 1947. One room of the small building is a tiny museum where the paneled walls are covered with stark photographs of the Holocaust. On one wall are two small memorials to the parents of the Merfelds. The second room is a permanent sukka. The memorial room has six steps at its entrance, six lights on its porch, and six small trees in an adjacent garden—all symbolic references to the six million victims of the Holocaust. Admission is free, however, most visitors leave a donation which is used by Hadassah to carry out its program.

Sullivan County Hall of Fame, in the Monticello Raceway, honors leading citizens of the county or citizens who were once employed there and then achieved outstanding prominence. Among those represented in the gallery with silver statuettes are: Barney Ross, who held two world boxing championships; Arnold 'Red' Auerbach, long-time coach of the Boston Celtics team of the National Basketball Association; Benny Leonard, one of the greatest lightweight fighters in boxing history; Jay Goldberg, a former U.S. Assistant Attorney General; Jacob Grumet, jurist and former chairman of the N.Y. State Crime Commission; Jerry Lewis, actor and producer; Milton Kutsher, of Kutsher's Country Club and three-term president of the Sullivan County Hotel Association; Danny Kaye; and Moss Hart, playwright.

Monticello, county seat of Sullivan County, which has a substantial year-round Jewish population, is the focal point of the Catskill Mountain resort area. It has been called at different times, "the borscht belt," "the sour cream sierras," or "the Jewish alps." The area is bounded roughly by Ellenville on Route 52 through Fallsburgh to Liberty and beyond, then south past Swan Lake, back east to Monticello, and along Route 17 back to the Ellenville area. Once there were more than 1,200 hotels and nearly as many rooming houses in and around Hunter and Tannersville, in Greene County; Ellenville and neighboring communities in Ulster County, and Fallsburgh, Livingston Manor, Ferndale, Kiamesha Lake, Liberty, and others in Sullivan County. Generations of Jewish families from New York, Philadelphia, and New Jersey came every summer for periods ranging from two weeks to the whole summer. Kosher cooking and Jewish-style cuisine, Jewish comedians, entertainers, and Broadway stars, many of whom got their start in the "borscht circuit," were the principal attractions. The area featured fresh air and more swimming pools, golf courses, tennis courts, and other recreational facilities per square mile than in any other comparable area in America. Of the estimated 500 hotels that catered to Jews in the 1950s, all but about 75 went broke as a new generation of Jews, no longer concerned with kosher food, passed up "the mountains" for packaged vacations to Israel, Europe, the West Indies, and to prominent American resorts which formerly excluded Jews. Only the larger hotels survived and they became even bigger and more posh, offering more and more amenities. In prior years they were exclusively summer resorts. Presently they are vacations spots with skiing, tobogganing, ice skating, conventions, programs for "singles" and divorcees, and special weekends for guests with special interests ranging from bridge and the stock market to United Jewish Appeal and other Jewish organizations.

The Catskill Mountain region was the first "American summer Jerusalem" for upper middle-class German Jews who, in the 1880s and 1890s, found themselves excluded from such places as Saranac Lake, Lake Placid, and Saratoga Springs. At the turn of the century East European Jews fleeing the summer heat of the big cities and the sweltering ghettos came to this region as farmers. Many of them bought property from gentile farmers happy to get a good price for their land. Loans and technical guidance were provided by the Jewish Agricultural Society. When the Jewish farmers were unable to get fire insurance, they formed their own cooperative company whose regulations were drawn up in Yiddish. Unable to make a living from agriculture, the Jewish farmers eked out their income by catering to summer boarders. Abraham Brickman, founder of Brickman's Hotel, had been a beet farmer in Poland, bought a 320-acre dairy farm around South Fallsburgh. Joseph Slutsky, who started The Nevele, began by picking rocks for neighboring farmers at 5¢ a bushel until he saved enough to buy his own farm. Murray Posner, Brickman's grandson, sold his cows in 1920 and used the proceeds to build a new 30-room hotel. The Kutshers expanded from a ten-room farm house built in 1908 into a number of small buildings by 1921. The Grossingers also started as farmers and boarding house keepers.

Hundreds of small hotels opened in the 1920s, mostly white wooden structures offering little more than fresh air, kosher food, milk direct from the cow, and such simple pastimes as hiking and berry picking. In the 1930s the hotels added athletic and recreational facilities, a social staff, organized activities, music, and dancing. The entertainment was often by young performers who went on to become world famous. Though the building boom produced indoor plumbing and golf courses, some of the hotels went bankrupt during the depression.

The Concord, Grossinger's only rival in size, comfort, and range of amenities, was reborn during the depression when Arthur Winarik, who had become a millionaire selling hair tonic, foreclosed a mortgage he held on The New Concord Hotel. When it burned down in the 1940s, he built the present palatial Concord Hotel and Country Club. Luxury became the order of the day in the 1960s. At least 25 hotels each costing several million dollars were built anew with plush accommodations equal to those at any resort in the country. The opening of the New York State Thruway and the Quickway brought the Catskills within two hours driving time of the greater New York area, and stimulated a fantastic growth of the "Borscht Belt" where the larger places added night clubs, and convention and sports facilities. Despite the changed vacation habits of Jews, the bigger resorts are prospering due to smart merchandising. As people began taking shorter but more numerous vacations, the Catskill hotels encouraged weekend guests, especially for winter sports, and for Passover and Rosh Hashanah. But the most important asset has been conventions. About a third of the guests at the large hotels are non-Jewish. Though hotels made their reputation catering to Jewish families and providing kosher food, they found little objection to kosher or Jewish style cuisine on the part of guests who arrived as delegates to conventions such as the Knights of Columbus, Jehovah's Witnesses, Lutheran school teachers, Sons of Italy, gasoline dealers, IBM salesmen, etc. Grossinger's alone books 400 conventions a year. Many comedians playing the "Borscht Belt" no longer deal in Jewish ethnic humor.

Besides the resort giants like Grossinger's, The Concord, Kutsher's, The Nevele, Tamarack Lodge, Brown's Country Club, Brickman's, and The Pines, there are a number of other large places that still cater to exclusively observant Jews. Largest of these is the *glatt* kosher Pioneer Country Club, which receives no guests from sundown Friday to sundown Saturday, and where guests cannot pay their bills during the Sabbath. This hotel also has a separate synagogue building, a sukka seating 500 (with a plastic cover if it rains), "kosher" elevators automatically controlled to stop at each floor, and a *mikveh*. Some of the closed hotels have reopened as religiously oriented children's camps and camps that specialize in particular interests—sports, music, weight reduction, etc. There are said to be nearly 100 full-time summer camps for children in what were once small hotels. The convention business necessitated the opening of a jetport in an area between Grossinger's and The Concord. In many parts of the Catskills new ethnic communities have sprung up where Italians, blacks, French, Irish, Poles, Greeks, Russians, and Ukrainians have belatedly discovered the mountain resorts.

Temple Sholom, Port Jervis and Dillon Rds.

MOUNTAINDALE

Hebrew Congregation of Mountaindale.

MOUNT MARSHALL

The 25th highest peak (4,360 feet) in the Adirondack Mountains, is named for the late Robert Marshall, a well-known forester, explorer, and conservationist, who was a son of Louis Marshall.

NANUET

Nanuet Hebrew Center, 34 South Middletown Rd.

NAPLES

Morton Brodsky Reception Pavilion at the Warren Cutler Boy Scout Reservation was a gift of Morton Brodsky, a Rochester civic leader.

NEWBURGH

Cong. Agudas Achim, 25 William St.

Gomez House, the oldest structure built and occupied by Colonial Jews in North America and still standing, is located on U. S. Route 9W, 1.4 miles south of the village of Marlboro, on Millhouse Rd., and a little more than six miles north of Newburgh. It is now the residence of Jeffrey Starin, a Newburgh realtor. The stone house was erected some time between 1717 and 1720 by Lewis Gomez and his son, Daniel, as a combined trading post, blockhouse, and residence at the juncture of several Hudson River Indian trails. A wealthy merchant of Sephardic ancestry, he had lived in Spain, France, and England before he came to Colonial New York in 1705, with special privileges assigned to him by Queen Anne of England. An Indian trader who had extensive dealings with the tribes between New York and Albany, Gomez and his sons also provided goods to the British military forces north of Albany and in Canada. One of the seven Jews who contributed to the public fund raised for the erection of the steeple of New York's Trinity Church, Gomez was one of the leaders of the city's Congregation Shearith Israel, oldest existing Jewish congregation in North America. He was one of the five members who bought the site on which the congregation erected the first building designed as a synagogue in North America. When it was consecrated in 1730, Gomez was its president. When the present New York City building at Central Park West and 70th St. was dedicated in 1897, the president, Dr. Horatio Gomez, was a direct descendant of Lewis Gomez. The Gomez House was built in what was once known as the Devil's Dance Chamber, a hollow where Indians gathered for tribal rites. The stream that ran past the house and through northern Newburgh to join the Hudson River at Marlboro was for many year's known as Jew's Creek, and it was so identified on early maps and records. It is now known as Acker's Creek. The house is now a private residence to which a second story has been added. Gomez' sons sold it in 1748. One of Gomez' kinsmen was among the 24 founders of the New York Stock Exchange. Lewis Gomez' grandson, Isaac, was one of the Revolutionary War patriots who left New York rather than live there under the British occupation.

Jewish Community Center, 360 Powell Ave.

Stern Parking Plaza, between the Hudson River and Front St., on both sides of 4th St., is a memorial to Frederick Stern, merchant, civil leader, philanthropist, member of the board of education, and son of Ferdinand Stern, a founder of Temple Beth Jacob.

Temple Beth Jacob, 344 Gidney Ave.

United Jewish Charities, 360 Powell Ave.

NEW CITY

New City Jewish Center, Old Schoolhouse Rd.

Temple Beth Sholom, 228 N. Hempstead Rd.

NEW PALTZ

Cong. Ahavas Achim, 1 Main St.

Hillel Foundation at State College at New Paltz.

NEW SQUARE

Chasidic village of 1,300 named for the Ukrainian shtetl of Skvira, was founded in 1961 by the followers of the late Skvirer Rebbe, Rabbi David Twersky. Established on a former 130-acre dairy farm 40 miles north of New York City and close by the heavily Jewish town of Spring Valley, New Square was supposed to be named New Skvira but a clerk in the Ramapo Township office misspelled it and the name became New Square. A modern village of single family Cape Cod style homes and garden apartments, all outfitted with two stoves and two kitchen sinks, New Square is a recreated European shtetl whose residents live a sheltered life in order to practice their own form of ultra-Orthodox Judaism. All of the inhabitants dress in the familiar Chasidic style. There is no television anywhere, comparatively few radios, and only emergency vehicles are allowed on Saturdays and Jewish festivals. A gasoline station in one corner of the village is shut on Friday nights and Saturdays. The only public buildings are the Rebbe's house, the synagogue at 15 Roosevelt Ave., and two schools, one for boys and one for girls. The Rebbe's house has a special rear wing which serves as both a reception room, and, with its sliding roof open, as a sukka. The large and airy two-story synagogue is built in the style of the Chasidic *shtiebel*. Instead of pews in the main hall, there are long tables, flanked by low, backless benches. Another synagogue, known as "the mobile schule," leaves New Square every morning except Saturday, carrying men to work in New York City. The village-owned bus is outfitted as a synagogue and the passengers recite the morning and afternoon prayers going and coming. In New Square itself the only industries are a gem-cutting shop and a watch assembly plant. There is also a small supermarket. Some residents work in Jewish-owned establishments in nearby Spring Valley. Yiddish is the village's language but some residents speak Hebrew and Hungarian. All, however, are fluent in English.

NIAGARA FALLS

Jewish Federation, 309 United Office Bldg.

Robert Moses Niagara Power Plant, part of the huge Canadian-American hydroelectric power system, is named for the man who was chairman of the New York State Power Authority when the plant was completed in 1965. Robert Moses Parkway runs along the American side of the Niagara River.

Temple Beth El, 720 Ashland Ave.

Temple Beth Israel, Madison and College Aves.

NORWICH

Norwich Jewish Center, 72 S. Broad St.

OGDENSBURG

Cong. Anshe Zophen, 416 Greene St.

OLEAN

B'nai Israel Cong., 127 South Barry St., was founded by Jewish merchants attracted to the area by the short-lived oil boom of the 1870s in Allegheny and Cattaraugus Counties. A number of Jews worked in the oil fields and several became quite rich when their wells paid off.

ONEONTA

Temple Beth El, 83 Chestnut St.

ORANGEBURG

Orangetown Jewish Center, Independence Ave.

OSWEGO

Brith Shalom Cemetery, a fenced off section of a Christian cemetery about 1,000 feet beyond the city limits on Route 27, contains the graves of 15 Jewish refugees who died at Fort Ontario where the U. S. government established a temporary camp in 1945 for 1,000 specially selected refugees from Europe, among them many Jews. The cemetery, which has graves dating back to the 1840s, was established by Cong. B'rith Shalom, which went out of existence at the turn of the century.

Cong. Adath Israel, 35 East Oneida St.

Hillel Foundation at State College of New York at Oswego, Hewitt Union Bldg.

PALISADES

Cong. Gemiluth Chesed, Oak Tree Rd.

PARKSVILLE

Cong. Tifereth Israel Anshei Parksville.

PEARL RIVER

Beth Am Temple, 60 Madison Ave.

Henry Kaufmann Campgrounds, Mildred Goetz Site, 667 Blauvelt Rd., is one of three permanent day camp sites in the Greater New York area established through gifts of Henry Kaufmann, Pittsburgh philanthropist, and administered by the Federation of Jewish Philanthropies of New York. The 100-acre camp site serves children from YM & YWHAs in the Bronx, upper Manhattan, Westchester, and Flushing.

PLATTSBURGH

Hillel Foundation at State College of New York at Plattsburgh, 5 Adams Pl. N.

Temple Beth El, Marcy Lane and Bowman St., is the oldest Jewish congregation in the Adirondacks, dating from 1862. The Jewish settlement here had its beginnings in the 1840s.

POMONA

Pomona Jewish Center, Pomona Rd.

PORT JERVIS

Cejwin Camps, one of the pioneers in integrating Jewish education with summer camping, was founded in 1919 as an outgrowth of a summer vacation program of the Central Jewish Institute of New York, which went out of existence 30 years ago. The camp gets its name from the cable address of the founding group.

Temple Beth El, 88 East Main St.

POTSDAM

Cong. Beth El, 81 Market St.

POUGHKEEPSIE

Cong. Brethren of Israel (Vassar Temple), 140 Hooker Ave.
Cong. Shomre Israel, 18 Park Ave.
Hillel Foundation at Vassar College, 360 Hooker Ave.
Jewish Community Center, 110 Grand Ave.
Jewish Welfare Fund, 110 Grand Ave.
Temple Beth El, 130 Grand Ave.

PUTNAM VALLEY

Reform Temple of Putnam Valley, Church Rd.

RENSSELAERVILLE

Gladys and Roger W. Straus Institute on Man and Science, under-written by Mrs. Roger W. Straus, wife of the late financier and philan-thropist, is a center for advanced study in human relations. One of the institute's main buildings is the Guggenheim Pavilion, named for members of the family of mining tycoons and art patrons. Mrs. Straus, a member of the Guggenheim family, heads the Daniel and Florence Guggenheim Founda-tion.

ROCHESTER

Beth Joseph Center, 1150 St. Paul St.
Bureau of Jewish Education, 456 E. Main St.
Howard Cohn Memorial Building of David Kaufman Post of Jewish War Veterans of the U.S., 60 Grove St., occupies what was once the Zion-Concordia Lutheran Church.
Cong. A.A.A. Kipel Volin, 703 Joseph Ave.
Cong. Beth Israel, 184 Rhinecliff Dr.
Cong. Beth Sholom, 1161 Monroe Ave.
Cong. B'nai Israel-Ahavas Achim, 692 Joseph Ave.
Cong. Light of Israel, 206 Norton St.
Cong. Tifereth Israel, 271 Dartmouth St.
Hillel Foundation at Rochester Institute of Technology, Lomb Memorial Dr.
Hillel Foundation at University of Rochester, Interfaith Chapel, on east bank of Genesee River, facing the River Campus. Hillel at Monroe Community College is also located here.
Hillel School, 2131 Elmwood Ave.
Interfaith Chapel at University of Rochester, a nondenominational chapel that serves as a center for the university's religious program of worship, teaching, counseling, and service, is constructed on three levels, beginning at the river level and ascending to the campus level. Four concrete arches rise from a base into a tower of four large stained glass windows which gather light into the main sanctuary. The main sanctuary on the campus level seats 600. The "river chapel" on the lowest level seats 300. Attached to the

chapel are three wings of "meditation chapels."

Jewish Community Center, (see Brighton).

Jewish Community Federation, 440 E. Main St.

Jewish Family Service, 440 E. Main St.

Jewish Home and Infirmary, 1180 St. Paul St.

Jewish Ledger, 721 Monroe Ave.

Joseph Ave. is named for Joseph London who was a branch manager of the Genesee Valley Union Trust Co. for more than 40 years beginning in 1923.

Leopold St. Synagogue, 30 Leopold St., has a synagogue which dates from 1866 and which is registered as a national historic place.

Rush Rhees Library of the University of Rochester, River Campus, houses the letters and papers of the late Louis Wiley, business manager of the *New York Times* from 1905 until his death in 1935. He was one of the best known newspaper executives in the country. Kept in the Local History Room, the Wiley papers contain documents, letters, clippings, and other items relating to Wiley's relationship with notables in all walks of life. Wiley, who was born in Horning, N.Y., and studied at the University of Rochester, edited the *Jewish Tidings* in Rochester and worked on newspapers in that city for ten years. He was the founder of the Rochester Press Club in 1888.

Talmudical Institute of Upstate New York, 138 Pinnacle Rd.

Temple Beth David, (see Brighton).

Temple Beth El, 139 Winton Rd. S., has an Ark of Israeli Galilean marble standing 32 feet high and resembling an open Torah scroll. The Eternal Light is an antique silver lamp crafted in Hamburg, Germany, in 1699. Two great windows which frame the Ark are each 30 feet high and 8 feet wide. They illustrate the two major precepts of Judaism: the window on the left carries the legend in Hebrew, *And thou shall love the Lord, thy God;* the one on the right has the legend, *Thy shalt love thy neighbor as thyself.* Ten tall, narrow windows represent the Ten Commandments.

Temple Beth Hamedresh-Beth Israel, 1369 East Ave.

Temple Brith Kodesh, (see Brighton).

Temple Sinai, (see Brighton).

War Memorial, 100 Exchange St., honoring Rochester's war dead, houses athletic events, exhibits, and conventions. On the Broad St. side of the building, in an area used for annual Veterans' Day ceremonies, there is a plaque honoring the four chaplains of World War II who died aboard the USS *Dorchester*, a troop ship which was torpedoed on Feb. 3, 1943. There is a monument to the Four Chaplains in White Haven Memorial Park, a cemetery located at 210 Marsh Rd., in Pittsford, a Rochester suburb.

Workmen's Circle Center, 1076 Clinton Ave. N.

ROME

Cong. Adas Israel, 705 Hickory St.

ST. BONAVENTURE

St. Bonaventure University, a Catholic institution, has the Friedsam Library, named for Michael Friedsam, Jewish department store owner (B. Altman & Co., in New York City), who not only contributed the building but also an important art collection from his home, including two Rembrandts, a Rubens, a Bellini, an Aspertini, and a prized collection of Chinese porcelain. Friedsam's bequests also helped establish the Board of Jewish Education of New York City.

SARANAC LAKE

Jewish Community Center, 13 Church St.

William Morris Memorial Park and Children's Playground honors the well-known theatrical manager who founded the Jewish Community Center and established the Hebrew Memorial Cemetery.

Saranac Lake Free Public Library has the William Morris Collection of Adirondackana, a gift of the founder of the Jewish Theatrical Guild of America.

SARATOGA SPRINGS

Simon Baruch Research Institute, south of Marrin Ave., at the traffic oval, was erected by the New York State Commission that administers the Saratoga Springs Reservation, in honor of Dr. Simon Baruch, German-born physician, surgeon in the Confederate Army, public health pioneer, and the man responsible for the development of cardiac therapy at the Saratoga spa. Dr. Baruch, the father of Bernard M. Baruch, was one of the first practitioners of hydrotherapy in America. The institute houses a laboratory, library, little theatre, auditorium, and administrative headquarters of the entire spa. Bernard M. Baruch was chairman of a special committee created by the State Legislature in 1929 to study opportunities for converting Saratoga into a European-type spa. The commission's work led to the creation of the state reservation

Cong. Sharei Tefilla, 260 S. Broadway.

National Museum of Racing, Union Ave. and Ludlow St., opposite the Saratoga Race Course, has on permanent display a portrait of August Belmont, the House of Rothschild's 19th century representative in the U.S., who became the father of American horse racing. The museum's hall of fame honors jockey Walter Miller and trainers Hirsch Jacobs and Maxmillian "Max" Hirsch.

Temple Sinai, 509 Broadway.

SCHENECTADY

Cong. Adath Israel, 872 Albany St.
Cong. Agudath Achim, 2117 Eastern Pkwy.
Hillel Foundation at Union College, 1031 Hickory Rd.
Jewish Community Center, 2565 Balltown Rd.

Jewish Community Council, 2565 Balltown Rd.

Jewish World, 416 Smith St.

Schaffer Library at Union College was a gift of Henry Schaffer, Russian-born immigrant who became a millionaire through a chain of supermarkets (see also Albany).

Schenectady Museum, Nott Terrace Hts., has a plaque in the lobby recording the fact that Henry Schaffer made possible the acquisition of the museum's site.

Temple Gates of Heaven, 852 Ashmore Ave.

Union College's Nott Memorial Bldg., at the center of the campus, has in its dome a Talmudic verse inscribed in Hebrew. It is from Pirke Aboth: *The day is short, the work is great, the laborers are sluggish, the reward is much and the Master of the House is urgent.*

SENECA FALLS

Site of first convention for women's rights, commemorated by a state historic marker at the corner of Fall and Mynderse Sts., is a reminder that one of the early militant women's rights leaders was Ernestine Rose, who for some reason did not attend the historic 1848 conference. Long before this conference, however, Mrs. Rose, the rebellious, agnostic daughter of a Polish rabbi, had been one of the most active feminist leaders of America. From 1850-1869, when she left the U.S. for England, Mrs. Rose was at the side of Susan B. Anthony and the whole galaxy of women who fought to achieve the economic, political, and social emancipation of their sex. There was great surprise when Mrs. Rose was not included in the first election to the Women's Hall of Fame in Seneca Falls.

SHARON SPRINGS

This once fashionable turn-of-the-century spa that attracted the rich and rheumatic, is now a sleepy village of faded hotels and boarding houses, the majority of whose guests are European Jews of modest means who arrived in the U. S. after World War II.

SOUTH FALLSBURGH

South Fallsburgh Synagogue, P. O. Box 658.

Yeshiva Gedolah Limtzuyonim and Zichron Moshe High School, Laurel Park Rd.

SPRING VALLEY

Jews first came to Spring Valley in the 1930s when the area had more than a score of kosher hotels. The first, Singer's Lakeside Manor Hotel, was founded by the late Sarah Singer who settled here before World War I. Gradually, many of the summer guests became permanent residents who gave the community a decided Orthodox cast. The neighboring town of Monsey, which also has a large array of Orthodox institutions, has a growing

Jewish population that accounts for half the total population.

Cong. B'nai Yechiel, 80 Washington Ave.

Cong. Chachmei Sfard, 7 Fanley Ave.

Cong. Kehilath Israel, Old Nyack Tpke.

Cong. Ohev Sholom, 141 Linden Ave.

Cong. Ramat Sholom, Lomond Ave., is an unstructured, unaffiliated congregation of young families most of whom live in the well-to-do Dexter Park development. The congregation has no rabbi and uses lay leaders. It also extemporizes in developing its services. Most of the other congregations in Spring Valley are Orthodox.

Cong. Shaarey Tfiloh, 972 S. Main St.

Cong. Sons of Israel, 80 Williams Ave.

Cong. Zemach David of New Square, 13 Truman Ave.

Finkelstein Memorial Library, South Madison Ave., the town's public library, was built in 1941 by the Finkelstein Foundation, comprised of Mrs. Sarah Finkelstein and her sons, Charles, Robert, Jack, and Abraham. They gave the library as a memorial to Joseph N. Finkelstein, husband and father of the foundation members. A new wing erected in 1961 memorializes Abraham D. Finkelstein.

Hebrew High School of Rockland County, 250 N. Main St.

Jewish Community Center, 250 N. Main St.

Temple Beth El, 415 Viola Rd.

Workmen's Circle Center, 44 Decatur Ave.

Yeshiva of New Square, 91 Washington Ave.

Yeshiva of Spring Valley, 115 N. Main St.

Young Israel, 23 Union Rd.

SHUSHAN

Washington County Village of 275, near the Vermont state line, is named for the Persian city connected with the story of Purim.

SUFFERN

Cong. Sons of Israel, Suffern Pl.

SWAN LAKE

Cong. Ahavas Shulem.

SYRACUSE

Cong. Ahavath Achim, 356 Mountainview Ave.

Cong. Anshe Sfard, 2013 E. Genesee St.

Max Gilbert Hebrew Academy, 450 Kimber Rd.

Jewish Community Center, 2223 E. Genesee St.

Jewish Community Council, 201 East Jefferson St.

Jewish Family Service Bureau, 316 S. Warren St.

Jewish Home of Central New York, 4101 E. Genesee St. The Kaplan

Annex, providing housing for the Jewish aged, is next door.

Jewish War Veterans Building, 2000 E. Genesee St.

Jewish Welfare Federation, 201 E. Jefferson St.

T. Aaron Levy Junior High School, Fellows Ave. and Harvard Pl., is named for Professor T. Aaron Levy, a one-time president of the Syracuse Board of Education. A distinguished lawyer and active Jewish communal leader, Professor Levy was on the faculty of the Syracuse University Law School for more than 20 years.

Louis Marshall Building of the N. Y. State College of Forestry, south of the Hendricks Chapel, is named for the late Jewish leader, lawyer, and defender of the state natural resources and wildlife. Inside the foyer is an oil painting of Marshall. He was a passionate lover of the outdoors, and particularly of the Adirondack forests. He was for many years chairman of the board of trustees of the College of Forestry. Under his leadership it became recognized as the premier institution of its kind in the country. When Franklin D. Roosevelt was governor of New York in 1930, he recommended to the State Legislature an appropriation of $600,000 for a new building to be named for Marshall, who died a year earlier. Born in Syracuse in 1856, Marshall was already a well-known constitutional lawyer when he settled in New York in 1894. For 35 years he was involved in a great variety of cases concerned with basic constitutional principles. Among the hundreds of suits he argued before the highest Federal and state courts were those affecting the constitutionality of statutes on bonus payments for veterans, workmen's compensation, alien immigration, against segregation of blacks, naturalization of Orientals, inheritance taxes, abolition of private and parochial schools, and conservation of natural resources. Marshall's most famous legal victory was won before the United States Supreme Court which upheld his contention as to the illegality of an Oregon law denying Catholics the right to send their children to parochial schools.

Marshall was both a conservative Republican and a champion of civil rights for all. He was one of the defenders of the five Socialist members of the New York State Legislature when an effort was made to deny them their seats. He had a decisive role in settling the bitter 1910 and 1919 clothing strikes in New York. Marshall was said to have been the only New Yorker to sit in three of the state's constitutional conventions—1890, 1894, and 1915. A founder of the American Jewish Committee and its president from 1912 until his death in 1929, Marshall was one of the principal leaders of and spokesmen for American Jewry in the two decades before his death. His unique status as a force in American Jewish life was epitomized by a wit who remarked that American Jewry was "ruled by Marshall law." Marshall was a key figure in the successful fight to get Congress to abrogate the Treaty of 1832 with Russia because of her refusal to recognize the American passport in the case of Jews. He battled militantly against restrictive immigration laws and intervened with Presidents William Taft and Woodrow Wilson on behalf of Balkan Jewry. On the outbreak of World War I, Marshall became president of the American Jewish Relief Committee. When that body merged with the American Jewish Joint Distribution Committee, he continued as a leader of the new agency.

In the long struggle over the creation of an American Jewish Congress, Marshall opposed the nationalistic objectives of its advocates. Ultimately, he accepted the Congress idea with the understanding that the Congress was to be a temporary body that would disband after the peace treaties were adopted. It was at that time that he learned to speak and read Yiddish in order to work in closer harmony with Yiddish-speaking leaders. Marshall went to Paris as a delegate of the Congress and fought to achieve unity of action among the quarreling Jewish delegations from various countries. The minority clauses in the postwar treaties and in the League of Nations agreements were in a measure his achievement. After the war, Marshall fought the Ku Klux Klan and the anti-Semitism of Henry Ford. The auto magnate's public retraction of his anti-Jewish libels was addressed to Marshall. Never a Zionist, Marshall did support efforts to rebuild Palestine. Before the Balfour Declaration of 1917, he was giving aid to Haifa Technical Institute and the Jewish Agricultural Experiment Station. After the Balfour Declaration was issued, he urged the American Jewish Committee to endorse it. Marshall took part in the creation of the Palestine Survey Commission. On the strength of that body's report, he became an indefatigable advocate of an enlarged Jewish Agency to include Zionists and non-Zionists. His last public act was to sign the constitution of the new Jewish Agency in Zurich. A deeply religious man, Marshall was for many years president of New York City's Temple Emanu-El. Simultaneously, he was chairman of the board of the Jewish Theological Seminary of America. He was also one of the leaders of the Jewish Community Center movement, having helped to establish the predecessor of the National Jewish Welfare Board. He also helped make possible the establishment of the Hebrew Press of the Jewish Publication Society of America. □

A. Clement Silverman Public Health Hospital, Renwick Ave., is named for the late Dr. A. Clement Silverman, a pioneer in pediatrics and former deputy city health commissioner.

Suburban Jewish Center, Vine St., North Syracuse.

Syracuse University

Syracuse University has a number of places of specific interest: Coyne Stadium, a major practice football field on the university campus, was a gift of J. Stanley Coyne, president of Coyne Industrial Laundry, Inc.; ●Sol Feinstone Collection of Early Americana, a gift of Sol Feinstone of Washington Crossing, Pa., includes some of the Haym Salomon papers. It is housed in the Ernest Stevenson Bird Library, on the main campus, in the Feinstone Room; ●Arnold Grant Law School Auditorium, is named for a university trustee who gave the university nearly $1 million; ●Haft

Dormitory, 795 Ostrom Ave., is a cooperative women's living center that memorializes Dr. Henry H. Haft, soldier and teacher, whose brother, Morris, a New York clothing manufacturer, erected the building; •Joe and Emily Lowe Art Center, in the university's art exhibit area, honors Mr. and Mrs. Lowe; •Hillel Foundation, Hendricks Memorial Chapel. •S. I. Newhouse School of Public Communications in one of the great institutions of its kind, especially on the graduate, postgraduate, and research levels. The first unit of the $15 million complex was a gift of Samuel I. Newhouse, owner of some 20 dailies, a number of magazines, and radio and television stations. It was dedicated in 1964 by President Lyndon B. Johnson. The three main buildings of the school are known as Newhouse I, Newhouse II, and Newhouse III. Mr. and Mrs. Newhouse also gave the university several million dollars for Newhouse journalism scholarships. •J. Robert Rubin Experimental Theatre, 820 E. Genesee St., is a memorial to the late vice-president of Loew's, Inc., who also gave the university the William Rubin Law School Reading Room in memory of his brother. ☐

Temple Adath Jeshurun, 450 Kimber Rd.

Temple Society of Concord, 910 Madison St., is the second oldest congregation in the state outside of New York City, having been founded in 1839. A large bronze statue of Moses by Ivan Mestrovic stands in the lobby.

Young Israel, 2200 E. Genesee St.

THIELLS

Cong. B'nai Israel of Letchworth Village is the only synagogue for the mentally retarded. It is located on Willow Grove Rd., in the center of Letchworth Village, a state institution. One-fourth of the 4,000 residents are Jewish.

TONAWANDA

Temple Beth El, 2368 Eggert Rd., was the oldest Jewish congregation in Buffalo before it moved to the suburbs in the early 1960s, having been founded in 1847.

TROY

Cong. Beth Israel Bikur Cholim, 27 Centerview Ave.

Cong. Beth Tephila, 82 River St.

Daughters of Sarah Jewish Home, Upper Tibbits Ave.

Hillel Foundation at Rensselaer Polytechnic Institute, Chaplain's Office.

Jewish Community Center, 2500 21st St.

Jewish Community Council, 2500 21st St.

Temple Berith Sholom, 167 3rd St., dedicated in 1870, is the oldest synagogue building in the state.

Temple Beth El, 409 Hoosick St.

TUPPER LAKE
Cong. Beth Joseph, Mill St., cor. Lake St.

TUXEDO PARK
This once exculsive Protestant enclave for the rich, now has about 15 Jewish families, mostly professionals. One of them gave the village's first bar mitzvah party in April, 1974, following religious services at Cong. Sons of Israel in nearby Suffern.

UPPER NYACK
Cong. Sons of Israel, 300 N. Broadway, is known as the "temple in the park" because it is located at the core of a wooded area. In the sanctuary is a stained glass window 51 feet wide and 43 feet high.
Temple Beth Torah, 330 N. Broadway.

UTICA
Cong. House of Jacob, 14 Clinton Pl.
Cong. Tifereth Zvi, 313 James St.
Hillel Day School, 14 Clinton Pl.
Jewish Community Center, 2310 Oneida St.
Jewish Community Council, 2310 Oneida St.
Charles T. Stirin Home, Tilden Ave.
Temple Beth El, 1607 Genesee St.
Temple Emanu-El, 2710 Genesee St., has a facade of field stone broken by a huge replica of the Tablets of the Law, and an ingeniously wrought Star of David backed by cathedral glass.

WALDEN
Cong. Beth Hillel, 20 Pine St.

WARWICK
Kutz Camp Institute of Union of American Hebrew Congregations.

WATERTOWN
Cong. Degel Israel, 557 Thompson Blvd.

WAVERLY
Cong. Beth Israel, 325 Chemung St.

WAWARSING
"Sholam Road," appears on a small marker on a blacktop road in the town of Wawarsing, along New York City's Roundout Reservoir, 11 miles from Ellenville. It is the only reminder of the first Jewish agricultural colony in the United States, established in 1838. In the panic year of 1837, 11 Jews from New York City's Congregations Anshe Chesed and B'nai Jeshurun,

bought 489 acres of virgin land in the township of Wawarsing, Ulster County, as the site of a farm colony they named, sight unseen, Sholom. (Various writers, documents, and records also spell it Sholem and Sholam.) A twelfth purchaser acquired 187 more acres in 1840. The settlers arrived in 1838 and found their property was isolated, rock-strewn barren land, totally unsuited for farming. Nevertheless, they cleared the land, built roads, erected eight frame houses on stone foundations, set aside a burial ground, and built a tiny synagogue with a stone fence in front. The colony also boasted of an art museum and a general store with a reception room where customers were served tea and cakes. The synagogue was called Shomere Haberit, and it applied to Anshe Chesed Congregation for the loan of a Torah. The community had its own *shochet* and cantor, Marcus van Geldern, who had filled both posts at B'nai Jeshurun and Shearith Israel, and later served as president of Anshe Chesed. Poor soil, remote markets, and lack of agricultural know-how made the settlers' road thorny. Nine of the colonists lost their land by foreclosure in 1842. Three others sold out a year later, but several stayed on until 1851. The colony survived as long as it did because the settlers supplemented their meagre farm income by manufacturing goose quill pens and fur caps, by cobbling, tailoring, and peddling used clothing they acquired in New York City. Gradually, Sholom fell into ruins. Until 1905, a U.S. topographical map listed a place called "Sholam." Natives of the area point out Sholam Hill as the site of the now vanished colony. In 1921, Gabriel Davidson, director of the Jewish Agricultural Society of America, found furniture from Sholom's houses in possession of families in Naponach. Several Wawarsing families claim descent from the Sholomites. "Sholam Road" alongside the Roundout Reservoir leads to the ruins of the colony—a pile of stones that has been identified as the rubble from the synagogue's stone steps and fence. Still standing are two pointed granite slabs, remains of the Sholom cemetery. For many years after the Jews left, the synagogue was used as a dance hall by people from the neighboring villages. The ruins are located off a dirt road that runs into Sholam Road, which intersects with New York State Route 55, adjacent to the Roundout Reservoir.

WEST POINT

United States Military Academy

A good part of the site of the U.S. Military Academy was mortgaged to Eleazar Levy, a New York businessman, before it became a military reservation in 1778. In May, 1772, Levy lent 1,000 pounds on the land. In 1779, after the American army took over Levy's land, using the timber for fuel and fortifications, he appealed for redress to John Jay, president of the Continental Congress, and again to Congress in 1783. In 1779, Levy was promised action after the war, and in 1783 he was told "it is not expedient for Congress to take any order therein." So Levy was unable to ever collect his money or regain his property. Major David Salisbury Franks (see Ohio and Pennsylvania), an officer in the American Revolution, was appointed aide-de-camp to General Benedict Arnold before the latter received command of West Point in August, 1780. The Jewish officer, who was a member of Arnold's official family at West Point, was completely exonerated of any previous knowledge of Arnold's treason.

Academic Board Room, a vaulted administration building on Thayer Rd., has a massive carved stone mantel over the fireplace, a feature of which are bas-reliefs of nine warriors of history—three pagan, three Jewish, and three Christian. The three Jewish military leaders are Joshua, David, and Judas Maccabeus—side by side with Hector, Alexander, Caesar, King Arthur, Charlemagne, and Godfrey de Bouillon.

Old Cadet Chapel, the dominant structure of the academy, rising 300 feet above the Hudson River, has affixed to its inside left wall, facing the pulpit, a plaque commemorating the members of the first class of the U. S. Military Academy in 1802, Joseph G. Swift, a Christian, and Simon M. Levy, a Jew. The plaque was a gift of the American Jewish Tercentenary Committee in 1954. After obtaining his commission, Levy became an instructor at the Academy. Because of ill health he resigned in 1805 and died in 1807. There are many stained glass windows, with the upper panels depicting Old Testament figures. A number of books mistakenly reported that Levy had fought at the Battle of Maumee Rapids before entering the Academy. The error arose from the misapplication of a footnote in General Cullum's *Biographical Register of Officers and Graduates of the U.S.M.A.* The footnote about the battle applies to Walter K. Armistead, whose name follows immediately after that of Levy in the register. There is nothing to indicate that Levy ever participated in active military operations.

In the Academy Library there is a letter written on October 6, 1779 by George Washington from his headquarters at West Point to Gen. Nathaniel Greene informing him that "considerable" French sea and land forces had arrived to help fight the British. The rare document was presented to West Point in 1965 by Sol Feinstone, a naturalized American citizen who arrived alone in this country at the age of 14, in 1902, with one cent in his pocket. A well-known collector of American documents, Feinstone has given West Point a number of other letters of great historic value. The constitution of the Military Philosophic Society, which was organized in 1802 by ten former cadets, one of whom was Simon Levy, whose name is signed to the constitution, is occasionally displayed in the library as part of special exhibits.

Grave of Col. David "Mickey" Marcus, an American army officer and World War II hero, who was one of the creators of the Israeli army, is in the Academy's historic cemetery where notable figures in American life are buried. Son of a Romanian immigrant, Marcus was born in 1901 in the Brownsville section of Brooklyn, New York. He was graduated from West Point in 1924 but resigned from the Army after two years to study law. In

1940, New York's Mayor Fiorello LaGuardia named Marcus commissioner of correction in charge of the city's prison system. When the country entered the war in 1941, he was appointed a lieutenant-colonel, and served in the Pacific on the staff of General George C. Marshall and in Normandy with airborne troops. He accompanied President Franklin D. Roosevelt to Yalta and Teheran, and later went to Potsdam with President Harry S. Truman. In the closing weeks of the war he helped draw up the surrender documents for Italy and Germany, outlined the program of military government for the occupied areas, and was with the American column that first came to the Dachau death camp. By V-E Day, Marcus was a full colonel. He returned home in 1947 to resume his law practice. However, at that point, the Jewish Agency sought his help and smuggled him into Palestine where he dictated the first military manuals published in Hebrew. He set up officers' training schools and advised the Haganah on the purchase and use of arms. After completing the blueprint and training of the army, he returned home to Brooklyn. By April, 1948, he was back in Palestine, this time as a commander of troops in the Israeli War of Independence. He was killed while leading Haganah forces on the Jerusalem front on June 10, 1949, just before the Arab-Israeli cease-fire became effective. He was buried at West Point with military honors. Colonel Marcus held the Distinguished Service Cross, second highest American military award, and the Bronze Star Medal, both for gallantry in action. His epitaph reads "A Soldier For All Humanity."

The Post Chapel, used by Protestant members of the garrison and their families has a Four Chaplains Memorial Window honoring the four chaplains of World War II who went down with the troop transport *Dorchester*.

As of 1976 there was no Jewish chapel at the Academy although Jewish worship services are held regularly under the leadership of part-time Jewish chaplains designated by the National Jewish Welfare Board Commission on Jewish Chaplaincy. Plans for the erection of a Jewish chapel and religious center were announced in 1976. □

WILLIAMSVILLE
Amherst Synagogue, 504 Frankhouser Rd.
Temple Beth Am, Sheridan Dr.
Young Israel of Greater Buffalo, 88 Sudbury Lane.

WINGDALE
Camp Ramah in the Berkshires.

WOODBOURNE
Cong. B'nai Israel.

WOODRIDGE
Woodridge Talmud Torah and Cong. Ohave Sholem, Maurice Rose St.

WESTCHESTER COUNTY

Westchester County was the first suburban area in which Jews from New York City settled, probably because it could be reached by land via The Bronx, the only one of the five boroughs that is not an island. In the 1930s, when Westchester's Jews numbered 30,000, all but a handful lived in Mount Vernon, Yonkers, New Rochelle, and White Plains, the business centers of the county. Most of the heads of Jewish families were in retail trade, the professions, or self-employed artisans; only a few commuted to New York. A number of wealthy Jews—notably, the Lehmans, the Warburgs, and the Ochses—owned extensive estates in the hilly area and along Long Island Sound. When the established golf and yacht clubs barred even the most influential Jews, Westchester became the site of some of the earliest Jewish golf and country clubs. Houses and apartments in some sections of the county also excluded Jews. Bronxville was the last holdout.

In the 1970s, Westchester had 165,000 Jews, almost as many as in Manhattan and more than those in The Bronx, from which many West-chester Jews came. Nearly half of all Westchester Jews live in White Plains, New Rochelle, Mount Vernon, and Yonkers. The other half is widely scattered, with substantial concentrations in Larchmont, Scarsdale, Port Chester, Rye, Mamaroneck, Tuckahoe, Pelham, Tarrytown, Harrison, and smaller but growing communities in Yorktown Heights, Chappaqua, Purchase, Hastings-On-Hudson, and Ardsley. In the 1970s, Jews represented nearly 16 percent of the county's total population. Further increase is expected in the next decade as more middle and upper middle-income Jewish families leave New York City.

Jewish beginnings in Westchester date back to the decade between 1715 and 1725 when Moses Levy, a leading New York City merchant, was a substantial property owner in what is now Rye. The first known Jewish residents in the county were the six sons of Michael Hays, a Dutch Jew, who settled near New Rochelle in 1720. They are said to have come in their own ship, bringing with them servants, cattle, seeds, and tools. The Hays brothers, who established themselves as farmers and merchants, had extensive holdings around Rye and Mount Pleasant (Pleasantville). One brother, Jacob, founded a family identified with Westchester County for more than 150 years. Judah Hays lived in Rye until about 1730 when he moved to New York, where his brothers, Solomon, Isaac, and Abraham, had preceded him. All members of New York's Congregation Shearith Israel, they became the forebears of a long line of Jewish notables.

Jacob's sons, Michael and David, Jr., were born in Pleasantville in the 1730s. The latter served with George Washington's forces in the French and Indian War and is said to have been present when the French defeated General Braddock in western Pennsylvania. Michael Hays was a farmer and merchant at Northcastle on the eve of the American Revolution. Tories drove him from his farm in 1776 and captured supplies he had assembled for the American army. After the Revolution he became active in politics. He is said to have helped draft the first constitution of New York State. In 1788 he was elected assessor of Pleasantville.

Asser Etting, father-in-law of David Hays, Sr., one of the original six Hays brothers, was in business at Northcastle in 1752, about the same time that Ralph Jacobs engaged in farming at Rye, and Meyer Benjamin at Yonkers. Abraham I. Abrahams, the most popular *mohel* in New York during the mid-18th century, recorded that he had officiated at the circumcision of Benjamin's son in 1758 at Yonkers. While David Hays, Sr., was serving with the American forces at the Battle of Long Island, Tories burned his farm house at Bedford. Mrs. Hays was in bed with a newborn infant when her Tory neighbors put her house to the torch. She had refused to disclose the hideout of a party of patriots attempting to drive cattle through the enemy lines to the American encampment at White Plains. Her seven-year old son, Jacob, later to become New York City's police chief, was one of those engaged in this hazardous foray.

The infant Hays was Benjamin Etting Hays, who lived in Pleasantville for nearly 75 years. An observant Jew and a qualified ritual slaughterer, he was known to his neighbors as "Uncle Ben the Jew, the best Christian in Westchester County." He donated the land on which Pleasantville's first high school was built. Benjamin's son, David, who owned a kosher hotel at Pleasantville in the 1840s, was the maternal grandfather of the late Arthur Hays Sulzberger, publisher of *The New York Times*.

Since all of these early Westchester Jewish settlers were members of Congregation Shearith Israel in New York, the synagogue leaders worried over the fact that because they lived so far away, they might be less inclined to pay their assessments. In 1736, Shearith Israel adopted a resolution pointing out that the cost of maintaining the synagogue required the assistance of "our brethren living in the country, even if their business and residence was not in the city." Twenty years later another resolution cautioned Westchester members against laxity in ritual and Sabbath observances.

Long before Westchester County became the seat of a number of important Jewish child care, medical, and old age institutions, a son-in-law of David Hays, Sr., put forth a scheme to establish in Pleasantville "the American Jewish Asylum," a sort of combined orphan home and trade school for Jewish boys and girls from all parts of the world. In the 1820s, Jacob S. Solis, who had married Charity Hays in Pleasantville in 1811, sent out a circular announcing his plan, but it never progressed beyond that stage.

Other Jewish families settled in Westchester County—Solomon Levy lived in Peekskill in the early 1800s, Samson Simson, one of the wealthiest and most prominent New York City Jews, exiled himself to Yonkers in 1813 after being injured in a street assault. In the late 18th century, Simson's father had acquired an estate that extended from Palisade Avenue to what is now the Saw Mill River Parkway. To that barony the son retired, living there with his sister and two grandchildren until 1846. He established his own kosher kitchen, matzoth bakery, and synagogue, but kept aloof from the Jews of the city. He also took part in prison reform, Westchester politics, and charity. When Simson returned to New York, he became one of the chief founders of Mount Sinai Hospital in 1852. That same year he organized the Jewish Theological and Scientific Institution as a rabbinical seminary. Hoping to see it established in Westchester County, he contributed several lots in Yonkers. However, nothing came of his plan, and the property was converted into the first assets of the Jewish Theological Seminary of America.

The first permanent Jewish community in Westchester came into being in Yonkers. An item in a Yonkers newspaper in 1870 reported that "the Hebrews of Yonkers have leased and fitted up for a synagogue the entire fourth story of Anderson's building on Getty Square and the Reverend M. Bernstein has been engaged to minister to them." There is a record of another service in 1875 in the home of Herman Lyons. Public High Holy Day services were held in 1887 in the hall of the Young Women's Christian Temperance Union on North Broadway. Out of this service came Congregation Oheb Zedek, which was chartered in 1903. The chief founders were Aaron Rabinowitz and Adolph Klein. The latter, a Hungarian Jew who settled in Yonkers in 1884, recruited Jewish workers for the Alexander Smith Carpet Company, which moved from The Bronx to Yonkers in the early 1890s. In 1890, the Hebrew Benevolent Society of Yonkers bought Teutonia Hall as the city's first synagogue.

The first Jew to settle in Mount Vernon was Moritz Lowenstein, a Civil War veteran who lost a leg on the battlefield. An employee at the U.S. Customs Office in New York City, Levy commuted daily to his job for 40 years, and may well have been the first Jewish commuter. Between 1869 and

1885 other Jewish Civil War veterans, tradesmen, artisans, and peddlers established themselves in Mount Vernon, New Rochelle, Port Chester, Tarrytown, Ossining, Mamaroneck, and White Plains. Mount Vernon's first *minyan* met in the home of Louis Subitzky in 1882, residents of Wakefield, Woodlawn, and Kingsbridge having been invited to complete the *minyan*. This *minyan* became Congregation Brothers of Israel in 1891 when there were 50 Jewish families in Mount Vernon. Congregation Sons of Israel in Ossining also dates from 1891. Port Chester had a synagogue in 1892 and a year later there was one in Tarrytown. New Rochelle's oldest congregation, Anshe Sholom, goes back to 1898. In the early 1900s there were also small settlements with congregations in Hastings-on-Hudson, Mt. Kisco, Peekskill, Tuckahoe, and Mamaroneck. Yonkers had a YMHA in 1900, and Mount Vernon established one in 1909.

Virtually all of the first congregations were Orthodox. In the 1960s, there were 46 synagogues in Westchester County—11 Orthodox, 21 Conservative, and 14 Reform congregations. Fifteen years later, the comparable figures were 25 Reform, 25 Conservative, and 10 Orthodox. The post-World War II building boom throughout Westchester brought a large influx of Jews who established new synagogues and synagogue-centers, Hebrew schools, and other Jewish institutions.

At the end of the 1960s, the county's major cities began to lose population to the fast-growing towns in the county and to the newly-built areas in other parts of the county. Between 1960 and 1965, 8,000 residents of Mount Vernon left the city to escape racial tensions, crime and narcotics in the schools, and the influx of blacks. Many of the migrating families were Jews. In 1954 there were 25,000 Jews in Mount Vernon, and they comprised one-third of the city's population. By 1969 there were only 12,000 Jews, the others having moved to Riverdale in The Bronx, to Scarsdale, Larchmont, and other Westchester communities, or to Rockland County and Connecticut. The city's synagogues were hard hit by the migration. Mount Vernon's Sinai Temple declined from 1,200 families in 1959 to 250 a decade later. Many of the Jewish families that left were young parents who did not want to send their children to the Mount Vernon public schools, the very same schools that had first attracted these families in the 1930s. The Jews who left the county's four big cities were often the builders of new Jewish communities in as yet undeveloped areas of the county. In 1948, Yorktown Heights had four Jewish families, two of whom—Jack Schaffer and Samson Solomon—were farmers. In the 1970s there were 400 Jewish families in the area out of a total of 5,000.

The principal national Jewish organizations are represented by chapters in every Westchester town and city. Some of them have created countywide councils. Each community conducts an annual drive for the Joint Campaign of the United Jewish Appeal-Federation of Jewish Philanthropies. There are a Westchester Board of Rabbis, a Westchester Jewish Conference that serves as a county clearing house and provides information, a Westchester task force of Federation's Commission on Synagogue Relations, and a number of Federation agencies. The Westchester Jewish Community Services, Federation's family service agency, has branches in Yonkers, New Rochelle, Mount Vernon, and White Plains. There are three Jewish newspapers in the county, *The Mosaic*, published by the Mount Vernon Jewish Community Council; *The Jewish Chronicle*, published by the Yonkers Jewish Community Council, and *The Jewish Tribune*, a private enterprise. The Mid-Westchester YM-YWHA in Scarsdale is affiliated with the Associated YM-YWHAs of Greater New York. There are independent YMHAs in Yonkers, Mount Vernon, and Port Chester, and a Hillel Counselorship at Pace College, served by the rabbi of the Community Synagogue in Rye.

The influx of thousands of Jewish voters from New York City where they had usually supported Democratic candidates, made a small dent in the political complexion of Westchester County, which has long been solidly Republican. Jewish officeholders on the county wide level are rare in Westchester. In 1975, Samuel Fredman was elected chairman of the County Democratic Committee. Some of the county villages have had Jewish mayors. Eugene H. Lehman was mayor of Tarrytown in 1931, and H. S. Green succeeded him two years later. Monroe Steiner was mayor of Larchmont in 1930. In 1974, Richard Maas was acting-mayor of White Plains. State Supreme Court Justice Alvin R. Ruskin served as a judge of the County Family Court.

*****

ARMONK
Anita Louise Ehrman Recreation Center, High St., Byran Hill Rd. and Cox Ave., an 11-acre site donated to the town of North Castle by Mr. and Mrs. Frederick L. Ehrman, is a memorial to their daughter, Anita Louise.

BREWSTER
Temple Beth Elohim, Route 22.

BRIARCLIFF MANOR
Cong. Sons of Israel, 1666 Pleasantville Rd.

BRONXVILLE
Walter Rothschild House at Sarah Lawrence College is named for the former president of the Abraham & Straus stores.

CHAPPAQUA
Temple Beth El of Northern Westchester, 222 S. Bedford Rd.

CROTON-ON-HUDSON
Temple Israel of Northern Westchester, Glengary Rd.

DOBBS FERRY
Greenburgh Hebrew Center, 515 Broadway.

HARRISON
Louis M. Klein Middle School, Nelson and Union Aves., is named for a former superintendent of schools.

Temple Emanu-El (Jewish Community Center), Union Ave., features a splendid circular sanctuary 62 feet in diameter.

HASTINGS-ON-HUDSON
Temple Beth Shalom, 740 N. Broadway.

Westchester Hills Cemetery, 400 Saw Mill River Rd., has the unusual mausoleum in which showman Billy Rose is buried. Three stained glass windows depict a pen, a telephone, and the notes of songs to trace his career. On one of the windows there is a map of Israel and musical notes from the song *Without a Song*, for which Rose wrote the lyrics. The center window shows a copy of a medal given to Rose by Israel after he had donated $1 million worth of art for the Billy Rose Art Museum in Jerusalem, now part of the Israel Museum. The word "wolf" is written in Hebrew on the window, an affectionate term that David Ben-Gurion used for Rose. The granite structure overlooking the entrance to the cemetery is directly opposite the mausoleum of famed composer George Gershwin, and the grave of singer Judy Holliday.

HAWTHORNE
Cedar Knolls School of New York Board of Jewish Guardians, 226 Linda Ave.

LAKE CARMEL
Jewish Center, Yorktown Rd.

LARCHMONT
Cong. Beth Emeth, 2111 Boston Post Rd.
Larchmont Temple, 75 Larchmont Ave.

MAMARONECK
Westchester Jewish Center, Palmer and Rockland Aves., has an unusual free standing Ark in hardwood flanked on each side by Menorah stands joined to the Ark, and a circular exterior sculpture and Menorah.

Westchester Religious Institute and Day School, 856 Orienta Ave.

MOHEGAN LAKE
Martha Guinsberg Pavilion, a public recreation center, is named for the wife of a prominent resident.

Mohegan Park Jewish Center, Decatur Rd.

MOUNT KISCO
Cong. Beth Medrash Chemed, Pines Bridge Rd.

Cong. Bet Torah, 60 Smith Ave.

Training Farm of Nitra Yeshiva, Pines Bridge Rd., is a training center for Orthodox teenagers planning to settle on Orthodox kibbutzim in Israel.

MOUNT VERNON
Cong. Brothers of Israel, 10 S. 8th Ave.

Emanu-El Jewish Center, 261 Lincoln Ave.

Fleetwood Synagogue, 11 E. Broad St.

Free Synagogue of Westchester, 500 N. Columbus Ave.

Jewish Center of Mount Vernon, 230 S. Columbus Ave.

Jewish Community Council, 30 Oakley Ave.

The Mosaic, 30 Oakley Ave.

Residence of Jewish Child Care Assoc. of N.Y., 163 Esplanade.

St. Paul's Episcopal Church, 897 Columbus Ave., a national shrine of the Bill of Rights, has a pair of eight-branched brass candlesticks and a pewter sanctuary lamp which were once the property of the synagogue in Landau, Germany. They were brought to the U.S. by Joseph Levy, maternal grandfather of Adolph S. Ochs, late publisher of *The New York Times*, and presented to the church by Ochs' son-in-law and daughter, Mr. and Mrs. Arthur Hays Sulzberger, as a memorial to Ochs. St. Paul's Episcopal Church is associated with John Peter Zenger's struggle for freedom of the press in Colonial days. His accurate report in 1733 of a fraudulent election on the village green, where the church now stands, resulted in his arrest for libel and subsequent acquittal, an event which was a landmark in the battle for a free press.

Shalom Nursing Home, is a strictly kosher institution sponsored by the National Council of Young Israel, Clairemont Ave.

Temple Sinai, 132 Crary Ave.

Westchester Jewish Community Services, 2 Gramatan Ave.

Westchester Jewish Tribune, 113 S. 3rd Ave.

Y.M.H.A. of Lower Westchester, 30 Oakley Ave.

NEW CASTLE
Warburg Park, used by the town of New Castle as a public park and

recreation area, is a memorial to the late Felix Warburg, the noted Jewish philanthropist. The 37 acre site was donated by James N. and Bessie H. Rosenberg.

NEW ROCHELLE

Beth El Synagogue-Center, Northfield Rd. at North Ave., has a frontal view emphasizing a 50-foot tall column of limestone incised with a golden Menorah and the Ten Commandments. A Sukkot garden and terraced meditation park are also part of the exterior. The two stained glass windows that run the full height of the structure, represent the Biblical story of Joachim and Boaz and the two beacons of light guiding the Children of Israel, one by day and one by night. In the main foyer there hangs a sculpture, *The Living Star of David*, created by the Israeli artist, Yaakov Agam. The bimah chairs for the rabbi and other dignitaries are upholstered seats incorporated into a stone base, an idea adapted from the Seat of Moses in the ancient synagogue at Hazor. The *Wall of the Martyrs*, a monumental bronze sculpture by Luise Kaish, said to be the first work of such scope and dimension commissioned by an American synagogue, is a symbolic representation of Jewish martyrdom through the ages. It hangs in the synagogue's Hall of Martyrs. It was endowed by Mr. and Mrs. Harry Platt. The Menorah in the synagogue is an exact copy of the Menorah in the Second Temple in Jerusalem. In the upper lobby are 61 panels containing English translations of the 54 regular weekly portions of the Torah and seven double portions. It is claimed that this display is the only one of its kind in a synagogue.

Cong. Anshe Sholom, 50 North Ave.

Raizen Memorial Plaza, between Main and Huguenot Sts., honors the late Charles S. Raizen, a former president of Temple Israel, who was one of the city's leading civic leaders and philanthropists. A bronze sculpture of Raizen set in a fountain of water stands in the plaza.

Temple Israel, 1000 Pinebrook Blvd.

United Home for Aged Hebrews, 60 Willow Dr.

Westchester Jewish Community Services, 271 North Ave.

Young Israel of Westchester, 1228 North Ave.

OSSINING

Cong. Anshe Dorshe Emes Reconstructionist Synagogue, Albany Post Rd.

PEEKSKILL

First Hebrew Cong., 1821 E. Main St.

Hebrew Day School of Northern Westchester and Putnam County, 1821 E. Main St.

Temple Israel of Putnam Valley, Lake Dr.

Valeria Home, Furnace Dock Rd., a vacation resort "for people of education and refinement, belonging to the middle class who would not be justified in asking for or accepting charity, but who are, nevertheless, not able to pay the prices exacted for a sojourn in the usual health resorts or sanitaria," was founded in 1914 with a $4 million endowment by Jacob Langloth, German-Jewish banker, and named for his wife, Valeria.

Young Israel, Pinelake Park.

PELHAM MANOR

Jewish Center, 451 Esplanade.

PLEASANTVILLE

Pleasantville Cottage School of Jewish Child Care Association, Broadway.

PORT CHESTER

Cong. Kneses Tifereth Israel, 575 King St., is a rectangular synagogue set against an ellipse. The entrance is within the ellipse, and the sanctuary and other parts are within the rectangle. The first rises only part way against the facade, so that the two units do not compete for attention—the sanctuary is dominant. The synagogue is sheathed in an off-white pre-cast stone. Jewel-like colored glass is set into its slit masonry walls. These narrow panels, each of a luminous color, are distributed in five tiers across the facade.

Jewish Center of Port Chester and Town of Rye, 258 Willett Ave., displays in its lobby an oil painting entitled *Torah, Chuppa and Good Deeds*.

POUND RIDGE

Hiram Halle Memorial Library, Route 124, is named for the Jewish financier who donated the land and original building in which the library is housed.

PURCHASE

Roy R. Neuberger Museum at State University of New York, College at Purchase, Lincoln Ave. and Anderson Hill Rd., houses the multimillion dollar collection of 20th century American art contributed by Neuberger to the University's art center. The museum, which was the college's first building, houses Neuberger's collection of paintings and sculptures, as well as the Elaine and Raphael Malsin Collection of Oceanic Art, and the Aimee and Eliot Hirshberg Collection of African Art.

Pforzheimer Memorial Building, Purchase St., the home of the Westchester Academy of Medicine, is named for Mr. and Mrs. Carl Pforzheimer, philanthropists and bibliophiles, whose son, Carl, Jr., presented the mansion and ten acres as a memorial to his parents. The building and grounds were formerly the estate of the late Gov. Herbert H. Lehman.

The Peter Lehman Post of the Purchase American Legion is named for Lehman's son, who was killed in World War II while flying with the Royal Air Force.

PUTNAM
Reform Temple of Putnam Valley, Church Rd.

RYE
Community Synagogue, 200 Forest Ave.
Cong. Emanu-El of Westchester, Westchester Ave. and Kenilworth Rd.

SCARSDALE
Scarsdale Synagogue, 2 Ogden Rd.
Westchester Children's Schule, Greenville Community Church, Ardsley Rd. near Central Ave.
Westchester Reform Temple, 255 Mamaroneck Rd. The main wing of the building is shaped like a Star of David. The walls of the sanctuary building are of fieldstone and are twenty feet high. A 12-foot high triangular lobby extends from the building toward a driveway.
Y.M. & Y.W.H.A. of Mid-Westchester, 999 Wilmot Rd.
Young Israel of Scarsdale, 43 Barand Rd.

SHENEROCK
Hebrew Cong. of Somers, Cypress Lane.

SHRUB OAK
Workmen's Circle Jewish Culture School, United Methodist Church, E. Main St.

TARRYTOWN
Marc Chagall Windows (nine), in the Union Church of Pocantico Hills, 555 Bedford Rd., N. Tarrytown, illustrate passages from the Book of Genesis and the Prophets.
Sleepy Hollow Cemetery, 540 N. Broadway, made famous by Washington Irving's stories, is the last resting place of Samuel Gompers, founder and for two generations, president of the American Federation of Labor (see District of Columbia).
Temple Beth Abraham, 25 Leroy Ave., has a tall sculpture at its entrance which reaches from roof line toward the sky and can be seen at a great distance. A pylon whose design incorporates in bronze, steel, and stained glass, The Tablets of the Law, is based on two columns. The steel columns turn into two ladders as they pierce the roof, recalling the ladder of Jacob. They terminate in the curves of the Tablets of the Law which are topped by a series of opposing curves forming the Menorah.

TUCKAHOE

Genesis Hebrew Center, 25 Oakland Ave.

VALHALLA

Blythedale Children's Hospital, Bradhurst Ave.

WHITE PLAINS

Cong. Beth Am Shalom, 295 Soundview Ave.

Hebrew Institute, 20 Greenridge Ave.

Jewish Community Center, 252 Soundview Ave., a synagogue despite its name, is housed in a parabolic structure outside of which stands an abstract bronze sculpture.

Solomon Schechter Day School, 280 Old Mamaroneck Rd.

Temple Israel Center, 280 Old Mamaroneck Rd.

Westchester Jewish Community Services, 172 S. Broadway.

Woodlands Community Temple, 50 Worthington Rd.

YONKERS

Cong. Agudas Achim, 21 Hudson St., has a chapel named for the parents of Sid Caesar, stage and television star, who attended Hebrew school here and celebrated his bar mitzvah here.

Cong. Ohab Zedek, 7 Prospect St. and 63 Hamilton Ave.

Cong. Sons of Israel, 105 Radford St.

Greystone Jewish Center, 600 N. Broadway.

Hebrew Academy High School, 700 McLean Ave.

Hebrew Academy High School of Lincoln Park, 311 Central Park Ave.

Jewish Chronicle, 122 S. Broadway.

Jewish Community Center, 122 S. Broadway.

Jewish Community Council, 122 S. Broadway

Jewish Guild for the Blind Home, 75 Stratton Ave.

Lincoln Park Jewish Center, 311 Central Park Ave.

Mesivta of Yonkers, 63 Hamilton Ave.

Midchester Jewish Center, 236 Grandview Blvd., has on an exterior wall a huge bronze Menorah designed as a memorial to the 6,000,000 victims of the Nazi Holocaust. It was a gift of Mr. and Mrs. Fred Silberman.

Neustadter Convalescent Center of Mount Sinai Hospital, 700 McLean Ave.

Northeast Jewish Center, 11 Salisbury Rd.

Smith-O'Hara-Levine Park, Lawrence and Wolffe Sts., is named in part for Pfc. Daniel Ira Levine, who was killed in action in 1944 in France during World War II.

Temple Emanu-El, 306 Ramsey Rd.

Untermyer Park and Gardens, 919 N. Broadway, is a public park maintained by the city and named for the late Samuel J. Untermyer, the noted lawyer. Once part of Untermyer's palatial estate and gardens known as Greystone, the park was bequeathed to the city in 1940 by Untermyer. It includes a Greek garden and theatre and part of what was once the largest private gardens in the U. S. Son of a Confederate veteran, Untermyer, a native of Lynchburg, Va., practiced law in New York for 61 years. He handled thousands of cases involving corporate matters, defended labor unions, acted for various committees of Congress and the New York State Legislature in exposing the money trust, housing scandals, the New York Stock Exchange, and in unifying the New York City transit system. The public investigations to which Untermyer was counsel led to the creation of the Federal Reserve System, the Federal Trade Commission, and the Securities and Exchange Commission. A law partner of Louis Marshall (see Syracuse, N. Y.), Untermyer once headed the Palestine Foundation Fund (Keren Hayesod). Counsel to Herman Bernstein in the first suit brought against Henry Ford for his libelous statements about the Jewish people, Untermyer in his last years became the leader of the movement to boycott German goods after the advent of Hitlerism in 1933. He donated the Minnie Untermyer Memorial Theatre to the Hebrew University in memory of his wife.

United Home for Aged Hebrews, 60 Willow Dr.

United Talmud Torah, P.O.B. 203.

Westchester Jewish Community Services, 20 S. Broadway and 598 Tuckahoe Rd.

Yonkers Sports Hall of Fame Room, in the Administrative Building of the Department of Parks, Recreation, and Conservation, is dedicated to Abe Cohen, who originated the Hall of Fame.

YORKTOWN HEIGHTS

Jewish Center, 2966 Crompond Rd.

Temple Beth Am, 203 Church Pl.

NEW YORK
NASSAU and
SUFFOLK COUNTIES

Nassau and Suffolk Counties, New York City's largest suburb, have more Jews than any one of New York City's five boroughs, and, together, constitute the third largest Jewish community in the United States. Only New York City as a whole and Los Angeles County have more Jews.

In the 1930s, the two cities and 54 towns and villages of Nassau and Suffolk Counties counted barely 18,000 Jews. By 1963, however, there were 352,000 in Nassau County and 38,000 in Suffolk County. When the total population of the two counties reached the 2,000,000 mark for the first time at the end of 1962, Jews constituted about 20 percent of the total. In the 1970s, the Jewish population had grown to 605,000 (Nassau, 455,000, and Suffolk, 150,000), or about 22½ percent of the total population of the 2,715,000 in the two-county area.

Although a large percentage of the working residents of Nassau and Suffolk Counties actually work in the counties, the Long Island Railroad, mindful that a considerable number of its daily commuters to New York are Jews, uses a Hebrew calendar to make certain changes in its schedule. On the eve of the High Holy days and Passover, the railroad always adds extra trains to accommodate Jewish commuters homeward bound at an earlier time than usual. School principals and teachers consult the Hebrew calendar in setting dates for major school events, final examinations, school openings, and graduations.

The largest Jewish concentration is in the Town of Hempstead, which is made up of 33 villages and the city of Long Beach, where 275,000 Jews represent about 40 percent of the total population. This is the area that includes Levittown, Oceanside, Rockville Centre, Valley Stream, East Meadow, Westbury, Hempstead, West Hempstead, Wantagh, and the Five

Towns (Lawrence, Cedarhurst, Hewlett, Woodmere, and Inwood). The town of North Hempstead, which embraces the major North Shore communities of Great Neck, Manhasset, Port Washington, Roslyn, and the city of Glen Cove, had 100,000 Jews in the 1970s. In the town of Oyster Bay, which includes the villages of Bethpage, Jericho, Hicksville, Massapequa, Plainedge, Plainview, Syosset, and Westbury, there were 80,000 Jews. In Suffolk County, 90,000 Jews lived in the western segment, the one closest to New York; 50,000 in the central portion; and 10,000 in the eastern tip.

New York was still New Amsterdam when Jews were doing business in all three counties of Colonial Long Island—Kings (Brooklyn), Queens, which once included all of Nassau County, and Suffolk. "The whole island was familiar country to Colonial Jewry," Dr. Jacob R. Marcus points out in his book, *Early American Jewry.*

As early as the 1660s Jewish merchants had found their way to that part of Long Island beyond the New York City limits. The ubiquitous Asser Levy of New Amsterdam owned property on Long Island and, after his death, his family moved there in 1730. Oyster Bay's town records contain a document dated January 19, 1745 listing the sale of 19 acres by the widow of Samuel Myers Cohen. A former president of New York's Congregation Shearith Israel, Cohen had acquired the property in 1741 or even earlier. Hart Aaron and Jacob Cohen had stores at Islip and Jericho between 1759 and 1760. Levy Michael lived at South Haven in 1760 when his son, Michael, was circumcised there by Abraham I. Abrahams of New York. Joseph Jacobs came to Southampton in 1760. Isaac Moses and Isaac Isaacs, whose home was in Jamaica, also had business interests on Long Island before the Revolution.

The best known of the handful of Jewish residents on Long Island before 1800 was Aaron Isaacs, who settled at East Hampton around 1750. Isaacs, who had been a member of Shearith Israel, was one of Long Island's most prominent merchants and shipowners in the middle of the 18th century. He owned property in Montauk and East Hampton and was part-owner of a wharf at Sag Harbor. During the Revolution, when the British controlled Long Island, Isaacs fled to Connecticut with other patriots. In 1750, he married a Christian. All of his eleven children were baptized. One daughter became the mother of John Howard Payne who wrote *Home Sweet Home,* based on the memory of his grandfather's house. The "Home Sweet Home" is still one of East Hampton's landmarks. The salt-box house sits not far from where Isaacs is buried, in a Christian cemetery.

A scattering of Jews lived on Long Island in the first half of the 19th century, but they were never numerous enough to acquire even the smallest burial ground or to conduct Jewish religious services. Between 1870 and 1890, Jewish peddlers, storekeepers, and factory workers from New York City began establishing themselves in the principal trading villages— Lindenhurst, Sag Harbor, Greenport, Riverhead, Southampton, Jericho, Lynbrook, Hempstead, Bay Shore, Babylon, Rockville Centre, Glen Cove, and Port Washington. Simultaneously, well-to-do Jews from Brooklyn and New York started coming to Long Island for summer ocean breezes. Some of the latter acquired substantial estates which were later converted into parks. Belmont State Park was once the estate and horse farm of August Belmont, Jewish-born banker, diplomat, and one of the founders of American horse racing. The Guggenheims, Schiffs, and Kahns also built Long Island mansions. Some of the vacationers who became permanent residents joined forces with the resident Jewish merchants to establish the first Jewish communities east of the New York City line.

Adolph Levy, an immigrant from Russia, began peddling among the clam diggers in the waterfront shacks from Baldwin to Massapequa in the late 1880s. He used to spend the nights in an old hotel in Seaford. Tired of walking, he made the hotel his base of operations and later bought it. There he played host to other traveling salesmen before moving to Freeport where he opened a men's clothing store at the turn of the century. His oldest son, David, was elected the first Jewish councilman on the Hempstead Town Board in the 1930s. Another son, George Morton Levy, became one of Nassau County's best known lawyers and founder of Roosevelt Raceway.

In the early 1880s, Harry Goldstein and his brother set up their peddling operation in an Eastport farmhouse. In 1885 Harry opened a little store in town. The Goldstein brothers and their sons also did business from a horse and wagon with the farmers from Riverhead to East Hampton, bringing new appliances as they came on the market. The Goldstein Department Store is still in business, but some of the third generation Goldsteins changed their name to Gerard. A second generation Goldstein, Lawrence, recalled how he and his brothers met the train from New York every Thursday because it brought a package of kosher meat bought by their grandmother in New York.

The first of these was probably in Lindenhurst in the 1870s when that village was still known as Breslau. The Jewish residents peddled in the nearby villages or worked in a local button factory. The families took turns going into New York by train and trolley to buy kosher meat. In 1875 these early Lindenhurst Jews opened a synagogue and built a *mikveh*. This settlement did not endure; the present Lindenhurst Jewish community dates from 1912.

The oldest Jewish community in continuous existence is in Sag Harbor where the United Hebrew Brethren was organized in 1883. The death of a child in 1889 and the lack of a local burial place led to the formation of the Hebrew Cemetery Association out of which evolved Temple Adas Israel, Long Island's oldest congregation. A synagogue was erected in 1898 when the congregation had 50 members. A quarrel between Russian and Hungarian Jews led the latter to form their own congregation and to acquire their own cemetery. The dissidents came back in 1918 and together established Temple Adas Israel. The two cemeteries, however, still exist side by side just off the highway between Sag Harbor and East Hampton, separated only by an iron railing. "Schmerel" Heller, the first *shochet* in Suffolk County, ran a boarding house for peddlers. Morris Simon, the cantor of the congregation, sold tea and coffee in Heller's home, and later opened a crockery store before moving to Patchogue. Among the early Jewish families in Sag Harbor were the Spodicks, Max Ollswang, the Eisenbergs, Morris Meyer, T. Thomashefsky, of the famed family of Yiddish actors, Sam Rosenberg, and a German Jew who was the village policeman. Eisenberg opened the village's kosher butcher shop. "Schmerel" Heller was the congregation's fundraiser who went to New York City to raise money for the first synagogue building and came back with a donation from Jacob H. Schiff. Many of the first Jewish settlers in Sag Habor were brought there by Joseph Fahy, a non-Jewish manufacturer who imported 40 to 50 Jewish families directly from the Castle Garden immigrant station for work in his watchcase factory.

Congregation Tifereth Israel in Glen Cove and the United Hebrew Benevolent Society in Bay Shore were both founded in 1897. The Glen Cove congregation met in private homes until 1900 when it bought a building known as the "opera house," which it used as a synagogue until 1925 when its present sanctuary was dedicated. This is the synagogue that has served as the focal point for demonstrations, sit-ins, and pray-ins at the nearby Soviet residential compound. The North Shore Jewish Center, located in Port Jefferson Station since the 1970s, was established in East Setauket in 1893. Greenport held worship services in the 1890s in the home of Fannie Levine and Congregation Tifereth Israel was founded there in 1900 and a synagogue was opened in 1904 under the leadership of Nathan Kaplan, for whom one of the village's principal thoroughfares is named.

Barnett Salke, a Civil War veteran who came to Hempstead in the 1870s, was one of the group that joined Dr. Adolph Rosenthal in 1901 in an unsuccessful attempt to establish a congregation there. Failing in that, the town's Jewish merchants, like their contemporaries all over Long Island, traveled to New York or Brooklyn for the High Holy days. Mrs. Lester Appel, who was born in Hempstead in the late 1890s, a decade after her parents settled there, recalled that they had owned the village's first hotel, known as Roth's Hotel, a popular gathering place for Long Island society. The general store opened by Isaac Jacobson in Lynbrook in 1896 was closed by his daughter-in-law in 1971. He had been a peddler in the area since 1891. Sam Patiky, whose parents, Jennie and Elias, settled in Kings Park in the late 1890s and opened a small department store, was one of the founders of the Kings Park Jewish Center.

There were Jews in Huntington in 1900 and they organized a *minyan* in the home of William Teich. The first High Holy day services were held in an old fire house on Main Street, where Isaac Levenbron was fire chief. Eight men founded the Brotherhood of Jewish Men in Huntington in 1906 which became the Huntington Hebrew Center a year later. A cemetery was opened in 1908 and the first synagogue was dedicated in 1911 on Church Street. It drew members from Northport, Kings Park, and other nearby communities who stayed with local families for the holidays so they could walk to synagogue. Rabbi Mayer Israel Herman, who came to Huntington in 1930, is believed to have been the first ordained rabbi to officiate in Suffolk County. Prior to World War I, there were also synagogues in Patchogue (1903), Rockville Centre (1907), Hempstead (1908), Riverhead (1911), Great Neck, (1912), and Lindenhurst (1912). Long Beach, Cedarhurst, and Lawrence, to which Jews first came as summer residents, had no permanent congregation until the 1920s. Temple Israel, Lawrence's oldest synagogue, moved from Far Rockaway in 1930.

A few of the first 20th century Jewish settlers came originally as farmers. In 1905, the Jewish Agricultural Society opened a test farm at Kings Park, where 60 Jewish immigrants learned elementary agricultural skills. Some of these students later became farmers at Farmingdale, Riverhead, Center Moriches, Calverton and East Islip. In the 1970s, there were still a number of Suffolk Jews engaged in dairy and poultry farming and tobacco growing as well as some who handled farm produce on a wholesale basis. Harry B. Goldstein of East Islip was in the dairy and cattle business for 55 years. Great Neck, where some 60 percent of the 43,000 residents of the seven villages included in the general area are Jewish, traces its Jewish beginnings to Avram Wolf, a tailor. He was brought from New York in 1875 by W. R. Grace, the shipping magnate, because he wanted his tailor close by. Wolf later went into the real estate and insurance business. Because the Great Neck Playhouse, now a movie theatre, was a major theatrical tryout house in the 1920s, many stage celebrities made their homes there, among them Eddie Cantor and Groucho Marx. Some of the Great Neck villages openly barred Jewish homeowners until the 1930s. Kings Point, Great Neck's wealthy suburb, has a substantial Jewish population.

World War I introduced large numbers of Jews to Long Island for the first time and provided some of them with a reason for moving there. It was at Camps Yaphank and Upton, both near Patchogue, that thousands of Jewish draftees from the New York area received their military training in 1917 and 1918. Tired of the long weekend visiting trip to Patchogue, some of the draftees' families settled down in nearby towns for the duration. Many became permanent residents, as did numbers of the returning Jewish doughboys who recalled the pleasant homes and business opportunities they had seen on Long Island.

Meanwhile, permanent Jewish communities were growing up in Long Beach, when summer residents decided to stay permanently, and in Great Neck and the Five Towns, where successful Broadway personalities, wealthy garment manufacturers, and other businessmen built lavish homes. One of the latter was Charles A. Levine, "the flying junkman from Brooklyn," who invested part of the fortune he had made in salvaging World War I equipment in financing Clarence Chamberlain's nonstop flight from Roosevelt Field on Long Island to Germany in 1927. Flying with Chamberlain, Levine was the first transAtlantic airplane passenger. Dr. Henry

Walden, a Jewish dentist who designed and piloted the first American monoplane, flew it from Mineola in 1909.

Long before there was the "miracle mile" shopping area on the Manhasset segment of Northern Boulevard, Jaffe's department store was a North Shore landmark. Benjamin Jaffe, who came to Manhasset in the early 1890s, opened branch stores in Glen Cove, Locust Valley, and Valley Stream. His grandsons operated the business until 1975 when it closed. In 1920 a Zionist group was founded in Greenport, a forerunner of the present Eastern Suffolk Zionist District. Four years later, Israel Kramer bought a tract of land in West Babylon with the intention of establishing a Zionist colony there. He placed ads in all the Yiddish newspapers and rented buses to take prospects from the Lindenhurst station of the Long Island Railroad to the property. But there were no buyers. Ezra Park, the name given to the area by Kramer, is now populated largely by people of Italian origin, but the neighborhood's main street is called Herzel (sic) Boulevard. One of the first post-World War II synagogues on Long Island was erected in Riverhead in 1947. There had been a congregation called Beth Haknesses Anshe Riverhead for a number of years and in 1924, as Temple Israel, it built a one-room synagogue. During the war, when Rabbi Simon Reznikoff, now of Temple Gates of Prayer, Valley Stream, was a chaplain at the Suffolk County Army Air Field in Westhampton, he encouraged the community to plan for a new building.

After World War II, thousands of returning veterans from New York City began the mass Jewish movement to the suburbs. Attracted by the low-cost one-family houses on Long Island that sprang up like mushrooms in huge developments, young Jewish families of limited means poured into Nassau County. It was William J. Levitt and his sons who started to change the face of Long Island from potato farms to large scale housing. The Levitts built houses on belt lines, like ships and planes had been built during the war. The day the Levitts' sales office opened on March 7, 1949, there were more than 1,000 couples waiting in line. Some had been there three or four days and nights, living on coffee and doughnuts. When the doors opened, it was like the Oklahoma land rush of 1889, so eager were the young married couples to be among the first to buy one of the basic four-room houses for $6,990 or to rent one at $60 a month. Many of the buyers were Jews. A makeshift synagogue was opened in an abandoned airplane hangar. Land for Levittown's Israel Community Center was donated by the Levitts but its members did much of the work involved in the building. Ultimately, the Levitts built 18,000 single-family houses on 4,000 acres.

As new housing developments opened up, Jewish families became the first settlers in many of them, creating instant Jewish communities overnight or greatly enlarging older settlements. A second wave of Jewish migration from New York in the early 1950s carried the Jewish population to the North Shore, the far edges of Nassau County, and into the western part of Suffolk County. In 1952 there were only nine Jewish congregations in

Suffolk County. By 1963 there were 20, as Jewish settlements reached Montauk Point, the most eastern tip of Long Island.

As Jewish families climbed the success ladder, many of them began to leave the smaller, mass-designed houses in Levittown, Hicksville, Valley Stream, and East Meadow for more expensive individually-built homes on the North Shore and the Five Towns. In Levittown, where the total population was 65,000 in the 1970s, only 11,000 were Jews, and only 11 percent of these were affiliated with the local synagogue. Growth continued in newer areas of Nassau and Suffolk Counties until the mid-1960s as newcomers from New York bought the older houses or pushed on to the newer developments.

By the 1960s a new trend set in. Nassau County had run out of land for large scale housing developments but garden and cooperative apartments were beginning to sprout. Older families that had roots on Long Island and preferred to stay in the suburbs eagerly became renters once again. The concept of an apartment in the sun in the beach areas also attracted former Jewish homeowners to the new high rise apartments in Long Beach and to cooperative residences that went up in the larger villages. At the same time, communities that were once heavily Jewish became less so. Rockville Centre, which developed into a major Catholic community when it became the diocesan headquarters of a bishop, lost Jewish population. Other communities have had similar experiences. As Jewish families with grown children departed for the city, suburban apartments, or Florida and Arizona, and were replaced by non-Jews, synagogue membership on Long Island, once numbering 80 percent of the total Jewish population, began to fall off. Massive declines in elementary and secondary school enrollments were matched by a falling off in the number of students in Jewish religious schools.

The postwar influx of Jews had touched off a massive boom in synagogue construction. At first the newer congregations formed in every town and village met in fire houses, schools, churches, Masonic halls, and even stores. Most of the older Orthodox congregations changed to Conservative and Reform and almost none of the new congregations founded in the 1950s were Orthodox. In the 1960s and 1970s, however, a number of Young Israel congregations came into being. In 1963 there were 109 congregations in Nassau County, all with full-time rabbis and their own buildings, many with substantial school buildings and recreational facilities as well, and 20 in Suffolk County. In the 1970s there were 130 in Nassau County and 32 in Suffolk County, including one each at Fire Island and Mastic Beach. Synagogue membership, however, began to decline in the 1970s. Enrollment in Jewish schools, which had almost tripled to 40,460 between 1945 and 1968, experienced an 8 percent decline in the early 1970s and further declines were expected before the end of the decade. The biggest decline was in the one-day-a-week schools whose enrollment dropped from 20,000 to 14,700, reflecting a steady shrinkage in Long Island's school age population and the falling Jewish birthrate. Enrollment in Hebrew day schools rose from 1,050 to 2,600 and the number of such schools increased to 11. The Hebrew Academy of Nassau County, founded in 1953, was the first Long Island Hebrew day school.

In other phases of communal life, the Jews of Nassau and Suffolk Counties are closely tied to New York City. The Joint Campaign of the United Jewish Appeal and Federation of Jewish Philanthropies and the New York-based national Jewish organizations conduct intensive drives on Long Island and reach out there for leadership. There are several hundred branches on Long Island of the various national Jewish organizations, a Long Island Board of Rabbis, a Long Island Rabbinical Council (Orthodox), a Long Island branch of the teachers' institute of Hebrew Union College-Jewish Institute of Religion, a Long Island Committee for Soviet Jewry, a public affairs council of Reform synagogues, and Long Island councils of local units of national Jewish organizations. The United Jewish Ys of Long Island promote support for the five existing YM-YWHAs in Nassau County and encourage the establishment of new ones. There are a number of local and regional Jewish Community Councils.

The Federation of Jewish Philanthropies, of which the five Ys and the United Jewish Ys are beneficiaries, also maintains Long Island offices of its Jewish Association for Service to the Aged and Jewish Community Services, and Federation Employment and Guidance Service. The Board of Jewish Education serves over 100 religious schools on Long Island. Federation conducts a day camp for Long Island and New York YMHAs at the Henry Kaufmann Campgrounds and sponsors the Usdan Center for Creative and Performing Arts, both at Wyandanch. There is a Long Island Division of Federation's Commission on Synagogue Relations. The Long Island Jewish-Hillside Medical Center and its affiliated Jewish Institute for Geriatric Care are also Federation affiliates. In West Hempstead, the Orthodox Jews have created an *eruv*, an enclave of strung wires that permits Sabbath-observing Jews to engage in a variety of activities within its boundaries that they would not otherwise be permitted on the Sabbath, except in their own homes. A plan of the Long Island Jewish Hospital-Medical Center to move its South Shore Division, the former St. Joseph's Hospital, from Far Rockaway in New York City, to Lawrence, in Nassau County, ran into strong opposition from the residents of Lawrence and the plan was dropped. Efforts of Far Rockaway's Temple Shaaray Zedek, an Orthodox congregation, to move across the city line into Lawrence were balked by the opposition of Lawrence residents, many of them Jews.

Kosher butchers are easy to find on Long Island. *Newsday*, the Long Island Daily founded by the late Alicia Patterson and her late husband, Harry Guggenheim, carries numerous ads for the fundraising bazaars conducted by synagogues and Jewish women's organizations throughout Long Island. Chanukah menorahs in banks and at shopping malls, Chanukah greetings in Long Island Railroad stations, public libraries, and Chanukah clubs in banks are commonplace. The Nassau County Police have enough

Jews to warrant an organization called Magen (shield), with a rabbi as its chaplain. A number of Jewish organizations provide volunteers for social, recreational, and religious programs for Jewish patients at some of Long Island's 76 nursing homes.

In some Long Island communities zoning ordinances were invoked in futile efforts to bar the construction of synagogues. In some villages it took Jews quite a while to break through unwritten restrictions and narrowly interpreted zoning regulations. Some of this opposition was a carry-over from the days when Long Island was a hotbed of anti-Semitic feeling and Ku Klux Klan activity. During the 1940s and early 1950s, synagogue building sites were regularly desecrated by anti-Semitic vandals. As late as 1975, a new congregation in Seaford encountered difficulty in its effort to establish a synagogue because of zoning regulations. Anti-Semitic incidents in the schools were reported periodically to the Long Island offices of the Anti-Defamation League, American Jewish Committee, and American Jewish Congress.

When A. T. Stewart, the department store magnate, laid out Garden City in 1869 as a model village, he specifically barred Jews from buying homes there, but this ban has long since been lifted. As recently as 1915, Long Beach, now about 40 percent Jewish, had clubs and hotels that refused to admit Jews. Virtually none of the golf, country, and yachting clubs on Long Island used to admit Jews. In 1971 there were 60 such clubs for non-Jews, 20 for Jews, and one had a 50-50 membership. Long Island's leading yacht club, which always excluded Jews, changed its policy just in time to enable its first Jewish member to pilot the yacht that carried the United States to victory in the 1962 America Cup race with Great Britain. In the 1970s some Jewish merchants fell afoul of old Sunday closing laws when they kept their establishments open on Sunday to test the validity of the laws.

Coming largely from all-Jewish neighborhoods in New York City, the postwar Jewish settlers on Long Island found their first social contacts with Jewish neighbors or in the activities of synagogues and other Jewish organizations. Gradually, the Jewish residents developed relationships with non-Jews through PTAs, scouting, volunteer fire departments, public libraries, chambers of commerce, youth organizations, civic associations, and common concern with neighborhood improvements and rising taxes.

In the 1950s and 1960s, there was a good deal of excitement in some communities over the display of Christological symbols in public places, Christmas observances, and Bible reading in the schools. While Jews were in the vanguard of Long Island's struggle over school and housing integration, many resisted it. They had left New York City for the suburbs because their old neighborhoods were in or near the edge of growing black and Puerto Rican communities. The South Shore village of Roosevelt lost its entire Jewish population when it became 95 percent black in the late 1960s. Some Jewish businessmen and professionals remain but the Jewish Center was sold and the proceeds used to buy life memberships in other synagogues for the older members. In Freeport, also on the South Shore, where Jews constitute 10 percent of the 41,000 residents, Congregation B'nai Israel, oldest of the village's two synagogues, took the lead in a campaign to encourage Jews to move to Freeport. The synagogue membership raised a special fund to underwrite the effort which included a home-finding service to stem a Jewish exodus as the village's black population increased.

The Jewish Association for Service to the Aged reported in the 1970s that there were some 30,000 Jewish aged on Long Island, including 4,500 Jewish poor in Long Beach. JASA operates the Brookdale JASA Senior Citizens Center at Temple Beth El, Long Beach, and is engaged in a variety of projects for the Jewish aged. Long Island's first golden age club was founded in 1950 in the Five Towns by the Peninsula Section of the National Council of Jewish Women.

While most of the postwar Jewish settlers on Long Island earned their livelihoods in New York City, a substantial change developed in the 1950s and 1960s when a growing number of Long Island Jews went into business on the island as retailers, manufacturers of electronic components, and plastics; as store managers in the newly opened department store branches and retail shops that filled the massive new shopping centers. Others were employed at Brookhaven National Laboratories, as engineers, technicians, scientists, and aerospace specialists in the aviation plants. They became owners or executives in the printing, industrial, chemical, and pharmaceutical plants that dot Nassau and Suffolk Counties. Many were engaged in the expanding service industries required to meet the growing needs of more than 2,500,000 people, in the professions, and in public service as employees of the county, state, and Federal governments. Jews were well represented on the faculties of the state and private universities in Nassau and Suffolk Counties. The network of parkways, expressways, public parks, and beaches that made Long Island attractive to home owners, businessmen, and vacationers is a monument to the vision of Robert Moses, for years president of the Long Island State Park Commission.

The more than 30-fold increase in the Jewish population since the 1930s made Jewish voters a political factor for the first time on Long Island. Prior to 1940, Jewish officeholders on any level were rare. Cedarhurst had Jewish mayors from 1928-1937, and Long Beach elected four Jewish mayors between 1929 and 1941. Glen Cove had a Jewish mayor, and Morton Stein was mayor of Malverne in 1963. Several of the Great Neck and Five Towns villages also had Jewish mayors. At first the city-bred Jews who were expected to reduce the overwhelmingly Republican majorities disappointed the Democrats by voting as their new neighbors did. But since the 1950s the margin between Republicans and Democrats has been narrowing, largely because of new Jewish voters from New York.

Election of Jews to village boards of trustees and school boards has become fairly widespread. A number of villages have had Jewish presidents of school boards and boards of trustees. There have been quite a few Jewish county judges in both Nassau and Suffolk Counties. Nearly a fourth of the State Supreme Court Justices on Long Island were Jews in the 1970s including one woman. Two Jewish women served as county judges in Nassau. Two Jews served as district attorneys in Nassau. Three Jews have been elected to Congress from Nassau County, Herbert Tenzer, Allard Lowenstein, and Lester Wolff, who was in Congress in 1976. When Suffolk County adopted the county legislature form of government, one of the members elected was Jewish. The first woman elected to the State Senate from Long Island was a Jew. Three Jews have served as head of the Nassau County Democratic Committee. Sol Wachtler, now a justice of the State Court of Appeals, lost a close race as the Republican candidate for Nassau County Executive. Norman Blackman, a retired real estate developer, who ran unsuccessfully for County Executive in 1973 as an independent, is the founder of Aware, a watchdog agency that keeps an eye on political wrong doing.

Highly civic-minded, Long Island's Jews are in the vanguard of many island-wide cultural and educational enterprises. Jews serve on the boards of trustees of Hofstra and Adelphi Universities; a Jew was president of the Nassau-Suffolk YMCA; George Morton Levy, a prominent attorney who grew up in Freeport, was the chief developer of Roosevelt Raceway. Leo Kopelman is the director of the Nassau-Suffolk Regional Planning Board. Robert Bernstein is chairman of the Association of Nassau County Art Organizations, and Martin Drewitz is director of the Long Island Youth Orchestra. Seymour Lipkin has been conductor of the Long Island Symphony since 1963, and Oscar Chudinowsky has operated, since 1929, Oscar's Literary Emporium in Huntington, the island's largest book store. Three Jews served on the panel of 19 civic leaders that created the design for a Nassau County legislature. David Laventhol is editor of *Newsday*, Long Island's influential daily paper. When *Newsday* drew up a list of the 50 people who run Long Island, it included ten Jews prominent in real estate, law, politics, city planning, and social service.

*****

AMITYVILLE

Beth Sholom Center of Amityville and the Massapequas, 79 County Line Rd.

Temple Sinai (see Massapequa).

ATLANTIC BEACH

Jewish Center of Atlantic Beach, 100 Nassau Ave. and Park St., is the only Jewish institution in this suburban village between Long Beach and Far Rockaway, which has a Jewish population of about 1,000, half of the 2,000 year-round residents. During the summer the village caters to tens of thousands who come to the local beach clubs.

BABYLON

Belmont Lake State Park, one of the largest of the L.I. state parks, covers about a third of what was once the country estate and horse farm of August Belmont, Jewish-born banker, diplomat, and one of the founders of American horse racing. Born in Germany in 1816, Belmont was first employed by the House of Rothschild in Frankfurt-am-Main, Germany, and later in Naples. He came to the U.S. in 1837 as an agent of the Rothschilds but soon established his own banking firm. A leader of and one of the financial supporters of the Democratic Party from 1844 on, Belmont was appointed U.S. chargé d'affaires at The Hague in 1853 by President Franklin Pierce. A year later he was promoted to the rank of minister-resident—probably the first Jew to hold this rank in the American diplomatic service. He served until 1857. During the Civil War, Belmont took a leading part in financing the war loans of the Federal government through his European banking connections. He also raised and equipped a regiment of German-born troops from New York. Although Belmont separated himself from the Jewish community, his Jewish origin was repeatedly used by anti-Semitic writers to attack him, especially in the Southern papers during the Civil War. From 1860-1884 Belmont was a member of the National Democratic Committee and served as its chairman for several years. Owner of a famous racing stable (Belmont Park in New York City's Borough of Queens is named for him), Belmont headed the American Jockey Club for many years. He married the daughter of Commodore Matthew C. Perry, who was responsible for opening Japan to the West. This marriage made Belmont a nephew of Commodore Oliver Hazard Perry, victor of the naval Battle of Lake Erie with the British in 1813. His marriage to a Christian gave rise to the rumor that he had been converted. There is no proof of this, although he is buried in a Christian cemetery in Newport, R.I. Some writers have said that Belmont's family name was originally Schoenberg and that Belmont is the Gallic form of Schoenberg. Belmont's oldest son, Perry, was twice elected to Congress from the town of Babylon, the only person sent to Congress from that part of New York up to 1953.

Cong. Beth Sholom, 441 Deer Park Ave.

Robert Moses State Park is named for Robert F. Moses, creator of Long Island's network of parks and connecting parkways. As president of the Long Island State Park Commission, Moses was responsible for acquiring the sites for every one of Long Island's state parks and for converting them into beautiful recreation spots. Moses was also president of the 1939 New York World's Fair. He masterminded New York City's network of new bridges, parkways, tunnels, shorefront parks, and initiated and supervised the development of Jones Beach. Descended from an old Sephardic family, Moses was secretary of state of New York in 1927 and the losing Republican candidate for governor in 1934 when he was defeated by Herbert H. Lehman.

Babylon was once proposed as the site of a Zionist training colony. In

1924, Israel Kramer bought a large tract in West Babylon with the intention of forming a Zionist colony there. This effort proved unsuccessful. Later, Kramer built one-family houses in the area which he named Ezra Park. The wide main street of the development has a sign that reads, "Herzel (sic) Boulevard."

BALDWIN
Baldwin Jewish Centre, 885 East Seaman Ave.
South Baldwin Jewish Center, 2959 Grand Ave.
South Shore YM & YWHA, 806 Merrick Rd.

BAY SHORE
Jewish Center, 34 N. Clinton St.
Sinai Reform Temple, 39 Brentwood Rd.

BELLMORE
Bellmore Jewish Center, 2550 S. Centre Ave.
East Bay Reform Temple, 2569 Merrick Rd.
Temple Beth-El, 1373 Bellmore Rd. (North Bellmore).

BETHPAGE
Hebrew Academy of Nassau County, 42 Locust Ave.
Jewish Center, 600 Broadway.
Society of Jewish Science, Round Swamp Rd. and Claremont Ave., has an unusual Torah inscribed in 1791 and used by Jews in Asiatic Russia. The Torah is enclosed in an elaborate silver and wood case. It is of Oriental origin and came originally from Bokhara in central Russia. It is made of leather rather than the usual parchment and uses a type of Oriental script. The society's services are similar to those held by the Society of Jewish Science in Manhattan. Services are held Friday evening and Saturday morning.

BRENTWOOD
Jewish Center, 28 Sixth Ave.

BROOKVILLE
Benjamin Abrams Communication Center, C.W. Post College of Long Island University, Northern Blvd., is named for the president of the Emerson Radio and Phonograph Corp., a trustee of the university.
Charles and Gertrude Merinoff Center of Association for the Help of Retarded Children, 189 Wheatly Rd., honors a husband and wife team that made many important contributions to the Nassau County chapter of the association.

CEDARHURST
Abraham Adelberg Monument, in the village park facing Cedarhurst Ave., near the L. I. Railroad station, is a memorial to the man who was one of the developers of the village and its mayor from 1928 until his death in 1932. Erected by public subscription, the monument is a large boulder to which is affixed a bas-relief portrait of Adelberg and the inscription: "To the memory of a beloved citizen unselfish in his devotion to community betterment."

Sephardic Temple, Branch Blvd.

Temple Beth El United Community Center, Broadway and Locust Ave.

Young Israel of Lawrence-Cedarhurst, 26 Columbia Ave.

CENTER MORICHES
Jewish Center of Moriches, Main St. This congregation is an outgrowth of a program of social and welfare services provided by Center Moriches residents to GIs from Camp Upton and the East Moriches Coast Guard Station from 1939 until the end of World War II. Leaders of this service established a men's club after the war and this became the nucleus of the congregation.

CENTRAL ISLIP
Temple Etz Chayim, 312 E. Suffolk Ave.

COLD SPRING HARBOR
Kehillath Sholom, 58 Goose Hill Rd.

COMMACK
Jewish Center, 83 Shirley Ct.

Temple Beth David, 100 Hauppauge Rd.

DEER PARK
Suffolk Jewish Center, 330 Central Ave.

DIX HILLS
Jewish Center, Deer Park Ave., has in its sanctuary a ceiling whose beams are interlaced to form Stars of David.

I. L. Peretz School, Timburr Lane Day School, Burr's Lane.

Temple Beth Torah, 158 Carman Rd.

EAST HAMPTON
Home, Sweet Home Museum, on the east side of the village green next to the church, was the birthplace, in 1791, of John Howard Payne, author of the words to the famed song, *Home, Sweet Home*, and grandson of Aaron Isaacs, one of the first Jewish settlers on Long Island. Some of the

property Isaacs once owned is now part of the extensive lands in East Hampton owned by Evan Manning Frankel, a product of New York's Lower East Side, who retired as a millionaire in 1952 and settled down in East Hampton. In 1975 he was said to own more than 1,000 acres of choice residential property in addition to his 15-acre estate, Brigadoon.

Jewish Center of the Hamptons, 44 Woods Lane.

EAST HILLS
Traditional Cong. of Roslyn-Kehilath Masoret.

EAST MEADOW
East Meadow Jewish Center, 1400 Prospect Ave.

Israel Grove, in the Carillon area of Eisenhower Park, a stand of 27 trees, one for each year of Israel's existence and one as a memorial to those who fell in her defense, was dedicated in 1974 by David Rivlin, Israel Consul General in New York.

Long Island Advisory Board of Anti-Defamation League of B'nai B'rith, 2310 Hempstead Tpke.

Memorial to the 6,000,000, a marble block set in stone in the lake area of Eisenhower Park, honors those murdered by the Nazis. Affixed to the block is a bronze tablet inscribed, "a living remembrance to the Six Million Jews." The memorial was originally dedicated in 1968 by Temple Beth El, Bellmore; Bellmore Jewish Center; Merrick Jewish Center; Cong. B'nai Israel, Freeport; South Baldwin Jewish Center; and Wantagh Jewish Center. It was rededicated in 1973 on the 30th anniversary of the Warsaw Ghetto Uprising, together with a memorial tree.

I. L. Peretz Jewish School, 574 Newbridge Ave.

Suburban Park Jewish Center, 400 Old Westbury Rd.

Temple Emanu-El, 123 Merrick Ave.

EAST NORTHPORT
East Northport Jewish Center, 328 Elwood Rd., has a sanctuary covered by an airy A-framed roof, representing the tent used by ancient Hebrews.

EAST ROCKAWAY
Hewlett-East Rockaway Jewish Center, 295 Main St., has in its main lobby a Holocaust memorial depicting the burning bush with six pointed flames symbolizing the 6 million martyrs. The flames are of various sizes to symbolize children, adults, and the elderly, and the contorted shapes recall the tortuous experience of these victims.

ELMONT
Belmont Park, the famous race track opened in 1905, is named for

August Belmont, Jewish-born horse breeder, diplomat, and banker.

Jewish Center, 500 Elmont Rd. and Cerenzia Blvd., has five stained glass windows depicting the First Five Books of Moses.

Temple B'nai Israel, Elmont Rd. and Baylis Ave.

FARMINGDALE

Jewish Center, 425 Fulton St., has a 25 by 17 foot mural composed of two dozen separate panels dominated by a painting of Moses and the burning bush. Two inscriptions in Hebrew frame the painting—"Thou shalt love thy God and "Love thy neighbor as thyself." Depicted in the mural are the signs of zodiac, major Jewish Holy days, and the names of the 12 tribes of Israel.

FIRE ISLAND

Fire Island Synagogue, Midway and C Street., Seaview, was founded by Herman Wouk, the author, and Joseph S. Gershman.

Robert F. Moses Beach is named for the man who conceived the idea of developing the South Shore barrier beaches off Long Island. The bridge over Fire Island Inlet is also named for him.

FLORAL PARK

Bellerose Jewish Center, 254-04 Union Turnpike.

Floral Park Jewish Center, 26 N. Tyson Ave.

Temple Sholom, 263-10 Union Turnpike.

FRANKLIN SQUARE

Central Nassau YM & YWHA, 276 Franklin Ave.

Jewish Center, Pacific and Lloyd Sts.

FREEPORT

Cong. B'nai Israel, 91 N. Bayview Ave.

Union Reform Temple, 475 N. Brookside Ave.

GARDEN CITY

Hillel Foundation at Adelphi University, Religious Center, South Ave.

Jewish Center, 168 Nassau Blvd.

GLEN COVE

Cong. Tifereth Israel, Hill Dr. and Landing Rd., is one of the oldest congregations on Long Island, having been founded in 1897.

Denis Park, at foot of Town Path, Glen St., now called Heritage Park, flies the flag of every nation represented by descendants of immigrants in the very ethnic city of Glen Cove, including the flag of Israel.

North Country Reform Temple, Crescent Beach Rd.

GREAT NECK

American Jewish Congress, North Shore Division, 98 Cutter Mill Rd.

Cong. Shomrei Hadat, 558 Middle Neck Rd.

Great Neck Synagogue, 26 Old Mill Rd.

North Shore Hebrew Academy, 26 Old Mill Rd.

Reconstructionist Synagogue, 2 Park Circle.

Temple Beth El, 5 Old Mill Rd., is the oldest of the eight synagogues in Great Neck, which has one of the largest Jewish communities on Long Island. Of the 44,000 people who reside in the nine incorporated villages (Great Neck, Great Neck Estates, Great Neck Plaza, Kensington, Kings Point, Lake Success, Russell Gardens, Saddle Rock, and Thomaston) and a small unincorporated area that make up what is generally known as Great Neck, 60 percent are Jewish. Beth El has a stunning stark white bimah, wall, and ark created by sculptress Louise Nevelson, a symbolic portrayal of a white flame to memorialize the 6,000,000 Jewish victims of the Holocaust. The nonobjective sculpture, consisting of white boxes of wood that break up light and shadow, is 55 feet wide and 15 feet high, and includes a design for the Ark and the Eternal Light. Eight of the Torahs in the Ark are dressed in handsewn mantles designed by Mrs. Ina Golub, and produced by a committee of 20 women. The mantles use word concepts rather than representative design. The words depicted are: *tzedakah*, light; *chesed*, loving kindness; *mishpat*, justice; *kedusha*, holiness; *shalom*, peace; *simcha*, joy; and *emet*, truth. Beth El has an excellent collection of Hebraic art and ceremonial objects. Among the latter is a Vienna brass Menorah which was smuggled out of Austria during the Nazi era by refugees. The huge synagogue doors depict a profusion of Biblical themes in 36 panels wrought in silver, 18 on each side.

Temple Beth Joseph, 1 Linden Pl.

Temple Emanuel, 150 Hicks Lane.

Temple Isaiah, 35 Bond St.

Temple Israel, 108 Old Mill Rd. A glass-enclosed corridor linking old and new buildings serves as a museum. One wall displays ancient Judaic relics and artifacts from Jewish communities of the past.

GREENPORT

Kaplan Avenue is named for Nathan Kaplan, an early settler here.

Temple Tifereth Israel, 4th St.

GREENVALE

B. Davis Schwartz Memorial Library of the C. W. Post Center of Long Island University, Greenvale Campus, is named for a benefactor of the college and former trustee, who was active in a variety of Jewish causes. The

$6 million structure has a capacity of one million volumes. The library houses the Cassirer Collection of Minerals, contributed by Fred Cassirer, a world-famous German-born mineralogist. The college's Interfaith Chapel, a $1.2 million structure, is one of two such chapels on Long Island, the other being at the U. S. Merchant Marine Academy at Kings Point.

HAUPPAUGE

Hebrew Academy of Suffolk, 525 Veteran's Memorial Highway, has a 20-foot Menorah in front of its building. The Rabbi Joseph Lief Library is a memorial to the late Jewish chaplain at the Veterans Administration Hospital at Northport.

Temple Beth Chai, Townline Rd.

HEMPSTEAD

American Jewish Committee, Long Island Chapter, 134 Jackson St.

Cong. Beth Israel, 94 Fulton Ave.

Hillel Foundation at Hofstra University, 100 Fulton St., has a tree outside its main door planted in memory of President Harry S. Truman in a *Tu Beshvat* ceremony.

Jewish Community Services of Long Island, 50 Clinton St.

George Morton Levy, Sr., Law Library at Hofstra University Law School, is named for the prominent attorney, and president and founder of Roosevelt Raceway.

Long Island Jewish Week, 156 N. Franklin St.

Paul Radin Memorial, a bas relief portrait of the famed anthropologist, is in the Hofstra University Library's Paul Radin Collection of 5,500 items that include Radin's own writings and those of Dr. Franz Boas, under whom he studied. The 9th floor of the Library is the David Filderman Gallery of Art.

Howard L. and Muriel Weingrow Fine Arts Library, which occupies one floor of the Hofstra University Library, on Hempstead Turnpike, is a major research collection of 4,000 books, documents, manuscripts, graphics, and prints relating to the foundations of modern art movements. Weingrow, who bought the collection from Philip Kaplan, has been a trustee of Hofstra University, an advisor to President Lyndon Johnson in the Office of Economic Opportunity, and served as treasurer of the Democratic National Committee in 1972.

HEWLETT

American Jewish Congress, South Shore Division, 301 Mill Rd.

Cong. Beth Emeth, 36 Franklin Ave.

Yeshiva Toras Chaim, 1170 William St.

HICKSVILLE

Theodore S. Cinnamon Ltd., 420 Jerusalem Ave., is a Judaica bookseller and publisher.

Cong. Shaarei Zedek, New South Rd. and Old Country Rd.

"Gates of Paradise," massive bronze doors whose ten panels depict famous episodes from the Hebrew Bible, are the entrance to Trinity Evangelical Lutheran Church, 40 West Nicholai St. They are exact replicas of the famed doors which Lorenzo Ghiberti fashioned in the early 1400s in Florence, Italy, for the Baptistery of the Cathedral of San Giovanni Battista. During World War II, sculptor Bruno Bearzi of Florence removed the famous sculptures to conceal them from the Nazis. While they were in his possession, he made molds from them—the molds from which he later cast the Hicksville replicas. The scenes depicted are Creation, Cain and Abel, Noah and the Ark, Abraham, Isaac and Jacob, Joseph, Moses on the way up Mt. Sinai, Joshua crossing the Jordan, David slaying Goliath, and Solomon welcoming the Queen of Sheba.

Jewish Center, Maglie Dr. and Jerusalem Ave.

Jewish Community Services of Long Island, 76 N. Broadway.

Pioneer Women, Nassau-Suffolk Council, 386 Oyster Bay Rd.

Temple Beth Elohim, RFD 1.

HUNTINGTON

Church St. is said to have acquired its name from the fact that the town's first synagogue was built at 11A Church St. Shorn of any Jewish symbolism, this building still stands as an apartment dwelling.

Dix Hills Jewish Center, 900 Walt Whitman Rd.

Huntington Jewish Center, 510 Park Ave. A chapel dedicated in 1976 memorializes the late Rabbi Joseph H. Lief, the Jewish chaplain at the Northport Veterans Administration Hospital, who led the daily *minyan* at the Center for many years.

Mt. Golda is one of the oldest Jewish cemeteries on Long Island.

Temple Beth El, 660 Park Ave.

HUNTINGTON STATION

Sholem Aleichem Folk Shule, Lincoln School, East 9th St.

South Huntington Jewish Center, 2600 New York Ave.

Temple Beth Torah, 660 Park Ave.

INWOOD

Jewish Community Center, Bayswater Blvd. and Elm Rd.

ISLAND PARK

Cong. Beth Emeth Jewish Center, 191 Long Beach Rd.

JERICHO
Jewish Center, North Broadway and Jericho Rd. Its building is said to have been the first religious structure erected by any faith in Jericho since 1788. There is a seating area for 1,500 people.

Temple Or-Elohim, 18 Tobie Lane.

Women's American ORT, North Shore Division, 50 Jericho Tpke.

JONES BEACH
Sidney Shapiro Memorial, in the Jones Beach Theatre, Gate D lobby, is a bronze plaque honoring the late chief engineer and general manager of the Long Island State Park Commission, who designed and built Jones Beach State Park and other parks, parkways, and bridges during a 46-year career with the commission.

KINGS PARK
Jewish Center, Route 25A, East Main St.

Patiky Street is named for the late Sam Patiky, his father and brothers, who settled on a farm in nearby Elwood at the turn of the century. The Patikys were founders of the Jewish Brotherhood in 1907—the original name of the Jewish Center.

KINGS POINT
U.S. Merchant Marine Academy has an interfaith chapel where Jewish services are held for Jewish cadets. The Torah was a gift of Chaplain and Mrs. Joshua L. Goldberg in 1962 on the centennial of the Jewish military chaplaincy.

LAKE GROVE
Markman's Center, 2842 Middle Country Rd., handles Judaica and Israeli gifts.

LAKE RONKONKOMA
Cong. Ohr Torah-Jewish Center, 821 Hawkins Ave. (Lake Grove).

LAKE SUCCESS
Jewish Center, 354 Lakeville Rd.

LAWRENCE
Brandeis School, 25 Frost Lane.

Cong. Beth Sholom, 390 Broadway.

Hillel School, 33 Washington Ave.

Temple Israel, 140 Central Ave., is a large synagogue shaped like a Magen David.

Temple Sinai, 131 Washington Ave., has a procession of stained glass windows in its sanctuary. The theme was inspired by the Biblical account of the Jews in the Sinai Desert.

The Source, 307 Central Ave., is a Judaica bookstore.

LEVITTOWN

This preplanned community of 60,000 was carved out of a stretch of potato fields, later renamed Levittown in honor of Abraham Levitt and his son, William, who built the town. When the Levitts opened the town's first section in 1947, returning veterans, desperate for housing, queued up in lines to rent the first 150 two-bedroom Cape Cods at $60 a month. Later the Levitts built more houses for rental or purchase—some selling as low as $6,990. By the end of 1951 there were 18,000 houses dotting the one-time potato fields.

Israel Community Center, 3235 Hempstead Tpke., the only Jewish institution in Levittown, stands on land donated by the Levitts. Construction began with much of the manual labor done by the members. There are 11,000 Jews in Levittown which has a total population of 65,000.

LIDO BEACH

Lido Beach Jewish Center, Fairway Rd.

LINDENHURST

Lindenhurst Hebrew Cong., 225 N. 4th St.

LONG BEACH

Once a summer resort for affluent Jewish New Yorkers, Long Beach began to decline in the 1960s, as the vacation habits of middle-class Jews shifted. Some of the beach clubs that dotted the Long Beach shore were taken over by Nassau County. Many of the large private homes have been converted to retirement and nursing homes. A good many of the year-round Jewish residents who had settled down in one-family homes built in newer sections of the city, have left, owing to the changing social conditions in the community. Nevertheless, 65 percent of the total population of 33,000 is Jewish, making Long Beach the only city north of Miami Beach with a Jewish majority.

Al's Kosher Delicatessen and Restaurant, 897 W. Beech.

Beach YM & YWHA, 405 Long Beach Rd.

Cong. Bachurei Chemed, 210 Edwards Blvd., is a Jewish youth congregation, probably the only one of its kind in the United States. In 1946, a group of young people, dissatisfied with the religious observance of their parents, organized a congregation of their own, with the assistance and advice of their Hebrew teacher, Simon Solomon. Three years later, thirteen adults who had gathered after Hosha'ana Rabbah services decided to launch a campaign for funds for a synagogue for the Orthodox Jewish youth congregation. The synagogue is small but complete. In the center is a modern square *bimah* with Jewish symbols in its design. The Ark is in the form of two giant tablets of the Ten Commandments. There is a balcony for girls and women. Although adults attend services quite regularly and are given the honor of being called up to the Torah, the entire service is conducted by the youth; it is not, however, a junior congregation since nothing in the service is omitted. The entire service is in Hebrew; eight boys serve as readers of the Torah and four serve as cantors.

Cong. Beth Sholom, 700 East Park Ave.

Edwards Boulevard is named for Louis F. Edwards, who was mayor of Long Beach from 1937-1939 when he was murdered. Edwards was one of four Jews who have been mayor of this seashore city.

Hebrew Academy of Long Beach, 530 West Broadway.

Jewish Association for Services to the Aged, 74 West Park Ave., a branch of an agency of the Federation of Jewish Philanthropies of New York, serves many of the estimated 8,500 older Jewish residents who live in fading hotels, retirement homes, nursing homes, or in apartments. These residents represent the largest number of low-income Jews in the county.

Komanoff Extended Care Facility of Long Beach Memorial Hospital, 455 E. Bay Rd., honors Mrs. Isidore Komanoff, the first woman to be elected to the Nassau Board of Supervisors, and her husband, who were among the city's leading civic leaders for 30 years.

Lido Beach Jewish Center, 1 Fairway Rd.

Lido Hotel, opened in 1928 as a Riviera resort close to home for New York socialites, rigidly barred Jews until 1940 when it passed into Jewish ownership. Today the hotel is a *glatt* kosher establishment that caters to middle-aged well-to-do Jews.

Marron's Kosher Delicatessen Restaurant, 17 E. Park Ave.

Rabbinical College of Long Island, 205 West Beech St.

Sephardic Congregation of Long Beach, 161 Lafayette Blvd.

Tel Aviv Kosher Delicatessen and Restaurant, 51 E. Park Ave.

Temple Beth El, 570 West Walnut St., houses JASA-Brookdale Senior Citizens Center.

Temple Emanu-El, 455 Neptune Blvd.

Temple Israel, Riverdale Blvd. and Walnut St.

Temple Zion, 62 Maryland Ave.

YM & YWHA of Long Beach, 405 Long Beach Rd.

Young Israel, 158 Long Beach Rd.

LYNBROOK

Cong. Beth David, 188 Vincent Ave.

Temple Emanu-El, Ross Plaza.

Women's American ORT, South Shore Division, 381 Sunrise Hwy.

MALVERNE
Jewish Center, 1 Norwood Lane.

MANHASSET
Levitt Clinic of North Shore University Hospital, 300 Community Drive, a five-story diagnostic center serving as a referral center for Long Island's 4,500 physicians, is named for William I. Levitt, the noted builder and philanthropist, who contributed $1 million toward the $9 million cost.

Reconstructionist Synagogue, Friends Meeting House, Northern Blvd. and Shelter Rock Rd. When and if zoning problems are cleared up, the congregation will move to Glenwood Rd., Roslyn Harbor.

Temple Judea, 333 Searington Rd.

MASSAPEQUA
Cong. Beth El, 99 Jerusalem Ave.

Hillel Hebrew Academy, 1066 Hicksville Rd.

Temple Judea, Jerusalem and Central Aves., has a 3 by 10 foot multicolored tapestry depicting the Jewish holiday symbols. Created by members of the sisterhood, the needlepoint piece adorns a second story wall.

Temple Sinai, 270 Clocks Blvd.

MASTIC BEACH
Hebrew Center, Neighborhood Rd.

MELVILLE
L.I. Jewish World, Windsor Pl.

Temple Beth Torah, Bagatelle Rd.

MERRICK
Cong. Ohav Sholom, 145 S. Merrick Ave.

Mama Liga's Kosher Steakhouse, 2035 Merrick Rd.

Merrick Jewish Center, 225 Fox Blvd.

Temple Beth Am, Kirkwood and Merrick Aves.

Temple Israel of S. Merrick, 2655 Clubhouse Rd.

MIDDLE ISLAND
Stones with Hebrew lettering, on west side of Miller Place—Yaphank Rd., about 3 miles north of Middle Country Rd., used as a protection barrier on a sod farm, are not pieces of Jewish gravestones. They are old cemetery stones—not gravestones—that were once part of posts or arches erected many years ago by individuals or congregations to mark the entrances or boundaries of their plots in Mount Carmel Cemetery, Brooklyn. The stones were removed some years ago, with the permission of the owners, to allow for easier maintenance of the cemetery. The owner of the sod farm acquired large chunks of granite and cement from the cemetery. One large stone that

was probably used as an archway is inscribed, "Cong. Kehilath Jeshurun, East 85th St., N. Y." Some of the stones have names on them and others have Hebrew carvings.

MINEOLA

Cong. Beth Sholom, 261 Willis Ave.

Court House of N.Y. State Supreme Court, Trial Term Part One, displays portraits of retired Supreme Court Justices Bernard Meyer and Manuel Levine.

Jewish Association for Services to Aged, 158 3rd St.

Jewish Community Services of L.I., 158 3rd St.

NEW HYDE PARK

Jewish Community Center, 100 Lakeville Rd.

L.I. Institute for Jewish Studies (Hineni House), 76-48 26th St.

Long Island Jewish-Hillside Medical Center, 271-11 76th Ave., the largest voluntary hospital in Nassau County, is a merger of the Long Island Jewish Medical Center and Hillside Hospital, both agencies of the Federation of Jewish Philanthropies. Adjacent to the medical center and attached to it by an underpass, is the $25 million Jewish Institute for Geriatric Care, also a Federation agency, which was the nation's first medical-geriatric-psychiatric complex. On the grounds of the medical center is the metropolitan New York area's first major children's hospital.

Temple Emanuel, 3315 Hillside Ave.

Young Israel, 264-15 77th Ave.

NORTH BELLMORE

Temple Beth El, 1373 Bellmore Rd.

Young Israel of North Bellmore, 2428 Hamilton Rd.

NORTHPORT

Rube Goldberg's desk, at which the famed cartoonist did much of his work from 1940 until his death in 1971, is one of the prized possessions of the Department of Adult Education of the Northport Public Schools, 66 Laurel Rd. Goldberg lived at Asharoken in the Northport school district for many years and often shared his art for community causes. It was bequeathed by his widow to the Department.

NORTH WOODMERE

Cong. Ohr Torah, 410 Hungry Harbor Rd. This is also the headquarters of Hineni, a Jewish evangelistic organization led by Mrs. Esther Jungreis, wife of the congregation's rabbi. The congregation has the first Holocaust Museum on Long Island, housing artifacts and memorabilia of concentration camps, including items that were used or worn by survivors.

OAKDALE
B'nai Israel Reform Temple, Biltmore Ave. and Idle Hour Blvd.

OCEANSIDE
Sholem Aleichem School, 3980 Weidener Ave.
Cong. B'nai Torah, Oceanside Rd.
Cong. Shaar Hashamayim, 3309 Skillman Ave.
Jewish Center of Ocean Harbor, Weidner and Royal Aves.
Oceanside Jewish Center, 2860 Brower Ave.
Temple Avodah, 3050 Oceanside Rd.
Young Israel, 150 Waukena Ave.

OLD BETHPAGE
Synagogue of Jewish Science, 825 Round Swamp Rd.
Temple Beth Elohim, 926 Round Swamp Rd.

OLD WESTBURY
Westbury Hebrew Cong., 21 Old Westbury Rd.

OYSTER BAY
Jewish Center, Marion St.
Sagamore Hill National Historic Site, Cove Neck Rd., the former home of President Theodore Roosevelt, has on exhibit in the North Room, a pair of seven-branched Menorahs, a gift to the Roosevelts from a family friend.

PATCHOGUE
Temple Beth El, 45 Oak St.
Young Israel of Patchogue, 28 Mowbray St.

PLAINEDGE
Dr. Gerald Greenberg Museum in the Northedge Elementary School, Stewart Ave., north of Hempstead Tpke., is named for the school's late principal who helped create the museum.

PLAINVIEW
Jewish Center, 95 Floral Dr.
Malka's Jerusalem, 1103 Old Country Rd., is an Israeli nightclub.
Manetto Hill Jewish Center, 244 Manetto Hill Rd.
Mid-Island YMHA, Orchard St. (old Fern Place School).
Ruby's Delicatessen and Restaurant, 387 S. Oyster Bay Rd.
Young Israel of Plainview, 115 Northern Pkwy.

PORT JEFFERSON STATION
North Shore Jewish Center, 385 Old Town Rd.

PORT WASHINGTON

Community Synagogue, 150 Middle Neck Rd. (Sands Point). One of the synagogue's two buildings looks like a medieval castle. It was once part of the estate of former Gov. Averell Harriman. The congregation's Antique Judaica Museum contains 95 important ceremonial objects.

Daniel and Florence Guggenheim Elementary School, Port Washington Blvd., is named for the noted Jewish philanthropists.

Port Jewish Center, 1515 Middle Neck Rd. (United Methodist Church), had as its rabbi in 1974-75 Michal Seserman who was ordained in 1975 as the third woman rabbi in the United States.

Temple Beth Israel, Temple Dr. A tapestry composed of 161,280 knots hooked by 318 persons hanging in the sanctuary, illustrates the concepts of the Sabbath as "the culmination of creation." At the base of the exterior of the building, a tower that forms an extension of the bimah area, is a framed window containing an illuminated Menorah. The building was designed by the well-known architect, Percival Goodman.

RIVERHEAD

Suffolk County Historical Society, 300 W. Main St., has on exhibit the famous John Hulbert Flag, said to be the first American flag with stars and stripes, which also contains 13 six-pointed white stars on a field of blue. Made a year before the Betsy Ross emblem, the Hulbert Flag was carried by Capt. John Hulbert of Bridgehampton and his company of Minute Men during the first year of the Revolutionary War.

Temple Israel, 490 Northville Tpke.

ROCKVILLE CENTRE

Barasch Memorial Field, a part of Lister Park on Sunrise Highway, is named for Samuel Barasch, who was the village's recreation director from 1940-1952.

Central Synagogue of Nassau County, 430 DeMott Ave.

Hebrew Union College—Jewish Institute of Religion School of Religion Extension, 430 DeMott Ave.

Temple B'nai Sholom, 100 Hempstead Ave.

ROOSEVELT FIELD

A 16-foot Menorah, on the Fountain Mall, South End, of this well-known area, is lighted daily during Chanukah.

ROSLYN

Lincoln Kosher Delicatessen, Inc., 29 Lincoln Ave.

Solomon Schechter Day School, Roslyn Rd., (Roslyn Heights).

Shelter Rock Jewish Center, Shelter Rock and Searingtown Rds.

Temple Beth Sholom, Roslyn Rd. and Northern State Pkwy. (Roslyn Heights).

Temple Sinai, 425 Roslyn Rd., (Roslyn Heights), has a junior chapel dedicated to the memory of Anne Frank, the celebrated Jewish martyr and diarist.

ROSLYN HARBOR

Reconstructionist Synagogue of North Shore, plans to occupy its own building on Glenwood Rd. when and if it can overcome present zoning problems.

SAG HARBOR

Temple Adas Israel, Elizabeth St. and Atlantic Ave., is believed to worship in the oldest existing synagogue building on Long Island, its sanctuary having been erected in 1898. Its old cemetery is on Route 114, on the way to East Hampton.

SANDS POINT

Benjamin and Rita Kaufman Learning Center of the Maimonides Institute.

Sands Point Park and Preserve is a 200-acre Nassau County nature preserve bequeathed to the public by Harry Guggenheim in 1971. Scion of the famous family of industrialists, mining tycoons, and philanthropists, Guggenheim was an aviator in World Wars I and II, served as U.S. Ambassador to Cuba, and was cofounder and publisher of *Newsday*, the famous L.I. daily newspaper. "Falaise," a 26-room Norman mansion containing many art treasures, was also bequeathed by Guggenheim. Hempstead House, Guggenheim's former residence, houses exhibits on Daniel Guggenheim, Harry's father. In this house Charles A. Lindbergh found refuge after his historic flight in 1927, and where he and other noted fliers were often guests. Harry Guggenheim was one of the chief supporters of the rocket and astronautic experiments of Dr. Robert Goddard. Among the exhibits in Hempstead House are some of Harry Guggenheim's uniforms and the horseracing trophies he won.

SAYVILLE

Temple Shalom, 225 Greeley Ave.

SEAFORD

Jewish Center, 2343 S. Seamen's Neck Rd.

Mid-Island YMHA, 3833 Jerusalem Ave., is a branch of the main building in Plainview.

SETAUKET

Hillel Foundation at State University of New York at Stony Brook, 75 Sheep Pasture Rd.

SMITHTOWN

Hebrew Academy of Suffolk County, 525 Veterans Highway.

Jewish Community Services of L.I., 22 Lawrence Ave.

Suffolk County Institute of Jewish Studies, meets weekly in St. Anthony's High School, St. John Ave.

Temple Beth Shalom, Edgewood Ave. and River Rd.

The Melting Pot, Hillside Shopping Plaza, Route 111, is a Kosher-style restaurant.

West Suffolk YM-YWHA, 22 Lawrence Ave.

STONY BROOK

Hillel Foundation, State University, (see Setauket).

L. I. Hall of Fame, a sculpture garden in the Stony Brook Museum, has a smiling bronze likeness of Robert F. Moses, who was among the first three Long Islanders elected to the Hall of Fame.

State University of New York at Stony Brook has a Benjamin N. Cardozo College for Men, named for the late justice of the U. S. Supreme Court (see Albany, New York); •Ruth Benedict College honoring the late anthropologist who trained Margaret Mead; •a dormitory named for Bernard M. Baruch, adviser to Presidents; •and the Roth Quadrangle, named for Emery Roth, Jr., the noted architect.

Temple Isaiah, 1404 Stony Brook Rd.

SYOSSET

Central Hebrew High School, 330 S. Oyster Bay Rd.

East Nassau Hebrew Cong., 310A South Oyster Bay Rd., has two giant stained glass windows, each 32 feet high by 30 feet wide, on the entire eastern wall of the sanctuary, that depict the Ten Commandments. Superimposed are huge flames that leap up and around the letters, representing the Burning Bush, as a symbol of eternal religious freedom. The windows are framed in tiny blue tiles that glow at night on the Northern Pkwy. Two huge arches frame the windows on the outside, representing the Tablets of the Law. On the synagogue grounds is an apple tree that is pruned into the shape of a Menorah.

Midway Jewish Center, 330 South Oyster Bay Rd.

North Shore Synagogue, 83 Muttontown Rd.

UNIONDALE

Hebrew Academy of Nassau County, 215 Oak St., occupies a site that was once part of Mitchell Field.

Jewish Center, 760 Jerusalem Ave.

UPTON

Brookhaven National Laboratory, the largest atomic laboratory in the nation, is dedicated to basic research on the peaceful uses of atomic energy. Among the founders was Dr. I. L. Rabi, Columbia University Nobel laureate in physics.

VALLEY STREAM

Gertrude Wachtler Cohen Hearing and Vertigo Center at Franklin General Hospital, 900 Franklin Ave.

Cong. Beth Sholom (Sunrise Jewish Center), 550 Rockaway Ave.

Jewish Center of Alden Terrace (Cong. Tree of Life), 502 N. Central Ave.

Temple Gates of Zion, 322 N. Corona Ave.

Temple Hillel (Southside Jewish Center), 1000 Rosedale Rd.

Temple Judea, 195 Rockaway Ave.

WANTAGH

Federation Employment & Guidance Service, 3521 Jerusalem Ave.

Jewish Center, 3710 Woodbine Ave.

Jewish Community Services, 3521 Jerusalem Ave.

L. I. Pedagogic Center of N. Y. Board of Jewish Education, 3521 Jerusalem Ave.

South Shore YM & YWHA, 806 Merrick Rd.

Suburban Temple, 2900 Jerusalem Ave.

United Jewish Ys of L. I., 3521 Jerusalem Ave.

WESTBURY

Community Reform Temple (Temple Beth Avodah), 275 Ellison Ave.

Israeli Doll Collection, among a collection of more than 1,000 dolls, is on view in the home of Mr. and Mrs. Alfred Marcus, 17 Lace Lane.

Temple Beth Torah, 243 Cantiague Rd.

Temple Sholom, 675 Brookside Court.

WEST HEMPSTEAD

Hebrew Academy of Nassau County 609 Hempstead Ave.

Jewish Community Center, 711 Dogwood Ave.

Nassau Community Temple, 240 Hempstead Ave.

Young Israel, 640 Hempstead Ave., paid $1 to Francis T. Purcell, a Catholic who was presiding supervisor of the town of Hempstead, for a 20-year lease to a square mile of West Hempstead as "common ground for the purpose of carrying." The synagogue is within that mile square area and its Orthodox members are permitted to carry prayerbooks, talethim, and other items to and from the synagogue on the Sabbath. This "fenced in" area is known as an *eruv*. The Talmud bars such carrying except on common ground surrounded by a wall, in this case an encirclement of telephone poles.

WOODMERE

Cong. Sons of Israel, 111 Irving Pl., has a series of five stained glass windows depicting the first five books of the Hebrew Bible.

Young Israel, 859 Peninsula Blvd.

WOODSBURGH

An almost all-Jewish village of 830 residents in 217 houses, tucked away among the better known Five Towns villages of Hewlett, Woodmere, and Cedarhurst, has only five known non-Jewish residents.

WYANDANCH

Usdan Center for the Creative and Performing Arts, 185 Colonial Springs Rd., named for Suzanne and Nathaniel Usdan, and the Alice N. Proskauer Site of the Henry Kaufmann Campgrounds are situated on 231 acres of woodlands and rolling hills on one of the highest elevation points on Long Island. This country day camp is equipped to serve 2,400 children daily from the Jewish Community Centers and YMHAs of New York City, Nassau, and Suffolk Counties. The first multi-agency country day camp to be developed on the outskirts of New York City with permanent structures, the Henry Kaufmann Campgrounds provide city youngsters with a true camping experience in a natural, rustic environment. Sponsored by the Federation of Jewish Philanthropies of New York, the Henry Kaufmann Campgrounds has pioneered the fast-growing trend of country day camping during the last decade.

NEW YORK CITY

New York Jewry Today

In 1976 there were 1,998,000 Jews in the five boroughs of New York City and the adjacent suburban counties of Nassau, Suffolk, and Westchester. This is a decline of 357,000 since 1963. Once the Jews of Greater New York represented 40 percent of all the Jews in the country but now they represent slightly less than 30 percent of the 5,731,685 in the United States.

In the city proper, the Jewish population in 1975 was reported to be 1,228,000, a drop of 600,000 over the 1963 figure and a loss of 886,000 over the all-time high of 2,115,000 reached in 1957. In the three suburban counties there were 770,000 Jews compared with 500,000 in 1964.

Manhattan has 171,000 Jews, a figure that surpasses only The Bronx's 143,000 and Staten Island's 21,000. The Jewish population of The Bronx, which reached a peak of 585,000 in 1930 when it accounted for 38 percent of all the Jews in the city, fell to 493,000 in 1937, declined again to 396,000 in 1960, and is now only 143,000. Brooklyn, which had 765,000 Jews in 1964, now has 514,000. Queens' Jewish population dropped from 450,000 in 1964 to 379,000 today. Staten Island's Jewish population rose from 13,000 in 1964 to 21,000 today.

Nassau County, with 455,000 Jews, has more Jews than any county except Brooklyn. Suffolk County, east of Nassau County, has 150,000 Jews, while Westchester County, just north of The Bronx, has 165,000 Jews.

Manhattan, the seat of the city's major business establishments and principal governmental, cultural, communications, entertainment, and transportation centers, is also the headquarters of every city-wide Jewish organization and of all national Jewish agencies and institutions located in New York.

New York is also the command post of American Jewry. All but three national Jewish organizations have their headquarters there. This concentration enables the national Jewish organizations and their apparatus to exercise a greater influence on the city's Jewish communal agencies than any local Jewish agency except the Federation of Jewish Philanthropies and the United Jewish Appeal of Greater New York.

While American Jewish life relies heavily on the leadership and philanthropic activities of New York Jewry, it is not really a community but more like "a collection of communities—religious, residential, commercial, intellectual—with interlocking ties, a diverse society that pervades and enriches the entire city." Unlike all other American cities with substantial Jewish populations, New York does not have an overall unified fundraising community-planning or representative body acting and speaking for all Jews.

The Federation of Jewish Philanthropies plans and raises funds for some 130 local health, welfare, medical, educational, and recreational agencies affiliated with it. The United Jewish Appeal of Greater New York, operating out of separate offices from the national United Jewish Appeal, is the principal local fundraising agency for overseas needs, and also provides New York's share of the budgets of several national organizations. Since 1974, Federation and the UJA of Greater New York have combined their annual campaigns into a single joint campaign.

The New York Board of Rabbis, with many members outside the Greater New York area, concerns itself with religious and interreligious matters. The Board of Jewish Education of New York is the central service agency for elementary and secondary Jewish education. The metropolitan area council of the National Jewish Welfare Board unites the city's Jewish Community Centers and YM-YWHAs, some of which are part of the Associated YM & YWHAs of Greater New York. A city-wide Jewish Community Relations Council that will coordinate the efforts of local councils in various parts of the city and also coordinate community relations activities of the metropolitan units of some of the national agencies affiliated with the National Jewish Community Relations Advisory Council and a number of other agencies with community relations programs was created in 1976.

There are also a number of city-wide federations, councils, and chapters of national organizations and thousands (the exact figure is unknown), of local voluntary associations ranging from synagogues, schools, and charitable societies to cultural and social clubs and neighborhood branches of national agencies.

Jews outside of New York regard New York Jewry as a prize example of organized chaos. They grumble at the influence it wields in national Jewish affairs and complain that it does not always meet its full share of national communal responsibilities. Virtually all national Jewish organizations were once headed by New Yorkers; today more and more top national Jewish leadership is drawn from other cities. Although New York is a major convention city, few national Jewish conclaves meet here. When Jewish communities beyond the Greater New York area are asked to support a national or international movement or institution, they always make inquiries as to how much New York will give, and usually insist that the city accept one-third of the quota.

Jews represent 2.8 percent of the American population, but they are seven times as numerous in New York as in the country as a whole. They are overwhelmingly English-speaking and native born, economically middle and upper middle-class, with a large proportion college educated. The Jewish birthrate in New York is falling but the percentage of intermarriage is far lower than in other cities.

Jews in New York earn less on the average than their coreligionists elsewhere in the United States but somewhat more than their Catholic fellow townsmen. Twenty-seven out of 100 gainfully employed New Yorkers are Jews. They account for 41 percent of all New Yorkers in trade, 30 percent in amusement, 35 percent in manufacturing, but only 14 percent of construction workers, 13 percent of transportation workers, 12 percent in finance, and 4 percent in public utilities. Not all Jewish businessmen are merchants and not all Jewish professionals are doctors, lawyers, dentists, or accountants; 26.5 percent of them are self-employed.

A 1973 study by Federation found that 15.1 percent of the city's Jews are poor or near poor, with incomes under $6,000 for a family of four, representing 140,000 families including 272,000 individuals. There were 316,800 one-person Jewish families of which 72,900 were below the poverty level. Half of the Jewish poor were aged couples or individuals.

The 1970 census reported that 543,000 New Yorkers still listed Yiddish as their mother tongue, including 189,000 American-born, 600 blacks, and 65 Puerto Ricans. In New York the municipal hospitals all provide kosher food on request. Often mobile synagogues manned by Chasidic rabbinical students are parked at the city's busiest corners and Jewish passersby are urged to try on phylacteries and to accept gift *mezuzahs*.

In New York the public schools are officially closed on Jewish High Holy Days because about half the teachers are Jewish. There are 800 members of the Shomrim, an association of Jewish policemen, about 200 in the Ner Tomid Society, a similar organization of Jewish firemen, and 15,000 Jewish employees in the Post Office. One out of every seven municipal employees is a Jew. New York Jews show a higher percentage of skilled and semi-skilled workers than do Jews in other parts of the country.

In the vast aggregation of New York Jews there are bankers and truck drivers, United Nations officials and kosher butchers, Nobel Prize winners and actors, policemen and professors, labor union leaders and salesmen, teachers and manufacturers, cabbies and bagelmakers, writers and caterers, rabbis and advertising executives, social workers and garment workers, builders and intellectuals, editors and brokers, and employees of Jewish organizations.

They live in duplex apartments on Park and Fifth Avenues and on Sutton Place, in the huge public, private, and cooperative housing developments, in one and two-family houses in the city and the suburbs, in high rise apartments, and in deteriorating tenements. Some commute by railroad and others are part of the daily subway and bus throngs. They are synagogue-goers of every theological belief, agnostics and atheists, weekend golfers, and *payot*-wearing Chasidim. They are successful novelists, playwrights, fashion designers, teenagers wearing yarmulkas in the subway, businessmen planning a real estate deal, cabbies who speak Yiddish and Hebrew, bankers who collect modern art, bearded Chasidim who drive trucks, and students at every college and university.

In New York one may find a Loyal League of Yiddish Sons of Erin which marches in the St. Patrick's Day parade; advertising banners that span main streets from building to building urging contributions to the United Jewish Appeal and Federation, or the purchase of Israel bonds; street solicitors collecting for Jewish schools, homes, and orphanages; full page advertisements in the *New York Times* for major philanthropies; newspaper travel sections crammed with ads of kosher and Jewish-style resorts; Hanukah clubs and Menorahs in banks and Hanukah greetings in railroad stations; extra cars on commuter trains to accommodate Jews rushing home on the eve of Jewish holy days; and kosher food ads containing Hebrew words in the daily newspapers.

The telephone directories require more than 40 pages just to list the Cohens, Levys, and Goldbergs; the social register has its quota of identifiable Jews; telegraph offices provide special blanks to encourage Jews to send holiday greetings by wire; every politician carries a black and white yarmulke in his pocket—black for luncheons and white for dinners and bar mitzvahs; bagels are available in the United Nations cafeteria; cries of "barata, barata" (bargains, bargains) resound on the Lower East Side as Jewish merchants call out to Puerto Rican shoppers; nearly 100,000 Israeli residents make New York "Israel's fourth city;" mini-food trucks bedecked with Hebrew lettering dispense *glatt* kosher hot dogs and snacks on city streets; and the Hebrew calendar can be followed in the window displays of department stores and candy shops.

In New York there are rabbinically supervised kosher Chinese restaurants with such piquant names as Shang-Chai, Moshe Peking, and Jerusalem East; an Irish pub called the "Irish Yarmulke;" the open-air diamond market on West 47th Street where a gem can be bought from bearded Chasidic Jews, the deal closed with a simple *Mazel tov* and perhaps a lunch at the diamond center's *glatt* kosher restaurant; a guide to the Jewish community of New York used by police in neighborhoods with a large Orthodox Jewish population; truck signs that read, "no passing" on the right, and "Happy Passover" on the left; "Wong Fat, Kosher Butcher" in a shop window in Chinatown; and "Se Habla Yiddish" in a fruit market in Spanish Harlem.

The size of the Jewish population and its impact on the city have fascinated, startled, irked, and impressed foreign and domestic observers since the turn of the century. Jew and New Yorker became synonymous in American folklore in the 1880s when New York's Jewish residents first began to excite comment. Widespread Jewish association with the easily identifiable and widely imitated New York products of the world of fashion, entertainment, and ideas sometimes saddled Jews with the envy and ill will the city engendered in other sections of the country.

Henry James wrote in 1907 that he was shocked at "the Hebrew conquest of New York" which he feared would transform the city into "a new Jerusalem." A visiting Englishman in 1910 found that the Jews, along with other non-British stock, constituted the city's chief audience for the offerings of opera and concert music—an observation that is still valid. Some Americans stated that, "New York would be all right if it were not for the damned Jews." A cliche current in the 1920s was that New York was built by the Italians, run by the Irish, and owned by the Jews. What this really meant was that Italian immigrants provided most of the labor for subways and skyscrapers, that Irish immigrants and their descendants dominated the police force and key political offices, and that immigrant or native born Jews were the city's leading merchants and department storeowners.

Ford Madox Ford, the noted British writer, observed in 1926 that New York owes "its intellectual vividness partly to the presence of an immense Jewish population . . . the only people . . . in New York . . . who really loved books with a real passionate yearning that transcended their attention to all terrestrial manifestations." Another foreigner found in the 1920s that "Israelite support of the arts was the difference between hardly supportable indigence and just bearable comfort for the city's creative talents."

The magazine *Fortune*, in a 1960 issue entirely devoted to New York, brought the picture up-to-date when it declared that "the great Jewish population gives New York much of the dynamism and vigor that make the city unique among all the cities on earth . . . Jewish elan has contributed to the city's dramatic character—its excitement, its originality, its stridency, its unexpectedness."

In 1963, the eminent Jewish sociologist, Nathan Glazer, in his book *Beyond the Melting Pot*, described the Jews of New York as "a group that may never act together and that may never feel together, but that does know it is a single group, from which one can be disengaged only by a series of deliberate acts. Only a minority are 'Jews' if we use some concrete defining index. Only a minority belongs to synagogues, is sent to Jewish schools, deals with Jewish welfare agencies, is interested in Jewish culture, speaks a traditional Jewish language, and can be distinguished by dress and custom as Jews. But, added together, the overlapping minorities create a community with a strong self-consciousness and definite character." A song in a Broadway musical put it this way: "When you're in New York, the whole world seems Jewish and the moon is yarmulke high in the sky."

How It All Began

In the first week of September, 1654, four men, two women, and 17 children, landed in the tiny Dutch outpost of New Amsterdam. They were the founders of New York Jewry. These 23 were the first permanent Jewish settlers in North America, although not the first Jews in the American colonies. Perhaps a score of others are known to have been in the English, Dutch, and French settlements before 1650, and even earlier in the Spanish domains in Florida and New Mexico, where they lived as secret Jews.

The journey for the 23 began in May, 1654, in Brazil. Marranos, or secret Jews, had found a tenuous haven in Catholic Brazil for more than a century, after fleeing the inquisition in Spain and Portugal when those lands expelled the Jews at the end of the 15th century. When the Dutch conquered northern Brazil in 1624, the Marranos established the first public Jewish communities in the Americas at Bahia and Recife.

After the Portuguese recaptured northern Brazil in 1654, they gave the Dutch colonists the option of staying and pledging allegiance to Portugal, or leaving within three months. Choosing exile to Portuguese rule, the 600 Jews of Brazil disposed of their property at a huge loss and sought a new refuge. Most of them headed for Holland, where there was an influential colony of Portuguese Jews. A smaller group sailed for the British, French, and Dutch islands in the Caribbean.

One Netherlands bound ship, carrying 23 Jews and a party of Dutch Calvinists, was captured by Spanish pirates. En route to a Spanish port in the West Indies, the buccaneer vessel was seized by a French privateersman and towed to the French West Indies. Stranded in a strange port, the pauperized refugees had only 933 guilders, and some clothing and house furnishings. When the French captain demanded 2,500 guilders for passage to New Amsterdam, the Jews agreed, and pledged themselves to be collectively responsible for the debt, with all their belongings to be forfeited if the full amount was not paid.

Whether they decided to go to New Amsterdam because they knew it was a Dutch colony whose motherland was a haven for religious dissenters, or whether their coming to New Amsterdam was accidental is still a matter of speculation. So is the name of the ship. The Reverend Johannes Polhemus, pastor of the Dutch Reformed Church in Brazil, one of its passengers, referred to it as the *St. Charles*. The old Dutch minutes of New Amsterdam are too faded in some places for a positive identification, but an English translation published in 1884 called the vessel the *Ste. Catherine*.

The "Jewish Mayflower" reached New Amsterdam a year after its incorporation as a city of 800 inhabitants whose houses were clustered at the tip of Manhattan Island. To collect the balance of the passage money, the ship's captain had the Jews' property sold at public auction. Three of the six adults were imprisoned as debtors when the sale left them still owing 495 guilders. Obliged to pay the daily board of the debtors, as well as special court costs, the Frenchman agreed to their release when his crew consented to wait for their share of the debt until the Jews heard from their kinfolk in Holland.

The Dutch burghers who had bought the Jews' belongings at bargain rates returned them to their owners and took some of the Jews into their own homes. But most of them camped in the open. The minister of New Amsterdam's Dutch Reformed Church grumbled about it, but during the bitter winter of 1654-55 he used church funds to feed "some Jews, poor but healthy," who came "several times to my house, weeping and bewailing their misery."

One, and possibly two, Jews preceded the 23 to New Amsterdam. Solomon Pietersen, counsel for the Jews in the ship captain's action against them, was identified as a Jew in the Dutch records, but Jewish historians are skeptical. But Jacob Barsimson, who arrived on July 8, 1654, was a Jew. The Dutch minutes noted his coming on the ship *Peartree* as "Jew, debtor," who owed 36 guilders for passage and board. He was either an agent of the Amsterdam Jews, exploring the possibility of extensive immigration to New Amsterdam, or a trader in the employ of the Dutch West India Company.

New Amsterdam's Governor Peter Stuyvesant made the Jews' impoverishment an excuse to demand that they "be not allowed further to infest and trouble this new colony." The peg-legged tyrant informed the Dutch West India Company that he intended to order the Jews out, "fearing that owing to their present indigence they might become a charge in the coming winter." Repeatedly, he sought to persuade his superiors that since "we have Papists, Mennonites and Lutherans among the Dutch," and "also many Puritans or independents among the English under this government, who conceal themselves under the name of Christians, it would create still greater confusion if the obstinate and immovable Jews came to settle here."

In January, 1655, the Jews appealed to the Dutch West India Company to revoke Stuyvesant's ouster order. In their plea for permission to stay, the Jews predicted that "the more of loyal people that go to live there (New Amsterdam) the better it is in regard to the payment of various excises and taxes which may be imposed there, and in regard to the increase of trade, and also to the importation of all the necessities that may be sent there."

On April 26, 1655, the Company replied to the Jewish plea in a letter of instructions to Stuyvesant. While agreeing with his fear that the presence of the Jews would create difficulties, the Company reminded the governor that the Jews had suffered heavy losses in Brazil out of loyalty to Holland and that their coreligionists were substantial investors in the Company. For these reasons Stuyvesant was told that "these people may travel and trade to and in New Amsterdam and live and remain there, provided the poor among them shall not become a burden to the Company or to the community, but be supported by their own nation." A year later the Company also directed Stuyvesant to allow the Jews to trade and buy real estate throughout New Netherland.

Tolerated but never really welcome in New Amsterdam, the Jews remained a tiny handful. In March, 1655, they welcomed the arrival of Abraham de Lucena, who brought the first Torah Scroll, and a few other adults. These newcomers and most of the first 23 were Sephardim, the name given to Jews of Spanish and Portuguese origin. Barsimson was probably of Ashkenazic, or German ancestry, as was Asser Levy, one of those imprisoned for failure to pay the passage debt.

Because most of the first settlers left for Holland or the Dutch West Indies, the Jewish community numbered not more than a dozen families until the 1680s. In 1660, when de Lucena departed, taking his Torah with him, there turned up a family of seven whose four daughters produced many of the Jews of Colonial New York. A few Jews trickled in from London and the British West Indies after the British captured the city and changed its name to New York. Before 1700 a handful of French Jews and a few from Holland arrived. By then the community was about equally divided between Sephardim and Ashkenazim, but the latter became the majority by 1729.

Although the Sephardim spoke Spanish and Portuguese and the language of the Ashkenazim was Yiddish or German, a common religious outlook and close family and business ties bound the two groups into a tightly-knit community. They numbered hardly more than 100 a century after the first settlement out of a total population of less than 25,000. But they had already made an impact on the city's business and civic life, and established the framework of community organization and a tradition of public service on which succeeding generations built.

From its beginnings in Manhattan, one of the five boroughs into which New York is divided, the Jewish community, like the city itself, spilled over into the four other boroughs—Brooklyn, Queens, The Bronx, and Richmond. Jewish settlement in Brooklyn, a separate city prior to its annexation to New York in 1898, began in 1834. In the 1660s and 1670s, however, Asser Levy owned considerable property in "Bruecklen." Kings County (Brooklyn) archives preserve a 1683 record of the purchase of a slave by Peter Strijker of Vlackbos (Flatbush) from "the worthy Abraham Franckfoort, a Jew residing in N. Jorck (New York)," who did business in the village of Mitwout (Midwood). Eighteenth century documents indicate that other Jews also traded in the Brooklyn villages and owned summer estates there.

In the Queens villages of Flushing, Jamaica, and Newton there were at least four Jewish merchants before 1760. Three circumcisions were performed in Jamaica between 1756 and 1781. A Jewish community did not develop until after the Civil War when peddlers, storekeepers, and farmers settled in the communities joined to New York City in 1898. Part of Forest Hills was once "Goldberg's Dairy Farm."

Manhattan Jews also had business interests in what is now The Bronx before 1700 but the permanent Jewish community only dates from the 1840s. It was founded by artisans, peddlers, and shopkeepers attracted to the area during the construction of the Harlem and Hudson River railroads and the High Bridge that carried the Croton Aqueduct across the Harlem River. Jewish settlers first reached Richmond in the 1850s.

All of what is now suburban Long Island, Nassau, and Suffolk Counties, east of Brooklyn and Queens, was familiar country to 18th century New York Jewry. Asser Levy's family settled at Oyster Bay in 1730 on property he had owned there before 1700. Before the Revolution, Jewish merchants and shipowners were well-known at South Haven, Islip, Jericho, Southampton, Sag Harbor, East Hampton, and Montauk. A handful of Jews lived on Long Island all through the 19th century but they did not become numerous enough to create communal institutions until 1890.

In Westchester County, north of The Bronx, there were Jewish farmers and storekeepers around Pleasantville and Rye as early as 1720 but a Jewish community did not develop in this suburban area until 1870.

Ten Generations of Immigration

One of the most remarkable episodes in the growth of New York has been the gathering together within its borders of more Jews than have ever been congregated in one city in the history of the world.

Massive immigration from the Russian and Austro-Hungarian regions of Eastern Europe was the salient factor in the creation of this unprecedented concentration of Jews. Between 1880 and 1924 more than 2,000,000 Jews reached the United States in flight from pogroms, revolution, war and postwar upheavals, economic discrimination, and social degradation. They came by whole families and often by entire communities. Landing in New York, few of them went further because they found in the great city other Jews who shared their religious traditions and social mores, and help in getting their first foothold in the new world.

When the great migration began, the Jews of New York numbered 85,000, the product of earlier but smaller waves of immigration. By 1800 New York was already the largest Jewish community in North America although few Jews migrated to the United States before then. The limited immigration—chiefly French families from Santo Domingo and a sprinkling of individuals from England and Holland—plus natural growth, barely balanced the inroads of intermarriage. So widespread was the defection from Judaism among the early Jewish settlers in the 17th and 18th centuries that there might not have been any Jews in New York today if immigration had been halted at the beginning of the 19th century instead of in the 1920s. There were only 306 Jews in the city in 1806 and barely 500 in 1812.

A trickle from the Polish province of Posen, newly annexed to Prussia, that began during the Napoleonic Wars, swelled into a stream of Yiddish and German-speaking immigrants in the 1820s and 1830s and reached major proportions in the 1840s. Mostly unlearned in Hebrew but attached to Jewish traditions, the immigrants came chiefly from Bavaria and Posen, where Jews were subject to galling restrictions and heavy taxes in the wake of the post-Napoleonic reaction, and from Poland after the abortive revolt of 1830.

Extremely poor, most of them arrived with only clothing and household goods. Many had their passage paid by relatives or Jewish communities abroad. A second wave of Jewish immigrants, including a good many of culture and means, poured into New York after the collapse of the 1848 revolutions in Germany, Austria, Bohemia, and Hungary.

Of the 6,000 Jews in the United States in 1825, less than 10 percent lived in New York, but by 1848 New York was the home of more than half the country's Jewish population of 13,000. Germans and Poles outnumbered the native-born, but the descendants of the pioneer Sephardim and those Ashkenazim who had married into Sephardic families constituted the upper crust of New York Jewish society until the 1850s.

The native-born had few contacts with the German and Polish Jews, while the Americanized English and Dutch Jews, who had come in the first decade of the 19th century, looked down on their fellow-Ashkenazim from Germany. To divert the Germans and Poles from peddling, unsuccessful attempts were made to settle them in agricultural colonies.

The Bavarians had little in common with the more cultured refugees from the abortive 1848 revolutions. All the German Jews considered themselves superior to those from Posen, while Germans and Poles sneered at the Galicians, Lithuanians, and Romanians, who began coming after 1860. The Germans, in whose synagogues German was used until the late 1870s, displayed similar arrogance toward the East Europeans in the 1880s. Intermarriage between the various groups in the community during the mid-and-late 19th century was frowned upon, and even burial in the same cemetery was usually avoided.

The community was predominantly German in origin in 1871 when the migration of German Jews to the United States virtually ceased, following their emancipation in the newly-united Germany. Although the German-Sephardic elite was at first shocked and dismayed by the tremendous influx from Eastern Europe that began in the 1880s, there had been a steady trickle since 1865 of Jews from Romania and the Russian provinces bordering on Germany. Before 1880, 25,000 East European Jews had reached the United States, and most of them stayed in New York.

But the older community neither recognized nor was prepared to cope with the beginning of a folk exodus that was to transplant one-third of East European Jewry to the United States in a generation and a half. The tidal wave from Eastern Europe swelled New York's Jewish population to 200,000 by 1890, and to 600,000 by the end of the century. By then the Lower East Side had become "a seething, human sea, fed by streams, rivulets and rills of immigration fleeing from all the Yiddish-speaking centers of Europe."

Sons and grandsons of German-Jewish peddlers of the 1840s and 1850s who worried lest the newcomers make American Jewry "a nation of peddlers," sought to settle them in other parts of the country. An Industrial Removal Office offered free transportation to families willing to go to smaller towns and cities. A Yiddish-speaking rabbi, who was a popular East Side orator, was employed to meet the newcomers at Ellis Island to persuade them not to remain in New York. A Jewish Immigrants Information Bureau was set up in Europe to encourage immigrants to take passage for Galveston, Texas, rather than for New York, thus facilitating the settlement of some in the South and Middle West. A number of short-lived agricultural colonies were founded in a futile effort to make farmers of the East Europeans. Those who were established as dairy and tobacco farmers in southern New Jersey, Connecticut, and the Catskill Mountain region of New York laid the foundation for the popular Jewish summer resorts in the seashore area and "Borscht Belt."

A second Sephardic immigration brought several thousand Ladino-speaking Jews from Greece, Syria, Turkey, and the Balkans between 1908 and 1914 in the wake of the Balkan Wars. Descendants of 15th century refugees from Spain and Portugal who had found a haven in the Turkish Empire, were kin of the Sephardim who had come to New Amsterdam in 1654.

More than half of the 250,000 Jewish refugees from Germany and Hitler-occupied Europe admitted to the United States between 1933 and 1945 remained in New York, where German was again heard in synagogues and a flourishing German-Jewish weekly appeared. After World War II, 125,000 concentration camp survivors arrived in New York where they became the backbone of the Chasidic community. The Hungarian revolution of 1956, anti-Semitism in Egypt and North Africa, and an exodus of Jews from Castro's Cuba added additional waves of Jewish immigration to the city's population. In the 1970s considerable numbers of Syrian Jews, and some 10,000 Russian Jews arrived in New York. Most of these new immigrants were aided by United HIAS Service in reaching the United States and were assisted in their resettlement in New York by the New York Association for New Americans. The American ORT Federation continued to maintain a trade school for immigrants in New York to provide vocational rehabilitation.

The 1970 census showed a marked decline over the 1960s in the number of New Yorkers of European birth or parentage, but during the 1960-1970 decade the net emigration of 950,000 whites, including many Jews, was offset by the immigration of 450,000 persons of other races. At the beginning of the 1970s, blacks in the city increased from 1,088,000 to 1,668,000 and during the same period the Spanish language population grew from 700,000 to 1,278,000, with the result that blacks and Hispanics together outnumbered Jews in New York City.

Each layer of Jewish immigration either created its own institutions or modified existing ones to meet its special needs of time and place. Out of their diverse origins, traditions, and experiences, each generation of newcomers poured its own quality, variety, color, and unique contribution into the mainstream of the life of New York and its Jewish community. Enriched and influenced by each other, all of the waves of immigration gradually fused to create the present Jewish community of New York.

The Rise of the Jewish Community

Though short of a religious quorum of ten adult males, the founders of New York Jewry conducted the first Rosh Hashanah services in North America on September 12, 1654, worshipping secretly, probably in an attic or in a borrowed room behind a shop. This was the beginning of Congregation Shearith Israel (the Spanish and Portuguese Synagogue), oldest existing Jewish congregation in North America.

The first community act of the Jews of New York was the acquisition of ground for a cemetery in 1656. No trace remains of this earliest Jewish burial ground referred to as a "little hook of land" north of what is now Wall Street. But a second one, originally a plot 52 by 50 feet, opened in 1682, was never completely effaced by the onward march of the city. One of the city's oldest historic sites, the old cemetery just south of Chatham Square is now hemmed in by buildings on three sides. Part of it was leased in 1746 to John Roosevelt, great-great-great-grandfather of Theodore Roosevelt and great-great-great-great-grandfather of Eleanor Roosevelt, at an annual rental of three peppercorns. Franklin D. Roosevelt's great-great-grandfather sold the Jews a piece of ground adjoining the cemetery in 1784 when they began restoring it after the Revolutionary War.

Public services began in 1673 in a rented room on Beaver Street. The existence of a synagogue was first reported in 1682 by the Reverend Henricus Selyns, a Dutch clergyman, who wrote "we have Quakers, Jews, and Labadists, all of whom hold their separate meetings." John Miller's map of New York in 1695 indicated the existence of a synagogue which was described in a real estate deed of 1700 as a house on Mill Street, "commonly known by the name of the Jews' synagogue."

New York Jewry was the only one in America with any community life in 1728 when efforts began to erect the first building constructed for synagogue purposes. The site, just west of the rented wooden frame house then used as a sanctuary, was bought for £100, one loaf of sugar, and a pound of tea. Because the Dutch Reformed Church and Episcopal Trinity Church were still the only religious bodies legally recognized and therefore entitled to own real estate, the lot was acquired in the name of four individual trustees. Appeals for financial help to Jews in the West Indies and Europe brought £223 of the £600 it cost to build the synagogue. Forty-five percent of the balance was contributed by 15 percent of the donors, 70 percent of whom were in the lowest income bracket, proof that the arithmetic of Jewish philanthropy has not essentially changed.

The one-story brick structure, 35 feet square and 11 feet high, was dedicated on Passover, 1730, and remained in use for nearly a century. White lead and "sundries" were bought from John Roosevelt. The bricks were sold by a G. Stuyvesant. Negro slaves provided the unskilled labor. Only the Dutch Reformed Church, Trinity Church, and the Lutheran, French, and Presbyterian churches ante-dated the first synagogue. Its president at the time of dedication was Jacob Franks, a merchant of Ashkenazic origin, one of whose daughters eloped with Oliver deLancey, member of one of New York's most prominent families which gave its name to Delancey Street.

Portuguese was used in the congregational minutes until 1736 and in financial accounts until 1745. After 1735 English was widely used because the Jewish immigrants from central and eastern Europe were mostly Ashkenazim who knew neither Portuguese nor Spanish. In 1757 Shearith Israel sought a *hazzan* (cantor) "who will be able to teach children Hebrew with translation into English and Spanish." After 1762 the *hazzan* (a lay minister), was required to know only Hebrew and English. Spanish was dropped from the curriculum of the congregation's parochial school in 1766.

In the absence of state-supported public schools, the community's Hebrew school, founded in 1728, was expanded in 1755 into a Jewish parochial school, in which secular and Hebrew education were combined.

The city's first Jewish schoolhouse, erected in 1731, was part of a communal shelter that included the residences of the cantor, ritual slaughterer, and beadle, as well as room for occasional visitors. In 1759 the community received its first overseas emissary seeking contributions for the Jews of Palestine. The first national Palestine appeal in America was conducted in 1770 when members of Shearith Israel raised £32 for their coreligionists in Hebron, compared with lesser amounts by the Newport and Philadelphia communities.

Synagogue funds also cared for the local poor, transients, widows and orphans, the sick and victims of epidemics; provided free matzoth, wood, medical care, and burial, interest-free loans; and maintained a pension plan for aged and chronically ill members. The yellow fever epidemic of 1798 so depleted the synagogue's treasury that a separate charity organization was formed by members of the congregration for the first time. This society published the earliest known campaign literature on Jewish philanthropy in New York in 1806—a printed circular appealing for $5,000 to erect a poorhouse and hospital.

Not until the first substantial influx of German and Polish Jews, and smaller numbers from England and Holland, in the early 1820s, was there any great burden on charity funds or the need for additional synagogues. Mostly Ashkenazim, they found Shearith Israel's Sephardic ritual strange, and sought unsuccessfully to organize within the mother synagogue a separate Ashkenazic service. The secession from Shearith Israel that led to the establishment of Congregation B'nai Jeshurun in 1825 (the first rift between the native-born Sephardim and older Ashkenazic families), was led by English and Dutch Jews and supported by some of Polish and German ancestry.

Social and language differences, conflicts over cemeteries, and minor ritual changes, rather than population growth, led to the proliferation of synagogues and their organizational offshoots between 1830 and 1850. Dutch, Polish, and German seceders from B'nai Jeshurun organized Anshe Chesed in 1828. Further splits led to the formation of Ohabei Zedek (1835) by Germans, Shaarey Zedek (1839) by Poles, and Shaarey Hashomayim (1839) by Germans. Other Germans who quit Anshe Chesed and Shaarey Hashomayim organized Rodeph Sholom in 1842. Beth Israel (1843) was founded by Poles withdrawing from Shaarey Zedek. Wealthier Germans moving toward substantial ritual reform founded Emanu-El in 1845. Another secession from B'nai Jeshurun in 1845 created Shaarey Tefilah. Multiplication by division rather than new congregations organized by newly-arrived immigrants gave New York 27 synagogues to serve 50,000 Jews before the Civil War.

Except for their Ashkenazic ritual, all of the synagogues founded before 1850 were at the outset as Orthodox as Shearith Israel. While the latter held fast to the Sephardic form of Orthodoxy, the newer congregations began modifying their practices even before the city's first ordained rabbi, Leo Merzbacher, arrived in 1842. Until then the only religious leaders were *hazzanim*. Merzbacher was called from Germany to serve both Anshe Chesed and Rodeph Sholom at $200 a year.

English preaching, heard only at Shearith Israel before 1840, was introduced at B'nai Jeshurun by its *hazzan*, Samuel Myer Isaacs, an Englishman. Jacques Judah Lyons, Shearith Israel's minister from 1840–1877, was also a *hazzan*. When Isaacs became minister of the new Shaarey Tefilah, he was succeeded at B'nai Jeshurun in 1849 by Morris Raphall, another Englishman, whose fame as an orator brought throngs of Christians and Jews to hear him preach.

Denied reengagement by Anshe Chesed in 1845 because he spoke against women wearing *sheitels* (ritual wigs), Merzbacher helped form Emanu-El, New York's pioneer Reform congregation, where he introduced sweeping changes in ritual and practice that made his synagogue a citadel of Reform Judaism. Max Lilienthal, the city's second ordained rabbi, was brought from Russia in 1845 by the three leading German synagogues to succeed Merzbacher at a salary of $1,000 a year. Lilienthal also broke with tradition by establishing the custom of confirmation both for boys and girls. The first synagogue formed by East European Jews was Beth Hamadresh Hagodol, founded in 1852. Its earliest rabbi was the Russian trained Abraham Joseph Ash, who served without pay because he was a successful manufacturer of hoopskirts until he went bankrupt in the Panic of 1873.

Religious bickering and social and economic differences, reflecting a growing struggle for community leadership between immigrants and native-born Jews, led to the establishment of multiple and rival charities, mutual aid, and cultural societies. This, in turn, gradually shifted leadership of communal affairs from the synagogues to the philanthropic organizations as they became independent of the congregations out of which they were born.

The two principal philanthropic agencies were the Hebrew Benevolent Society, founded in 1822 by leaders of Shearith Israel and dominated by native-born English and Dutch Jews, and the German Hebrew Benevolent Society, organized in 1844. Legend has it that the older group originated with a visit by a committee of synagogue elders to a hospitalized Jewish veteran of the Revolution. The $300 left in the fund raised for his care gave impetus to the formation of the society when he died.

In the 1840s and early 1850s, the Hebrew Benevolent Society was helping 200 people a year. This increased tenfold in 1858 when its expenditures totaled $3,500. Aiding only German Jews, the German society spent three times as much that same year. The first appeal to all Jews to contribute to a fund for needy immigrants started in 1837 when there was a door-to-door solicitation for food, clothing, fuel, and cash. In 1839 a New York Hebrew Assistance Society was created to aid immigrants. Old-line Jews sponsored a benefit concert of Italian opera in a Christian church in 1849 to raise funds for the relief of newly-arriving German Jews. Organization of a Bachelors Hebrew Benevolent Loan Society, a Young Men's Hebrew Benevolent Fuel Association, and a host of other mutual aid societies between 1830 and 1855 demonstrated that the Dutch warning to Jews to take care of their own, had become the bedrock on which Jewish communal life was being built.

The need for an orphanage and a hospital where Jews would be free from conversionist efforts by Christian clergymen as well as the inability of the community to cope with the mounting number of needy and sick immigrants, spurred unification of Jewish charitable efforts in the 1850s. The two major societies, which did not merge until 1859, were planning "an asylum for the aged and sick of the Hebrew persuasion" in 1851, but were by-passed by a group of individuals who incorporated Jews' Hospital in 1852. Opened in 1855 on 28th Street between 7th and 8th Avenues, the hospital admitted only Jews in its early years, except for accident cases. The words "Jews' Hospital" in English, and *Bet Holim* in Hebrew were emblazoned in big letters over the front of the four-story building. The hospital became nonsectarian in 1864 and the name was changed to Mount Sinai Hospital two years later. In the ensuing century it became a great medical center with a decisive role in the development of the city's network of Jewish-sponsored health services, and in the major changes that characterized medical care in the 20th century. An immediate result of the consolidation of the two benevolent societies was the establishment in 1859 of the first Hebrew Orphan Asylum, whose successor is the Jewish Child Care Association.

Forerunner of the women's groups that now raise huge sums annually for Jewish institutions and causes at home and abroad was the Female Hebrew Benevolent Society, founded by the ladies of Shearith Israel in 1820. The Ladies Association for the General Instruction of Children of the Jewish Persuasion was another pioneer among the women's charity societies organized in the 1840s and 1850s. By 1860, New York had 35 Jewish burial, mutual aid, and charitable organizations. These organizations accounted for the fact that Jews were seldom found in the New York Poor House. In 1858, Mayor Tiemann said that in three years he had heard of only three Jews seeking aid at city institutions.

Out of the mutual aid societies grew the first fraternal orders and cultural groups. B'nai B'rith, oldest national Jewish membership organization, was founded in New York in 1843, mostly by German Jews. The latter also established the Free Sons of Israel in 1849, and the United Order of True Sisters, the first women's organization independent of the synagogue, in 1852. These fraternal societies were important instruments for Americanizing the immigrants and in giving them the security of social, economic, and cultural opportunities. The first B'nai B'rith lodges were opened at Covenant Hall on Orchard Street in the 1850s, where they maintained a library and Jewish Community Center. The Harmonie Club, established by German Jews in 1847 on Ludlow Street as a social and cultural headquarters, was the pioneer Jewish town club. Temple Emanu-El was an outgrowth of the Cultus Verein, founded by synagogue dissenters in 1843. Young people's choirs at Shearith Israel in 1818 and B'nai Jeshurun in 1828 were the predecessors of Jewish young men's literary societies and Jewish military companies in the 1850s. These in turn paved the way for New York's first YM and YWHA in 1874.

This growing network of communal institutions was financed largely from the proceeds of fairs, theatrical benefits, Purim and Chanukah balls, and dinners, which were the major social events in the Jewish community calendar.

Elementary Jewish education in New York before 1851 was provided largely by synagogue sponsored all-day or parochial schools. Immigrant and native-born Jews alike were reluctant to expose their children to the strong Protestant influences that pervaded the early free elementary schools, where education was meagre at best. After the State Legislature empowered local school boards to choose their own texts from approved lists, Jewish pupils poured into the free public schools in great numbers as the books objectionable to Jews were eliminated in Jewish neighborhoods. The fee-charging separate Jewish schools then went out of existence. In their place the synagogues opened afternoon Hebrew and Sunday schools. Wealthier Jews sent their children to private Jewish day and boarding schools. Rabbi Lilienthal presided over a "Hebrew, commercial and classical boarding school" and some Christian private schools sought to attract Jewish students by offering Hebrew studies.

Matzoh-baking and the preparation of kosher meat were also under synagogue supervision until the 1840s. This control broke down because of the proliferation of congregations, the increase in the number of Jewish butchers, and the emergence of Jewish matzoh bakeries operating independent of synagogue supervision. Machine matzoh-baking was introduced by Moses S. Cohen, one of the five matzoh-makers in New York in 1855.

The first Hebrew calendar printed in America appeared in New York in 1850. Eight years later the preacher at Beth Hamedresh Hagodol produced the first full Hebrew book published in the United States. Most printed Jewish literature in mid-19th century New York consisted of prayer books, polemics, and speeches. Religious appurtenances, from Torah Scrolls to prayer shawls, were hard to come by, most of them being imported or brought as gifts by the stream of messengers from Palestine seeking funds among the Jews of New York.

New York Jewry established itself as the leader of the American Jewish community in 1840 when it organized the initial public effort on behalf of persecuted coreligionists abroad. Outraged by the arrest and torture of Jews in Damascus used to force them to confess to ritual murder, New York's Jews held a protest rally at which they called upon the United States government to intercede with the Sultan. This meeting led to the first intercession by the United States to succor Jews abroad when President Martin Van Buren instructed the American consul in Damascus to use his good offices to protect the Jews there.

The rally had been held at B'nai Jeshurun because Shearith Israel's trustees opposed it. There was a reluctance on the part of the native-born Jews to participate in joint communal undertakings lest they be swamped by the German, Polish, and English Jews. Emanu-El, a rival of the mother synagogue in status and influence due to the rising power of the German Jews, also stood apart from early efforts to unite the Jewish community. Opposition in New York also blocked later plans, originating in Philadelphia and Cincinnati, to federate American synagogues.

All the New York synagogues, however, supported the protest against the Mortara Affair in Italy. Shocked by the news that a Jewish child named Edgar Mortara had been secretly baptized by a Catholic nurse in the Mortara home in 1854 and then kidnapped in Bologna with the connivance of Papal officials, the Jews of New York staged a giant demonstration in Mozart Hall in 1858. More than 2,000 people attended, including many Protestants who used the occasion to propagandize for the antialien, anti-Catholic Know-Nothing party.

Although the Mozart Hall rally's demand that President James Buchanan intervene with the Vatican was rejected by the State Department, the protest stimulated the organization of the Board of Delegates of American Israelites in 1859. The first national representative body of synagogues, the Board's aim was to protect Jewish rights at home and abroad. Shearith Israel and Emanu-El did not participate and the Reform synagogues outside of New York also boycotted the new body. It survived until 1878 when it merged with the Union of American Hebrew Congregations, the federation of Reform synagogues. New York was "definitely established as the center of Jewish life in America" when the Board made its headquarters there.

Communal affairs were dominated by descendants of the old Sephardic families and by first and second generation Germans in the 1860s and 1870s when the first trickle of Jews from Russia and Romania gave rise to a new array of philanthropic, cultural, and religious institutions. New York's first *landsmanschaft*, a uniquely European Jewish self-help society based on local origin, but unknown among the earlier immigrants from Germany, was chartered in 1864 as the Bialystok Mutual Aid Society. By 1877 there were five more, providing small loans and funeral and cemetery benefits, as well as 22 East European synagogues.

The German-Jewish community made no organized attempt to aid the post-Civil War immigrants until 1870 when a Hebrew Emigrant Aid Society was formed. It was short-lived because of the belief that the new immigration would be temporary. The Hebrew Free School Association, founded in 1864 to counteract proselytizing among immigrant children, survived as part of the city's first Jewish settlement house.

In 1874 the United Hebrew Charities came into being through an amalgamation of the old Hebrew Benevolent Society and four smaller groups. The new organization created the Hebrew Sheltering Guardian Society in 1879 to care for needy children, and a year later established the Hebrew Technical School for Girls. Through subsequent mergers, the United Hebrew Charities emerged in 1917 as the Federation of Jewish Philanthropies, a huge philanthropic and social welfare complex which in the last decade alone has poured $200,000,000 into the maintenance of 130 institutions, plus tens of millions more spent on new facilities.

The first Home for Aged and Infirm Hebrews opened in 1870. Four years later the native-born and German-Jewish leadership founded the 92nd Street YM and YWHA, now the country's oldest existing Jewish Community Center, to provide cultural and recreational activities for young people. Montefiore Hospital, an outgrowth of a home for chronic invalids established by Mt. Sinai and the United Hebrew Charities to cope with the growing number of chronically Jewish sick who refused to go to city institutions, came into being in 1884.

Out of deep-seated religious differences, immense social and cultural cleavages, and wide economic disparities between the older community and the masses of East Europeans who arrived after 1880, there grew up parallel Jewish communities. Many uptowners were contemptuous of and sometimes hostile to the zealous efforts of their Yiddish-speaking downtown coreligionists to recreate old world institutions, to maintain the minutiae of Orthodoxy, and to cling to their own folkways. The East Europeans equated the Reform synagogues and modernized Orthodox congregations with churches and regarded the Americanized Jew as a thinly disguised missionary. Many of the German Jews denigrated the newcomers as "uncouth strangers" who threatened the status of the older community by giving impetus to the rising antialien sentiment. Some repudiated the "miserably darkened Hebrews" with whom "the thoroughly acclimated American Jew . . . has no religious, social, or intellectual ties."

Responsible uptown leaders, recognizing that they could not ignore the plight of fellow Jews without rejecting their own Jewishness, brought all elements of the community together in the Russian Emigrant Relief Society in 1881. Reorganized as the Hebrew Emigrant Aid Society, this group struggled for 18 months to meet the needs of daily shiploads of destitute Jews dumped in the vast domed shed of Castle Garden, New York's old immigration station. Hundreds slept on floors and temporary benches, crowded into narrow, unsanitary quarters, until a former lunatic asylum on Ward's Island was converted into the Schiff Refugee Center, where hot meals and medical care were provided. There the poet Emma Lazarus, who came from an old Sephardic family, had her first contact with the "huddled masses yearning to breathe free," whom she immortalized in her sonnet on the Statue of Liberty.

When the Hebrew Emigrant Aid Society suspended operations in 1884, its work was taken over by the United Hebrew Charities, which was, at first, not too sympathetic to the East Europeans. This prompted the older established Russian Jews to organize their own relief societies. In 1882 they had formed the Hebrew Emigrant Auxiliary Society. A Hebrew Sheltering Society, which opened temporary immigrant shelters in 1882, and the Hebrew Emigrant Aid Society, founded in 1902 as the Voliner Zhitomirer Aid Society to provide burial for Jews from Zhitomir who had died on Ellis Island, became the predecessors of United HIAS Service, the world-wide immigrant agency.

These societies furnished lawyers and interpreters to help the immigrants through the red tape of Ellis Island, which in 1890 replaced Castle Garden as the principal immigration inspection depot. They provided kosher food for steerage passengers who had not eaten any cooked meals since leaving Europe, temporary housing, and employment information. The United Hebrew Charities provided relief for those needing it after clearing Ellis Island. It even outfitted many with new clothing before sending them to their first jobs. The National Council of Jewish Women operated a port and dock department at Ellis Island to curb exploitation of girls and women arriving alone and penniless.

Once the newcomers were housed and provided with jobs, the older community made strenuous efforts to Americanize them through a network of social service agencies, vocational training programs, kindergartens, and classes in English. The most influential Americanization force was the Educational Alliance. Opened in 1883 as the YMHA's downtown branch and then expanded through a merger with the Hebrew Free School Association and the Hebrew Technical Institute, the Alliance was the first settlement house in the United States.

Its volunteer teachers included some of the city's most cultured Jews, among them Emma Lazarus, the poet; Oscar S. Straus, the diplomat; and Julia Richman, first woman assistant superintendent of schools. Henry M. Leipziger, founder of the Board of Education's adult education system, was the first principal of the Educational Alliance's adult classes.

Out of the Alliance's classes came a long line of eminent citizens. David Sarnoff, radio and television tycoon, and Sir Louis Stirling, his British counterpart, learned English there; Eddie Cantor's career began as an amateur entertainer at the Alliance's summer camp; Morris Raphael Cohen tested his philosophic concepts as a youthful Alliance orator; Sir Jacob Epstein, Jo Davidson, Chaim Gross, William Auerbach-Levy, and Abraham Walkowitz paid three cents a lesson at the Alliance's Art School. When Jacob Epstein was knighted, Walkowitz said to the sculptor's brother, "I see Jake is Sir Jake now." "Pfui," retorted the brother, "Jake was knighted at 102 Hester St.," where Epstein found his first models among pushcart peddlers.

Many East European Jewish lawyers, doctors, engineers, and dentists, who fled Russia before getting their degrees, were able to complete their professional education through student loans from the Baron de Hirsch Fund. With the millions bequeathed by Maurice de Hirsch, French railway magnate, the leading New York Jews who managed the Fund created the Baron de Hirsch Trade School, the Clara de Hirsch Home for Immigrant Girls, underwrote the Alliance classes, and opened settlement houses in other parts of the city. Before it was turned over to the Board of Education, the school had graduated more than 9,000 students. The home is now a women's residence dormitory affiliated with the 92nd Street YM & YWHA.

Galled by patronizing philanthropy and denied a voice in the organizations established for their benefit, the East Europeans fashioned their own pattern of communal services while recreating their intense old world religious life. Because kosher food was unavailable at Mt. Sinai Hospital, where Yiddish-speaking physicians were often snubbed, the East Europeans established Beth Israel Hospital in 1890, the first under Orthodox auspices. They also founded the Jewish Maternity Hospital, Lebanon Hospital, in the Bronx, orphanages, old folks homes and, with the backing of uptown leaders, the Hebrew Free Loan Society in 1902.

Hundreds of *landsmanschaften* organized as mutual aid societies also filled important social and cultural needs. Several hundred thousand Jews belonged to these societies before they were outmoded by Americanization, social security, and commercial insurance. Of the 600 new synagogues established in New York between 1880 and 1914, the majority were of the storefront or back-room variety, organized according to old country town of origin. Each little congregation supported its own rebbe brought over from Europe, and struggled to maintain a separate elementary Hebrew school because the Hebrew Free School Association was not considered sufficiently Orthodox. These one-room schools, usually housed in a tenement flat or basement, were gradually replaced by more modern Talmud Torahs and parochial schools, Talmudic academies, Hebrew classes fostered by the early Zionist societies, and Yiddish schools created by secularists.

Itinerant preachers such as Hirsch Masliansky, the "Yiddish Henry Ward Beecher," Chaim Zhitlovsky, a radical Yiddishist, and the modern services at the People's Synagogue in the Alliance attracted large audiences. Breadwinners in hundreds of families earned their livelihoods as religious functionaries—ritual slaughterers, cantors, sextons, scribes, translators, ritual circumcisers, and itinerant preachers. The omnipresent *pushka*, or charity box, reflected the concern of even the poorest household for needy Jews at home and abroad.

Secularism gradually eroded the Orthodoxy of many of the first and second generation immigrants. Under the impact of poverty, sweatshop conditions, and radical political movements, houses of prayer lost ground to trade unions and lodges. The Yiddish press, stage, and lecture platform became more influential than revered rabbis. Even the strict Sabbath closing was breached. By 1913, sixty percent of East Side stores and pushcarts were open on Saturday. The Keepers of the Sabbath Society gave up its boycott of the antireligious *Jewish Daily Forward*, and Yiddish theatres played to standing room only audiences on Friday nights and Saturday matinees.

Immigrants who resisted Americanization as a threat to their way of life found themselves in conflict with American-born or educated children who rejected the customs and values of their parents as obstacles to Americanization. The struggle between German-Jewish manufacturers and the Jewish trade unions was carried over into the communal arena. As a result of the hostility for nearly a generation to the organized Jewish community control by uptowners, the Jewish labor movement formed separate secular Yiddishist cultural institutions, relief societies, and Zionist parties.

The first big influx of Orthodox East Europeans coincided with the split between Reform and Orthodoxy in the United States. Reform had taken root as an essentially German movement under the influence of European-ordained rabbis. The limited changes in ritual and practice they had encouraged in the New York congregations founded by German immigrants broadened into Reform Judaism as it became Americanized under the leadership of Rabbi Isaac Mayer Wise of Cincinnati and Rabbi David Einhorn of New York's Temple Beth El.

Having accepted some innovations, many of the older New York congregations and their rabbis occupied a middle ground between radical Reform and unchanging Orthodoxy. The hope that the Hebrew Union College, opened in Cincinnati in 1873 as a Reform rabbinical seminary, might train rabbis for all congregations, vanished with the final break in 1885. It was precipitated by a radical declaration of principles adopted by a conference of Reform rabbis convened by Dr. Kaufman Kohler, Rabbi Einhorn's son-in-law and successor at Beth El. This platform repudiated Talmudic regulations and most of the Mosaic code, including the dietary regulations, in favor of the prophetic ideals of the Bible, less stringent Sabbath observance, and rejection of the idea of a return to Zion.

Opponents of this course countered in 1886 by establishing the Jewish Theological Seminary in New York to disseminate the tenets of Traditional Judaism, the original name of Conservative Judaism. The Seminary's founders differed from their Orthodox East European coreligionists only in the use of English in pulpit preaching, religious instruction for the young, greater decorum in the service, and some prayer book modifications. The Conservatives even joined the larger East European synagogues in forming the Union of Orthodox Jewish Congregations in 1898.

Convinced that European Orthodoxy could not thrive in America, the majority of second and third generation Orthodox leaders set out to provide American-educated rabbis for the growing number of non-Reform English-speaking synagogues. When the Seminary opened in 1887, there were only 12 American-ordained rabbis—all Reform.

The East Europeans, whose religious leadership came from Yiddish-speaking old world rabbis, rebuffed the Seminary. Although it had graduated 17 English-speaking rabbis by 1902, most of them immigrants or sons of immigrants, the Seminary was in danger of closing because of meagre support from its founding congregations. Reform Jews put it on a sound footing in the hope that the Seminary would "westernize" the Judaism of the immigrants by fostering an Americanized Orthodoxy without Yiddish, among those to whom Reform Judaism was anathema.

A $500,000 endowment fund raised under the leadership of Louis Marshall, president of Temple Emanu-El, and Jacob H. Schiff, head of Kuhn, Loeb & Co., made it possible to invite Dr. Solomon Schechter, world-renowned savant at Cambridge University, to become the Seminary's president. Dr. Schechter surrounded himself with men who not only made enduring contributions to Jewish scholarship but whose teaching and inspiration gave impetus to Conservative Judaism by molding its rabbinic leadership and constituency.

Dr. Mordecai M. Kaplan, ordained by the Seminary in 1903, became perhaps the single most influential force in American Jewish religious life. As dean of the Seminary's Teachers' Institute and for a generation a professor at the Seminary, he became the mentor of thousands of rabbis, educators, social workers, scholars, and laymen. Founder of Reconstructionism, which advocated substantive changes in Jewish life, and author of significant religious works, Dr. Kaplan and his disciples precipitated a great theological ferment which animated creative changes in all branches of American Judaism.

Under Dr. Schechter's successors, Drs. Cyrus Adler, Louis Finkel-stein, and Gerson Cohen, the Seminary, as the fountainhead of Conservative

Judaism, and the congregations affiliated with the United Synagogue of America, began an era of great expansion. Some first and second generation East Europeans who had not rejected the synagogue remained with those East European congregations that moved to newer neighborhoods. The majority joined the newer synagogues led by Seminary graduates that sprang up in all parts of the city, as well as the older congregations. There they found less of a break with tradition than in the anti-Zionist Reform temples whose adherents were drawn from the more well-to-do element. As the East Europeans, once regarded as the wards of Conservatism, scaled the economic ladder, they gave strength and permanence to the movement.

The East European Orthodox community at first relied on its preponderant numbers and constant replenishment through immigration to offset heavy losses to secularism and Conservatism. When both of these bulwarks were breached and it became evident that the Talmudic scholarship of European-trained rabbis had little impact on American-born Jews, the Orthodox established the Isaac Eichanan Rabbinical Seminary. Under the guidance of Dr. Bernard Revel, this Seminary expanded into Yeshiva University. Under his successor, the late Dr. Samuel Belkin and the latter's successor, Rabbi Norman Lamm, it has become the focal point of modern Orthodoxy in America.

Reform made little headway among the Jewish masses of New York until well into the 1930s, although much of the Jewish community's leadership was in the hands of wealthy members of Temple Emanu-El. Reform congregations began attracting considerable numbers of East Europeans after 1936 when the Reform rabbinate adopted a new program that repudiated the 1886 platform. Gradually the Reform synagogues reinstituted ceremonials and Friday evening and Saturday morning worship, added more Hebrew to the service, restored the Bar Mitzvah rite, and turned to active support of Palestine. Sons and grandsons of East Europeans ultimately dominated the Reform rabbinate and acquired influence and status among the Reform laity.

Reform achieved its most phenomenal growth in New York after World War II when children and grandchildren of Yiddish-speaking immigrants began a return to the once rejected Jewish folkways. The leap from secularism to membership in Reform synagogues was made easy as Jews, who had never before belonged to a synagogue in the city, moved into the suburbs in great numbers. The removal of the Union of American Hebrew Congregations (Reform synagogue federation) headquarters to New York in 1951, under the leadership of Dr. Maurice Eisendrath, was followed by a merger of the Hebrew Union College with the Jewish Institute of Religion, founded in New York in 1922.

Before Reform altered its course, New York's most eloquent spokesmen of the compatibility between Jewish tradition and Americanism were Judah L. Magnes and Stephen S. Wise, both Reform rabbis. As secretary of the Federation of American Zionists from 1905-1908 and a leader in the protests against Czarist anti-Semitism, Dr. Magnes won the respect and affection of the East Side Jews. As rabbi of Emanu-El, of which his brother-in-law, Louis Marshall, was president, he openly advocated Zionism in the face of congregational hostility. From the pulpit he denounced a temple trustee who had marched down the aisle of St. Patrick's Cathedral to give away his daughter in marriage to a Hungarian count. His insistence on more traditional forms cost him the pulpit and he became rabbi of B'nai Jeshurun.

Stephen S. Wise, who began his career in this same Conservative congregation in 1893, had little contact with the East European masses until he became the first secretary of the Federation of American Zionists in 1898. From the pulpit of the Free Synagogue, which he organized in 1906 after rejecting an invitation from Emanu-El under the conditions laid down by Marshall, Wise's prophetic mood and oratory attracted wealthy Jews who had been flirting with Unitarianism and Ethical Culture, as well as Yiddish-speaking radicals and Zionists who had broken with Orthodoxy.

"God's angry man," Wise excoriated evil in the synagogue, the Jewish community, business, industry, and politics. Preaching a liberal Judaism that rejected the kind of Reform that was the "center of wealth and fashion," he created a social service division to put Jewish teachings into practice as part of congregational life. When Zionism had only a marginal following among the Jews of New York, Wise was its most passionate spokesman. His sermon on "Jesus the Jew" created such a furor in 1925 that the Orthodox rabbinate excommunicated him as a heretic and narrowly failed to oust him as chairman of the United Palestine Appeal. To prepare rabbis for congregations of all denominations, he organized the Jewish Institute of Religion, which became a focus of significant Jewish scholarship and religious experimentation. He also led the American and World Jewish Congresses.

In their efforts to bridge the chasm between the two Jewish communities in New York, Wise, Magnes, and other like-minded rabbis had potent allies among the more understanding German-Jewish spokesmen who respected the traditions of the East Europeans. Jacob H. Schiff and Louis Marshall were the dominant figures of this group. Despite his German ancestry and membership in Emanu-El, the East Side Jews sensed that Schiff was their friend. Though he contributed princely sums to higher education and philanthropic causes, his principal interest was Jews.

Schiff fought vigorously for the protection of Jews overseas. The relief fund for the victims of the 1903 Kishinev pogrom was organized on a private basis by Schiff before he, Oscar S. Straus, and Cyrus L. Sulzberger formed the National Committee for the Relief of Sufferers of Russian Massacres. The Educational Alliance and the Henry Street Settlement were among his earliest beneficiaries. He was the prime mover in the reorganization of the Jewish Theological Seminary, in the underwriting of the Jewish Encyclopedia, in the establishment of the Jewish Division of the New York Public Library, and the Jewish collection in the Library of Congress. Schiff built the first home of the 92nd Street YM & YWHA, helped organize the

National Jewish Welfare Board, and was the key figure in the formation of the American Jewish Joint Distribution Committee.

For more than a generation Kuhn, Loeb partners, like Schiff, were to the Jewish community of New York what the Morgans and Rockefellers were to the non-Jewish community. Schiff's son-in-law and daughter, Mr. and Mrs. Felix M. Warburg, his son, Mortimer, and granddaughter, Dorothy Schiff, continued the tradition of Jewish community leadership. The third generation of Schiffs were less involved and the Warburgs do not play a leading role in Jewish affairs. Jacob Schiff's grandson was married in a Protestant church in 1963, as his father had been before him. Otto H. Kahn, another Kuhn, Loeb partner, though never prominent in Jewish affairs, supported the Yiddish theatre and helped bring the Habimah Theatre to the United States.

The son of Benjamin Buttenweiser, also a Kuhn, Loeb partner, whose family has been actively associated with many Jewish causes, married the daughter of Isidor Lubin, son of an East European immigrant, and one-time United States Commissioner of Labor Statistics. Rear Admiral Lewis L. Strauss, who gave up his Kuhn, Loeb partnership to enter public service, was president of the Jewish Agricultural Society and Temple Emanu-El, and headed the board of the Jewish Theological Seminary.

Louis Marshall was drawn into the conservative German-Jewish circle when he came down from Syracuse in 1898 to join the Guggenheimer and Untermeyer law firm. His membership in a committee in investigate East Side slum conditions and sponsorship of a Yiddish daily shaped his sympathetic attitude toward the problems of the East European Jews. One of the principal founders of the American Jewish Committee in 1906, Marshall headed the successful fight to abrogate Russia's commercial treaty with the United States in protest against the refusal of the Czar's government to recognize American passports held by Jews. When the treaty was allowed to lapse, Marshall emerged as the recognized leader of American Jewry. The years of his dominance were often called "the era of Marshall law," and he was dubbed "Louis XIX."

Marshall endeared himself to the Jewish masses of New York by his vigorous advocacy of civil rights, unrestricted immigration, and Jewish education. He defended the right of the Yiddish press to publish in wartime, spoke up for Negroes and Chinese, and represented the Catholic Church in its legal fight against an Oregon antiparochial school law. Marshall, a native-born Jew, was for years the chief exponent of unrestricted immigration, while Samuel Gompers, an immigrant Jew, was the leading spokesman for immigration curbs. During the "red hysteria" of the 1920s, Marshall championed the five New York City Socialists who had been denied their seats in the State Assembly. Simultaneously president of Temple Emanu-El and the board of the Jewish Theological Seminary, he fought for greater support of Jewish education and scholarship and the establishment of Jewish Community Centers. Although he had led the fight against the World War I

American Jewish Congress, advocated by Zionists and Yiddish nationalists, he was won over and headed the Jewish delegation to the Versailles Peace Conference. After the war, Marshall helped establish the Palestine Survey Commission which brought non-Zionists into cooperation with the World Zionist Organization and created the Jewish Agency for Palestine.

The forceful leadership of Marshall, Schiff, and their associates in the German-Jewish community to halt Czarist persecution and to stem the rising tide of antialienism, helped break down many of the barriers between the East European and German-Jewish communities. The 250th anniversary of Jewish settlement in America, observed in 1905, brought pride and dignity to both elements. The decisive intercession of uptown leaders in the great needle trades strikes before World War I helped draw the Jewish working class masses into the main stream of Jewish community life.

The uproar created in 1908 when Police Commissioner Theodore A. Bingham charged in an article in the *North American Review* that New York's 1,000,000 Jews, representing a fourth of the total population, accounted for half the city's criminals, led to the first citywide agency to represent the totality of Jewish life. Confronted with the facts that disproved his charges, Bingham retracted, apologized, and resigned, but all elements of the Jewish community were so outraged by the incident that they joined forces in creating the New York Kehillah. It was intended to cope with the complex religious, educational, cultural, and community relations of the entire Jewish community. Under the chairmanship of Rabbi Magnes, the Kehillah undertook to supervise kashruth and Sabbath observance, standardize Jewish education, arbitrate disputes between Jewish workers and Jewish employers, combat juvenile delinquency, and compile communal statistics. Despite influential leadership and wide support, the Kehillah went out of existence during World War I, having failed to overcome deep-seated institutional and religious rivalries.

A more enduring consolidation of Jewish forces in New York grew out of common obligations to suffering Jews in the war zones of Europe early in 1914. Three separate agencies at first undertook relief efforts for the stricken Jews of Eastern Europe. The Orthodox and East Europeans set up the Central Relief Committee, the German Jews formed the American Jewish Relief Committee, and the Jewish unions sponsored the People's Relief Committee. Their merger in 1915 into the American Jewish Joint Distribution Committee (JDC), under the chairmanship of Felix M. Warburg, set in motion the machinery for the first united Jewish war relief campaign. Record breaking sums were collected as volunteers and professionals of the two communities forged an unprecedented alliance. What began as an emergency program grew into American Jewry's major overseas relief and rehabilitation agency. From its New York headquarters JDC raised and administered tens of millions of dollars for war and postwar relief, medical care, economic, religious and cultural reconstruction, refugee resettlement, and aid to Israel.

In the process, the JDC produced a galaxy of notable leaders and set new standards of philanthropic giving that contributed immeasurably to the integration of differing points of view in the Jewish community. Under the pressure of unforeseen tragedy for European Jewry, many of the JDC leaders who had opposed Zionism became important factors in the economic and cultural developments in Palestine after 1921.

Until 1914 Zionism was sneered at by the uptown Jews as an "East Side affair" because the bulk of the members of the Zionist Organization of America were immigrants. One of its founders, however, was Dr. Gustav Gottheil, senior rabbi of Emanu-El, whose son, Richard, a Columbia University professor, served as the first president of the American Federation of Zionists. On her return from the second World Zionist Congress, where Theodor Herzl had urged her to mobilize Jewish women of America for the Zionist cause, Mrs. Richard Gottheil joined the Daughters of Zion. This group had been organized as a discussion club by East Side women even before the first World Zionist Congress in 1897. Gradually it developed chapters throughout the city and in 1912 it became the ladies auxiliary of the Zionist Organization of America. Signatories to the invitation to organize a national body included Henrietta Szold and Mrs. N. Taylor Phillips of Congregation Shearith Israel, and the organizing meeting was held in Emanu-El's vestry hall. The New York chapter of the Daughters of Zion took the name Hadassah, later adopted by the national organization of women Zionists.

When the world Zionist movement shifted its headquarters temporarily to New York during World War I and Louis D. Brandeis took over leadership of the American Zionists, Zionism began to grow in stature and membership as it enlisted broader elements of the New York community. Much Zionist history was made in New York. The Biltmore Platform calling for the establishment of a Jewish commonwealth in Palestine was adopted in New York in 1942. The American Jewish Conference, a democratically elected body of delegates from all parts of the country, which convened in New York in 1943, supported this position and mapped a postwar program of Jewish reconstruction. The United Nations' decision to partition Palestine into Jewish and Arab states and the admission of Israel to the United Nations were both voted on in New York.

Until 1939, the principal Zionist fundraising instrument was the United Palestine Appeal, whose headquarters was in New York. Then the JDC, the United Palestine Appeal, and the National Refugee Service united to create the United Jewish Appeal. For the next 35 years, UJA, from its New York headquarters, became the central American Jewish fundraising organization for the settlement of Jews in Israel and elsewhere, and for aid to needy Jews throughout the world. Between 1939 and the Yom Kippur War of 1973, UJA raised over $2 billion. In 1951, the Israel Bond Organization, also headquartered in New York, began its sales effort.

UJA's annual campaign in the spring, and the fall drive of the

Federation of Jewish Philanthropies—which were united in a joint annual campaign in 1974—together with numerous independent appeals for local, national, and overseas causes and institutions, have made fundraising a major enterprise of the New York Jewish community. Sheer numbers and access to a pool of talented volunteers, professionals, and big donors in the headquarters town of American Jewry, combined to make New York the principal source for raising Jewish philanthropic dollars and a potent force in determining where and how they are spent. The Jews of New York have made philanthropy an art and a science. Federation and UJA showed the way in organizing donors on an industry, trade, profession, and neighborhood basis, a technique now widely emulated by all major philanthropic endeavors.

Federation itself is the largest local philanthropic undertaking in the world under private auspices. Founded in 1917 to serve only Manhattan and The Bronx, it later incorporated the Brooklyn Jewish Federation, established in 1909. At the time of the merger, there were 3,637 separate Jewish institutions in New York City—schools, recreation and cultural agencies, multi-service societies, correctional agencies, hospitals, old age homes and orphanages, child care and family agencies all competing for contributions through a maze of wasted effort, time, money, and duplication of service. In the 1970s there were 130 agencies affiliated with Federation in the city proper and in the three adjacent suburban counties. These included hospitals, old age homes, child care agencies, family services, Jewish Community Centers and YM-YWHAs, camps, medical research centers, adoption agencies, Jewish education agencies, and facilities for the care of the mentally ill.

Most Federation-supported institutions and services are an outgrowth of those originally created to meet the needs of an immigrant generation. As the Jewish population of the city became overwhelmingly native-born and its economic status moved strikingly upward, the community's philanthropic agencies changed their emphasis. They became heavily involved in meeting the medical, residential, and social needs of the aged, supporting recreational and cultural services, underwriting Jewish educational programs, foster homes, homemaker and child adoption services, care for the chronically ill and mentally disturbed, and family services. Jewish family agencies that grew out of the special problems of immigrants now serve one-fourth more people than they did in 1946, including the immigrants of the 1970s. Jewish hospitals, opened initially to provide training for Jewish doctors when they were barred from the staffs of most New York hospitals, now have a large proportion of non-Jewish patients while non-Jewish hospitals have as many Jewish doctors on their staffs as do the Jewish hospitals.

In the 1970s, Federation turned its attention to meeting the urgent needs of the Jewish poor, who were estimated to number over 300,000 and to represent some 15 percent of the city's total Jewish population. More than half of the Jewish poor were elderly. The Federation-funded Metropolitan New York Coordinating Council on Jewish Poverty was created to coordinate community services for the Jewish poor and a new Federation agency, the Jewish Association for Services to the Aged, had a key-role in coping with the housing, relocation, legal aid, social, and communal problems of the aged poor. Other Federation agencies intensified their services to families, the poor, and the aged. Federation also established the Jewish Association for College Youth to initiate new programs for college-age young people and to give them an opportunity to serve other Jews, especially the aged. A number of Federation joint service centers were opened in neighborhoods with substantial numbers of Jewish aged and Jewish poor.

The Federation Employment and Guidance Service stepped up its services on behalf of job seeking Jews affected by the depression and for Jewish young people seeking career and vocational counseling. Branch offices of Federation-supported Jewish family and child care agencies were opened in the suburbs and in newly established neighborhoods with large Jewish populations. The Federation's Commission of Synagogue Relations focused action-producing attention on problems of drug and alcohol addiction, divorce, intermarriage, and the special needs of divorced and widowed parents, the unmarried, and other groups of singles. The phenomenon of black Jews, including some who were properly converted, seeking membership in synagogues and the admission of their children in synagogue religious schools and yeshivas was another concern of the Commission on Synagogue Relations. There were said to be some 3,500 black Jews scattered around the city, who worship at one of the ten or 12 black synagogues in Harlem, Brooklyn, and The Bronx.

Institutions and services established for the immigrant generations also gave rise to professional Jewish social work. Children of the immigrants became the first real Jewish social workers. Pioneering in child care, adoption, family relations, juvenile delinquency, mental hygiene, recreation, and rehabilitation, they sowed the seeds for the flowering of the community's philanthropic program.

Unified philanthropic efforts during World War I paved the way for the community's religious forces to combine to provide religious and welfare services to American Jewish soldiers. Setting aside sectarian differences, rabbinical and congregational groups joined the Council of Young Men's Hebrew Associations and Kindred Associations to form the National Jewish Welfare Board in 1917. Under its banner an agreement was reached on a common servicemen's prayer book, a uniform system of selecting Jewish chaplains, and a program of providing cultural activities, religious literature, and kosher food. This collaboration was enlarged during World War II and has continued as a unique manifestation of interdenominational unity coordinated by the secular National Jewish Welfare Board. World War I also brought thousands of Yiddish-speaking draftees from New York into contact for the first time with American Jews of other backgrounds and set in motion a process of amalgamation that was strengthened during World War II and by the subsequent growth of suburban Jewish communities.

Communal unification was also fostered by the Bureau of Jewish Education, set up by the Kehillah in 1910. Under the direction of Drs. Samson Benderly and Israel Chipkin, this Bureau modernized teaching methods in Jewish schools, adapted the Talmud Torah to American life, encouraged professional teacher training, and stimulated communal responsibility for the support of Jewish education. In 1939 the Bureau was absorbed by the new Jewish Education Committee of New York, founded through a legacy of Michael Friedsam, head of B. Altman & Co. An agency of Federation, the JEC (now known as the Bureau of Jewish Education), has been a major influence in improving Jewish elementary and secondary Jewish education.

The Jewish Communal Register of New York City, published in 1918 by the Kehillah, provided the first statistical picture of the community. It listed 3,637 separate organizations for a population of 1,500,000. Of the 858 congregations, 784 occupied their own houses of worship, 730 were Orthodox synagogues on the lower East Side or in the new ghettos of Brooklyn and The Bronx, 32 were Conservative, and 16 Reform. There were also 2,168 mutual aid societies, 164 philanthropic and social service institutions, and 69 Jewish schools.

In 1927 congregations had increased to 1,044, with 656 owning sanctuaries and 575 supporting full-time rabbis. Notwithstanding the synagogue building boom of the 1920s in the newer areas of settlement, less than one-third of the city's Jewish families were synagogue members in the 1930s. Between 1918 and 1930 the second generation of East Europeans, transformed from essentially a working class group to an increasingly middle-class community, had become the "lost generation" of New York Jewish life.

The flight from Judaism was halted and gradually reversed by the surge of religious and communal activity on the part of the third generation East Europeans after World War II. In the 1930s and 1940s the German-Sephardic and Russian communities had begun to fuse into a native-born generation that had shared the dislocations of the depression, the shock of anti-Semitic agitation, the unifying impact of the war, concern for the victims of Nazism, and pride in the rebirth of Israel. This generation's "reassertion and reinforcement of Jewish identity through religious affiliation" was reflected in the return to the synagogue by war veterans and their families, and by the children of antireligious Yiddishists.

In 1963, there were 630 synagogues in the five boroughs and 153 in the adjacent three suburban counties. Of the 494 Orthodox congregations in the city in that year, some 80 percent were tiny congregations, much like those established in the 1880s. Conservative and Reform congregations numbered 91 and 45, respectively, in 1963 in the city. In 1975 the total number of congregations in the city had dropped to 541. Of these, 375 were Orthodox,

100 Conservative, 46 Reform, and one Reconstructionist.

The reduction in the number of synagogues in the five boroughs was due to two developments: heavy population growth in the suburbs and the closing or sale of many synagogues to blacks and Puerto Ricans as a result of the exodus of Jews from such neighborhoods as Brownsville and East New York in Brooklyn, the entire South Bronx and much of the Grand Concourse and Tremont neighborhoods of The Bronx, and in a number of sections of Manhattan. Among the synagogues that went out of existence were a number of small and older Orthodox sanctuaries in the first and second areas of Jewish settlement. On the other hand, new congregations sprang up in and around the high-rise housing projects in Brooklyn (Starrett City), Queens (Lefrak City), The Bronx (Co-Op City), and Manhattan (Lincoln Center). Orthodox groups such as Young Israel were particularly active in creating new congregations of young married couples who were products of the Hebrew Day schools.

While there are no reliable statistics of synagogue membership, about 40 percent of the Jews in New York City and nearly 50 percent of those in the suburbs belonged to congregations in the mid-1970s. The New York Board of Rabbis claimed 700 members but these included some with congregations in nearby New Jersey, Pennsylvania, Connecticut, and upstate New York.

While synagogue membership declined at the beginning of the 1970s, concern for more intensive Jewish education became widely apparent. The Bureau of Jewish Education turned to tested advertising techniques to encourage enrollment in Jewish schools. The synagogue schools of all denominations expanded their curricula and hours of study, experimented with new approaches, updated curricula, developed more effective texts, and used new teaching tools. Federation began to allocate considerably greater sums to Jewish educational agencies, including Hebrew day schools. Travel to and study in Israel by teenagers became increasingly widespread, encouraged and stimulated by Israeli-oriented agencies and the Jewish educational institutions.

Probably the most striking development in Jewish education in New York during the 1960-1970 decade was the growth of the Hebrew day school. Thirty years ago most American Jews regarded the Hebrew all-day school, which combined secular and Jewish educational programs on the elementary and secondary levels, with considerable distaste. In the 1930s Hebrew day schools in New York had only 3,000 pupils. In 1963, there were 179 in New York, with an enrollment of 40,000, out of a total of 154,342 attending all types of Jewish elementary and secondary schools. In 1975 there were 54,000 pupils enrolled in these schools—128 elementary and 73 high schools. All but 17 of these schools were under Orthodox auspices, and many were sponsored by Chasidic groups in Williamsburg, Borough Park, and Crown Heights in Brooklyn. But there were also such schools conducted by Conservative synagogues and one was under the aegis of a Reform congregation. A considerable number of the children in the Hebrew day schools did not come from Orthodox homes. They left the public schools because of parents' uneasiness over attacks on Jewish children and teachers. By 1972, half the city's white children were attending parochial schools—Jewish, Catholic, and Lutheran.

The Hebrew day schools, formerly found only in the older neighborhoods, have penetrated middle-class areas as well as the suburbs. Their growth in numbers and enrollment created growing Jewish sentiment for government support of parochial schools in contradiction to the general opposition to such aid by the national Jewish community relations organizations and most of the congregational bodies. In the 1970s, sponsors of the Hebrew day schools made common cause with Catholics in seeking state and federal funds for their parochial schools. Financial problems continued to plague the Hebrew day schools as unfavorable court decisions banned the use of state and federal funds for parochial schools. All told there were 700 Jewish schools of all types in the metropolitan New York area in the 1970s, and they enrolled 135,000 children. Most of these schools received educational aids, pedagogical material, and counseling from the Board of Jewish Education.

Establishment of the State of Israel spurred greater interest in Hebrew in the city's public schools. Hebrew now ranks fifth in popularity among the languages offered in some 60 junior and senior high schools. Attendance at congregational Jewish high schools and Hebrew-speaking camps sponsored by national agencies has also increased.

Because of its stress on Jewish education in depth, Orthodox Judaism regained some of its lost ground in New York in the 1960s and 1970s. The efforts of Young Israel synagogues, often led by scientists, professors, and highly educated Jewishly laymen, the impact of the immigrants from Hungary, Syria, Russia, and North Africa who are ultra-Orthodox, the leadership of English-speaking American-educated rabbis associated with Yeshiva University's Isaac Elchanan Rabbinical Seminary, and the Rabbinical Council of America have also strengthened Orthodoxy. Yarmulke-wearing young people in public places have become a common sight. Increased observance of kashruth and the greater availability of kosher food products in supermarkets are also manifestations of increased Orthodox feeling and observance. New York also has several ultra-Orthodox seminaries and rabbinical organizations. The world headquarters of the Lubavitcher Movement and a network of social and economic institutions maintained by other Chasidic communities which isolate themselves from the rest of the community, are located in New York. The presence in New York of the national headquarters of the Reform (Union of American Hebrew Congregations), Conservative (United Synagogue of America), and Orthodox (Union of Orthodox Jewish Congregations of America) movements and their related rabbinical seminaries—Hebrew Union College-Jewish Institute of Religion,

Jewish Theological Seminary of America, and Isaac Elchanan Rabbinical Seminary of Yeshiva University—are a great asset to Jewish life in New York City.

Religious differences among New York Jews have become as much economic as theological. Broadly speaking, Jews in the higher income bracket are more likely to be members of either a Conservative or Reform synagogue. While most of New York's Orthodox Jews are in a low-income group (many of them are among the city's thousands of poor and aged Jews), there is a substantial middle-class and well-to-do Orthodox community. Children and grandchildren of Orthodox immigrants constitute the bulk of membership in Reform and Conservative congregations. For the first time, conversion to Judaism is being encouraged by the Jewish community. The Reform group maintains a school for them at the House of Living Judaism, and the Conservatives have a method of dealing with serious-minded Christians seeking to embrace Judaism. Even the Orthodox are no longer entirely hostile to conversion provided it is accomplished in accordance with the Halacha.

GROWTH OF NEW YORK CITY JEWISH POPULATION

Year	Population
1695	100
1760	100
1795	300
1806	380
1812	500
1825	600
1840	15,000
1850	50,000
1860	60,000
1870	75,000
1880	85,000
1890	200,000
1900	600,000
1910	1,252,000
1920	1,643,000
1930	1,825,000
1940	1,785,000
1950	1,996,000
1957	2,114,000
1960	1,836,000
1975	1,228,000

Changing Neighborhoods

Until well after the American Revolution, most of the city's Jews lived within shouting distance of the spot where the refugees from Brazil had landed in 1654. Clustered in the vicinity of the first synagogue on Mill Street, long known as Jews' Street or Jews' Alley (now South William Street), the Jews had their homes and places of business on Stone, Beaver, and Broad Streets, Hanover Square, and lower Broadway, in the heart of what is now the financial district.

As the city began expanding northward, the Jews started moving toward what is now the City Hall area and Greenwich Village. At about 1820, the majority of Jews had settled around West Broadway. The wealthier lived along Greenwich, Laight, Greene, Pearl, Water, Wooster, and Crosby Streets, the poorer on Broome, Houston, Canal, and Franklin Streets. A year before the oldest congregation moved into its second synagogue on Crosby Street in 1834, only one Jewish family was left in the Mill Street neighborhood. When the second congregation was established in 1825, its synagogue was a converted Negro church on Elm Street.

The Lower East Side first became a Jewish neighborhood in the late 1830s and 1840s when German and Polish immigrants settled on Bayard, Canal, Elm, Baxter, and Mott Streets, and Chatham Square, around what is now Chinatown. From there they pushed east into Division, Allen, Christie and Henry Streets, and north to Stanton, Ludlow, Clinton, Attorney, Rivington, Pitt, Ridge, and Houston Streets. By the 1850s Jews had moved as far north as 20th Street on the east side and to 34th Street on the west side.

After the Civil War, the more prosperous German-Jewish families and the remnant of the Sephardim quit the older Jewish neighborhood, moving en masse to the middle east side between 30th and 57th Streets, and to the west side between 59th and 96th Streets, where they occupied the then luxurious brownstones. Working class and lower middle-class German and Hungarian Jews took up residence north of Houston Street, along the numbered streets between Avenue B and the East River, while others began settling in Harlem.

The exodus of the older families and their synagogues from the Lower East Side was virtually ended by 1880 when the Jewish community was still "hardly more than a subject for idle curiosity." Because each new contingent of Jewish immigrants went first to the Lower East Side, where they took over houses and synagogues abandoned by their predecessors, this section remained heavily Jewish until the final break up of the area as the heart of New York Jewry. The 20 city blocks of the Lower East Side, between Houston Street and East Broadway, east of the Bowery, were "an immigrant Jewish cosmopolis," jammed with nearly 600,000 people by 1910. Most all of these were from Eastern Europe except the Levantine Jews, who took root between Allen and Christie Streets.

There was, however, a steady exodus from the Lower East Side. As "those whose lot improved moved out, they were replaced constantly by new arrivals" from Europe. As early as the 1890s the trek was on from the Lower East Side to Yorkville, between 72nd and 100th Streets, east of Lexington (now part of the Barrio of the Puerto Ricans), and then north to Harlem, where the German Jews had preceded them.

Higher wages won by the garment unions and the opening of the subways enabled Jews to leave the East Side tenements for brighter homes in Washington Heights in northern Manhattan, the lower Bronx, and the Brooklyn neighborhoods of Brownsville, East New York, Borough Park, and Bensonhurst. As the East Side sweatshops were eliminated, and the clothing factories began moving north to Madison Square and then towards Times Square, there was no longer any need for Jews who could afford to live elsewhere to remain on the Lower East Side.

The Lower East Side began to fade as the city's principal Jewish quarter in the 1920s about the time when the German Jews and the more successful East Europeans were taking root on Riverside Drive, West End Avenue, and Central Park West. In the 1930s, when Harlem was abandoned to the Negroes, the Lower East Side had fewer Jews than in 1900, while Washington Heights became known as "the fourth Reich" because of an influx of refugees from Nazism. Until the 1940s, the west side, from 70th to 125th Streets, and from Central Park West to Riverside Drive, was the most important Jewish neighborhood. The brownstones on side streets from 72nd to 96th Streets were heavily populated by middle-class Jews until the 1930s. When these residences became economically unviable, the Jews withdrew to the large apartment houses on the main thoroughfares.

In the 1950s a substantial Jewish exodus began from this section to which blacks and Puerto Ricans had been moving in great numbers. Temple Israel and the West End Synagogue, two of the oldest Reform synagogues in the area, shifted to the middle east side. A third, Rodeph Sholom, reported that its west side membership had fallen, while its east side membership accounted for a third of the total. Older members tended to remain, but their children moved. Shearith Israel, the Free Synagogue, B'nai Jeshurun, the Jewish Center, and the Society for the Advancement of Judaism have remained on the west side.

The Columbia University-Jewish Theological Seminary-Union Theological Seminary cultural complex between 116th and 123rd Streets, from Amsterdam Avenue to Riverside Drive, encourages young professionals, academicians, and older families to stay in that neighborhood despite serious problems resulting from ethnic changes in the area. The Jewish Theological Seminary silenced rumors that it might move because it was unable to obtain urgently needed space by completing a new dormitory. The first New York chavurah, founded in 1969, rented a Morningside Drive apartment near Columbia University where its adherents sought to redefine their own Judaism on a personal level through communal sharing, discussion, and prayer. Widows, retired people living on pensions and Social Security, and owners of neighborhood retail businesses also stayed on the west side because they were reluctant to leave rent-controlled apartments, notwithstanding an increase in crime in the area. The major rebuilding around Lincoln Center in the west 60s, and the erection of new middle and low-income housing projects between West 80th and 90th Streets, gave rise to something of a Jewish revival on the west side.

The Jewish middle-class exodus from the west side in the 1950s and 1960s created new Jewish communities on the middle and upper east side. The 92nd Street YM & YWHA had discussed moving until the 2nd and 3rd Avenue elevated lines were razed, and the new high-rise apartment houses that replaced slum dwellings from Madison Avenue to the East River between 34th and 96th Streets, revitalized the entire area. Temple Emanu-El added a large school wing. A new Reform congregation was established on East 35th Street where it shares quarters with the Community Church. The Park East Synagogue on East 67th Street added an eight-story building. The Park Avenue Synagogue added a multi-use structure. The established Orthodox and Conservative synagogues in the area enjoyed new growth. Central Synagogue remained fixed at 55th Street and Lexington Avenue despite the shifting tides of Jewish population, and added a center annex.

The new east side Jewish settlement also drew from residents on upper Fifth and Park Avenues, Beekman and Sutton Place cooperatives, from older families returned from the suburbs who moved into high-rise cooperatives in the 60s, 70s, and 80s between Fifth and Second Avenues, employees at the United Nations, and executives with firms occupying the skyscraper office buildings on 6th and Park Avenues who reside at neighboring apartment houses. A number of national Jewish organizations have headquarters in buildings between East 52nd and East 84th Streets. The Federation building is on East 59th Street.

On the lower west side, where Jews rarely lived, there is a growing Jewish community in the Chelsea area, south of Pennsylvania Station, thanks to new middle-class cooperative and public housing developments. Luxury apartments on lower Fifth Avenue and modernized tenements in Greenwich Village have brought back middle-class families, students, and intellectuals. Several new synagogues have been formed in Greenwich Village in the last five years. Some Jews have moved into SoHo, between Houston and Canal Streets, where artists' studios and apartments have taken root in old warehouses.

There has also been a return of lower and middle-income Jews to the east side, south of 23rd Street. Since the city's first public housing project, Knickerbocker Village, opened in the 1930s, younger families of limited means have gone back to the first area of Jewish settlement. Peter Cooper Village, Stuyvesant Town, and the network of public housing along the East River have given rise to a new Jewish community. There is a YMHA at the corner of 14th Street and Second Avenue. New Reform and Conservative synagogues have been opened in the area, finding members among the residents of new high-rise apartment houses that sprang up along First,

Second, and Third Avenues between 14th and 23rd Streets, after the elevated lines came down. Some of the older Orthodox congregations in this area gained new members from the refugees from Hungary, Cuba, and Syria who first settled there on their arrival.

The old Lower East Side, the portal to America for hundreds of thousands of Jews, with its crowds of pious Jews, Hebrew schools, kosher butchers, colorful cafes, open air pushcarts, and all the "warming images of the Jewish ghetto" are gone forever. There are still some 20,000 Jews left on the Lower East Side, most of whom live in the public and private cooperatives along Delancey Street, Grand Street, and East Broadway. Many of this Jewish remnant are old and poor, some are pensioners living on social security. There is also a younger Jewish element living in the eight residential developments built on the Lower East Side between 1956 and 1966. The neighborhood is now a daily ethnic confrontation of Puerto Ricans, Chinese, and blacks, as well as Jews. There have been bitter struggles between Jews and Puerto Ricans over rights to apartments in new housing complexes, over the appointment of an anti-Semite as local school superintendent, and over the continued vandalism of the remaining synagogues in the area.

Yiddish and Hebrew signs are still evident but are now outnumbered by those in Spanish, Chinese, Italian, and Greek. Whenever a Jewish storekeeper sells out, the buyer is never a Jew. But the neighborhood is still a Jewish marketplace. Along three blocks of Orchard Street, suburban descendants of yesterday's immigrants converge in search of bargains and nostalgia at shops that sell a great variety of merchandise at bargain prices. Some Jewish merchants employ Spanish-speaking salesmen for their Puerto Rican customers. The throngs of buyers are so dense on Sundays that Orchard Street between Delancey and Houston Streets is reserved for pedestrians from 8 A.M. to 6 P.M. The remaining handful of synagogues are architectural relics of the bygone past where worshipers often pray in the dark, lest lights attract vandals and hoodlums. The synagogues that are still in use are badly in need of repair and their worshipers struggle just to keep them open. The Yiddish writers, poets, playwrights, novelists, scholars, labor leaders, and journalists who once wandered in and out of the *Jewish Daily Forward* building on East Broadway have long since vanished. In 1975 the *Forward* too, left East Broadway, moving uptown to East 33rd Street in the new home of the Workmen's Circle, which also departed from the East Side. With their departure a large part of the remnant of the old East Side faded.

The Educational Alliance, founded for the first immigrants of the 1880s era, is still at East Broadway and busier than ever, serving Jews and the minorities that have taken over the East Side. The Henry Street Settlement, founded in 1893 to serve poor Jewish immigrants, now serves mostly Puerto Ricans, but the executive director and many of the board of directors are Jews, as are nearly half of the old people who come to the

Settlement for a variety of programs. The Settlement sponsors a Jewish theatrical group and serves kosher lunches with menus printed in English and Spanish and prepared by a black dietician.

The Washington Heights area, in northwest Manhattan, is another neighborhood where changes have converted a once important Jewish area into one now predominantly black, Puerto Rican, and Cuban. In the 1920s the neighborhood became one of the areas in which Jews leaving the Lower East Side settled in substantial numbers in new elevator apartment houses. In the 1930s Washington Heights became known as "the fourth Reich" because so many Jewish refugees from Hitler Europe settled there, including the family of Henry Kissinger, who grew up there. In the 1970s the Jews numbered less than one-fourth of the 187,000 people who dwell in Washington Heights. In the 1960s they were one-third of the population. Fear of crime and environmental issues such as noise, dirty streets, and deteriorating schools drove families with school age children away. The remaining Jewish residents included a good many aged poor. Washington Heights is the home of the main campus of Yeshiva University, a YM-YWHA, several Hebrew day schools and synagogues, and a Jewish community council. The latter has had a safety patrol cruising the streets after dark to protect Jewish residents.

Forty years of population shifts and urban redevelopment dropped Manhattan from first to third place as the borough with the largest number of Jews. The latest figures for Manhattan's Jewish population was 171,000. Manhattan's loss of Jewish residents first showed up as huge increases in Brooklyn and The Bronx during the 1930s. By the 1960s, Manhattan's continued loss of Jewish residents was reflected in the growth of the Queens, Long Island, and Westchester Jewish settlements.

The Struggle For Equality

The 23 unwanted refugees who arrived in New Amsterdam in 1654 found no freedom. They fought to achieve it for themselves and others.

The first victory over Peter Stuyvesant's bigotry that permitted the Jewish Pilgrim Fathers to stay was more than an entering wedge for the achievement of further civil rights. It also paved the way for other religious sects to assert and win their rights and set a precedent which succeeding generations of New York Jews emulated in supporting the struggle of other disfranchised and oppressed minorities.

In 1655 when Stuyvesant ordered the Jews exempt from military training and guard duty but imposed a special monthly tax on them in lieu of such service, Asser Levy and Jacob Barsimson challenged this discrimination. Told by the city fathers to "go elsewhere" if they did not like it, the two simple workmen successfully appealed to Holland which ordered Stuyvesant to allow them to help defend the city. When Levy stood guard in defiance of the local authorities, he became the first Jewish soldier in America. Three years later, when Barsimson failed to appear in his own defense in a court action, "no default is entered against him as he was summoned on his Sabbath."

In 1655, Abraham de Lucena was fined for violating the ban on retail selling by Jews, but Asser Levy and Moses de Lucena, the first Jews to be licensed as butchers, were excused in 1660 from killing hogs on grounds of their religion. Levy was admitted to the burgher right in 1657.

That same year the Jews won the right to share in the defense of the city and to own property. But public worship, the vote, retail business, and the practice of any trade but that of butcher were not permitted. They could exercise their religion "in all quietness . . . within their houses for which end they must without doubt endeavor to build their houses close together in a convenient place on one or the other side of New Amsterdam—at their choice." This hint to create a ghetto was ignored, but the Jews did settle in the neighborhood of Mill Street where the first synagogue was opened.

The rights wrung from the Dutch permitted the Jewish settlement to enjoy a decade of reasonable security despite the harassment of Stuyvesant and his successors. All economic disabilities against the Jews were lifted by the English. Freedom of religion began in 1674 when the Duke of York instructed his governor in the colony renamed for him "to permit all persons of what religion so ever, quietly to inhabit within the precincts of yo're jurisdictions without giving them any disturbance or disquiet whatsoever for or by reason of their differing opinion in matter of religion." Another governor decreed in 1685 that "publique worship" was a privilege limited to those "that professe faith in Christ," but the earlier order was reaffirmed in 1686.

Until after the Revolution, all sects remained subject to a special assessment by the Colonial Assembly for the support of Trinity Church. As late as 1730 even "the Jew synnagogg" paid four shillings and nine pence for support of the Church of England ministry.

Saturday was the day New York's householders had to clean the street in front of their residences until 1702 when it was changed to Friday. In 1727 the Jews were permitted to omit the words "upon the true faith of a Christian" in taking the loyalty oath. Fifty Colonial Jews, many of them from New York, were recognized as freemen between 1687 and 1769. Samuel Myers Cohen, a butcher, was the first Jew to become a citizen in 1740 when the British Parliament passed a naturalization law that gave aliens of seven years residence all the rights of native-born British subjects. The right of Jews to vote was questioned in 1737 when a defeated candidate for the Colonial Assembly challenged the outcome on the plea that Jews had all voted for his opponent. The protest was upheld by the legislature which declared votes cast by Jews null and void.

With the adoption of New York State's first constitution in 1777 the Jews were granted full citizenship and complete equality. This final emancipation set a precedent for the other states and paved the way for the achievement of similar rights by Catholics.

The right of rabbis to be Army chaplains, the last battle for Jewish religious equality in the United States, first established during the Civil War, was won chiefly through the efforts of the Reverend Arnold Fischel, the Dutch-born reader at Shearith Israel. As the representative of the Board of Delegates of American Israelites, he negotiated with members of Congress and the War Department and persuaded President Abraham Lincoln to recommend that Congress amend the law to permit the appointment of rabbis as chaplains. Rabbi Ferdinand Sarner, chaplain of the 54th New York Volunteers, was the only one of the three rabbis commissioned under the amended act of 1862 to serve at the front.

Before the Civil War discrimination against Jews in employment in New York and sporadic anti-Semitic incidents were not uncommon and "specific individuals were abused as Jews by those who opposed, hated, or envied them." It was, however, "not a common habit to attack all Jews for whatever anyone found wrong with life in the United States. That remained for the Civil War period."

Even some of the most respectable New York City newspapers "spoke as though all the Jewish bankers in the world, with Belmont in the lead, were joined together for the support of the Confederacy." August Belmont, Democratic party spokesman and banker, who married into the family of Commodore Oliver Hazzard Perry, reared his children as Christians and had nothing to do with the Jewish community, was the particular target of the Republican press. But all Jewish businessmen were regularly denounced as gold speculators and war profiteers.

The leading role played in the Confederacy by Judah P. Benjamin, a Jew, and Senator David Yulee of Florida, who had left the Jewish fold, "provided a convenient slur with which all Jews could be defamed." Anti-Semites who attacked Belmont as a Confederate sympathizer ignored the fact that he aided the United States Treasury in securing the support of European capital and that he had recruited and equipped the first German-American regiment in New York.

Anti-Jewish sentiment was further aggravated by General Ulysses Grant's notorious Order No. 11, expelling all Jews "as a class" from the Department of Tennessee. The "most sweeping anti-Jewish regulation in all American history," the Order was in effect from December 11, 1862 until January 7, 1863 when President Lincoln ordered it rescinded. Issued as part of the Union Army's attempt to halt trading with the Confederacy and the ensuing widespread profiteering, the Order created indignation among native-born Jews, alarm among the German immigrants, and blackened the reputation of all Jewish businessmen. It even played a role in the 1868 presidential election when it prompted many ordinarily Republican New York Jewish voters to switch to the Democrats. Grant, who always regretted the Order, sought to make amends when he became president by appointing Benjamin F. Peixotto, a New York attorney and president of B'nai B'rith, as United States consul general to Romania in 1870, in the hope he would be able to halt the anti-Jewish policies of that country.

Grant's order contributed greatly to the postwar American stereotype of the Jew as peddler and profiteer when he also became equated with a parvenu. Coupled with the rising antialien sentiment of 1870-1890 and the agrarian revolt against Wall Street, these prejudices became the seed-bed of American anti-Semitism.

The "no Jews allowed" pattern of restrictions at resorts and hotels, which took form in the 1870s, claimed as its most prominent victim Joseph Seligman, banker, friend of Lincoln, and the leader of the Jewish community. His exclusion from the Grand Union Hotel in Saratoga Springs in 1877, on orders of its owner, Henry Hilton, created a national sensation. A boycott by Jews and non-Jews of A. T. Stewart & Co., of which Hilton was trustee, ruined the firm's wholesale trade, and only a take-over by John Wanamaker saved the retail establishment.

The Reverend Henry Ward Beecher's famous sermon, "Jew and Gentile," preached from Plymouth Church, Brooklyn, in 1877, was not just an attack on Hilton but a classic repudiation of anti-Semitism. Beecher's denunciation was also aimed at Austin Corbin, a real estate promoter, who publicly announced that he wanted no Jewish patrons at his lavish new resort at Manhattan Beach. A. T. Stewart, when he laid out Garden City, on Long Island, as a model village in the 1870s specifically excluded Jewish property owners.

The New York City Bar Association rejected a Jewish applicant in 1877 solely because he was a Jew. Before the Jews swamped the Lower East Side, the principal property owner on Second Avenue would not rent to Jews. Discrimination by insurance companies against Jewish merchants was so widespread during this period that New York Jews seriously considered forming a company that would accept only Jewish policy holders. While some Jews gained entry to high society clubs and exclusive hotels, most Jews sought social outlets in all-Jewish clubs and patronized resorts where Jews were in a majority. The exclusion of Jews from college fraternities at the end of the 19th century gave rise to Jewish Greek letter societies at the New York colleges.

Jew-baiting of a more violent character was fairly common on the Lower East Side, especially where Irish neighborhoods bordered Jewish sections. The worst anti-Semitic incident in the city occurred in 1902 when the funeral procession of Rabbi Jacob Joseph was attacked by workers in the printing press factory of R. Hoe & Co., which employed no Jews. More than 125 Jews were injured.

Biased or sensation-seeking journalists contributed to the rise of anti-Semitism by drawing a distorted picture of the East Side as a neighborhood of squalor, poverty, and pushcarts, peopled by wild-eyed radicals, bizarre foreigners, and ill-kempt children. Henry James spoke of the East Side as "a vast aquarium in which innumerable fish, of over-developed proboscises, were to bump together, forever, amid heaped spoils of the sea." Visitors who failed to recognize that on the sidewalks of the East Side was flowering a fertile seed-bed of great talents, translated the sights and sounds and smells of the East Side into subtle anti-Jewish feeling.

Only a few perceptive non-Jewish observers—Jacob Riis, reporter and reformer; Hutchins Hapgood; and Lincoln J. Steffens, whose muckraking articles greatly influenced muncipal reforms—sensed the ferment of progress on the East Side.

At the very time when Czarist persecution was bringing almost daily shiploads of Jews to New York, American racists and anti-Semites began assailing the "Hebrew conquest" of New York. Foes of immigration made the Jews their principal target, denouncing "the great Jewish invasion" of the metropolis, which they said, threatened to make it "a city of Asiatics."

The struggle against overt anti-Semitism first took organized form in New York in 1859 with the establishment of the Board of Delegates of American Israelites. This body was replaced in 1906 by the American Jewish Committee. Differences of opinion over tactics and techniques created other national agencies in this field. The Anti-Defamation League of B'nai B'rith, founded in the midwest in 1913, moved to New York in the 1930s. New York is also the headquarters of the American Jewish Congress, the Jewish Labor Committee, and the National Jewish Community Relations Advisory Council.

A small beginning in outlawing discrimination was made in New York in 1913 with a state law forbidding places of public accommodation from advertising their unwillingness to admit anyone because of race, creed, or color. Before World War I, Adolph S. Ochs, publisher of *The New York Times* wrote to all daily newspapers reminding them that the word "Jew" is a noun, and was not to be used as an adjective or adverb, as in "Jew-down" or "Jew-boy." Similar efforts ended the practice of identifying criminals by religion, nationality, and race, and eliminated offensive Jewish characters from stage and screen. These modest efforts gradually eliminated the coarser manifestations of anti-Semitism but it took another generation of education before the Jews of New York could work, study, live, and play without restrictions.

In the 1920s and 1930s, a quota system sharply curtailed the number of Jewish students in the city's private colleges and universities. It barred all but a handful from the city's five medical colleges, and held down their number at the city's leading law schools. Not until the state outlawed discrimination in higher education did Jewish medical, law, and dental students get a better break in New York's colleges.

This discrimination impelled many New York Jewish students to seek admission to colleges out of the city and even abroad for the first time. One of the first major victories against Jew-baiting came in 1927 when Henry Ford addressed to Louis Marshall a public apology for seven years of vilification of the Jews in *The Dearborn Independent*.

Few white collar or clerical jobs were open to Jews in New York in the

1920s and 1930s. The big downtown law offices seldom engaged Jewish law clerks. Banks, insurance companies, and public utilities turned away Jewish applicants. Jewish graduates of the City's public high schools found their high academic standing meant little in the face of quotas applied by Ivy League colleges and out-of-town medical schools. Even when they could afford it, few Jews could rent or buy housing in the better neighborhoods. Membership in the influential social clubs was closed to them and summer resorts flaunted "Christian only" signs and advertisements.

Beekman Place, Sutton Place, and the Carl Schurz section were resisting Jewish tenants in the 1920s and 1930s as much as Fifth and Park Avenues did just before World War II. Some luxury cooperatives and the Westchester village of Bronxville still continue this practice today. Once no Jew could rent in the exclusive apartments north of Grand Central Station any more than he could in Forest Hills, Queens, or Bay Ridge, Brooklyn. Coney Island, Brighton Beach, Manhattan Beach, and Sheepshead Bay, once exclusive Brooklyn seaside resorts which barred Jews, now have large Jewish populations. Sea Gate, a segment of Coney Island that was once a Gentile millionaire's preserve, became a middle-class Jewish enclave.

As late as 1915, Long Beach, in Nassau County, now about half-Jewish, was dotted with clubs and hotels that refused to admit Jews. Most golf and country clubs or resorts on Long Island and in Westchester were not open to Jews, and a few are still barred to them. Long Island's leading yacht club, which always excluded Jews, reversed its policy just in time to enable its first Jewish member to pilot the yacht that carried the United States to victory in the America Cup race with Great Britain in 1962. In 1963 one of the largest Long Island country clubs publicly asked Jewish organizations to help it enroll more non-Jewish members to create a better balance. Indignant denials were made when the president of Temple Emanu-El charged in 1963 that a Fifth Avenue cooperative was not available to him only because he was a Jew. Zoning ordinances were invoked in efforts to bar the construction of synagogues in some Long Island and Westchester communities in the 1940s and 1950s, and even in the 1970s, and it took some time before Jewish home-buyers broke through unwritten restrictions.

The 1930s also saw Nazi Bundist parades and rallies, Christian Front meetings, and noisy Coughlinites peddling anti-Semitic literature on street corners. Despite great provocation the Jewish community resisted attempts to outlaw such demonstrations because of its deep commitment to civil rights for all. The close association of such New Yorkers as Sidney Hillman, David Dubinsky, Samuel Rosenman, and Benjamin Cohen with Franklin D. Roosevelt led to attacks on the New Deal as "the Jew deal," and inspired campaign slogans with anti-Semitic overtones, such as "clear it with Sidney." More recent anti-Jewish meetings by latter-day Nazis and the rash of swastika daubings on Jewish public buildings in the 1950s created concern but no panic.

Most overt anti-Semitism in New York is now largely a thing of the past, thanks to state and city antidiscrimination and fair employment legislation fought for by the Jewish community relations agencies. Their programs of intergroup action, information, education, research, public opinion, and determined pressure for remedial laws reduced incidents of anti-Semitism to its lowest level in history in the 1950s and early 1960s, while paving the way for the profound changes toward civil rights and equal opportunities for all minorities. Discrimination still exists, of course, but it is confined largely to the executive suite—where great progress has been made in opening the doors to employment for qualified Jews—a few clubs, some luxury cooperative apartments, and occasional employers. The National Jewish Commission on Law and Public Affairs of the Union of Orthodox Jewish Congregations dealt effectively with many cases of discrimination against Jewish Sabbath observers.

The community relations problems of New York's Jews in the 1960s and 1970s grew less out of anti-Semitism as such, and more from differences with Catholics and Negroes. Christmas observances in the public schools, displays of Christological symbols in public places, child adoption policies, abortion, and public funds for parochial schools were issues on which Catholics and Jews did not always see eye-to-eye. Catholic-Jewish relations, however, were greatly improved as a result of numerous joint educational and research projects involving Catholic clergymen and educators. Sunday closing laws aligned some Protestant groups against Jewish merchants as part of a legal struggle that began more than 200 years ago. It started in New Amsterdam in 1665 when Abraham de Lucena was fined for keeping his shop open during the Sunday church sermon. It ended in 1963 when the City Council enacted a Fair Sabbath Law that gave Sabbath-observing Jewish family-operated establishments the right to open their places of business on Sunday.

Anti-Semitism in the black and Puerto Rican communities, a by-product of the militant black and Puerto Rican struggle for employment, housing, and educational opportunity, became a matter of serious concern for the first time in the 1960s. Long the most vigorous champion of minority rights, the Jews of New York were taken aback by the Jew-baiting of the Black Muslims—now a thing of the past—and by the anti-Semitic statements of some black newspapers and leaders. Charges of discrimination against blacks levied against the Jewish leadership of the International Ladies Garment Workers Union were especially disturbing. While similar charges were made against other unions, Jewish unionists were the first targets because of the blacks' feeling that more was to be expected from Jews than from other whites.

Conflicts between black and Puerto Rican advocates of local school control and Jewish teachers during the 1968 school strike led to anti-Semitic outbursts by various black militants and an angry backlash by Jews. Black publications attacked what they called "exploitation" by Jews of blacks and Puerto Ricans in the school system. Anti-Semitism became an issue in the

1969 mayoralty election when Democratic candidate Mario Procaccino accused Mayor John Lindsay of fostering an "upsurge in anti-Semitism" by his actions during the teachers' strike when there were frequent confrontations between black parents and Jewish teachers. A panel of experts appointed by Lindsay to study bigotry in the city concluded that propaganda and threats used by black extremists during the teachers' strike and the struggle over decentralization of the school system contained "a dangerous component of anti-Semitism."

The charges and countercharges of black anti-Semitism and white racism seriously strained the long-time black-Jewish alliance forged during the years of the civil rights struggle. Facing one another across picket lines at schools on the Lower East Side, Brooklyn, and at housing projects in Queens, mutual recriminations and threats seriously exacerbated black-Jewish tensions. Because much of the black-Jewish conflict occurred in communities where blacks were recent arrivals, some sociologists saw the conflict as due in part to the "normal" conflict between the remnants of a departing group and the upwardly mobile efforts of a new group. Ethnic polarizations over school busing in the Ocean-Brownsville and Canarsie areas, anti-Semitism by a Puerto Rican district school superintendent on the Lower East Side, the bitter and partially successful struggle of the Jews of Forest Hills to prevent the building of a massive low-income housing project in their neighborhood, and discrimination against the Jewish poor by black administrators of local antipoverty programs combined to create great bitterness between blacks and whites.

Affirmative action programs that were designed to give minorities a better break in government employment, often turned out to be undermining the idea of merit in public employment, some sectors of private employment, and in the schools and colleges, were regarded as reverse discrimination against Jews. One of the by-products of affirmative action in the public schools was an almost 50 percent loss of jobs by Jewish school supervisors between 1968 and 1973 as a result of the decentralization of school districts. City College, which three generations of New York Jews used as a stepping stone to a better life, became involved in the black-Jewish conflict when its standards of admission were lowered to make room for more minority students. The idea of racial quotas in civil service, further embittered black-Jewish relations.

Blacks and Puerto Ricans resented the flight of Jews from neighborhoods into which they moved and the transfer of thousands of Jewish children from the public to private and Jewish day schools. The Jews, on the other hand, were fleeing the city because of growing crime, deteriorating schools, street violence, and fear. The president of the Rabbinical Council of America, noting the abandonment of Orthodox synagogues and Hebrew schools in various parts of the city, urged the Jews to remain in changing neighborhoods. The Orthodox were usually the last to leave such areas, with the result that there was greater conflict between them and the newly arrived black and Puerto Rican residents. In one year, 75 Orthodox synagogues were abandoned or sold in Brownsville, East New York, Crown Heights, Williamsburg, the lower Bronx, the upper West Side, and Jamaica.

All of this gave rise to a new mood of anger and militancy on the part of rank and file Jews who refused to believe that the decline of old Jewish neighborhoods was not a deliberate policy of the city government during the years of urban renewal. Long-time Jewish activists and supporters of a wide variety of good causes, Jewish organizations, and many liberal movements, suddenly began to look at programs and projects with an eye as to whether they were good or bad for Jews. Jewish ethnicity, long confined to religion, education, and philanthropy, came to the fore in such areas as housing, poverty, public education, and school busing. This previously unknown Jewish militancy nurtured local Jewish security squads such as the Maccabees in Brooklyn. The Jewish Defense League was founded in 1968 for the specific purpose of protecting Jews from physical attack, especially school teachers and yeshiva students. In its early years the JDL went into Harlem to protect Jewish storekeepers from harassment by the Black Panthers.

As a sense of fear and frustration began to pervade growing segments of the Jewish community, they became more parochial in their concerns and adopted more conservative stances on public issues and gave their support to conservative candidates. The Jewish Rights Council was organized as an outgrowth of the Jewish protests against low-income housing in Forest Hills. The new Jewish militancy also expressed itself in strong demands for Jewish rights to a fair share of poverty funds, food stamps, and jobs created with Federal funds. In the 1970s, some 35 local Jewish community councils sprang up in many neighborhoods concerned with local Jewish interests. With the support of Federation, these councils became instruments for preserving the viability of neighborhood Jewish communities, caring for the needs of the elderly left behind by the exodus of younger families to the suburbs, encouraging the Jewish poor to apply for welfare benefits to which they are entitled, and protecting their legal, civil, and cultural rights. Dissatisfied with the Federation-sponsored efforts for the Jewish poor, a small independent group called Association of Jewish Anti-Poverty Workers was founded and they operate a store-front center in Brownsville. In 1975 there were signs of a resumption of close ties between Jews and blacks.

Businessman and Workingman

Jewish enterprise, innovation, and a sense of social justice were potent factors in New York's rise to commercial, business, and financial eminence, and in its unique role in the emancipation of the workingman.

Handicapped by Dutch restrictions, the early Jewish settlers earned their livelihood chiefly as Indian traders or butchers. Asser Levy built an abattoir with a Christian partner in the 1660s on what is now Wall Street and was also engaged in a flourishing business in furs. By 1700, however, Jewish merchants had made their influence felt in the city's trade and commerce.

The governor of the colony wrote the London Board of Trade "that were it not for one Dutch merchant and two or three Jews that have lent me money, I should have been undone." Nevertheless, most Jewish businessmen were still itinerant traders or retailers of such modest means that few were listed as taxpayers.

Hayman Levy, the best known Jewish merchant in Colonial New York, is reputed to have given the fabulous John Jacob Astor, a non-Jewish immigrant, his first job beating peltries at a dollar a day. A hogshead of rum supplied by Levy also launched the mercantile career of Nicholas Low, ancestor of a future mayor and president of Columbia University.

Jacob Franks, Levy's son-in-law, was chief purveyor of goods to the British during the French and Indian Wars. Another son-in-law, Isaac Moses, owned ships that plied the American coast from Montreal to Savannah and sailed to Europe and India. A privateersman whose captains harassed French shipping, Moses was a partner of Robert Morris, Revolutionary patriot, and, with Samson Simson, also a shipowner, was among the founders of the New York Chamber of Commerce in 1768.

New York's Colonial Jews also included a jeweler, Benjamin Franks, who had sailed with Captain Kidd in 1696; three of the signers in 1705 of a mercantile petition seeking the establishment of a fair standard of value for foreign coins; and Lewis Gomez, a dealer in rum, slaves, and furs, in whose Greenwich Village home the Colonial Assembly met in 1746 because of an epidemic in the commercial quarter of the city. A number of Jewish merchants were engaged in the slave trade with the West Indies.

Rodrigo Pacheco was one of the five merchants chosen to voice New York's protest against the Molasses Act of 1733. Every Jewish merchant in the city pledged himself not to import goods subject to the Stamp Act of 1765. Six risked British retaliation by signing the Non-Importation Resolutions of 1770.

Except for a few Loyalists, every Jew left New York when it was occupied by the British during the Revolution. Uriah Hendricks and Barrak Hays were among the Loyalist merchants whose presence kept the British from confiscating the synagogue. Another was Alexander Zuntz, a sutler with the Hessian troops, who later became president of Shearith Israel.

The 60 identifiable Jewish names in the city directory of 1799 included merchants and brokers, a scattering of shipowners, coppersmiths, soap-boilers, harness-makers, carpenters, tobacconists, accountants, auctioneers, a boat pilot, a mantilla-maker, and a bookseller. Shearith Israel's records first mentioned a tailor in 1819. The wealthiest Jew in New York at the beginning of the 19th century was Ephraim Hart, a partner of John Jacob Astor. Hart, Isaac Gomez, Alexander Zuntz, and Benjamin Seixas were among the 24 founders in 1792 of the Stockbrokers Guild, out of which grew the New York Stock Exchange.

Before the first wave of immigration from Germany and Poland early in the 19th century, most of the old line families were in retail business, stock brokerage, manufacturing, the professions, and public service, but there were also a good number of self-employed artisans. Bernard Hart, grandfather of Bret Harte, the writer of western tales, furnished arms and clothing to the citizens' army formed to defend the city during the War of 1812, and served as secretary of the Stock Exchange. Harmon Hendricks owned a pioneer copper smelter which supplied Paul Revere's foundry and provided some of the metal used in building Robert Fulton's steamboat, the *Clermont,* and the historic warship, USS *Constitution.* Isaac Baer Kursheedt, who had led the secession from Shearith Israel that launched Congregation B'nai Jeshurun, was a manufacturer of lace goods as well as the city's most learned Jew.

The immigrants who were not artisans or professionals turned overwhelmingly to petty trade, particularly peddling and the sale of used clothes. Of the 6,000 peddlers in the United States in 1860, most were said to have been Jews.

Chatham Street, center of the second-hand goods trade in the 1830s and 1840s, was sneeringly called "Jerusalem from the fact that the Jews do most if not all the business on this street." Cheaper and of better quality than the shoddy ready-to-wear men's clothing first introduced after 1820, the renovated used apparel sold by the Jewish immigrants not only found a ready market in New York, but was eagerly sought after in the south and west as the discarded fashions of the style-setting east. Moving around the country with hard-to-get merchandise, many of the second-hand dealers and the omnipresent peddlers became the nuclei of new Jewish communities in the south and west—the founders of great mercantile and industrial enterprises and ancestors of eminent Americans. One second-hand dealer, Levi Straus, who failed in the California gold rush, came back to New York to manufacture a special kind of pants for the miners and to add the word Levis to the English language.

From the second-hand trade and peddling it was a short step to retailing, importing, jobbing, wholesaling, and manufacturing of clothing, drygoods, and other consumer goods. From Chatham Street the Jews moved their establishments to Grand Street and the Bowery, and later, further uptown. The eerie silence that today settles over many business sections of New York on Rosh Hashanah and Yom Kippur was already noticeable more than a century ago. In 1847 the *New York Drygoods Reporter* said that because Jewish customers account for 25 percent of all sales by wholesalers, "some suspended business on the Jewish holidays rather than do without this increasingly influential element."

The *New York Commercial List* in 1853 recorded 2,751 wholesale firms, of which 105 were Jewish; half of these were in the clothing, drygoods, or related fields. An 1859 roster of 3,300 wholesalers and bankers contained 141 firms with Jewish names in the garment and affiliated industries.

The German Jews, who first gave the community the strength of numbers, were quickly absorbed into the middle class because the rags-to-riches saga was more common among those who arrived between 1830 and 1850 than among any other previous immigrant group. In the expanding post-Civil War economy, many of the peddlers, second-hand dealers, artisans, and storekeepers of the 1830-1860 era became well-to-do New York merchants, department store owners, real estate investors, bankers, industrialists, and manufacturers.

From the German-Jewish generations came the Lehmans, Guggenheims, Lewisohns, the Strauses of Macys, the Gimbels, Altmans, Sterns, Bloomingdales, Schiffs, Speyers, and Seligmans. Some of the oldest New York banking houses such as Speyer & Co. (1854), J. W. Seligman (1862), Kuhn, Loeb & Co. (1865), and Lehman Bros. (1868), founded on earnings from jobbing, clothing manufacturing, and cotton goods, were established by immigrants with links to German banks eager to invest in the American economy.

The leading figures of this generation were two former pack peddlers, Joseph and Jesse Seligman, who went into banking after clothing the Union Army. Horatio Alger probably got the idea for his "rags to riches" books, while serving as a tutor in the household of Joseph Seligman. The Seligmans, who sold nearly $200,000,000 worth of American bonds through their German branch when French and English bankers were reluctant to buy these securities during the most critical days of the Civil War, also underwrote some of the first railroads in the west and southwest. Joseph, who was instrumental in getting a pension for President Lincoln's widow, was the first chairman of the city's rapid transit commission and declined President Grant's appointment as Secretary of the Treasury. Jesse, who twice refused the Republican nomination for mayor, was the father of the eminent Columbia University professor of economics, Edwin A. Seligman.

James Speyer, whose immigrant father and uncle founded the banking firm of Speyer & Co. in the 1850s, was the moving spirit in the creation of the Museum of the City of New York and the Provident Loan Society. Albert Speyer, broker for James Fisk and Jay Gould when they tried to corner the gold market in 1869, paid off every dollar to his customers while his principals repudiated their debts.

Jacob H. Schiff, who came here from Germany in 1865 and married the daughter of a Kuhn, Loeb founder, was one of the key figures in American banking from 1885 until his death in 1920. As head of Kuhn, Loeb & Co., his influence was second only to that of J. P. Morgan. As part of the Rockefeller combine, Schiff successfully challenged Morgan in the underwriting of vast industrial enterprises and the railroad projects of James P. Hill and E. H. Harriman. In 1905, when other bankers hesitated, Schiff floated a $50 million loan for Japan, which helped bring about Russia's defeat in the Russo-Japanese War.

Lazarus Straus, who came to New York from Georgia in 1865 to pay off long-forgiven ante-bellum debts, was the father of the remarkable Straus brothers—Isidor, Oscar, and Nathan—who built Macy's from a crockery shop on Chambers Street. Oscar, the first Jewish Cabinet member, served as Theodore Roosevelt's Secretary of Commerce and Labor. Nathan was the city's most beloved philanthropist, and Isidor was a member of Congress. Benjamin Altman, the department store magnate who left a multimillion dollar art collection to the Metropolitan Museum, was the son of an immigrant. The Lewisohn Stadium, once famed for its summer concerts, but torn down in the 1970s, was a gift from Adolph Lewisohn, a German immigrant who made a fortune in metal mining.

Emanuel Lehman (father of Herbert H. Lehman, New York's only Jewish governor and former United States Senator), and his brother, Mayer, were immigrants who became Confederate patriots before they established Lehman Bros. in New York. The Guggenheims, celebrated for their art and literary fellowships, art museum, and support of aeronautical research, are the heirs of a 19th century immigrant who struck it rich when he invested the profits from lace manufacturing in silver and copper mines. The first segment of the now torn down 3rd Avenue elevated line was built in 1878 by Henry I. Hart, of English-German ancestry. Andrew Freedman, son of an immigrant, who developed large stretches of upper Fifth Avenue and The Bronx, was extensively involved in the construction of the first subway system.

The late Arthur Hays Sulzberger, publisher of *The New York Times*, was the grandson of a German-Jewish merchant whose son married into one of the old Sephardic families. Robert Morgenthau, Democratic candidate for governor against Nelson Rockefeller in 1962, and United States Attorney in New York in 1975, is the grandson of Henry Morgenthau, Sr., who came from Germany in 1856 and became wealthy in upper Manhattan and Bronx real estate. The elder Morgenthau helped Woodrow Wilson win the presidential nomination in 1912 and served as ambassador to Turkey.

When the wave of East European immigration began in the 1880s, the German Jews dominated the men's clothing and tobacco industries. Of 241 clothing factories in New York in 1888, 234 were Jewish-owned, as was 80 percent of the retail clothing outlets. Jews were also important factors in the manufacture of shirts, hats, hosiery, metal and leather goods, house furnishings, glass and paint products, in the processing of furs and hides, wholesale meat, and the grocery, wine, and liquor trades. German-Jewish manufacturers were also heavily represented in the women's ready-to-wear field when it began to replace the home and custom-made industry.

The need for cheap and docile labor by the expanding needle trades industry and the religious beliefs of the East Europeans combined to lead many of them into the garment trades. Although the earlier arrivals included many skilled craftsmen and artisans, until 1900 nearly one-third of the East Europeans in New York were employed in the clothing industry. Preferring to work where they could observe the Sabbath and kashruth, they sought employment with Jews who might be more sympathetic to demands for time off for afternoon and evening prayers or absences on the Sabbath and holy days.

Some Jewish employers did not scruple to force Jewish workers to accept lower pay for such privileges. Others who were active on immigrant aid committees combined business with philanthropy by leading immigrants directly to their factories. Harry Fischel, a Russian immigrant of 1865 who erected some of the first tenements in Harlem, Brooklyn, and The Bronx, encouraged Jewish workers in the building trades with half pay for no work on Saturday. Reuben Sadowsky's cloak factory acquired a certain fame because the work schedule was arranged to permit prayers three times daily.

From 1880-1900, most clothing manufacturers employed few workers except highly skilled cutters, who were then largely Germans or Irish. Bundles of unfinished cuttings were turned over to petty entrepreneurs, known as contractors, who finished the garments in their own outside shops. Some contractors handed this work over to subcontractors whose savage competition for bundles led to price cutting and exploitation of the workers through wage cuts and longer hours.

The outside shop became the horrible sweatshop, a sunless tenement flat which doubled as living quarters and factory. Until the contractor became prosperous enough to open an inside shop in a loft building, his workers were often members of his own family or fellow-townsmen. Most of the contractors and subcontractors were also East European immigrants who went into business for themselves as soon as they accumulated some capital. At Ellis Island they met and recruited relatives and former neighbors for the sweatshops.

In the front room of tenement flats tailors, basters, and finishers bent over rented sewing machines that covered every inch of floor space. Piles of finished and half-finished garments filled the bedroom. The red hot stove and blazing grate of glowing flat irons in the kitchen, where the pressers sweated, gave birth to the name "sweatshop." Parents and children worked side-by-side. Payment was by the piece and the longer they worked the more they earned. The working day often began at 4 a.m. and did not end until ten at night. Sanitary conditions were appalling, and the sweatshop became synonymous with disease-breeding tenements occupied by exploited workers.

At the turn of the century, the sweatshops and clothing factories had created a chaotic industry in which more than 200,000 Jewish workers depended for their livelihood on enterprises owned and operated by other Jews. The workers lived on the Lower East Side despite its squalor and congestion because of its proximity to the clothing factories and because it offered cheap housing. They also felt at home in the Yiddish-speaking milieu of relatives and fellow-townsmen where they could sustain their religious life.

A far smaller proportion of the post-1880 immigrants took to itinerant peddling than was the case among their German predecessors because the changing economy had narrowed the market for the peddlers' wares. Most numerous were the pushcart peddlers, whose number was estimated at 25,000 in 1900. They "converted whole blocks of the East Side into a street bazaar where their high-piled carts lined the curb," selling everything from tin cups to bananas and from fish to small articles of clothing. With a five dollar stock of shirts, socks, shoes, pots and pans, and a rented pushcart, an immigrant became a budding Wanamaker. Sometimes he went into business with only 75¢ in cash by peddling pickles, roasted sweet potatoes, soda water, Indian nuts, and halvah. These uncovered wagons started many on the road to uptown success and chain store operations.

For more than a generation the old East Side resembled a *yarid*, or old world market. Hester Street was known as the *chazermark*, or pig market, because it was the center of pushcart operations and an open air labor exchange where workers jostled each other every Saturday for hiring by contractors for clothing manufacturers.

While the stereotype of the East Side Jew was that of a pushcart peddler, a study of 135,000 East European Jews in New York in 1890 showed that 75 percent of those gainfully employed were workers and craftsmen. The other 25 percent included not only peddlers but owners of countless kosher butcher shops, bakeries, fish, vegetable and fruit stands, soda kiosks, delicatessens, small clothing and drygoods stores, and vendors of religious articles and Yiddish and Hebrew books.

The mounting demand for kosher meat among the immigrants helped keep New York an important center of the meat slaughtering and packing industry. Half of the city's 4,000 meat retailers and 300 of the wholesalers were Jews in 1890.

There were 500 Jewish bakeries, many of them ritually supervised, on the East Side in 1900. Some grew into the city's largest baking firms, such as Levy's, Messing, Goodman, and Gottfried. The immigrants' nonalcoholic drinking habits were responsible for flourishing sales of seltzer water, "East Side champagne."

Some thrifty sweatshop workers, peddlers, junkdealers, and petty tradesmen pyramided tiny accumulations of capital into successful clothing manufacturing, real estate, and mercantile enterprises. Most of the first generation East Europeans, however, never climbed beyond the wage worker level. The better educated immigrants escaped the sweatshops as real estate, insurance, and Singer sewing machine agents, salesmen, clerks, and teachers. On the whole, however, the East Europeans needed two generations to achieve what the German Jews had accomplished in one.

The most dynamic force to emerge from the sordid conditions under which the East Siders lived and worked was the Jewish labor movement that began with an outburst of "righteous discontent on the tenement-sweatshop frontier" in the early 1880s. From "the corner of pain and anguish," as Morris Rosenfeld, the ghetto's Yiddish poet laureate, called it, came first laments, then protests, and finally unions.

Individual Jews had participated in the New York tailors' strikes in the 1850s. German-Jewish capmakers joined German and Irish girls in the 1873-74 strike against German and Polish-Jewish manufacturers. German, Hungarian, and Galician Jews and the first Russian Jews employed in clothing factories in 1870 helped form Knights of Labor locals in New York. Many of the 2,000 Jews employed in the Keeny Bros. factory took part in the cigarmakers strike of 1877-78, led by Adolph Strasser, a Hungarian Jew. His chief lieutenants in the International Cigarmakers Union were Ludwig Yablonovsky, a Polish Jew, and Samuel Gompers, an English Jew, who was 13 when he came to New York in 1863. A full-fledged union member at 14, Gompers was one of the founders and first president of the American Federation of Labor in 1881. Except for one year, he headed the AFL continuously until his death in 1924.

The Jewish labor movement originated in the Yiddish section of the Socialist Labor party, formed in 1882. Failure of the first spontaneous strikes against the degradation of the sweatshop demonstrated that the party's Russian-speaking intellectuals could make no headway with the Yiddish-speaking masses. Ab Cahan made the first Socialist speech in Yiddish in August, 1882, in a hall behind a German saloon. He also printed the first Yiddish Socialist handbills to recruit party members.

The first Jewish labor organization was formed in 1885 through an alliance of the Socialist Labor party's Russian and Yiddish sections with some Jewish leaders of German-dominated unions. Known as the Jewish Workingmen's Association, it started an "anti-sweating league" and founded 14 different unions in the garment trades and among other workers. It published the first Yiddish leaflet demanding the eight-hour day, sponsored East Side clubs in support of Henry George's mayoralty campaign in 1886, and launched the *Yiddish Folkszeitung*, the first durable Yiddish labor weekly. The Association disbanded in 1887 and its feeble unions disintegrated in the wake of the antilabor hysteria generated by the Haymarket Riot of 1886 in Chicago.

The remnants of the Socialist Labor party's Yiddish section became the nucleus of the United Hebrew Trades, established in 1888 as a federation of Yiddish-speaking locals of the United German Trades and of new unions in trades and industries where Jewish workers predominated. In 1890, when the United Hebrew Trades took part in the first May Day parade in the United States, its 40 affiliates included unions of Jewish clothing workers, actors, musicians, bank clerks, writers, bakers, seltzer bottlers, painters, bookbinders, printers, grave-diggers, chorus girls, and ragpickers. There were also independent unions of Jewish newsboys and bootblacks.

Despite some minor but short-lived strike victories, many of the unions melted away during the depression of 1893. Their early failures were also due to the union's involvement in the efforts of Daniel de Leon (a Jew of Marrano ancestry), who was head of the Socialist Labor party, to capture the

Knights of Labor and the American Federation of Labor. When de Leon ordered members of the Jewish unions to quit the older labor federations and join his separatist Socialist Labor Alliance, the Jewish unions gradually withered. The militant atheism of de Leon's chief Jewish associates, who staged Yom Kippur demonstrations in front of East Side synagogues, undermined the party's influence among the Orthodox masses.

When de Leon's party split in 1899, most of the Jewish Socialists, led by Morris Hillquit, Morris Winchevsky, Meyer London, Louis Miller, Isaac Hourwich, and Ab Cahan, shifted their support to Eugene V. Debs' new Socialist party. This same group founded the *Jewish Daily Forward* in 1897, and in 1900 the Workmen's Circle, a workers' insurance-fraternal order. With the United Hebrew Trades this trio became a principal factor in the rise of the Jewish labor movement. The plight of the exploited East Side workers had aroused wide public sympathy, but it was the victims themselves who broke the sweatshop system by forming stable and powerful unions "born of despair, with poverty as the midwife."

The International Ladies Garment Workers Union was founded in 1900, followed by the Capmakers Union in 1901, the Fur Workers Union in 1904, and the Amalgamated Clothing Workers Union in 1914. The mass strikes of 1909-1914, known as "the great revolt," and the 1911 Triangle Shirtwaist factory fire that took the lives of 143 girls, were the great turning points in the history of the Jewish workers.

The first general strike in the needle trades began November 22, 1909 when 20,000 Jewish factory girls, makers of blouses and skirts, walked out. The city hummed Charles Harris' tune, "Heaven Will Protect the Working Girl," as upper and middle-class women joined the picket lines after strikers were routed by mounted police. The following year the entire garment industry was paralyzed by the city's biggest strike when 60,000 cloakmakers downed their tools. Dismayed by the bitterness of the struggle between Jewish workers and Jewish employers and by the use of Jewish thugs to assault strikers, the uptown Jewish community helped bring about a settlement. Louis Marshall and Jacob H. Schiff enlisted the aid of Louis D. Brandeis who came down from Boston to serve as chairman of the mediation board which drafted "the protocol of peace."

A milestone in the history of industrial relations, the settlement sounded the death knell of the sweatshop by abolishing homework and inside contractors' shops. It also gave the workers shorter hours, higher wages, decent working conditions, and set a precedent for peaceful resolution of labor conflicts in other industries by creating permanent arbitration machinery.

The great outcry of sympathy and protest that followed the Triangle fire brought state legislation that provided for factory fire prevention and building inspection, sanitary working conditions, workmen's compensation and liability insurance, and shortened hours of labor for women and children.

Strike gains and legislative reforms solidified the Jewish unions behind leaders who modified the militant radicalism of their predecessors into industrial democracy and moved the Jewish workers into the mainstream of the American Labor movement. Abraham Rosenberg, Benjamin Schlesinger, Max Pine, Rose Schneiderman, Abraham Shiplacoff, Joseph Schlossberg, Max Zaritsky, and Morris Sigman, principal architects of the 1909-1920 needle trades strikes, anticipated the trailblazing union practices that became part of the social welfare revolution of the 1930s.

Under the later leadership of Sidney Hillman, David Dubinsky, and Jacob Potofsky, the needle trades pioneered the 40-hour, five-day week, paid vacations, unemployment and health insurance, retirement pensions, workers medical care, education and recreation, and cooperative and low-rent housing. The garment workers also raised a generation of trained labor organizers, economic analysts, lawyers, and editors who played significant roles in developing new patterns of collective bargaining and labor-management partnership in all segments of industry. In the 30 years from 1942 to 1972, employers in the once foul sweatshop industry contributed more than one and a half billion dollars to 127 health, welfare, and union benefit funds.

The Jewish unions also had an important political influence in New York. As the backbone of the Socialist party, they elected Meyer London to Congress, seated several Socialists in the state legislature, and enabled Morris Hillquit to make a remarkable showing in the 1917 mayoralty election. Dubinsky, Hillman, Zaritsky, and Alex Rose were the prime movers in the organization of the American Labor party in the 1930s which rallied pro-Roosevelt but anti-Tammany Jewish workers behind the Democratic state ticket. When the Communists captured the American Labor party, the same leadership created the Liberal party, which became a major force in local and state elections. John L. Lewis found his strongest support among the Jewish leaders of the needle trades unions when he began organizing the CIO in the 1930s; they were equally prominent in the CIO-AFL merger. In 1976, the Amalgamated Clothing Workers Union of America merged with the Textile Workers Union of America under the name of the Amalgamated Clothing and Textile Workers Union. Three of the four top officers of the merged group were Jews.

Today, however, the Jewish trade union movement is nearing its end. Once an overwhelming majority of wage workers, the Jewish population of the city is now predominantly middle and upper middle class, despite the large pockets of Jewish poor and near-poor. Children and grandchildren of factory workers are now professionals, retailers, small manufacturers, civil service workers, executives, scientists, professors, editors, artists, entertainers, and school teachers. About half of the city's school teachers are the offspring of garment workers from whom they imbibed trade union tradition. This accounts for the fact that half the leadership of the United Federation of Teachers is Jewish, with Albert Shanker as its best known leader. Barred from banking, insurance, and other major areas of white collar employment in the 1930s and 1940s, the children and grandchildren of the immigrants from Eastern Europe at the turn of the century went into teaching and civil service positions. Recruited just before and during World War II, these public employees now find themselves threatened by affirmative action programs that discriminate against whites.

The garment center, once almost entirely Jewish and Italian in its workers and ownership, now employs mostly blacks, Puerto Ricans, Greeks, Chinese, and Italians. The Jews are a vanishing minority in the needle trades because as older Jewish garment workers retire or die, they are almost always replaced by non-Jews. Highly skilled Jewish and Italian workers have largely left the industry and have been replaced increasingly by semiskilled blacks and Puerto Ricans, as the industry becomes more mechanized. Jews are still a major factor in the ownership of women's clothing firms and in union leadership. But here too change is under way. There are fewer sons taking over from Jewish fathers in the business. Many garment firms are now part of conglomerates. The man elected president of the International Ladies Garment Workers Union in 1975 predicted that he would probably be the last Jew named to that post. Similar ethnic change is under way in the character of the once all-Jewish fur industry. In both industries Jewish workers account for only a tiny fraction of the total. The ILGWU's Yiddish paper, *Gerechtigkeit*, was discontinued as far back as 1957. The United Hebrew Trades still exists but its unions have mostly non-Jewish workers.

The East European Jews were "one generation proletarians, in most cases neither sons nor fathers of workers" who looked to self-employment or education as the escape route from the wage worker class. The majority of them hailed from communities where tailors, shoemakers, bakers, and other artisans were on the lowest rung of the social and communal ladder. Because they considered such occupations a humiliation, they and their children slaved and saved to achieve something better.

Only the steady influx of large numbers of immigrants before 1924 blurred the fact that the East Europeans and their children had always been "graduating out" of the clothing factories and other working class jobs. From the working class they moved into the lower middle-class occupations, retail trade, and the bottom rungs of the professions and white collar employment and then gradually climbed upward into manufacturing, wholesaling, real estate, building construction, and the communication and mass entertainment fields.

The heavy representation of East European Jews in insurance brokerage began when the big insurance companies hired clothing workers as agents in the tenements and factories, where business was transacted in Yiddish. Billposters, ushers, bookkeepers, and booking agents employed in the Yiddish theatre did well in the budding movie industry. Immigrants who had scooped up junk in backyards and alleys accumulated enough capital to become speculative builders. Coal, wood, and kerosene dealers with a one-horse-and-wagon trade expanded into fuel distribution and subway construction. Marcus Loew and Adolph Zukor, a couple of ex-furriers, fashioned an empire of movie palaces and film production out of penny arcades. East Side newsboys, such as the late David Sarnoff of the Radio Corporation of America, and Samuel Newhouse, who owns the country's biggest newspaper chain, had a special penchant for success. Helena Rubenstein and Hattie Carnegie also started on the East Side.

Manhattan's skyline, which began to take form before World War I, reflected, to a considerable extent, the enterprise and daring of former East Siders who learned the construction business by erecting apartment houses and two-family dwellings in Brooklyn and The Bronx. The Jewish builders who dominated the medium-priced apartment building field beginning in the 1920s erected what sociologist Marshall Sklare dubbed "Jewish avenues" along Eastern Parkway and Ocean Parkway in Brooklyn, Grand Concourse in The Bronx, and later on Queens Boulevard in Queens. These were apartments erected by Jews largely for Jews. Louis Horowitz, who came here from Poland at 13, covered Manhattan with $600,000,000 worth of new skyscrapers, including the Woolworth, Chrysler, and Paramount Theatre buildings, and the Waldorf-Astoria Hotel. A. E. Lefcourt, a one-time newsboy, was the prime mover in the relocation of the garment industry north of 34th Street and south of 42nd Street in the 1930s and 1940s. By 1929, Lefcourt, Paul Singer, Henry and Irwin Chanin, Abraham Bricken, George Backer, and Henry Mandel were raising new skyscrapers on Fifth, Madison, Lexington, and Seventh Avenues, and on the side streets where the garment center was growing. The late Abraham Eli Kazan, who grew up on the East Side, helped rebuild its tenements with the first union-backed cooperatives, and pioneered in building middle-income cooperatives such as Co-Op City in The Bronx, Rochdale Village in Queens, and Penn Station South in Manhattan.

A new generation of Jewish builders led the way in the residential and office building boom which altered the face of Manhattan in the 1960s and 1970s, and changed the life of many of the suburbs. William Zeckendorf, responsible for some of the city's biggest private housing projects, assembled the land on which the United Nations buildings were erected. The 18,000 single-family houses built by William J. Levitt between 1947 and 1951 on 4,000 acres of former Long Island potato land grew into the bustling community of Levittown. Samuel J. Lefrak and Marvin Kratter erected many of the huge residential developments in upper Manhattan, Queens, and Brooklyn. Lefrak built Lefrak City in Queens. The Tishman brothers led off the building transformation on Park Avenue. The Uris brothers were the city's leading builders of office skyscrapers, accounting for 13 percent of all those erected in Manhattan since World War II. The 59-story $100,000,000 Pan Am Building is a monument to the late Erwin Wolfson. The Weilers, Fisher brothers, Minskoffs, Richard Ravitch, Saul Horowitz, Jr., and Sol Atlas were other creators of the new city skyline.

The city's biggest industry, the $7 billion women's ready-to-wear trade, is in a sense a monument to the vanishing Jewish needle trades worker. Seventh Avenue, a generic name for the garment center, is the home of the city's women's and children's apparel industry employing 175,000 people. In the enclave between 35th and 40th Streets, and 6th and 9th Avenues, are designed and produced three out of every four women's dresses, coats, suits, children's garments, and women's sportswear made in the United States. The industry is the city's largest private employer. Many of the manufacturers are sons or grandsons of former union members and organizers who now deal with the unions their ancestors founded. On the streets south and the avenues east of the garment center, other Jewish entrepreneurs dominate the processing of the garment industry's raw materials and the manufacture of millinery, textiles, hosiery, furs, leather goods, underwear, and costume jewelry.

The *shmata* (Yiddish for rag) business, as it is jokingly called, has stimulated folklore and fiction that reflects its Yiddish-speaking origin. Plays and novels such as "The Fifth Season," "Seidman and Son," "I Can Get It For You Wholesale," and "Enter Laughing" depicted the industry's impact on Jewish life, the intergeneration squabbles to which it gave rise, and its mordant humor and bitter competitiveness.

Making clothes and setting dress styles for half the nation at prices within reach of all, the garment industry's verve and enterprise are credited with strengthening American democracy by "eliminating differences in dress that were once a mark of class distinction."

Linked to the garment center through retailing and merchandising are some of the liveliest Jewish contributions to the city—the great department stores in the city proper and in the suburbs, the women's speciality shops, and the discount stores. R. H. Macy's, Gimbels, Bloomingdale's, Lord & Taylor, Saks Fifth Avenue, B. Altman, Franklin Simon, Ohrbach's, and Abraham & Straus are shoppers' paradises. Saks Fifth Avenue and Bergdorf Goodman are landmarks among the high-fashion shops, as are the salons of the leading custom designers—Hattie Carnegie, Molly Parnis, and the late Tobe Coller Davis. Lane Bryant, who made maternity clothes big business and stylish, got its name from an error in Lena Bryant's first bank deposit slip.

Gene Ferkauf, whose name in Yiddish means "to sell," fathered the E. J. Korvette discount stores, which began a merchandising revolution. Bargain-hunters thronged to S. Klein, on Union Square, and its suburban branches, until they went out of business, as they do to the neighborhood department stores of the Alexander's, Gertz, and the May chains in Brooklyn, The Bronx, Queens, and the suburbs. Among the success stories of the post-World War II immigration is that of Stephen Klein, who started the Barton's chain of candy shops which are closed on Friday at sundown and remain shut on Saturday and Jewish holy days.

Creators of the City

Inextricably woven into the entire tapestry of New York's history, Jews have had a large hand in shaping the city's civic, cultural, and professional life and in coloring its liberal, social, and political outlook. In every generation they were distinguished for community responsibility, a passion for social and political reform, a zest for culture, and a gift for expressing the city's uniqueness in word, song, and art.

1. *In the People's Service*

The liberal political bent of Jewish voters in New York goes back to the days when Thomas Jefferson coalesced the opponents of the domestic and foreign policies of the Federalist party into a new political alignment. Samson Simson, first Jewish member of the New York Bar, was among the founders and a vice-president of the Jeffersonian Democratic party in 1795. He and Naphtali Judah were early members of the Society of St. Tammany (Tammany Hall), which began as a social group supporting Jefferson. In 1798, the Reverend Gershom Mendes Seixas, first native-born minister of Shearith Israel, preached a sermon sharply at variance with the views of the other clergy who supported the Federalists in their denunciations of the republican regime in France. Mordecai Myers took an active part in helping the Democratic-Republicans win a state election in 1800 that paved the way for Jefferson's presidential victory in the fall.

Mordecai M. Noah, friend and political ally of Presidents Andrew Jackson, Martin Van Buren, and William Harrison, was grand sachem of Tammany in 1820 and the Jewish community's spokesman for more than 40 years. When he was appointed sheriff of New York County in 1822 there were protests against the likelihood that a Jew might have to execute Christians. "Pretty Christians that they should require hanging at anyone's hands," was his retort. Noah's successor in the Tammany hierarchy was Emanuel Hart, a sachem for half a century, who was elected to Congress in 1851. Jonas N. Phillips, president of the City Council in 1857, was acting-mayor for a time.

Because they opposed slavery, many of the native-born and most of the immigrant Jews quit the Democrats in the 1850s to join the new Republican party. In local elections, however, most of the immigrant generation stayed with the Democrats, who were more friendly to immigrants, until the Tweed Ring scandals of 1871.

Jonathan Nathan was one of the founders of the Republican party in New York and J. Solis Ritterband was the first president of the New York Young Men's Republican Club. Sigismund Kaufmann and Dr. Joseph Goldmark, refugees from the 1848 revolutions in Europe, were among the organizers of the Republican party in Brooklyn. In 1856 Kaufman campaigned for John Fremont, first Republican presidential candidate. J. Dittenhoefer was a Lincoln presidential elector in 1860 and 1864. Kaufmann, a Lincoln elector in 1864, was a power in Republican circles because of his influence with the German immigrants. This earned him the Republican nomination for lieutenant governor in 1870. Joseph and Jesse Seligman, who declined all municipal and national offices, were among the sponsors of the pro-Lincoln rally at Cooper Union that paved the way for Lincoln's nomination in 1860.

Although there were many prominent Jews in the Democratic party at the time of the Tweed Ring exposures, most of them were associated with the reform group of the party. Joseph Seligman and Joseph Blumenthal served on the Committee of 70 that exposed the Tweed machine, and Simon Sterne was the committee's secretary. Samuel A. Lewis and Adolph Sanger were elected president of the Board of Aldermen as anti-Tammany Democrats in 1874 and 1885, respectively. Sanger was acting-mayor when the Statue of Liberty was accepted by the city in 1886. Anti-Tammanyite Theodore Myers was elected city controller in 1887, and reelected in 1891 as the Democratic and Republican nominee. Oscar S. Straus was secretary of the committee of Democratic reformers that returned William R. Grace as anti-Tammany mayor in 1884. Albert C. Cardozo, the first Jew elected to the State Supreme Court, resigned in 1872 to escape impeachment when he was implicated with the Tweed Ring.

Like other newcomers to the city, the immigrant Jews at first accepted the help of Tammany and gave it their support. Anti-Tammany reformers were regarded as alien uptowners, but Yiddish-speaking saloon-keepers allied with Tammany had the influence needed to do petty favors for those strange to American ways. Petty Jewish politicians could be counted on to provide food baskets, jobs for breadwinners, and help for youngsters in trouble and for peddlers entangled with the law.

De Ate, as the immigrants called the 8th Assembly District, became a Tammany stronghold after 1892 when its Republican assemblyman, "Silver Dollar" Smith, a Jewish saloonkeeper, switched to the Democrats in protest against immigration curbs enacted by a Republican Congress. In the Tammany-controlled wards where the Jewish immigrants were the balance of power, Democrats and Republicans sought Jewish votes by picking Jewish candidates. Henry Goldfogle, Tammany's East Side spokesman for many years, was elected to Congress by the Democrats in 1900, the first Jew from the East Side so honored. The following year Tammany made Jacob Cantor president of the Borough of Manhattan, the first of seven Jews to hold this post, and named Aaron J. Levy as Democratic leader of the State Assembly. The Republicans elevated Otto Rosalsky and Gustav Hartman to the bench, and in 1908 elected Samuel Koenig Secretary of State and New York County chairman. Edward Lauterbach had filled the same office in the 1890s.

As they acquired political sophistication, the Yiddish-speaking masses joined other elements of the Jewish community in supporting political reform movements, regardless of party. The Citizen's Union had a number of Jews among its founders when it was formed in 1897 to war on Tammany corruption. During the 1901 fusion campaign, when the cleanup of East Side graft and rackets was a major goal, William Travers Jerome, anti-Tammany candidate for district attorney, deluged the ghetto neighborhoods with Yiddish circulars and a Yiddish newspaper. Uptown Jewish notables joined forces with sweatshop workers and synagogue leaders to elect Seth Low, president of Columbia University, as fusion mayor. In Low's reelection campaign wealthy uptown Jews and Christians invested a small fortune in an East Side Yiddish daily in a vain attempt to reelect Low. William Randolph Hearst, a champion of the oppressed Jews of Russia, carried the East Side in his unsuccessful race for mayor as an anti-Tammany candidate, and again in his losing the race for governor in 1906. In both elections he employed Yiddish inserts in his newspapers to win Jewish votes.

The fact that no Jew was elected mayor of the city until 1973 despite the large number of Jewish voters, indicated that they usually supported a non-Jewish liberal in preference to a Jewish conservative. A Jew was first nominated for mayor in 1892, when Edwin Einstein, who had served in Congress, was the defeated Republican candidate. Eight years earlier Tammany had tried to clean its house by nominating for mayor the popular philanthropist, Nathan Straus, but he refused to run. Jonah J. Goldstein, a lifelong Democrat, was the losing Republican nominee in 1945. Rudolph Halley and Harold Riegelman, Liberal and Republican standard-bearers, respectively, lost to Robert F. Wagner in 1953 for the office of mayor. The latter defeated a prominent Jew, State Controller Arthur Levitt, in the 1961 Democratic primary, and then defeated State Attorney General Louis Lefkowitz in the election. In 1965, Abraham Beame, the Democrat, was beaten by John Lindsay, the Republican, in a three-man race in which many Jews among the Reform Democrats voted for Lindsay on the Liberal Party line, while many Catholic Democrats voted for the independent candidate, a Catholic. In 1969 Beame was elected City Controller and four years later he became the first Jewish mayor of the world's largest Jewish-populated city.

Until the Socialist party became a major political force on the East Side, its Jewish masses usually voted Democratic locally, divided in state contests, and were partial to Republican candidates for president. Theodore Roosevelt was their particular favorite. As police commissioner, he had assigned a company of Jewish policemen to protect a notorious European anti-Semite during his visit to the city. As President, he fought immigration curbs, intervened with Romania against its anti-Semitic policies, and protested against Russian pogroms. His appointment of Oscar S. Straus, a former ambassador to Turkey and later a judge of the Permanent Court of Arbitration at The Hague, as Secretary of Labor on the eve of the 1906 gubernatorial election probably cost William Randolph Hearst the governorship.

The Straus appointment was an event of great import to all Jews because no Jew had previously sat in the Cabinet, and the immigrant generation swelled with pride at the honor to the son of a pack peddler. William Howard Taft campaigned for president on the East Side before a huge Jewish audience in 1908. In the 1912 gubernatorial election the East Side faced a dilemma. Roosevelt's Progressive party had named Oscar Straus to oppose Tammany's William Sulzer, a non-Jewish Congressman from the East Side who, as chairman of the House Foreign Affairs Committee, led the fight for the abrogation of the Russo-American treaty of commerce. Although Straus lost, he won over Sulzer in the Jewish districts and ran ahead of Roosevelt, the party's presidential candidate, throughout the state.

Sweatshop exploitation that turned many immigrants to socialism, made the Socialist party the strongest on the East Side by 1910. The party's political titans were Morris Hillquit and Meyer London. Both repeatedly scared the Democrats with strong runs for the legislature and Congress before London was elected to the House in 1910. Thereafter the Republicans put up a single Jewish candidate against him, beating him twice. He was reelected in 1916 and 1920 despite bitter opposition from uptown Jews and many downtowners who attacked him as an atheist and an anti-Zionist. Backed by the Jewish unions in 1917, Hillquit made a remarkable showing as an antiwar candidate for mayor in a three-way race during which the most prominent Jewish leaders warned Jewish voters against him.

In 1912 William Howard Taft said that Jews "make the best Republicans," and 40 years later Adlai Stevenson said they make the best Democrats. Each was right, in his own day. Despite their changed economic status, New York's Jewish voters returned to the Democratic party after 1920 because of the liberal social legislation fathered by Alfred E. Smith and Robert F. Wagner, Sr. The progressive program of Governor Franklin D. Roosevelt strengthened the Democrats' hold on the liberal and international-minded Jewish electorate whose socialist residue settled in the New Deal, Fair Deal, and the Liberal Party.

Smith's closest advisors were Mrs. Belle Moskowitz and Joseph Proskauer, who had met Smith while doing settlement house work on the East Side. Proskauer managed Smith's first three gubernatorial campaigns and joined with him in founding the anti-New Deal American Liberty League when Smith broke with Roosevelt. Key figures in the state Democratic party in the 1920s were Henry Morgenthau, Sr. and Bernard M. Baruch, who had helped elect Woodrow Wilson, Max D. Steuer, Samuel Untermyer, Nathan Burkan, and Herbert H. Lehman. Together with Jesse Straus, later ambassador to France, and Laurence Steinhardt, a future ambassador to Russia and Canada, they raised the money that helped James J. Farley line up the delegates for Roosevelt's victory in the 1932 presidential nomination. Baruch, head of the War Industries Board in World War I, held key posts in World War II, and developed America's first position paper on control of the atomic bomb.

When Roosevelt agreed to run for governor in 1928, he insisted on Herbert H. Lehman as the candidate for lieutenant-governor. Lehman had been active in the Democratic party but was better known as a banker and a

388 — NEW YORK CITY

leader of the Jewish community. Roosevelt's opponent was Albert Ottinger, son of a German-Jewish immigrant, who had twice been elected attorney general in the face of Democratic sweeps. Rabbi Stephen S. Wise's opposition to Ottinger is said to have been a decisive factor in Roosevelt's narrow victory. In this campaign Samuel L. Roseman plied Roosevelt with facts and figures and then became the governor's speech writer and counsel before moving on to Washington as head of the White House "brain trust."

Dr. Wise was a potent force for political reform, although he never held office. A long-time foe of Tammany, in 1930 Wise and Dr. John Haynes Holmes were the prime movers in the action that led to the resignation of Mayor Jimmy Walker. Wise and Holmes teamed up again to back the fusion campaign of 1933 that elected the Yiddish-speaking Fiorello LaGuardia mayor, and Bernard S. Deutsch, president of the City Council. LaGuardia, raised as a Protestant, was, through his mother, a Jew, related to Luigi Luzzatti, Italy's first Jewish prime minister.

In 1932, Lehman succeeded Roosevelt as governor, the first Jew to hold this office in New York. One of the best and most popular chief executives in the state's history, his "little New Deal" put New York in the vanguard of progressive social legislation. Reelected four times, he resigned in 1942 to become the first director of the United Nations Relief and Rehabilitation Administration in war-torn Europe. In 1949 he was elected to the United States Senate where he led the fight for civil rights and sparked the move to condemn Senator Joseph McCarthy. Long actively identified with major Jewish causes, he returned to the sidewalks of New York when he was past 80 to join Eleanor Roosevelt in a successful battle to reform the city's Democratic party. His death in 1963, the day before he was to receive the Medal of Freedom in a White House ceremony, evoked nationwide regret. His funeral was attended by President Lyndon B. Johnson.

Robert Morgenthau, son of the late Secretary of the Treasury Henry Morgenthau, Jr., who was elected District Attorney of New York in 1973, and former Supreme Court Justice Arthur J. Goldberg, were the defeated Democratic candidates for governor in 1968 and 1970, respectively. Robert Moses was the defeated Republican candidate for governor in the 1930s.

When Jacob K. Javits, a liberal Republican, won the Senate seat vacated by Lehman in 1956, he defeated Mayor Wagner in a tight race. Overwhelmingly reelected in 1962, 1968, and 1974, Javits was the first Republican to carry New York City in a statewide campaign. A product of the East Side where his father was a janitor who did petty favors for Tammany, Javits became a Republican because he was outraged by Tammany venality. A popular member of Congress from 1946-1954, Javits gave up his House seat in 1954 when he won an upset victory over Franklin D. Roosevelt, Jr., in the campaign for State Attorney General.

Most Jews prominent in Republican affairs were also aligned with the party's liberal wing. Among these were former Attorney General Nathaniel Goldstein, Manhattan Surrogate George Frankenthaler, the late Stanley

Isaacs, long the only Republican on the City Council, and Judge Caroline Simon, the first woman nominated for citywide office when she ran for president of the City Council. She later served as New York's Secretary of State. Although Jews have been important factors in the Tammany wing of the Democratic party (two Jews headed Tammany Hall), they have been even more prominent in good government and political reform movements in the Democratic party. Among the founders of the Liberal party, which has been allied in most elections with the Reform Democrats, is Alex Rose, a prominent labor union leader, who remains a force in his party's political deals and endorsements. Sanford Garelik, former chief inspector of the Police Department, was elected president of the City Council in 1969 on the Liberal party ticket.

All boroughs of the city except Staten Island have had at least one Jewish borough president. Manhattan Borough Presidents included Jacob Cantor, Marcus Marks, Hugo Rogers, Julius Miller, Stanley Isaacs, Edgar J. Nathan, Jr., and Samuel Levy. Abe Stark was Borough President of Brooklyn and Sidney Leviss was the first Jewish Borough President of Queens. In 1975, Donald Manes and Robert Abrams were serving their second terms as Borough Presidents of Queens and The Bronx, respectively.

While 85 percent of the city's Jewish voters are registered Democrats, they no longer automatically vote for any Democrat or even for a liberal of any party. The first sign of a more conservative vote occurred in 1966 when 55 percent of the Jews voted against the creation of a civilian review board to check on actions of the police. Jews also voted heavily for the conservative Democratic mayoralty candidate in 1969. In the 1972 presidential election there was a 17 percent drop in the Jewish vote for the Democratic candidate, George McGovern, against President Richard Nixon. In New York City, Jewish voters are regularly wooed by politicians of all parties. Mayor John Lindsay was the first mayor to have a full-time Jewish expert attached to his staff. Lindsay also broke precedent by having a sukkah erected on public property for a reception honoring Prime Minister Golda Meir. The Jewish swing to the right was a reaction to an assault on Jewish interests and on Israel by the New Left and by some black militants. Although Jews are now less than one-fourth of the total population, they represent 32 percent of all voters. This is due to the fact that Jews register to vote and actually vote more consistently than other citizens. The polls often find that a large proportion of voters reporting themselves undecided is highest in predominantly Jewish neighborhoods. The Jewish vote "is the ballgame," as one candidate noted. In recent years the Chasidic rabbis have developed considerable political clout in local elections.

2. *In Pursuit of Learning*

The impact of Jews on education and the cultural arts in New York has been compared to "a sort of cosmopolitan galvanic battery" that is always charging up an intellectual ferment.

The fruitful association with learning dates from 1787 when the Reverend Gershom Mendes Seixas, the community's religious leader, was elected a trustee of King's College (Columbia College). One of the 168 citizens who launched New York University in 1831 was Mordecai M. Noah. Annie Nathan Meyer founded Barnard College. The Ethical Cultural movement with its progressive schools was created by Dr. Felix Adler, son of a rabbi, when he broke with organized Judaism in the 1870s. The science of anthropology received its greatest impetus in the United States from Dr. Franz Boas, geographer and explorer, who taught many of the early American specialists in that field at Columbia University.

Dr. Joel Hart was one of the founders of the New York County Medical Society in 1806. In the 1830s, Dr. Daniel L. M. Peixotto edited the *New York Medical and Physical Journal*, and Dr. Isaac Nordheimer taught medicine at New York University. Dr. Abraham Jacobi, one of the first attending physicians at Mt. Sinai Hospital, had a profound influence on the development of pediatrics. Dr. Simon Baruch, father of Bernard M. Baruch, was a pioneer in hydropathic medicine and the earliest exponent of physical medicine. The city's leading 19th century opthalmologist was Dr. Emil Gruening, father of Ernest Gruening, Alaska's first United States Senator.

Although the struggle for an economic foothold and the conflict with rebellious children tarnished the dream of "the goldene medina" (the golden land) for many first generation East Europeans, they took full advantage of every opportunity for the educational advancement of the second generation. As soon as they learned English, East Side youngsters crowded the public elementary schools, the public libraries, and the free lectures of Cooper Union's People's Institute. They did amazingly well in high school and college. An 1889 report noted that for the previous ten years each graduating class at City College had contained 25 percent Jews. One out of five graduates of the New York Normal College for Teachers in 1889 was a Jewish girl. By 1900 children of immigrants were a majority in the city's free institutions of higher learning. A 1907 study of the secondary schools was "struck with the large percentage of Jewish scholars and their relatively high rank."

City College was long known as "the Jewish college of America." From 1900 on Jews heavily outnumbered non-Jews in its student body. Jews once accounted for 95 percent of its student body and its alumni roster reads like a roll call of the country's leading figures in law, business, art, science, literature, and philosophy. In the 1970s the Jewish enrollment dropped to about 40 percent when scholastic standards, once on a par with those at Harvard, plummeted with the inauguration of an open admissions policy for minorities. From Bernard M. Baruch and David B. Steinman, builder of bridges, to Jonas Salk, developer of the anti-polio vaccine, Arthur Kornberg, Nobel Prize winner, and Mayor Abe Beame, the achievements of Jewish New Yorkers who began their higher education at City College are written large in the history of the 20th century.

Henry Leipziger, father of the city's public adult education program, was once acting president of City College, and Moses J. Stroock headed its board of trustees. The first Jewish president of an American college (not under Jewish auspices), was Dr. Paul Klapper, for many years the dean of City College's School of Education. An immigrant from Romania, Klapper became president of Queens College when City College's Queens branch achieved independent status. In the 1970s, Robert E. Marshak was president of City College, and Jews held the number two administrative posts at Columbia University and New York University. A number of the presidents of colleges in the City University of New York system were also Jews.

Perhaps the two most distinguished immigrant alumni of City College were former Supreme Court Justice Felix Frankfurter, who was born in Austria, and Russian-born Professor Morris Raphael Cohen, one of the few original philosophers America has produced. A legal prodigy, and one of the few Jewish law school graduates engaged as a clerk in a major New York law office before World War I, Frankfurter was dean of the Harvard Law School and mentor of a host of public figures before being appointed to the Supreme Court. Cohen, who went hungry as an East Side teenager in order to rent books, read Gibson's *Decline and Fall of the Roman Empire* while working in a pool hall. A student of William James and Josiah Royce at Harvard, Cohen was head of City College's philosophy department for a generation. Brilliant teacher, liberal crusader, and Socratic gadfly, he was one of the most popular and influential of contemporary American thinkers.

Working in sweatshops by day and attending professional schools at night, the East Side Jews turned in great numbers to medicine, dentistry, pharmacy, law, and teaching. Out of the immigrants' ambition for professional careers for their children came the now familiar boast, "my son the doctor" and "my son the lawyer."

Immigrants and their children contributed greatly to early medical research at Mount Sinai and Montefiore Hospitals and made pioneering discoveries. Joseph Goldberger found the cause of pellagra. Drs. Phoebus Levine and Samuel J. Meltzer were part of the original six-man staff of the Rockefeller Institute, opened in 1910. Selman Waksman won the Nobel Prize for isolating streptomycin, and Isidor Rabi received the same honor for his accomplishments in nuclear physics. Dr. Sigismund S. Goldwater, who served as New York's commissioner of health and hospitals, fathered the medical administration profession when he became superintendent of Mt. Sinai in 1904. Many of the first East Side physicians practiced group medicine as lodge doctors, caring for *landsmanschaften* members, and establishing new facilities for Yiddish-speaking patients who refused to go to Bellevue or Blackwell's Island where they would be wardmates of alcoholics. The first new medical school established in New York State in a generation was the Albert Einstein College of Medicine, sponsored by Yeshiva University, which is the oldest liberal arts college under Jewish auspices. Mount Sinai

Hospital also established a medical school in the 1970s. Yeshiva University opened the Benjamin Cardozo Law School and a new and small Jewish college known as Touro College, has announced plans for a law school.

The campuses of New York's public and private colleges and universities as well as the Jewish institutions of higher learning and research are studded with graphic reminders of the generosity of sons and grandsons of Jewish immigrants. The Guggenheim School of Aeronautics at New York University, Bronx campus (now Bronx Community College); Columbia University's School of Mines, a gift of Adolph Lewisohn; Benjamin Javits Hall at Fordham University's Law School; the Loeb Student Center at New York University; and City College's Aaron Davis Hall for Performing Arts, are but a few examples of this generosity.

The New School for Social Research was expanded in the 1930s by Jewish philanthropists to provide academic posts for noted refugee professors from Nazi Europe. Its graduate faculty was known as "the University in Exile." The original endowment fund of $500,000 for Long Island University came from Nathan Jonas, first chairman of the university's board and a founder of Brooklyn College. William Zeckendorf, board chairman in the 1960s, spurred Long Island University's postwar expansion.

3. The Cultural Ferment

Eagerness to use talents pent up by centuries of oppression also galvanized and stimulated American culture. The role of Jews in the New York world of the theatre, music, literature, art, and mass entertainment has been described as "sometimes strident, generally exciting and often original and profound."

In 1859 a New York newspaper said that "if any segment of the population makes extensive sacrifices on behalf of newspapers, the theatre and scholarly and artistic efforts, it is first and foremost, among all immigrants, the New York Jews." This referred to the cultural interests of the German Jews, but the older families had set the precedent.

One of the most prominent artists of 18th century New York was Myer Myers, a leading silversmith, whose work is still preserved in museums. Two of the city's late 18th century bookdealers and publishers were Benjamin Gomez and Naphtali Judah. Mordecai M. Noah and Samuel B. H. Judah were successful playwrights in the 1830s and 1840s, and Henry B. Phillips was a popular actor.

The first permanent Italian opera company in the city was established in 1843 by Max Maritzek, who introduced 36 operas. Moritz Strakosch, who conducted for Maritzek, married Amelia Patti and discovered the vocal gift of her sister, Adelina. The New Orleans-born pianist, Louis Gottchalk, was the city's musical sensation between 1853 and 1863.

Leopold Damrosch and Oscar Hammerstein were the pioneers in establishing New York as the musical capital of the world. Damrosch, friend of Wagner and Liszt, came to New York in 1871 as Temple Emanu-El's musical director. In 1873 he founded the Arion Society, predecessor of the New York Philharmonic Society, and later became conductor of the newly-opened Metropolitan Opera House. The Metropolitan's first impresario was Heinrich Conried, a leader of the New York Germania Theatre, founded by Adolf Neundorf, Temple Emanu-El's musical director. Maurice Grau, Conried's successor, made the Metropolitan pay when he hired Damrosch. The latter introduced German opera because his backers did not know the difference between the more costly Italian stars and the lesser-known Germans. Damrosch's son and successor, Walter, persuaded Andrew Carnegie to build Carnegie Hall.

Oscar Hammerstein, grandfather of Oscar Hammerstein II, of Rodgers and Hammerstein fame, first introduced operas in English in his Harlem Opera House. Later he became the king of vaudeville with his celebrated Victoria Theatre and the huge Olympia Hall. When this combined music hall, theatre, and cabaret opened in 1895 on what was then Longacre Square, but is now known as Times Square, the area became the capital of show business. The profits from this venture were put into the new Manhattan Opera House and competed with the Metropolitan for four years. When he agreed to sell out to the Metropolitan, Otto H. Kahn became the chairman of the Metropolitan's board.

What Damrosch and Hammerstein were to the world of music Charles, Daniel, and Gustave Frohman, and David Belasco were to the theatre. The Frohmans produced over 700 plays and introduced some of the stage's greatest stars, while Belasco, the Frohmans' chief competitor, was both producer and playwright.

The East European Jews found their cultural outlet in the Yiddish theatre, organized in 1882 by Boris Thomashefsky, a choir singer in an East Side synagogue. The first production, Abraham Goldfaden's *Koldunya* (The Witch), was staged by an amateur troupe from London in an East 4th Street hall. Four years later he starred in a stock company that staged plays in Bowery Hall. By the turn of the century, he was the most popular actor, playwright, director, and producer in the Yiddish theatre, and the matinee idol of the sweatshop girls. Michael T. Thomas, the rising young orchestra conductor, is Thomashefsky's grandson.

Jacob P. Adler, who brought over the first company of experienced Yiddish actors in 1890, teamed up with playwright Jacob P. Gordin to usher in the most exciting epoch of Yiddish drama. In the heyday of the Yiddish theatre its greatest stars in addition to Adler and Thomashefsky were David Kessler, Bertha Kalish, Morris Moscovitch, Sigmund Mogilescu, Jennie Goldstein, Ludwig Satz, and Rudolph Schildkraut. Adler's children—Stella, Luther, Celia, Francis, and Julia—all began their acting careers in Yiddish plays.

Adler's Grand Theatre, opened in 1904 as the first built especially for Yiddish productions, and Thomashefsky's National Theatre, whose curtain went up in 1911, made Second Avenue the Yiddish Rialto. At the height of its popularity the Yiddish theatre filled four houses Monday through Thursday via a benefit system through which the *landsmanschaften* bought blocks of tickets. Some claim that the modern theatre party, backbone of Broadway hits, was invented by East Side Jews who seldom said they were going to theatre, but always to a benefit.

In its latter years the Yiddish theatre produced such Broadway and Hollywood stars as Molly Picon, Paul Muni, Edward G. Robinson, Joseph Schildkraut, Menashe Skulnik, Hershel Bernardi, and Maurice Schwartz. The latter's Yiddish Art Theatre began a new era of modern plays and productions in 1918. *Eli Eli*, composed by Jacob Sandler for a Thomashefsky Passover production, became the most moving Jewish melody. *Bei Meir Bist du Schoen*, was written by Sholom Secunda for a Yiddish musicale. He sold the song for thirty dollars and it earned millions for the buyers. Not until the copyright came up for renewal did he earn additional money.

The movies, to which the immigrants flocked, dealt the first body blow to the Yiddish stage from which it never recovered. The end of immigration heralded the doom of Yiddish drama. In 1928 there were 11 Yiddish theatres in New York. In the 1970s, there were three Yiddish theatrical companies enjoying a modest revival of interest with its productions housed in Broadway theatres.

Samuel Rothapfel, better known as Roxy, who built the now demolished Roxy Theatre in 1926, and Mitchell Mark, who opened the Strand in 1914 as "a Cathedral of motion pictures," were as much landmarks of the Great White Way as their theatres.

From the earliest days of radio and television in New York those media counted the Sarnoffs, Paleys, Flamms, and Strauses among their most enterprising leaders.

In the heyday of vaudeville and radio and in the early years of television, the most popular headliners were comedians and singers whose roots were on the East Side. Eddie Cantor, George Burns, the Marx Bros., the Ritz Bros., Jack Pearl, Phil Silvers, Sid Caesar, Milton Berle, Joey Bishop, Fannie Brice, Danny Kaye, and those adopted New Yorkers, Al Jolson, Ed Wynn, and Jack Benny, rose to the top without reliance on Jewish gags. Part of Coney Island's fame as the playground of the masses was attributable to the showmanship of Samuel Gumpertz, who has a permanent niche in show business history as the godfather of the sideshow, and more particularly the genuine freak. Unlike P. T. Barnum's frauds, Gumpertz scoured the world for genuine bizarre people.

The ethnic Jew of vaudeville, who disappeared with the "Dutch act" of Joe Weber and Lew Fields, children of the tenements, and the demise of the "Potash and Perlmutter" variety of humor, was replaced by *Abie's Irish Rose*, which charmed audiences in the 1920s. The daily life of the Goldbergs of The Bronx, as recounted by Gertrude Berg, occupied the regular attention of millions of Americans on radio for 25 years, and later on television. Comics like Sam Levenson, Jerry Lewis, Shelly Berman, Danny Kaye, Alan King,

Myron Cohen, and some of the "sickniks" found their humorous foils in the environment out of which they came.

The city's musical life has been enriched in special abundance by Jews. First of the East Side kids to put the spirit of America to music was Irving Berlin. Son of a synagogue cantor, Berlin was a Bowery saloon song plugger whose first tune earned him 37¢. His earliest songs were about immigrants—*Marie from Sunny Italy, Oh How That German Could Love,* and *Yiddishe Eyes. Alexander's Ragtime Band,* a musical landmark, set him on the road to fame in 1910. Millions of Americans marched off in World Wars I and II singing his *Oh, How I Hate to Get Up in the Morning* and *God Bless America.* The latter, which has become virtually a second national anthem, is one reason why Berlin's more than 1,000 folk tunes have been called "a continuous obbligato to American history."

George Gershwin had the same relationship to jazz and modern American music. The composer of *Porgy and Bess, Rhapsody in Blue,* and other notable works was a self-taught pianist whose first job was playing for rehearsals in a Second Avenue Yiddish theatre. Some of the biggest hits to come out of Tin Pan Alley were written by such East Side tunesmiths as Irving Caesar, Gus Kahn, Gerald Marks, Jack Yellen, Wolfie Gilbert, Ira Gershwin, Harold Arlen, Richard Rodgers, Oscar Hammerstein, II, and Burt Bacharach.

The Jewish musicians who began arriving from Russia in large numbers in the 1890s, after the expulsion of Jews from Russia's big cities, paved the way for a flock of Russian-born Jewish virtuosi and later for native-born artists of world-renown. For years the violin was synonymous with Jewish musicianship, as Berlin's 1908 tune, *Yiddle on Your Fiddle, Play Some Ragtime,* indicated. Jewish artists who made their debut in Carnegie Hall constitute a who's who of 20th century musicians. An early product of the Julliard School was Sophie Braslau, a contralto star at the Metropolitan from 1920-1934, whose father was an East Side doctor. Another was the Romanian-born Alma Gluck. Regina Reznik, Rosa Ponselle, Leonard Warren, Richard Tucker, Jan Peerce, and Robert Merrill were all raised on the East Side. Aaron Copland, one of America's great 20th century composers, grew up in Brownsville. Leonard Bernstein, the ex-Bostonian wunderkind, vitalized music in New York as composer, conductor of the New York Philharmonic, and musical director of the Metropolitan Opera. WASPS, however, still predominate in the control of the Metropolitan, whose board has only two or three Jews. But at the New York City Opera, where Beverly Sills became a great star after being denied a chance at the Metropolitan, Jewish board members outnumber WASPS two to one.

The Naumburgs and the John Simon Guggenheim Foundation have done much to encourage the flowering of the city's musical talents. The Guggenheim fellowships, handed out for nearly 40 years, have become a kind of intellectual knighthood to musicians, artists, writers, scholars, and scientists of promise, as the Guggenheim Museum is a mecca for followers of modern art. The New Friends of Music, which provides chamber music concerts, was founded by Ira Hirschman. Julius Bloom, as director of the Brooklyn Academy, turned a white elephant into the borough's cultural and musical oasis. As executive director of Carnegie Hall, Bloom and violinist Isaac Stern were among those who saved Carnegie Hall from the wrecker's ball in the 1960s. Avery Fisher Hall at Lincoln Center, home of the New York Philharmonic, is not only named for a Jew whose money created it, but it is filled night after night with heavily Jewish audiences. George Wein is the impresario who annually brings the Newport Jazz Festival to the city.

Outdoor music first acquired its enormous impact when the Stadium Concerts were started in 1918 in the now razed Lewisohn Stadium by Mrs. Charles S. Guggenheimer. The Goldman band concerts, begun in 1918 by Edward Franko Goldman on the Columbia University Green, and now conducted by his son, Richard Franko Goldman in Central and Prospect Parks, have been supported since 1924 by the Guggenheim family. The late Sol Hurok, the immigrant who first "presented" anybody when he prevailed upon Efraim Zimbalist to appear before a Jewish cultural society in Brownsville, brought to America the greatest names in music, dance, opera, and ballet.

The new American art form called musical theatre owes much to Jewish lyricists and composers. Marc Blitzstein's *The Cradle Will Rock*, and Harold Rome's *Pins and Needles*—first of the musicals of social significance—and Jerome Kern's *Showboat*, paved the way for the musical plays of Lorenz Hart, Oscar Hammerstein, II, Richard Rodgers, Frederick Loewe, and Alan Lerner. These grassroot operas displaced the musical extravaganzas and revues which Florenz Ziegfeld, an adopted New Yorker, had made Broadway's dominant type of entertainment.

As producers, playwrights, directors, and stage designers, Jews have been among Broadway's most important innovators and trailblazers. From the "star factory" era of the Frohmans and the successive hits of the Schuberts, to the present, the theatre has been enriched by a long line of Jewish luminaries: Elmer Rice, George S. Kaufman, Moss Hart, Lillian Hellman, Sidney Kingsley, Arthur Miller, Sam and Bella Spewack, Clifford Odets, Dore Schary, S. N. Behrman, Lee Strasberg, Max Gordon, David Merrick, Kermit Bloomgarden, Neil Simon, and David Susskind, among others. The Theatre Guild and the Group Theatre, directed almost entirely by Jews, were a major force in transforming taste and style in the American theatre. Lawrence Langner, Philip Moeller, Theresa Helburn, and Lee Simonson of the Theatre Guild gave a stage to Eugene O'Neill and introduced the realism of Ibsen, Gorki, Shaw, and Strindberg. The Neighborhood Playhouse, an offshoot of the Henry Street Settlement, which pioneered off-Broadway drama, was backed by Irene and Alice Lewisohn. Shakespeare in Central Park was the brainchild of Joseph Papp, one-time king of the off-Broadway theatre, who did more than anyone else to bring Shakespeare to the masses. In the mid-1970s, he headed the Public Theatre downtown and the two theatres in Lincoln Center. Many of the off- and off-off (sic) Broadway playwrights and producers have been young Jews. Neil Simon, who has authored a long list of Broadway hits, depicted with good humor and perception the character of New York as he first encountered it in his native Bronx.

The 92nd Street YM & YWHA, which marked its 100th year in 1975, continued to be the city's "little cultural center" for concerts, poetry readings, recitals, chamber music, and the modern dance. Allan Ginsburg was the poet of the beat generation whose adherents once crowded Greenwich Village where Maxwell Bodenheim once presided as high priest of the Bohemians. Bob Dylan, born in Minnesota, caught the tone of restless rebelling youth in his music.

When former President Richard Nixon was quoted in the Watergate tapes as warning his daughter Tricia "to stay away from the arts" because "they're Jews," he was quite right so far as New York is concerned. It was Alfred Stieglitz who first championed the new and daring world of modern art. One of the great photographic artists of his time, he fostered and encouraged the modernists. In 1908, Stieglitz introduced Max Weber, whose work bore the stamp of his East Side boyhood. The same was true of Jo Davidson, Sir Jacob Epstein, William Zorach, Ben Shahn, Abraham Walkowitz, and Maurice Becker. Perhaps one third of the city's art galleries are owned or managed by Jews. The Jewish Museum on Fifth Avenue and the new museum on the uptown campus of Yeshiva University, are among the most popular in the city. Joseph Hirshhorn, a former slum kid who became rich mining uranium in Canada, is one of the leading cultural innovators whose purchases stimulated the new school of art. Most of his multimillion dollar collection is now housed in the Hirshhorn Museum in Washington, D. C.

Barney Josephson opened the city's first integrated night club, "Cafe Society," in Greenwich Village in the mid-1930s, and it became an important incubator of musical talent. Upstairs at the Downstairs, the nightclub founded by Irving Haber, was the breeding ground for some of the country's best comedy and musical talents. Many of the Greenwich Village cafes have been the first step on the road to fame for Jewish entertainers. There are now a number of Israeli nightclubs and coffeehouses: El Avram, where the telephone operator greets you with a *shalom* when you call for reservations; Cafe Feenjon, where Israeli, Arab, and Greek music and food are available, and where Puerto Rican youngsters gave birth to shouts of *nochamol, nochamol* (again, again) when they liked a performance; and Cafe Yaffo, in the heart of the old Gashouse district.

New York's Jewish book publishers and critics have long been influential in molding national literary and cultural tastes. Mavericks like Alfred A. Knopf, Benjamin A. Huebsch, Charles Boni, the Guinzbergs of Viking Press, Horace Liveright, Bennett Cerf, and the Max L. Schuster-

Richard L. Simon duo, dynamically changed the book publishing industry after World War I. They introduced European authors, encouraged new American writers, produced books more attractively, and were responsible for enlarging the American reading audience. The first book clubs and the first paperbacks in America were other innovations of Jewish literary entrepreneurs. Literary critics such as Waldo Frank, James Oppenheim, Louis Untermeyer, Babette Deutsch, Alfred Kazin, John Simon, and Paul Rosenfeld, and the philosophic concepts of Horace Kallen, Sidney Hook, Irving Kristol, Irving Howe, Irwin Edman, David Riesman, Daniel Bell, and Nathan Glazer helped shape American literary and cultural taste and thought. Robert Silvers, as founder-editor of the *New York Review of Books*, Jason Epstein as one of its backers, Norman Podhoretz as editor of *Commentary*, and Norman Mailer, were important literary and cultural influences in the 1960s and 1970s.

Max Abramovitz, associate of Wallace Harrison in designing the United Nations headquarters, was the architect of the Lincoln Center for the Performing Arts. The Coliseum, another city landmark, is the work of Lionel and Leon Levy. Robert E. Blum and David Keiser helped bring Lincoln Center into being. The Lehman Children's Zoo and the Wollman Ice Skating Rink are among the many Central Park reminders of the civic responsibility of the city's Jews.

In the public sector of the city's rebuilding no one accomplished more than Robert F. Moses. President of the 1964 New York World's Fair, he masterminded the city's network of new bridges, parkways, tunnels, shorefront parks, and planned the Jones Beach development on Long Island. Descended from one of the Sephardic families and son-in-law of New York's commissioner of education in 1900, Moses was Secretary of State of New York in 1927. In 1934 he was the losing Republican candidate for governor against Herbert H. Lehman.

4. *The Fourth Estate*

Mordecai M. Noah, founder, editor, or publisher of seven different dailies between 1820 and 1840, was the first eminent Jewish figure in New York journalism. On his *Enquirer* he employed James Gordon Bennett, who, according to legend, started the *Herald* with $100 borrowed from Noah.

Noah's uncle by marriage, Solomon H. Jackson, launched *The Jew*, the earliest known English language Jewish publication in the United States in 1823. Married to a Presbyterian minister's daughter, Jackson started his paper to counteract the widespread efforts to convert the Jews. Twenty different groups were trying to convert the Jews of New York to Christianity in the 1820s. From 1825, when *The Jew* suspended publication, until 1849 there were no other Jewish journals in the city. *Israels Herold* had a brief existence as the first German-Jewish weekly. *The Asmonean*, an English language weekly, appeared from 1849 to 1858. *The Jewish Messenger* founded in 1858, was followed by a succession of weeklies in English, or

German and English. Many of them were absorbed by *The American Hebrew*, established in 1879, which itself was merged into the *American Examiner*. The latter, under the new name of *The Jewish Week and American Examiner*, came under new ownership and editorship in 1970, and became the largest, most widely read, and probably the most influential American Jewish weekly. The Greater New York area also had a number of other Jewish weeklies and fortnightlies in English, as well as the weekly English language, Orthodox-oriented *Jewish Press*.

Noah's successor as the city's most controversial newspaperman was Joseph Pulitzer. His innovations and unorthodox methods on *The New York World*, which he acquired in 1883, involved a bitter war with other publishers. Son of a Jewish father but raised as a Protestant, Pulitzer was assailed by Charles A. Dana of *The New York Sun* as a renegade Jew whose "face is repulsive not because the physiognomy is Hebraic but because it is Pulitzeresque." Pulitzer's relentless battle against political corruption and his struggle with Hearst's jingoistic efforts which led to the Spanish-American War have been forgotten. New Yorkers know his name only as the founder of the Pulitzer Prizes and as the donor of Columbia University's School of Journalism.

Adolph S. Ochs, too, has been forgotten by most New Yorkers but he built an enduring memorial in *The New York Times*. A one-time Tennessee printer's devil, Ochs acquired the bankrupt *Times* in 1896 and built it into the country's most influential newspaper. His high standards of journalistic ethics, enormous energy and resourcefulness, and capacity for choosing brilliant associates made the *Times* synonymous with complete and impartial news coverage and a symbol of honest and socially responsible journalism.

The New York Post, the city's oldest daily, is published by Mrs. Dorothy Schiff, a granddaughter of Jacob H. Schiff. The late Herbert Bayard Swope was the managing editor of *The New York World* when it was the city's most exciting paper. One of its most popular features was *The Conning Tower*, conducted by Franklin P. Adams, better known as F.P.A. Much of New York's flavor is savored in the memorable *New York Times* stories of Meyer Berger, a dead end kid who became a newspaperman of legend, and in the slanguage of Walter Winchell and his columnist colleagues, Mark Hellinger, Louis Sobel, and Leonard Lyons.

Frederick B. Opper, political lampoonist for the Hearst press and *Puck*, who created the cartoon characters, "Happy Hooligan" and "Alphonse and Gaston," was the ace newspaper cartoonist of an earlier generation and a forerunner of Rube Goldberg, Milton Gross, and Al Capp.

Walter Lippmann and Walter Weyl, described in a moment of annoyance by President Theodore Roosevelt as "two uncircumcised Jews," helped found *The New Republic*. Alfred A. Knopf published *The American Mercury* when it was the happy hunting grounds of H. L. Mencken and George Jean Nathan. Hugo Gernsbach created the science fiction magazines. *The Reporter* and *The New Leader* were launched by Jewish liberals.

Norman Cousins was the prime factor in the success of *The Saturday Review* and *Variety*, the Bible of show business, was founded by Sime Silverman.

One of the most colorful episodes in New York journalistic history was the rise of the Yiddish press. It began in 1871 when a Jewish politician published *The Jewish News*, in English, German, Yiddish, and Hebrew, to win votes. Two more enduring weeklies, Kasriel Sarasohn's *Yiddish Zeitung* and Henry Gersoni's *Juedische Post*, appeared in 1872. The first daily, *The Yiddishe Tageblatt* (Jewish Daily News), was founded by Sarasohn in 1885. (*Tageblatt* later became a generic term for any Yiddish newspaper.)

The second daily, *The Teglicher Herold* (1891), merged into *The Warheit* in 1905, which was absorbed by *The Day* in 1917. When *The Forward* was launched in 1897 as the third daily, the city boasted of 12 Yiddish journals reflecting viewpoints from anarchism on the left to Orthodox Judaism on the right. The first morning paper, *The Jewish Morning Journal*, appeared in 1901 as the spokesman of the Orthodox, non-radical community. Merged with *The Tageblatt* in 1928, it was consolidated in the 1950s with *The Day*. There were also numerous weeklies, monthlies, and quarterlies published by political parties, unions, *landsmanschaften*, and cultural groups and a few devoted to literature and humor.

Created by and for immigrants, the Yiddish press flourished so long as mass immigration continued. The Yiddish press taught the immigrants about the ideals and traditions of the bewildering new world, kept them in touch with happenings in the old world, and was influential in molding their political, cultural, and social integration.

The Forward, edited by Ab Cahan from 1902-1951, rose to great influence on the tidal waves of immigration. Cahan made *The Forward* the largest and most influential newspaper in the Jewish world and a major weapon in the rise of the Jewish labor movement and in the Americanization of two generations of immigrants. A successful writer in English, he helped America learn about the Jewish immigrant, and as a Yiddish journalist and Socialist organizer taught the immigrant about America. As a mediator between Yiddish and American cultures he "helped infuse the one with the other and thus had a share in creating a Jewish American culture."

When some of Cahan's Socialist colleagues objected to editorials urging mothers to keep their children supplied with clean handkerchiefs, Cahan asked, "Since when is Socialism opposed to clean noses?" He published simple lessons in civics, history, and American government, and through *The Forward's* letter column, "The Bintel Brief " (bunches of letters) created the most popular immigrant open forum.

By opening its columns to old and new writers, the Yiddish press also encouraged and enriched Jewish cultural creativity. *The Forward* published the works of virtually every notable Yiddish author. Working class poets, essayists, and novelists, such as Solomon Bloomgarden (Yehoash), who first translated the Bible into Yiddish, Morris Rosenfeld, Abraham Reisen, and

H. Leivick, poured out their anguished protests against the sweatshops in the Yiddish press. Rosenfeld's poem, *The Machine*, has been compared to Markham's *The Man With the Hoe*. The works of Peretz, Mendele Mocher Seforim, Sholom Aleichem, Sholom Asch, Zalman Schneur, Israel J. Singer, Isaac Bashevis Singer, and Elie Wiesel all first appeared in Yiddish papers.

The Yiddish press was at the acme of its influence in 1915 when New York's five Yiddish dailies reached a peak circulation of 526,000. By 1921 it had dropped to 400,000. To the first generation of East Europeans, the Yiddish paper had been a household necessity but their children had little need for it, particularly when they began to shun Yiddish as the language of greenhorns. Every reader the Yiddish dailies helped Americanize became a lost reader. English pages and columns and English-Yiddish photo captions were added in the late 1920s in a futile effort to halt an irreversible trend.

The postwar Yiddish-speaking DPs from Europe provided only a temporary shot in the arm. During the 1962-63 New York newspaper strike the Yiddish dailies were crammed with advertisements of public events, job opportunities, Civil Service examinations, and Broadway shows. At the end of 1963, the circulation of *The Forward, Day-Morning Journal*, and the Communist *Freiheit* was down to about 100,000, and still falling. In the early 1970s, the *Day-Morning Journal* suspended publication. It was replaced by a Yiddish weekly, *Allgemeine Zeitung*. *The Forward* also encountered difficulties and in 1975 it made a public appeal to Jews for financial support.

The Hebrew press, which never achieved the status of its Yiddish counterpart in New York, antedated it. The first Hebrew journal, *Hatzofeh Baaretz-Hahadashah*, appeared in 1870 when the first Hebraists began arriving from Europe. One of these was Judah D. Eisenstein, who edited the first Hebrew encyclopedia and translated the Declaration of Independence and the Constitution of the United States into Hebrew and Yiddish. Later Hebrew editors, such as Reuben Brainin, Menahem Ribalow, and Chaim Tzchernowitz, gave rise to the Histadruth Ivrith in 1913, which stimulated Hebrew-speaking societies, publications, and programs. *Hadoar*, now the only Hebrew weekly in the United States, started as a New York daily in 1921. One of the early New York Hebraists was Naphtali Herz Imber, a vagabond genius and poet, who wrote *Hatikvah* in 1886 when it was an anthem without a country.

5. *Their Brother's Keeper*

From the days when they were still only a tolerated minority with a precarious foothold in New Amsterdam, Jews have given leadership and support to almost every liberal, humane, and forward-looking movement. It began with Asser Levy, who gave 100 florins to the fund raised to defend New Amsterdam against the British invasion in 1664. Seven years later he advanced money to the Lutherans to help them build their first church. A public subscription taken up in 1711 to complete the Trinity Church steeple included seven Jewish donors. Gershom Mendes Seixas' lectures on Judaism at St. Paul's Church in 1800 set an enduring example of interfaith amity in the city where the National Conference of Christians and Jews was born in the 1920s.

Moses Judah helped liberate 50 slaves as an active member of the New York Manumission Society from 1799-1809. The Society's records contain the names of many Jews who emancipated their own slaves and helped maintain the underground railway for runaway slaves. Ernestine Rose, who came from Poland, was one of the reformers who began the struggle for women's rights in the 1830s. During the Irish famine relief appeal of the 1840s Shearith Israel conducted a fundraising rally among its members.

Most of the Jewish immigrants from Germany, Bohemia, and Austria sided with the abolitionists. Philip J. Joachimsen, an assistant United States District Attorney in New York, secured the first conviction of a slave trader. When Rabbi Morris Raphall preached a sermon from the pulpit of B'nai Jeshurun early in 1861, attempting to justify slavery on Biblical grounds, he was bitterly assailed in Jewish circles.

Felix Adler, who founded the city's first kindergarten on the East Side, joined with Isaac N. Seligman to erect the first model tenement on Cherry Street in 1885. For a generation he warred on firetraps until he persuaded the state to create a tenement house commission. A generation later the Fred L. Lavanburg Foundation anticipated the public housing program by building the city's first low-rent apartments. Dr. Simon Baruch prodded the city into opening the first public baths on the East Side. The free pasteurized milk stations opened by Nathan Straus were credited with saving the lives of thousands of babies and lowering the city's death rate.

The horrible housing, health, and social conditions on the Lower East Side after 1880 impelled dedicated reformers to establish the Henry Street, University and College Settlements, and Clark and Madison Houses. In the house on Henry Street, founded by Lillian D. Wald, and in the other East Side settlements, uptown Jewish volunteers were introduced to practical social welfare and imbued with the liberal concepts that were converted into legislation by Alfred E. Smith, Franklin D. Roosevelt, Robert F. Wagner, Sr., and Herbert H. Lehman. In these islands of hope for the slum dwellers Lehman, Henry Morgenthau, Jr., Belle Moskowitz, Gerard Swope, and Joseph Proskauer, among others, worked side by side with Eleanor Roosevelt, Frances Perkins, and Harry Hopkins in battling for housing reforms, parks, playgrounds, cleaner streets, and public health services. Thousands of Jewish teachers, lawyers, musicians, artists, and public figures came under the wholesome influence of the settlements where they acquired their social, political, and cultural attitudes.

The social idealism that brought uptown Jews to the East Side as settlement house workers and then involved them in wider communal efforts never waned. Dr. Stephen S. Wise, Lillian D. Wald, Joel and Arthur Spingarn, and Dr. Henry Moskowitz were among the founders of the National Association for the Advancement of Colored People. Arthur

Spingarn was for many years president of NAACP. Professor Edwin R. A. Seligman of Columbia University was the first chairman of the Urban League. A recent president was Theodore Kheel, the labor arbitrator. Columbia University's Franz Boas began the struggle against racism in 1911. Pauline Goldmark and Maud Nathan organized the Consumer's League and were pioneers in the women's suffrage movement. Dr. Abraham Jacoby was advocating birth control in 1912. Alice Davis Menken and Anna Moskowitz Kross led the fight for juvenile courts and night courts for women and wayward minors. Felix Adler headed the National Child Labor Committee.

From the pulpit of the Free Synagogue, Dr. Stephen S. Wise defended the 1919 steel strikers. Abraham Epstein and Isaac M. Rubinow were the trailblazing sociologists whose work contributed enormously to the enactment of the Federal social security program. For years Arthur Garfield Hays was chief counsel of the American Civil Liberties Union and was succeeded by Aryeh Neier. Leo Cherne heads the International Rescue Committee for Victims of Political Oppression. In the struggle for better housing and schools, parks, fair employment practices, school and housing desegregation, and social legislation, there were and are no more vigorous fighters than the descendants of peddlers and sweatshop workers who take American democracy seriously.

6. *Defenders of Freedom*

As defenders of the freedoms they fought so hard to establish and enlarge, the Jews of New York distinguished themselves in every war since Asser Levy and Jacob Barsimson insisted on their right to defend New Amsterdam.

The first Jew to bear arms for the British in North America, Joseph Isacks, enlisted in the New York militia in 1689 on the outbreak of King William's War. Isaac Myers organized a company of volunteers in the Rising Sun Inn and led it across the Alleghenies during the French and Indian War.

Almost all the Jews of New York were on the side of independence when the Revolutionary War began. Four, who were in the ranks when George Washington read the Declaration of Independence to his troops in New York, shared the hardships of the Battle of Long Island, which was fought in Brooklyn. Tory neighbors burned the Bedford (Westchester County) farmhouse of one of these soldiers because his wife refused to disclose the hideout of a band of patriots attempting to reach the American camp at White Plains.

Haym Salomon, the patriotic broker, who had come from Poland in 1775, joined the Sons of Liberty in New York and was later imprisoned by the British. Released to serve as an interpreter to the commander of the Hessian troops, Salomon became an underground agent for the Americans in the New York area, risking his life to help French and American prisoners escape British jails and to induce Hessians to desert. The Continental

Congress voted its thanks to Isaac Moses whose privateersmen wrought havoc on British shipping.

The most ardent advocate of independence in the Jewish community was the Reverend Gershom Mendes Seixas. Anticipating the city's occupation by the British, he took Shearith Israel's ritual objects and records and led a majority of the congregation to Stratford, Connecticut, rather than live under the British. At the age of 68, he vainly petitioned Congress for permission to form a military company during the War of 1812, insisting he "could stop a bullet as well as a younger man." His powerful sermons helped rally public support for the war. Samuel Noah, one of the first Jewish graduates of West Point, was one of the builders of the defenses of Brooklyn against an expected British attack in 1812.

More than half of the 6,000 Jews who volunteered for military duty in the Civil War on the Union side were with New York City regiments. Benjamin Levy, who enlisted at 16, won the Congressional Medal of Honor. Colonel Leopold C. Newman, of Brooklyn, who was mortally wounded at Chancellorsville, received a deathbed visit from President Lincoln. Brigadier General Philip J. Joachimsen organized and commanded the 59th N.Y. Volunteers, and Colonel William Mayer recruited the "Perkins Rifles."

New York's synagogues and Jewish charity societies participated actively in fund-raising projects for the United States Sanitary Commission, which distributed medical supplies, food, and clothing to sick and wounded Union troops. To care for the families of Jewish soldiers the Jewish community raised special relief funds. Several of Mt. Sinai Hospital's wards were converted to military purposes. Dr. Israel Moses, attending surgeon at Mt. Sinai, was in the medical corps where he invented the "Moses Wagon," which was used to transport the wounded. The Jewish hospital became a sanctuary for the wounded during the New York draft riots of 1863.

During the brief Spanish-American War many Yiddish-speaking immigrants volunteered for Army duty in the hope of striking a blow against the nation that had driven out its Jews in the 15th century. General John J. Pershing, commander-in-chief of the American Expeditionary Forces in World War I, paid high tribute to the heroism of Jewish doughboys from New York. Representing 40 percent of the 77th Division, which bore the brunt of the Meuse-Argonne battle, they included two Medal of Honor winners, Sydney G. Gumpertz and Benjamin Kaufman.

The World War II story is graphically recorded in *American Jews in World War II*, a book of over 600 pages devoted to listing the names of New York Jews killed, wounded, or missing in action as well as those decorated for bravery. Among these were Colonel David Marcus, a staff officer who later organized Israel's Army; Lieutenant Meyer Levin, bombardier of the plane that almost sank the first Japanese warship; and Solomon Isquith, who directed the rescue of the USS *Utah* at Pearl Harbor. Thousands of New York Jews served in all branches of the armed forces during the Korean and Vietnam wars.

Manners and Mores

In the 322 years since a handful of refugees found a grudging haven in New Amsterdam, the Jews of New York have risen from an immigrant, low income, embattled group to a largely native-born, well-educated, mostly middle-class community accepted as an inseparable element of the nation's greatest city.

More widely dispersed than ever before throughout the city and its suburbs, yet more densely concentrated, Jews have settled in new neighborhoods which are often as distinctly Jewish as the old Lower East Side was 75 years ago. Never dissolved in the melting pot but imbedded in two cultures, Americanism and Judaism, the Jews fully accept Will Herberg's conclusion that "to be a Protestant, a Catholic or a Jew are today the alternative ways of being an American."

In their new city or suburban areas of residence the Jews have adopted the manners and mores of their non-Jewish neighbors but they have also held on to many of the habits of their parents and grandparents. Despite its poverty and wretched living conditions, the Jewish working class of the immigrant generations was middle class in moral and health standards, in its almost worshipful adoration of education and eagerness to escape from the slums.

Exposés of the old East Side always mentioned its disease-breeding tenements, but the 10th ward, an almost 100 percent Jewish neighborhood, had the lowest mortality rate in the city in 1894. Yiddish-speaking mothers took avidly to health education programs, and welcomed the summer camps sponsored by the settlement houses, the penny luncheons of the public schools, and the pasteurized milk stations of Nathan Straus.

Contemporary descriptions of life on the East Side painted a generally accurate picture of the dismal conditions but seldom mentioned the lack of crime or absence of drunkenness, venereal disease, drug addiction, and illiteracy. Jewish paupers were strangers to the New York Almshouse. No Jew was ever buried in Potter's Field. Most crime and violence on the East Side was not committed by immigrants; they were usually its victims. The few Jewish toughs who came to public attention were children of immigrants. It was never dangerous to walk at night through the slum streets inhabited by Jews, even though most East Side kids belonged to gangs. They warred with neighboring Irish and Italian youngsters who attacked and insulted Jews, knocking over pushcarts and tweaking beards. Bearded and caftaned Jews, the favorite prey of Irish toughs, found protectors in the children of greenhorns. Theodore Roosevelt, when he was police commissioner in the 1890s, first encouraged Jews to become policemen by seeking out "the fighting Jewish type."

Some Jewish gangs did become breeding grounds for criminal rings and the Jewish neighborhoods had their share of poolroom operators, brothel-keepers, and petty grafters. Eddie Cantor told how he helped a gang break into a bicycle shop and was paid off "with a cup of coffee and two doughnuts" and "a nickel carfare home." As a "strongarm" member of a gang of strikebreakers, Cantor was once paid "three bucks a day." Irving Berlin recalled being beaten by neighborhood toughs when he ventured beyond Jewish-controlled streets. The settlement houses and strong Jewish family ties, even where strained by American ways, were prime factors in deflecting Jewish youngsters from gang influence.

The first Jewish athletes were prize fighters who learned boxing to defend themselves from Irish kids on the Bowery who invaded the Jewish East Side. Joe Bernstein, first hero of East Side Jewish youth, achieved fame as Joe Choynski when he battled Bob Fitzsimmons for the heavyweight crown. Jewish fighters from the East Side often took Irish names (Al McCoy, Mushy Callahan, Sid Terris, Leach Cross, etc.) because most fight fans were Irish and Jews regarded prizefighters as bums. When East Side fighters with unmistakably Jewish names—Benny Leonard, Abe Attell, Al Singer, Ruby Goldstein, Benny Jeby, and Barney Levinsky—became title contenders and champions, the crowds yelled "kill the kike" or "hit the Hebe." Later, non-Jewish fighters took Jewish names to attract Jewish fans.

John J. McGraw beat the minor league bushes in a vain search for a "Jewish Babe Ruth" on the theory that a Jewish star in a Giants' uniform would be baseball's greatest box office attraction. When he finally found Andy Cohen, in Texas, Jews who had never before seen a baseball game, jammed the Polo Grounds. Hank Greenberg, the first New York Jew to achieve big league stardom, made it in a Detroit uniform, while Sandy Koufax, who grew up in Brooklyn, hit the top with the Dodgers only after they had moved to Los Angeles. Ronnie Blomberg, the slugging New York Yankee who grew up in Atlanta, was cheered as "the kosher boomer" by Yankee fans.

Though Jewish parents frowned on athletics as the pastime of loafers, immigrant kids took to sports with avidity. Hirsch Jacobs, who sent over 3,000 racing thoroughbreds across the winning line at tracks all over the country, began with the only racers that could find moving room in the slums—pigeons. Mike Jacobs rose from the East Side to transform boxing into big business. Lon Myers and Abel Kiviat wore the colors of the old Irish-American A.C. when they represented the United States in Olympic track and field events. Sammy and Joe Renick, who never knew horses were used for anything but delivering milk when they attended a Bronx Hebrew school, became the country's leading jockeys. Sid Luckman, one of the all time greats of collegiate and pro football, learned the game in Brooklyn.

The East Side schools raised a host of basketball players for City College and St. John's University when their teams ruled the collegiate courts, and the Brooklyn and Bronx schools contributed many Jewish stars to college and professional basketball. Nat Holman, "Mr. Basketball," long the City College coach, learned the game at P.S. 62 whose alumni helped make basketball a rival of baseball as the national sport. Maurice Podoloff, an East Side boy, led the National Basketball Association for 16 years and made the professional game a major sport.

New York area Jewish high school kids still star in sports but most of them now come from the suburbs. Jewish parents now encourage their youngsters to compete and are not unhappy when a prowess in sports yields a college scholarship or a professional contract. The city's Jewish parochial high schools have their own basketball league and Yeshiva University fields a fair team in intercollegiate play. In the Orthodox neighborhoods of Brooklyn it is not strange to see youngsters in yarmulkas playing basketball on YMHA courts.

No matter where the Jews have moved in New York, their dietary predilections have influenced the eating habits of the whole city and of a growing segment of the nation as well. Only a minority of New York Jews keep strictly kosher homes, but many buy kosher food. It is easier today than a generation ago when few kosher items were available in stores. The kosher food industry, concentrated in New York, has become a multimillion dollar enterprise, and the demand is rising.

More than 2,000 different kosher products are made by some 400 companies. Most of them have accepted the rabbinical supervision of the Union of Orthodox Jewish Congregations. The Union's kosher certification service, which guarantees the kashrut of a product, is identified by the "U" symbol, available only to firms meeting strict requirements. The sales promotion value of this symbol has encouraged food packers to turn out everything from unsalted kosher margarine, fruit pie fillings and hard cheeses to kosher spaghetti and baby food. The Heinz Company promoted its kosher ketchup in full page newspaper ads headlined "my brother is a schlemihl."

Manufacturers of kosher products that do not subscribe to the UOJC's service label them "K," or identify them by the Star of David or with some Hebrew words. Frozen or precooked kosher foods are available on planes leaving New York airports, and in hospitals which do not have kosher kitchens. All of the city's newer hotels and most of the larger older hostelries have separate sets of dishes and cutlery for use at kosher affairs. The New York Hilton can serve 3,700 from its own Kosher kitchen.

Kosher catering establishments are highly successful with weddings and bar mitzvahs. Some maintain lavish establishments with synagogue-like names. The innumerable "manors" and "mansions," where so many bar mitzvahs and Jewish weddings are held, originated with Clinton Hall and New Irving Hall, where the East Side congregated for major social events, political rallies, *landsmanschaften* meetings, benefit parties, and even dancing classes. Most of the larger synagogues of all denominations depend heavily on income from their official caterers who use synagogue facilities. Some caterers have succeeded in preparing kosher food that is indistinguishable from non-kosher dishes, including a kosher sukiyaki and glazed "kosher ham."

The scope of the kosher food business in New York gave rise to frequent scandals involving rabbis and dealers who falsely certify restaurants, caterers, and products as kosher. Racketeers have offered kosher ritual food tags to non-kosher caterers. Unethical practices and price gouging in the New York kosher poultry business led to one of the most famous decisions of the Supreme Court of the United States. When the Live Poultry Code of NRA (National Recovery Administration), was created in the 1930s to govern the fiercely competitive all-Jewish industry, a wholesaler by the name of Schechter brought suit, and in the "sick chicken case" succeeded in having the whole NRA declared unconstitutional.

In 1944 New York became the first state to set up a separate division to maintain an on-going inspection of meats sold under kosher auspices. The kosher law enforcement bureau handles 2,500 cases a year, and spot checks every place where kosher meat is slaughtered, manufactured, processed, sold, or served. Eight inspectors and supervisors cover New York City to prevent any establishment from claiming or advertising that it sells or serves kosher meat products unless it is supervised by a competent rabbinical authority. In 1975, it became illegal to advertise products or establishments as "kosher style."

Kosher food products crowd supermarket counters in almost every neighborhood. Candy chains feature chocolate matzos for Passover, chocolate *hamantashen* for Purim, candy *dreidels* for Chanukah, and assorted sweets for other Jewish holidays. Radio and television commercials and newspaper ads plug Jewish bread, kosher wine, and a long list of Jewish delicacies, including a herring *maven*. When bagelmakers strike, it is a municipal disaster. Stores offer gefilte fish, lox, and bagels as Lenten substitutes. Kosher Chinese food is available for home delivery and kosher hot dogs can be bought at Yankee Stadium and Madison Square Garden. Popular restaurants include Passover dishes on their menus, together with non-Passover staples. Department stores feature Passover table settings and window displays of Chanukah gift objects. One daily newspaper publishes a special Passover and Rosh Hashanah section devoted largely to kosher recipes and advertisements for kosher foods and Jewish resorts.

The popularity of kosher and Jewish-style food among non-Jews has been attributed to the city's cosmopolitan tastes and to the fact that many of them tried and liked Jewish delicacies in Jewish homes or as delegates to conventions held in "Borscht-Belt" hotels. The easy availability of ready-to-serve kosher foods, on the other hand, may explain the absence of more than a handful of genuinely kosher restaurants. The city and suburbs are studded with non-kosher eating places that offer Jewish delicacies and dairy restaurants where Runyonesque-type waiters serve traditional non-meat Jewish dishes. None ever acquired the fame of the now vanished Cafe Royale on 2nd Avenue, "the downtown Sardi's," where Yiddish literati and uptown Jewish communal leaders gathered.

Non-Jewish epicures who relish the gastronomic pleasures of what has been called "belly Judaism," also know and use many Yiddish words and expressions. While Yiddish is declining as a spoken and printed language in New York, it has won a place as a piquant element in American "slanguage." The linguistic amalgam known as New Yorkese has spilled into American English through many expressive words and phrases that come straight from the East Side by way of the garment center, Broadway, radio, television, and the columnists.

Little surprise is evoked when New Yorkers of Irish or Italian extraction refer to a *"zaftig"* girl who may be a *"shikse,"* or who describe a legal arrangement as *"kosher"* and identify a fool as a *"shlemihl."* The tunesmiths of Tin Pan Alley have poured Yiddish phrases into the stream of American popular music. Comedians who tested their routines in the "Borscht Belt" made words like *"gelt," "Mazuma," "momser," "kibitzer,"* and *"meshuggah"* part of the lingua franca. Al Capp's "shmoo" is related to the Yiddish *"schmaltz"* and *"shmo,"* and the latter is an abbreviation for a Yiddish obscenity. The Yiddish deprecatory prefix *"shm"* found its way into the New Yorkese in such descriptive phrases as, "cancer schmancer" and "fancy-shmancy," and even a First National City Bank ad that starts with "wampum, schwampum."

In New York, politicians and reporters talk about a political *mish-mash* and of situations that are not *kosher*. Policemen refer to jaywalkers as *schlemiehls*. *Kibitzers* flourish everywhere and *shlock* and *shmattas* have become synonyms for junk and rags. Shrewish women are called *yentas*. A *tsimmes* is not a dish but a lot of noise about nothing. A *gontze metziah* is no great bargain. Advertisers cash in on such slogans as "dress British and think Yiddish," and "you don't have to be Jewish" to relish this or that product associated with Jewish palates, such as rye bread, matzoth, borscht, and Passover wine. A manufacturer of heating units advertised that his product worked best when treated with "a Jewish mother's love." A delicatessen asked in a newspaper ad "what's wrong with kosher delicatessen at your Xmas party." A department store used a full page ad to promote a whole line of *mavens*. Most New Yorkers know the meaning of *chutzpa* and do not need a dictionary to get the meaning of *gantze mishpocha, gantze megillah*, and *mishegas* as used by television comedians and the advertising business. Because so many New York Jews still speak Yiddish, the Department of Agriculture printed and distributed 200,000 copies of a leaflet in Yiddish explaining how poor Jews can qualify and apply for food stamps.

Once the language of the vociferous masses, Yiddish is now chiefly the tongue of scholars, researchers, poets, new immigrants from the Soviet Union, and a passing older generation. It is in no immediate danger of dying, however. There are still a number of important Yiddish cultural journals and party organs in New York, besides the two Yiddish dailies. The Sholom Aleichem Schools of the Workmen's Circle report a growing number of American-born children studying Yiddish in suburban classes. Yiddish is being taught in many universities and some New York Jews are first learning Yiddish terms from television comedians.

The amazing success of Allan Sherman's *My Son the Folksinger* among Jews and non-Jews indicated that the city could still be intrigued by the flavor of the East Side when recaptured by playwrights, novelists, and musicians. While immigrant parents and Jewish garment workers have almost vanished from real life, sentimental portraits of their idiosyncracies and relations with American-born children and grandchildren became more common. "Matzo-ball soup operas"—Jewish family situation comedies and dramas—once the chief stock in trade of the Yiddish theatre, became great Broadway successes. Plays and musicals such as *A Majority of One*, *Dear Me the Sky Is Falling*, *Enter Laughing*, *Come Blow Your Horn*, *The Tenth Man*, *Milk and Honey*, and *Cafe Crown* resemble in theme and appeal the plays that brought the immigrant generation thronging to the Yiddish theatre. Although nostalgic sentiment characterizes all of these shows, American-born Jewish audiences, and large numbers of non-Jews, too, have made them great hits, as witnessed by the huge success of *Fiddler on the Roof*.

The story of the New York Jewish immigrant and his descendants became a best seller through the novels and short stories of Herman Wouk, Bernard Malamud, Saul Bellow, Philip Roth, Bruce Friedman, Herbert Gold, Chaim Potok, and the translations of Isaac Bashevis Singer. The body of fiction by and about the Jews of New York provides a continuing insight into the changing patterns of Jewish life and history in the city. The East Side and its impact on Jewish and American life have intrigued writers for half a century. Ellis Island and the ghetto as the Jewish immigrant's frontiers were the themes of Ab Cahan's *The Rise of David Levinsky*, and Mary Antin's *The Promised Land*. The tears and whimsy of Fannie Hurst and Montague Glass were succeeded by the idealized clichés of Leonard Q. Ross' *The Education of Hyman Kaplan*, Milt Gross' *Nize Baby*, and Arthur Kober's *Having A Wonderful Time*. The proletarian novels of disenchantment by Mike Gold, Isidor Schneider, Henry Roth, Joseph Freeman, Albert Halper, and Leona Zugsmith presaged the debunking and self-hatred of Ben Hecht, Jerome Weidman, Budd Schulberg, and the novels of wartime anti-Semitism by Irwin Shaw, Arthur Miller, and Norman Mailer. The books of Harry Golden and Sam Levenson of East Side reminiscences and the recent Jewish novels with New York characters completed the cycle in which New York Jews were no longer pathetic strugglers, victims or *schlemiehls*, but ordinary Americans of middle-class status.

The new *Encyclopedia Judaica* summed up the Jewish role in New York in these words: "So complete was the Jewish involvement in New York cultural life in the middle decades of the 20th century that it would be impossible to imagine practically any aspect of the latter without it. Moreover, this involvement was not at all restricted to the realms of 'high' culture and the arts. It made itself felt most heavily in numerous areas of every day New York life, in its impact on local speech, gestures, food, humor and attitudes. It is doubtful, indeed, if anywhere else in the history of the

Diaspora has a large Jewish community existed in so harmonious a symbiosis with a great metropolis without either ghettoizing itself from its surroundings or losing its own distinct sense of character and identity.

"Nor can the relationship be thought of as having been merely one-way. If the Jews gave to New York unstintingly of their experience, energies and talents, they received in return an education in urbanity and a degree of cosmopolitan sophistication unknown to any other Jewish community of similar size in the past. It is little wonder that many Jews developed an attachment to New York that bordered on the devotional. Above all, when 20th century New York Jews thought of the city they lived in, they did not simply consider it a great capital of civilization that had generously taken them in. Rather, they thought of themselves, and with every justification, as joint builders of this greatness and of its main continuing supports. Such a relationship marks a unique moment in Jewish history and one that given the current political, demographic and cultural trends in the U.S. and the world at large is not likely to recur again."

*****

MANHATTAN

LOWER MANHATTAN

BATTERY PARK *(at southern end of Manhattan–east or west side IRT subway local to South Ferry station)*. At Whitehall and State Sts., there is a flagpole that commemorates the settlement in 1654 of the first group of Jews in the United States. Set in a small landscaped plot, a stone's throw from the spot where the first Jewish settlers landed, the flagstaff rises from a 7-foot-high granite base on which a bronze commemorative plaque is mounted. The inscription reads:

ERECTED BY THE STATE OF NEW YORK
TO HONOR THE MEMORY
OF THE TWENTY-THREE MEN, WOMEN
& CHILDREN WHO LANDED IN SEPTEMBER
1654 & FOUNDED THE FIRST JEWISH
COMMUNITY IN NORTH AMERICA

A Star of David at the top of the plaque is flanked by the Lions of Judah; the seal of the American Jewish Tercentenary adorns the bottom. The flagpole was presented to the City of New York at a ceremony during which the plaque was unveiled by Judge Edgar J. Nathan, Jr., a descendant of Abraham de Lucena, an early Jewish settler. ●There is another plaque in the Park honoring Emma Lazarus, noted Jewish poetess. The plaque is set in Israeli granite. ●The East Coast Memorial, a war monument, commemorates the 4,596 Christian and Jewish Americans who died in World War II.

FRAUNCES TAVERN, Broad and Pearl Sts., was once the home of Phila Franks, sister of David Franks and aunt of Rebecca Franks of Philadelphia. Phila lived here after she had eloped in 1742 with the socially prominent Oliver deLancey of New York. In 1783, George Washington said farewell to his officers in the tavern's Long Room, which was faithfully restored in 1907 by the Sons of the Revolution.

SITE OF ASSER LEVY HOUSE, Broad and Stone Sts., was the home of Asser Levy, one of the original settlers, who waged a successful fight to stand guard in the defense of New Amsterdam (now New York). Jews at first were prohibited from this duty and were, instead, burdened with a special tax.

SITE OF CONGREGATION SHEARITH ISRAEL, Broad and S. William Sts. (originally Mill St.). A modern garage at 26 S. William St. occupies the site of the first synagogue in North America. This was Congregation Shearith Israel's (Spanish and Portuguese Synagogue) first building. A plaque marking the site of the first synagogue in North America was dedicated on Sept. 12, 1976. Because of the concentration of Jewish population in this area, the street was informally called "Jews' Alley" or "Jews' Street." Nearby is the site of the home of Abraham de Lucena.

NEW YORK STOCK EXCHANGE, Broad and Wall Sts. The Exchange had its beginnings in 1792, when 24 brokers, five of whom were Jewish, drew up a trading agreement under a buttonwood tree at what is now 68 Wall St.

KUHN, LOEB & CO., 40 Wall St., is an investment banking firm that played a role in the financial history of the U.S. Among its partners were Jacob H. Schiff, Otto Kahn, and Felix and Paul Warburg. In 1914, Kuhn, Loeb & Co. and J. P. Morgan & Co. joined forces to come to the rescue of New York City when it found itself unable to meet a $100 million obligation to England, payable in gold. In 1931, the two firms again rescued the city by organizing a banking group to set up a huge revolving credit.

THE STATUE OF LIBERTY (boats depart from Battery Park to Liberty Island in upper New York Bay daily from 9 a.m. to 4 p.m. The ferry can be reached by taking a Broadway bus or the IRT or BMT subway to South Ferry).

This world-famous statue has been the symbol of freedom and hope for millions of immigrants. It is 151 feet high and stands on a pedestal of about the same height. Affixed to the base is the sonnet, *The New Colossus*, by the American Jewish poet, Emma Lazarus. The poem, a tribute to liberty and to America as the haven of the oppressed, follows:

Not like the brazen giant of Greek fame,
With conquering limbs astride from land to land;
Here at our sea-washed, sunset gates shall stand
A mighty woman with a torch, whose flame
Is the imprisoned lightning, and her name
Mother of Exiles. From her beacon-hand
Glows world-wide welcome; her mild eyes command
The air-bridged harbor that twin cities frame.
"Keep, ancient lands, your storied pomp!" cries she
With silent lips. "Give me your tired, your poor,
Your huddled masses yearning to breathe free,
The wretched refuse of your teeming shore.
Send these, the homeless, tempest-tost to me,
I lift my lamp beside the golden door!"

In 1885, as the drive to raise $300,000 for the statue's pedestal was faltering, a wide variety of fund-raising methods were used—from penny collections among school children to high-pressure campaigns in Wall St. Artists and writers were invited to donate works which could be auctioned off for the benefit of the pedestal fund. Among those who contributed original manuscripts were Walt Whitman, Mark Twain, and Bret Harte. But Emma Lazarus, then 34 years old and already known for her poetry, essays, and outspoken advocacy of Jewish rights, submitted a special sonnet for the occasion—*The New Colossus*.

It almost went unwritten. Emma at first refused to contribute to the exhibition, saying that she was unable to write to order. But Constance Cary Harrison, a leading citizen who planned to publish the manuscripts and sketches in a portfolio—a 19th century version of a souvenir journal—personally called on the poetess to persuade her with the following argument: "Think of the Goddess of Liberty standing on her pedestal yonder in the bay, and holding the torch out to those refugees you are so fond of visiting at Ward's Island." Two days later Constance Harrison received *The New Colossus*. Emma Lazarus' sonnet yielded $1,500 for the pedestal fund. For 20 years the poem was all but forgotten. In 1903, Georgiana Schuyler, a New York artist, came across a copy of the portfolio and was so taken with the sonnet that she had it inscribed on a bronze tablet and received permission to have it affixed inside the base of the Statue of Liberty. In 1945, the tablet was moved from the second-story landing to the entrance of the statue.

Among Emma Lazarus' relatives were the Rev. Gershom Mendes Seixas, *hazzan* of the Spanish and Portuguese Synagogue and Revolutionary patriot; Maud Nathan, suffragette; Annie Nathan Meyer, a founder of Barnard College; Robert Nathan, poet and novelist; and Supreme Court Justice Benjamin N. Cardozo.

After Emma Lazarus had seen Jewish refugees huddled at Ward's Island in the East River, her works about her people saw new life. *Century Magazine* in May, 1882, published a passionate prose protest against persecution of all kinds, in answer to a previous article by a Madame Ragozin, who tried to whitewash the Russian pogroms against Jews. For the closing exercises of Temple Emanu-El's religious school, Emma wrote the poem *The Banner of the Jew*, a clarion call for a new Ezra to arise and lead his people. In *The Dance of Death*, a poetic drama based on an incident in the persecution of Germany's Jews in the Middle Ages, she wrote, "I have no thought, no passion, no desire, save for my people." Her activity on behalf of Jewry was climaxed in a series of 16 articles called *Epistles to the Hebrews*, appealing for united Jewish action to help the persecuted Jews of Europe, for economic restratification of Jewish life, for changes in Jewish education, and for the restoration of what was then Palestine as the Jewish homeland. The articles were published in the *American Hebrew.* □

ELLIS ISLAND, through which millions of immigrant Jews passed en route to American settlement, was proclaimed by President Lyndon B. Johnson a part of the Statue of Liberty National Monument, and it is now open to tourists.

AMERICAN MUSEUM OF IMMIGRATION, located within the walls of old Fort Wood at the outer base of the Statue of Liberty, is dedicated to those Americans who came from other lands and contributed so largely to the country's cultural and physical development. There are 38 permanent exhibit units in a major exhibit hall enclosed within a terrace. The exhibits tell the story of immigration beginning with the Indians, who originally came to America from Asia. There is a small exhibit entitled "The Seed of Abraham." Of special interest is the Torah used at the first Jewish services held at both Dachau and Mathausen after these concentration camps were liberated in 1945. Other exhibits are devoted to the story of the Statue of Liberty itself. The museum includes dioramas, silk-screen enlargements, photographs, audio-visual aids, murals, and other items.

LOWER EAST SIDE

In this area once lived the largest Jewish community in the world. More than 1,562,000 Jews—most of them from East Europe—arrived in America between 1881 and 1910. The vast majority settled here on the Lower East Side, creating what amounted to a voluntary ghetto.

Life for the immigrants was hard. They lived in tenement houses and eked out a living mostly as peddlers or in the expanding needle trades. Workshops set up in the tenements exploited and enslaved whole families; the sweatshop era had begun, with its disease and degradation. Out of these depths the labor movement developed and grew.

In addition to the settlement houses, which were created to help the immigrants adjust to their American environment, the newcomers organized their own societies to meet their varied needs and gave their overwhelming support to the Yiddish press and Yiddish theatre. Most of these are now memories. A few of the institutions, however, are still in business at the same old stands, but the clientele has changed. Nevertheless, there are a number of kosher dairy or meat restaurants serving blintzes, *varnishkes*, *kishke*, gefilte fish, delicatessen, etc. One can still see Hebrew and Yiddish signs, and wander through stores specializing in Jewish books and ceremonial objects.

Though the population has changed, a significant percentage is still Jewish—the rest mostly Puerto Rican, black, Italian, and Chinese. The pushcarts are gone, and the tenements are giving way to modern housing developments. The great Yiddish theatre and its stars are no more.

ESSEX STREET MARKET, Delancey and Essex Sts. *(IND "D" train to Delancey St.)*. This market features items of virtually every kind of Jewish cuisine. There are large numbers of kosher butcher shops and fish stands where giant carp are whittled into manageable portions for gefilte fish by capable dissectors, mostly sturdy, Yiddish-speaking women.

CONGREGATION BETH HAMEDRASH HAGODOL, 60 Norfolk St., is the oldest Russian Orthodox synagogue in the country. Founded in 1852, its first building was on Allen St. The present synagogue, formerly a Methodist church, was acquired and remodeled in 1885. It has been designated a landmark by the city's Landmark Preservation Commission.

CANAL STREET AND EAST BROADWAY. This area contains many shops specializing in Jewish books in Hebrew, Yiddish, and English; skullcaps; prayer shawls; phylacteries; Torah Scrolls and covers; Menorahs; Jewish records; prayerbooks; Israeli jewelry; and other items.

EDUCATIONAL ALLIANCE, 197 E. Broadway (corner Jefferson St.), is the famous pioneer Jewish Community Center—Settlement House which helped Americanize three generations of Jewish immigrants. In the lobby are photographs of some of the Alliance's famous alumni. David Sarnoff learned English here and Arthur Murray learned to dance. William Auerbach-Levy, Jo Davidson, and Jacob Epstein paid three cents a week to study art, using pushcart peddlers or bearded patriarchs for models. Work of the students of Moses Soyer, another artist who developed his talents at the Alliance, is also on exhibit in the lobby. Eddie Cantor acted in Alliance-sponsored plays. Chaim Gross, world-famous sculptor, and Isaac Soyer, Moses' brother, also studied here. Morris Raphael Cohen discussed philosophy in the settlement's *Comte Synthetic Circle*. As a member of the Alliance, Sholom Aleichem wrote many of his works here, lectured in the auditorium, and discussed literature and world Jewish themes with other members. In 1906 Sholom Aleichem and Mark Twain appeared together at the Isidor Straus Theatre of the Alliance. It was here that Sholom Aleichem was introduced as the "Jewish Mark Twain," after which Twain replied, "I am the American Sholom Aleichem."

The Alliance was built in 1893 to help Jewish immigrants become integrated into American society. It was also hoped that the settlement house would overcome the activities of conversionist missions on the East Side. Tablets in the Alliance lobby mention philanthropists who helped make the work of the Alliance possible. Here are the names of such distinguished persons as Jacob H. Schiff; Nathan, Isidor, and Ida Straus; Henry Morgenthau; Benjamin Altman; Adolph and Leonard Lewisohn; Isaac J. and Henry Bernheim; Mayer and Babette Lehman; Isaac N. Seligman; and members of the Guggenheim, Bloomingdale, Stern, Loeb, Greenbaum, Bernheimer, Wolff, Lavanburg, and Dreyfuss families. Andrew Carnegie, the Christian multimillionaire, is also listed.

At one time the Educational Alliance had an all-Jewish membership. Today, while its sponsorship and staff are still mostly Jewish, it provides services to substantial numbers of Christians. The Alliance has a new two-story Israel and Leah Cummings Recreation Center and Gymnasium, and a ten-story apartment house for the elderly, known as the David L. Podell Apartment House. ☐

NATHAN STRAUS SQUARE, diagonally opposite the Alliance, honors the memory of the philanthropist who made it possible for the poor and young to have pastuerized milk, thereby saving thousands of lives. In 1920, there were 300 Nathan Straus milk stations in 36 cities in America.

B'NAI B'RITH'S birthplace at what used to be Sinsheimer's Cafe, 60 Essex St., is permanently marked by a plaque at the site across the street from Seward Park High School, Ludlow St., bet. Broome and Grand Sts. B'nai B'rith was founded there on Oct. 13, 1843.

SEWARD PARK, next to Nathan Straus Square, was for many years the Lower East Side's main social, recreational, and cultural center. Across from Seward Park is the Garden Cafeteria, where Yiddish writers and actors once congregated.

BIALYSTOKER CENTER AND BIKUR CHOLIM and BIALY-STOKER HOME AND INFIRMARY FOR THE AGED, 228 E. Broadway.

BIALYSTOKER SYNAGOGUE, 7 Willet St., is one of the city's few surviving ecclesiastical buildings from the Federal period. It was originally erected as the Willet Street Methodist Church in 1826 and became a synagogue in 1908. It has been designated a city landmark.

CONGREGATION KAHAL ADAS JESHURUN ANSHE LUBETZ, 14 Eldridge St., has an unusual and spectacular interior.

HENRY STREET SETTLEMENT, 265 Henry St. (now known as the Urban Life Center), was founded in 1893 by Lillian D. Wald, pioneer social worker. The agency was originally called the Nurses' Settlement, and Lillian Wald was the head worker. She is credited with having helped to found the Federal Children's Bureau in 1912. Lillian Wald was a nurse as well as a social worker and, together with other nurses, organized what is still known today as the Visiting Nurses' Service, which has treated thousands of sick people in their homes. The Settlement has the Harry DeJur Playhouse, named for a Russian immigrant who was a Henry St. Settlement boy. He died in 1972 and left funds for the theatre. The Settlement is now a national historic landmark.

RABBI JACOB JOSEPH SCHOOL, for years at 165 Henry St. until it moved late in 1976 to Staten Island, is an all-day yeshiva named after the only Chief Rabbi the Jews of New York ever had. The rabbi's great-grandson, a Marine officer who was killed at Guadalcanal in World War II, is memorialized in the Captain Jacob Joseph Playground next to the school.

SCHIFF PARKWAY, Delancey St. from Chrystie to Clinton Sts., is a parkway named for the famed philanthropist, Jacob H. Schiff.

CONGREGATION SHAAREI SHAMAYIM, Rivington St., is the first Romanian congregation in New York.

CONGREGATION ANSHE SLONIM, Norfolk and Stanton Sts., is the oldest synagogue in New York City (1849).

NAPHTALI HERZ IMBER TABLET, 140 E. Second St., is a memorial bronze tablet on the building dedicated to Naphtali Herz Imber, composer of *Hatikvah*, which was the official anthem of the world Zionist movement for more than a generation and is now the national anthem of Israel.

GUSTAVE HARTMAN SQUARE, (a triangle) at Houston St., Ave. D, and Second St., is named for Judge Gustave Hartman, who spent his life on the Lower East Side as teacher, legislator, and humanitarian.

PERETZ SQUARE, Houston St., between First Ave. and Ave. A, is a small park named for the famous Yiddish writer, Isaac Loeb Peretz.

SECOND AVENUE (lower) was once known as the Yiddish Rialto. There are just a few theatres remaining which produce Yiddish plays, (see also ENTERTAINMENT).

CHATHAM SQUARE CEMETERY, St. James Pl. off Chatham Sq., contains the remains of the first cemetery of the Spanish and Portuguese Synagogue, Congregation Shearith Israel. A tablet over the gateway reads, "what remains of the first Jewish cemetery in the United States." The cemetery, which may still be seen, was acquired in 1682 (see also HISTORIC JEWISH CEMETERIES. For places to dine in this area, see DINING OUT).

CITY HALL, has in the Aldermanic Rooms a portrait of Jacob Hays, the last High Constable of New York City, who was often referred to as the first modern detective. From 1802 to 1849 he was in effect chief of police. ●In a side lobby on the main floor there is a collection of Israeli artifacts in two glass cases. ●Room has been made in the Mayor's Reception Room for a portrait of Abraham Beame, who, when elected in 1974, became the city's first Jewish mayor.

CIVIC CENTER SYNAGOGUE, 49 White St., is an Orthodox synagogue.

MIDTOWN

THE NEW YORK PUBLIC LIBRARY, 5th Ave., at 42nd St., has 120,000 volumes of Judaica in its Jewish Division (see also LIBRARIES AND MUSEUMS).

ISRAEL DISCOUNT BANK, 5th Ave. and 43rd St., has bronze doors cast from an original clay relief by Nathan Rapoport, Israeli sculptor. The name of the bank appears in Hebrew over the doorway. Traditional and contemporary fine arts and crafts from Israel are integrated in the bank's interior design, and a wall-length mural depicts the cultural and industrial life of modern Israel. There are also samples of Israeli minerals and other items.

DIAMOND CENTER runs from the lower forties to the lower fifties, east and west of 5th Ave. The main street, however, is 47th Street between 5th and 6th Avenues. Shops specializing in diamonds and expensive jewelry line both sides of the street. Above these shops are the offices of nearly 400 registered diamond dealers and workshops of over 200 diamond-cutting firms, in addition to sawyers, setters, and equipment suppliers. Many of the activities and transactions of the Center are conducted by Hasidim. It is quite an ordinary sight to see these bearded Hasidim, dressed in traditional Jewish garb, carrying a large fortune of diamonds on their person. A robbery occurs infrequently since 47th St. is one of the best protected streets in Manhattan. In addition to police patrols on the street, detectives are employed by each of the jewelry arcades. The main trading centers are the Diamond Trade Association, 15 W. 47th St., and the Diamond Dealers Club, 30 W. 47th St. The Club is almost entirely Jewish, and this is where most, if not all, the Hasidic "curbstone" diamond dealers transact their business. The Association, which is 90 percent Jewish, was founded by Jews from Belgium. Each organization has a central room that provides booths, lockers, tables, telephones, kosher canteen, bullet-proof windows, and burglar-alarm-studded walls. Above the Club is a small synagogue where dealers can go for the afternoon *mincha* service.

AMERICA-ISRAEL CULTURE HOUSE, 4 E. 54th St., is a showcase for Israel's contribution to the arts. It is also the office of the America-Israel Cultural Foundation.

ISRAEL GOVERNMENT TOURIST OFFICE, 488 Madison Ave.

HARMONIE CLUB, 4 E. 60th St., is the oldest Jewish social club in America. It was founded in 1852.

HOUSE OF LIVING JUDAISM, 838 5th Ave., is the headquarters of the Reform lay movement in America. Here are housed the offices of the Union of American Hebrew Congregations; the National Federations of Temple Brotherhoods, Sisterhoods and Youth; and the New York Federation of Reform Synagogues. Across the east wall of the building are the words from the Bible: "Love Thy Neighbor as Thyself," etched in stone. A Magen David is carved in an attractive stone design above the massive oak entrance doors. The limestone façade is capped by the Tablets of the Law with Hebrew abbreviations of the Ten Commandments in bronze letters. Along the south wall of the building are inscribed Micah's words: "Do Justly, Love Mercy and Walk Humbly with thy G-d." A plaque to the left of the entrance notes that this is the home of the Union of American Hebrew Congregations. A plaque on the right reads: "Moritz and Josephine Berg Memorial," commemorating the parents of Dr. Albert A. Berg, noted surgeon and philanthropist. The vestibule is of rose Cassina marble. Twelve marble pillars that symbolize the Twelve Tribes of Israel support the two-story lobby. In the high arches between the pillars, blue and gold wall plaques illustrate the major Jewish holidays. In the center of the lobby in bronze is the Union seal—*Talmud Torah K'neged Kulom* (The Study of Torah Transcends All). Two pieces of sculpture stand in opposite corners. One is by Walter Midener and the other by Moses Ezekiel. Through the archway to the left is the Sisterhood Lounge. A wood sculpture by Erna Weill stands in the corner of the lounge. In the southwest corner of the lobby is the Union Book Shop, with materials published by the Union of American Hebrew Congregations and its affiliates. Books, filmstrips, records, and games are available. There is a small chapel at the far end of the lobby where daily services are conducted by the UAHC staff. Above the doorway is a sculptured replica of *The Hands Raised in Priestly Benediction.* On the doors are small carvings in bronze representing various rituals of Judaism. Four stained glass windows ablaze with light symbolize four phases of Jewish history and the history of the synagogue. The doors of the Ark bear a gold replica of the Tree of Life resting upon the Scrolls of the Law, guarded on either side by the Lions of Judah. The candelabrum is an emblem of the light that devotion to the moral law affords. Above the Ark are tablets with the Ten Commandments surmounted by the crown of the Torah. The Torah Scrolls within the Ark were rescued from a German synagogue destroyed by the Nazis.

TEMPLE EMANU-EL, 5th Ave. and 65th St., is the largest Jewish house of worship in the world. In plan, the temple follows the basilica common in Italy. The exterior walls are of variegated limestone. The dominating feature of the exterior is the great recessed arch on Fifth Ave., enclosing the rose window with its supporting lancets and the three entrance doors. On the exterior the motifs of the carved decorations have been drawn in general from Hebrew symbols. The symbols of the Twelve Tribes of Israel appear on the front of Beth El Chapel, which adjoins the main temple on the north. The chapel is a two-domed structure reminiscent of the Byzantine churches of the Near East (see also HISTORIC SYNAGOGUES).

STEPHEN WISE CONGRESS HOUSE, 15 E. 84th St., is the home of the American Jewish Congress.

YIVO INSTITUTE FOR JEWISH RESEARCH, 1048 5th Ave., housed in the old Vanderbilt Mansion, is the headquarters of YIVO. This worldwide scholarly institution engages in research on various aspects of Jewish life. The building has been designated a landmark by the New York

Community Trust. YIVO's archives include over 2,000,000 items. Its library contains more than 300,000 volumes in 15 languages (see also LIBRARIES AND MUSEUMS).

SOLOMON R. GUGGENHEIM MUSEUM, 5th Ave. and 89th St., is the only museum in New York named for a Jew. A broad vertical band inscribed "The Solomon R. Guggenheim Museum" ties the two parts of the museum together. This unique structure, set in foliage, was called "a little temple in the park" by Frank Lloyd Wright, its eminent architect. Guggenheim was a metallurgist, mining executive, and patron of the arts. When he died in 1949, he left $8 million to the foundation that bears his name, with $2 million of it earmarked for the museum. There is little of intrinsic Jewish interest in the museum, with the exception of a number of Chagall paintings.

THE JEWISH MUSEUM, 5th Ave. and 92nd St., has a three-story wing, the Albert A. List building, and a sculpture garden. An unusual modern structure connects the wing to the museum proper on each of the first three stories, thus binding a modern structure to a Gothic mansion (built in 1908). A glass facade and special lighting enable passers-by to see exhibits in the wing from the street. The sculpture garden is a memorial to Felix M. and Frieda Schiff Warburg. Situated on land adjacent to the Jewish Museum, the garden features a monumental bronze exhibit entitled *Procession*, consisting of four figures observing a religious ceremony. The first figure carries a Torah; two others hold prayerbooks; and the fourth bears a Menorah (see also LIBRARIES AND MUSEUMS).

MOUNT SINAI HOSPITAL, 99th-101st Sts. and 5th Ave. (originally called "Jews' Hospital"). In 1866, the hospital became, by a special act of the legislature, the Mount Sinai, to emphasize its nonsectarian services.

MEMORIAL PLAQUE FOR THE GHETTO RESISTANCE, Riverside Park at 83rd St., honors the memory of the defenseless Jews who rebelled against the Nazi war machine.

HISTORIC SYNAGOGUES

ORTHODOX

SPANISH AND PORTUGUESE SYNAGOGUE (Congregation Shearith Israel), 8 W. 70th St. *(IND local or West Side IRT to 72nd St., Central Park West or Columbus Ave. bus to 70th St.).* Guided tours of groups are conducted but arrangements must be made in advance. Call TR-3-0800. For more than three centuries, Congregation Shearith Israel has been intimately identified with the history of New York. It has also had many connections with other historic American congregations such as Yeshuat Israel (Touro Synagogue), in Newport, R. I., and Mikveh Israel in Philadelphia. To this day, the congregation holds the legal title to Newport's historic Touro Synagogue. For use of the Touro Synagogue, the Newport

Jewish community pays the New York congregation one dollar a year for rent.

The present building was erected in 1897. In the cornerstone, laid in 1896, there are Jewish ritual articles, earth from the Holy Land, and extensive historical information. The cost of the building exceeded $250,000, an impressive sum in those days. At the dedication on May 19, 1897, the doors were ceremoniously opened by Dr. Horatio Gomez, a great-great-grandson of Lewis Moses Gomez, president of the congregation in 1730, when its first synagogue on Mill Street was dedicated. The Greek Revival style of the building was designed by the noted architect Arnold Brunner. In the north entrance hall there are two massive millstones, five inches in thickness, dating back to a mill erected in the latter part of the 17th century where Mill St. became Mill Lane. These were brought to the synagogue in 1894. These stones recall the mill in the spacious quarters above which the Dutch Church of Manhattan held its services from 1628-1633 and in later years, as tradition has it, the earliest synagogue services in the city were held.

The synagogue keeps a separate gallery for women, as has been traditional in Jewish houses of worship since ancient days. In the earliest days of Congregation Shearith Israel in New Amsterdam, it evoked no comment from Dutch Reformed neighbors, who also seated men and women separately. Tribute is paid to women in the present synagogue by the tablets set up in the L. Napoleon Levy Auditorium in memory of Amelia Barnard Lazarus Tobias "whose beneficence knew no creed," said Sara Lyons, principal of the Polonies Talmud Torah School of the congregation from 1898-1934. To assure that the Reader's words will be heard, the reading desk is set near the center of the synagogue. Symbolizing the desire of the congregants to stand in prayer where their forefathers stood, the boards making up the floor of the present reading desk were transferred from the reading desk of the Nineteenth Street Synagogue. They had been brought from the Crosby Street Synagogue of 1834, and it is said, originally from the Mill Street Synagogue building of 1730.

Three of the Torah Scrolls in the Ark come from the Sephardic congregation in The Hague and were rescued from the Nazis. The oldest pair of bells crowning the Scrolls bear the Hebrew date 5497 (1737). Another pair bear the name of Myer Myers (1723-95), the famous Colonial silversmith. Two of the pointers used in reading the Torah are inscribed with the date of 1846, although others may be older than these. The beaten brass lamp that is kindled during Chanukah may well be 300 years old. The four lamps hanging on the eastern wall of the synagogue were rededicated in 1921 to the memory of four men of the congregation who gave up their lives in World War I. Along the western wall of the synagogue auditorium are a number of memorial tablets. One of these, affixed in 1905 on the 250th anniversary of the congregation, commemorates the ministers, as they were then known, from Saul Pardo, who came to New York from Newport in 1685, to Jacques

J. Lyons, who died in 1877. Two other tablets, originally set up in the Crosby Street Synagogue, honor Abraham Touro, "whose practical efforts to cherish the religion of his fathers were only equalled by his munificence which showered his blessings without sectional distinction," and Washington Hendricks, another philanthropist who was one of the principal supporters of the congregation. Another tablet in the L. Napoleon Levy Auditorium below the synagogue recalls Hendricks' "liberal bequests to the Ladies of the Association for the Moral and Religious Instruction of Children of the Jewish Faith." A tablet in the center of the west wall is dedicated to the memory of Jacques J. Lyons, who was *hazzan* of the congregation from 1839-1877. Another was affixed by the Hebra Hasses Va-Amet on its centennial anniversary in 1902 in tribute to its founder, Gershom Mendes Seixas, the *hazzan* of the congregation, a Jewish minister during the American Revolution, and an incorporator of Columbia College.

The Little Synagogue is a Colonial chapel. Known as the Little Synagogue to distinguish it from the main synagogue, it is a composite of the synagogues occupied by Shearith Israel for more than three centuries under three flags: a decade under the Dutch, a century under the British, and since 1783 under the United States. The chapel is 31 x 24 feet, not much smaller than the first American synagogue erected in 1730, the lines of which it closely follows. Here, tangible reminders of our Colonial heritage and ancient religious artifacts come together as symbols of religious freedom. The Reader's desk was used in 1730. The original railing around it, with its exquisite spindles, holds four candlesticks that are the oldest items in the Little Synagogue. The designs on these candlesticks represent a *Havdalah* set. Made of Spanish brass, the candlesticks may date from the 15th century. They have been in use since 1730. The tablet of the Ten Commandments from 1730 is set above the Ark. Next to it are two very old brass urns with the almond blossom motif in their ornamental carving. In Biblical days, almond sprigs were brought to a synagogue and placed in vases on each side of the Ten Commandments. When sprigs were not available, the urns remained empty. Two of the scrolls were damaged during the British occupation of New York during the Revolutionary War. The interior of the Ark is lined with crimson silk damask, as it was in the 1730 Mill Street Synagogue. The *rimmonim* (Torah headpieces) from the first synagogue of Shearith Israel resemble those used by Sephardim in the 13th century. They consist of a turret with open arches in which gold bells hang.

The *Ner Tamid* (Perpetual Light) in front of the Ark has been in continuous use since 1818. The *bancas* (benches) on each side of the Ark were made in 1834 for the congregation's Crosby Street Synagogue. Along the south wall are three pews from the Mill Street Synagogue with full backs edged with mahogany. They are hand-wrought benches with lockers in which books and *taleisim* (prayer shawls) of the congregants are kept. The other benches were made in 1834 for the Crosby Street Synagogue. In those days members provided themselves with individual seat cushions of various shades and materials. Two memorial lamps are in the alcove on the north wall. One was the *Ner Tamid* of the Nineteenth Street Synagogue. It was remodeled slightly during the restoration to make it match the Davis Memorial Lamp next to it. In the center of the west window hangs the Sabbath Lamp of the Seven Wicks, an interesting and lovely lamp from the 1730 synagogue. The two candlesticks on the window sill and the sconces are from the Crosby Street Synagogue. The stained glass windows were made by Tiffany in 1896 and are reminiscent of the stained glass windows from Crosby Street. The Omer Board, made before 1730, has a movable parchment scroll that is set daily to count the days of the seven-week period between Passover and Shavuot. The ancient Chanukah Menorah of beaten brass was made in Holland prior to 1730. The four chandeliers were created for the Little Synagogue in 1896, in the design of the Byzantine oil lamps used in old synagogues of Europe and Asia (see also UNIQUE SYNAGOGUES AND SERVICES). ☐

WALL STREET SYNAGOGUE, 47 Beekman St. On the grass-green roof is a replica of the first synagogue in North America which was erected on Mill Street (now South William St.) in 1730. The original synagogue had only one room and resembled a log cabin. Its replica seats 20 persons. Built of fireproof material, it has rustic wood on the inside, as in the original synagogue. At one end of the 12 x 20 foot room stands the *bimah*.

Modern in construction, the synagogue below seats 180 people—110 men on the main floor and 70 women in the balcony. The synagogue has a kosher luncheon club patronized by stockbrokers and insurance executives whose offices are nearby. ☐

JEWISH CENTER, 131 W. 86th St., is an Orthodox synagogue, despite its name. The sanctuary on the second floor has a beautiful marble altar framed by two lovely stained glass windows recessed on either side. The parchment Scrolls of the Torah, some of which are hundreds of years old, have exquisite silver ornamentation. The synagogue is open every day from 8 a.m. to 7 p.m.

CONGREGATION OHAB ZEDEK, 118-124 W. 95th St., was founded on the Lower East Side and incorporated as the First Hungarian Congregation Ohab Zedek. With the migration uptown of many of its members to what was then fashionable Harlem, Ohab Zedek purchased its third building in 1906 at 18 W. 116th St. and built a beautiful synagogue with facilities for an expanded Talmud Torah and social assembly. In 1912 the world-famous Yossele Rosenblatt was engaged as cantor, and he officiated in the Harlem synagogue for many years. On May 9, 1926, the cornerstone of the present building was laid. Several years later Cantor Rosenblatt was reengaged and he served until 1935. Early in 1938 the former Chief Rabbi of Frankfurt-am-Main, Dr. Jacob Hoffman, became the synagogue's spiritual leader. The following year the Beth Hillel Hebrew Institute was dedicated on a site adjoining the synagogue. It is now called the Dr. Hillel Klein Center of Jewish Education.

YOUNG ISRAEL OF THE WEST SIDE, 210 W. 91st St., is in a building formerly occupied by Reform Temple Israel.

CONGREGATION RAMATH ORAH, 550 W. 110th St., had as its rabbi Dr. Robert S. Serebrenik, who was Grand Rabbi of Luxembourg when the Nazis conquered it. Brought in the spring of 1941 to Gestapo headquarters in Berlin, he faced Adolf Eichmann and bargained for the life of the Jewish people of Luxembourg and other communities. He testified at the Eichmann trial in Jerusalem.

CONGREGATION K'HAL ADATH JESHURUN, 85 Bennett Ave., is a prominent congregation composed mostly of Jewish immigrants from Frankfurt-am-Main. The synagogue's social hall is at 90 Bennett Ave. A day school, the Yeshiva Rabbi Samson Raphael Hirsch, is at 91 Bennett Ave., and a *mikveh* is at 536 W. 187th St. The synagogue's Rika Breuer Teachers Seminary for Girls offers a complete course of studies leading to teacher certification and a course of advanced Jewish studies leading to a general certificate.

CONGREGATION SHAARE HATIKVAH, 715 W. 179th St., was organized in 1935 by Jews who fled from Nazi persecution. CONGREGATION BETH HILLEL OF WASHINGTON HEIGHTS, 571 W. 182nd St., was also organized by refugees from Germany.

CONGREGATION EZRATH ISRAEL (better known as the Actors' Temple), 339 W. 47th St. For more than a quarter of a century, actors, directors, and producers made this temple their spiritual headquarters. Orthodox services are held daily.

RADIO CITY SYNAGOGUE, formerly on 6th Ave., is now at 110 W. 48th St. Among its early supporters were Walter Winchell, the late George Sokolsky, and other well-known professionals.

GARMENT CENTER CONGREGATION, 205 W. 40th St. (in the Brotherhood House). Founded in the 1930s in the vicinity of Macy's, Saks, and Gimbels, the congregation took an active interest in the public life of the city.

FUR CENTER SYNAGOGUE, 228 W. 29th St., is in the heart of the city's fur industry. The synagogue has a reading room, the gift of three mink ranchers' organizations.

CONGREGATION ORACH CHAIM, 1459-63 Lexington Ave. Among its rabbis were Simon Langer, who received the Legion of Honor from the French government, and Dr. Joseph Hertz, formerly Chief Rabbi of England.

CONGREGATION KEHILATH JESHURUN, 125 E. 85th St., is the sponsor of Ramaz School, a private Jewish day school that is modern and progressive in its approach. Religious and secular studies are alternated and, when possible, are correlated and integrated. The school was the inspiration of Joseph H. Lookstein, rabbi of Congregation Kehilath Jeshurun and principal of Ramaz. It is named for Moses Zebulun Margolies, grandfather of Rabbi Lookstein and for 31 years the congregation's rabbi. He was known as

Ramaz—a name coined from the Ra-M-Z of Rabbi Moses Zebulun. The school is coeducational, with classes from kindergarten through 12th grade. The "Ramaz Plan" has excited educators across the nation and the school has become a model for many others.

FIFTH AVENUE SYNAGOGUE, 5 E. 62nd St. This is the only Orthodox synagogue in this area. Immanuel Jakobovits, Chief Rabbi of the British Commonwealth, was once its rabbi.

CONGREGATION TALMUD TORAH ADERETH EL, 133-135 E. 29th St., is over 100 years old.

MARINERS' TEMPLE, 3 Henry St. (on the Lower East Side), has been designated a landmark of New York by the New York Community Trust.

PARK EAST SYNAGOGUE (Congregation Zichron Ephraim), 163 East 67th St., directly across the street from the Soviet Mission to the United Nations, is a colorful city landmark of Byzantine-Moorish architecture. Bulbous cupolas, set at different levels, are surmounted by a slender shaft supporting a Star of David. The façade of the main structure rises from behind an elaborately arched portico. At either wing there is a decorative square tower, one higher than the other, each richly carved, arched, and star-crowned. Standing out in bold relief are the synagogue's stained glass windows. There are two circular windows—one above the Ark, rich pink, blue, and silver, called the Moon, and the other, known as the Sun, in the rear wall facing the street. The Ark is intricately carved, with loops and pointed cupolas leading the eye to the vaulted, spangled, and delicately buttressed roof. A large outdoor plaque has inscribed: "Hear the Cry of the Oppressed—the Jewish Community in the Soviet Union." Construction is under way for a $6 million cultural center and day school. The congregation was founded in 1888 by the late Jonas Weil, its first president.

LINCOLN SQUARE SYNAGOGUE, Amsterdam Ave. and 69th St., is in the shape of a Star of David and is designed to recapture the centrality of the Torah.

CONSERVATIVE

PARK AVENUE SYNAGOGUE, 50 E. 87th St., attracts visitors from all over the world. Founded in 1882 by a group of German and Hungarian Jews, the congregation developed out of the amalgamation of Congregation Agudath Jeshorim, an Orthodox synagogue on East 86th Street; a Reform temple on East 82nd Street; and the Congregation Bikur Cholim on 72nd Street and Lexington Avenue. It is now a Conservative congregation. Its members include some of the most distinguished Jewish civic and communal leaders in the city. It was the congregation of the late, beloved Rabbi Milton Steinberg, who is memorialized in the adjoining Milton Steinberg House, a five-story civic and educational center. The current rabbi, Judah Nadich, was General Eisenhower's adviser on Jewish affairs in

Germany. Sabbath services begin at 5:45 p.m. on Fridays and at 10 a.m. on Saturdays. The synagogue is open every day for individual prayer and meditation. The architecture of the Milton Steinberg House is contemporary, yet designed to blend with the traditional design of the adjacent synagogue. The façade of stained glass windows, designed by the eminent artist Adolph Gottlieb, depicts Jewish traditions and holidays in an overall abstract mural. The design embodies 1,300 square feet of glass comprised on 91 individual window panes covering the four floors. One-third of the glass is designed and painted to contain 21 individual abstract paintings portraying the religious holidays and traditions. Each of the paintings is repeated four or five times at different points on the façade, forming a checkerboard pattern against a background of traditional, diamond-shaped stained glass panes that compose the remainder of the façade. The paintings are on antique glass imported from Europe; the diamond-shaped panes are of American marine antique glass. In the lobby is *The Altar*, a painting by Moshe Castel, an Israeli artist. Other interesting features of the building are a uniquely sculptured pair of bronze Ark doors and a beautiful candelabrum executed by the sculptor, Calvin Albert.

THE BROTHERHOOD SYNAGOGUE (Congregation Beth Achim), 28 Gramercy Park South, is located in the former Friends Meeting House, a New York City landmark built in 1859. The interior is of classical, formal elegance and spare simplicity. The building is what the Victorians called the Italianate style—a melange of near-Renaissance motifs strong on cornices, pediments, and round-headed windows. The building was designated a New York landmark in 1965. It has a long record of social as well as religious usefulness. During the Civil War, its members took an active interest in the cause of the Negro or "Freedman," as they were called, by supplying garments from a sewing room on the third floor. The congregation calls itself "Liberal Conservative."

CONGREGATION B'NAI JESHURUN, 257 W. 88th St., is the oldest Ashkenazic congregation in New York City. It was established in November, 1825, as an offshoot of Congregation Shearith Israel, by a group of English and Dutch Jews who wished to follow the Ashkenazic (English and German) rather than the Sephardic (Spanish and Portuguese) ritual. Among the founders of B'nai Jeshurun were John I. Hart, son of the Reverend Judah Hart of Portsmouth, and Abraham Mitchell, one of a handful of Jews who served in the War of 1812. Haym M. Salomon, son of the famous Haym Salomon of Philadelphia, presented a Hebrew Bible when the first house of worship was consecrated in 1827, on Elm Street. As the city grew, the population moved northward. By 1849 the old synagogue had been outgrown, and a new house of worship was dedicated on Greene Street. The period beginning with the dedication of the Greene Street Synagogue ushered in a flourishing career for the congregation, whose members took active parts in the communal agencies that had begun to grow and develop. In 1865, a new synagogue was dedicated on 34th Street, west of Broadway, on the present site of Macy's. Dr. Morris J. Raphall, first of B'nai Jeshurun's famous rabbis, was the son of the banker to the king of Sweden. He was the first Jewish minister to open a session of the United States House of Representatives with prayer. The congregation's fourth house of worship, on Madison Avenue at 65th Street, was erected in 1885. In 1893, Stephen S. Wise, aged 21, became rabbi of the congregation and served it until 1900, when he went to Portland, Oregon. Another distinguished minister was the Reverend Dr. Judah L. Magnes. The present synagogue was erected in 1918. It has been called "an architectural masterpiece embodying the spirit of ancient Semitic art." Its façade is of a striking composition featuring a tall romanesque portal; the interior is decorated with intricate polychrome ornament. Rabbi Israel Goldstein became the rabbi a few months after the dedication of the present building. In 1928, a six-story community building adjoining the synagogue was dedicated. The congregation's Institute of Adult Jewish Studies, under Rabbi William Berkowitz, attracted nation-wide attention.

TEMPLE ANSCHE CHESED, 251 W. 110th St., was founded in 1876.

CONGREGATION SHAARE ZEDEK, 212 W. 93rd St., is over 100 years old.

SUTTON PLACE SYNAGOGUE, 225 E. 51st St., is called the Jewish Center for the United Nations. Its façade of rough stone blocks matches that of the adjoining Greenacre minipark. The themes of Judaism, world peace, and universal brotherhood are reflected in the building and particularly in the stained glass windows. Across the front of the red-carpeted sanctuary is a design in the shape of an open Torah Scroll upon which are inscribed the words of Isaiah: "And they shall beat their swords into plowshares."

THE LITTLE SYNAGOGUE, 27 E. 20th St., is a unique congregation which calls itself "modern Hasidic" but follows the Conservative ritual. Its rabbi, the Reverend Joseph Gelberman, is a religious and psychological counselor and a devotee of Martin Buber. Lectures are given Wednesday evenings throughout the year. With the exception of the summer months, services are held every other Friday evening.

MILLINERY CENTER SYNAGOGUE, 1025 6th Ave., conducts services frequently during the day for those who need to say *kaddish*.

REFORM

TEMPLE EMANU-EL, 5th Ave. and 65th St., is open from 10 a.m. to 5 p.m. daily. *(East Side IRT local to 68th St., BMT to 5th Ave., or 65th St. crosstown bus to 5th Ave.)* A guide is available, call RH-4-1400. Friday night services begin at 5:15 p.m. throughout the year, and from the first week in November and the last week in March, additional services are held on Friday evenings at 8:30. On Saturdays, services begin at 10:30 a.m. The temple has a choir and an organ. It also has a special Sunset Service, conducted from Sunday through Thursday at 5:30 p.m., in the Beth El Chapel under the sponsorship of the Men's Club. Its Friday evening services are broadcast from 5:30 to 6:00 over stations WQXR and WQXR-FM.

This imposing edifice, on the site of the old Vincent Astor residence, is the congregation's fourth building. Its first building, which it purchased in 1847 after worshipping in a private home on the Lower East Side for two years, was at 56 Chrystie St. In November, 1862, an imposing structure at 5th Avenue and 43rd Street was selected as Emanu-El's new home. The building was described by *The New York Times* as the "architectural sensation of the city." Louis Marshall, lawyer, civic leader, and Emanu-El's president, led the fight for a new temple and laid the cornerstone of the present magnificent building in May, 1928. Marshall died in Switzerland on September 11, 1929. His funeral was the first service held in the present structure. Judge Irving Lehman, who succeeded him as president, dedicated Temple Emanu-El on January 10, 1930. It has been a Reform congregation since its beginning in 1845. The temple's vestibule walls and floors are Siena Travertine; the ceiling is walnut. The walls of the building are actually self-supporting, while the buttresses of the exterior and the trusses of the interior are, respectively, the stone and plaster covering the structural steel members necessary to bridge the span of the great nave. The main body of the temple's auditorium is 77 feet wide between piers and 150 feet in length, from the east wall of the vestibule to the sanctuary steps, with a height of 103 feet to the underside of the ridges of the ceiling. The walls of the auditorium are covered from the top of the stone base to the ceiling with acoustic tile. The side galleries are supported by marble columns. French Vaurion stone was used for the flooring of the aisles. The temple seats 2,500 people. The sanctuary is 30 feet in depth and just over 40 feet wide, with a marble floor and marble (and mosaic) wainscot on the sides. Below the arch is the Ark, with columns of French Benou Jaume marble. The Ark doors are bronze, and the frame of the opening is of Siena marble with mosaic insets. The columns are crowned with small bronze tabernacles. The abbreviated version of the Ten Commandments is on the Ark's bronze grille, while on both sides of the Ark are beautiful seven-branched candlesticks. The Shield of David is repeated in the mosaics and windows of the temple; the Lion of Judah and the Royal Crown of the Torah are also pictured. Twenty-five feet above the sanctuary is the choir loft, cut off by a pierced railing surmounted by marble columns of varied colors carrying arches that conceal the organ, part of which is placed over the choir gallery and part above the sanctuary vault. The great organ, located above the chancel, is four manual, having 116 speaking stops, 50 couplers, 7,681 speaking pipes, 32 bell chimes, and 61 celesta bars. Under Temple Emanu-El is the Isaac M. Wise Memorial Hall, which seats 1,500 and has a stage, kitchen, and banquet facilities.

Just outside the Temple, a "Garden of Freedom" was dedicated during the American Bicentennial in 1976. A Vermont marble bench surrounded by plants, a tree, and shrubbery, has the following inscription: "This garden is dedicated to the people of the United States in grateful recognition of 200 years of religious freedom—1776-1976." □

BETH EL CHAPEL, which adjoins the temple on the north, is named for Temple Beth El, which merged with Congregation Emanu-El in 1927. Over the door of the chapel is the verse from Genesis: "This is none other than the house of G-d." The inscription in the exterior frieze of the chapel is from Isaiah: "And the work of righteousness, quietness and security forever." The two domes of the chapel are supported by six columns of pink Westerly granite, while the side walls rest on arches springing from columns of Breche Oriental marble. Verdello marble is used for the wainscots and for the pierced side walls. The sanctuary arch, in which blue is the dominant color, has a golden brown mosaic background with the Ten Commandments inscribed in blue, against which the Ark of wrought steel is set. The chapel is lit by two great chandeliers finished in silver and enamel. The seating capacity is 350. An eight-story community house adjoins Temple Emanu-El to the east. Over the grouped entrance doors is a verse from the 78th Psalm: "Give ear, O my people, to my instructions, incline your ear to the words of my mouth which we have heard and know, and which our fathers have related to us." The community house contains the Ivan M. Stettenheim Library, with thousands of volumes of Judaica and other literature; an assembly room that seats 750; the rabbis' studies; a paneled meeting room for the trustees; the temple's offices; smaller assembly rooms; and other facilities. Adjoining the community house is a religious school building. The building contains eight huge stained glass windows, each of which has more than 1,000 pieces of glass. Illustrating the traditional symbols of Judaism, the windows are divided into four groups—the Ten Commandments, the *shofar*, the Star of David, the Burning Bush, the Eternal Light, the Tree of Life, the Menorah, and the Book of Jewish Laws.

JUDGE IRVING LEHMAN MEMORIAL MUSEUM, in Temple Emanu-El's religious school building foyer, contains a valuable collection of Jewish ceremonial objects that the distinguished jurist and former president of the congregation gathered during his travels in many parts of the world. Judge Irving Lehman was the older brother of Senator Herbert H. Lehman.

CENTRAL SYNAGOGUE, 652 Lexington Ave., was built in 1870. The cornerstone was laid by Dr. Isaac Mayer Wise on December 14, 1870. No other temple in New York in use today has been on its current site that long. In 1846, 18 young men, most of whom had come from Bohemia, met in a hall in Coblenzer's Hotel on Ludlow Street and conducted their own services. They looked to the Book of Micah for their congregation's name and chose Ahawath Chesed—"Love of Mercy," (from "Do Justly, Love Mercy, and Walk Humbly with Thy G-d"). When the little congregation outgrew its home in 1849, it moved seven blocks east, to Ridge Street, having transformed the upper part of two houses into a synagogue at a rental of $100 a year; dues were $1.50. The ritual in those days was Orthodox. In 1854, the congregation bought a house on narrow Columbia Street, which it remodeled. Its next move, in 1864, was to the southwest corner of Fourth Street and Avenue C. Rabbi Isaac Mayer Wise, who was to lay the cornerstone of the congregation's present structure and whose son was to become its rabbi, spoke at the dedication ceremonies. In 1870, with the movement of the population, the congregation decided to acquire the property at 55th Street and Lexington Avenue. This is said to be the second largest synagogue in New York. It was designed by Henry Fernbach, the first Jewish architect in America. The synagogue seats more than 1,300 persons. The Eternal Light above the Ark was lit in 1872 when the building was opened and was not extinguished until 1946 when gas was replaced by electricity during the 100th anniversary restoration. This light has probably burned continuously longer than any other in New York. In 1898 Congregation Shaar Hashomayim merged with Ahawath Chesed and the new name was Congregation Ahawath Chesed Shaar Hashomayim. This name continued in use until 1920, when it was changed to Central Synagogue. One of the synagogue's rabbis was Dr. Alexander Kohut, who had come from Hungary as one of the leading authors, scholars, and religious leaders. In 1925, Rabbi Jonah B. Wise, the son of Rabbi Isaac Mayer Wise, was offered the pulpit, which he served until 1958. Central Synagogue has taken part in interfaith Thanksgiving services with Central Presbyterian Church and the Congregation of Christ Church Methodist. The ministers rotate in preaching the sermons and conducting services. Central Synagogue was designated a landmark of New York by the New York Community Trust. A plaque on the building reads:

LANDMARKS OF NEW YORK
CENTRAL SYNAGOGUE
THIS IS THE OLDEST SYNAGOGUE BUILDING IN
CONTINUOUS USE IN NEW YORK CITY. THE
CONGREGATION WAS ESTABLISHED IN 1846 AND
THIS TEMPLE, DESIGNED BY HENRY FERNBACH,
WAS COMPLETED IN 1872. THE STYLE IS MOORISH
REVIVAL, THE ARRANGEMENT GOTHIC.

More recently, Central Synagogue was designated a National Landmark.
JONAH B. WISE COMMUNITY HOUSE, 55th St. near Park Ave., is the Central Synagogue's $2,500,000 structure.
TEMPLE ISRAEL OF NEW YORK CITY, 112 East 75th St., is one of the better known temples in New York. It moved from the West Side after having been there many years and now has a $2 million sanctuary. Among its most impressive features is its huge cylindrical Ark.
CONGREGATION SHAARAY TEFILA, 250 East 79th St., once familiarly known as the West End Synagogue, has a new temple. The sanctuary grew out of the shell of a Trans-Lux Theatre that occupied the site

when it was purchased by the congregation. While the structure was completely renovated, certain features were retained, such as the sloping auditorium and the airconditioning system. In the building's four stories and mezzanine are classrooms, offices, an assembly hall, and recreation and meeting rooms. Its original name was the name it now uses exclusively— Shaaray Tefila ("Gates of Prayer). It started as an Orthodox congregation in humble circumstances. In 1847, its struggling Wooster Street congregation frequently paid "worshippers" to insure the required *minyan*. After nearly two decades on Wooster Street, the congregation moved to Broadway and 36th Street. In 1869, an imposing new edifice was consecrated on 44th Street west of 6th Avenue. Ten years later, the congregation voted to abandon Orthodoxy in favor of Reform Judaism. In two decades the congregation made another move, to 82nd Street, east of Amsterdam Avenue. There, it became familiarly known as the West End Synagogue, although its corporate name has always been Congregation Shaaray Tefila.

METROPOLITAN SYNAGOGUE (in the Community Church building), 40 E. 35th St., is well-known for its fine music during services. Its cantor, Norman Atkins, has appeared with opera companies throughout the country and with all of the major symphony orchestras. Leonard Bernstein is the synagogue's honorary music consultant. Special events at the synagogue have included the world premiere of *The Golem* by Abraham Ellstein, presented by the New York City Center Opera Company; a coast-to-coast televised brotherhood service conducted by the Metropolitan Synagogue Choir and the Choir of the Church of the Master; a service of music and prayer dedicated to Ernest Bloch; *Gideon*—a dialogue between Arthur Cantor, producer of the play, and the synagogue's spiritual leader, Rabbi Judah Cahn; the recording of Bloch's *Sacred Service*, with Leonard Bernstein conducting the New York Philharmonic and Rabbi Cahn singing with the Metropolitan Synagogue Choir; and joint Thanksgiving services with the Community Church. Outside the synagogue, on the church building, is a large sculpture of the Prophet Isaiah. Isaiah's right arm holds a shard of sword broken off near the haft; his left arm rises straight up, the hand gripping the blade. The plowshare beside him rounds out the line from the Book of Isaiah that inspired the sculpture: ". . . and they shall beat their swords into plowshares." Below the large figure of Isaiah is a smaller piece of sculpture in the form of an open book. On the right-hand side is a smaller figure of Isaiah; on the left is the "swords into plowshares" passage. Friday evening services are held throughout the year at 8:30 p.m. Services on Saturday begin at 10:45 a.m. In addition to the Sabbath service, there is a Saturday morning period of adult education.

THE STEPHEN WISE FREE SYNAGOGUE, 30 W. 68th St. Founded in 1907 by Rabbi Stephen S. Wise, the synagogue uses the word "free" because the pulpit is free—not subject to control. The pews are free since seats are never sold or reserved. Contributions are voluntary, and there are no fixed membership dues. Rabbi Wise founded the Free

Synagogue partially in reaction to a dictum he received when he was offered the pulpit of Temple Emanu-El in New York. Louis Marshall, an officer of the temple, made it clear that "the pulpit should always be subject to and under the control of the board of trustees." Rabbi Wise then rejected the offer, declaring in part:

A free pulpit, worthily filled, must command respect and influence; a pulpit that is not free, howsoever filled, is sure to be without potency or honor. In the pursuit of the duties of his office, the minister may from time to time be under the necessity of giving expression to views at variance with the views of some or even many members of the congregation. Far from such difference proving the pulpit to be wrong, it may be and ofttimes is found to signify that the pulpit has done its duty in calling evil evil and good good, in abhorring the moral wrong of putting light for darkness and darkness for light.

Rabbi Wise founded the Free Synagogue also in reaction to what he saw as a lack of vitality and influence on the part of the Reform movement of his day. In a lecture at the Hudson Theatre on West 47th Street, he declared:

What is a Free Synagogue? A Synagogue! A Synagogue, a Jewish society, for I am a Jew, a Jewish teacher. The Free Synagogue is not to be an indirect or circuitous avenue of approach to Unitarianism; it is not to be a society for the gradual conversion of Jewish men or women to any form of Christianity. We mean to be vitally, intensely, unequivocably Jewish. Jews who would not be Jews will find no place in the Free Synagogue, for we, its founders, wish to be not less Jewish but more Jewish in the highest and noblest sense of the term.

The response was gratifying. Some attended out of curiosity. Some were seeking a kind of Jewish affiliation they could not satisfy in existing institutions. On April 15, 1907, more than a hundred "religious pioneers" met at the Hotel Savoy for the purpose of organizing a Free Synagogue. Henry Morgenthau, Sr., presided, and Charles E. Bloch served as secretary. Morgenthau reported that 192 persons had announced their intention of joining and contributed $9,300. Among those who joined together with Morgenthau and Bloch were Jacob H. Schiff, Adolph Lewisohn, Isaac N. Seligson, M. J. Stroock, and J. B. Greenhut. Services were first held Sunday mornings at the Universalist Church of the Eternal Hope on West 81st Street, and attracted as many as a thousand people. Beginning with Rosh Hashanah eve on October 3, 1910, services were held at Carnegie Hall, giving the Free Synagogue the largest seating capacity of any Jewish congregation in the country. In 1911, the brownstone houses on West 68th Street were bought to accommodate the school, social service department, executive offices, and studies. Branches of the Free Synagogue were organized on the Lower East Side. (Sabbath eve services were conducted at Clinton Hall, near Grand Street; in The Bronx at 929 Southern Blvd.; in Washington Heights at Corrigan Hall; in Flushing, and in Newark, New Jersey.) A synagogue house was built in 1922 at 40 West 68th St., as temporary quarters. When it became apparent that the needs of the congregation could best be served by the more traditional Sabbath eve service, the Sunday morning services at Carnegie Hall were discontinued, and Carnegie Hall was used only for the High Holy Days. The current five-story structure was dedicated on January 20, 1950. The cornerstone is from the Holy of Holies in Jerusalem. It was presented to Rabbi Wise by Brigadier Sir Wyndham Deedes in 1922. The adornments in the interior of the synagogue were designed by the noted Jewish artist, A. Raymond Katz, who was assisted in the execution of the decor by Louis Ross, an expert in the technique of gesso. Above the portals of the entrance are inscribed the words: "Blessed be he who comes in the name of the Lord. We bless you out of the House of the Lord." The proscenium arch, which spans the choir screen, bears Katz's interpretation of the holidays. At the lower left is the letter *shin*, standing for *Shabbat*. Within the letter are the ritual objects of the Sabbath services in the home—the candles, the *kiddush* cup, the *challah*, and the traditional fish. Masks, the crown of Ahasuerus, and the *megillah* depict Purim. Passover is represented by the cup of Elijah, the pyramids the Hebrews built in slavery, the wheat of the matzo, and the four cups of wine. The Tablets of the Law and the blossoms of spring portray the mood of *Shavuot*. The top of the arch bears the Hebrew inscription: "Know before Whom thou standest." At the top of the right-hand side of the arch are the *dreidel* and the eight branched candelabrum, symbols of Chanukah. Succoth is represented by the *lulav* and *etrog*. Yom Kippur is depicted by the Book of Life. The *shofar* is the central symbol of Rosh Hashanah. At the lower right of the arch are the twisted candle, the *kiddush* cup, and the spice box—symbols of the *Havdalah* service, which concludes the Sabbath day. Six panels on either side of the Ark express the ideals of Judaism—gratitude for G-d's goodness, Torah, labor, good deeds, love of neighbor, prayer and praise of the Lord, ethics, joyousness, truth, peace, justice, freedom, the love of Zion, and study. On the Ark doors are carved hands, in the palms of which are the Ten Commandments. The Ark is surmounted by the words that are the heart of Jewish belief: "The Lord is Our G-d, the Lord is One." The Perpetual Light is fashioned of two Hebrew letters—the *zayin* which stands for *zikaron* or "remembrance," and the *shin*, which, in this instance, stands for *Shaddai*, or the Almighty. The design on the pulpit is a variation on the two letters. The form of the Menorah is also the letter *shin*, standing for *Shaddai*; each branch is crowned with the letter *yod*, which again suggests the name of the Lord. There is a chapel under the east balcony that accommodates smaller groups for special services. □

CONGREGATION HABONIM (German-Liberal), 44 West 66th St., was founded in 1939 by a group of refugees from Nazi Germany. The sanctuary has 12 stained glass windows created by Robert Sowers. The whole ensemble may be seen as an image of the life cycle, from youth on the left, represented by slender, shoot-like forms thrusting upward out of deep reddish soil; through the vigor of young manhood in the center, where the long, figure-like forms in bronze seem to join hands, and in so doing create the primordial shelter—the Ark, the temple, the family hearth; on to the extreme right, where the simple, white shield-like form of maturity sets off the more somber hues of the firmament. The three panels just to the left of the center window contain symbols that may be read as the torch of knowledge and as covered scrolls standing in a row. The three panels just to the right of the center window contain a series of forms that to some may suggest a star, to others the Cloak of Many Colors, to still others just the laborious effort of the human being to combine simple elements in this precarious world into a durable structure. In the center window's upper right-hand section, there is a form very much like a letter of the Hebrew alphabet. This form, since it is not an actual letter, appears in bronze on both the inside and the outside of the window. Yet it is in the spirit of the actual characters of the alphabet. This same form may also be read as the head, a rather king-like bearded head in profile, of one of the figure-like forms previously mentioned, while these forms may themselves be seen in another sense as forming between them the letter H. At the bottom of the window, where they are most evident from the outside, are two more bronze forms that recall the Tablets of the Law. From the inside, the whole light center area of the window, with its fiery core of color and its bronze forms, grows upward from the Ark. The faceted backgrounds at both ends of the design are based on the form of the Star of David. While the congregation is affiliated with the Reform movement, it calls itself "German-Liberal," and its male congregants wear *taleisim* and head coverings. Fragments of temples destroyed on *Kristalnacht* have gone into a monument which memorializes the Nazi victims. Behind the monument, in the temple's lobby, is a modernistic representation of the Tree of Life.

CONGREGATION RODEPH SHOLOM, 7 W. 83rd St., was founded in 1842. One of its ministers, Rabbi Aaron Wise, who served from 1875-1897, was the father of Rabbi Stephen S. Wise. The current building, erected in 1930, was designed by Charles B. Myers, for many years architect for the City of New York.

EAST END TEMPLE, 398 Second Ave., is in a former bank branch. There are two museum-type window display cases, each about four and a half feet square and a foot deep, facing 23rd Street. The exhibits vary from month to month. The temple has some silver Torah ornaments made by native craftsmen in Mexico. Its library has over 1,700 volumes of Judaica, almost all of them in English. Sabbath evening services are held at 8:40 p.m. the year round.

HEBREW TABERNACLE OF WASHINGTON HEIGHTS, 605 W. 161st St., is a Reform synagogue, although its male congregants wear hats or *yarmulkas* and *taleisim* and it observes two days of Rosh Hashanah and eight days of Passover and Succoth.

THE INTERNATIONAL SYNAGOGUE, Tri-Faith Plaza of John F. Kennedy International Airport (see Queens, New York).

UNIQUE SYNAGOGUES AND SERVICES

SYNAGOGUE OF THE SOCIETY FOR THE ADVANCEMENT OF JUDAISM (Reconstructionist), 15 W. 86th Street. Sabbath services begin at 6 p.m. on Fridays, and at 10:15 a.m. on Saturdays. One of the unique features here is that both men and women are called up to the Torah. In the Society for the Advancement of Judaism, women have complete equality with men not only in the synagogue service but also on the board of trustees and in the bat mitzvah ceremony. Founded in 1922 by Dr. Mordecai M. Kaplan, the society, which is the fountainhead of the Reconstructionist movement, conducts not only a synagogue but also a school, in the Joseph and Nellie Y. Levy Building, at 32 W. 86th St. It cooperates with the Park Avenue Synagogue and Congregation B'nai Jeshurun in the Milton Steinberg Central High School of Jewish Studies and offers a comprehensive adult education program.

Covering the south wall of the synagogue are murals depicting Palestinian life and the story of Israel's rebirth in the Holy Land. The contrast between ancient Jewish life and modern Zionist activity forms the theme of panels covering more than 180 square feet. The central panel, almost 20 feet long and 5 feet high, deals with present-day agricultural aspects of the Holy Land. Two flanking panels are vertical. In the upper right-hand corner of the panel at the right is the old city of Tiberias. Emerging from the city are some Hasidim in their traditional garb, dancing with the Holy Scroll with expressions of joy and ecstasy. Three Jews are shown at prayer by the Wailing Wall. At the bottom and to the left, children of the yeshiva sit at their studies. To the right a diversified crowd is seen passing through the narrow arched streets of the old city of Jerusalem. The vertical, left-handed panel deals with new elements in the Holy Land. The city of Haifa with its new port is in the upper left corner. To the right is Mount Scopus, dotted with olive trees; and there stands the Hebrew University, in all its glory. Below is Technion-Haifa, Israel's great scientific institute. Two mains from the Ruttenberg Electrical Works lead directly to the young worker who is in the center of the panel. Other laborers at the lower right symbolize the building activity in the land. To the left are suggestions of Tel Aviv's modern architecture, and below, a group of enthusiastic, spirited, singing youth. The murals are the work of Temima N. Gezari, a Jewish artist. □

CONGREGATION SHEARITH ISRAEL (Spanish and Portuguese Synagogue), 8 W. 70th St. The services and practices at this congregation are rather unique. The prayers are read in Sephardic Hebrew rather than Ashkenazic. Upon entering the synagogue it is customary to bow and to recite the following words in Hebrew: "Lo, in Thy abundant love I enter Thy house; in reverence to Thee I bow toward Thy holy temple." As congregants approach the doors to leave the synagogue, they turn about momentarily, face the Ark, bow and say, "Lord, lead me in Thy righteousness . . . make Thy path straight before me." A suitable head covering is worn at all times. At morning services, the *talis* (prayer shawl) is worn by all males. The congregational services emphasize the participation of all in chanting the prayers of the synagogue. Special prayers are added on Sabbath days that commemorate the consecration of one of the earlier synagogue buildings; the present synagogue is commemorated on Rosh Hodesh, Jewish festivals, and the High Holy Days. On these commemoration days and other special occasions, the Ark is opened before the *Baruh Sheamar* by one of the worshippers, and the scrolls can be seen blanketed with cloaks of different colors. On the seventh day of Passover and on *Shabbat Shirah*—the Sabbath of Song—the *Az Yashir* (Song of Moses), is chanted during the Torah reading. The *Nishmat* (The Soul of Living) is sung by the choir and congregation, after which the services continue in much the same fashion of antiphonal response that characterized the earlier part of the service. The *hashcaboth* are the memorial prayers recited every Sabbath.

The Reader announces the name of those who are called upon to participate in the ceremony of taking the Torah Scroll from the Ark. The honors to be bestowed include those of opening the Ark, carrying the scroll, removing the bells and band after the scroll has been carried to the reading desk, lifting up the scroll, and accompanying the scroll. The *mitzvot* of removing the bells and band from the scroll generally go to two boys, except on festivals and holy days when they are given to young men. One boy removes the bells from the scroll and places them atop the reading desk. The other boy removes the band and returns to his seat. The first boy then removes the cloak from the Torah, and it is then brought forward to the reading desk, and the bells are placed atop the scrolls. The Torah is unrolled so that five or six columns of its writing are seen and held aloft by the *levantador*, who, after raising the scroll, turns counter-clockwise to the four sides of the synagogue. Many worshippers then hold their hands up, point to the Torah, and chant, "This is the Torah that Moses set before the children of Israel. Moses commanded us our Law, the heritage for the congregation of Jacob." The *hazzan* responds with the following: "The way of G-d is perfect, the word of the Lord is true-tested. A shield is He to all who trust in Him." The Torah reading follows. On being called to the Torah, each person bows to the presiding officer as he approaches the reading desk and says the Hebrew words for "the Lord be with you." The congregation responds, "the Lord bless thee." Then the blessing for the Torah is recited. After the blessing and immediately before the *hazzan* begins to read, the one who is called turns and bows to the previous one who had the *mitzvah,* at which point the latter leaves the reading desk. At the close of the Torah portion, the one who is called says the word *emet* ("truth") or *Torat mosheh emet* ("the Law of Moses is truth"), and the concluding blessing is recited.

After the special announcements and the chanting of the section beginning with the words, *Yehi Hasdeha,* the Torah is returned to the Ark. As the Reader says, "Have I not commanded thee?" the *Sefer*-carrier approaches the reading desk and rests the scroll upon it. The *hazzan* chants *Yimloh,* which is sung antiphonally twice by the *hazzan* and the congregants. Then follows what is one of the most beautiful and impressive parts of the service: As the choir chants Psalm 29, the *Sefer*-carrier slowly begins to leave the reading desk followed by the *hazzan,* who bows ceremoniously to the others on the reading platform, before taking leave; the *parnas* also bows to those on the platform, and then the others fall in. All of these proceed in measured pace behind the *Sefer*-carrier, who returns the *Sefer* to the Ark as the closing strains of Psalm 29 are chanted. At this point in the service, anyone who wishes to express a prayer of gratitude or wants to mark the anniversary of one departed can make an offering before the Ark. Services are held daily at 7:30 a.m. and 6 p.m., with certain exceptions.

Services on any of the festivals or holy days are equally interesting. On the eve of Yom Kippur, the congregants arrive just before sunset, and the men, many of whom come in full dress with white tie and tails, cover themselves with the *talis.* Before the *Kol Nidre* is read, the scrolls, covered in cloaks of white, are carried from the Ark to the reading desk by a number of men, dressed in formal attire, in a beautiful and solemn procession.

On Succoth, Shearith Israel erects a beautiful *succah* that embodies within itself the principle of "a beautiful dwelling," and some of the members eat and study there and "do all that would normally be done within the home." On the evening preceding *Hosha'ana Rabbah,* the *Mishmarah,* a special service, is held in the *succah.* Some congregants remain awake throughout the night and continue reading from the Psalms, the *Zohar,* and other religious books for added spiritual uplift in order to merit blessing in the year ahead. On the following morning, the entire synagogue is bedecked in white. At the conclusion of the *Musaf* service, seven scrolls are carried from the Ark to the reading desk and are held there while seven circuits are made about them by men and boys, carrying the *lulav* and the *etrog* in their hands.

Passover is observed in much the same manner as in other Orthodox synagogues. Of special note is the *Tikkun ha-Tal* (the prayer for dew), in which the congregation and the choir participate with the Reader in the chanting of the beautiful prayers set in lovely poetic form.

On Shavuot, the entire synagogue is decorated with greens and the steps leading to the Holy Ark are covered with an abundance of colorful flowers and plants reminiscent of the fruits that were brought as offerings in Temple days.

On the black fast day of *Tisha b'Ab* the synagogue is draped in black and the services are not read from the reading desk but from a table set especially low in front of the reading desk, as a sign of sadness and mourning.

This table is also draped in black and has chairs for the *hazzanim* and the presiding officer. The twelve white tapers that surround the reading desk are covered in black, and the Ark also has a black covering. The reading light permitted for the evening service should come from the candles; however, because of fire hazards, flashlights have been used in recent years. Small candlelights are placed upon the table for the *hazzanim*. There is virtually no other source of light. All is shrouded in darkness to commemorate one of the most mournful events—the destruction of the Temple in Jerusalem. The *hazzan* begins the service with the chant of Psalm 137, "By the rivers of Babylon there we sat, yea, we also wept . . ." The melody with its sorrowful intonation sets the mood for the entire service. One of the unusual aspects of the service is that often the accentuation in the reading is purposely incorrect. This emphasizes all the more the unusually sorrowful occasion and the fact that everything is changed for the worse on this sad day. Before the closing dirge is read, the Reader announces the number of years passed since the destruction of the Temple. The solemnity and the sadness of the occasion are made more vivid on the following day when even the *Sefer* is covered in black, and the beautiful silver bells that normally adorn the scroll are replaced with two black coverings.

Congregation Shearith Israel has held services on Thanksgiving day without interruption since 1781. ☐

ETHIOPIAN HEBREW CONGREGATION and the COMMAND-MENT KEEPER'S CONGREGATION, 1 West 123rd St., *(7th Ave. IRT to 125th St.)*. The congregants claim to be Ethiopian Hebrews who trace their descent to Solomon and Sheba, and who observe *kashruth* and circumcision. As the congregation is unique, so is the synagogue. On the front wall near the Ark hangs a photograph of one of the rabbis with a partially opened Torah in his arms. There is a stained glass window with two Stars of David; the star on top has an eye in the center, while the lower one has a pointing hand. A plaque on a side wall pays honor to the Rev. Matthew and identifies him as "Chief Rabbi of the Ethiopian Hebrews of the Western Hemisphere." The order was founded 46 years ago with eight people. Ethiopian Hebrews now claim to number 350,000 throughout the Western Hemisphere. On the same wall there is a mizrach, a paper with numerous drawings representing a variety of Bible stories. People from all over the world come to see the synagogue and take part in the services, which start mid-morning on Saturdays. The congregation calls itself Orthodox. Men and women sit separately, the first three rows being reserved for men. The Philips' Hebrew Prayer Book, used by many Orthodox congregations, is also used here. Services are conducted in Hebrew and English. The congregation has a choir, composed of both men and women. The women in the choir are all dressed in white with royal blue headdresses. The Hebrew word for Zion is embroidered on their garments, and some of them wear the *Magen David*.

The service itself is interesting. After the opening prayer and response in Hebrew, the prayers are recited antiphonally in English, the rabbi chanting a portion of a sentence and the congregants responding with the following portion, at a quick pace. Instead of ending the prayers with "Amen," the congregants chant fervently, "Halleluyah, Amen!" The chants are punctuated with notes from the piano, which has a harpsichord attachment to give it the effect of an organ. The prayers alternate with hymns sung by the choir. The high point comes when the Torah is read. In Orthodox and Conservative synagogues seven men are called up to the Torah on Saturday mornings; each one recites the opening blessing, the Reader then reads a portion of the Torah, after which each man recites the closing blessing. At the Commandment Keepers' Congregation, however, there is no limit to the number of men who are called up. The rabbi announces their names and tribes, and each man says both blessings as he is called up. The rabbi assigns the tribes, unless the man has already been assigned a tribe or known whether he is a Levi or a Cohayn (generally the tribes mentioned are limited to Levi, Judah, Reuben, Naphtali, and Simeon). Male visitors will be able to go up, too, since after the male members of the Congregation have been called up, the rabbi asks visitors, "Would any of you gentlemen like to be called up? You have that privilege." After all of the men say their blessings, one of the rabbis reads an entire section of the Torah. Then the Torah Scroll is rolled up, tied, and covered. With the Torah in his arms, the Chief Rabbi leads all of the male congregants in a march around the synagogue and everybody sings hymns and claps his hands. After the Torah is put back in the Ark, the rabbi addresses the congregation. Occasionally he is interrupted with shouts of "Halleluyah," "Holy G-d," and "Halleluyah, Amen." After the rabbi's sermon, the mourner's *kaddish* is recited, not by the mourners alone, but by the entire congregation. The rabbi explains: "This is an example of united prayer. We hope that someday there will be united brotherhood." To which the congregation responds, "Halleluyah, Amen!"

The principal beliefs of the Royal Order of Ethiopian Hebrews were codified by Rabbi Matthew and published under the title: *The Twelve Principles of the Doctrines of Israel with Scriptural Proof* about 1940 in the minute book of the Commandment Keepers. This book also includes the curriculum of the Ethiopian Hebrew Rabbinical College and an article, "Anthropology of the Ethopian Hebrews." □

SOCIETY OF JEWISH SCIENCE, Steinway Hall, 113 W. 57th St., holds services every Sunday at 11 a.m. Organ music is played until all are seated. The Reader recites the *Borchu* in Hebrew and the congregants respond; the same procedure is then followed in English. The *Shma* is recited in unison, after which Deuteronomy VI, 4-10 is read in English. Members rise to sing a hymn from the Jewish Science service pamphlet, accompanied by a piano. There is an exposition of a Psalm by the leader, followed by a piano solo and a lecture by the leader on a topic of religious significance. Following this, the group is asked to repeat aloud the following affirmations:

1. "The G-d Consciousness in me expresses itself in health, in

calmness, in peace, in power, and in happiness";

2. "I am calm and cheerful; I hate no one; I envy no one; there is no worry or fear in me; I trust in G-d all the time." An oral exposition by the leader follows each affirmation. A healing period of silence follows the affirmations. The congregants are told to relax, close their eyes, and to concentrate on the one thing they need most. They are told to present a mental picture of this request to G-d. During the healing period there is complete silence. The healing period usually lasts seven or eight minutes and is the outstanding feature of the service. The remainder of the service consists of the singing of another hymn, a discourse by the leader on Judaism, a collection to further the work of the Jewish Science group, the recitation of *kaddish* when the entire congregation is asked to rise, and the playing of organ music as the congregants leave the hall. The entire service lasts about one hour. During the service an Ark containing a Torah Scroll is on the stage of the hall, but it is never opened.

The Society of Jewish Science was founded in 1922 by Rabbi Morris Lichtenstein. Born in Lithuania in 1889, he was raised in an atmosphere of strict Orthodoxy. He came to the United States when he was 17 and enrolled at the Hebrew Union College-Jewish Institute of Religion in Cincinnati. In 1922, he formed the Society to end the movement of Jews to Christian Science, by showing that what they were searching for was available to them in Judaism. Jewish Science preaches that there is no conflict between their beliefs and medicine. "Medical science can effect cures for some diseases; prayer and correct thinking can effect cures for others." They do not claim to be a new faith or creed but an attempt to reawaken the Jewish consciousness in each Jewish person; it draws its material solely from Jewish sources. Among the ten fundamentals of Jewish Science are these: Prayer, when properly offered, never goes without answer; the individual must keep calm at all times, be cheerful, seek to eliminate anger and hate from his heart and not envy others; worry and fear destroy men, and they must never have a place in anyone's psychology; trust in G-d's goodness is to be cultivated; death is not an end to life but merely a state in the development of the human spirit; and G-d is the source of health, and He heals. □

NEW YORK SOCIETY FOR THE DEAF, 344 E. 14th St., conducts worship services in the sign language during the High Holy Days and one Sabbath each month.

LIBRARIES AND MUSEUMS

THE JEWISH MUSEUM of the Jewish Theological Seminary of America, 5th Ave. at 92nd St., is open from noon to 5 p.m., Mondays through Thursdays and from 11 a.m. to 6 p.m., Sundays; Thursday evenings from 7 to 9 o'clock; closed Friday and Saturday.

Starting in 1904 with a collection of 26 ceremonial objects donated by Judge Mayer Sulzberger, the Jewish Museum has become the repository of the largest and most comprehensive collection of Jewish ceremonial objects in the world. First housed on Morningside Heights, the museum moved to its present location on New York's "Museum Row," in 1947, after Mrs. Frieda Warburg, widow of the prominent banker, presented her six-story mansion to the Jewish Theological Seminary of America as a "tribute to the men of my family, my father (Jacob H. Schiff), my husband, and my brother Mortimer, who each in his own way has done so much to build up the Seminary toward its present effective usefulness."

Before entering the museum itself, the visitor can see a sculpture garden and a wing, and the Albert A. List Building, which enables the museum to mount many more major exhibitions than it had in the past. The first floor has a lobby and large exhibition area; a large gallery, which is occasionally used as an auditorium, is on the second floor; the third floor has three exhibition galleries and a storage area. The Tobe Pascher Workshop, where contemporary Jewish ceremonial objects are made, is in the basement.

Among the most interesting items on display are a predominantly blue mosaic wall from a 16th century Persian synagogue; a 17th century gold *kiddush* cup; the "Friedberg Tower"—an unusually fine silver spice container of the 16th century; a large wooden Chanukah Menorah made by a boy in a concentration camp; a Torah Scroll made of deerskin; a spice container of silver filigree; several unique Torah Arks; a Torah Ark curtain with the representation of the vision of the Prophet Zechariah; a Chanukah lamp in the form of a richly decorated Torah Ark; a pewter Chanukah lamp; a *shofar* in the shape of a fish with an open mouth; a Torah wrapper, painted on linen, with glass pearls; a curtain for the Ark, embroidered on a net, from the synagogue of Pitigliano, Italy; marriage contracts *(ketubot)*; panels of the famous frescoes of Dura Europos, Syria; mosaics from ancient synagogues; a variety of Torah crowns, breastplates, and pointers. The museum's collection of Jewish medals is the largest and most comprehensive ever assembled, and the Harry Stein Collection of ancient Hebrew coins is the most outstanding private collection of its kind outside of Israel. The Jewish Museum conducts a varied program of lectures, concerts, courses, and guided tours. ☐

YIVO INSTITUTE FOR JEWISH RESEARCH, 1048 5th Ave., is the only secular Jewish research institute in the world outside of Israel. Founded in Vilna in 1925, YIVO was moved to New York in 1940 to escape the ravages of the Nazis. It is dedicated to the scholarly exploration of historical, sociological, economic, literary, linguistic, and other phases of Jewish life. YIVO maintains the world's largest collection of original documentary material on Jewish life. There are an estimated three million letters, photographs, and manuscripts ranging from Theodor Herzl's diary to former top-secret documents of the Ministry of Foreign Affairs of the Third Reich. The YIVO library has over 300,000 volumes, and the museum contains the most extensive and complete collection of material on the Yiddish theatre, including thousands of photographs, announcements, manuscripts, music sheets, and other memorabilia. Recognized as the world center for Yiddish research, YIVO has the most complete record of Jewish life in Eastern Europe. Among its collections are the S. Niger Collection, the H. Leivick Collection, the Dr. Khayim Zhitlowsky Collection, the Kalman Marmor Collection, the Dr. Joseph Rosen Collection, the HIAS-HICEM Collection, the Joint Reconstruction Collection, the collections of the Lodz and Vilna Ghettoes, the Vilna Collection, the so-called Berlin Collection, and the DP Collection. Among the specific items of interest are a tractate of the Talmud handwritten by Anshel Rothschild in 1722, which was handed down through five generations of Rothschilds; a handwritten manuscript of Sholom Aleichem that gives a rare insight into the technique of a literary genius; a once-secret Nazi document presented by the prosecution at the trial of Adolf Eichmann; 350 memoirs regarding the development of the American Jewish community today; a rare trilingual Jewish periodical published in the United States in 1871; a Bible printed in Mantua, Italy, in 1742; other materials on Eichmann and the Grand Mufti; the files of Rabbi Schneer Zalman Schneerson on the underground rescue activity of the Orthodox movement in Nazi-occupied France; the archives of Meyer Birman dealing with Jewish life in the Far East; the personal archives of the philosopher Dr. Horace M. Kallen; and the archives of the National Conference of Jewish Communal Service. YIVO not only provides documents and other items for researchers and scholars, it also engages in original research, the results of which are printed and circulated, and conducts a training program for students. Visitors and scholars are welcome at the Atran Exhibition Room and the library reading and reference room.

THE NEW YORK PUBLIC LIBRARY, Jewish Division, 5th Ave. at 42nd St., has more than 140,000 volumes dealing with Jewish subjects, including medieval and modern literature, Talmudic and *midrashic* writings and commentaries. The Division has one of the largest collections of Jewish periodicals ever assembled in this country, as well as extensive files of the more important Yiddish newspapers, both American and foreign, available on microfilm. There are also early Hebrew books—the first one printed in 1475 in Hebrew characters. Available also is literature on the Yiddish theatre both here and abroad, and the history and lore of Jewish people in all parts of the world. The Jewish Division was started in November, 1897, when Jacob H. Schiff, the noted philanthropist, donated $10,000 for the purchase of Semitic literature. The A.M. Bank Collection, which incorporated the Leon Mandelstamm Library and the Meyer Lehren Collection, was purchased, and this was the nucleus from which one of the finest collections of Judaica developed.

The Division started as a reference library for scholars. It became a multi-service, multi-level archive used by people from all over the world. Jewish philanthropists, along with others, helped build up the New York Public Library to its present size. Jacob Schiff, Dr. Albert A. Berg, and Louis M. Rabinowitz were among the library's major benefactors. Their names and others are inscribed on the marble pylons in the library's main lobby. In 1940 Dr. Berg, an outstanding surgeon, donated his collection of English and American literature to the library as a memorial to his brother, Dr. Henry W. Berg. Later he bought and donated the collection of W. T. H. Howe of Cincinnati, and then added, by joint gift, the collection of Owen D. Young. The Berg Collection now has more than 50,000 items, dating from the end of the 15th century. These include two of the eleven known copies of Edgar Allan Poe's first published work, *Tamerlane*. Dr. Berg left the library an endowment of $2 million for the care, servicing, and expansion of his original gifts. Portraits of the Bergs are in the Berg Memorial Room. Jacob Schiff gave, in addition to his other contributions, 317 James Tissot's Old Testament paintings. Louis M. Rabinowitz, New York manufacturer, gave the library 79 incunabula (works printed before 1500). The widow of Simon Guggenheim, the industrialist and former senator from Colorado, donated 1,000 19th and 20th century books, letters, and documents, among them a letter from Theodore Roosevelt, written in 1915, expressing some misgivings about the ultimate success of the women's suffrage movement. □

ZIONIST ARCHIVES AND LIBRARY of the Palestine Foundation Fund (Keren Hayesod), 515 Park Ave., is located in the Jewish Agency for Israel building. Here are more than 50,000 books and pamphlets on Israel, the Middle East, Zionism, and Jewish life. The archival collection consists primarily of materials on American Zionism. There are thousands of photographs, slides, films, filmstrips, and microfilms; in addition, there are hundreds of recordings, including Israeli folk music and symphonic scores. The Zionist Archives and Library, which also serves as an information service, has the Herzl, Gottlied, Brandeis, DeHaas, and Friedenwald Collections, as well as the collection of the late President Franklin D. Roosevelt on material related to Zionism.

NEW YORK UNIVERSITY LIBRARY OF JUDAICA AND HEBRAICA, 2 Washington Sq. N. The library contains the Mitchell M. Kaplan Collection of manuscripts, incunabula, and rare editions, including a treatise on Cabbalah; the *Book of Cusari* by Yehuda-ha-Levi, printed in 1594 in Venice; an encyclopedia on Jewish rituals and customs printed in 1489 in Lisbon; Maimonides *Guide to the Perplexed*; and a 13th century manuscript of a Passover *Haggadah*. Also: the William Rosenthal and Israel Matz Collections of Current Judaica and Hebraica; the Lagarde Collection; the Abraham I. Katsh Collection of microfilms of rare Hebrew manuscripts in the Soviet Union—the only collection of its kind in the United States; an exceptional collection of German Judaica; several ancient Torahs, one of which is 3 feet wide and 50 feet long; and the David Kaufmann Collection of Rare Manuscripts—some dating back to the 11th century. There is a portrait of Albert Einstein in the library showing the famous scientist seated in characteristic attire—a sweater and open-collared shirt; with a pencil in his right hand and papers on his lap. The painting was done from life by the artist, Max Westfield.

MORRIS RAPHAEL COHEN LIBRARY of City College, (the north end of the South Campus), 135th St. between St. Nicholas Terrace and Convent Ave. The $3,500,000, three-story, glass-enclosed library is named for the noted philosopher and member of the college's faculty for more than 30 years. It is of a contemporary design of glass blocks and wide expanses of beige masonry outside and subdued tones and simple decor inside. It provides shelf space for the college's collection of 850,000 volumes, including Dr. Cohen's personal library and papers. The Davidson Collection of Judaica contains 7,000 volumes in Hebrew, Yiddish, French, German, Italian, Arabic, and Aramaic. There are many rare works of medieval Hebrew poetry and Talmudic, *midrashic*, and rabbinic lore, liturgy, rites, and folklore. Professor Israel Davidson, for whom the collection is named, was an alumnus of the college and a professor of Medieval Hebrew Literature at the Jewish Theological Seminary from 1905-1939.

BUTLER LIBRARY, THE JUDAICA COLLECTION, Columbia University, 116th St. and Broadway. This collection includes the Temple Emanu-El Library of Biblical and Rabbinic Literature, presented to the university by Emanu-El in 1892, and the library of Professor Richard Gottheil. There are 6,000 Hebrew books and pamphlets, 1,000 manuscripts, 28 incunabula, and 12,000 volumes of Judaica. The university has a three by five inch psalter printed in Hebrew in 1685 at Cambridge University, England. The psalter was used by Samuel Johnson at the graduation of the first seven candidates for bachelor's degrees at King's College on June 21, 1758. The Hebrew psalter is in the King's College Room, as is a 1708 edition of *The History of the Jews, from Jesus Christ to the Present Time*. The Professor Edward A. Seligman Collection on Economics and the Spinoza Collection are in the Special Collection Department of Butler Library. (For information on the libraries of the Jewish Theological Seminary, Yeshiva University, and the New York branch of the Hebrew Union College-Jewish Institute of Religion, see PLACES TO VISIT—SEMINARIES.)

MUSEUM OF THE CITY OF NEW YORK, 5th Ave. at 104th St., has a tablet, at the right of the entrance, dedicated to James Speyer, German Jewish philanthropist and moving spirit in the creation of the museum. Speyer selected as the museum's motto the following quotation from Lincoln: "I like to see a man proud of the place in which he lives. I like to see a man live so that his place will be proud of him." In the north wing on the first floor there is a portrait of Moses Levy (1665-1728). The museum displays the work of Myer Myers, well-known early American Jewish silversmith. In addition, there is a portrait of Isaac Moses, prominent Jewish merchant and ardent patriot who fitted out, at his own expense and in association with Robert Morris, eight privateersmen to prey on British commerce, and who helped bolster American credit at a crucial point during the American Revolution.

HISPANIC SOCIETY OF AMERICA, Broadway between 155th and 156th Sts., has a tile with a Star of David glazed in white on a black and white background. The tile, made in Toledo, Spain, in the second half of the

15th century, hangs on the west wall of the museum's staircase. It was once part of the decoration in the synagogue of Toledo, which, after the Jews were expelled in 1492, became the Church of El Transito. The museum also has a 15th century Hebrew Bible inscribed in Spanish. The Hispanic Society was established to advance the study of the Spanish and Portuguese languages, literature, history, and culture.

METROPOLITAN MUSEUM OF ART, 5th Ave. between 80th and 84th Sts. Jewish men and women have played an important role in the museum's development. In addition to the bequests left to the museum by Amelia B. Lazarus, Jacob H. Schiff, and Stanley A. Cohen, the museum's priceless collections have been enriched by a number of Jewish patrons of the arts, among them Benjamin Altman, Michael Friedsam, George Blumenthal, who gave $1,000,000 to the museum, and was its president from 1934 until his death in 1941. Among the Jewish artists whose works are in the museum are Jacob H. Lazarus, Josef Israels, Henry Mosler, Max Lieberman, Lewis Cohen, Bernard Karfiol, and Leon Kroll. Jacob Epstein, Isadore Konti, and Maurice Sterne are among the Jewish sculptors whose works are represented. ●The Robert Lehman Wing houses the multi-million dollar collection of modern art assembled by the late banker and bequeathed to the Museum. One room in the wing was taken intact from Lehman's townhouse.

NEW YORK PUBLIC LIBRARY, Aguilar Branch, 174 E. 110th St., is an outgrowth of the library established by Jacob Schiff and the 92nd Street YM & YWHA. It is named for Grace Aguilar, Anglo-Jewish novelist of the 19th century. Much of her writing was devoted to explanations of Jewish ritual. She placed particular emphasis on a knowledge of Jewish history and the Hebrew language. Her major works include *The Magic Wreath, The Vale of Cedars*, and *The Women of Israel*. For some time before her death at the youthful age of 31, she was mute. Her last words, expressed in sign language, were: "Though He slay me, yet will I trust in Him" (Job 13:15).

NEW YORK PUBLIC LIBRARY, Lincoln Center Branch, 111 Amsterdam Ave., has the Benedict Stambler Archive of Recorded Jewish Music—a collection of some 4,000 Jewish phonograph records. The collection is part of the Rodgers and Hammerstein Archives of Recorded Sound. Included is a disc of Sholom Aleichem reading from his own work. Mr. Stambler devoted the last 20 years of his life to the gathering, preservation, and dissemination of Jewish music on records.

NEW YORK PUBLIC LIBRARY, Nathan Straus Young Adult Library of Donnell Branch, 20 W. 53rd St., is named for the philanthropist and pioneer advocate of pasteurized milk.

NEW YORK PUBLIC LIBRARY, Bloomingdale Branch, 150 W. 100th St., is named for Samuel Bloomingdale, department store owner and philanthropist.

YESHIVA UNIVERSITY MUSEUM, housed in Yeshiva University's Mendel Gottesman Library, at the Main Center, 2520 Amsterdam Ave., is devoted to Jewish art, architecture, and history. Endowed by Erica

and Ludwig Jesselson, the Museum's salient feature is its permanent display
of scale models of "Synagogues Through the Centuries," which includes 10
synagogue models ranging from the 3rd to the 19th centuries and important
for their style and place in history. Other permanent features are a
reproduction of the frescoes found in the ruins of the Dura-Europos
Synagogue, 3rd century, Syria; a 17-foot long electronic map tracing the
migration of Jews since the time of Abraham; and two audio-visual shows,
"The Story of the Synagogue" and "The Story of the Temple." Also on exhibit
are the Torah Scroll of the Baal Shem Tov; the first book of Psalms written in
Hebrew and printed in Barbados, 1742; a book by Menasseh ben Israel, the
renowned 17th century Dutch rabbi; and other historic religious appurtenances and artifacts.

NEW YORK ACADEMY OF SCIENCES, 2 East 63rd St., has a
bust of Dr. Paul Ehrlich, German-Jewish scientist, in its lobby. Dr. Ehrlich,
who was noted for his discoveries in immunology and antibiotics, won the
Nobel Prize in 1908.

LEO BAECK INSTITUTE LIBRARY, 129 E. 73rd St., specializes
in material about Jewish life and history in Germany, Austria, and other
Germanic-speaking areas of Europe. It houses unique collections of documents, books, manuscripts, photographs, letters, memoirs, clippings, and
personal papers about the great and near-great among German Jewish
authors, scientists, rabbis, communal leaders, statesmen, industrialists, and
public figures.

AMERICAN MUSEUM OF NATURAL HISTORY, Warburg Hall,
Central Park West at 79th St., which houses the "Man and Nature" exhibit,
is named for the noted Jewish philanthropist and banker. (see also
SEMINARIES AND OTHER INSTITUTIONS OF HIGHER LEARN-
ING, THE STATUE OF LIBERTY, and the Midtown section.)

HISTORIC JEWISH CEMETERIES

CHATHAM SQUARE CEMETERY, St. James Place below
Chatham Sq. A plot of land in lower Manhattan which is the famous cemetery
of Congregation Shearith Israel. A plaque over the gateway to the cemetery
has the following inscription:

This Tablet Marks What Remains of
The First Jewish Cemetery
In the United States
Consecrated in the Year
1656
When It Was Described as
"Outside the City"

The tablet refers to the cemetery that was located on a plot of ground
granted to the Jews of New Amsterdam by Peter Stuyvesant in answer to a
petition by Abraham de Lucena, Salvador Dandrada, and Jacob Cohen

Henricques. The site of this cemetery can no longer be identified.

The ground of Chatham Square Cemetery, known also as the New Bowery Cemetery and the Oliver St. Cemetery, was acquired in 1682. Benjamin Bueno de Mesquita, who died in 1683, was the first person to be buried there.

The cemetery played a part in the American defense of New York in 1776. General Charles Lee placed several guns in what he called the "Jew Burying Ground," and the tablet over the gateway states that the cemetery "during the War of the Revolution" was "fortified by the patriots as one of the defenses of the city." Among the graves in the cemetery are those of 18 Revolutionary soldiers and patriots. These include Hayman Levy and Jonas Phillips, signers of the Non-Importation Resolutions of 1770; Isaac Moses, signer of bills of credit for the Continental Congress; and Gershom Mendes Seixas, minister of Congregation Shearith Israel, who closed the synagogue and removed the scrolls of the Torah to Stratford, Connecticut, when British forces occupied New York.

A second cemetery of the Spanish and Portuguese Synagogue is located in a small enclosed triangle of land on 11th Street, a few yards east of 6th Avenue. It was consecrated on February 27, 1805, as Beth Haim Sheni (The Second Cemetery). Shortly after the yellow fever scourge of 1822, it became the only Jewish cemetery in New York that could be used. In 1830, the city opened 11th Street to development and condemned the entire burial ground. The congregation successfully petitioned the city for that part of the cemetery that would not interfere with the street. Among the few still buried in this cemetery is the American soldier and patriot, Ephraim Hart, who was one of the founders of the New York Stock Exchange. □

BETH HAIM SHELISHI, West 21st St., west of 6th Ave. is the third Spanish and Portuguese cemetery. Consecrated on August 17, 1829, the graveyard served Congregation Shearith Israel for almost 22 years. Mordecai Manuel Noah, the playwright and colorful character who tried to found a Jewish colony on Grand Island in the Niagara River, was one of the last persons to be buried here. Also interred here are three soldiers of the American Revolution. On Memorial Day each year, the graves of the Revolutionary soldiers and patriots in all three cemeteries are decorated with the American flag. (See also Brooklyn and Queens.)

SEMINARIES AND OTHER INSTITUTIONS OF HIGHER LEARNING

Rabbi Isaac Elchanan Theological Seminary, Amsterdam Ave. and 186th St., (Orthodox), is thought of by many as Yeshiva University. However, Yeshiva University, which is the nation's oldest and largest university under Jewish auspices, has 17 schools and divisions of which the seminary is one. At the Main Center are the seminary, the Yeshiva High School, Yeshiva College for Men, Teachers Institute for Men, the Bernard Revel Graduate School, Harry Fischel School for Higher Jewish Studies, Cantorial Training Institute, and the Graduate School of Science. The other schools are located elsewhere in Manhattan, The Bronx, and Brooklyn.

In September, 1886, a small group of immigrants on the Lower East Side enrolled their children in America's first Jewish day school—Yeshiva Eitz Chaim. Classes were held in a second-floor loft on East Broadway. Ten years later, the Rabbi Isaac Elchanan Theological Seminary was established, and this, too, was a first—the first school on the American continent for the advanced study of Torah. In 1915, Eitz Chaim became part of the seminary setup, and four years later was approved by the New York State Board of Regents as the Eitz Chaim Talmudical Academy, which combined a high school education with the study of the Talmud. Thus Eitz Chaim became the first high school in America under Jewish auspices.

In 1921, the institution moved to larger quarters and merged with the Teachers Institute, which had been founded by the Mizrachi Organization of America in 1917. In 1928, Yeshiva College was established—the first college of liberal arts and sciences under Jewish auspices in America. That same year Yeshiva moved to uptown Manhattan. In 1945, the state of New York granted Yeshiva university status. □

YESHIVA UNIVERSITY, 500 West 185th St. The historic Main Building was erected in 1928 at the Main Center at a cost of $2,500,000. It is one of the outstanding examples of Byzantine architecture in Greater New York. Its towering dome has become an upper-Manhattan landmark. ●In the Main Building is the Nathan Lamport Auditorium, whose architectural motifs include twelve pillars representing the Tribes of Israel and other themes. ●The Harry Fischel Synagogue-Study Hall is also in the Main Building. ●The Mendel Gottesman Library, which has a large collection of Judaica, is on the second floor of the Main Building. This library is especially noted for its rabbinic literature. ●The Yeshiva University Museum occupies the ground level of the library, with approximately 4,000 square feet of space devoted to the exhibition area. (See also MUSEUMS and LIBRARIES.) ●Pollack Library, south of the Main Building, is one of the university's five principal library collections. Other collections are the Aaron Etra Collection of historical, synagogal, and rabbinical documents; the Nathan Isaac, Gitelson, and Peter Wiernik Collections; the Kraus Library; the library of the late Julius Streicher, member of the Nazi's Third Reich government; and the Hershey Collection of Versailles Conference Papers which represents 5,000 documents related to the peace treaties of World War I. ●Wurzweiler School of Social Work, 55 5th Ave., is named for Gustav Wurzweiler. ●Benjamin F. Cardozo Law School, 55 5th Ave., named in honor of the late justice of the Supreme Court, is the first law school named for a Jew. □

HIGH SCHOOL RESIDENCE HALL of Yeshiva University, Amsterdam Ave. and 185th St., is a $3,500,000 seven-story residence hall and student center. ●At the corner of Amsterdam Ave. and 185th St. stands the classroom-administration building. Built at a cost of $3,000,000, it has 35 modern classrooms that serve the seminary and colleges, graduate schools, and institutes at the Main Center. This building also contains an electronic language laboratory that can transmit foreign language tapes to students in three different languages simultaneously while broadcasting hi-fi tapes to the music study room on another floor. ●The graduate center and other facilities are at 55 5th Ave.

LEAH AND JOSEPH RUBIN RESIDENCE HALL of Yeshiva University, Amsterdam Ave. and 185th St., serves as a dormitory for college students. Here is the university's cafeteria which serves more than 10,000 meals a week. ●The residence hall faces the Danciger Campus, traditional site of the university's June graduation ceremonies.

STERN COLLEGE FOR WOMEN and TEACHERS INSTITUTE FOR WOMEN of Yeshiva University, 253 Lexington Ave. The building houses laboratories, lecture halls, an auditorium, library, classrooms, and a cafeteria which is open to the public for lunches.

THE JEWISH THEOLOGICAL SEMINARY OF AMERICA, Broadway between 122nd and 123rd Sts. (Conservative). The library has one of the largest collections of Judaica in the world. Housed temporarily in a pre-fab construction, in what was the Seminary quadrangle (the Tower stacks having been destroyed in the April, 1966 fire), the library will be located in a new academic building.

On either side of the main entrance are carved the names of Sabato Morais and Solomon Schechter. In January, 1886, Morais, an Italian-born Jew who succeeded Isaac Leeser as rabbi of the historic Mikveh Israel Congregation in Philadelphia, and six other rabbis issued a call for "an institution in which Bible and Talmud shall be studied to a religious purpose." This led to the founding, on January 2, 1887, of the Jewish Theological Seminary in the Nineteenth Street Synagogue of Congregation Shearith Israel. Morais became the seminary's first president and professor of Bible. Schechter, a world-renowned Jewish scholar, was the seminary's president from 1902 until his death in 1915. Under Schechter's guidance, the seminary acquired a reputation for leadership and scholarship throughout the world. One of the accomplishments Schechter is particularly famous for is his discovery, in Cairo, Egypt, of a *Genizah* (a special hiding-place where unusable but forbidden-to-be-destroyed Hebrew books, letters, and documents are kept) that had some 100,000 manuscripts and fragments which had been buried for centuries. Schechter's portrait hangs in the seminary's dining hall. The names of other founders and leaders of the seminary are carved on the pier caps of the columns of the arcade leading into the inner court. These include Mayer Sulzberger, Morris Loeb, Abraham P. Mendes, Alexander Kohut, Mortimer L. Schiff, Joseph Blumenthal, Adolphus S. Solomons, Louis Marshall, Newman Cowen, and Sol M. Stroock.

A set of beautifully constructed wrought iron gates guard the large, vaulted passageway leading through the main entrance. There is an inscription noting that "These gates were presented in 1934 by Mrs. Felix M. Warburg in memory of her parents, Jacob H. and Therese Schiff." The inscription is flanked by the Lions of Judah. Directly above the center of the gate is a solidly forged Menorah, copied from one found on the Arch of Titus in Rome, which was a contemporary replica of the Menorah used in the Temple in Jerusalem. ●The Harriet and Mortimer M. Marcus Rare Book and Manuscript Room has 10,000 rare books, 8,000 manuscripts, some 25,000 fragments from the *Genizah*, and thousands of notes, letters, and documents. There is a Chinese translation of one of Sholom Aleichem's books; a Hebrew edition of *Profiles in Courage*, autographed upside-down by the late President John F. Kennedy; a High Holiday *machzor* shaped to fit inside the sleeve of a toga; *The Long Megillah*, an inch-high Purim *megillah* that stretches out like a tape measure; manuscripts, fragments of manuscripts, and letters written in Maimonides' own handwriting; books used in concentration camps; the *Book of Esther* from one of the original Gutenberg Bibles; a Jewish *Code of Laws*, published in Italy in 1475, believed to be the oldest extant book printed in Hebrew; the *Almanac* of Abraham Zacuto (1440-1510), a celebrated Spanish-Jewish astronomer whose astronomical tables helped Columbus frighten the natives of what is now British Jamaica with a "permanent loss of moonlight," thus making them agree to sell the explorers food; Pentateuch leaves written in Egypt in the 10th century and fragments from the Prophets written in Persia; the first edition of the Pentateuch with Targum and Rashi, printed in Bologna in 1482; Avicentna's *Medical Encyclopedia*, printed in Naples in 1491-1492; a treatise on the plague, believed to be the only copy in existence, which was printed about 1510; the ancient French prayer book *Mahzor Vitry*, written in the 13th century; some manuscripts of the *Zohar*, predating the first edition; the first complete 15-volume set of the Babylonian Talmud with commentaries printed by Daniel Bomberg in Venice between 1520 and 1523; five books of Jewish interest from the libraries of Tsars Alexander III and Nicholas II and of the latter's son, Alexei, all bearing the insignia of the imperial dynasty; and other rare books, pamphlets, manuscripts, and prints. ●The Louis Ginzberg Microfilm Collection includes Judaica and Hebraica from the major libraries of the world.

The library has more than 250,000 volumes. Included are books of 16 languages that were transliterated in Hebrew characters: Arabic, English, French, German, Greek, Italian, Persian, Polish, Portuguese, Provencal, Samaritan, Spanish, Syriac, Tataric, Ukrainian, and Yiddish. The library grew from small beginnings. On the 70th birthday of Dr. Morais in 1893, it was decided to set up the Morais Library at the seminary. The library then owned about 1,000 volumes, to which was added the collection of Dr. David Cassel of Berlin. After Morais' death in 1897, the library received his collection of more than 700 volumes. When the seminary was reorganized in 1902, Judge Mayer Sulzberger of Philadelphia donated his collection of 2,400 rare volumes and almost 500 manuscripts. He later donated the library of the bibliophile, Solomon J. Halberstamm of Berlitz, Austria. In 1907, Jacob H. Schiff donated the collection of the bibliographer Moritz Steinschneider, 60 percent of which was lost in the 1966 fire. In 1921 when his son Mortimer L. Schiff gave the library the Israel Solomons Collection, the seminary library had become second only to the Anglo-Judaica collection in the British Museum. The seminary synagogue is an unusual place of interest. It is Conservative, but in many respects its services resemble an Orthodox service. Actually, it has been described as right-wing Conservative. The Reader and cantor face the Ark instead of the audience, and men and women sit separately. One week out of every year, the Seminary *sukkah*—which extends for a full city block—attracts many visitors, and is used by students, faculty members, etc. ●The Mathilde Schechter Residence Hall, 415 W. 120th St., the Seminary's first residence hall for non-rabbinical students, was made necessary by the growing enrollment of students seeking degrees in Jewish education and history. ☐

HEBREW UNION COLLEGE-JEWISH INSTITUTE OF RELIGION (New York Branch), 40 W. 68th St. (Reform). The campus, principal building, library, and museum of the Hebrew Union College-Jewish Institute of Religion are in Cincinnati, Ohio, where the institution was founded. The five-story structure in New York is the local branch of the HUC-JIR. Founded in 1922 as the Jewish Institute of Religion by Rabbi Stephen S. Wise, the school merged with the Hebrew Union College in 1950. ●In the lobby of the New York school are busts of the "Two Wise Men"—Rabbi Isaac Mayer Wise and Rabbi Stephen S. Wise. There is also a large auditorium. ●The Emil Hirsch-Gerson Levi Library on the fifth floor has approximately 75,000 volumes, including valuable Hebrew manuscripts; autographed manuscripts of Italian and German rabbis from the 16th to the 19th centuries; manuscripts and plays by Cantor Isaac Offenbach and a liturgical composition for the High Holy Days by his son, Jacques Offenbach; seven incunabula; 200 volumes of 16th century editions of Hebraica; the best modern Hebrew literature collection; a fine collection of scholarly periodicals from Europe, Israel, and the Jewish press of America; and proceedings and publications of early American Zionist societies. The library was begun in 1922 with Rabbi Stephen S. Wise's own library and that of his father. Added to these were the Brann Collection from the Jewish Theological Seminary of Breslau, part of the Kohut Library, and the Hirsch and Levi Collections. ●The Wise-iana collection has personal letters and documents of Rabbi Stephen S. Wise, including addresses, articles, sermons, statements, and copies of Rabbi Wise's letters to Presidents Woodrow Wilson and Franklin D. Roosevelt. ●The New York branch of HUC-JIR also has a School of Education and Sacred Music for the training of teachers, principals, and cantors.

HERZLIAH-JEWISH TEACHERS SEMINARY, 69 Bank St., consists of the Jewish Teachers Seminary and People's University—the only Yiddish teachers college in America offering diplomas and the degree of Bachelor of Jewish Literature. There is also a Jewish music division training cantors, music teachers, and folk singers; a graduate division offering the degree of Doctor of Jewish Literature; and the training of men and women to teach Yiddish, Hebrew, and Jewish social studies in colleges and universities. ●The Horace Kallen Academy, a nondenominational junior and senior high school teaching English, Hebrew, and Yiddish under the Seminary's auspices, is a pioneering effort in Jewish education. ●The Jewish Teachers Seminary and People's University was established in 1918 and Herzliah Hebrew Teachers Institute in 1921. These strongholds of Yiddish and Hebrew culture combined in 1967, and in 1971 acquired their own building which also houses the Dr. Abraham and Ann Goodman Hebrew-Yiddish-English Library comprising over 40,000 volumes, including the Israel Matz Collection of Haskalah Literature.

NEW SCHOOL FOR SOCIAL RESEARCH, 66 West 12th St., is famous for its "University in Exile." The "University's" faculty was drawn from among the most brilliant scholars, and political and religious exiles from Nazi Germany. It was organized in 1934 by Dr. Alvin Johnson, president of the New School. Through the School's efforts, these renowned figures were rescued and given the opportunity of teaching in America. During the period from 1934 to 1941, scholars from many of the countries conquered by the Nazis were also brought over. The "University in Exile" was the nucleus of the school's Graduate Faculty of Political and Social Science. Endowment funds for this humanitarian effort were provided by Lucius N. Littauer and many other Jewish philanthropists. Dr. Horace Kallen, the well-known American philosopher, taught here for many years.

NEW YORK UNIVERSITY, Washington Sq. The University's graduate program in the Hebrew language, culture, and education is a unique course of studies for the training of teachers and community leaders in Hebraic studies. In 1933, the University introduced courses in modern Hebrew, and that marked the beginning of the Department of Hebrew Culture and Education, the first and only one of its kind in America. The department has both graduate and undergraduate courses. ●The Washington Square College of Arts and Sciences has its own program of Hebrew instruction. ●Courses in the Hebrew and Arabic languages are also taught in the Division of General Education and Extension Services—a non-credit division of the University. ●The Department of Hebrew Culture and Education sponsors summer sessions and summer workshops in Israel. ●The Jewish Culture Foundation, 2 Washington Sq. ●Murry and Leonie Guggenheim Foundation Institute for Dental Research, 339 E. 25th St. ●Samuel Rubin International Hall, 35 5th Ave. ●Salomon Brothers Center for the Study of Financial Institutions, 90 Trinity Pl. ●Weinstein Center for Student Living, 5 University Pl.

One of the founders of New York University in 1831 was Mordecai M. Noah, who was among the 168 prominent citizens who answered a call in 1830 to discuss the establishment of a university in New York "on a liberal and extensive foundation." ☐

LOEB STUDENT CENTER of New York University, Washington

Sq. South. This luxurious $5 million structure is sheathed in aluminum and glass except for a brick-enclosed auditorium wing jutting from the facade. A gift of $1 million toward the construction of the center was made by Mrs. Alan H. Kempner, and John L., Carl M., Jr., and Henry A. Loeb in memory of their parents. The 1,000-seat assembly hall is named the Eisner and Lubin Auditorium for Joseph I. Lubin and the late Joseph Eisner, business partners and alumni of the University.

NEW YORK UNIVERSITY-BELLEVUE MEDICAL CENTER, 550 1st Ave. The Goldberger Memorial Laboratory is named for Dr. Joseph Goldberger, who is noted for his work on pellagra. ●The Henry W. and Albert A. Berg Institute of Experimental Physiology, Surgery, and Pathology adjoins the building on 30th Street, east of 1st Avenue. The Institute's greenhouse is called the Enid A. Haupt Children's Garden, after its donor, Enid Haupt, editor and publisher of *Seventeen* magazine. The plants in the greenhouse are set on benches of graduated heights so that children or adults, in wheelchairs or standing, can work on them. There is a wading pool so designed that even children in wheelchairs can roll themselves to its edge and swing around to dabble their toes without assistance. A special feature is a long plant box, designed for blind children, containing cacti without spines and a patch of a variety of fragrant herbs. The greenhouse also has decorative birds and an aquarium. A children's pavilion at Bellevue was made possible by a $1 million gift from the William J. Wollman Foundation.

ROCKEFELLER UNIVERSITY, 1250 York Ave., one of the world's great medical and scientific institutions, has portraits of and memorial plaques to Dr. Simon Flexner, Dr. Phoebus Levine, and Dr. Samuel J. Meltzer. Flexner, a world-famous authority on epidemiology, was the first director of the Rockefeller Institute, out of which the university grew. Dr. Levine was a noted biologist, and Dr. Meltzer was a celebrated physiologist and pharmacologist. A number of the scientists at Rockefeller University who have won Nobel Prizes in medicine, chemistry, and physics were Jews.

PACE UNIVERSITY, Schimmel Center, Pace Plaza (in downtown Manhattan), is named for Michael Schimmel, who donated what is said to be the only theatre in this district.

COLUMBIA UNIVERSITY, Broadway between 116th and 124th Sts. In 1762, King's College, as Columbia University was then called, was in financial straits and launched a drive to raise £10,000. Phila Franks used her influence in England to obtain money for the struggling college and enlisted the support of her brother, Moses, a leading Philadelphia merchant. Together they raised £4,000. Since then, many Jewish citizens have played an extensive role in the development of the university. These include Gershom Mendes Seixas, one of the incorporators when King's College was reincorporated as Columbia College after the American Revolution, and a trustee from 1787-1815; Sampson Simson; Jesse and Isaac N. Seligman;

James Speyer; Adolph Lewisohn; Arthur Hays Sulzberger, publisher of *The New York Times;* and Herbert Bayard Swope, editor of *The New York World* in the 1920s. In 1887 Temple Emanu-El set up a fund for the salary of a professor of rabbinic literature. This led to the establishment of a Department of Semitics, which was first chaired by Professor Gustav Gottheil and later by his son, Professor Richard J. H. Gottheil.

EARL HALL, Columbia University, is the interfaith center where Jewish student organizations Seixas, Menorah, and the Jewish Graduate Society meet. A portrait of Rev. Gershom Mendes Seixas hangs in Earl Hall, with the following inscription:

Gershom Mendes Seixas
1745
Regent, University of the State of New York 1784-1815
Trustee of Columbia College 1787-1815
Minister of Congregation Shearith Israel

A required part of the fourth year's study at King's College was an intensive course in Hebrew grammar and Biblical Hebrew, and its first president, Samuel Johnson, knew Hebrew. The official seal of Columbia has the word *Adonai* in Hebrew in a triangular glory above the head of a woman seated upon a throne with three nude children at her knees. To the left of her mouth is a ribbon with the Hebrew words *Ori El*—"G-d is my Light."

BARNARD COLLEGE, 606 W. 120th St. Annie Nathan Meyer, a relative of Emma Lazarus and Benjamin Cardozo, is credited with having originated the idea of a college for women under the wing of Columbia University. Her letter proposing the college, which appeared in the January 1, 1888 issue of *The Nation*, was called the "first broadside in the campaign for the founding of Barnard College." As a bride of 20, Annie Meyer pushed doorbells asking for contributions to the first Barnard College budget; her husband, Dr. Alfred Meyer, gave $500 and signed the lease for the original building at 343 Madison Ave. ●Annie Nathan Meyer Drama Library, 3rd Floor, Barnard Hall. Mrs. Meyer's portrait hangs in the College Parlor. An inscription beneath the portrait refers to Annie Meyer as the "Author of the Original Plea for the Establishment of Barnard College (and) Organizer of the First Board of Trustees." She served as a trustee of the college for over half a century. ●A portrait of Jacob Schiff also hangs in the College Parlor. The inscription beneath it states that he was the donor of Barnard Hall, trustee of the college from 1889-1897, and treasurer from 1889-1893. Barnard Hall has been referred to as "Jake." "Meet me on Jake" is a familiar phrase. A round tablet on the floor of the reception area of the Hall bears an inscription stating that the building is the gift of Jacob Schiff. ●Adele Lehman Hall-Wollman Library, Barnard College, was built from funds from the Wollman Foundation, an additional donation from Adele Lehman, and contributions from other individuals.

CITY UNIVERSITY OF NEW YORK, 139th St. and Convent Ave., has the largest enrollment of Jewish students in any institution of higher learning in the world. There are a number of memorials to Jewish individuals, among them Albert Einstein; Rubin Goldmark, composer; Gustave Hartman, jurist; Paul Klapper, educator and administrator; Mark Eisner, educator; Alfred Stieglitz, photographer; David B. Steinman, engineer and bridge builder; Felix S. Cohen, attorney, philosopher, and author; and Henry Leipziger, the pioneer of free public lectures. •There is also the Davis Center for Performing Arts.

CITY UNIVERSITY OF NEW YORK—BARUCH COLLEGE OF BUSINESS AND PUBLIC ADMINISTRATION, 17 Lexington Ave., is named after Bernard Baruch. There is a black granite park bench bordering the front of the library dedicated to him. •The Arthur M. Lamport House, 25 E. 22nd St., is a social and recreational center for Baruch students. The college also has a B'nai B'rith Hillel Foundation.

HUNTER COLLEGE, 695 Park Ave., has a valuable collection of Judaica. •Also: The Samuel J. Silberman School of Social Work, 129 E. 79th St., is named for a former president of the Federation of Jewish Philanthropies.

NEW YORK MEDICAL COLLEGE, 5th Ave. at 106th St., has the Sophie D. and William W. Cohen Research Building which was established through a $2 million bequest from the late Sophie D. Cohen, prominent philanthropist whose husband William has been a stockbroker and Congressman. In her will, she gave as the reason for her bequest, "It has come to my attention that the New York Medical College, Flower and Fifth Avenue Hospitals, in New York City, is an institution that does not discriminate against Jewish students and selects its student body from among those most qualified, and has among it a very large percentage of Jewish students who are fully capable and equipped, and that its faculty is likewise chosen upon the same principles."

FORDHAM UNIVERSITY AT LINCOLN CENTER, 140 W. 62nd St., has the Benjamin A. Javits Halls of Law. The buildings house the university's law school and law library. Benjamin Javits, a 1918 graduate of Fordham University Law School, is a well-known attorney and brother of Senator Jacob K. Javits.

TOURO COLLEGE, 30 W. 44th St., is the newest institution of higher learning in New York under Jewish auspices.

INFORMATION FOR JEWISH LIVING: JEWISH ORGANIZATIONS, THEIR FUNCTIONS AND SERVICES

For the benefit of persons wanting assistance, advice, or information, major organizations are listed in this section according to the area of service for which they are best known. This is not a complete listing. Readers wanting more information about Jewish organizations should consult the *American Jewish Year Book* or *American Organizations Directory.*

MAJOR COMMUNITY RELATIONS AGENCIES

AMERICAN JEWISH COMMITTEE—INSTITUTE OF HUMAN RELATIONS, 165 E. 56th St., is the national headquarters of this pioneer human relations organization. The American Jewish Committee pursues a varied program to combat bigotry, protect the civil and religious rights of Jews in all countries, and aims to improve human relations for all people everywhere. A wall inscription in the lobby reads: "Dedicated to man's understanding of his fellow man." ●The Blaustein Library is named in honor of the industrialist and philanthropist Jacob Blaustein and his wife. Its contents consists of over 40,000 volumes, numerous periodicals, information files, and special collections in the areas of the Committee's current concerns. Though primarily intended for staff use, it is open to qualified researchers and writers, on application. ●The William E. Wiener Oral History Library is an ever-expanding collection of tapes and transcripts which document the American Jewish experience during the 20th century. ●The Joseph M. Proskauer Room is a legal reference library, named after the eminent jurist. ●*Commentary*, the noted monthly opinion journal, and *Present Tense*, the quarterly journal of Jewish world affairs, have their offices here. ●The editorial office of the *American Jewish Year Book* is also located here.

THE ANTI-DEFAMATION LEAGUE OF B'NAI B'RITH, 315 Lexington Ave. The prime objective of this organization is "to counter the defamation of Jews and assaults on their status and rights." Its three major areas of operation are education, legislation, and monitoring of activities of harmful and potentially harmful organizations and individuals. It is also the headquarters of the American Federation of Jewish Fighters, Camp Inmates, and Nazi Victims. This building is also the headquarters of a variety of citywide and regional B'nai B'rith groups and the New York office of national B'nai B'rith projects.

JEWISH LABOR COMMITTEE, 25 E. 78th St., (in the Atran Center for Jewish Culture), seeks to combat anti-Semitism and racial and religious intolerance abroad and in the United States, in cooperation with organized labor.

METROPOLITAN NEW YORK COORDINATING COUNCIL ON JEWISH POVERTY, 21 E. 40th St.

NATIONAL JEWISH COMMUNITY RELATIONS ADVISORY COUNCIL, 55 W. 42nd St., is the national consultative, advisory, and coordinating council of nine national Jewish organizations and some 100 local Jewish councils.

STEPHEN WISE CONGRESS HOUSE, 15 E. 84th St., the former Ogden Reid home, is the headquarters of the American Jewish Congress. This organization fights all forms of racial and religious bigotry and works to defend religious freedom and the separation of church and state. The Martin Steinberg Cultural Center, dedicated in 1976, is separated from Congress

House by a garden. It is designed as a gathering place for young Jewish artists, writers, musicians, and film-makers. It contains the Charles and Bertie Schwartz Jewish Reading Room and Library and the Bernard L. Madoff Jewish Music Library, a screening room for film presentations, and exhibition space for work by Jewish artists and sculptors. Mrs. Betty Ford, wife of the President, participated in the dedication ceremony.

UNITED JEWISH COUNCIL OF THE LOWER EAST SIDE, 235 E. Broadway, is an umbrella organization for all Jewish organizations on the East Side.

AGENCIES RELATED TO ISRAEL

AMERICA-ISRAEL CULTURAL FOUNDATION, 4 E. 54th St., helps support about 40 cultural institutions in Israel. It conducts a two-way program of cultural exchange between the United States and Israel, and awards scholarships in the performing arts to talented young Israelis for study in Israel and abroad. Among the groups it supports are the Israel Philharmonic Orchestra, the Habimah Theatre, the Inbal dancers, Bezalel National Museum, and the Rubin Academy of Music. It conducts an annual "Music Under the Stars" program at Madison Square Garden featuring the top talent of America.

AMERICAN JEWISH JOINT DISTRIBUTION COMMITTEE (JDC), 60 E. 42nd St., organizes and administers welfare, medical, and rehabilitation programs and distributes funds to needy Jews overseas for relief and reconstruction; in Israel, JDC conducts an extensive program, Malben, which includes institutions to help the aged, youth, handicapped, and others.

AMERICAN JEWISH LEAGUE FOR ISRAEL, 595 Madison Ave., is dedicated to the welfare of Israel as a whole. It is not affiliated with any class or party.

AMERICAN MIZRACHI WOMEN, 817 Broadway, sponsors social service, child care, and vocational education programs in Israel—all conducted within the framework of traditional Judaism. It also conducts a program of cultural activities in America geared to spread Zionist ideals and strengthen traditional Judaism.

AMERICAN ZIONIST FEDERATION, 515 Park Avenue.

AMERICAN ZIONIST YOUTH FOUNDATION, 515 Park Avenue.

BNAI ZION, 136 E. 39th St., is a fraternal Zionist organization. It seeks to spread Hebrew culture in America; offers insurance and other benefits to its members; and sponsors settlements, medical clinics, and youth centers in Israel. The building is called the America-Israel Friendship Building.

BRITH ABRAHAM, 853 Broadway, is a fraternal order that sponsors Zionist activities and conducts a program of civic defense, mutual aid, and philanthropy.

CONSULATE GENERAL OF ISRAEL, 800 2nd Ave. The Israeli Mission to the United Nations is located here.

FARBAND HOUSE, 575 6th Ave., is the home of Farband—Labor Zionist Order—an organization that provides members and families with low-cost fraternal benefits, seeks to spread Jewish education and culture, and supports the State of Israel in keeping with the ideals of Labor Zionism.

HADASSAH, 50 W. 58th St., is the women's Zionist organization of America. The building is fronted by four archways. Its interior is blue and white and lined in part with Jerusalem marble.

THEODOR HERZL INSTITUTE, 515 Park Ave.

ISRAEL GOVERNMENT OFFICE, 850 3rd Ave., houses such Israeli government offices as the Office of the Economic Minister, Ministry of Defense, Treasury Department, etc.

JEWISH AGENCY FOR ISRAEL, INC., 515 Park Ave., administers funds for programs in Israel related to immigration, colonization, public health, housing, absorption, labor, and public works. Over the entrance of the building is a Menorah, symbol of modern Israeli and Jewish tradition and culture, which indicates the purpose to which the building is dedicated. The design of the Menorah, which also appears on Israel's tenth anniversary stamps and commemorative coins, is a modern adaptation of a Menorah carved upon the walls of the necropolis of Beth Shearim in the third or fourth century. The murals in the lobby of the building are the work of the Israeli artist Perli Pelzig, who uses the Italian *sgraffito* technique by which the picture is carved out of superimposed layers of cement and lime concrete of different colors. The first panel as you enter is devoted to *aliyah*, the Hebrew term for "ascent," which refers to immigration. In contrast to the other murals, the first panel is dominated by human faces and figures. The second panel depicts the life of the pioneers. The third panel depicts barren soil and stubborn rock giving way to flourishing farm communities. On the fourth panel are symbols of teeming cities and the ships that carry Israel's flag across the seven seas. Israel's artistic, spiritual, and scientific life is the subject of the fifth panel (on the lobby's eastern wall). Another panel by Perli Pelzig in the second-floor auditorium shows a group of young Israeli pioneers dancing the *hora*. Though set apart from the murals in the lobby, the 25-foot panel in a sense completes the cycle of a people who rose from the dispersion to redeem and rebuild itself and its ancient homeland and at last has learned to dance and sing again.

JEWISH NATIONAL FUND, 42 E. 69th St., raises money to buy, develop, and reclaim the soil of Israel.

LABOR ZIONIST ALLIANCE, 575 6th Ave., supports labor and progressive forces in Israel and works for the democratization of American Jewish community life, the expansion of civil rights, and the progress of organized labor. The Alliance includes organizations devoted to Labor Zionism.

NATIONAL COMMITTEE FOR LABOR ISRAEL (Israel Histadrut Campaign), Histadrut House, 33 E. 67th St. The committee, headquartered in the former Vanderbilt mansion provides funds for various social welfare and other services of Histadrut for the benefit of workers and immigrants. It works to promote an understanding among Americans of the aims and achievements of Israel labor. Of special interest to visitors are photo exhibits of Israeli personalities, lectures and films on Labor Israel, and an exhibit of the Afro-Asian Institute.

NATIONAL YOUNG JUDEA, 817 Broadway, is concerned with the development of a Jewish youth movement dedicated to Zionism and Israel and pledged to service on behalf of the Jewish people in America and Israel.

PALESTINE ECONOMIC CORPORATION, 511 5th Ave., promotes the economic development of Israel through investments.

PIONEER WOMEN, 315 5th Ave., is the women's Labor Zionist organization of America. It offers a program of social services to Israeli youth through agricultural training schools; to women and children through vocational training, kindergartens, and day nurseries; and to Arab women through special clubs and vocational training. It also provides guidance and training for new immigrant women.

POALE AGUDATH ISRAEL OF AMERICA, INC., 156 5th Ave., seeks to educate and prepare youth to become Orthodox *halutzim* in Israel.

RELIGIOUS ZIONISTS OF AMERICA *(Mizrachi-Hapoel Hamizrachi)*, 26 West 26th St., seeks to promote a close relationship between religious Jewry of America and Israel; supports, maintains, and establishes schools and yeshivas in Israel; establishes all-day schools in America; and fosters a youth program through the Bnei Akiva and Mizrachi Hatzair.

STATE OF ISRAEL BOND ORGANIZATION, 215 Park Ave., provides investment funds for the economic development of Israel through the sale of Israel bonds.

UNITED JEWISH APPEAL (national), 1290 Ave. of the Americas.

UNITED JEWISH APPEAL OF GREATER NEW YORK, 220 W. 58th St., conducts a joint campaign with Federation of Jewish Philanthropies.

WOMEN'S LEAGUE FOR ISRAEL, 1860 Broadway.

WORLD ZIONIST ORGANIZATION-American Section, 515 Park Avenue.

ZIONIST ARCHIVES AND LIBRARY, 515 Park Ave.

ZIONIST ORGANIZATION OF AMERICA, 4 E. 34th St., assists in the economic development of Israel and works to strengthen a sense of Jewish identity. The building is known as ZOA House.

ORGANIZATIONS WORKING FOR SOVIET JEWRY AND OTHER REFUGEES

GREATER NEW YORK CONFERENCE ON SOVIET JEWRY, 11 W. 42nd St.

HIAS, 200 Park Ave. S., is an international migration agency. Founded in 1884 as the Hebrew Immigrant Aid Society, the organization's original purpose was to provide shelter and assistance in finding employment for Jewish immigrants. It later became international in scope and character, covering all phases of immigrant aid. Since its founding, the organization has helped rescue more than three million Jews from oppression and persecution, resettling them in lands of freedom and security. They help settle Russian Jewish immigrants to the U.S., outside of New York, among other activities.

NATIONAL CONFERENCE ON SOVIET JEWRY, 11 W. 42nd St.

NEW YORK ASSOCIATION FOR NEW AMERICANS, 15 Park Row, settles Jewish immigrants in New York. The most recent immigrants have been from the Soviet Union.

STUDENT STRUGGLE FOR SOVIET JEWRY, 200 W. 72nd St.

THE JEWISH PRESS

ALGEMEINER JOURNAL, 404 Park Ave. South, is a Yiddish weekly.

AUFBAU, 2121 Broadway, is a paper for German Jews.

THE JEWISH DAILY FORWARD, 45 E. 33rd St. (originally on the Lower East Side), has a bust of Abraham (Ab) Cahan in the lobby. Cahan built the *Forward* from a journal of 6,000 readers to a modern, lively Yiddish newspaper with a paid circulation of 200,000. He was responsible for introducing many human interest features, one of which was the "Bintel Brief" (Bundle of Letters), which carried letters describing problems of the East European Jewish immigrants. The *Forward* was credited with being the principal force in organizing thousands of Yiddish-speaking immigrants in the needle trades union. It was also a chief instrument in the Americanization of the newcomers. Cahan was the author of the novel *The Rise of David Levinsky*. He had many critics and enemies and was an anti-Communist. The Workmen's Circle, a labor-oriented fraternal organization, is housed in this building.

JEWISH TELEGRAPHIC AGENCY, 165 W. 46th St., is a Jewish wire service serving not only Jewish newspapers in America, but throughout the world.

THE JEWISH WEEK, 3 E. 40th St., is one of the liveliest American Jewish weeklies in the country. Lists most important Jewish happenings in the city.

JEWISH EDUCATION AGENCIES

AMERICAN ASSOCIATION FOR JEWISH EDUCATION, 114 5th Ave., coordinates, promotes, and serves Jewish education nationally through community programs and special projects. The National Council on Jewish Audio-Visual Materials, which is sponsored by the AAJE, lists, evaluates, and originates audio-visual materials.

ATRAN CENTER FOR JEWISH CULTURE, 25 E. 78th St., is the headquarters for the women's division of the Jewish Labor Committee, the Central Yiddish Culture Organization, the Congress for Jewish Culture, Inc. and its World Bureau for Jewish Education, and the International Jewish Labor Fund. The Center has art exhibits from time to time and has a cafeteria serving home-cooked Jewish lunches. ●The William Green Human Relations Library contains published and unpublished material on human relations with special emphasis on labor's role in furthering civil rights.

BETH JACOB SCHOOLS, 142 Broome St.

BOARD OF JEWISH EDUCATION OF NEW YORK, 426 W. 58th St., is the city's central bureau of Jewish education, serving well over 700 schools. BJE works for better teacher training and higher standards in religious schools; sponsors the Jewish Theatre for Children, art exhibits, and music and dance festivals; publishes *World Over* and various booklets; promotes the study and appreciation of the Hebrew language, literature, and culture; conducts an intensive program of adult education; and researches and disseminates information about Jewish education. The BJE library is a specialized pedagogic collection for the use of teachers, principals, social group workers, and lay educational leaders. A trained librarian is available for information, reference, and bibliography work. An unusual illuminated mosaic wall decorates the BJE building. The wall, eight by twelve feet, consists of 20 Venetian glass mosaic panels. They were individually designed by students of 17 Jewish schools, unified through color and dedication to a central theme. The 20 panels offer a multi-colored panorama of Jewish history. From about the middle of March to the end of June there is an exhibit of children's artwork from all types of Jewish schools.

DOWNTOWN TALMUD TORAH, 149 E. Broadway.

HEBREW ARTS SCHOOL FOR MUSIC AND DANCE, 15 W. 65th Street.

THE HEBREW ARTS FOUNDATION, 120 W. 16th St. The building which houses this organization and Histadruth Ivrith of America, known as Hebrew House, has a central Hebrew library, an exhibition hall for Israeli books and art objects, and a Hebrew theatre.

HISTADRUTH IVRITH OF AMERICA, 120 W. 16th St., emphasizes the importance of Hebrew in Jewish life, culture, and education; conducts Hebrew courses for adults; publishes Hebrew books; sponsors the

Hebrew-speaking Masad camps, the Hebrew Academy; and Noar Ivri, a youth group on campuses and in cities throughout the United States.

MESIVTA TIFERETH JERUSALEM, 145 E. Broadway.

TORAH UMESORAH (The National Society for Hebrew Day Schools), 229 Park Ave. S., helps set up Jewish day schools throughout the country. It places teachers and administrators in these schools, conducts teaching seminars and workshops, and publishes textbooks and supplementary reading material.

YESHIVA HEICHAL HATALMUD OF TEL-AVIV, 217 E. Broadway.

YESHIVA HEICHAL HATORAH, 630 Riverside Drive.

YESHIVA OHR TORAH, 308 W. 75th St.

YESHIVA RABBI MOSES SOLOVEICHIK, 560 W. 185th St.

YESHIVA RABBI SAMSON RAPHAEL HIRSCH, 91 Bennett Avenue.

HILLEL FOUNDATIONS

BERNARD M. BARUCH COLLEGE, 144 E. 24th St.

CITY COLLEGE OF NEW YORK, 475 W. 140th St.

HUNTER COLLEGE, 49 E. 65th St. This Hillel unit is known as the Roosevelt Memorial because it is housed in the former home of President Franklin D. Roosevelt and his mother, Sara.

COMMITTEES FOR INSTITUTIONS OF HIGHER LEARNING

AMERICAN COMMITTEE FOR WEIZMANN INSTITUTE, 515 Park Ave.

AMERICAN FRIENDS OF BAR-ILAN UNIVERSITY, 641 Lexington Ave.

AMERICAN FRIENDS OF BEN-GURION UNIVERSITY OF THE NEGEV, 342 Madison Ave.

AMERICAN FRIENDS OF HAIFA UNIVERSITY, 500 5th Ave.

AMERICAN FRIENDS OF HEBREW UNIVERSITY, 11 East 69th St.

AMERICAN FRIENDS OF TEL AVIV UNIVERSITY, 342 Madison Ave.

AMERICAN SOCIETY FOR TECHNION-ISRAEL INSTITUTE OF TECHNOLOGY, 271 Madison Ave.

BRANDEIS UNIVERSITY HOUSE, 12 East 77th St.

MOUNT SINAI SCHOOL OF MEDICINE, 5th Ave. and 100th St.

FRATERNAL ORDERS

B'RITH ABRAHAM, 853 Broadway, was founded in 1883.

FREE SONS OF ISRAEL, 932 Broadway, was founded in 1849.

UNITED ORDER OF TRUE SISTERS, 150 West 85th St., was founded in 1846.

WORKMEN'S CIRCLE, 45 East 33rd St., a Yiddish-oriented fraternal order that was founded by East European immigrants in 1900, it now has many English-speaking branches. It sponsors secularist Yiddish schools for children, and a Jewish educational program. In its lobby is a 7½ foot high model of the sculpture to be created by Nathan Rapoport as a memorial to the Holocaust victims and the Warsaw Ghetto partisans. The sculpture is to be dedicated in 1978 on the 35th anniversary of the Warsaw Ghetto Revolt.

COORDINATING AGENCIES

CONFERENCE OF PRESIDENTS OF MAJOR AMERICAN JEWISH ORGANIZATIONS, 515 Park Ave.

COUNCIL OF JEWISH FEDERATIONS AND WELFARE FUNDS, 315 Park Ave. South, provides national and regional services in Jewish community organization, campaigns and interpretation, budgeting, planning for health and welfare, and cooperative action by Jewish welfare funds and federations in the United States and Canada.

COUNCIL OF JEWISH ORGANIZATIONS IN CIVIL SERVICE, 20 W. 43rd St.

FEDERATION OF JEWISH PHILANTHROPIES OF NEW YORK, 130 E. 59th St., is the "community chest" of Jewish-sponsored agencies in the metropolitan New York area, providing philanthropic support to 130 affiliated institutions. Federation occupies five floors of its 17-story modern office building, with 12 floors leased to commercial tenants. •The Warburg Room on the 7th floor has a 50-foot stained glass memorial wall and a scroll of remembrance. The memorial wall, designed by Irv Koons, one of the nation's top artists, and beautifully illuminated, symbolically depicts, in a series of seven nine-foot high panels, various aspects of Federation's philanthropic activity. The scroll of remembrance is of parchment and is engraved with the names of those who have left legacies to Federation. An electrical device turns the giant scrolls to reveal any one of the 2,600 inscribed names •Behind the Warburg Room is the Sulzberger Room, and on the sixth floor, there is the Madeleine Borg Meeting Room. •The Personal Service Department is, in effect, an information center for people who want to know which Federation agency offers the type of help they need. In a sense, Federation can be considered a miniature "Jewish City Hall," for communal planning, consideration of social welfare legislation, and religious affairs. Federation conducts a joint campaign with the United Jewish Appeal of Greater New York.

JEWISH COMMUNITY RELATIONS COUNCIL OF GREATER NEW YORK, 111 W. 40th St., is a citywide agency that seeks to unify the Jewish community's response to critical community relations problems.

VOCATIONAL AGENCIES

AMERICAN ORT FEDERATION (Organization for Rehabilitation Through Training), 222 Park Ave. South, trains Jewish men and women in the technical trades and agriculture, and organizes and maintains vocational training schools throughout the world.

BRAMSON ORT TRADE SCHOOL, 222 Park Ave. South, is the only specifically Jewish vocational training school in the United States. Its purpose is to teach needle-trade skills to Jewish refugees and other newcomers to enable them in obtaining employment.

FEDERATION EMPLOYMENT AND GUIDANCE SERVICE, 28 E. 21st St.

NATIONAL ASSOCIATION OF JEWISH VOCATIONAL SERVICES, 114 5th Ave., is a national body of vocational agencies.

WOMEN'S AMERICAN ORT, 1250 Broadway.

COMMUNITY CENTERS

ASSOCIATED YM & YWHAs OF GREATER NEW YORK, 130 E. 59th St. YM & YWHA branches serve neighborhoods in four of the five boroughs of New York City and Westchester County.

ASSOCIATION OF JEWISH CENTER WORKERS, 15 E. 26th St.

EDUCATIONAL ALLIANCE, 197 E. Broadway, is an agency that has played an important part in the teeming life of one of the fabled communities of the world—the ever changing, ever exciting Lower East Side. The Educational Alliance has been expanded and now maintains an apartment residence for the aged. (See also section on Lower East Side.)

EMANU-EL MIDTOWN YM-YWHA, 344 E. 14th St., includes facilities for the Jewish Society for the Deaf.

JWB, 15 E. 26th St., is the Association of YM & YWHAs and Jewish Community Centers and camps in the United States and Canada. It is the only Jewish agency accredited by the United States government to serve the religious, cultural, social, and recreational needs of Jewish military and naval personnel and their dependents. It also serves hospitalized veterans, and is the Jewish member agency of the United Service Organizations (USO). JWB encourages appreciation of Jewish culture through its Jewish Book Council, Jewish Music Council, and JWB Lecture Bureau, and has a wide variety of Israel-related activities.

92ND STREET YM & YWHA, Lexington Ave. and 92nd St., is the

largest and oldest Jewish Community Center in continuous existence in the United States. The only YMHA in the United States that has dormitory facilities, this Y has the Henry Kaufmann Building with its Clara de Hirsch Residence Hall, providing comfortable living quarters for about 300 girls. Jacob H. Schiff, one of the first to recognize the importance of Jewish Community Centers, gave the Y its first buildings. A bas-relief of Schiff hangs in this lobby. •In addition, the Y has a new Theresa L. Kaufmann Auditorium, Kaufmann Art Gallery, the Felix M. Warburg Lounge, and Buttenwieser Hall. With its varied program of activities in music, dance, drama, and the arts, the Y is an important cultural center for all New Yorkers.

WORLD FEDERATION OF YMHAs AND JEWISH COMMUNITY CENTERS, 15 E. 26th St.

YM & YWHA OF WASHINGTON HEIGHTS AND INWOOD, 54 Nagle Ave., is a strikingly modern and functional social, recreational, cultural, and educational center serving people of all ages. It rises three stories high at its main entrance and four stories at the rear. A unique feature of its multi-purpose auditorium which seats 400 persons, is a glass wall facing West 196th St. which opens out into a protected garden. The building has a roof play area of approximately 7,000 square feet.

INSTITUTIONS FOR THE AGED AND HOSPITALS

BETH ISRAEL HOSPITAL, 10 Nathan D. Perlman Pl., was founded in 1890 when 40 immigrants each contributed 25¢ to open a clinic for the sick, impoverished people of the Lower East Side. Its present location is its fifth. It is now one of the largest hospitals in New York and one in which dietary laws are observed. •The $2 million Charles H. Silver Clinic is designed to care for about 100,000 patients annually. •On the operating-room floor of the hospital is a statue and plaque honoring Dr. Jonas E. Reinthaler, whose contribution to the development of medical education in the United States was primarily in connection with the furthering of nurses training schools. A 300-bed private and semi-private pavilion meets increased demands for beds on the rapidly growing East Side, where other facilities are inadequate or obsolete. •Nathan D. Perlman Place is named for the late Judge Perlman, who was a Congressman from 1920-1927, and judge of the New York Court of Special Sessions from 1936 until his death in 1952. He was a vice-president of Beth Israel Hospital.

CENTRAL BUREAU FOR THE JEWISH AGED, 31 Union Square W.

HOME FOR AGED AND INFIRM HEBREWS, 121 W. 105th St., is a 410-bed structure with convertible facilities to accommodate the well and the chronically ill aged.

HOME OF THE SAGES OF ISRAEL, 25 Willett St.

HOSPITAL FOR JOINT DISEASES, 1919 Madison Ave., is another Federation agency.

JEWISH ASSOCIATION FOR SERVICES TO THE AGED, 222 Park Ave. S.

JEWISH HOME AND HOSPITAL FOR THE AGED, 120 W. 106th Street.

JEWISH HOME FOR CONVALESCENTS, 853 Broadway.

JEWISH MEMORIAL HOSPITAL, Broadway and 196th St., serves the communities of Washington Heights and Inwood. The hospital includes a two-story laboratory and research building.

MOUNT SINAI HOSPITAL, 5th Ave. from 99th to 101st Sts., was originally known as "Jews' Hospital" and was founded by Sampson Simson, probably the first Jew admitted to the New York Bar; the Rev. Samuel M. Isaacs; John I. Hart; Benjamin Nathan; John M. Davies; Henry Hendricks; Theodore J. Seixas; and Isaac and John D. Phillips. It became the Mount Sinai Hospital in 1866 by a special act of the legislature. Mount Sinai was New York's first great medical center among the non-municipal hospitals to place emphasis on research. ●A plaque in the entrance foyer of the hospital's main building at 100th Street pays tribute to George Blumenthal for "his inspired leadership and unparalleled contribution to the development of (Mount Sinai) during forty-six years as trustee and twenty-seven as president." Mr. Blumenthal gave almost $2 million to the hospital. ●On Madison Avenue, between 98th Street and 99th Street, stands the seven-story Atran Laboratory. This building is named for Frank Z. Atran, textile manufacturer and philanthropist, whose $1 million gift made completion of the structure possible.

CHILD CARE INSTITUTIONS

JEWISH BOARD OF GUARDIANS, 120 W. 57th St. This mental health agency, headquartered in its own building—The Edwin B. Elson Building—provides a variety of diagnostic and treatment services for emotionally disturbed youngsters and their parents. Jewish Board of Guardians facilities include:

● MADELEINE BORG CHILD GUIDANCE INSTITUTE, provides out-patient service with its licensed mental hygiene clinics in Manhattan, Brooklyn, and The Bronx.

● CHILD DEVELOPMENT CENTER in Manhattan provides out-patient service.

● HAWTHORNE-CEDAR KNOLLS and LINDEN HILL SCHOOLS, Hawthorne, N.Y., serves severely disturbed adolescents.

● HENRY ITTLESON CENTER FOR CHILD RESEARCH, 5050 Iselin Ave., Riverdale, has a day treatment center for severely disturbed boys and girls.

• STUYVESANT RESIDENCE CLUB, 74 St. Marks Place, is for boys from 15 to 18 years of age.

The agency also conducts a children's court and other community services. Volunteers involved in the activities of JBG are called Big Brothers and Big Sisters.

JEWISH CHILD CARE ASSOCIATION, 345 Madison Ave. The agency provides foster home care and foster family day care, and operates two schools—the Pleasantville Cottage School (Pleasantville, Westchester County), and the Edenwald School (The Bronx). One of the first cottage-plan orphanages in the United States and the first such institution under Jewish auspices, The Pleasantville Cottage School today is considered one of the best residential and treatment centers for emotionally disturbed children from eight to sixteen years old. Edenwald, a smaller school, cares for and trains mildly retarded (educable and trainable), and emotionally disturbed children. Edenwald differs from other schools for educable retarded children in that it serves children who would require separation from families even if they were not retarded. Professional persons—doctors, psychologists, social workers, and teachers—may arrange to visit the Pleasantville Cottage School by calling JCCA's community relations department. JCCA also has group residences for boys and girls who, while able to live and attend school in the community, cannot adapt to foster home living. Of the institutions, four are the Hartman-Homecrest residences which consolidated with JCCA in 1962.

AGENCIES FOR THE HANDICAPPED

ALTRO HEALTH AND REHABILITATION SERVICES, 225 Park Ave. South, retrains, under the supervision of doctors and social workers, the post-mentally ill, cardiac, and tubercular patients to return to full-time jobs. The Altro Workshop has been expanded.

JEWISH BRAILLE INSTITUTE OF AMERICA, 110 E. 30th St., seeks to further cultural, educational, and religious welfare of the Jewish blind. It publishes Hebrew and English prayer books in Braille and teaches Hebrew Braille. It has the largest Jewish Braille and talking-book library in the world.

JEWISH GUILD FOR THE BLIND, 15 W. 65th St., maintains a home for the blind at 75 Stratton St., Yonkers. The Guild helps blind and visually handicapped persons, regardless of race, religion, age, or economic status, to participate in the community on a self-supporting basis. Among its services are teaching the skills of daily living, preparing the blind to travel alone, vocational rehabilitation, sheltered workshops, mental health services, Braille library facilities, student training program, and other services.

ASSISTANCE WITH PERSONAL AND FAMILY PROBLEMS

AGUDATH ISRAEL OF AMERICA, 5 Beekman St., has a variety of social and legal services for the poor and elderly.

HEBREW FREE BURIAL ASSOCIATION, 1170 Broadway.

HEBREW FREE LOAN SOCIETY, 205 E. 42nd St., is a unique institution founded in 1892 with a capital of $95. Here, individuals, employed or not, can get interest-free loans of up to $500 without being investigated and without putting up any collateral. All that is required is the endorsement on each loan of one or two responsible persons who have checking accounts and who do business in Greater New York (on loans of $100 or less, only one endorser is required). Loans must be repaid in a maximum of ten months.

JEWISH CONCILIATION BOARD OF AMERICA, 33 W. 60th St., is an agency to which members of Jewish families torn by internal strife take their problems for arbitration. The decisions of this unusual, non-judicial body—made up mostly of rabbis, judges, businessmen, and lawyers—are binding upon the disputants and enforceable in the civil courts. Referred to as "the court of first resort," the Jewish Conciliation Board sits in regular session. A panel of board members hear disputants plead their own cases. The board's work has been praised by Supreme Court Justice William O. Douglas and other prominent persons. Cases are initiated when a complaint is registered at the office of the JCB; it is then arranged that both parties appear at a fixed session of the board. All sessions are private. An arbitration agreement must be signed by both parties before the hearing.

It is interesting to observe why persons would place themselves under the jurisdiction of a board that may rule against them although no legal case exists. Its officers say that it is because "our people have a great moral sense. They want to do the right thing." The board was originally founded to keep quarrels involving Jews out of the courts and to help immigrants avoid costly litigation. The services of JCB are free. It is a descendant of the *Beth Din*, a religious court in which Jews were allowed to resolve their own differences. In addition to marital difficulties, which comprise 80 percent of the board's work, problems are heard involving the support and maintenance of older parents. The JCB sees itself as more than an arbitration tribunal. It is a Jewish communal institution that aims "to carry out the Jewish ideal of justice simply, without the encumbrances of complicated procedure. Its field of service includes the amicable adjustment of disputes arising between Jewish persons and Jewish religious, communal, fraternal, and benevolent organizations as well as differences arising between individual parties; such differences, by mutual consent, are submitted for conciliation." An important adjunct of the board is the Social Service Department where relief, advice, and guidance are provided for those who are in need. As a rule, problems involving marital relationships, aged parents, and rebellious or indifferent children are resolved in private through this department. □

JEWISH FAMILY SERVICE, 33 W. 60th St., provides consultation centers, a homemaker service, a family location and legal service, a family mental health clinic, a family counseling center, a crisis unit, a youth services unit, and other services.

LOUISE WISE SERVICES, 12 E. 94th St., conducts adoption services and the Jewish Unmarried Mothers Service. It was founded by the late Louise Waterman Wise, who was the wife of Rabbi Stephen S. Wise and the mother of Justice Justine Wise Polier of the Domestic Relations Court.

SYNAGOGAL AND RABBINIC BODIES

CENTRAL CONFERENCE OF AMERICAN RABBIS, 790 Madison Ave., represents the Reform movement. (See also: UNION OF AMERICAN HEBREW CONGREGATIONS.)

EDUCATORS ASSEMBLY, 155 5th Ave. (Conservative).

HOUSE OF LIVING JUDAISM (see Midtown section).

NATIONAL CONFERENCE OF SYNAGOGUE YOUTH, 116 E. 27th St. (Orthodox).

NATIONAL FEDERATION OF TEMPLE YOUTH, 838 5th Ave. (Reform).

NEW YORK BOARD OF RABBIS, 10 E. 73rd St., located in the former Berg Mansion, is a body of Orthodox, Conservative, and Reform rabbis. It provides chaplains for local civilian hospitals, penal institutions, and other agencies. It is also a center for information about Judaism.

RABBINICAL ASSEMBLY OF AMERICA, 3380 Broadway, represents the Conservative body.

RABBINICAL COUNCIL OF AMERICA, 220 Park Ave., S., is a body of Orthodox rabbis.

SYNAGOGUE COUNCIL OF AMERICA, 432 Park Ave., S., represents synagogues and rabbis of all three wings on a national level.

UNION OF ORTHODOX JEWISH CONGREGATIONS OF AMERICA, 116 E. 27th St.

UNITED SYNAGOGUE OF AMERICA, 155 5th Ave., represents Conservative synagogues.

UNITED SYNAGOGUE YOUTH, 155 5th Ave. (Conservative)

JEWISH WOMEN'S ORGANIZATIONS

NATIONAL COUNCIL OF JEWISH WOMEN, 15 East 26th St., conducts a program of service and education for social action in the fields of social legislation, international affairs, contemporary Jewish affairs, community welfare, overseas service, and assistance to the foreign-born.

THE COUNCIL WORKSHOP FOR SENIOR CITIZENS, 915 Broadway, is an agency of the National Council of Jewish Women. The New York Section is located at 9 E. 69th St.

NATIONAL FEDERATION OF TEMPLE SISTERHOODS, 838 5th Ave., is located in the House of Living Judaism.

NEW YORK JEWISH WOMEN'S CENTER, 299 Riverside Dr., (Apt. 3D), sponsors a women's school in Judaica, a monthly minyan, an outreach campus program, and a monthly Sunday seminar.

UNITED ORDER TRUE SISTERS, INC., 150 W. 85th St., is a fraternal, philanthropic women's organization providing a cancer-treatment program.

WOMEN'S AMERICAN ORT, 1250 Broadway.

WOMEN'S BRANCH, UNION OF ORTHODOX JEWISH CON-GREGATIONS OF AMERICA, 84 5th Ave.

WOMEN'S LEAGUE FOR CONSERVATIVE JUDAISM, 48 E. 74th St.

(For other women's organizations, see listing under other categories.)

JEWISH COMMUNAL PROFESSIONAL ORGANIZATIONS

NATIONAL CONFERENCE OF JEWISH COMMUNAL SER-VICE, 15 E. 26th St., conducts an annual meeting for professionals in various fields of Jewish communal service and publishes the *Journal of Jewish Communal Service*. Affiliated with it are: Association of Jewish Center Workers, National Council of Jewish Education, National Association of Jewish Family, Children's and Health Professionals, Association of Jewish Community Relations Workers, Association of Jewish Community Organization Personnel, National Association of Synagogue Administrators, and National Association of Jewish Homes for the Aged.

HOUSING DEVELOPMENTS

AMALGAMATED DWELLINGS, 570 Grand St., the first housing development built in Manhattan under the pioneer State Housing Law of 1926, is a cooperative built by the Amalgamated Clothing Workers of America. Within the complex are houses named for Louis D. Brandeis (see Louisville), Edward Filene (see Boston), and Meyer London, who was elected to Congress as a Socialist in 1914 from the Lower East Side.

BARUCH HOUSES, 100 Columbia St., is named for Bernard M. Baruch, advisor to Presidents and chairman of the War Industries Board during World War I, and for his father, Dr. Simon Baruch, a physician in the Confederate Army who later devoted himself to improving public health facilities in N.Y.C.

GOMPERS HOUSES, 50 Pitt St., is named for Samuel Gompers, one of the founders and first president of the American Federation of Labor.

HOLMES-ISAACS HOUSES, 403 East 93rd St., memorializes in part Stanley Isaacs, a leading advocate of public housing and one-time president of the Borough of Manhattan.

LEHMAN VILLAGE, 1605 Madison Ave., is named for the late

Senator and former Governor, Herbert H. Lehman.

STRAUS HOUSES, 228 East 28th St., is named for Nathan Straus, philanthropist, whose milk fund was credited with saving the lives of thousands of babies and lowering the city's death rate.

VLADECK HOUSES, 366 Madison St., is named for B. Charney Vladeck, general manager for many years of the *Jewish Daily Forward* and a member of the first N.Y.C. Housing Authority.

WALD HOUSES, 54 Avenue D, is named for Lillian Wald, founder of Henry Street Settlement and the pioneer of public nursing.

WISE TOWERS, 124 West 91st St., is named for Dr. Stephen S. Wise, noted rabbi, Zionist leader, civic reformer, and president of the American and World Jewish Congresses.

ENTERTAINMENT

THEATRE, MUSIC, AND ART

Although the Yiddish theatre has long passed its peak productions and attendance, it is by no means dead. The following are a number of groups which stage productions from time to time:

THE ANDERSON YIDDISH THEATRE, 66 2nd Ave.

THE EDEN THEATER, 189 2nd Ave.

FOLKSBIENE PLAYHOUSE (in the auditorium of the Central Synagogue), 123 E. 55th St.

THE MAYFAIR THEATER, 235 W. 46th St.

ROOSEVELT YIDDISH THEATRE, 100 W. 17th St.

For the past several years there have been four shows a season. Some of these are shown daily, while others are seen on weekends only. Some of the plays use a musical comedy format with English and Yiddish mixed, and some are modernized versions of old Jewish stage hits by such masters as Abraham Goldfaden, Jacob Gordon, and Z. Libin. The Folksbiene Theatre features an earnest group of amateur performers with professional polish who have been putting on plays for a half century. It is the oldest organization of its kind and is devoted to serious theatre. The Folksbeine season starts in November and performances run for 20 weekends: Saturdays at 8 p.m., Sundays at 2 p.m. and 5:30 p.m. □

EDUCATIONAL ALLIANCE, 197 East Broadway, offers concerts, plays, dance recitals, operas, film programs, forums, and festival activities in its Isidor Straus Theatre.

THEODOR HERZL INSTITUTE, 515 Park Ave., provides lectures and forums on virtually all aspects of Judaism. The institute holds both morning and evening programs with the exception of Friday evenings and Saturdays. In addition to the lectures, there are courses, public functions, conferences, audio-visual presentations, and special events. During the summer months, the institute conducts the Ulpan course in Hebrew, but most other activities are suspended. The institute's art exhibits are always interesting.

JEWISH THEATRE FOR CHILDREN, Franklin Playhouse, 154 W. 93rd St. This group is sponsored by the Board of Jewish Education of New York. It produces original full-length plays based on Jewish themes. Productions can be seen every Sunday afternoon from November through March.

YM & YWHA, 92nd St. and Lexington Ave., features a variety of programs, such as dance recitals, lectures, seminars, concerts, plays, and poetry readings. Some programs are of specifically Jewish interest; most are of interest to all New Yorkers, who frequently visit the Y auditorium.

NIGHTCLUBS

CLUB CAESAREA, 2 E. 86th St., is an Israeli nightclub, featuring *glatt* kosher cuisine. There are two shows nightly and dancing. (Open every evening except Friday). Papa Lou's, a kosher Italian restaurant, is located here.

CAFE FEENJON, 117 Macdougal St., is a nightclub featuring Middle-Eastern, Jewish, and Israeli entertainment.

CAFE YAFFO, 450 W. 42nd St., is a restaurant and night spot designed to give its patrons a taste of Israel. It has experimented with full-length Israeli films shown to diners at no extra charge.

DAVID'S HARP, 131 W. 3rd St., is an Israeli nightclub featuring Middle-Eastern food.

EL AVRAM, 80 Grove St., is an Israeli kosher nightclub and restaurant featuring American-Israeli cuisine and Russian, Yiddish, and Israeli entertainment. In addition to its Israeli owner, Avram Grobard (a singer and accordionist), there is an Armenian oud-player and an Israeli-Arab chef. (Open every night but Monday).

GOLDA'S NIGHTCLUB, near Bleecker and Jones Sts., off 7th Ave.

SABRA EAST, 232 E. 43rd St., is an Israeli supper club. There is a choice of Middle Eastern or traditional *glatt* kosher cuisine. It also features entertainment and dancing.

SIROCCO, 29 E. 29th St., is an Israeli-Greek nightclub.

TEL-AVIV CAFE, 100 W. 72nd St., has nightly entertainment.

DINING OUT

The opportunity to get "a good Jewish meal" to suit every palate and pocketbook makes eating out one of New York's principal pleasures for Jews and non-Jews alike. Whether one's taste runs to blintzes with sour cream, *varnishkes*, *pirogen*, cream cheese and lox, *maatjes* herring, gefilte fish, *matzo-brei*, hot pastrami or corned beef, chopped liver, *flanken*, stuffed derma, *tzimmes*, stuffed *miltz*, *lungen* stew, *kreplach* soup, *pitcha*, or any other kind of Jewish food—all are available in New York. There are even restaurants specializing in kosher Chinese food. In recent years a number of Israeli restaurants have opened.

The listing that follows includes not only kosher and Israeli restaurants, but also those with a history of Jewish interest, special atmosphere, or particular Jewish clientele. Prices and hours of some of these restaurants are listed, but these are subject to change. It is wise to check by phone prior to planning a visit to these restaurants.

MEAT RESTAURANTS—MIDTOWN

In an area where 25 to 30 percent of the population is Jewish, it is inevitable that many restaurants will serve dishes with a special appeal to Jews such as gefilte fish, chopped liver, chicken soup, delicatessen, cheese blintzes, etc. Among the many restaurants in this area offering these and other dishes, some of the best known are:

DIAMOND CENTER DELICATESSEN AND LUNCHEONETTE, 71 W. 47th St.

DUBROW'S CAFETERIA, 515 7th Ave., is a garment center landmark, where a wide selection of Jewish specialties are part of the daily menu.

ESKOW'S, 225 W. 57th St.

HECTOR'S, 1506 Broadway.

HELLO DELI, 460 W. 42nd St., features kosher delicatessen.

HOUSE OF TAAM, 968 6th Ave., serves deli and kosher Chinese dishes.

KOSHER WORLD, Broadway at 32nd St., sells pizza and falafel and other Middle Eastern dishes. *Shomer Shabbat. Cholov Yisroel.*

LA DIFFERENCE (Roosevelt Hotel), Madison Ave. and 45th St., has a French menu.

MACCABEEM, 147 W. 47th St., has a Middle East menu.

MIDTOWN, 52 W. 47th St., is a *glatt* kosher restaurant.

MOSHE PEKING, 40 W. 37th St., serves *glatt* kosher Chinese and Continental cuisine.

NATHAN'S JEWELRY CENTER RESTAURANT, 36 W. 47th St.

PAPA LOU'S, 2 E. 86th St., is a kosher Italian restaurant, which is also where Club Caesarea is located.

ROSOFF'S, 147 W. 43rd St.

LOU G. SIEGEL, 209 W. 38th St. (near Broadway, open Sunday through Friday, 12 noon to 8:45 p.m., kosher). The specialty of this restaurant, located in the heart of the garment center, is delicatessen, served in generous portions, Hungarian stuffed cabbage is also a specialty. They also feature stuffed derma, *tzimmes*, meat *lungen*, and *miltz* stew. Known since 1917, Siegel's attracts patronage from all over the world. The firm provides kosher catering to TWA and Pan Am Airways. It is one of the few Jewish restaurants open during Passover.

SOLOWEY'S, 431-433 7th Ave.

STAGE DELICATESSEN AND RESTAURANT, 834 7th Ave. (north of Shubert Alley), is frequented by actors, dancers, and musicians.

TIP TOP, 491 7th Ave., is a *glatt* kosher restaurant.

MANNY WOLF'S CHOP HOUSE, 49th St. and 3rd Ave.

YAHALOM, 49-55 W. 47th St., is a *glatt* kosher restaurant and cafeteria. It is in the heart of the Diamond Center. It features American and Hungarian cuisine.

MEAT RESTAURANTS—UPPER WEST SIDE

FASS' RESTAURANT AND DELICATESSEN, 4179 Broadway, is a *glatt* kosher restaurant.

FINE AND SCHAPIRO, 138 W. 72nd St., (open 7 days a week, from 11 a.m. to midnight). The restaurant is kosher, although it does not have rabbinical supervision, as does Lou Siegel's. Their specialties are gefilte fish, boiled beef flanken, stuffed cabbage, potato *kugel*, stuffed derma, and prune *tzimmes*. Also: mushroom and barley soup or lentil soup with frankfurters. They are known for their hot strudel for dessert. The restaurant is conveniently located near the Spanish and Portuguese Synagogue, Temple Emanu-El, etc.

STERN'S RESTAURANT AND CATERERS, 666 West End Ave., (in Hotel Windermere, is open daily from 5 to 8:30 p.m.; Sundays, from 4:30 to 8:30 p.m.). This restaurant is open Friday, but closed Saturday. Money is not handled on the Sabbath. After reservations are made, the Sabbath meals must be paid for in advance.

TOV M'OD LUNCHEONETTE, 2549 Amsterdam Ave.

MEAT RESTAURANTS—LOWER EAST SIDE

BERNSTEIN-ON-ESSEX-STREET, 135 Essex St. (open 12 noon to 10 p.m., except Friday night and Saturday.) This was the first kosher Chinese restaurant in New York and claims to be the originator of kosher Chinese foods. The diner will be served by Chinese waiters wearing black *yarmulkas*. Specialties are won ton soup (Chinese *kreplach*); egg rolls; spare ribs; sweet and pungent veal; Chicken Bernstein (chicken stuffed with minced bamboo shoots and water chestnuts); and pastrami and Chinese vegetables. They also feature a choice of non-Chinese food such as hot corned beef, pastrami, or frankfurters—all of which come from the factory of the owner's famous father, Schmulka Bernstein. The factory is located at 107 Rivington St.

CROWN KOSHER RESTAURANT AND DELICATESSEN, 157 E. Houston St.

G & M KOSHER CATERERS, 41 Essex St., serves kosher meats and spaghetti, as well as the traditional *cholent, kishke,* and *kreplach.*

GLUCKSTERN'S STRICTLY KOSHER RESTAURANT, 135 Delancey St., (open seven days a week, 11 A.M. to midnight). This restaurant specializes in boiled beef *flanken*, steaks, and chops. Pollack's is now an annex to Gluckstern's.

HENRY'S KOSHER DELICATESSEN AND RESTAURANT, 195 E. Houston St. A sign in the window calls attention to the fact that "this is the only kosher restaurant in the vicinity."

KATZ'S DELI, 205 East Houston St., is a popular kosher-style establishment.

MIFGOSH, 830 8th Ave., specializing in Israeli-Yemenite cooking, serves Israeli-American kosher food. *Mifgosh* in Hebrew means a "meeting place where friends meet."

SAM'S KOSHER DELICATESSEN, 158 E. Broadway (closed Saturday).

SECOND AVENUE KOSHER DELICATESSEN AND RESTAURANT, INC. 156 2nd Ave.

Since it is not possible to list all the kosher delicatessen shops in Manhattan, look for the following to ascertain whether the eating establishment is truly kosher:

1. The word "kosher" should be printed in Hebrew; however, this may mean that only the delicatessen is kosher.

2. Check whether milk or milk products are served.

3. For the especially observant, inquire whether the establishment is closed on Saturday.

DAIRY RESTAURANTS—MIDTOWN

BLUM'S KOSHER DAIRY RESTAURANT, 10 W. 47th St.

DIAMOND KOSHER DAIRY LUNCHEONETTE, 4 W. 47th St., on the mezzanine in the Jeweler's Exchange. *Cholov Yisroel.* Full-course suppers are served from 5 to 7 p.m.

ESTHER'S KOSHER DAIRY RESTAURANT, 165 Madison Ave.

FARMFOOD RESTAURANT, 142 W. 49th St., emphasizes health and vegetable salads, but also serves a variety of fish and soups.

GEFEN'S KOSHER DAIRY RESTAURANT, 297 7th Ave., serves *Cholov Yisroel* upon request. (*Cholov Yisroel* is milk that has been produced and tested under the supervision of a recognized Jewish authority.) *Mehadrin* ("zealous") cream available. All cooking and baking are done on the premises. Full-course dinners are served from 4:30 to 8:30 P.M.; special club breakfasts are served from 6 to 10 a.m. (Closed Friday night, Saturday, and Jewish holidays).

R. GROSS DAIRY AND VEGETARIAN RESTAURANT, 1372 Broadway.

HAMIZNON KOSHER DAIRY RESTAURANT, 44 W. 30th St.

DAIRY RESTAURANTS—UPPER WEST SIDE

FAMOUS DAIRY RESTAURANT, 222 W. 72nd St., specializes in blintzes or vegetables with sour cream, soups, fish, and salads.

DAIRY RESTAURANTS—BELOW 23rd STREET

BROWNIE'S, 21 E. 16th St., is a fish and vegetarian restaurant.

CALDRON RESTAURANT, 308 E. 6th St., serves natural foods and has a bakery and natural food store featuring their specialties, *(Shomer Shabbos)*.

HAMMER DAIRY RESTAURANT, 243 E. 14th St.

RATNER'S, 138 Delancey St., is one of the best-known dairy restaurants in New York. They serve a variety of different types of blintzes as well as *kasha varnishkes*, soups and fishes. The tables are laden with a variety of rolls and breads and the bold waiters will undertake to advise the diner on what to order.

YONAH SCHIMMEL KNISHERY, 137 E. Houston St., is an interesting place to visit. There are over a dozen varieties of knishes available, as well as *potatoniks (kugel)*, strudel, *latkes*, sour milk, borsht, cheese bagels, and coffee. They advertise that it is the original Yonah Schimmel's Knishery and a picture of the founder is in the window. They are open from 7 a.m. to 10 p.m.

INSTITUTIONAL RESTAURANTS

ATRAN CENTER FOR JEWISH CULTURE, 25 E. 78th St., has a cafeteria which serves Jewish lunches.

B'NAI B'RITH BUILDING, 315 Lexington Ave., has a kosher counter service.

JEWISH THEOLOGICAL SEMINARY OF AMERICA, 3080 Broadway, and Rubin Hall at YESHIVA UNIVERSITY, 185th St. and Amsterdam Ave., both maintain cafeterias.

STERN COLLEGE FOR WOMEN, 253 Lexington Ave., an affiliate of Yeshiva University, has a kosher cafeteria where lunch is served.

WALL STREET SYNAGOGUE, 47 Beekman St., has a kosher restaurant that serves meals from 11 a.m. to 3 p.m.; also Passover meals.

SHOPPING

BOOKS AND RELIGIOUS OBJECTS

BEN ARI ARTS, LTD., 11 Ave. A, trades in Jewish art, antique Judaica, Israeli gift items, and synagogue supplies and decorations.

BEHRMAN HOUSE, 1261 Broadway. The visitor to this publishing house will find a homey atmosphere, replete with a large comfortable library in which to browse leisurely while sipping coffee. Behrman House stocks almost every book of Jewish interest. It caters to professional people in Jewish life—rabbis, student rabbis, Jewish teachers and principals, cantors, administrators, writers, etc.

JAKER BIEGELEISEN, 83 Division St., carries a supply of Hebrew books, but his specialty is Hasidism. He also has books on Judaica and Jewish religious articles.

BLOCH PUBLISHING CO., 915 Broadway. This firm was founded in Cincinnati in 1854 by Rabbi Isaac Mayer Wise and his brother-in-law, Edward Bloch. Rabbi Wise had always been eager to address a nationwide audience, and when he moved to Cincinnati, he took steps the very first month to start a newspaper. His young brother-in-law, who had experience in printing was seeking a similar job in Cincinnati, and thus was born Bloch and Company, Publishers and Printers. They published in several languages and distributed their material. Their first publication, the *American Israelite*, a weekly printed in English, was the counterpart of *Die Deborah* in German. In 1901 the firm moved to New York. Charles Bloch, present publisher, is the fourth generation Bloch in the business. The firm publishes and distributes a wide variety of English Judaica and Hebraica and also sells ritual objects and religious novelties made in America and Israel. Though the firm began under Reform Jewish auspices, it has become prominent in the publication of *Haggadahs* and daily and holiday prayer books.

EASTERN JEWELRY MFG. CO., 39 West 19th St., carries Jewish religious goods, gold charms and novelties.

RABBI MOSES EISENBACH, 13 Essex St., carries *Sifrei* Torah, books, *tefilin*, and *taleisim*.

PHILIPP FELDHEIM, 96 East Broadway, has a large stock of German Judaica, and a collection of rare and old volumes. Mr. Feldheim is also a publisher as well as a bookseller.

GIMBEL'S DEPARTMENT STORE, Broadway and 33rd St., has an unusually large display of Israeli stamps, coins, covers, and albums.

HEBREW PUBLISHING CO. AND BOOKSTORE, 314 Grand St., prints a large percentage of Hebrew and English books in the United States and Jewish greeting cards. The firm has monotype machines in Hebrew and groups may arrange in advance for a tour of the premises to see how Hebrew is set into type. The store is spacious, and contains a large variety of books in English, Yiddish, and Hebrew. There are also greeting cards, Torah covers and ornaments, Ark curtains, *kiddush* cups, pointers, original paintings from Israel, spice boxes, candlesticks, *taleisim*, *tefilin*, and an assortment of other items rarely found elsewhere.

NISSIM HIZME HEBREW JEWELRY, INC. 37 Eldridge St. Hizme, a Yemenite Jew, is noted for his original, hand-crafted Hebrew jewelry and religious items. He also designs original Hebrew monograms that may be made into pins or used on personal stationery, or wedding and bar mitzvah invitations. The firm carries an assortment of charms, cufflinks, *kiddush* cups, *talis* clips, *mezuzahs*, etc.

ISRAEL ART DESIGN IMPORT CORP., 21½ Essex St., has Torahs and other Scrolls, *taleisim, tefilin,* and unusual arts and crafts.

ISRAEL RELIGIOUS ART, INC., 32 W. 61st St., imports ancient and modern art and carries other items such as Sephardi Torahs from Egypt.

THE JEWISH ART GALLERY, 11 Essex St., has Jewish oil paintings, lithographs, and prints.

KTAV PUBLISHING HOUSE, 75 Varick St., corner Canal St., publishes juvenile books and textbooks, and manufactures an array of articles. It is the world's largest manufacturer of *dreidels.*

J. LEVINE CO., 58 Eldridge St., calls itself "The Synagogue Beautiful" Department Store. It manufactures flexible hooked Torah binders with interlocking woods, scrolls of remembrance, Torah covers, and other religious regalia. It is the sole agent in the United States and Canada for the Yad Vashem Memorial Lights. Once a neighborhood store, its business now is largely mail-order, with customers all over the world. It specializes in synagogue essentials and general Judaica.

MIRIAM RELIGIOUS SUPPLIES MANUFACTURING CO., 54 Canal St., makes pure linen "eternal cloths," *parochet* (Ark Curtains), matzo and *challah* covers, Torah mantles, *yarmulkas,* and gowns. They sell bronze tablets and "earth from Israel" for the use of religious Jews at burial rites.

MOSES PARNES, 41 Essex St., sells scrolls, *tefilin,* and books (both retail and wholesale).

POLLAK'S BOOK STORE, 54 Canal St., sells *taleisim, tefilin,* books, and Israeli goods.

SOLOMON RABINOWITZ HEBREW BOOK STORE, 30 Canal St.

REINMAN'S SEFORIM CENTER, INC., 29 Essex St., is a center for copies of the Talmud and other Judaica.

SEPHARDIC PUBLISHING CO., 7 Rivington St.

ASHER SHALLER, 1495 St. Nicholas Ave., sells bar mitzvah sets, books, records, Ark curtains, book bindings, jewelry and Israeli imports.

LOUIS STAVSKY, 147 Essex St., specializes in religious articles for homes, congregations, and schools. They also carry a large selection of books of Jewish interest.

STM SCRIBES, INC. 220 W. 80th St., specializes in Hebrew lettering, invitation, etc., and has *Sifrei* Torah, *tefilin,* and bar mitzvah sets.

TIV TOV EMBROIDERY CO., 48 Eldridge St., carries Torah covers, *yarmulkas,* and *taleisim.*

UNITED NATIONS GIFT SHOP stocks items from Israel.

EMANUEL WEISBERG, 45 Essex St., sells bar mitzvah sets, Hebrew religious articles and antique Judaica (wholesale and retail).

M. WOLOZIN, INC. 38 Eldridge St., manufactures and sells *taleisim* and Hebrew religious articles and books.

YANKEE TALLIT WORKS, 175 5th Ave., produces and sells denim

prayer shawls, *yarmelkes,* and *tallit* bags. The *tallit* is both uniquely American and 100% kosher. Inspired by the American Bicentennial, they appeal to young people who believe that prayer can and should be a less formal experience without having to deviate from tradition or *halacha.*

ZION TALIS MANUFACTURING CO., 48 Eldridge St., is probably the leading manufacturer of silk, woolen, and rayon prayer shawls. It also imports and distributes Hebrew religious regalia for synagogue and home use. In its retail store it carries a large selection of items ranging from skullcaps to a *Sefer* Torah. Conducted tours through its plant where the *taleisim* are made can be arranged. Religious school students can visit the plant and see how the actual *talis* is made and the *sofrim* at work repairing or retracing parts of the Torah.

The following specialize in Israeli jewelry, gifts, and other imports:

ABADA CHEN HEBRON LTD. ISRAEL, 94 Canal St.

ARTISTIC ISRAELI JEWELRY MFG. CO., 4 W. 37th St.

EASTERN ORIGINS, 435 Park Ave. South.

FAR-N-WIDE, INC., 175 E. 86th St.

FINKELSTEIN ENTERPRISES, 350 Hudson St.

ILAN IMPORTS, 342 Madison Ave., features handmade silver jewelry.

MEDITERRANEAN TRADING CO., 9 W. 57th St.

THE UNDERGROUND JEWELER, 147 E. 86th St.

JEWISH MUSIC

METRO MUSIC CO., 54 Second Ave., has the largest selection of music and recordings of Jewish interest in the world. Included are popular and folk music; theatrical, art, liturgical, and ethnic music; dances; Hasidic music; language instruction; stories and Biblical readings for children; dramatic works; and solo, choral and instrumental classical music.

RIVINGTON MUSIC CENTER, 106 Rivington St., specializes in Israeli and Yiddish records.

(Jewish records can also be purchased at stores selling Judaica, several department stores, and record shops.)

KOSHER CANDIES AND BAKE GOODS

BARRICINI'S AND LOFTS, with branches throughout the Metropolitan area, sell candy and cookies designed for some of the Jewish holidays.

BARTON'S BONBONNIER, (executive offices at 80 DeKalb Ave., Brooklyn, N.Y.), has 21 stores in Manhattan, 14 in Brooklyn, 3 in The Bronx, 8 in Queens, and 4 in Nassau, Suffolk, and Westchester Counties. (Some of these stores are franchised and do not observe the Sabbath.) Barton's manufactures a full line of candies, cakes, pastries, and other confections for Rosh Hashanah, Chanukah, Purim, and Passover. All of these are packaged in specially designed holiday boxes containing an illustrated explanation of the symbols and customs of the particular holiday. Copies of these leaflets and others explaining various aspects of the Jewish heritage are available without charge at the stores. Most stores also carry a selections of gifts made in Israel. All Barton products are manufactured under the supervision of the Union of Orthodox Jewish Congregations of America and carry the organization's seal of *kashruth*.

GERTEL'S BAKE SHOPPE, 53 Hester St., has cake and other baked goods for the Sabbath and Jewish holidays, in addition to their regular bakery products. There are tables in the shop where coffee and tea are served. (Closed Saturdays and Jewish holidays.)

MOISHE'S HOMEMADE KOSHER BAKERY, 181 E. Houston St.

STERN'S KOSHER PASTRY SHOP, INC., 490 Amsterdam Ave., specializes in wedding cakes.

STREIT MATZOTH CO., 150 Rivington St.

KOSHER CHEESES

CHEESE UNLIMITED, 1263 Lexington Ave., is a small store carrying kosher and non-kosher cheeses. They also carry cheeses from Israel, Poland, Romania, Czechoslovakia, etc.

CHEESES OF ALL NATIONS, 153 Chambers St., carries kosher and Israeli cheeses, as well as non-kosher varieties. Most of the Israeli cheeses are made from sheep's milk with the exception of feta, which is made from goat's milk. The kosher cheeses are made under rabbinical supervision. They also carry gift boxes of kosher cheeses for Passover and Chanukah.

LEIBELS' KOSHER SPECIALITIES, INC. 27½ Essex St., carries kosher cheeses.

MILLER'S CHEESE, 13 Essex St., sells only kosher cheese and is under the supervision of the Union of Orthodox Jewish Congregations of America. They carry eight different varieties of cheese—all made from sheep's milk.

MISCELLANEOUS PUBLIC PLACES

CENTRAL PARK, which runs from 59th to 110th Sts., from 5th Ave. to Central Park W., has among its many recreational attractions the following:

• Herbert H. Lehman Children's Zoo, named for the former senator and governor.

• Wollman Memorial Rink, a popular ice skating area, was a gift of Kate Wollman.

• Michael Friedsam Merry-Go-Round, named for the merchant, art patron, and philanthropist.

- Elkan Naumburg Bandstand, is named for the philanthropist.
- 72nd St. Boathouse and Restaurant was a gift of Mr. and Mrs. Carl M. Loeb, Sr.
- The Sophie Irene Loeb Fountain in the Heckscher Playground.
- The Lionel Sutro Playground is named for a friend of the park system.
- Pulitzer Memorial Fountain, is named for Joseph Pulitzer, famed journalist whose father was Jewish. ☐

CHAPELL MUSIC PUBLISHING CO., 810 7th Ave., has in the lobby of its building a large photo collage depicting such noted Jewish composers as George and Ira Gershwin, Richard Rodgers, Bob Dylan, Julie Styne, and Maurice Hamlisch.

DAMROSCH PARK, (in front of Lincoln Center), is named for the later Walter Damrosch, conductor of the New York Philharmonic, whose father was the music director at New York's Temple Emanu-El.

FELT FORUM, Madison Square Garden's 5,000-seat amphitheatre, 8th Ave. and 33rd St., is named for Irving Mitchell Felt, one-time campaign chairman of the Federation of Jewish Philanthropies, board chairman of Madison Square Garden, and board chairman of the National Conference of Christians and Jews.

AVERY FISHER HALL, Lincoln Center, is named for a one-time book designer who acquired an international reputation as founder of Fisher Radio, maker of high quality high fidelity instruments. He donated $4 million for the Center's main auditorium, the home of the New York Philharmonic.

HADASSAH'S BIRTHPLACE is marked by a plaque in the lobby of the building at 521 5th Ave., which occupies the site of the old Temple Emanu-El at 5th Ave. and 43rd St., in whose vestry room Hadassah was founded in 1912.

JERUSALEM GROVE, adjoining Castle Clinton National Monument, in Battery Park, is a collection of 15 Atlas cedars, similar to those grown in Israel. It was planted by the City of Jerusalem in 1976 as a gift to New York City on the American Bicentennial.

CAPTAIN JACOB JOSEPH PLAYGROUND, next to school at 165 Henry St., is named for a Marine who was killed in action at Guadalcanal during World War II. Captain Joseph was the grandson of Chief Rabbi Jacob Joseph, and the son of Lazarus Joseph, City Comptroller.

LOEB PLAYGROUND, E. Broadway, Market, and Henry Sts., is named for Sophie Irene Loeb, pioneer social worker.

SOPHIE IRENE LOEB FOUNTAIN, Heckscher Playground, 63rd St. and West Drive.

MENORAHS in Cathedral of St. John the Divine, Amsterdam Ave. from Cathedral Pkwy. to 113th St. Each is 12 feet high, following the design of those that stood in King Solomon's Temple. The first of their kind to be used in a Christian cathedral, the Menorahs were a gift of the late Adolph S. Ochs in 1930. One of the Cathedral's two great bronze doors contain tableaux depicting the exploits of Jewish prophets and patriarchs of the Bible.

PALEY PARK, (east of) 5th Ave. at 53rd St., one of the city's growing number of vest-pocket parks, was established by William Paley, chairman of the board of Columbia Broadcasting System, and named for his father, Samuel, a Philadelphia cigar manufacturer and owner of one of the city's first radio stations.

PERLMAN PLACE, (off) 2nd Ave. near 17th St., where Beth Israel Medical Center is located, is named for the late Congressman and Supreme Court Justice, Nathan D. Perlman.

ADOLPH S. OCHS BUST, in the lobby of *The New York Times*, 229 W. 43rd St., memorializes the man who, as publisher, built the *Times* into one of the world's greatest newspapers.

The following schools were named after prominent Jews:

• Louis D. Brandeis High School, 151 W. 84th St., is named for the first Jew appointed to the U.S. Supreme Court.

• Simon Baruch Intermediate High School, 330 E. 21st St., is named for Dr. Simon Baruch, physician, surgeon in the Confederate Army, and pioneer in public health and cardiac therapy. He was the father of Bernard M. Baruch.

• William Ettinger High School, Madison Ave. at 106th St.

• Julia Richman High School, 317 E. 67th St., is named for the first woman to be appointed district supervisor in New York City's school system. She is credited with the establishment of the first P.T.A. in New York and with setting up classes for mentally retarded children.

• Arthur A. Schomburg High School, 2005 Madison Ave.

• Robert E. Simon High School, 600 E. 6th St. ☐

STATUE OF MOSES is one of the heroic-sized statues of famous lawgivers that ring the top of the exterior of the building of the Appellate Division of the State Supreme Court, Madison Ave. and 25th St. The Moses statue is in the center on the 25th St. side.

STRAUS PARK, 106 St. and West End Ave., is a triangular area containing a fountain in memory of Ida and Isidor Straus, philanthropist husband and wife who went down with the *Titanic*. Mrs. Straus remained with her husband after refusing to leave with the other women and children.

HENRIETTA SZOLD PL., at right angles with East 11th St., is named for Henrietta Szold, founder of Hadassah (see Baltimore, Md.).

The following theatres are named for prominent Jews:

Vivian Beaumont Theatre, Lincoln Center, is named for a daughter of Commodore Beaumont, philanthropist and department store tycoon, whose father was a pioneer merchant in Leadville, Colo.

Martin Beck Theater
Belasco Theater
Billy Rose Theatre

Brandt Theater chain
Loew Theater chain
Minskoff Theatre
Morosco Theatre
Mitzi E. Newhouse Theatre, Lincoln Center, is named for the wife of Samuel Newhouse, newspaper publisher.
Morton Robbins Theatre
Rugoff Theatre chain
Selwyn Theater
Shubert Theatre
Uris Theater chain

LILLIAN WALD PLAYGROUND, Monroe St., east of Montgomery, is named for the social work pioneer and founder of the Visiting Nurse Service.

UNITED NATIONS

UNITED NATIONS, 42nd to 48th Sts., from 1st Ave. to the East River. The permanent headquarters of the United Nations occupies 18 acres. The glass Secretariat building houses offices of approximately 4,000 employees of member nations. The shallow-domed General Assembly is the meeting place of the representatives to the organization. A limited number of tickets to various meetings are available on a first-come, first-served basis on the day of the meeting. Guided tours are conducted daily from 9:15 A.M. to 4:45 P.M.

Few visitors to the United Nations do not see the connection between the international peace organization and Jewish contributions to world civilization, but inscribed on the wall of the Plaza stairway (43rd St. and 1st Ave.), across the street from the UN enclave, are the words of the Prophet Isaiah: "They shall beat their swords into plowshares and their spears into pruning hooks. Nation shall not lift up sword against nation, neither shall they learn war any more." Only recently was Isaiah's name added to the inscription, largely due to the efforts of Sam Brown, who conducts tours to New York sites of Jewish interest. Isaiah's vision of a war-free world has become a universal ideal; so universal, in fact, that the same idea is expressed on the base of a statue the Soviet Union donated to the UN. The statue, an impressive nine-foot sculpture of a man beating a sword into a plowshare, stands on a broad, granite base in the rose garden north of the General Assembly building. The work of Russian sculptor Evgeniy Vuchetich, the statue won the "Grand Prix" diploma at the Brussels World Exhibition in 1958. On the base is inscribed part of the same verse from Isaiah, "We shall beat our swords into plowshares." The late Secretary General Dag Hammarskjöld, in accepting the statue from the Soviet representative, said that the "dream of world peace" was Isaiah's and that the statue "gives symbolic expression" to Isaiah's words. □

• UNITED NATIONS ABRAHAM H. FELLER READING
ROOM, UN Building, 42nd St., has a 7,000-volume legal library of the
United Nations, named after the first principal director of the organization's
legal department—the late Abraham H. Feller. It contains Feller's collection of books on international organization and international law. There is
also a portrait of Feller and a bronze commemorative plaque with a quotation
from his last book, *The United Nations and World Community:* "The
Charter bears the seeds of a greater growth, which, if nourished by
governments and peoples, can be made to give forth the fruit of deliverance
from our age-long perils." Abraham Feller was one of the principal architects
of the UN Relief and Rehabilitation Administration (UNRRA). In 1944-45,
he served as general counsel and as UNRRA representative to the
International Labor Organization Conference, and to the Bretton Woods
Monetary Conference in 1944; in 1949 he became the first American lawyer to
appear before the International Court of Justice at The Hague. He was
General Counsel of the UN from February 1946 until his death on November
13, 1952.

• Drawing the attention of the thousands of visitors to the UN is the
gift of Israel—4,000 square feet of stone slabs from the Kastel Hills near
Jerusalem. The stones are in a special garden patio within the open area that
connects the UN's three major structures: the Secretariat building, the
Conference building, and the General Assembly building.

• The United Nations Meditation Room is a darkened room where
people of all faiths can enter, sit on a stone bench and meditate in silence. Just
outside the door is a bronze plaque commemorating the 37,000 servicemen
who died while fighting under the United Nations' unified command.

• In front of the Secretariat building stands a 21-foot bronze
sculpture memorializing the late Dag Hammarskjöld, Secretary General of
the UN. It was a gift of the Jacob and Hilda Blaustein Foundation. Jacob
Blaustein, a former member of the American delegation to the UN and
honorary president of the American Jewish Committee, was a close friend
of Hammarskjöld. The sculpture, titled *Single Form,* is the work of the
well-known British sculptress, Barbara Hepworth. It is mounted on a
granite plinth. ☐

BROOKLYN

The 514,000 Jews who lived in the 88.8 square miles of Brooklyn in 1976 accounted for 42 percent of the city's total Jewish population and more than the combined total in 42 states. Brooklyn has more Jews than all of Europe excluding the Soviet Union, France, and Great Britain. A few square blocks of Brooklyn house as many Jews as there are in Detroit, St. Louis, or Cleveland.

In 1923 Brooklyn became the borough with the largest Jewish population, reaching 740,000 while Manhattan's fell to 706,000. A peak of 920,000 was reached in 1950 after which Brooklyn's Jewish population began to decline as the tide of Jewish settlement shifted to Queens and the suburban counties. By 1958 it had declined to 854,000, and in 1963 to 765,000.

Permanent Jewish settlement in Brooklyn can only be traced to 1834, the year it received its municipal charter as a separate city, but the history of Brooklyn Jewry begins much earlier. Asser Levy owned substantial property in the 1660s and 1670s in what used to be called Bruecklen. The archives of Kings County preserve a document dated August 15, 1683, recording the purchase of a slave by Peter Strijker of Vlackebos (Flatbush) from "the worthy Abraham Franckfoort, a Jew residing in N. Jorck (New York)." The sale was made in the village of Midwout (Midwood) and the seller signed himself "Aberham Franckfort."

Town records of New Utrecht, New Lots, Gravesend, Williamsburg, and other villages later incorporated into Brooklyn indicate that other Jews also did business there in the early 18th century. Jacob Franks, one of the presidents of Manhattan's Shearith Israel, owned a summer estate in Flatbush in the mid-1700s. Several Jews from New York and Philadelphia shared the hardships of the Continental Army during the Battle of Long Island, which was fought in Brooklyn. Samuel Noah, a kinsman of Mordecai M. Noah and a graduate of the 1807 class at West Point, helped build the defenses of Brooklyn against an anticipated British attack during the War of 1812.

The Jewish community began in the 1830s with separate but almost simultaneous settlements around lower Fulton Street, in what is now the Borough Hall section, and in Williamsburg, then an independent town north of Brooklyn. The founding fathers were immigrants from Bavaria and Alsace who set up small retail establishments. The 1838 Brooklyn directory lists Benjamin Levy as owner of a variety store; Daniel Levy, cartman; another Benjamin Levy, auctioneer; and a Moses family—all with Fulton Street addresses. The first known Jewish settler in Williamsburg was Adolph Baker, who arrived in 1837. By the middle 1840s, there was a good-sized Jewish settlement around Grand Street. Emanuel Pike, a Dutch Jew who had a haberdashery shop in downtown Brooklyn in the late 1840s, was the father of Lipman Pike, the first professional baseball player.

The 1850 census showed Jews prominent in the feed business, tailoring, dry goods, cigarmaking, and meat packing, as well as a scattering of laborers, machinists, watchmakers, ropemakers, pharmacists, and junk dealers. The 1850s saw the establishment of Samuel Liebman's brewery, now Rheingold, the Katz brewery, and the Eagle Fireworks Co., founded in Williamsburg in 1856 by Philip Licht, who made signal rockets for the Union Army during the Civil War. The meat packing industry along Bushwick Avenue was started when a kosher slaughtering house was opened there in 1851 by Ernest Nathan. The dry goods emporium founded in 1865 by Abraham Abraham and Joseph Wechsler became Abraham & Straus, Brooklyn's largest department store. The present name was adopted in 1893 when Isidore and Nathan Straus, who built Macy's, joined the firm. The Namm and Loeser stores, now out of business, both began in the late 1870s. By then, half of Brooklyn's clothing manufacturers were Jews. They also dominated the dry goods field and were important factors in tobacco manufacturing and baking.

An apocryphal tale made up by a couple of Jewish newspapermen in the 1930s gave rise to the legend that Jews from the Borough Hall and Williamsburg sections used to row across the East River to New York on Friday afternoon for worship services and return to Brooklyn on Sunday. Private services in homes or stores began in the 1840s. Public worship by Jews was unknown in Brooklyn until 1851. In that year, Kahal Kodesh Beth Elohim, the first Jewish congregation in Brooklyn and in all Long Island, was organized by Louis Reinhardt, Elias Adler, Isaac Mayer, Moses Kessel, and Isaac Eisman. New York's Congregation Anshe Chesed loaned the Brooklyn group its first Torah. David Barnard, Beth Elohim's first cantor, was listed in Williamsburg's 1849 directory as "Hebrew teacher" and "fancy grocer." Brooklyn's earliest Jewish school was opened behind Barnard's grocery on Grand Street.

A rented hall on what is now Marcy Avenue was Beth Elohim's first house of worship after it outgrew Kessel's home. Its first synagogue, erected on Keap Street in 1876, was Brooklyn's second synagogue. The first was dedicated in 1862 at the corner of Boerum Place and State Street by Congregation Baith Israel, formed by a Borough Hall group in 1854 under the leadership of Morris Ehrlich, Solomon Furth, Morris Hess, and Mark Marks.

Most of the other congregations founded in Brooklyn before the 1880s were offshoots of Beth Elohim and Baith Israel. Williamsburg's Beth Elohim was consolidated in 1921 with Temple Israel, established in 1869, to form Union Temple. In 1861 secessionists from Beth Israel created another Beth Elohim—Brooklyn's first Reform congregation. It is now known as the Garfield Place Temple. Beth Israel's first rabbi was Aaron Wise, father of Dr. Stephen S. Wise. The municipal traffic court at Lafayette and Bedford

Avenues is the former synagogue of Temple Israel, two of whose rabbis, Judah L. Magnes and Nathan Krass, were "promoted" to the pulpit of Emanu-El in New York. Congregation Ahabath Achim, founded in 1868, and Beth Jacob, formed in 1867 in Williamsburg and later merged with Anshe Sholom, were also offshoots of Beth Israel.

A Jewish community also developed around 1850 in Greenpoint where the established settlers were hostile. Jewish funeral processions going through Greenpoint and Williamsburg before the Civil War were frequently attacked by hoodlums. The first Jewish cemetery in Brooklyn, Union Fields in Cypress Hills, was opened in 1848 by the pioneer congregation in Williamsburg. When burials were banned in Manhattan, Congregation Shearith Israel of New York bought a seven-acre tract on the heights of Cypress Hills overlooking Jamaica Bay, about five miles from Williamsburg. Many New York Jews first visited Brooklyn to attend funerals. The huge Washington Jewish Cemetery, on the edge of Bensonhurst, was originally a nondenominational burying ground but later became exclusively Jewish. The oldest section of the Jewish cemetery at Cypress Hills has a monument to Jewish Civil War veterans. Nearby are the graves of Supreme Court Justice Benjamin N. Cardozo, Emma Lazarus, Commodore Uriah P. Levy, and Rabbi Judah L. Magnes. In a newer section, owned by the Workmen's Circle, is a pantheon of Jewish labor leaders and literary figures. Side by side lie Sholom Aleichem, Meyer London, Max Pine, general secretary of the United Hebrew Trades; Morris Rosenfeld, poet of the sweatshops; and Benjamin Schlesinger, one of the founders of the International Ladies Garment Workers Union.

Several of the pre-Civil War Jewish residents of Brooklyn were important personalities. Sigismund Kaufmann, a refugee from the 1848 revolutions in Europe, who settled in Brooklyn in 1849, taught French and German and studied law while working in a pocketbook factory. He and Dr. Joseph Goldmark, also a '48er, helped organize the Republican party in Brooklyn. Goldmark owned a Brooklyn factory that made percussion caps and cartridges. When draft rioters set the factory on fire in 1863, one of those detailed to protect the premises, where ammunition for the Union Army was being produced, was Solomon Furth, Beth Israel's first president, who was a member of a National Guard cavalry regiment. Goldmark's daughters married Dr. Felix Adler, founder of the Ethical Culture movement, and Louis D. Brandeis. Kaufmann, who campaigned for John Fremont in the 1856 presidential election, was one of the draft board judges in 1863 when New York and Brooklyn were bedeviled by antidraft riots. A Lincoln presidential elector, Kaufmann lost a race for the State Senate from Brooklyn in 1869. He presided over the meeting that led to the formation of the Brooklyn Hebrew Orphan Asylum in 1878. Michael Heilprin, a political refugee from Hungary and a foe of slavery; Col. Leopold C. Newman, who lost a foot at the Battle of Chancellorsville in 1863 and who is said to have received a deathbed visit from Lincoln; and Morris Hess were among

Brooklyn's leading supporters of Lincoln.

When Brooklyn still had only a handful of Jews, the Reverend Henry Ward Beecher, whose sister, Harriet Beecher Stowe, wrote *Uncle Tom's Cabin*, created a national stir by defending them from the anti-Semitism of Judge Henry Hilton, the department store king. Beecher's sermon in Plymouth Church, Brooklyn, in 1877, entitled "Jew and Gentile," remains a classic of philo-Semitism. Beecher's denunciation of anti-Semitism was also aimed at Austin Corbin, a real estate promoter who had publicly proclaimed a wish that Jews would not patronize his new and lavish resort at Manhattan Beach, which he hoped would become "the most fashionable and magnificent watering place in the world." But, he added, "we cannot bring the highest social element to Manhattan Beach if the Jews persist in coming." Many Christian patrons of Corbin's hotel, led by the celebrated atheist orator, Robert G. Ingersoll, bitterly assailed Corbin.

A piece of doggerel popular at the time indicates that Coney Island and Manhattan Beach were not only attractive to middle-class Jews from New York but also to Jewish peddlers:

> On ev'ry path, by almost every turn,
> Industrious Israelites a living earn,
> By selling colored specs to screen the eye,
> Which would not serve an idiot to disguise.

Corbin hated Jews, but he thought it good business to lure away Jules Levy, cornetist in the rival Oriental Hotel, by raising his salary from $350 to $750 a week to get him to play at the Manhattan Beach Hotel. Levy was adored by the ladies who swooned over him as teenagers of later generations did over crooners.

After the turn of the century, when Coney Island became the summer playground of the masses of New York, part of its fame was attributable to the showmanship of Samuel Gumpertz, who has a permanent niche in show business history as the godfather of the sideshow, and more particularly the freak. From 1906-1930, Gumpertz brought to Coney Island countless oddities and outlandish human beings he found all over the world. Unlike P. T. Barnum's frauds, Gumpertz located genuinely bizarre people on trips to Borneo, Java, and Africa. He was also the organizer of midget sideshows and performances by child acrobats, staged Buffalo Bill's Wild West exposition, and exploited the talents of Harry Houdini.

When the famous Dreamland burned before World War I, Gumpertz put together the Dreamland sideshow, developed the Surf Avenue concessions, bought Barnum's Eden Musee on 23rd Street in New York, and set up the Coney Island waxworks. Later, he was managing director of the Barnum & Bailey Circus. Dr. Moses Bluestone, the first Jewish doctor in the Coney Island area, was for years the personal physician to Gumpertz's freaks. Robert Moses and Paul Moss, the New York City license commissioner, wrote finis in 1938 to Coney Island's ballyhoo artists by outlawing the spielers and ending its raucous era.

In the summer of 1915, Nathan Handwerker, who managed a small downtown Manhattan restaurant, went to work for Feltman's famous shore restaurant at Coney Island. Within a year, Handwerker had opened his own stand, pioneering the nickel hot dog. Until the subway reached Coney Island, he almost went broke. He made his fortune when he picked a choice location between the new boardwalk and the subway terminal. The "follow the crowd to Nathan's" sign became a landmark. At first Handwerker had to hire ten bums clothed in white suits and carrying stethoscopes to line up at the stand, above which was a sign, "If doctors eat our hot dogs, you know they're good." From then on Nathan's was an institution. "Make mine Nathan's" became a national slogan and the hot dog became a national habit. Campaigning for the governorship of New York in 1958, Nelson Rockefeller, while eating a hot dog at Nathan's, blurted out, "no one can hope to be elected in this state without being photographed eating a hot dog at Nathan's Famous." Since then scores of candidates for city, state, and even national office have included Nathan's in their New York vote-gathering itinerary.

Corbin's old domain ultimately became almost as solidly Jewish as the old East Side. In the 1960s more than half the residents of Coney Island, Brighton Beach, and Manhattan Beach, once fashionable resort areas and the meccas of the sporting world, were Jewish. Sea Gate, that portion of Coney Island, west of 37th Street, once a millionaire's preserve and where non-Jews made their last stand on New York's beaches, became a middle-class enclave of 8,000 residents. Most of them were Jewish professionals and business people who lived behind a 12-foot high wire fence and maintained their own synagogue and center. Today Sea Gate is a polyglot middle-class community, still largely white, whose fence has become "a fortification of chain link and barbed wire," and where many fewer Jewish families now reside. The Coney Island beach area, once a rival of Atlantic City as the nation's summer entertainment capital, is now but a shell of its past glory. Central Coney Island, which once housed a predominantly white Jewish population, is now a mixed community of blacks and Puerto Ricans, second generation Italians, and a remnant of poor and elderly Jews seeking to live out their years in familiar but increasingly hostile surroundings. New high rise housing projects are occupied largely by low income families, but Coney Island as a whole is a poverty area and one of the most dilapidated in the city. The Jewish senior citizens fear to go out at night, but in the day time and in good weather they crowd the boardwalk benches. The Jewish Association for Services to the Aged has built the Scheuer House, a residence for elderly Jews, a block from the boardwalk.

Brighton Beach, which is adjacent to Coney Island, has the largest elderly population in the city. While persons over 65 account for 12 percent of the city's population, in Brighton Beach they are 35 percent of the 27,300 residents, almost all of whom are Jews. Many have lived there for 35 to 40 years. They live for the most part in apartment houses of 1930 vintage, rooming houses, one and two-family houses, and winterized bungalows. The quarter of a mile from Brighton First Street to Coney Island Avenue is a tiny Yiddish-speaking shtetl where the old sit day after day in good weather on folding chairs or benches and talk about yesterday.

The Brighton Beach community has been called "the Fort Lauderdale of the senior set" because it is a community of aged and retired former shopkeepers, garment workers, union activists, Yiddishists, widowed housewives, and widowers, all living on Social Security and small pensions. The Shorefront YM & YWHA has 1,400 senior citizens in its programs. The Jewish Association for Services to Aged maintains a community service there which collaborates with the Y in serving the aged. The area has recently been nicknamed "Odessa-by-the-sea" because it has attracted many of the newly-arrived Russian Jews who settled in New York. The Brighton Beach community is very Orthodox, so much so that its pizza parlors have signs assuring patrons that the tomato sauce and ersatz pepperoni are prepared under strict rabbinical supervision.

On the other hand, the Brighton Beach Baths, a private club, is the Rose Bowl and World Series of handball, because its courts have produced an endless number of national champions, most of them Jewish. Manhattan Beach, once described as the Newport of the city's bathing areas, has many high rise apartment houses where large numbers of middle-class Jews live. The same is true of Sheepshead Bay, just east of Manhattan and Brighton Beaches.

Brooklyn attracted few East European Jews until the late 1880s. Right after the Civil War, Greenpoint, a largely German and Irish neighborhood, had as its Republican boss Benjamin Raphael. Half a mile away, in Williamsburg, Ernest Nathan and Jacob Brenner, both German Jews, held the same office. Abraham Oppenheimer succeeded Nathan and was in turn succeeded by Israel Fisher, who in 1894 became the first Jew elected to Congress from Brooklyn. One of the last German Jews of influence was the late Meir Steinbrink, Kings County Republican leader in the 1920s, subsequently a State Supreme Court judge and national chairman of the Anti-Defamation League of B'nai B'rith.

While the older German-Jewish settlement was still concentrated in Williamsburg, Borough Hall, and Greenpoint, the flood of East European immigrants to New York began to spill over into Brooklyn for the first time. Hundreds of refugees from Czarist pogroms were temporarily sheltered in 1881 at hastily erected barracks in Greenpoint.

The earliest large-scale Jewish settlement was in Brownsville. It began when Jacob Cohen, a New York clothing manufacturer, bought a house in Brown's Village in 1885 because his wife needed the fresh country air. A tiny farm village beyond Brooklyn's city limits, its bucolic quiet was broken forever when Cohen moved his factory to Brown's Village and was followed by many of his Jewish workers. After the opening of the Fulton

Street elevated line, other East Side sweatshop operators moved to Brownsville and thousands of their workers followed suit. Farmers cut up their land into building lots which were sold to speculators who in turn sold to realtors and builders. Tailors became landlords and some early Jewish fortunes were based on the Brownsville real estate boom. Louis Horowitz and the Chanin brothers, who later helped change the New York skyline, did their first building in Brownsville and Williamsburg.

By 1900, Brownsville was a worse slum than the East Side. Unpaved streets and walks, homes without drains and sewers, only one public bathhouse, and streets that were morasses in wet weather, made the area unhealthy. Yet, between 1890 and 1900 more than 15,000 Jewish sweatshop workers lived there, attracted by cheap rents and the accessibility of work in a rural atmosphere. The Jewish peddlers of Brownsville formed the American Hebrew League of Brooklyn in the 1890s to protect themselves from neighboring toughs. The same labor union ferment that stirred the East Side boiled up in Brownsville. Abraham Shiplacoff, a Brownsville sweatshop worker, who studied law at night, became secretary of the United Hebrew Trades and labor editor of the *Jewish Daily Forward*. In 1916, Brownsville sent him to the State Legislature as the first Socialist assemblyman. A leader of the 1921-22 clothing workers' strike, Shiplacoff was general manager of the Amalgamated Clothing Workers of America. In his last years, he managed the Brownsville Labor Lyceum.

The most influential civic factor in Brownsville was the Hebrew Educational Society, founded in 1899 with the aid of the Baron de Hirsch Fund. The first Jewish Community Center in Brooklyn, the HES opened milk stations, baby clinics and manual training classes, established farm gardens, organized a branch of the Public Library, and promoted the public evening school system. Patterned after the East Side's Educational Alliance, the Brownsville center encouraged Jewish traditions and cultural activities while furthering Americanization.

By 1917, Brownsville rivaled the East Side as an almost all-Jewish community. On the eve of World War I, over 150,000 Jews lived there. Isolated from the rest of the city, Brownsville not only had its own synagogues and Jewish educational institutions, but a growing class of professional men, educators, merchants, and artists. Except for public school teachers and policemen, the average Jew in Brownsville rarely encountered non-Jews. The area even had a flourishing Yiddish theatre, now a black Baptist church.

Out of this milieu came a notable array of eminent American Jews. Among the teachers in Brownsville's Hebrew schools were the late Rabbi Solomon Goldman of Cleveland and Chicago; Dr. Solomon Grayzel, for many years editor of the Jewish Publication Society of America; and Dr. Louis Finkelstein, for a generation chancellor of the Jewish Theological Seminary of America, whose father was a Brownsville *shochet*. On the teeming streets of the Brownsville ghetto there grew up David Kominsky, known to the world as Danny Kaye; Max Weber, the noted sculptor; Aaron Copland, one of the creators of modern American music; Alfred Kazin, the literary critic; Sol Hurok, whose first presentation occurred when he prevailed upon Efrem Zimbalist to play before a Jewish cultural society in Brownsville; Mortimer Caplin, later United States Collector of Internal Revenue, whose father peddled brushes and second hand shoes from a pushcart; and Joseph H. Hirshhorn, uranium king and art collector, whose collection is housed in the Hirshhorn Museum in Washington.

"Murder, Inc." also came out of the Brownsville slums, but the majority of the immigrant children raised in Brownsville were a credit to the city and nation, just as their contemporaries on the East Side were. A Brownsville cloakmaker was the father of Dr. Arthur Kornberg, who shared the 1955 Nobel Prize in medicine. Sylvia Porter, widely syndicated columnist, was born in Brownsville. So were Colonel David "Mickey" Marcus, the West Pointer who organized and led Israel's army; Lt. Commander Solomon Esquith, who won the Navy Cross for directing the rescue of the USS *Utah* at Pearl Harbor; and Meyer Berger, the *New York Times'* legendary reporter who had a love affair with New York.

Other well-known figures from Brownsville were Sid Luckman, one of the all-time greats of college and pro football; Vic Hershkowitz, the greatest all-around handball player of the century, who learned the game at the Hebrew Educational Society; Sid Gordon, who starred for the New York Giants baseball team at the Polo Grounds; and Al McCoy, neé Al Rudolph, who shared the middleweight boxing title in 1914-17. Abe Stark, long the unofficial mayor of Brownsville, was elected Borough President of Brooklyn, the first Jew to hold this office. He had previously served as president of the New York City Council. The Brownsville Boys Club which Stark built is now part of the city park system. New York's first Jewish mayor, Abraham Beame, is also a native of Brownsville.

That Brownsville is no more. In the 1970s, the historic Jewish neighborhood had become a four-mile area of blight that resembled a bombed-out city. When younger Jewish families began moving out in the mid-1960s, private houses and tenements fell into disrepair and poor blacks and Puerto Ricans began moving in. Gradually, the area became a dumping ground for evicted tenement dwellers from urban renewal projects elsewhere, and for welfare clients. The last Jewish institution to close in Brownsville was the Stone Avenue Talmud Torah, the last of 200 synagogues in the area. Of the 400,000 Jews who once lived in Brownsville, only a tiny remnant of some 1,500 were left in 1976. They had been trapped by age, illness, extreme poverty, and the inability to cope with bureaucratic systems. Federation's Coordinating Council on Jewish Poverty sought to aid the remaining Jews in Brownsville through a variety of projects involving a volunteer escort service manned by college volunteers, a transportation service operated by the Jewish Association for Service to the Aged, and other activities. The independent Council for the Jewish Poor set up a store-front center as a combined meeting place and synagogue. The Hebrew Educational Society, for so long the principal cultural agency of the Jewish community, relocated to Canarsie.

The arrival of hundreds of thousands of additional East European Jews after 1900 and the razing of whole blocks of East Side slums to make way for the Williamsburg Bridge in 1903 and the Manhattan Bridge in 1909, caused a great surge of Jewish migration to Williamsburg, directly across the river from the East Side. While the German Jews gradually retreated to Greenpoint, the Bedford-Stuyvesant area, and the streets around Prospect Park, the newcomers established their own synagogues and Jewish schools. Newly-built elevated and subway lines that brought Williamsburg and other close-in sections of Brooklyn within easy reach of Manhattan's factories and the erection of inexpensive one and two-family dwellings and modern apartment houses in the period between 1910 and 1920, gave impetus to recurring waves of Jewish migration from Manhattan and the older sections of Brooklyn. The move to Williamsburg, and later to Borough Park, Crown Heights, and Bensonhurst was often the first step up the ladder from the East Side tenements.

Each population shift created new institutions as the larger synagogues followed their congregants to the new neighborhoods, but in each old neighborhood there always remained a substantial community, flourishing synagogues, and Jewish schools. The middle-class Jews were the first to quit Williamsburg, their exodus having begun in the 1930s. The more Orthodox Jews stayed on despite rapid neighborhood changes. When the ultra-Orthodox Chasidim, survivors of the Holocaust, arrived after World War II, most of them settled in Williamsburg and later in nearby Crown Heights, both of which became Chasidic strongholds. The older Orthodox residents of Williamsburg, not considered Orthodox enough by the Chasidic newcomers, moved out as blacks and Puerto Ricans moved in, transferring their Orthodox institutions to Queens and Long Island. A mile-square area of Williamsburg, on the edge of the almost all-black Bedford-Stuyvesant area, became known as the "Jerusalem of America." There the Chasidim under the rule of rabbinic dynasties tried to "make paths of heaven out of grimy streets."

The replacement of slum dwellings with public housing projects, where the Chasidim would not live because they would not use elevators on the Sabbath, and the increasing influx of blacks and Puerto Ricans pushed some of the Chasidim out of Williamsburg and into Crown Heights and Borough Park. The Chasidim who remained in Brooklyn—two groups established separate colonies in upstate New York (see New York)—erected their own community buildings, established their own medical services, opened their own stores, and organized an ambulance and bus service, in addition to synagogues, yeshivas, and *glatt* kosher butchers. Many of the Chasidim were counted among the city's poor Jews, and on their behalf Federation created a Commission on Chasidic Affairs to help this community achieve its legitimate health and welfare needs.

A three-story red brick house on Eastern Parkway in Crown Heights is the world headquarters of the Lubavitcher Chasidim, who first established themselves in Williamsburg, in 1941, with the arrival of Rabbi Joseph Isaac Schneersohn, a direct descendant of the founder of Chasidism. To anchor the Chasidic community in Crown Heights, the Lubavitchers bought houses in their neighborhood with the aid of loans from the Hebrew Free Loan Society. During the early 1960s, many of the Jews of Crown Heights abandoned the area, those remaining decided to stand fast in the neighborhood. The Lubavitcher Rebbe called on his followers and other Jews to stay in the neighborhood. Many listened and some even moved back from other areas. Because the Lubavitcher Chasidim have not sealed themselves off from secular activities, they have acquired political clout in the neighborhood. In the 1970s, the police began diverting vehicular traffic on Saturdays between 9 A.M. and 9 P.M. from Crown Heights streets on which Lubavitcher synagogues are located and where there is heavy foot traffic by Chasidim.

The Crown Heights Community Corporation, an anti-poverty center financed by public funds, was headed by a rabbi in the 1970s, staffed by Orthodox youths, served both Jews and blacks, and was professionally directed by Simon Levine, a non-Jewish black. Although there has been some conflict between the Chasidim and blacks in Crown Heights, on the whole, both groups have accommodated themselves to each other. For a time police dressed in Chasidic garb were assigned to Crown Heights, Borough Park, and Williamsburg in an effort to apprehend hoodlums who specialized in molesting Chasidic rabbis and students. In the 1960s, Rabbi Samuel Schrage organized the Maccabees as a Jewish auxiliary patrol manned by bearded Jews and armed only with large flashlights in an effort to fight a crime wave against Jews in Crown Heights and to protect Jewish schools and synagogues from vandals.

An even more important Jewish neighborhood in Brooklyn is Borough Park, which has been a major area of Jewish residence since the 1920s. Nearly 60 to 75 percent of the 80,000 to 90,000 people there are Jewish and the rest are of Italian and Hispanic origin. There were 140 Jewish organizations in the area in 1976. Dozens of stores display signs announcing that they are closed on Saturdays. *Glatt* kosher establishments are common. Many stores advertise "Sabbath clocks" that control electrical appliances on the Sabbath. Borough Park's 13th Avenue from the 30s to 50th Street is a mile of lower middle-class Jewish businesses reminiscent of a shtetl. Though many younger Jews have moved to Queens and the suburbs, this loss has been balanced by Orthodox Jews from Williamsburg and Crown Heights. Thirteenth Avenue is crowded with stores that sell prayer shawls, black hats for rabbinical students, *kiddush* cups, Yiddish and Hebrew records, and kosher food stores of all kinds. A bus line operated by Sabbath-observing drivers links the Jewish communities of Williamsburg, Crown Heights, and Borough Park. It does not run on Saturdays or Jewish holidays. Borough

Park's Jewish community is diversified. There are settlements of Yemenite, Lebanese, Egyptian, and Syrian Jews there, although the latter are more numerous in adjacent Bensonhurst and in Forest Hills, Queens. The Yemenites have their own synagogue, restaurants, and social clubs. Some of them have recently moved to Queens. Borough Park's kosher pizza parlors are run by Yemenites.

East Flatbush, once a solid middle-class Jewish neighborhood, underwent rapid change in the early 1970s as the area became about 15 percent black and Puerto Rican. Flatbush and East Flatbush had been settled before World War I by the children of Jewish immigrants who were raised in the tenements of the East Side, Brownsville, and Williamsburg, and who followed the new subway lines into the farmlands of eastern Brooklyn. When people in Brooklyn referred to Flatbush in the 1970s, they meant a neighborhood into which blacks had not yet moved. However, by 1976, there were blacks in Flatbush and some Jews began leaving. A mosque for Albanian Moslems was opened in Flatbush in the 1970s. The exodus of middle-class Jews from East Flatbush to Canarsie, Queens, and the suburbs, left behind a large elderly Jewish population. Black, Puerto Rican, and Haitian families filled the vacancies left by the departing Jews. Bensonhurst, with its thousands of private homes, remained a largely lower middle-class area, 85 percent white, and equally divided between Jews and Italians.

East New York, once the home of 80,000 Jews, numerous synagogues, societies, and Jewish owned retail businesses, now has only a tiny pocket of old and poor Jews left. The former Jewish residents were largely working people, mostly Orthodox, who moved away under the impact of blockbusting by unscrupulous real estate brokers who panicked Jewish home owners into selling their property with stories that the "blacks are coming." In 1972, the East New York YM-YWHA, the area's major Jewish institution, moved to Queens.

Since World War II, the Jewish population of Brooklyn has shifted several times. Thousands of new households established by war veterans filled the middle-income apartments along the ocean front from Fort Hamilton to Canarsie and from Manhattan Beach to Coney Island, where new clusters of high rise buildings and one and two-family dwellings were heavily tenanted by Jews. Some Jews also began moving back to downtown Brooklyn, Brooklyn Heights, and to the civic center area, either as tenants in new co-ops or as owners of remodeled town houses.

Canarsie, once a sparsely settled marshland, became the center of a fast growing new Jewish community in the 1960s and 1970s. In 1976 there were 75,000 Jews in the area which had ten synagogues and the Hebrew Educational Society. Part Italian and part Jewish, Canarsie exploded in the 1970s over accepting minority students bussed in from East Flatbush. The opening of the new Starrett City housing development for middle-income families, stretching along both sides of Pennsylvania Avenue, between Flatlands Avenue and Shore Parkway, gave rise to a brand new Jewish community. A tent city synagogue opened by Congregation B'nai Israel was the first Jewish organization in this new complex. It was established in 1975, but since then a number of other Jewish groups have been formed to serve the needs of Jewish residents in the 46-building housing development.

Much of the postwar new building in Brooklyn was by Jewish developers, notably the Lefraks, who replaced Luna Park and Steeplechase Park in Coney Island with giant apartment houses, and Marvin Kratter who bought and tore down Ebbets Field, once a Brooklyn sports shrine, and built the Ebbets Houses on the site. George Klein of the Barton Candy Corp. is helping to rebuild Brooklyn's downtown shopping area. A number of new shopping malls in Brooklyn were built by Jewish entrepreneurs.

Although Brooklyn has been part of New York City since 1898, Jewish communal institutions developed independently of those in Manhattan. A Hebrew Benevolent Society organized by the German Jews of Williamsburg in 1868 to care for the local needy, became an important instrument in providing social welfare needs in Brownsville after 1890. Out of this society grew the Brooklyn Federation of Jewish Philanthropies in 1909. During the depression, the New York Federation of Jewish Philanthropies came to the aid of the older Brooklyn agency in order to preserve its service, and in 1937 the latter was merged into the New York Federation. There are a number of local Jewish community councils, as well as a borough-wide Jewish Community Council, and Brooklyn federations of the local units of national Jewish organizations. The Jewish Hospital, an outgrowth of the Hebrew Hospital Dispensary founded in 1895, is Brooklyn's oldest Jewish medical institution. The first Hebrew Home for the Aged was established in 1907, a year after the first YMHA was organized.

After World War I, the synagogue-center movement gained great impetus in Brooklyn among Conservative Jews. The largest of such institutions is the Brooklyn Jewish Center on Eastern Parkway. About half of all the synagogues in New York City are located in Brooklyn, and the great majority of them are Orthodox. There are over 100 Hebrew day schools and elementary and secondary yeshivas in Brooklyn, and a number of ultra-Orthodox rabbinical seminaries.

Jewish voters played an important part in making Brooklyn one of the most heavily Democratic voting areas in the state. Abraham D. Beame, who had served as City Controller before his election in 1973 as the city's first Jewish mayor, was for many years one of the key leaders of the Democratic Party in Kings County. Arthur Levitt, a Brooklynite who has been elected State Controller five times, twice winning reelection as the only Democratic to gain state office during gubernatorial victories by Nelson Rockefeller, failed to win the Democratic mayoralty nomination in 1961 against Robert F. Wagner, Jr. Stanley Steingut, who was elected speaker of the State Assembly, a post previously held by his father, the late Irwin Steingut, was Kings County Democratic leader in the 1960s. Emanuel Celler, who served in Congress from Brooklyn for 50 years, lost his seat in 1972 when he was defeated in the Democratic primary by Elizabeth Holtzman, who in 1976 was one of the two Jewish women serving in Congress, the other being Bella Abzug of Manhattan.

Some of Brooklyn's principal cultural institutions owe much to the leadership of Jews. The late Nathan Jonas was one of the founders of Long Island University. His $500,000 gift constituted the university's original endowment fund. He was the first chairman of the university's board of trustees and played a key role in the establishment of the Brooklyn branch of City College, now Brooklyn College. Jonas' contribution of $1 million fostered the merger of the Brooklyn and New York Federations. William Zeckendorf, Long Island University's board chairman in the 1960s, was a key factor in its postwar expansion into Long Island.

Simon Rothschild, of the Abraham & Straus Department Store, and his son, Walter Rothschild, were among Brooklyn's most influential civic leaders. The late Joe Weinstein, an immigrant who built a tiny Fulton Street store into the Mays department store chain, was known as "Mr. Brooklyn" because of the millions he gave to educational, religious, and philanthropic institutions. Julius Bloom, former director of the Brooklyn Academy of Music, the city's oldest performing complex, turned this perennial white elephant into the borough's cultural and artistic mecca. In his capacity as executive director of the Academy during the 1970s, he was mainly responsible for its renaissance. Under his direction, the Academy became Brooklyn's principal center for all the arts—from ballet to theatre and jazz. Siegfried Landau was director and conductor of the Brooklyn Philharmonic, the borough's only professional symphony orchestra, from 1955-1972.

New York sees, hears, enjoys, and reads the products of an unusually talented group of Jews who were raised in Brooklyn—playwright Arthur Miller, singer Barbra Streisand, writer Norman Mailer, novelist Bernard Malamud, actor Zero Mostel, opera star Beverly Sills, and a long list of vaudeville, radio, television, and nightclub comics such as Henny Youngman, Alan King, Sam Levenson, Phil Foster, Abe Burrows, Buddy Hackett, and Phil Silvers.

* * * * *

Of the many places of Jewish interest in New York City, Williamsburg in Brooklyn is perhaps one of the most fascinating, though it too, like other sections, has undergone vast changes. *(BMT Broadway subway to Hewes Street or Marcy Avenue; by car: across the Williamsburg Bridge to Keap or Hooper Streets.)*

The area is no longer the Williamsburg of yesteryear—it is run down but still unique in many respects. There are the Hasidic Jews, more Orthodox than those of a generation ago; there is also a large number of

Christians. Between the Hasidim and the non-Jewish community, there is a non-Hasidic Jewish community that serves as a "social wall" to deflect the values of the outside world before they can penetrate to the Hasidim.

In the Hasidic neighborhoods, there is no blare of the television set or the radio from any of the Jewish homes, since the Hasidim are not allowed to own a set. They do not read any of the regular Yiddish newspapers. They are frowned upon because the Hasidim feel "the editors are unsympathetic toward the Hasidic Jews and spread lies about them," and "the Yiddish papers are published on the Sabbath, and what can a religious Jew expect from desecrators of the Holy Sabbath?"

The visitor to the area can see Hasidic men with beards, *payot*, long black coats, and broad-brimmed hats; little boys with side-curls and *yarmulkas*; married women—all wearing wigs. Unmarried women and girls are not distinguishable from other single girls with the exception that they dress more modestly. Their dresses are high-necked and long-sleeved, and they always wear hose. Boys and girls are segregated from each other at a very early age, and they never attend any school or participate in activities in which the sexes are mixed.

The Hasidic Jews consider the garments they wear to be the traditional Jewish garments that were once the apparel of all Jews. The types of Hasidic clothing and the appearance of the Hasidim change from class to class, and serve as identifying symbols of social rank. The Hasidic garments vary from *zehr Hasidish* (extremely Hasidic) to *modernish* (modern). Those whose religious observances are less frequent and less intense, wear *modernish* clothing. This may be a long-outmoded dark double-breasted western suit that buttons from right to left.

To recognize the rank of a Hasid, the visitor must note the following: the *yiden* have the fewest Hasidic status symbols and wear *modernish* clothing; the *balebatishe yiden* have, in addition to the clothing, beards and side-locks (some beards are never cut or trimmed and some sidelocks are never cut or shaved, a symbol of still higher status); the *talmidei hachamim*, in addition to having beards and side-locks, also wear *biber* hats (large-brimmed black hats made of beaver); the *sheine yiden*, the next highest in rank, have all of these plus the *kapote*, a long overcoat, usually black, worn instead of a jacket; one rung higher is the *shtickel rebbes* who wear, in addition, the *shtreimel* (a fur hat made of sable) and the *bekecher*, a long Hasidic coat made of silk or a silky material in which the pockets are in the back; and highest are the *rebbes*, whose attire includes that of all the others plus *shich*, slipper-like shoes, and *zocken*, white knee socks into which the breeches are folded.

There are a profusion of Hasidic synagogues in Williamsburg, the most prominent of which is the Congregation Yetev Lev D'Satmar, 152 Rodney Street, headed by the renowned Satmar Rebbe. Within a radius of 40 square blocks there are 32 synagogues of varying sizes. Some of these are

Hasidic and others are non-Hasidic *(Mitnagid)*. The contrast is striking and interesting. Among these are the following:

ADAS YEREIM, Lee Ave., corner of Roebling St.
AHAVATH TORA BEIT YITZCHOK, 657 Bedford Ave.
CONG. AGUDATH ISRAEL, 240 Keap St.
CONG. AHAVATH ISRAEL, 240 Keap St.
CONG. ANSHEI BRISK D'LITAH, 274 Keap St., built in 1876, is the oldest shule in the area. It was also known as "Keap Street Shule."
CONG. ARUGATH HABOSEM, 559 Bedford Ave.
CONG. ATZEI CHAIM, 152 Jewes St.
CONG. BETH HAKNESETH CHOFETZ CHAIM, 284 Rodney St.
CONG. BETH JACOB OHEV SHALOM, 284 Rodney St.
CONG. BETH YEHUDA, 904-8 Bedford Ave.
CONG. OHEL MOSHE CHEVRA THILIM, 569 Willoughby Ave.
CONG. SHTIPANESHTER KALUS NUSSACH SFARD, 355 Keap St.
CONG. TIFERETH ISRAEL, 491 Bedford Ave.
CONG. ZEMACH DAVID CHASIDE SQUARE, 571 Bedford Ave.
SHOTZER SASSOWER CONG., 143 Rodney St.
YOUNG ISRAEL OF BROOKLYN, 563 Bedford Ave.
YOUNG ISRAEL OF WILLIAMSBURG, 730 Willoughby Ave.

In the midst of these synagogues is the only Jewish Community Center in the area, the YM & YWHA of Williamsburg, 575 Bedford Ave.

There are also many separate Hasidic religious schools for boys and girls. Numerous other schools are located all along Bedford Avenue and other streets in the area. The children in these schools attend classes from early morning to evening. There is a strong emphasis on the beliefs, rituals, and practices of Hasidism in addition to their secular studies.

LUBAVITCHER HIGH SCHOOL, 770 Eastern Parkway (Crown Heights), is also the office of the United Lubavitcher Yeshivoth and the Lubavitch World Headquarters.

YESHIVAH TORAH VODAATH AND MESIVTA, 425 E. 9th St. (Flatbush), is a preparatory school. The seminary, students' hall, alumni association, and executive offices of the organization are also at this address.

The kosher butcher shops and catering establishments in Williamsburg may look the same to the visitor as they do elsewhere, but they, too, are different. The meat must be *glatt* kosher (kosher beyond a doubt); the butcher must be a Hasid himself (no one else is trusted). Most of the *glatt* kosher butcher stores carry the name of the sponsoring rebbe or of the rebbe's organization, and avow that its net profit goes for the maintenance of the religious school.

KAHAL ARUGAT HABOSEM (Zehlimer Butcher Store), 61 Lee Avenue.

KAHAL TORAT HAIM (Wisnitzer Butcher Store), Ross St.

KAHAL YETEV LEV D'SATMAR, 174 Rodney St.

YITZHAK LEVY'S MEHADRIN GLATT KOSHER COMPANY, is a *glatt* kosher sausage factory.

Glatt kosher catering establishments not only serve *glatt* kosher meats but also have a room where a skylight can be opened above the canopy during wedding ceremonies.

BETH RACHEL HALL, Heyward St. near Bedford Ave.

THE CONTINENTAL, Rutledge St. near Wythe St.

KINGS TERRACE, Rutledge St. near Bedford Ave.

The Williamsburg area is dotted with stores that sell a variety of merchandise. There are numerous *shmura* matzo bakeries producing handmade matzos that have been guarded from the time of harvesting (the "most zealous of the zealous" will eat only handmade matzo that has been so guarded). Stores specializing in wigs and turbans for women to keep their hair covered, Hasidic dairy companies, *mikvahs*, Hasidic clothing shops, religious objects, hardware stores carrying kosher ritual baths for dishes and other objects, can be seen in this neighborhood. Among some of the more interesting are:

APPEL'S EGG MARKET, advertises unwashed eggs for Passover, which assures the buyer that the eggs were not washed in solutions containing *hometz* (leaven).

SUKKAT SHALOM WOODWORKING, 175 Lee Ave., sells portable *sukkahs*.

TIV-TOV HARDWARE STORE, 125 Lee Ave., sells *shabbos zeigers* used for turning house appliances on or off on the Sabbath.

WELHELM'S, 157 Division Ave., sells *shabbos zeigers* and other interesting religious items.

ZEIGER AND FARKAS CORP., 181 Marcy Ave., sells portable *sukkahs*.

A number of Hasidim have left Williamsburg for better sections of the city, the suburbs, uncrowded areas in New Jersey, and Israel. Physically, many parts of the area are slums. The high-rise housing developments pose a problem to the Hasidim, who refuse to ride elevators on the Sabbath. Those who do live in these new developments will only rent apartments on the lower floors.

The visitor to Williamsburg will sense the spirit that pervades the area, especially on such holidays as Purim, Simhas Torah, or just before Passover. On Purim, the young children masquerade either as characters in the Purim story, prominent personalities of today, or figures out of fairy tales. Hasidic men hurry arm in arm, carrying *shaloach manos* (Purim gifts), of food, including *hamantaschen,* or other items for their relatives, friends or others who are poorer than they. On Simhas Torah, streets are closed off for a gay celebration, with the Hasidim dancing and singing in the streets. Just before Passover, one can visit a matzo bakery and see how *shmura* matzo is made.

Another unusual occasion is a Hasidishe wedding. After the ceremony itself, the festivities start out slowly, gradually building up to an almost overwhelming crescendo of dancing, singing, clapping, and laughing. Men and women do not touch each other; even the bride and groom dance apart, each holding the end of a handkerchief between them. At all Hasidic festivals, men dance and dine with men, and women with women; a screen or wall generally separates the two sexes.

In the 1920s and 1930s the Williamsburg area was predominantly Jewish. Bedford Avenue was the main street for strollers to show off their finery. Jewish people from the Lower East Side moved to Williamsburg as a step upward on the social ladder. Starting in the 1940s, the Jewish people who prospered, began to move to Borough Park and Bensonhurst. The building of the Brooklyn-Queens Expressway in 1957 destroyed many houses and displaced hundreds of people in Williamsburg who then moved to Crown Heights and adjacent areas. The empty apartments that remained were taken over by many ultra-Orthodox Jews who had arrived from Hungary in the 1940s. These are the Williamsburg Hasidim of today.

Whether one goes to Williamsburg on special occasions or just at ordinary times, the visitor will be impressed with the inner religious spirit and joy rather than with the outer form; this is what the Hasidim themselves emphasize, and it is so.

SYNAGOGUES (Brooklyn—General)

ORTHODOX

AHI EZER CONG., 1885 Ocean Parkway.

CONG. BETH-EL OF BORO PARK, 4802 15th Ave., has a magnificent domed structure, with the lights on the inside of the dome forming the pattern of a Star of David.

CONG. ZICHRON RABBI ELIEZER MESKIN, 725 Crown St., was founded by black Jews, with the cooperation of white Jews, and is open to all.

MAGEN DAVID COMMUNITY CENTER, 34 Avenue P, is the center of cultural and social activities of the Syrian Jews.

CONSERVATIVE

BROOKLYN JEWISH CENTER, 667 Eastern Parkway, is one of the two oldest synagogue-centers in the country. Its $1 million structure has been a Brooklyn landmark since 1920. It was the first synagogue in Brooklyn with complete facilities for cultural, social, educational, and athletic activities, and its program set the pattern for the establishment of other large synagogue-centers.

BOULEVARD JEWISH CENTER, 1380 Linden Blvd., has a unified interior and exterior design with the milk-and-honey theme of the Bible as the motif. Over the entrance to the synagogue is a stylized 16-foot-high, seven-branched candelabrum, tipped by soft lights, as symbolic of both the ritual and of the motto that in unity there is strength.

CONGREGATION BAITH ISRAEL Anshei Emes, 236 Kane St., was organized by 12 men who, according to legend, grew tired of rowing across the river to Manhattan every Friday afternoon to attend Sabbath services. In 1862 they built the first synagogue in Brooklyn, at State and Boerum. It was near a stable of race horses, and soon there were complaints about "that loud praying from the synagogue" disturbing the horses. The minutes kept by the congregation reflect its changing nature. The first minutes were in English, written by Jews of Dutch and Portuguese descent. Later, they were written in German, after the wave of immigration from Germany. The German gave way to Yiddish, reflecting the flood of immigrants from Eastern Europe. Prior to the turn of the century, the minutes were again written in English, and have been since. The synagogue's congregation was originally Orthodox, but became Conservative during the Civil War. In 1905 the synagogue acquired its present building on Kane Street near Court. The high ceiling of the interior is painted almost white, and has finely wrought columns, an organ loft, balcony, and stained glass windows. It was originally built as a Dutch Reformed Church in 1846.

EAST MIDWOOD JEWISH CENTER, 1625 Ocean Ave., contains a tablet honoring the memory of the six million Jewish victims of Nazism. The tablet, measuring 8½ by 20 feet, is made of Italian marble with brass lettering; six lamps burn constantly at its base. It was the gift of Paul Lewis, a building contractor of Dallas, Texas, who has given similar memorials to other synagogues. The tablet is on the wall of the synagogue's lobby.

REFORM

CONG. BETH ELOHIM, 8th Ave. & Garfield Place, is popularly known as the Garfield Place Temple. It was founded in 1861 as Brooklyn's first Reform congregation by dissenters from Cong. Beth Israel.

PROGRESSIVE SYNAGOGUE, 1395 Ocean Ave., has a stained glass window which memorializes the six million Jews slain by the Nazis. The window design, executed by A. Raymond Katz, incorporates a figure representing a concentration camp survivor, the Nazi crematoria, and chimneys topped by the four freedoms in Hebrew.

UNION TEMPLE, 17 Eastern Parkway, is a 12-story building—possibly the tallest synagogue in the world. The temple is a union of Temple Israel of Lafayette and Bedford Aves., with Temple Beth Elohim (Keap Street Temple), as well as a union of the Reform Jews of the Williamsburg and Bedford sections. The temple contains, in addition to its sanctuary, an auditorium with a frescoed ceiling, social rooms, classrooms, and athletic facilities. The ceiling depicts the history of the synagogue, beginning with the Tabernacle in the Wilderness.

CEMETERIES

MOUNT CARMEL CEMETERY, Cypress Hill St. and Cypress Hill Ave., Workmen's Circle section, is a pantheon for outstanding figures in Jewish labor and Yiddish literary circles. Among those buried here are Sholom Aleichem, the Yiddish humorist; Meyer London, Congressman; B. Charney Vladeck, general manager of the *Jewish Daily Forward* and member of the first New York City Housing Authority; Abraham Cahan, noted editor of the *Forward;* Benjamin Schlesinger, founder of the International Ladies Garment Workers' Union; Max Pine, secretary of the United Hebrew Trades and a founder of the American Jewish Joint Distribution Committee (JDC); Abraham Shiplacoff, general manager of the Joint Board of the Amalgamated Clothing Workers of America; Morris Rosenfeld, Yiddish poet; and A. Litwak (Hayim Helfand), journalist and author. Before he died, Sholom Aleichem had said, "Let me be buried among the poor, that their graves may shine on mine and mine on theirs." His name in Hebrew is above the Yiddish poem he wrote for his own tombstone:

> *Here lies a simple-hearted Jew*
> *Whose Yiddish womenfolk delighted;*
> *All the common people, too,*
> *Enjoyed the stories he recited.*
> *Life to him was but a jest,*
> *He poked fun at all that mattered;*
> *When other men were happiest,*
> *His heart alone was bruised and shattered.*

TEMPLE BETH EL OF BORO PARK CEMETERY, near the Workmen's Circle section of the New Mt. Carmel Cemetery, has the grave of Mendel Beilis, who was accused of having murdered a Christian boy to use his blood for Passover. Beilis' trial took place in Kiev in 1913. Although the Czarist government fabricated evidence against Beilis, he was acquitted. Beilis settled in the United States in 1922 and died 12 years later.

UNION FIELDS CEMETERY, Jamaica Ave. and Crescent St. On August 3, 1851, Congregation Shearith Israel consecrated a tract of nearly seven acres on the heights of Cypress Hills overlooking Jamaica Bay, not far from Cypress Hills Cemetery. The following day, Abigail, the 80-year-old daughter of Aaron Lopez of Newport, R. I., and widow of Isaac Gomez, Jr., was the first to be buried there. The cemetery was chartered by the Legislature in 1853. A monument to Jewish soldiers in the Civil War was erected in the 1890s by the Hebrew Union Veterans Association, forerunner of the Jewish War Veterans. Buried in this cemetery are such Jewish notables as: Justice Benjamin Cardozo, Jacob de Haas, Bernard Hart, Emanuel B. Hart, Naphtali Judah, Israel Baer Kursheedt, Emma Lazarus, Commodore Uriah P. Levy, Dr. Judah L. Magnes, Benjamin Franklin Peixotto, and Adolphus S. Solomons. A plague with the words of *The New Colossus* is at the grave of Emma Lazarus.

MUSEUMS

BROOKLYN MUSEUM, Eastern Parkway and Washington Ave., has five symbolic statues representing Hebrew culture in a frieze on the outside of the left front of the building. The statues are not portraits, but representations of the "Hebrew Lawgiver," the "Hebrew Psalmist," the "Hebrew Prophet," and the "Hebrew Apostle." The names of Moses, David, Jeremiah, and Isaiah are cut in below the frieze. ●The Edward C. Blum Industrial Design Laboratory is a memorial to the late president of Federated Department Stores. ●The Frieda Schiff Warburg Memorial Sculpture Garden is named for the noted philanthropist. ●The museum has busts of comedians Alan King and Danny Kaye. ●The Worgelt Study, an extraordinary Art Deco room-within-a-room, is named in memory of Ethel Worgelt, who commissioned the room.

SCHOOLS AND SEMINARIES

SHOLOM ALEICHEM FOLK SHUL, 5013 10th Ave.
BETH EL TALMUDIC INSTITUTE, 1219 Ave. T.
BETH JACOB OF BORO PARK, 1371 46th St.
BETH JACOB TEACHERS SEMINARY OF AMERICA, 132 S. 8th St.
BIALIK SCHOOL, 500 Church Ave.
ISAAC BILDERSEE SCHOOL, 966 East 82nd St., is named for one of the Jews to be appointed a district school superintendent.
BOBOVER YESHIVA, 1533 48th St.
CENTER FOR HOLOCAUST STUDIES, 1605 Ave. J, has tapes of interviews, slides, movies, diaries, letters, posters, photographs, and clothing—all relating to the Holocaust. It was founded and is directed by Dr. Yaffa Eliach, professor of Judaic Studies at Brooklyn College—herself a survivor of the Holocaust.
CENTRAL YESHIVA BETH JOSEPH RABBINICAL SEMINARY, 1427 49th St.

FIRST HEBREW DAY NURSERY AND NEIGHBORHOOD HOUSE, 321 Roebling St.

GEORGE GERSHWIN THEATRE, Walt Whitman Hall, Brooklyn College.

GUR ARYEH INSTITUTE FOR ADVANCED JEWISH SCHOLARSHIP, 1373 President.

HARRY HERSKOWITZ INSTITUTE of Mesivta Torah Vodaath, 425 E. 9th St., at Cortelyou Rd., is an Orthodox rabbinic academy. The institute's two buildings, erected at a cost of $4 million, includes a residence hall, four libraries, an auditorium, outdoor and indoor gymnasiums, 35 classrooms, and two science laboratories. Harry Herskowitz, for whom the institute is named, was a prominent tax expert and educational philanthropist who died in 1954.

KAHAL KENESSETH SCHOOL, 723 Eastern Parkway.

KAMENITZER YESHIVA U'MESIVTA, 960 49th St.

MEYER LEVIN SCHOOL, 5909 Beverly Rd., is named for one of the first heroes of World War II.

LONG ISLAND UNIVERSITY EXTENSION, 385 Flatbush Ave. Nathan Jonas, lawyer and philanthropist, was one of the principal founders of L.I.U. in 1926, his gift of $500,000 constituting its original endowment. The university's first board chairman, he also played a major role in the creation of the Brooklyn branch of City College which became Brooklyn College. Jonas gave $1,000,000 in 1930 to make possible the merger of the Brooklyn and New York Jewish Federations of Philanthropies.

MACHZIKE TALMUD TORAH SCHOOL OF BORO PARK, 4622 14th Ave.

COL. DAVID MARCUS SCHOOL, 210 Chester St., is named for an eminent public servant and World War II intelligence officer who helped create Israel's army.

MESIVTA RABBI CHAIM BERLIN, 321 Ave. N.

MIRRER YESHIVA CENTRAL INSTITUTE, 1791 Ocean Parkway.

NER ISRAEL RABBINICAL COLLEGE, 599 Empire Blvd.

NEW HEBREW SCHOOL, 461 Empire Blvd.

DAVID PINSKY'S HEBREW FOLK SCHOOL, 1180 Brighton Beach Ave.

SIMON ROTHSCHILD SCHOOL, 300 Adelphi St., is named for one of the founders of the Abraham & Straus department store, who was one of Brooklyn's leading communal figures.

SHULAMITH SCHOOL FOR GIRLS, 1353 50th St.

STONE AVENUE TALMUD TORAH AND HEBREW FREE SCHOOL, 400 Stone Ave.

YESHIVA UNIVERSITY HIGH SCHOOL FOR BOYS, Church and Bedford Aves.

YESHIVA UNIVERSITY HIGH SCHOOL FOR GIRLS, 2301 Snyder Ave.

UNITED LUBAVITCHER YESHIVOTH, 770 Eastern Parkway.

HILLEL FOUNDATION

BROOKLYN COLLEGE, 2901 Campus Rd. This unit occupies the Abe Stark House, named for a former Brooklyn borough president.

JEWISH COMMUNITY CENTERS

EAST FLATBUSH-RUGBY YM & YWHA, 555 Remsen Ave., has the Henry Kaufmann Building, which offers an expanded program to a highly congested area with limited play space for children.

HEBREW EDUCATIONAL SOCIETY, 9502 Seaview Ave., is the oldest Jewish Community Center in Brooklyn, having been founded as a social and cultural center for newly-arrived immigrants who had settled in Brownsville. The Society organized the first reading room in the neighborhood; a penny provident fund; a kindergarten; and classes in English, citizenship, sewing, and music. The H.E.S.'s Young Peoples Fellowship is housed in an attractive colonial-style building at 1212 East New York Ave.

HENRIETTA AND STUARD HIRSCHMAN BUILDING of the YM & YWHA of Coney Island, 3330 Surf Ave. The Shorefront YM & YWHA is at 330 Coney Island Ave. The Kings Bay YM & YWHA, 3643 Nostrand Avenue.

JEWISH COMMUNITY HOUSE OF BENSONHURST, 7802 Bay Parkway, has been a hub of communal activity since it was established in 1906. It has been in its present building since 1927.

YM & YWHA OF BORO PARK, 4912 14th Ave.

YM & YWHA OF WILLIAMSBURG, 575 Bedford Ave.

HOMES AND HOSPITALS

BROOKDALE HOSPITAL MEDICAL CENTER, Linden Blvd. and Rockaway Parkway, has, in its Theodore Shapiro Residence Hall, a bronze plaque that was cast from the sculpted reproduction of *The Oath of Maimonides*.

BROOKLYN WOMEN'S HOSPITAL, 1395 Eastern Parkway.

FIRST UNITED LEMBERGER HOME FOR AGED, 8629 Bay Parkway.

INFANTS HOME OF BROOKLYN, 1358 56th St.

JEWISH CHRONIC DISEASE HOSPITAL, now known as Kingsbrook Jewish Medical Center, 86 E. 49th St.

JEWISH HOSPITAL AND MEDICAL CENTER OF BROOKLYN, 555 Prospect Pl., was the first Jewish medical institution established in Brooklyn. It was an outgrowth of the Hebrew Hospital Dispensary, which was founded in Williamsburg in 1895.

LONG ISLAND COLLEGE HOSPITAL, Henry and Pacific Sts.,

has a memorial room dedicated to Edward C. Blum, well-known Brooklyn merchant and civic leader.

MAIMONIDES MEDICAL CENTER, 4802 10th Ave., is Brooklyn's largest voluntary general hospital. The hospital also has a mental health center and a community services center.

MENORAH HOME AND HOSPITAL FOR AGED AND INFIRM, 871 Bushwick Ave.

SEPHARDIC HOME FOR THE AGED, 2266 Cropsey Ave.

UNITY HOSPITAL, 1534 St. Johns Pl.

HOUSING PROJECTS

SCHEUER HOUSE, 3601 Surf Ave., Coney Island, is a housing community for senior citizens developed by the Jewish Association for Services for the Aged, a member agency of the Federation of Jewish Philanthropies. It is named for S. H. Scheuer and family.

STARRETT CITY, a huge middle income 46-building development built on 150 acres of former marshes and landfill along Jamaica Bay in southeastern Brooklyn, has a large Jewish population among its 25,000 residents. A number of synagogues have been established and several national Jewish organizations have branches here.

COORDINATING AGENCIES

BORO PARK JEWISH COMMUNITY COUNCIL, 4910 14th Ave.

BROOKLYN JEWISH COMMUNITY COUNCIL, 16 Court St.

CROWN HEIGHTS JEWISH COMMUNITY COUNCIL, 387 Kingston Ave.

JEWISH WAR VETERANS MEMORIAL HALL, 220 Sullivan Pl.

ENGLISH-JEWISH PRESS

The Brooklyn Jewish Journal, 16 Court St.

The Jewish Press, 338 3rd Ave., is an Orthodox newspaper in the English language. It contains a wealth of Jewish educational material.

PARKS AND RECREATION AREAS

MONROE COHEN PARK, in area bounded by East 102nd and East 104th Sts., and Seaview Ave., is named for the late member of the City Council who represented the Canarsie area.

HERMAN DOLGIN PLAYGROUND, in Sheepshead Bay Housing Project, is named for a World War II hero.

FOX SQUARE, Flatbush Ave., Nevins St., Fulton St., and Flatbush Ave. Extension, is named for William Fox, movie tycoon and the theatre he opened here in 1931.

LOEW SQ., at intersection of Pitkin and Barrett St., in Brownsville, is named for Marcus Loew, pioneer movie producer and theatre owner, who opened one of the first penny arcades showing films in Brownsville.

COLONEL MARCUS PLAYGROUND, Ocean Pky. and Ave. P, is named for Col. David "Mickey" Marcus (see West Point, N. Y.).

PROSPECT PARK has the Michael Friedsam Memorial Merry-Go-Round at the Empire Blvd. entrance, a memorial to the noted merchant and philanthropist. In the Music Grove there is a eucalyptus tree that was flown from Israel in 1953 and planted in the park on the fifth anniversary of Israel's independence.

SHIPLACOFF PARK AND PLAYGROUND, Sackman and Powell Sts., is named for Abraham J. Shiplacoff, one-time sweatshop worker, who became labor editor of the *Jewish Daily Forward*, secretary of the United Hebrew Trades, and the first Socialist ever elected to the N. Y. State Assembly (from Brownsville) in 1916. He led the 1921-22 clothing workers strike.

LOUIS SOBEL PARK, Lee and Division Aves. and Roebling St., in the Williamsburg section is named for a World War I hero.

PUBLIC PLACES

EMANUEL CELLER FEDERAL COURTHOUSE, 225 Cadman Plaza East, is named for former Rep. Emanuel Celler, who served in Congress from a Brooklyn district for 49 years and 63 days, from 1923 to 1972. He was chairman of the House Judiciary Committee for 23 years in which capacity his name appears on four amendments to the Constitution and on nearly 400 bills that became law, including every major civil rights bill since 1940. In the lobby of the courthouse there is a bust of Celler.

MANHATTAN BRIDGE, completed in 1909 as the third span linking Brooklyn and Manhattan, was designed and built by Leon S. Moisseiff, a Russian-born, Yiddish-speaking engineer.

RESTAURANTS

MEAT

BERGER'S, 1427 Coney Island Ave. (*glatt* kosher).

BUFFET BY THE SEA, 2815 Flatbush Ave. (dining and entertainment).

CHAPANOSH, E. 15th St., corner of Ave. M (Flatbush) and 5413 New Utrecht Ave. (Borough Park).

CROWN GLATT KOSHER CATERERS AND RESTAURANT, 4904 13th Ave.

GOTTLIEB'S RESTAURANT, 352 Roebling St. (*glatt* kosher).

GREIFER'S KOSHER RESTAURANT AND DELICATESSEN, 4904 13th Ave.

GUTTMAN'S, 53rd St. and 13th Ave.

HY-TULIP DELICATESSEN AND RESTAURANT, 1980 86th St.

ISRAEL KOSHER RESTAURANT, 1412 Coney Island Ave. (closed Saturday).

JAFFA, 4210 18th Ave.

KOSHER COUNTRY, 1501 Surf Ave. and Whitehead Hall, Brooklyn College.

LANDAU'S DELICATESSEN AND RESTAURANT, 65 Lee Ave. (*glatt* kosher).

MOSHE PEKING II, 1760 Utica Ave. (Kosher Chinese cuisine—closed Friday and Saturday).

NATHAN PINCUS' KOSHER DELICATESSEN, 1405 Nostrand Ave.

PRUZANSKY'S GLATT KOSHER RESTAURANT AND DELICATESSEN, 954 Eastern Parkway. (Open daily and Sunday, 10 A.M. to midnight.) Special *parve* dinners are served during the period of abstinence (when observant Jews eat no meat), and sorrow commemorating the breaching of the walls of the Temple by the Romans.

ROSENBLOOM AND ROSETTI, 4127 18th Ave., is a *glatt* kosher Italian restaurant.

S & G KOSHER RESTAURANT, 306 Brighton Beach Ave.

SCHNEIDER'S KOSHER DELICATESSEN, 226 Roebling St.

SHANG-CHAI, 2189 Flatbush Ave., is a kosher Chinese restaurant.

ISRAEL SKILOWITZ & SONS, 4914 13th Ave.

TEL AVIV CATERERS, 2915 Ocean Parkway.

DAIRY

FAMOUS DAIRY RESTAURANT, 13th Ave. and 48th St.

WEISS' DAIRY RESTAURANT, Coney Island Ave. between Ave. J and K. *Cholov Yisroel. Shomer Shabbos.*

PIZZERIAS (KOSHER)

CHAIM'S KOSHER PIZZA, 954 Nostrand Ave., features kosher pizza and Israeli *falafel.* The owner, Chaim Najjar, a Yemenite Jew, was raised in Israel and came to America in 1952. While working in a bakery, he took note of the American penchant for pizza. He also noticed that Orthodox Jewish areas did not have any restaurants serving these exotic foods. He opened a pizza parlor in 1959 at 5113 13th Ave., featuring a kosher kitchen.

L & M RESTAURANT, 1817 Ave. M, features pizza, knishes, cookies—all kosher.

LEE AVENUE KOSHER PIZZA SHOP, 108 Lee Ave., features pizza, falafel, knishes, and french fries.

NATHAN'S FAMOUS, Surf and Stilwell Aves. A list of Brooklyn's Jewish eateries would not be complete without sampling the food at the world's largest and most celebrated hot dog stand. Called the "spiritual home of the American hot dog," Nathan's sells more than eight million frankfurters a year. The founder, Nathan Handwerker, came to America from Poland in 1912 and four years later opened his hot dog stand at Coney Island with a capital of $300. Nathan's also sells sea food and Orthodox Jews will not eat there.

ENTERTAINMENT

JEWISH THEATRE CO., housed in Temple Beth Abraham, 301 Seabreeze Ave., Brighton Beach, is an ensemble company presenting Yiddish and English language plays on Jewish themes.

SHOPPING

ABRAHAM & STRAUS, 420 Fulton St., carries items for some of the holidays—Seder trays and plates, *Haggadahs*, bagel holders and cutters, as well as many items from Israel.

REBECCA BENNET PUBLICATIONS, INC., 5409 18th Ave., specializes in the Babylonian Talmud in Hebrew and English, with complete or individual tractates.

CENTER OF JEWISH BOOKS, 1660 Ocean Parkway.

CROWN HEIGHTS HEBREW BOOK STORE, 382 Kingston Ave.

FRANKEL'S HEBREW BOOK STORE, 4904 16th Ave.

MILLER'S HEBREW BOOK STORE, 349 Utica Ave.

THE BRONX

Historically "the top of the escalator" on which successive waves of New York Jews "rose from the cheap slum housing on the East Side," The Bronx was for a generation, the symbol of the Jewish lower middle-class to the millions of Americans who listened to Bronx-bred Gertrude Berg describe *The Rise of the Goldbergs* on network radio. In the 1930s, when Brooklyn had the largest Jewish population, there were sections of The Bronx as solidly Jewish as the old East Side and Brownsville had once been.

The Jewish population of The Bronx reached a peak of 585,000 in 1930 when it accounted for 48 percent of all Jews in the city. Since then it has lost

Jewish population steadily. From 538,000 in 1940, the Jewish population fell to 493,000 in 1957, and to 396,000 in 1960. It was then the borough with fewer Jews than any other except Staten Island, although it contained 22 percent of the city's total Jewish population and accounted for 38 percent of the total population of The Bronx. The decline continued into the 1970s when there were only 143,000 Jews in The Bronx, or slightly less than 12 percent of the total population.

Jewish settlement in The Bronx began in the 1840s. The first arrivals were German and Hungarian storekeepers, artisans, and peddlers who came in the wake of Irish immigrants as they moved in to work on the construction of the Harlem and Hudson River Railroads and the stone High Bridge that carried the Croton Aqueduct across the Harlem River.

Individual Jews, however, had business connections in what is now The Bronx before 1700. Jewish traders from New York who did business in Connecticut as early as 1670 traveled there via the Boston Post Road, a principal highway to New England that passed through the east Bronx. This was the road taken by the leaders of New York's Congregation Shearith Israel during the American Revolution when they closed the synagogue and carried the Torah Scrolls to the safety of Stratford, Connecticut. Jewish merchants who developed important commercial ties in northern New York State a decade before the Revolution, journeyed via the Albany Post Road through the west Bronx.

There is no evidence that any of these travelers through The Bronx ever lived there, even temporarily. Neither did the descendants of Jewish farmers and merchants who settled in Westchester County in the 18th century, although they may have been 19th century property owners in the independent southern Westchester villages that later became The Bronx.

The railroad that first linked downtown New York with Westchester County gradually changed from a sparsely populated farming region to one of the city's earliest suburbs and stimulated the settlement of artisans and tradesmen. Isaac Blumenstiel, a shoemaker who acquired some lots in 1849 in Morrisania, also owned a house and shop on Fordham Avenue. Joseph Loewenstein, a peddler, and Daniel Eichler, tailor, were located on the same street. Jacob S. Abrams, merchant, and Leopold Lehman, clockmaker, were in business on Fulton Avenue.

The Morrisania directory for 1853-54, which listed establishments in the area now embraced by Hunts Point, Mott Haven, Kingsbridge, West Farms, Tremont, and Jerome Avenues, and the Grand Concourse south of Fordham Road, included a number of Jewish names. Jacob Cohen, one of New York's first Jewish real estate speculators, who in 1871 had published a short-lived Yiddish paper in support of his campaign for supervisor, owned Karl's 23rd Ward Park, a popular Bronx summer garden, in the 1860s. The 1872 directory for the same area listed new Jewish names: Julius Epstein, clerk; Louis Falk, builder and fire department trustee; H. Friedman, liquors; Angus Goldstein, pianomaker; Selig Hecht, tailor; Isadore Isaacs, restaurant owner; Richard Kohn, peddler; Henry Levy, fancy store; Gustavus Levy, lawyer; and Israel Ritter and Samuel Sandstein, cigarmakers.

There was no synagogue included in the 1872 directory's roster of 22 houses of worship. The early Jewish settlers belonged to congregations in Manhattan until a Jewish community began growing up in Morrisania, Kingsbridge, and West Farms after 1874 when these townships were annexed to New York City. The first considerable number of Jews settled in The Bronx in the late 1880s and early 1890s, following the extension of the elevated line from Harlem, the completion of bridges linking Harlem with the lower Bronx, and the inclusion of all of The Bronx in New York City.

J. Clarence Davies, who organized the Bronx Board of Trade in 1893, probably sold more Bronx real estate for housing purposes than any other man. Henry Morgenthau, Sr., who founded the Bronx House in 1911 as a Jewish settlement house, became wealthy through the sale of Bronx parcels on which vast stretches of apartment houses were erected at the turn of the century. Before Williamsbridge in the northeast Bronx became part of New York City, Abraham Mogilesky was selling building sites there.

Temple Adath Israel, organized on East 169th Street by German Jews in 1889 and for two generations a landmark on the Grand Concourse (it was sold to blacks in the 1970s), is believed to have been the first Jewish organization in The Bronx. Beth Hamedrash Hagodol Adath Jeshurun was founded in 1892. Lebanon Hospital and Congregation Bachurim Anshei Hungary were organized in 1893. Congregation Zichron Israel (1894), Congregation B'nai Jacob (1895), and Congregation Hand-in-Hand (1895) were other pioneer institutions in the Mott Haven and Prospect Avenue areas.

In his *Memories of an American Jew*, Philip Cowen, editor and communal worker, whose father was Newman Cowen, the first Russian Jew of influence in New York, touched on the beginnings of the Jewish community in the Mount Hope section around Tremont Avenue. Among the first Jewish residents there were Mr. and Mrs. Joseph Herzog (the latter a sister of Dr. Cyrus Adler, the second president of the Jewish Theological Seminary of America). The nearest Jewish religious school was at Congregation Hand-in-Hand and many of the scattered Jewish residents in Mount Hope were sending their children to nearby Christian Sunday schools.

When Cowen moved in 1896 to Mott Haven and 149th Street, at the lower end of what is now the Grand Concourse, he organized a free Hebrew school in rented quarters on Washington Avenue and 177th Street. A grant of $300 from New York's Congregation Shearith Israel helped the school get started. One of the first teachers was Mordecai M. Kaplan, later celebrated as the founder of Reconstructionism. The Baron de Hirsch Fund encouraged Jewish settlement in The Bronx in 1898. As part of a plan to get Jews out of the crowded East Side, the Fund bought 16 lots for $69,000 on 137th and 138th Streets, between Willis and Bronx Place, facing St. Mary's Park (now the heart of a Puerto Rican slum area), as the proposed site of model tenements and clothing factories. The scheme failed but it helped to enlarge the Jewish population of the borough.

By the turn of the century, more than a dozen synagogues were clustered around the Tremont, Mott Haven, and Mount Hope areas. Opening of the first subway line to The Bronx in 1904 set off a mass migration of Jews from the Lower East Side and Harlem to the lower Bronx, Tremont and Fordham sections. Later population tides moved to the Grand Concourse and University Heights, where Jewish builders erected block after block of apartment houses right after World War I. Between 1916 and 1925, four of the city's most populous Jewish neighborhoods were in The Bronx. The Tremont section was then nearly 96 percent Jewish. The Bronx YM-YWHA, oldest in the borough, moved to the Grand Concourse in the 1950s from its original site on Fulton Avenue, where it was founded in 1909.

New subway lines opened in the 1930s and 1940s gave impetus to large-scale public and private housing developments in new areas and caused a major movement of Jews to Pelham Bay Park, Edenwald, Wakefield, Gun Hill Road, Williamsbridge, Olinville, Eastchester, Unionport, Throggs Neck, and Woodlawn. The Parkchester development, erected in the 1930s by the Metropolitan Life Insurance Co., was long heavily tenanted by Jews. It occupies the site of the old Catholic Protectory Oval, where Hank Greenberg, the first Jew elected to baseball's Hall of Fame, started his career playing for James Monroe High School. Bess Myerson, whose parents came to The Bronx before World War II, is the only New York girl and the only Jew to be chosen Miss America (1945). Al Schacht, the clown prince of baseball, was born a stone's throw from Yankee Stadium. Sammy and Joe Renick, who never knew horses were used for anything but delivering milk when they went to a Bronx Hebrew school, became the country's leading jockeys.

There have been comparatively few Jews of note in the political life of The Bronx where Jewish voters have traditionally aligned themselves with the majority Democratic party. Bernard S. Deutsch, a Democrat, was elected president of the Board of Aldermen in 1933 on the LaGuardia Fusion ticket. Isidore Dollinger and Burton Roberts, both Democrats, served as district attorneys of Bronx County. Robert Abrams was twice elected Borough President, and in 1976 was serving his second term. In 1974, Abrams ran a close race for state attorney general against the incumbent Republican, Louis Lefkowitz.

New York University, whose main campus used to be in the University Heights section of The Bronx (it is now the site of Bronx Community College), had Jews among its founders and benefactors. The Guggenheim School of Aeronautics, established on the New York University campus by Daniel Guggenheim, was the first in the United States. ●Julius Silver Residential Hall is named for the chairman of the Polaroid Corporation's board, who was graduated from New York University with scholarship aid.

The only Bronx monument to a Jew is a bas-relief portrait of Heinrich Heine on the Lorelei Fountain in Joyce Kilmer Park, Grand Concourse and 164th Street. Rice Stadium in Pelham Bay Park is a memorial to Isaac L. Rice, inventor of the opening in chess known as Rice's Gambit, who was a successful industrialist, lawyer, and editor. Alexander's Department store on Fordham Road is the borough's best known retail establishment. One of its owners, Mrs. Ruth Farkas, served as United States Ambassador to Luxembourg from 1973-76. The late Dr. Morris Meister founded the famed Bronx High School of Science, which has graduated many leading space age scientists, and also the Bronx Community College, of which he was the first president.

Two of the city's major medical institutions are in The Bronx: the Albert Einstein Medical College of Yeshiva University and Montefiore Hospital.

The most remarkable aspect of Jewish history in The Bronx in the last 25 years has been the mass exodus of the Jewish population. As the earliest sections of the south Bronx became overcrowded, Jewish families who could afford it, left for Pelham Bay Parkway, Williamsbridge, Wakefield, and the Grand Concourse—that wide tree-lined boulevard became *the* social address for lower and middle-class Jews. The great depression of the 1930s and the years of World War II brought almost a complete halt to house building. As the cheap tenements erected in the 1920s or earlier became run-down and their Jewish tenants left, they were replaced by working-class blacks and Puerto Ricans. The latter were attracted to the south Bronx from Harlem by cheap housing and proximity to jobs in Manhattan—the same advantages that had attracted the earlier groups of the Irish, Jews, and Italians. As the suburban housing boom got under way in the 1940s, there was an almost mass exit of Jews from the south Bronx and later from the Tremont, Morrisania, Hunts Point, and Intervale areas. By the 1960s the east Tremont and south Bronx areas were among some of the city's worst slums. One after another old established synagogues began to close as the Jewish exodus left them with greatly reduced memberships. The number of synagogues dropped from 125 to less than 70.

The Grand Concourse, lined with squat, solid apartment houses for 4½ miles from east 138th Street to Mosholu Parkway, sparked a massive building boom when it opened in 1909. The opening of the Jerome Avenue and Concourse subway lines in the 1930s gave further impetus to building, and by World War II, the Concourse south of Fordham Road was an almost solid Jewish neighborhood. In the 1970s, however, the Concourse south of Tremont Avenue had become an urban slum occupied mostly by blacks and Puerto Ricans who replaced the departing Jews. The same trend occurred in the University Heights area and further east in the Hunts Point, Morrisania, and Intervale sections. The well-known Intervale Jewish Center, built in the 1920s by the father of Herman Wouk, the novelist, was cut down to one story. Twenty aged Jews worship there on Saturdays, surrounded by deteriorating buildings where 100,000 Jews once lived. What is left of the synagogue looks like a fortress, with double locked steel doors and wire hatches protecting its windows. The 10,000 people, mostly Jews, who lived in five and six-story tenements on East Tremont Avenue, were forced to find new homes when many houses were torn down to make way for the Cross Bronx Expressway. This enforced Jewish migration is believed by many to have touched off the Jewish exodus from The Bronx.

The Sephardic Jews left The Bronx en masse when their center was sold to blacks and migrated to Queens in 1973 and 1974 where a new center is being built. The Hebrew Institute of The Bronx, on University Heights, closed its doors in the early 1970s. The brand new $3,000,000 Salanter-Akiba-Riverdale Academy, which opened in 1975 in Riverdale, is a merger of three day schools from the east Bronx. The Bronx YMHA has opened a branch in Riverdale where it will ultimately move its main building, now on the Grand Concourse.

Federation maintains a service center at the Y to seek out the more than 3,000 elderly Jewish poor who have resisted moving from deteriorated neighborhoods where they have spent much of their lives. The city's second largest pocket of Jewish poverty is in The Bronx. The aged Jewish poor, many of them widows, who still remain in the Morrisania and Tremont areas, are often beaten, robbed, and occasionally murdered.

The continuing exodus of lower middle-class Jews from once stable neighborhoods gave rise to the new Jewish community in Co-Op City, a huge cooperative housing development whose 35 apartment towers cover 210 acres in the northeast Bronx and house some 75,000 people, nearly 75 percent of them Jews. Almost all of Co-Op City's residents are middle and lower income families headed by teachers, civil service employees, small businessmen, hospital personnel, skilled craftsmen, a sprinkling of doctors, lawyers, dentists, and accountants, and a large proportion of retirees, widows, and widowers living on fixed incomes.

Long before the first tenants moved into Co-Op City in 1968, neighboring synagogues had planned on moving into quarters provided by the management which is closely related to the labor movement. In the mid-1970s, Co-Op City had six synagogues on the premises and one or more units of virtually every major national Jewish organization. Federation provides coordinated services through an on-the-spot office maintained by the Jewish Family Service. The nearby Bronx House, on Pelham Bay Parkway, sponsors a coordinated program with and for the Jewish residents of Co-Op City. The Montefiore Medical Center, an affiliate of Montefiore Hospital, has its own clinic in Co-Op City. The two weekly newspapers that serve Co-Op City (one a private enterprise), are packed with news about Jewish programs, projects, meetings, and fundraising. The Co-Op City Jews constitute a Jewish community larger than those in Denver, Cincinnati, Houston, Berlin, Rome, Vienna, and Amsterdam. There is an active Jewish Community Council and fundraising campaigns for the Joint Campaign of the

UJA-Federation, Hadassah, ORT, Histadrut, Jewish War Veterans, Farband, and B'nai B'rith. Co-Op City siphoned off thousands of Jews who were ready to leave older Bronx neighborhoods but who could not or would not settle in the suburbs. Most could not afford the more expensive apartments and houses in Riverdale, the upper middle-class area in the northwest corner of the borough.

The Jewish settlement in Riverdale dates from the years following World War I when a few Jewish families from Yonkers, in adjacent Westchester County, began moving in. Riverdale was then a rural corner of The Bronx of mostly palatial estates, some large houses, and private schools. In the 1970s it was the home of Manhattan College and the College of St. Vincent (both Catholic), the Hebrew Home for the Aged, several well-known private elementary and secondary schools, and the Salanter-Akiba-Riverdale Academy, which occupies the site of the former Arturo Toscanini estate.

The high percentage of synagogue affiliation that developed in other new Jewish communities in Greater New York or those which grew rapidly on the base of older settlements was missing in Riverdale. The Jewish population was estimated in the 1970s to be between 40,000 and 60,000 out of a total of some 92,000. Whichever figure is accepted, Riverdale has more Jews than all but a dozen or so American Jewish communities. All but 20 percent of them live in high rise apartment houses, although large segments of the community are strictly zoned for detached private homes. When the first apartment houses were built in the 1950s, the home owners resented them because they diluted the semirural environment for which Riverdale is noted. A bitter zoning fight erupted when the Bronx YM-YWHA sought to build its main headquarters in Riverdale. At the end of 1975 the Y still lacked an approved site, although the community raised no objections to the erection of a Soviet residential compound in the area. Few of Riverdale's residents like to admit that they live in The Bronx, but since a separate post office was established, mail must now be addressed Bronx, New York, with an appropriate Riverdale zip code.

Riverdale's first Jewish settlers were well-to-do businessmen, manufacturers, officeholders, and professionals who wanted rural living within the city limits. The first Jewish worship services were held in 1924 at 61 Marble Hill Avenue in the home of Morris Nacht in the Kingsbridge area, once an independent town of which Riverdale was a part. An Orthodox group broke away in 1934 and formed Kenneseth Israel of Riverdale in 1938. A Reform group broke away in 1933. In Riverdale proper, the Riverdale Temple (Reform) was founded in 1946 although a Sunday school had been established in 1941. The Conservative Synagogue of Riverdale dates from 1954, and the Riverdale Jewish Center (Orthodox) was organized in the same year. The Hebrew Tabernacle of Washington Heights (in northern Manhattan) maintains a Sunday school in Riverdale for children of its members who have settled there, and is discussing the possibility of moving to Riverdale.

The opening of the Salanter-Akiba-Riverdale Academy attracted a growing number of Orthodox Jews who belong to the Beth Midrash Horeb Congregation, the Ahavath Tsedek Congregation in Kingsbridge, the Young Israel of Riverdale, Congregation Levi Isaac Riverdale Torah Center, and Ohel Torah, which moved to Riverdale from the Bronx in 1967. Despite the large number of congregations, their regular membership represented less than 10 percent of the total Jewish population in the 1970s.

The Pelham Bay Park area contained some 50,000 Jews in 1976, living in well-kept apartment houses and private houses between Bronx Park and Williamsbridge Road and between Waring Avenue and Bronxdale Road. This section has some of the characteristics of the one-time close-knit Jewish neighborhoods that have been abandoned. A number of Russian Jewish refugees have settled in the neighborhood which has many synagogues and yeshivas. Bronx House, the principal communal Jewish institution in the area, has created a Russian American Neighborhood Action Committee as well as programs for the many Yiddish-speaking older residents in the neighborhood. The Mosholu Parkway area had a large Jewish settlement in the 1970s, sharing the five and six-story apartment houses with the Irish, Italians, and a growing number of blacks who work at the nearby Montefiore Medical Center. Jews have been leaving this area in growing numbers because of their fear that the quality of the neighborhood and public schools is declining. Some interracial violence in the schools stimulated younger families to move to Westchester and Rockland Counties.

The 100 or more synagogues that dotted The Bronx in 1964 have been reduced to about 70, many of them occupying old and deteriorating buildings or store front quarters. In 1976 most of the remaining congregations were Orthodox, however, there were still ten Conservative and eight Reform congregations in the borough.

* * * * *

SYNAGOGUES

ORTHODOX

B'NAI ISRAEL OF EDENWALD, 1014 E. 227th St.
CHOTIMER JEWISH CENTER, 2256 Bronx Park E.
CONG. ANSHE AMAS, 713 E. 222nd St.
CONG. B'NAI ISRAEL, 1570 Walton Ave.
CONG. MOUNT HOREB, Falasha Synagogue, 1042 Stebbins Ave.
JEWISH CENTER OF WAKEFIELD & EDENWALD, 641 E. 233rd Street.
KINGSBRIDGE CENTER OF ISRAEL, 3115 Corlear Ave.
KINGSBRIDGE HEIGHTS JEWISH CENTER, 124 Eames Pl.
MOSHOLU JEWISH CENTER, 3044 Hull Ave.

RIVERDALE JEWISH CENTER, 3700 Independence Ave., has an ultra-modern structure. The congregation was launched with the aid of Yeshiva University, which assigned a "rabbinical Daniel Boone" to the Riverdale area with no more than a slip of paper bearing the names of five local residents who had contacted Yeshiva for aid.

SEPHARDIC, SHA-RE RAHAMIM, 100 Co-Op City Blvd.

YOUNG ISRAEL MESILATH YESHURIM, 1921 Walton Ave.

YOUNG ISRAEL OF ASTOR GARDENS, 1328 Allerton Ave.

YOUNG ISRAEL OF CO-OP CITY, 147-1 Dreiser La.

YOUNG ISRAEL OF KINGSBRIDGE, 2620 University Ave.

YOUNG ISRAEL OF MOSHOLU PKWY., 100 E. 208th St.

YOUNG ISRAEL OF PARKCHESTER, 1375 Virginia Ave.

YOUNG ISRAEL OF PELHAM PARKWAY, Barnes and Lydig Aves.

YOUNG ISRAEL OF RIVERDALE, 547 West 239th St.

YOUNG ISRAEL OF THE CONCOURSE, Grand Concourse at 165th St.

CONSERVATIVE

CONG. AHAVATH TSEDEK, 3425 Kingsbridge Ave.

CONSERVATIVE SYNAGOGUE OF RIVERDALE, 250th St. & Henry Hudson Pkwy.

CO-OP CITY JEWISH CENTER, 900 Co-Op City Blvd.

PELHAM PARKWAY JEWISH CENTER, 900 Pelham Pkwy. S.

JACOB H. SCHIFF CENTER, 2510 Valentine Ave.

SHIELD OF DAVID INSTITUTE, 1800 Andrews Ave.

TEMPLE EMANUEL AT PARKCHESTER, 2000 Benedict Ave.

REFORM

RIVERDALE TEMPLE, 246th St. & Independence Ave., has a chapel made of four components—wood, stone, glass, and metal. One side of the chapel is made up of great stones reminiscent of those of the wall of Jerusalem; on the opposite side are large windows. The pulpit has a mosaic wall in multi-colors of Jewish ceremonial symbols in Venetian glass. The symbols are a Torah Crown, a ram, phylacteries, a *kiddush* cup, a fish and a Torah. In the center of the wall is the Ark with doors about 12 feet high in the form of the Tablets of the Law hammered in sterling silver; the Ten Commandments are in 22 carat gold Hebrew letters. Over the Ark is the Eternal Light in the form of a Star of David with the word *Shaddai* (The Almighty), in its center. Under the Ark the mosaic is black and white, suggestive of the *talis*. A modern Menorah graces the pulpit, in front of which are boxes for plants and flowers. The doors leading into the chapel are beautifully carved with reproductions of the open Torah and other religious symbols. Every phase of the temple was executed by the architect, Simon B. Zelnik.

SINAI CONGREGATION OF THE BRONX, 2011 Grand Concourse.

TEMPLE JUDEA, 615 Reiss Place.

TREMONT TEMPLE BETH-EL OF CO-OP CITY BRANCH, 920 Baychester Ave.

TREMONT TEMPLE—CENTER OF MERCY, 2064 Grand Concourse.

SCHOOLS AND OTHER EDUCATIONAL INSTITUTIONS

BETH JACOB-BETH LEAH SCHOOL FOR GIRLS, 1779 E. 172nd Street.

BETH JACOB-BETH MIRIAM SCHOOL, 1570 Walton Ave.

BETH JACOB SCHOOL FOR GIRLS, 2126 Barnes Ave.

ALBERT EINSTEIN COLLEGE OF MEDICINE of Yeshiva University, Eastchester Rd. and Morris Park Ave., is the first medical school established under Jewish auspices in America (founded in 1955). The main building is a ten-story, glass-faced structure of contemporary design. •The three-story D. Samuel Gottesman Library, which has room for 200,000 volumes, is adjacent to the college's nine-story science building. One side of the entire length of the library's reading room is glass and faces the main campus and the white brick, seven-story Abraham Mazer Student Residence Hall. •The ten-story, twelve-sided, tower-like building at Morris Park and Newport Aves. is the Ullmann Research Center for Health Sciences. •Among the other facilities are the fan-shaped Mary and Karl Robbins Auditorium and the Max L. and Sadie Friedman Student-Faculty Lounge.

The college is named for the famous physicist, mathematician, and Nobel Prize winner. An original 20-page manuscript by Einstein containing one of his early attempts to find a unified field theory is among the important Einstein papers in the Gottesman Library. Although the college is under Jewish auspices, it is nonsectarian and selects students and faculty solely on the basis of scholarship and ability.

The college is the heart of a $100 million medical center that includes a $40 million hospital center constructed by the City of New York and a $45 million psychiatric hospital established by the State of New York. The hospital center includes the Abraham Jacobi Hospital, named for Dr. Abraham Jacobi, famous for his contributions to the science of pediatrics. He opened the first pediatric clinic, invented the laryngoscope, and was elected president of the American Medical Association on his 80th birthday in 1910. Although visitors are welcome at the campus, the Albert Einstein College of Medicine is not open to the public. ☐

SAMUEL GOMPERS VOCATIONAL HIGH SCHOOL, 455 Southern Blvd., is named for the founder and first president of the American Federation of Labor.

GOULD MEMORIAL LIBRARY, on campus of Bronx Community College, has over the entrance to its main hall, a Hebrew inscription which translated reads: "The beginning of wisdom is the fear of the Lord" (Psalm 111:10). The same saying appears on the wall in six other languages. In the Library's reading room there are Hebrew inscriptions from the Torah, Maimonides, and Isaiah.

GUGGENHEIM SCHOOL OF AERONAUTICS, the first in the U.S., founded by Daniel Guggenheim, is on the campus of Bronx Community College.

HERBERT LEHMAN COLLEGE of City University, Bedford Park Blvd. and Goulden Ave.

HEBREW INSTITUTE AT RIVERDALE, 3333 Henry Hudson Pkwy., W.

SALANTER AKIBA RIVERDALE ACADEMY, 655 W. 254th St.

LUBAVITCHER YESHIVA ACHEI TMIMIM, 3415 Olinville Ave.

YESHIVA TORAH V'EMUNAH, INC., 1779 E. 172nd St.

JEWISH COMMUNITY CENTERS

BRONX HOUSE, 990 Pelham Pkwy., S., was founded in 1911 by Henry Morgenthau, Sr., as a neighborhood settlement.

BRONX RIVERDALE YM-YWHA, 450 West 250th St.

BRONX YM & YWHA, 1130 Grand Concourse.

MOSHOLU-MONTEFIORE COMMUNITY CENTER of the Associated YM & YWHAs of Greater New York, 3450 DeKalb Ave., is on the grounds of Montefiore Hospital. In addition to its regular program of social group work with people of all ages, the Center conducts a variety of projects with the hospital. One outstanding example is its work with orthopedically handicapped children. The Center has a permanent art exhibit, a roof playground, and a nursery school.

PELHAM PARKWAY BRANCH OF BRONX HOUSE, 2222 Wallace Ave.

HOMES AND HOSPITALS

BETH ABRAHAM HOME FOR THE CHRONICALLY ILL, 612 Allerton Ave., is one of the largest homes of its kind. Beth Abraham Hospital is at the same address.

BRONX HOME FOR SONS AND DAUGHTERS OF MOSES, 990 College Ave.

BRONX-LEBANON HOSPITAL CENTER, Grand Concourse and East Mt. Eden Ave.

EDENWALD SCHOOL FOR BOYS AND GIRLS of Jewish Child Care Association, 1250 East 229th St.

ANDREW FREEDMAN HOME, 1125 Grand Concourse, is a home for the aged founded in 1916 by Andrew Freedman, subway contractor and one-time owner of the New York Giants.

HENRY ITTLESON CENTER FOR CHILD RESEARCH, 5050 Iselin Ave., an affiliate of the Jewish Board of Guardians, studies causes of severe childhood emotional and psychological disorders.

HEBREW HOME FOR THE AGED, 5901 Palisade Ave.

HEBREW HOME FOR THE CHRONIC SICK-CHEVRA MISH-NAIS, 1776 Clay Ave.

MONTEFIORE HOSPITAL AND MEDICAL CENTER, 210th St. and Bainbridge Ave., was founded in 1884 on the centennial of the birth of Sir Moses Montefiore, famous Anglo-Jewish leader and philanthropist. It was originally a home for incurable invalids, but it has since become the nation's largest privately-supported general hospital for the scientific treatment of prolonged illnesses, and it is now a great medical center. The hospital's vast medical complex includes the Henry L. Moses Research Institute, an expanded Solomon and Betty Loeb Memorial Center for intensive post-hospital nursing care, an ambulatory services building, an emergency suite, a diagnostic and treatment center, and basic science laboratories. It was at Montefiore Hospital that cobalt 60 (radioactive isotopes) was first used early in 1953 in the fight against cancer.

WORKMEN'S CIRCLE HOME FOR THE AGED, 3155 Grace Ave.

HILLEL FOUNDATION
LEHMAN COLLEGE, 55 Rudolph Terrace, Yonkers.

HOUSING DEVELOPMENTS
AMALGAMATED APARTMENTS, 8 Van Cortlandt South, is a cooperative project erected in 1927-32 by the Amalgamated Clothing Workers of America, then an almost solidly Jewish union. The buildings were the first low-rent apartments built and operated under the New York State Housing Law.

CO-OP CITY, the world's largest cooperative housing development, in northeast Bronx, where the New England Thruway and the Hutchinson River Parkway intersect, has as many Jewish residents as Atlanta or Indianapolis, and more than New Orleans, Des Moines, and Wilmington, Delaware, put together. It is virtually a community unto itself, with eight synagogues on the premises, one or more branches of virtually every national Jewish organization, and offices of local Jewish welfare, family service, and child care agencies. A large proportion of the Jewish residents are elderly people, living on pensions and social security, while others are lower middle class, many of whom moved from the older decaying areas of The Bronx.

RESTAURANTS
SCHWELLER'S KOSHER RESTAURANT AND DELICATES-
SEN, 3411 Jerome Ave.

SHOPPING
PELHAM PARKWAY HEBREW BOOK STORE, 781 Lydig Ave.

PUBLIC PLACES
HALL OF FAME FOR GREAT AMERICANS, on campus of Bronx
Community College, has busts of noted American Jews elected by public
ballot every five years—Rabbi Isaac Mayer Wise, father of Reform Judaism
in America; Louis D. Brandeis, first Jew named to the U.S. Supreme Court;
Dr. Albert Michelson, physicist and first American to win the Nobel Prize in
physics; and Lillian D. Wald, founder of Henry Street Settlement and
pioneer of public nursing service.

LORELEI FOUNTAIN, recalling the legendary siren of Heinrich
Heine's *Die Lorelei*, is located in Joyce Kilmer Park, Grand Concourse and
164th St. On the south side of the fountain is a bas-relief fountain of Heine,
the great German Jewish poet. Completed in 1893 as a gift to Duesseldorf,
Heine's birthplace, it was refused by the German government. German-
Americans in New York then purchased the fountain and presented it to the
city.

ISAAC L. RICE STADIUM in Pelham Bay Park, was established
with a $1,000,000 gift from the widow of Isaac L. Rice, a musician, editor,
inventor, lawyer, industrialist, and chess master. Rice organized railroads,
lectured at Columbia University Law School, invented the opening in chess
known as Rice's Gambit, founded electric storage battery and boat companies, and developed many inventions in the electric, rubber, and transportation fields.

SOCIAL SERVICE AGENCIES
ALTRO WORKSHOP, 3600 Jerome Ave., a non-sectarian rehabilitation center for patients cured of cardiac diseases where they are helped to
return to productive life. It is an affiliate of the Federation of Jewish
Philanthropies.

STREETS AND PARKS
DEUTSCH PLAZA, University Ave., just south of Tremont Ave., is
named for Bernard S. Deutsch, who was elected president of the N.Y.C.
Board of Aldermen in 1933 in the election triumph of Fiorello H. LaGuardia
as mayor. Deutsch served as president of the American Jewish Congress. He
died in 1935.

CPL. IRWIN FISCHER PL., south of W. 170th St., bet. Nelson and
Shakespeare Aves., was named in 1949 for a soldier killed in World War II.

GLADSTONE SQ., at Westchester Ave. and Southern Blvd., is

named for Benjamin Gladstone, a member of the New York State Assembly, who served in World War I.

LATKIN SQ., at intersection of East 169th St., Home St., Intervale Ave., and Tiffany St., is named for David Latkin who was killed in World War I.

QUEENS

The 379,000 Jews who live in the borough of Queens constitute the fourth largest aggregation of Jews in any county of the United States with only Kings (Brooklyn), Nassau, and Los Angeles Counties having more Jews. Queens and Staten Island are the only two boroughs in which the Jewish population has shown some growth. The rise of the Queens Jewish community is one of the most remarkable aspects of the historic Jewish population shifts in New York City.

At the end of World War I, when Queens had barely 400,000 people, its Jewish population was 10,000. This rose to 50,000 in 1923, more than doubled to 115,000 in 1940, and almost doubled again by 1950 when it reached 223,000. The heaviest increase, reflecting the post-World War II exodus from Brooklyn, Manhattan, and The Bronx, occurred between 1950 and 1957. In the latter year Queens passed Manhattan as the borough with the third largest Jewish population. Growth slowed somewhat in the 1960s when Queens passed The Bronx as the borough with the second largest Jewish population, topped only by Brooklyn.

Individual Jews lived in what is now Queens before the Revolution and were doing business in Jamaica, Flushing, and Newtown more than a century before these villages were incorporated into the City of New York. There is a record of at least four Jewish merchants in Queens between 1759 and 1770. The firm of Hart Aaron and Jacob Cohen had branches in Jamaica, Flushing, and Newtown in 1759 and 1760. Levy Moses and Isaac Isaacs, both with families, were in business in Jamaica in the 1760s.

Isaacs' sons, Joseph and Henry, were born in Jamaica and circumcised there by Abraham I. Abrahams, the most popular *mohel* in the New York area in the mid-18th century. Abrahams' registry of circumcisions performed from June, 1756 to January, 1781 shows that he officiated three times in the Jamaica prison. In each instance the occasion was the birth of one of the sons of Levy Moses, who was regularly jailed for debt.

A Jewish community did not develop, however, until after the Civil War when Jewish peddlers, storekeepers, and a few farmers began settling in the Long Island villages that were annexed to New York City in 1898. One section of Forest Hills stands on what was once known as Goldberg's Dairy Farm in the early 1870s. Among the first Jewish arrivals were the Miller and Exiner families, who established themselves in Jamaica in 1868. The Worms, Frank, and Brandon families came to Newtown, now known as Jackson Heights, in the early 1880s. Emanuel Brandon owned a cigar factory and was elected judge of the Court of County Sessions. Samuel Worms served as one of Newtown's first excise commissioners. The earliest known Jewish institution in Queens was the Hebrew Sanitarium, established in Far Rockaway in 1876.

German-Jewish vacationers who began spending summers in the seaside villages on the Rockaway Peninsula in the 1880s organized what was probably the first Jewish worship services in Queens. An Orthodox congregation was formed in Hammels around 1890, while the summer service held over the drygoods store of A. Louis Nebenzahl, who had peddled all over Long Island from 1879-1882, grew into Temple Israel in 1900.

Astoria's Congregation Mishkan Israel was founded in 1894 by a group of Jewish storekeepers. Two years later, Flushing's Gates of Prayer was formed by merchants who had been in business in Flushing since the 1880s. Jamaica's Congregation Ahavas Israel, organized in 1900, originated with a *minyan* that began meeting in the home of Emil Spitzer in the 1890s. Other early Jewish settlements were made in Corona (1900), Maspeth (1904), Long Island City (1904), Middle Village (1908), Richmond Hill (1909), and Ridgewood (1910). Some of these communities were created by peddlers turned storekeepers who had crossed from the Jewish neighborhoods in Brownsville and East New York in Brooklyn.

The opening of the Queensboro Bridge in 1909 brought the first sizable influx of Jews who established new communities in Ozone Park, Woodhaven, Woodside, Queens Village, and Hollis. The first subway lines to reach Queens during the 1920s gave impetus to Jewish settlement in Sunnyside and Jackson Heights, particularly in the newly-built two-family homes erected by the Metropolitan Life Insurance Co. to meet the post-World War I housing shortage. The late Clarence S. Stein, chairman of the New York State Housing and Regional Planning Commission, planned the Sunnyside Gardens development which was occupied in the 1930s by many Jewish newlyweds.

The first large Jewish concentration of Jews in Queens developed in the Rockaways, which accounted for nearly 36 percent of the borough's Jewish population in 1923. Separate communities grew up in Far Rockaway, Averne, Edgemere, Belle Harbor, Neponsit, and Rockaway Beach, each with its own synagogues and societies. In the 1930s, the Rockaways were still the most populous Jewish neighborhood and the only one where Jews represented more than 40 percent of the population.

Once a model community and a popular summer resort for lower middle-income families, the Rockaways were described as a disaster area in 1964 by its Congressman. Huge housing developments that attracted low income welfare families, a decaying beachfront, and the razing of wooden bungalows and old hotels as part of some future urban renewal project, created slum conditions. The population, however, increased from 68,000 in the 1960s to over 100,000 in the 1970s. Some of the population increase came from the residents of nursing homes. In the 1970s, 40 percent of all the nursing homes in Queens and ten percent of those in New York City were in the Rockaways. The nursing homes were the biggest employer on the Rockaway Peninsula. The Rockaways became a dumping ground for infirm elderly persons and discharged mental patients in nursing homes, while many of the new high rise apartment houses were occupied by poor blacks and Puerto Ricans.

Many of the elderly residents of the Rockaways were poor Jews who were often attacked by anti-Semitic hoodlums. The Anti-Defamation League recruited auxiliary police to increase the safety and security of the Jewish population in the housing developments. Edgemere and Rockaway Beach established units of the Maccabees to protect Jews. In the 1970s there was occasional fighting between Black Panthers and members of the Jewish Defense League. Federation has opened a center for the aged in Far Rockaway. The Jewish Association for Service to the Aged, has built a 22-story apartment house for 547 aged families. Others are planned.

In Far Rockaway, which adjoins the village of Lawrence, in Nassau County, there is a growing Orthodox Jewish community of some 2,500 families. The first of them arrived in the 1950s. They now maintain ten synagogues, several yeshivas and day schools, and support numerous kosher food stores. In 1975 they completed an *eruv*—a halachically-approved enclosure by means of wires atop telephone poles—bounded by the L.I.R.R. tracks on the north, Rockaway Turnpike on the east, the ocean on the south, and Beach 19th St. on the west. This enclosure permits them to carry items within the area, thus getting around the halachic ban on carrying any parcel from one domain or *eruv* to another on the Sabbath.

By the end of the 1930s, Sunnyside began to lose its Jewish population, as did some of the other older Jewish settlements, while new middle-class settlements began to develop in Jamaica, Laurelton, Springfield Gardens, and St. Albans. These four neighborhoods were almost 20 percent Jewish by the 1940s. A decade later Springfield Gardens and St. Albans had become predominantly black while the first signs of change became evident in Jamaica. Laurelton, on the edge of Nassau County, was an all-white community until the mid-1960s. Blockbusting by unscrupulous real estate brokers created a panic and by 1966 Laurelton had become 20 percent black as Jewish families began leaving, as did other white families. The Jewish Community Council in Laurelton and the local synagogue struggled to maintain the delicate racial balance by an intensive effort to bring in new Jewish families. Many of the Jewish families who refused to abandon Laurelton favored an integrated community. The Jewish Council of Southeast Queens, representing the synagogues in Cambria Heights, Laurelton, Rosedale, and Queens Village sought to attract new Jewish families by offering potential buyers who lacked enough cash for down payments, interest-free loans of up to $3,000 payable in three years. In exchange for the loans, provided by the Hebrew Free Loan Society, the buyers were expected to become synagogue members as part of the effort to strengthen Jewish institutions.

This undertaking was only partly successful. The Federation of Jewish Philanthropies gave the Laurelton Jewish Community Council a $10,000 grant to fight panic selling and to help preserve the Jewish community. A series of open houses to which potential new Jewish residents were invited was held and the Council set up a home finding service. Nevertheless, the Jewish population of Laurelton, which had accounted for 90 percent of all residents in 1954, declined to 40 percent in 1974.

Rochdale Village, in southeast Queens, had a similar experience. Among the original 24,000 residents of the 20 identical 14-story buildings, were thousands of middle-income Jews but they, like many other whites, have moved out, largely because of crime and dissatisfaction with local schools. Jackson Heights, one of the older areas of Jewish settlement, still has a considerable Jewish community, but there too, in a neighborhood of apartment houses and private houses, an organized effort to attract younger Jewish families was undertaken in the 1970s. Many of the Jewish residents were older families while many of the newcomers to Jackson Heights were Hispanics.

The big change in the Jewish residential pattern in Queens began after World War II when the new rapid transit lines and automobile parkways made it easy to reach Queens from the older sections of Manhattan, Brooklyn, and The Bronx. Many Jews from the older Jewish neighborhoods in the other boroughs had first visited Queens during the 1939 World's Fair and found it appealing. When returning Jewish war veterans found a housing shortage in their home neighborhoods, they poured into the new apartment houses that had begun to rise in Queens.

Instant Jewish neighborhoods were born as Jews moved from the Jewish sections of Brooklyn, The Bronx, and from older areas of Queens. Miles of new high rise apartment houses along the main avenues, boulevards, and streets, as well as garden apartments and private houses were rented and bought by Jews of all economic levels in Fresh Meadows, Bayside, Queens Village, Elmhurst, Jamaica, Flushing, Long Island City, College Point, Whitestone, Rosedale, Douglaston, Little Neck, Rego Park, Kew Gardens, and Forest Hills. The Forest Hills-Rego Park area, which had less than 500 Jews in the 1920s when most apartments there were closed to them, was less than two percent Jewish in the 1930s. Douglaston and Little Neck, bordering Great Neck in Nassau County, had virtually no Jews in the 1920s and 1930s.

By the end of the 1950s, the Forest Hills-Rego Park area was more than half Jewish and had superseded the Rockaways as the principal Jewish neighborhood.The South Flushing and Fresh Meadows sections were each nearly 40 percent Jewish. The Laurelton-Rosedale neighborhood was still 30 percent Jewish, but Astoria, Ridgewood, Maspeth, Richmond Hill, Ozone Park, and Corona had become minor Jewish concentrations. In the Rockaways, where hotels and clubs which had refused to admit Jews in the early 1900s later became all-Jewish establishments. A new year-round Jewish middle-class community developed in the high rise apartments erected along the seashore in the 1960s. In 1976, over 65 percent of all the Jews in Queens lived in six neighborhoods: Forest Hills-Rego Park, Kew Gardens and Kew Gardens Hills, South Flushing-Fresh Meadows, Bayside-Oakland Gardens, Douglaston-Little Neck, and the Rockaways. At the end of 1975 a new Jewish community sprang up on Roosevelt Island in the middle of the East River where the first Jewish residents in a massive new housing complex organized the Congregation of Roosevelt Island.

Most of the immense postwar growth of the Queens Jewish population consisted of younger families who had not been previously affiliated with synagogues. In the new child-centered life that developed in Queens in the 1950s and 1960s, these families flocked to the synagogue in tremendous numbers. Because the existing congregations could not accommodate the newcomers, new synagogues were established in every neighborhood. Some of the older congregations erected new buildings or additions. All of the new congregations embarked on construction programs. Millions of dollars were raised and spent in Queens for new synagogues and religious schools between 1948 and 1960. In 1963 there were 110 synagogues in Queens—56 Orthodox, 43 Conservative, and 11 Reform. The comparable 1976 figures were 78 Orthodox, 45 Conservative, and 12 Reform.

Some of the Orthodox congregations from Brooklyn and The Bronx have moved to Queens, which is dotted with Hebrew day schools and yeshivas. Kew Gardens Hills has had a special attraction for the Orthodox. In 1976 it had eight Orthodox synagogues, a number of *glatt* kosher butchers, a couple of kosher restaurants, and kosher bakeries and pizza parlors. In 1951 when Young Israel organized in Kew Gardens Hills, the neighborhood was 20 percent Jewish but it was nearly 80 percent in 1976, and half of that is accounted for by Orthodox Jews. More Orthodox Jews are being attracted to the area because it now has an *eruv*, a network of pole-strung wires that marks off a given area and binds it to the household of its residents, thus enabling Orthodox Jews to push baby carriages on the Sabbath and to engage in activities which would not otherwise be permitted except within the bounds of their own homes. The Hillcrest-Flushing area also has an *eruv*.

Because so many Israelis live in Queens—an estimated 75 percent of all the 100,000 Israelis in New York City—the borough has been dubbed "the fourth city of Israel." Queens Boulevard is virtually a Jewish promenade. Hebrew newspapers are on sale at newsstands. Israeli foods are available in the supermarkets. There is a proliferation of Israeli restaurants and retail establishments owned by Israelis. Some local merchants speak Hebrew. The Bank Leumi has a branch in Queens. The 1970 census showed that Queens had the highest proportion of residents of foreign origin in the city. Half of its over 2,000,000 people were either born abroad or had one foreign-born parent. Most of the borough's foreign-born are concentrated in Forest Hills-Rego Park, Jackson Heights, and Flushing. The third largest group comes from Russia, which usually means Jews, and the fourth largest comes from Germany and Austria, which reflects the large number of German-Jewish refugees in the area. A substantial majority of the 100,000 people in Forest Hills and the 25,000 in Rego Park are Jewish.

Most Forest Hills Jews are refugees from other parts of the city who fled to Queens when the influx of low-income minorities and welfare families led to an increase in crime and violence, lowered school standards, and a deterioration of neighborhoods. The move to Forest Hills, Rego Park, and Kew Gardens was a search for safety in the streets, schools, elevators, and corridors. Queens Boulevard is lined with tall apartment houses that became the dominant feature of Queens housing when the type of building shifted from single family houses and six-story apartment houses. The largest housing development in Queens is the $150 million Lefrak City, built by Samuel Lefrak. It houses 25,000 people, many of them Jews, in 5,000 apartments in 20 duplicate brick structures spread out over 40 acres. Lefrak City has two synagogues and among its security guards are some who speak Yiddish.

Lefrak City's tenants are typical of the polyglot populace of the Rego Park-Forest Hills area. Besides the tens of thousands of Israelis, the neighborhood has colonies of Yemenite, Russian, Egyptian, Yugoslavian, Moroccan, and Bokharan Jews. In the mid-1970s, the area became an important center for Sephardic Jews who moved from Brooklyn and The Bronx. Many Greek and Turkish Jews who had resided in The Bronx moved to Queens in anticipation of the relocation of the Sephardic Jewish Center of The Bronx, which sold its building and moved to Forest Hills-Rego Park. Pizza shops run by Yemenite Jews in the area are popular gathering places for Israelis. The East New York YM-YWHA disposed of its building in 1972 in Brooklyn and moved to Queens. It was renamed the Central Queens YMHA. It conducts branch programs in Lefrak City, Howard Beach, and Rego Park pending the erection of a large main building in the Forest Hills area.

In 1972, the largely middle-class Jewish community of Forest Hills exploded in anger and bitterness over the city's plan to erect three 24-story buildings containing 840 apartments in Rego Park which were to be occupied largely, if not entirely, by low income and welfare families. The huge complex was designed to establish low income housing for minorities within a middle-class neighborhood and away from ghetto areas—the so-called scatter housing approach. Fearing an influx of poor blacks with the resultant strain on neighborhood schools, traffic, police, fire, and health facilities, and the likelihood of a major change in the neighborhood, a large majority of the area's Jews lined up against the project. When construction began there were inflammatory speeches, sit-downs on Long Island Expressway, and confrontations between Jews and blacks on opposite sides of the street at the project site.

The Jewish fight against the housing project was ostensibly aimed at the environmental dangers it threatened. In effect, however, they were saying by their opposition that Forest Hills-Rego Park was a secure place to live and they did not want welfare cases and minorities undermining that sense of safety. The older residents remembered the neighborhoods they had built in Brooklyn and The Bronx and from which they had fled as those areas deteriorated from increased crime and squalor. The fight created wide division in the Jewish community. A minority, including some rabbis, supported the project, but the bulk of the Jewish population—residents, businessmen, public officials, and employees of various enterprises—fiercely opposed the project. The rabbinate too, was divided, with the majority opposed, reflecting the view of their congregants. One synagogue whose rabbi supported the housing development was invaded by congregants of a neighboring synagogue who interrupted the service and threatened the rabbi.

The major national Jewish community relations agencies became involved in the controversy because their Forest Hills members were involved. The American Jewish Committee opened an office in Forest Hills to help allay fears, to develop a senior citizens tenants association, and to undertake a variety of educational programs for use when the project opened. The Queens Jewish Community Council was born out of the conflict. It openly charged the Lindsay administration with trying to destroy the Forest Hills Jewish community. The Council was backed by the Orthodox Rabbinical Association of Queens which called on all rabbis to denounce the project from the pulpit during the High Holy Days. Pro-project rabbis received threatening calls and letters after some of them had called attention to the irony of Jews opposing the admission of minorities in an area where Jews themselves had once had to fight housing restrictions. Oddly enough, the first Chasidic families who settled in Forest Hills and Rego Park also encountered some opposition from Jewish residents who feared another Williamsburg might develop.

The controversy led to many Jewish families moving out of the Forest Hills-Rego Park neighborhood but the majority that remained were finally resigned to the project. In a compromise, the project plans were reduced to three buildings of 12 stories, with a total of 430 apartments. The entire complex was converted into a low income cooperative with some 40 percent of the occupants being low income aged, which in practice would mean elderly Jews already living in the area. At the end of 1975 when the first tenants moved in, there was a vestige of fear over the potentially negative impact on the neighborhood. These fears were intensified when the Board of Education began busing black and Puerto Rican students from other areas into Forest Hills High School.

Notwithstanding its size, Queens Jewry developed no independent borough-wide Jewish institutions until the housing fight gave rise to the Queens Jewish Community Council. There are borough-wide federations of local units of national Jewish organizations and temporary committees that conduct area appeals for the Joint Campaign of the United Jewish Appeal of Greater New York-Federation of Jewish Philanthropies. The Associated YM & YWHAs of Greater New York has established branch Ys in Far Rockaway and the Douglaston-Little Neck section. Long Island Jewish-Hillside Medical Center, on the Queens-Nassau border, a merger of Hillside Hospital and Long Island Jewish Hospital, is a major Federation agency. The Federation-supported Long Island Jewish Community Services and the Federation Employment and Guidance Service also operate in Queens. At John F. Kennedy International Airport, the New York Board of Rabbis maintains the International Synagogue.

A good deal of the heavy residential construction that has changed the face of Queens was accomplished by Jewish builders. The biggest of these is Samuel J. Lefrak, who boasts that one out of every 16 New Yorkers lives in a Lefrak-built apartment house. He is the largest single property owner in Queens and the borough's single biggest taxpayer. In addition to Lefrak City, he has blueprinted Satellite City, to be erected over the Sunnyside yards of the Long Island Railroad, where he would move the entire garment industry and provide housing for 17,000 families. He already owns twin 20-story apartment towers that straddle the railroad tracks at Kew Gardens. He also built large housing projects in Seaside and Hammels on the Rockaway Peninsula.

The Jamaica, Flushing, and Queens Boulevard retail shopping areas were also largely the creation of Jewish businessmen. The Gertz department store, largest in Queens, was founded in Jamaica by Benjamin Gertz at the turn of the century, and now has branches in the suburbs. The ten-block area of Rego Park, just west of Forest Hills, has been converted into central Queens' "downtown" area. Within walking distance of the Long Island Expressway, this new shopping center has office buildings, luxury condominiums, and branch stores of Alexander's, Korvette's, Macy's, and Ohrbach's. In downtown Jamaica there are Macy's and May stores in addition to Gertz's.

The large Jewish population helped change Queen's political complexion from solidly Republican to Democratic, and considerable support for the Liberal party. Since the 1950s, Jewish voters who used to help pile up huge Democratic majorities in Brooklyn and The Bronx, have greatly strengthened the Democrats in Queens County. The first Jew to attain borough-wide political status was a Republican, Benjamin Marvin, a municipal court judge in the 1920s. He owned the *Long Island Daily Press*, now known as the *Long Island Press*, one of the links in the nationwide newspaper chain owned by Samuel Newhouse. The two Jews elected to Congress from Queens in the 1950s and 1960s won with Liberal Party backing, although one was a Democrat (Benjamin Rosenthal) and the other a Republican (Seymour Halpern). Halpern did not run for reelection in 1974 but Rosenthal was still in the House in 1976, together with another Democrat, Lester Wolff, whose district includes a slice of eastern Queens and the Great Neck area of Nassau County.

In 1963, the Democrats were the first major party to designate a Jew as county leader, Moses Weinstein. Melvin Klein and Sidney S. Hein were Republican county leaders. Queens has had two Jewish Borough Presidents, Sidney Leviss and Donald Manes. In 1975 the Queens Interfaith Clergy Council chose a rabbi as its first Jewish president. David Katz was the founder of the Queens Chamber of Commerce. Queens College, the borough's major higher educational institution, has a Yiddish section in its Paul Klapper library, named for its first president, offers courses in Yiddish, and is the home of the semiannual magazine, *Yiddish*.

*****

SYNAGOGUES

ORTHODOX

CONG. AHAVATH SHOLOM, 75-02 113th St., Forest Hills.
CONG. CHOFETZ CHAIM, 92-15 69th Ave., Forest Hills.
CONG. EMUNA SHLEIMA, 69-69 Main St.
CONG. KNESETH ISRAEL, 728 Empire Ave., Far Rockaway, familiarly known as "the White Shule." At one time it numbered among its congregants about 35 ordained, non-pulpit rabbis. The congregation has no *hazzan*. Instead it uses a battery of its own unusually gifted *baaley tefilah*, who work in rotation.
CONG. SHAARAY TEFILA, 1295 Central Ave., Far Rockaway. Both this congregation and Cong. Kneseth Israel help make Far Rockaway a unique Jewish community—predominantly Orthodox. Traffic on the Sabbath and Jewish holidays virtually ceases on some streets, where Jewish all-day schools are common (the best known is Hi-Li—the Hebrew Institute of Long Island). It is not unusual to see bearded men in Hasidic garb and boys with side-locks. The community has a high proportion of religiously-educated

laymen. The building is designed in the tradition of New York's Spanish and Portuguese Synagogue and is geared more to the entire Jewish community than to the Jewishly-educated. All told, there are 19 synagogues and nine yeshivas in Far Rockaway. There are also *eruvs* in the Wavecrest-Bayswater area and the eastern-most section, enabling the Orthodox to carry on the Sabbath and wheel carriages without violating the sanctity of the Sabbath.

CONG. SONS OF ISRAEL, 33-21 Crescent St., Long Island City.

CONG. TIFARETH AL-OZER V'YESHIVAS DEGEL-HATORAH, 82-61 Beverly Rd., Kew Gardens.

KEW GARDENS SYNAGOGUE-ADATH YESHURUN, 82-17 Lefferts Blvd., Kew Gardens.

MASPETH JEWISH CENTER, 66-64 Grand Ave.

QUEENS JEWISH CENTER AND TALMUD TORAH, 66-05 108th St.

SEPHARDIC JEWISH CONGREGATION AND CENTER, 101-17 67 Drive, Forest Hills.

TIFERETH ISRAEL OF JACKSON HEIGHTS, 88th St. & 32nd Avenue.

YOUNG ISRAEL OF FOREST HILLS, Yellowstone Blvd. & Burns Street.

YOUNG ISRAEL OF HILLCREST, 169-07 Jewel Ave.

YOUNG ISRAEL OF JACKSON HEIGHTS, 86-15 37th Ave.

YOUNG ISRAEL OF KEW GARDENS HILLS, 150-01 70th Rd.

YOUNG ISRAEL OF SUNNYSIDE, 41-12 45th St.

CONSERVATIVE

BAYSIDE JEWISH CENTER, 203-05 32nd Ave.

BAYSIDE-OAKS JEWISH CENTER, 56-40 231st St.

BAYSWATER JEWISH CENTER, 2355 Healy Avenue, Far Rockaway.

BAY TERRACE JEWISH CENTER, 209th St. & Willets Point Boulevard.

BELLEROSE JEWISH CENTER, 254-04 Union Turnpike.

BELL PARK JEWISH CENTER, 231-10 Hillside Ave.

CLEARVIEW JEWISH CENTER, 16-50 Utopia Parkway, Whitestone.

FOREST HILLS JEWISH CENTER, 106-06 Queens Blvd., has an Ark designed by Arthur Szyk in the form of a *tzitz* (the breastplate of a Torah Scroll). The pattern includes the symbols of the Jewish festivals, the emblems of the Twelve Tribes, and a series of 39 jewels representing the 39 books of the Bible. The borders carry Biblical verses praising the Torah. The whole majestic design rises to a peak that forms the two tablets of the Ten Commandments, and these are capped by the Crown of the Torah.

HILLCREST JEWISH CENTER, 183-02 Union Turnpike, Flushing, has for its façade a mural executed in ceramic tile consisting of five eight-foot-high panels, each expressing a particular theme: the Sabbath, peace, the fruitful life, righteousness, and eternity. A mural in the lobby, *Jacob's Dream*, depicts the Twelve Tribes in stars. Both the exterior and the lobby murals were designed by Anton Refregier, a non-Jewish artist. On the doors of the Ark in the sanctuary there is a charming miniature mosaic by A. Raymond Katz blending a few traditional motifs into its largely abstract play. The sanctuary itself is intimate, and one structural detail that contributes to this intimacy is a niche behind the Ark that broadens upward and outward to become a kind of canopy. The hung ceiling has a large glass panel bearing a wooden Star of David.

JAMAICA ESTATES HEBREW CENTER, 182-69 Wexford Terrace.

JEWISH CENTER OF JACKSON HEIGHTS, 34-25 82nd St., has a chapel dedicated to the memory of the six million victims of Nazism.

REGO PARK JEWISH CENTER, 97-30 Queens Blvd., has a 6 by 36-foot mosaic panel over its main entrance executed in Venetian glass. The motifs in the panel are of the nine Jewish festivals and the symbols of the name of G-d. The fingers of a hand holding a ram's horn also form the letter *shin* (standing for *Shaddai*, the Almighty). A huge Star of David hangs above the mosaic. A. Raymond Katz, who designed the mosaic, also designed the synagogue's two sets of stained glass windows, one of which represents the ethical, religious, and national significance of the three Patriarchs—Abraham, Isaac, and Jacob. The Ark and its setting are an elaborate composition in wood and marble.

SUNNYSIDE JEWISH CENTER, 45-46 43rd St.

TEMPLE GATES OF PRAYER, 38-20 Parsons Blvd.

REFORM

CONG. BETH HILLEL OF JACKSON HEIGHTS, 23-38 81st St.

FREE SYNAGOGUE OF FLUSHING, 136 Sanford Ave., has in its building some marble from the dismantled Vanderbilt mansion on 5th Ave. The congregation's community house was originally the home of a Long Island railroad executive and its designer was the famous architect, Stanford White.

ROOSEVELT JEWISH CONG., serves the Jewish residents of the

housing developments on Roosevelt Island, which is located in the middle of the East River.

TEMPLE BETH-AM, 120-43 166th St.

TEMPLE BETH SHOLOM, 171-39 Northern Blvd., Flushing.

TEMPLE EMANU-EL OF FAR ROCKAWAY, 1526 Central Ave.

TEMPLE EMANU-EL OF QUEENS, 91-15 Corona Avenue, Elmhurst.

TEMPLE ISAIAH, 75-24 Grand Central Pkwy., Forest Hills, has etched in stone on the left side of the façade, the famous quotation from Micah: "What does the Lord require of thee? Only to do justly, love mercy, and walk humbly with thy G-d." Above the entrance the words "The righteous lives by his faith" are inscribed in Hebrew and English. In the sanctuary the Ark doors are handcarved by Milton Horn, well-known sculptor. Stained glass windows on each side wall depict the various Jewish festivals. An innovation at Temple Isaiah is the closed circuit televised High Holy Day services in the auxiliary sanctuary.

TEMPLE ISRAEL OF JAMAICA, 188-15 McLoughlin Ave., was designed by Percival Goodman. There is a mosaic in the west wall designed by Goodman and an outstanding oil-burning Menorah and Eternal Lamp designed by Arnold Bergier.

TEMPLE JUDEA, 82-17 153rd Ave.

TEMPLE SHOLOM, 263-10 Union Turnpike.

TEMPLE OR OF THE DEAF, holds services in the sign language for the deaf in Temple Israel, 188 Grand Central Pkwy., Hollis.

SCHOOLS AND SEMINARIES

BENJAMIN CARDOZO HIGH SCHOOL, 57-20 223rd St., Bayside, named for Supreme Court Justice Benjamin N. Cardozo, has a monument of Cardozo on its front lawn.

ISRAEL MEYER HA-COHEN RABBINICAL SEMINARY OF AMERICA, 92-15 69th Ave., Forest Hills.

HEBREW ACADEMY OF WEST QUEENS, 86-15 37th Ave.

MAX AND ROSE HELLER HEBREW ACADEMY, 203-05 32nd Ave., Bayside.

LEXINGTON SCHOOL FOR THE DEAF, 30th Ave. and 75th St., Jackson Heights, is a $6 million center on a seven-acre tract. The center includes a school for 300 deaf students, a graduate studies institute, facilities for research, and an out-patient hearing and speech clinic. The first school in America to teach the deaf to speak and to read lips, the Lexington School is one of many affiliates of the Federation of Jewish Philanthropies. In addition to the wide variety of vocational shops, training facilities, and courses, the school is planning a treatment and diagnostic center.

SOLOMON SCHECHTER SCHOOL, 76-16 Parsons Blvd. Flushing.

BENJAMIN SCHLESINGER PUBLIC SCHOOL, 133-25 New York Blvd., Jamaica, is named for an eminent leader of the labor movement.

YESHIVA OF FLUSHING, 71-50 Parsons Blvd.

YESHIVA RABBI DOV REVEL OF FOREST HILLS, 71-02 113th Street.

YESHIVA TIFERETH MOSHE, 83-06 Abingdon Road, Kew Gardens.

JEWISH COMMUNITY CENTERS

CENTRAL QUEENS YM & YWHA, 108-05 68th Rd., Forest Hills.

GUSTAVE HARTMAN YM & YWHA OF THE ROCKAWAYS, Hartman La. and Beach Channel Drive, Far Rockaway.

NORTH HILLS YM & YWHA (Samuel Field Bldg.), 58th Ave. and Little Neck Parkway, Little Neck.

SEPHARDIC JEWISH CENTER, 62-67 108th St., Forest Hills, was under construction in 1976, replacing a building in The Bronx.

YM & YWHA OF GREATER FLUSHING (Abraham and Dora Felt Bldg.), 45-35 Kissena Blvd.

HILLEL FOUNDATION

QUEENS COLLEGE, 152-45 Melbourne Ave., Flushing.

HOUSING PROJECTS

BROOKDALE VILLAGE, Beach 119th St., bet. Seagirt Blvd. and the Boardwalk, the largest non-profit senior citizen housing complex in New York State, is sponsored and operated by the Jewish Association for Services for the Aged. A retirement community of 1,600 residents, Brookdale Village comprises four high-rise apartment towers and an adjoining community center.

COORDINATING AGENCIES

JEWISH COMMUNITY SERVICES OF LONG ISLAND, 97-45 Queens Blvd., Rego Park.

QUEENS JEWISH COMMUNITY COUNCIL, 86-82 Palo Alto St., Holliswood.

HOMES AND HOSPITALS

Goldwater Memorial Hospital, Welfare Island, is named for Dr. Sigismund S. Goldwater, hospital administrator and public health authority. Goldwater was the New York City Commissioner of Hospitals from 1934-1940. Earlier he had been superintendent of Mount Sinai Hospital and Health Commissioner of New York City.

MISCELLANEOUS

HOROWITZ BROS. & MARGARETEN (kosher foods), 29-00 Review Ave., Long Island City

LONG ISLAND ZIONIST HOUSE, 132-32nd Ave., Kew Gardens.

MUSEUMS AND LIBRARIES

KLAPPER MEMORIAL LIBRARY at Queens College, 65-30 Kissena Blvd., Flushing, honors Dr. Paul Klapper, the college's first president and believed to be the first unconverted Jew to be named president of any non-rabbinical institution of higher learning. An immigrant from Romania, he rose to be dean of City College's School of Education and became president of Queens in 1937, serving until 1948. He helped lay the ground work for the establishment of the State University of New York.

RESTAURANTS AND NIGHTCLUBS

ARELE'S, Long Island Expressway at 162nd St., is a nightclub under rabbinical supervision featuring dining, dancing, and floor shows.

CAFE BABA OF ISRAEL, 91-33 63rd Drive, is a *glatt* kosher nightclub.

THE FLAME LAPID, 97-04 Queens Blvd., serves Israeli food.

LUIGI GOLDSTEIN'S, 72-24 Main Street, is a kosher Italian restaurant.

JERUSALEM WEST, 117-18 Queens Blvd., is a kosher Chinese restaurant.

KARMEL'S KOSHER BURGERS, 19-03 Cornaga Avenue, Far Rockaway.

KOSHER CHEF, 17-29 Seagirt Blvd., Far Rockaway.

KOSHER KORNER, 67-03 Main St., Flushing.

KOSHER PIZZA-FALAFEL, 71-24 Main St.

LEVY'S KOSHER PIZZA & ISRAELI FALAFEL, 68-28 Main St. (*Shomer Shabbat*).

LINDEN HILL KOSHER DELICATESSEN AND RESTAURANT, 29-22 Union Turnpike, Flushing.

NEW FOREST RESTAURANT, 64-20 108th St. Forest Hills.

PATIO KOSHER DELICATESSEN & RESTAURANT, 78-16A Linden Blvd., Howard Beach.

PHIL'S BROADWAY KOSHER DELICATESSEN & RESTAURANT, 30-05 Broadway, Astoria.

SHOPPING
CONTINENTAL ART GALLERY, 72-21 Austin St., sells works of Israeli artists.

GIFT WORLD, 72-20 Main St., sells books of Jewish interest.

HOUSE OF ISRAEL, 90-05 150th St., Jamaica.

THE JONATHAN DAVID CO., 68-22 Eliot Ave., Middle Village, publishes books of sermons and commentaries on various aspects of Judaism, books of instruction and psychology, some fiction and juvenile works, and sells numerous items for use in synagogues and religious schools. Among the articles to be found here are medals, charms, pins, plaques, certificates, albums inscribed with a Magen David, and just about everything for the synagogue, including furniture.

JOHN F. KENNEDY INTERNATIONAL AIRPORT
Opened in April, 1964, the International Synagogue at the airport is part of Chapel Plaza, located on a lagoon in the central area of International Park adjoining the Protestant and Catholic chapels. The plaza is the first tri-faith chapel development at an American airport. The main sanctuary of the synagogue is modeled after the first synagogue built in America. A museum containing religious objects from Jewish communities throughout the world, a Jewish information center, and a library reading room have been set up within the synagogue, which is sponsored by the New York Board of Rabbis. The structure is dominated by the two tablets of the Ten Commandments, which rise 40 feet from their base in the lagoon. The tablets are flanked on both sides by sculptured stained glass windows depicting the Twelve Tribes of Israel. The foyer of the synagogue contains a tablet of states, on which the sponsoring congregations and individuals from the 50 states have been inscribed.

Among the items displayed in the International Museum are replicas of famous copper plates given by the ruling Hindu king to Joseph Rabban, the leader of the Cochin Indian Jewish community; a 200-year old *shofar*, serpentine in shape and about two feet long; two reed-like leaves on which is inscribed in Malayan a contract between a money-lender and a synagogue that borrowed 1,000 rupees; and other interesting articles. The copper plates, engraved in old Tamil script, were made sometime between 379 B.C.E. and the 9th or 10th century C.E.

Inside the imposing arched concourse of the International Arrivals Building is a large, gray-black marble plaque bearing a raised torch with an excerpt from the same poem by Emma Lazarus that is etched into the base of the Statue of Liberty:

> . . . *Give me your tired, your poor,*
> *Your huddled masses yearning to breathe free*
> . . .
> *Send these, the homeless, tempest-tost to me,*
> *I lift my lamp beside the golden door!*

One line of the poem was omitted: "The wretched refuse of your teeming shore," on orders of Austin J. Tobin, executive director of the New York Port Authority, which operates the airfield. Tobin said the deleted line "had meaning during the mass migrations of the nineteenth century, but it has no meaning now and might be offensive to the fine people of Europe—they might not regard themselves as 'wretched refuse,' " Inside the building the flag of Israel hangs alongside the flags of other nations.

The east wall of the EL AL Airlines Terminal is covered with a mural *Man's Aspiration of Flight*, by Zvi Gali, one of Israel's leading artists. It uses the Italian Renaissance technique of *sgraffito*, which gives the mural a sculptured effect. On the opposite wall, Bezalel Schatz, another Israeli artist, used simple bars of silver to profile capitals served by EL AL and to show their time by silver clock arms.

STATEN ISLAND

Although the Jewish population of the borough of Richmond is growing faster than the general population, fewer Jews lived there in 1976 than in three or four of the giant apartment house developments in The Bronx, Brooklyn, and Queens. In 1963 there were 11,000 Jews on Staten Island, about half of one percent of the total population. In 1975 the Jewish population was 21,000 out of a total of some 350,000. Most of the Jews live in St. George and Port Richmond but there are also sizeable settlements in New Dorp, Tompkinsville, Castleton Corners, New Brighton, Tottenville, Roseville, Stapleton, and South Beach.

Geography and limited transportation facilities have kept Staten Island and its Jewish community small. The opening of the Verrazano Narrows Bridge from Brooklyn to Staten Island in 1965 brought a building boom to Staten Island and a considerable influx of new residents, including Jews. But in 1976 there were no indications that the Staten Island Jewish community would assume the proportions of the older settlements in Queens and Brooklyn.

Though the first white settlers occupied Staten Island in 1661, there is no trace of Jewish residents or even property-owners and merchants before the 1850s. Moses Greenwald, a German immigrant, is believed to have been the earliest Jewish resident. His son, Abram, was born on Staten Island in the 1860s. Several other families established themselves at St. George, Tompkinsville, Port Richmond, and New Brighton before 1880.

Among the first European Jewish settlers were the Kiviats, who arrived from the East Side in 1892, bringing with them a six-month old boy named Abel. Abel Kiviat, who learned to run in the open fields of Staten Island, became one of the great track and field stars of the country, winning national titles in the 600 and 1,000 yard runs, the mile, and cross-country racing from 1910-1915. He was a close contender in the 1912 Olympic 1,500-meter race.

Jewish religious services were first held around 1882 in the home of Simon Raunes, 7 Richmond Turnpike, now 49 Victory Boulevard. Congregation B'nai Jeshurun was the pioneer synagogue, having been founded in Tompkinsville in 1888. The Chevrah Agudath Chesed Shel Emeth, a charitable society, was organized in 1889. A second congregation, Agudath Achim Ansche Chesed, was formed at New Brighton in 1900, and Temple Emanu-El was organized in 1907. In 1916, when there were somewhat more than 3,500 Jews, a fourth congregation, Temple Tifereth Israel, was founded at Stapleton. In 1976 there were nine congregations, as well as a Jewish Community Center and a cluster of local branches of national Jewish organizations.

The Federation of Jewish Philanthropies maintains one of its Henry Kaufmann Campgrounds on Staten Island. It also sponsors a home for unmarried mothers.

The first substantial influx of Jewish residents began after World War II when white collar workers were attracted by the low-cost of new one-family homes. Some Jewish business and professional men from the heavily industrialized area around Bayonne, New Jersey also settled on Staten Island because they found homes there easily accessible. To reach Manhattan or Brooklyn without driving a car, Staten Island residents must take a ferryboat, and the lack of direct transportation links other than the Verrazano Bridge has discouraged mass migration to Staten Island.

*****

SYNAGOGUES

ORTHODOX

CONG. AGUDATH ACHIM ANSHE CHESED, 641 Delafield Ave., is the second oldest congregation on the island.

SYNAGOGUE OF THE YESHIVA OF STATEN ISLAND, 1870 Drumboole Rd., E.

YOUNG ISRAEL OF STATEN ISLAND, 835 Forest Hill Rd.

CONSERVATIVE

CONG. AHAVATH ISRAEL, 59 Sequine Ave.

CONG. B'NAI ISRAEL, 45 Twombley Ave.

CONG. B'NAI JESHURUN, 19 Martling Ave., is the oldest congregation on the island.

TEMPLE EMANU-EL, 984 Post Ave., is the third oldest congregation on the island.

TEMPLE TIFERETH ISRAEL, 119 Wright St.

REFORM

TEMPLE ISRAEL, 315 Forest Ave.

COMMUNITY CENTER

JEWISH COMMUNITY CENTER, 475 Victory Blvd.

SCHOOLS AND SEMINARIES

RABBI JACOB JOSEPH SCHOOL, 3495 Richmond Rd. This school was formerly located on the Lower East Side for over 76 years. It is an all-day school and is named after the only Chief Rabbi that New York City ever had.

YESHIVA OF STATEN ISLAND, 1870 Drumboole Rd., E.

YESHIVA TIFERET SCHMUEL EZRA-JEWISH FOUNDATION SCHOOL, 20 Park Hill Circle.

MISCELLANEOUS

BERNSTEIN INTERMEDIATE SCHOOL, Hylan Blvd. and Huguenot Ave., is named for a prominent local communal leader.

FLORA HAAS SITE of the Henry Kaufmann Campgrounds, 1131 Manor Rd., is a Federation agency which has a permanent day camping site for children from other borough community centers.

ABRAHAM LEVY MEMORIAL PARK, cor. Jewett and Castleton Aves., memorializes the first Staten Island soldier to die in World War I.

JEWISH FAMILY SERVICE, 114 Central Ave.

RICHMOND MEMORIAL HOSPITAL, 375 Sequine Ave., is a voluntary non-profit, general hospital located in a building donated by Berta E. Dreyfus as a memorial to her husband. Portraits of Dr. and Mrs. Louis A. (Berta) Dreyfus are in the lobby.

WAGNER COLLEGE, Grimes Hill, has a plaque in the lobby of its main administration building recording the establishment of its biological laboratories in 1940 in memory of Dr. Louis A. Dreyfus.

RESTAURANTS

WEINSTEIN DELICATESSEN, 816 Forest Ave.

PENNSYLVANIA

Who was the first Jew in Philadelphia, where did Pennsylvania's Jewish history begin? It might have been Isaac Israel, one of the Jews from New Amsterdam who had been given permission to trade along the Delaware River with the Indians in 1656 near what is now Wilmington. One of them may have gone up the river to the settlement of Wicaco, a collection of cabins that later became Philadelphia. There is a record that "the honourable councillor Israel was in charge of the trading post at Passayunk," a small settlement later incorporated into Philadelphia. If Israel was a Jew, which is far from certain, then he was not only the first Jew to have been in what is now Philadelphia, but also the first Jewish officeholder in Pennsylvania. One Isaiah Mesa, described as a Jew, is recorded as having been engaged in a business dispute in Philadelphia in 1657.

In a lecture before the Philadelphia YMHA in 1880, Hyman Polock Rosenbach, member of an old Jewish family and author of a history of the Jews of Philadelphia, said there was a tradition that there were Jews in Philadelphia before William Penn arrived in 1682 to administer the huge land grant he received a year earlier from the King of England. The only written record of any Jews in Pennsylvania during the colony's first two decades is an entry in the ledger of William Trent, one of Philadelphia's leading merchants, mentioning an account with one Jonas Aaron in 1703. There is no certainty that Aaron was a Jew. Old receipt books of the Quaker merchant Thomas Coates mention six Jews from the West Indies who were in Philadelphia on business between 1706 and 1719. These were Joseph Monteyro, Eleazar Valderde from the Barbados, Samuel Peres, Jacob Pinedo, Abraham Haim de Lucena, who came from New York eight times between 1715 and 1719, and Daniel Gomez, also of New York.

The first permanent Jewish settler in Philadelphia of whose Jewishness there is no doubt was Isaac Miranda, who arrived from Italy between 1710 and 1715. He first settled at Conoy Creek, in what is now Lancaster County, and became an Indian trader. In 1723 he represented the governor of the province in some matter concerning a mine near the Susquehanna, an action that brought protests from the settlers involved. James Logan, William Penn's agent in Pennsylvania, warned the protesters against Miranda to whom he referred "as an apostate Jew or fashionable Christian." In 1727 he again served as a government agent and was appointed a deputy judge of the court of vice-admiralty of the province. By then he was already a Christian and could take the oath of office on the faith of a Christian. By the time Miranda died in 1732, he was known as a rich landowner and hard-driving trader. Although he had converted, Miranda owned a Hebrew library from which he lent books to Logan. Logan, who was secretary of the province from 1701-1717 and governor from 1736-1738, was a devotee of Hebrew, and Jewish history and customs. Although he may have learned to read and write Hebrew at school in England, he studied it in Philadelphia with the aid of dictionaries, grammars, Hebrew Bibles, prayerbooks, and even a Shulhan Arukh. Logan's collection of Hebrew books is now in the Loganian Library in Philadelphia.

The first settler who was a professing Jew was Nathan Levy, who arrived in Philadelphia in 1735 as a merchant and shipper and settled there permanently two years later with his family and his brother Isaac. He was the son of Moses Levy, a prominent New York businessman and an officer of Shearith Israel Congregation. In its issue of January 3, 1738, the *Pennsylvania Gazette* reported that Nathan and Isaac Levy had sold a black slave. The death of Nathan Levy's child in 1738 led him to request permission to buy a small piece of ground for a cemetery on the north side of Walnut Street, between 8th and 9th Streets. The first Jew known to have died in Philadelphia was buried here. Two years later he acquired another plot at the same site for a permanent family burying ground which he later donated to the first congregation as a communal cemetery. The wooden gate at this burying ground, which still remains, has marks of British bullets. It was the custom of European armies to execute deserters at the gates of Jewish cemeteries, and the British followed that practice in Philadelphia during the Revolutionary War.

Acquisition of the cemetery marked the beginning of Jewish communal life in Pennsylvania, with Nathan Levy as the founding father. The year the cemetery was established marked the arrival from New York of David and Moses Franks, Levy's nephews. Levy and David Franks became partners in a variety of mercantile enterprises. In 1742, they were among 74 Philadelphia merchants and shopkeepers who met to establish a standard rate of exchange. This was the first known participation by Jews in general civic affairs, according to Maxwell Whiteman and Edwin Wolf, 2nd, in their illuminating book *The History of the Jews of Philadelphia from Colonial Times to the Age of Jackson.* Levy and Franks had extensive shipping interests and did regular business with London firms. They dealt in West Indies sugar and rum and sold a variety of imported goods at their warehouse. It was on one of their vessels, the *Myrtilla,* that the Liberty Bell, built in England, arrived in 1752. Levy had other talents, too. A Maryland physician who toured Philadelphia in the summer of 1744 reported that at a performance of a "tollerable concerto" only one of the performers was much good, he being "one Levy (who) played a very good violin." The fiddler was Nathan Levy.

Like most other merchants of the time, Levy and Franks had a western agent, Joseph Simon, Lancaster's leading businessman. A consortium of Simon, Levy and Franks became one of the major factors in the western trade which exchanged imported or domestic-made goods for furs. As early as 1749 Jewish traders were traveling in the wilderness of the Alleghenies. Simon sent his agents with "sundries for the Indians" from Lancaster to the forks of the Ohio. He himself made several trips to Fort Duquesne when it was still a French outpost, and later when it became Fort Pitt, a British post, to barter for furs at what is now Pittsburgh. Before the American Revolution, Simon, David Franks, and Levy Andrew Levy operated one of the larger trading posts at Fort Pitt.

Until after 1750 there were so few Jews in Philadelphia that all their names are known. Israel Jacobs arrived from London in 1739. Mathias Bush became a naturalized citizen in 1749, the year in which Moses Mordecai came. Solomon Heim Bonn, Midrach Israel, Isaac Rodriguez Santino, Naphtali Hart, and Benjamin Levy turned up about the same time. Another early arrival was Sampson Levy, who became a Christian, but, like Miranda, was always referred to by his contemporaries as a Jew. Sampson's son, Nathan, was circumcised, but his other sons, Sampson, Jr., and Moses, who became prominent attorneys, never regarded themselves as Jews. Moses Levy was so highly regarded as a lawyer that Thomas Jefferson considered appointing him attorney general. Together with Israel Israel, who was naturalized in 1752 under the name Midrach Israel, these were the only known Jews in Philadelphia between 1730 and 1750. An active patriot during the Revolution and a prominent Mason referred to in Masonic records as "an Israelite in whom there is no guile," Israel was the son of Michael Israel, a professing Jew who married a non-Jew. He was baptized and buried in a Christian cemetery.

Barnard Gratz, who arrived from Germany in 1753, was apprenticed to David Franks. Gratz's brother, Jacob, was already in business in Lancaster. Soon after, another brother, Michael, came to Philadelphia. The Gratzes learned much from David Franks who was an enterprising merchant. He ran a general store, conducted a commission business, freighted ships, underwrote marine insurance, and bought and sold commercial paper. Long before the Revolution he was associated with other businessmen in efforts to control the western fur trade all the way to the Mississippi River. At one time he was involved in ambitious land deals with speculators and government officials that reached to Ohio and Illinois. Franks and the brothers Gratz not only sent agents but often accompanied the pack trains of goods, clothing, foodstuffs, weapons, and ammunition needed by the isolated settlers who had pushed on to western Pennsylvania. The names of Gratz, Simon, and Levy were constantly linked in various business combinations and were associated with the leading non-Jewish traders in numerous enterprises.

During the French and Indian War (1754-63) David Franks and his father, Jacob, were official agents and supply contractors for the British army in America. They rounded up the supplies used in General Braddock's ill-fated attempt to capture Fort Duquesne in 1755. Three years later when another British expedition captured Fort Duquesne and rebuilt it as Fort Pitt, the Franks were again the major source of supplies. Frankstown Avenue in Pittsburgh is said to be named for these enterprising Jewish merchants.

Meanwhile, the Gratzes, who had gone into business for themselves, sent furs, grain, lumber, and cattle abroad in exchange for hard cash and consumer goods. Barnard engaged in the coastal trade from New Orleans to Quebec, while Michael sent cargoes to Canada, Georgia, and the Dutch and British West Indies. By 1768 the Gratzes were actively engaged in an Illinois land venture in which William Murray acted as their agent in the Mississippi River area. The same Murray also served as agent for David Franks in his army supply firm. Michael Gratz married Miriam Simon, one of the seven daughters of Joseph Simon of Lancaster. In 1759, Simon and Levy Andrew Levy established a fur trading post at Fort Pitt. Simon had been a business associate of Levy and Franks of Philadelphia since the English Jew first arrived in Lancaster in 1740. By 1747 there were ten Jewish families in Lancaster. This town became famous as the starting point for settlers heading west towards Pittsburgh and the Ohio, or south to Baltimore and Richmond. Simon was one of Pennsylvania's largest landowners. He owned trading posts at Fort Pitt, in the Ohio and Illinois country, and had interests in many parts of Pennsylvania.

Simon's partner in the manufacture of arms, the sale of hardware, and the export of iron bars in Lancaster was the eminent inventor, William Henry. Henry invented a rifle that was a prized possession in Colonial days. This master craftsman had joined forces with Simon after he had completed his apprenticeship as a gunmaker in 1750. Using equipment from the Simon and Henry forge, Henry, in 1763, built the first stern-wheeled steamboat in America, but the boat sank in Conestoga Creek. One of Henry's pupils, Robert Fulton, was more successful with his steamboat experiment than his teacher. Fulton had learned the art of draughting and gunmaking at the Simon and Henry forge. By 1768, Simon, the Gratzes, the Franks, and their non-Jewish associates had begun to merge their interests in the Indiana-Grant-Ohio-Walpole-Vandalia colony on the Upper Ohio. After the Revolution, the Gratz brothers resumed their fur trading around Pittsburgh.

Other pioneer Jews followed Simon's example and settled north, south, and west of Philadelphia. Elijah Etting, a son-in-law of Simon's, settled in York in 1760 and was one of the incorporators of the town in 1762, three years before he was naturalized. There were Jews in Reading as early as 1753. In 1750, when Easton was first surveyed, Myer Hart was already in business there, and he became the town's leading citizen. In Northumberland, Aaron Levy, a Dutch Jew, was the leading merchant in 1760. His name and that of Levy Andrew Levy, another son-in-law of Simon's, appear on the first county tax list in 1775. Moses Henry owned land in Pittsburgh in 1768 when he was granted permission to "occupy a lot" in the new town of Pittsburgh. In Lancaster, Simon was one of the founders of the public library and of the first fire department. He was also one of the backers of the Conewango Canal. The Colonial Jewish communities included many of Simon's seven sons-in-law. The Lancaster house Simon built for his daughter Miriam and her husband, Michael Gratz, was the birthplace of their daughter, the noted Rebecca Gratz. The Reverend Richard Locke who visited Lancaster in 1747 found ten Jews living there, including Dr. Isaac Cohen, a physician. By 1751 nine additional Jews were listed. There is a tradition of a Jewish settlement at Schaefferstown in Lancaster County early in the 18th century. These colonists were said to have been among the 150 German families who had fled their homeland because of economic crises, wars, and religious persecution. They first settled in New York's Upper Hudson Valley before moving into southern Pennsylvania in 1723.

On the eve of the American Revolution there were some 300 Jews in Philadelphia and probably 100 or more in the other towns of

Pennsylvania. When a group of Philadelphia merchants met in the State House on October 25, 1765 to fight British taxes and especially the hated Stamp Act, they agreed to boycott imported British goods through the Non-Importation Resolutions. The first to step forward to sign was Mathias Bush, who was then president of the city's first Jewish congregation. Out of the 25 known Jewish merchants in Philadelphia in 1765, ten were among the signers of the pledge to avoid importing British merchandise of any kind. Other signers were Barnard and Michael Gratz, Moses Mordecai, Joseph Jacobs, Benjamin and Sampson Levy, and David Franks. The latter was assigned by the Continental Congress to provide food and clothing for the British military prisoners and Tories held by the Americans at Easton, Lancaster, and Reading. This assignment created trouble for Franks, who with his father, Jacob, and his two brothers in England, had been the King's agent for the northern colonies before the war and purveyors to the British army for many years. In 1778 Franks was arrested by the American authorities on suspicion of having Tory sympathies. Before the year was out he had been ousted as commissary to the British prisoners held by the American troops. Later he was brought to trial but acquitted, only to be arrested again by the state authorities in Pennsylvania on a charge of corresponding with the enemy.

Franks had married into a prominent Episcopalian family when Margaret Evans, daughter of Philadelphia's registrar of wills, became his wife in 1743. Although all of his children were baptized, he continued annual contributions to Shearith Israel Congregation in New York, collected books on Jewish antiquities, and kept abreast of Jewish affairs in New York and Philadelphia. His sister, Phila, eloped with Oliver DeLancey, member of a socially prominent Christian family in New York, after whom Delancey Street on the Lower East Side is named. Franks and Sampson Levy, still a Jew in 1748, were members of the exclusive Assembly Ball, when it first began.

Half a dozen Philadelphia Jews were engaged in privateering against British shipping early in the Revolution. At the request of the Continental Congress, Michael Gratz provided blankets for the troops. So did Aaron Levy in Northumberland. Manuel Joseph secured guns, cutlasses, and bayonets, and Levy Andrew Levy of Lancaster and Barnard Gratz at Fort Pitt furnished other equipment. Samuel de Lucena provided saltpetre and sulphur. Joseph Simon outfitted several companies and manufactured rifles with his partner, William Henry, at Lancaster. Solomon Bush was a deputy adjutant general in the Pennsylvania State Militia which included at least eight other Jews. There were Jews with Washington in the Valley Forge encampment, among them Abraham Levy and Philip Russell. Russell had been a surgeon's mate under General Lee in 1775, and later was with the 2nd Virginia

Regiment encamped at Valley Forge, where he cared for the freezing, hungry troops. In Lancaster, five Jews joined in a pledge to maintain one or more messengers to ride between the town and Washington's headquarters. In Easton, Myer Hart was the supervisor of the prisoner-of-war camp. The *Journal of the Continental Congress* records numerous transactions of Jews furnishing military supplies. Jonas Phillips, who bought one of the first printed texts of the Declaration of Independence in 1776, mailed it with a letter in Yiddish to a friend in Amsterdam, sending it via the Dutch West Indies island of Eustatia to circumvent the British blockade. The letter was never received because the British intercepted it, and the enemy gained possession of the first printed copy of the Declaration of Independence. The Yiddish puzzled them and they assumed it was a secret code. The broadside containing the Declaration and the letter were filed away in the Public Records Office in London with other mail seized in the colonies. Phillips, who came to Philadelphia in 1775 from New York, was a tailor, auctioneer, and itinerant merchant, who later became leader of the Jewish community.

Two of the most colorful Jewish characters of Philadelphia during the years of the American Revolution and the period following it were Solomon Bush and Jacob Philadelphia.

Bush, the son of Mathias Bush, who had been engaged in trading in Philadelphia since 1749 and who was related by marriage to Barnard Gratz and Joseph Simon, had served with distinction during the early years of the Revolutionary War. His thigh shattered by a bullet during a skirmish in 1777, he was carried to his father's house in Chestnut Hill, near Philadelphia, shortly after the British occupied the city. He was discovered and imprisoned and the lack of medical care kept him from further service. Repeatedly he appealed to various state and federal bureaus for financial aid, and finally he was granted pay and rations equal to his rank of major. In 1779 he was promoted to lieutenant-colonel in the Pennsylvania State Militia, thus becoming the highest ranking Jewish officer in a combat unit of the Continental army. In 1785 he was granted a pension.

During and after the war Bush vainly sought various government appointments. He devoted his last years to intense work in the Masonic order. In 1781 he had been made deputy-inspector general of Masonry for Pennsylvania, and later was grand master of the state's Sublime Lodge of Perfection. To further relations with English Masonry, Bush made a trip to Great Britain. In a letter to the German Emperor Frederick the Great, who held high Masonic office, Bush described himself in these terms: "I, Solomon Bush, Grand Elect, Perfect and Sublime Knight of the East and Prince of Jerusalem, Sovereign Knight of the Sun and of the Black and White Eagle, Prince of the

Royal Secret, and Deputy Inspector General, and Grand Master over all Lodges, Chapters and Grand Councils of the Superior Degrees of Masonry in North American within the State of Pennsylvania, etc." He signed himself, "Your very humble and most affectionate brother."

Jacob Philadelphia, who was trained in the natural sciences, had been to England in the 1750s to work in the experimental laboratories of the Duke of Cumberland. Highly versatile, Philadelphia was a physicist, chemist, astrologer, expert mechanic, submarine pioneer, and prestidigitator. For a time he was acclaimed as one of Europe's most famous magicians. Philadelphia conceived the idea of a German-American trading company which would strengthen economic ties between the two countries. In 1783, he wrote a letter to Frederick the Great, outlining his plan. The letter fell into the hands of Frederick William von der Schulenberg, who never forwarded it to the emperor because he deemed the proposal inexpedient. Nevertheless, the following year, the state of Saxony tried to set up just such a company as Philadelphia had suggested, and in 1785 Prussia signed its first treaty of trade and amity with the fledgling United States.

There is a tradition that in the mid-1740s, observant Jews in Philadelphia banded together for worship in a house in Sterling Alley, with Nathan Levy as their leader. Occasionally this group was augmented by Jews from Lancaster and by travelers, but it totally lacked organization. The first Torah was brought to the city in 1761, by which time services were being held regularly. That same year the young community contributed to a fund for the relief of Jewish earthquake victims in Safed and two years later it came to the aid of the Jews in Hebron. In 1769, Emanuel Lyon advertised in a Philadelphia paper offering Hebrew lessons. In its issue of July 30, 1771, the *Pennsylvanisch Staatsbote* reported that "on last Saturday in Cherry Alley in this city was opened the first Jews synagogue, and Jewish divine services were held there." This was the first public notice of a permanent religious community of Jews in Philadelphia.

The earliest surviving Jewish record of a formal congregational body is dated February 22, 1773 when at a meeting of the "mahamed Kahal Kodesh Mikveh Israel" it was unanimously agreed to establish the congregation on a more solid foundation and to collect funds for the "uses of the synagogue." Barnard Gratz was the first president and Solomon Marache, who later moved to Lancaster, was treasurer. In 1776 Michael Gratz engaged a Hebrew teacher for his six children who also served as reader in the synagogue and *shochet*. Jonas Phillips, who arrived from New York in 1773 and emerged as the post-revolutionary leader of the community, had been the *shochet* of Shearith Israel Congregation in New York. There were also services held in Lancaster as early as 1776 in Joseph Simon's home. A portion of the Ark used then as well as other religious appurtenances from the Holy Congregation of Lancaster are preserved by the American Jewish Historical Society. The congregation's record book for 1781 is owned by the American Jewish Archives. There were 100 or more Jews in Lancaster in the 1780s and the synagogue had at least ten family members.

By 1780, the Jewish population of Philadelphia had grown to nearly 200 families and 1,000 persons. The need for a synagogue became an urgent matter. Jews from New York, Savannah, and Charleston who had come to Philadelphia during the early years of the war greatly enlarged the Jewish community and provided leadership. The Reverend Gershom Mendes Seixas, minister of Shearith Israel in New York, who had come to Philadelphia during the British occupation of New York after a brief stay in Connecticut, became Mikveh Israel's first spiritual leader, a post he held until 1784. The oldest existing minutes of Mikveh Israel show that in 1782 a formal congregation was organized and authorization given to buy an old bake house and adjoining lot on Sterling Alley as the site for a synagogue. When the Lutheran Church objected to a synagogue as a close neighbor, a new lot was bought on the north side of Cherry Street, midway in the block from 3rd Street to Sterling Alley. When the synagogue was dedicated on September 13, 1782, it was the first in Pennsylvania. There were sixty contributors to the building fund and forty members. Haym Salomon, the noted patriot and financier, who made the largest contribution to the building fund, headed the dedication procession that marched from the old rented quarters in Sterling Alley, and was given the honor of opening the door to the new synagogue.

Salomon, who was honored with a U.S. postage stamp in 1975 as part of the American Bicentennial celebration, has been the subject of a good deal of fictionalized history about his role in the Revolution. The record was set straight by Dr. Jacob R. Marcus in his book *Early American Jewry,* Volume II.

Born in Lissa, Poland, about 1740, Salomon came to America on the eve of the Revolution with a working knowledge of German, French, Italian, Russian, Polish, and English, an understanding of finance, and friends among bankers in Europe's major banking centers. In the summer of 1776, because of his known warm attachment to the American cause, Salomon was given permission by the commanding officer at Lake George to sell food and drink to the troops. This incurred the suspicion of the British who arrested him when they took New York and confined him to a prison ship. He escaped with the aid of a Hessian mercenary. Shortly before his arrest he had married 15-year old Rachel Franks, daughter of Moses B. Franks. Salomon was then 37. In New York, he used his knowledge of German to propagandize among the Hessian troops hired out to the British, but was betrayed and imprisoned. After his escape he fled to Philadelphia in 1778, and started as a commission merchant and bill broker. In 1787 he was engaged by the French armed forces in America to sell their bills of exchange. His immediate superior was John Holker, the French consul, who worked closely with Robert Morris, who in 1781 had accepted the post of superintendent of finance for the United States. Morris needed an able and honest broker to help sell the bills of exchange coming from Europe and engaged Salomon as his chief agent.

In August, 1781, when the drive to stop General Cornwallis in Virginia was being mapped by Washington and his staff, Morris was called upon to raise the necessary funds, and Salomon assisted him. Morris' diary mentions Salomon more than 100 times. After Cornwallis' surrender in October, 1781, Salomon continued to serve Morris, selling bills of exchange, negotiating drafts, and floating securities. In July, 1782, Morris accepted Salomon's offer to sell bills of exchange and a year later permitted him to advertise himself as "Broker to the Office of Finance," In his diary, Morris wrote: "This broker has been usefull to the public interest, and requests leave to publish himself as broker to the office to which I have consented, as I do not see that any disadvantage can possibly arise to the public service but the reverse, and he expects individual benefits therefrom." A monument in Chicago keeps alive the spirit of the deeds of Morris, Washington, and Salomon (see Illinois).

In an advertisement in *The Pennsylvania Packet* of Philadelphia, dated July 20, 1782, Salomon stated that he was broker not only to the office of finance but also to the consul general of France and to the treasurer of the French army. He emphasized that he bought and sold on commission all kinds of commercial paper and bonds from all parts of Europe, the West Indies, and the United States. He also lent money, discounted notes, and stored and sold on commission tobacco, sugar, and tea. In the summer of 1782 he undertook a new venture as a merchant and importer.

The multilingual and knowledgeable financier often lent money to certain delegates to the Continental Congress who were in desperate need, among them James Madison. In August, 1782, Madison wrote to Edmund Randolph, "I cannot in any way make you more sensible of the importance of your kind attention to pecuniary remittances for me than by informing you that I have for some time past been a pensioner on the favor of Haym Salomon, a Jew broker." At another time, Madison wrote Randolph, "The kindness of our little friend in Front Street, near the coffeehouse, is a fund which will preserve me from extremities, but I never resort to it without great mortification, as he obstinately rejects all recompense." Years after Salomon died, his heirs sought vainly to gain some repayment from the United States government for what they claimed was money owing him.

By the end of the war Jews were well established in Philadelphia. They were no longer only merchants but included cordwainers, soap and starch makers, glazers, tailors, peddlers, petty tradesmen, and artisans. One of the first members of the Library Company of Philadelphia was David Franks, and a generation or two later Jacob Gratz continued this tradition as one of the first directors of The Atheneum. In 1761, Mathias Bush contributed five pounds to the Pennsylvania Hospital, the first in the Colonies. The earliest records of the College of Philadelphia, founded in 1749 and later known as the University of Pennsylvania, included Jewish entrants and graduates. Franklin and Marshall College, founded at Lancaster in 1787, had four Jews in its first class. Jews held high office in Masonry. Solomon Bush was deputy inspector general of Masons for the entire state. Solomon Etting founded the first lodge in Lancaster. In the 1800s, Henry M. Phillips was grand master of the Grand Lodge of Pennsylvania. David Salisbury Franks was one of the original members of the Pennsylvania Society of the Cincinnati, the country's first veterans organization. Four Jews were among the first subscribers to the Chestnut Street Theatre, opened in 1792. Solomon Bush was one of the early members of the first abolitionist society founded in Philadelphia in 1774. Jonas Phillips was an active member of the Pennsylvania Society of Abolitionists. Benjamin Nones, David Nassy, and Moses Myers were among those who freed their slaves in 1794. The Society of the Sons of St. George, organized in 1772 as a mutual aid society, had ten Jewish members. On July 4, 1788, when Philadelphia held a great parade to celebrate the ratification of the new Constitution, the Reverend Gershom Mendes Seixas marched arm in arm with Christian clergymen. When the march ended and the paraders were invited to partake of refreshments, the Jews found one table set aside with kosher edibles.

In 1783, after the Continental Congress had left Philadelphia for Princeton, New Jersey, to escape mutineering soldiers demanding their back pay, ten Jews were among the 800 Philadelphia merchants who signed a petition urging Congress to return to Philadelphia. Isaac Franks, who rented his house in Germantown to George Washington, was lieutenant commander of the 2nd Regiment of the Philadelphia County Brigade sent to western Pennsylvania to put down the whiskey rebellion. During the yellow fever epidemic of 1793, Dr. David Isaac Nassy ministered to the stricken citizens. The first Jewish doctor to practice in Philadelphia as a trained physician, Nassy was the first Jew elected to membership in the American Philosophical Society. The city's first Jewish lawyer was Zalegman Phillips, admitted to the bar in 1790. In Pittsburgh, Jews were among the signers of a petition to the Pennsylvania State Legislature in 1787 calling for the creation of a new county to be known as Allegheny, with Pittsburgh, then in Westmoreland County, as county seat.

Notwithstanding their involvement in the mercantile, civic, cultural, and military affairs of the state for nearly three quarters of a century, it was not until 1790 that the Jews of Pennsylvania won complete civil and political equality. William Penn's Frame of Government of 1682 afforded the Jews full freedom of conscience and the right to the public exercise of their religion, But it also denied them the right to hold public office because they did not "possess faith in Jesus Christ." The convention of 1776 that adopted the state's first constitution at first voted to give the vote to anyone who took the oath of allegiance to the United States and who expressed belief in one God, but finally rejected this provision on the ground that it would give Jews and Turks the vote. Instead, the convention adopted another clause reserving political rights to Christians but requiring of all officeholders an oath acknowledging both the Old and New Testaments. In 1783, Mikveh Israel Congregation petitioned the State Council to remove the test oath. During the Constitutional Convention in Philadelphia in 1787, Jonas Phillips sent a letter to the delegates urging them not to include a religious test for public office in the Federal Constitution they were drafting. His plea was dated September 7, but since the convention sessions were not public, he could not have known that two weeks earlier the delegates had adopted Article 6 declaring that no religious test was to be required of Federal officers. Not until a new state constitution was adopted in 1790 was the religious test for state officers eliminated.

In 1790, the Board of Trustees of Shearith Israel Congregation in New York proposed that the country's other congregations in Philadelphia, Richmond, Newport, Charleston, and Savannah suggest language for a joint letter to the newly-elected President Washington on behalf of all Jews in the country. Newport felt it improper to write to Washington before the Rhode Island State Legislature had written; Savannah had already sent a letter. When Washington visited Newport, the congregation there presented an address to him. When Washington came to Philadelphia after the capital was moved there from New York, Mikveh Israel presented an address to him on behalf of the congregations in Philadelphia, New York, Charleston, and Richmond. Earlier, the Philadelphia Jews had joined in an address of loyalty to Congress.

When the Jews from New York, Savannah, and Charleston left Philadelphia after the Revolutionary War ended, Mikveh Israel was in danger of having to close its synagogue. A lottery and a public appeal were made to "their worthy fellow citizens of every religious denomination." Benjamin Franklin was among those who contributed. In 1784 Reverend Seixas left Mikveh Israel to return to Shearith Israel in New York, and he was succeeded by the Reverend Jacob Raphael Cohen. In 1795 the second congregation in Philadelphia was organized as the German Hebrew Society by post-Revolutionary immigrants from Germany, Holland, and Poland. In 1802 it dedicated its first synagogue, and in 1812 under the name of Congregation Rodeph Shalom became the first Jewish congregation to be chartered as a corporate body. This was the country's first Ashkenazic congregation.

New faces, among them the children and grandchildren of the community's founders, came to the fore in Philadelphia after 1800. Benjamin Nones, one of the last Jewish survivors of the Revolution in which he had distinguished himself, was one of the leaders of the Jeffersonian Democrats during the 1800 presidential election. He found himself denounced in scurrilous anti-Semitic terms in the Federalist press. His reply for himself and on behalf of all Jews and other respectable citizens, as he put it, was an eloquent rejoinder.

Some 30 Jews from Philadelphia volunteered for service in the War of 1812, among them Uriah P. Levy (see Virginia), a grandson of Jonas Phillips. Eight Jewish women were among the founders of the Female Association for the Relief of Women and Children in Reduced Circumstances in 1801. Among them was Rebecca Gratz, engaging in her first communal activity. Simon and Hyman Gratz, heirs of Michael Gratz, expanded from wholesale groceries into shipping, insurance, banking, and the building of toll roads, canals, and railroads.

Jews were among the founders of the Orphans Society, organized in 1814. A year earlier the first Jewish mutual aid society, the Society for Visitation of the Sick and Mutual Assistance, was established. The Female Hebrew Benevolent Society and the United Hebrew Beneficent Society were founded in 1819 and 1822, respectively. The city's second Jewish doctor, Abraham Solis, arrived in the city in 1800, announcing that "he will be happy to practice in the medical profession" with which "he is regularly acquainted." Dr. Manuel Phillips, one of Jonas Phillips' sons, was the first Jewish doctor to open a regular practice in the city. He was one of the 17 Jews who attended the University of Pennsylvania Medical School between 1792 and 1838. Jonas Horwitz, who graduated in 1815, was the first Jewish doctor named to a semipublic post in Philadelphia County, having been appointed attending physician at the Northern Liberties branch of the Philadelphia Dispensary, founded in 1786. One of the city's best known doctors in the first half of the 19th century was Dr. Isaac Hays, a grandson of Michael Gratz, one of the original managers of the Musical Fund Society and a leader in the Library Company. Hays was an early specialist in opthalmology. In 1827 he became editor of the

Philadelphia Journal of the Medical and Physical Sciences and after it changed its name to *American Journal of Medicine,* he continued as editor until 1869. This journal was the forerunner of the *Journal of the American Medical Association.* Hays had been one of the society's founders in 1847 and was the author of its code of ethics.

When Henry Solomon won a seat on the Philadelphia Common Council in 1818 he became the first professing Jew elected to public office in Pennsylvania. John Moss, a coal shipper, banker, importer and exporter, and builder of turnpikes, was elected to the Common Council in 1828. Moss, Hyman Gratz, and Zalegman Phillips, a lawyer, were the leading figures in Jewish communal affairs in the first 40 years of the 19th century. Abraham Hart, for many years president of Mikveh Israel, was long the city's leading bookseller and publisher. The firm of Edward L. Carey and Hart published the autobiography of Davy Crockett in 1833, one of America's first bestsellers. The Carey-Hart company also published James Fenimoore Cooper's popular novels.

The first of the notable group of lay and rabbinic personalities who were associated with Philadelphia in the 19th century was Dr. Isaac Leeser, who was only 23 when he became *hazzan* of Mikveh Israel in 1829. With him began a new era as he emerged as the city's leading Jew and ultimately one of the most prominent American Jewish figures. When he came to Philadelphia, the Jewish community was not quite a century old and still tiny compared to contemporary urban Jewish centers. A large part of the Jewish community could trace its origin to Colonial stock, with only 225 foreign born Jewish residents. By the 1830s, when large numbers of Jews began arriving from Germany, Bohemia, and Hungary, the foreign born outnumbered the native born Jews. Leeser wrote school books for children, prayer books for his congregation, treatises on Judaism, and translated the Hebrew Bible into English. He published *The Occident,* the first national Jewish magazine, organized the Hebrew Education Society and Maimonides College, the country's first rabbinical seminary, and promoted a plan to unite all Jewish congregations into a national union. Leeser was the prime mover in the creation of the first Jewish Publication Society and it was he who stimulated the establishment of new philanthropic and cultural institutions. His enterprising spirit influenced the Jews of the entire country.

Two of his Mikveh Israel congregants created major Jewish institutions: Hyman Gratz bequeathed the funds to establish Gratz College, and Moses Aaron Dropsie, the first president of Gratz College, endowed Dropsie University. A third congregant, Rebecca Gratz, was identified with many of the city's Jewish agencies as founder or prime mover. It was Leeser, in his capacity as secretary of the Board of Ministers of Hebrew Congregations in Philadelphia, who wrote to President Lincoln requesting the appointment of a Jewish Army chaplain. Congress in 1862 changed the law to permit the appointment of rabbis as chaplains. The first Jewish chaplain commissioned under this new law was Jacob Frankel, *hazzan* of Philadelphia's Rodef Shalom Congregation. Some 600 Jews from Pennsylvania served in the Union Army during the Civil War. The Union League Club, founded in 1864 as a bastion of Republicanism, had 14 Jewish founding members. A later generation of Philadelphia Jews, however, found that the club barred them.

The surge of the German migration between 1825 and 1850 led to the establishment of new Jewish communities in Pittsburgh, Lancaster, Easton, Reading, Wilkes-Barre, Allentown, Harrisburg, Honesdale, Chambersburg, and Pottsville. Jews lived in Pittsburgh since its incorporation in 1804. Newspaper files between 1800 and 1812 mention an Isaac Jacobs and an M. Levy. *Cramer's Almanac* for 1816 lists Charles Rosenbaum as a manufacturer of pianofortes. William Eichbaum, Jr., Pittsburgh's postmaster in 1829, was described as a Jew in an early book of travel, but he later became a Christian. His father came to the city as supervisor of the first glass works in the west. The city directory of 1826 lists Joseph Abrahams, currier, and Moses Stein, carpenter. The Harris directory for 1837 mentions Charles H. Israel as an alderman and Joseph Israel as a bricklayer. John H. Israel, publisher of *The Tree of Liberty,* organ of the Democratic party of Thomas Jefferson, was attacked in the Federalist *Gazette* as the publisher of "a Jew press" and his office was called "a synagogue." Solomon Schoyer was practicing law in Pittsburgh in 1834. By 1850 there were said to be 2,000 Jews in Pittsburgh.

The first Pittsburgh *minyan* was holding worship services in private homes as early as 1842. An historical sketch of Rodef Shalom Congregation, published in 1899, said that a small number of Jews from Germany settled in and around Pittsburgh between 1838 and 1844 and were joined by others in 1847 and 1852. The Bes Almon Society, a burial association, was founded in 1844 by the participants in the early *minyan*. Out of this society, which acquired a cemetery plot on Troy Hill, came the formation of a congregation in 1846. It took the name Ez Haim and began holding services in rented rooms on Penn Street. A quarrel over ritual between the German and Polish Jews led to a split that gave rise to a second congregation named Rodef Shalom in 1854. A young English Jew, Josiah Cohen, later an Allegheny County judge, headed Rodef Shalom's Jewish day school. In 1861 Rodeph Shalom erected Pittsburgh's first synagogue on Hancock Street (later 8th Street). A secession from Rodef Shalom in 1864 led to the establishment of Congregation Tree of Life. Only seven years later the first East European Jews in Pittsburgh founded Congregation Beth Hamedresh Hagodol, the city's first Russian congregation.

By the end of the Civil War there were four congregations in Philadelphia—Mikveh Israel, Rodeph Sholom, Beth Israel, and Knesseth Israel; two in Pittsburgh, Rodef Shalom and Tree of Life, and one each in Easton (1839), Lancaster (1847), Wilkes-Barre (1848), Harrisburg (1851), Scranton (1858), Erie (1861), and Reading (1864).

The Civil War brought the first Jewish philanthropic agency to Pittsburgh, the Hebrew Ladies Aid Society, founded in 1863 to care for soldiers and their families. During the agitation against the United States-Swiss Treaty of 1854, the still tiny Jewish community in Pittsburgh held a public mass meeting to protest discriminatory clauses against Jews. Philadelphia Jewry established the Jewish Foster Home (1855), the Jewish Hospital (1865), a home for the aged (1866), an orphan home (1868), the United Hebrew Charities (1869), and the country's second YMHA in 1875. The United Hebrew Relief Association of Allegheny County, founded in 1880, was the ancestor of the present federation.

On the eve of the great migration of Jews from Czarist Russia in the 1880s, there were 18,000 Jews in Pennsylvania, 12,000 of them in Philadelphia. By 1900 the East European Jews had become the majority among the state's 100,000 Jews. In 34 cities and towns besides Philadelphia and Pittsburgh there were then one or more Jewish institutions. Of the more than 1,000,000 Jewish immigrants from Eastern Europe between 1889 and 1910, some 108,000 settled in Pennsylvania. By then many of the most important national Jewish institutions had been founded in Philadelphia or by Philadelphia Jews. Rabbi Henry Berkowitz had created the Jewish Chautauqua Society. Rabbi Joseph Krauskopf founded the National Farm School and the Jewish Publication Society of America. Dr. Cyrus Adler organized the American Jewish Historical Society. Dr. Sabato Morais, who had succeeded Isaac Leeser at Mikveh Israel, was one of the two founders and the first president of the Jewish Theological Seminary of America. The Pittsburgh meeting of the Central Conference of American Rabbis adopted the first doctrinal code of American Reform Judaism. The first American Jewish Congress was organized in Philadelphia in 1916. The American Jewish Conference was born out of the Pittsburgh meeting of national Jewish organizations convened in 1943 by Henry Monsky, president of B'nai B'rith. Five years earlier, the late Edgar Kaufmann, Pittsburgh civic leader and department store tycoon, had convened a conference out of which came the General Jewish Council, the predecessor of the National Jewish Community Relations Advisory Council.

By 1917 there were 322,000 Jews in Pennsylvania. Only New

York had a larger Jewish population. Philadelphia, with 200,000 Jews, was topped only by New York City and Chicago. Pittsburgh, with 60,000 Jews, was the eighth largest Jewish community in the country. There were also 1,000 or more Jews in Chester, Erie, Harrisburg, Lancaster, McKeesport, Reading, Scranton, Allentown, Altoona, Braddock, Bethlehem, and Wilkes-Barre. There were 16 cities with between 150 and 900 Jews and 593 small towns and cities with a total of 27,366 Jews. Ten years later, Pennsylvania's Jewish population rose to 404,979 and it increased to 434,616 by 1937. It still had more Jews than any other state except New York, while Philadelphia, with 293,000 Jews, was still the second largest Jewish community. Pittsburgh counted 52,000, a falling off from the previous decade. By 1960, the Los Angeles metropolitan area with 400,000 Jews had displaced the Philadelphia metropolitan area with 331,000 Jews as the second largest concentration of Jews, while Pittsburgh's Jewish population fell off to 47,000. In 1975, California's 666,610 Jews made that state the one with the second largest Jewish population, while Pennsylvania with 470,000 dropped to third place. The Philadelphia metropolitan area fell back to fourth place among the major concentrations of Jewish population, being topped not only by the New York metropolitan area, but also by the Los Angeles metropolitan area and Long Island. In 1975, the Jewish population of the Greater Pittsburgh area was 52,638, with the largest concentrations in Squirrel Hill, South Hills, East End, and eastern suburbs.

Beginning in 1950, the Philadelphia Jewish population began to shift heavily towards the suburbs in Delaware, Montgomery, and Bucks Counties, Pennsylvania, and Camden County, New Jersey, across the Delaware River. Germantown, West Oak Lane, Oxford Circle, and Mt. Airy neighborhoods, once heavily Jewish, began to lose their Jewish population in the 1950s, and by the 1970s were becoming largely black. Some city neighborhoods such as northwest Philadelphia, gained Jewish residents, but the general trend was towards the suburbs to which many synagogues moved, while some in the city merged with neighboring congregations. In 1957, there were 256,000 Jews in the city of Philadelphia compared with 74,000 in Delaware and Montgomery Counties. In 1972 the city's Jewish population declined to 202,000 while the Jewish residents in the suburban counties rose to 150,000. By 1975, the major Jewish neighborhood in the city was northeast Philadelphia where some 80,000 Jews lived. Most of these Jews came from changing neighborhoods such as west Philadelphia, south Philadelphia, Strawberry Mansion, Wynnefield, West Oak Lane, Logan, and Parkside. In the early 1970s there was a noticeable rise in Jewish population in the inner city as older couples and many newlyweds moved into the new high rise apartment houses.

The Philadelphia and Pittsburgh communities played a major role in aiding the Jews of Wilkes-Barre when that city was inundated in 1972 by Hurricane Agnes. The two major cities in the state sent trained social workers, food, religious equipment, books, and other necessities as Wilkes-Barre's Jews sought to rebuild. In an unprecedented outpouring of help for American Jews in need, Jewish communities throughout the country raised over $3 million for emergency relief, business loans, and reconstruction.

More Jews (ten) have been elected to Congress from Pennsylvania than from any other state with the exception of New York. They are: Charles Lewis Levin (1845-51); Henry M. Phillips (1857-59); Myer Strouse (1863-67); Benjamin Golder (1925-33); Henry Ellenbogen (1933-38); Leon Sacks (1936-43); Samuel A. Weiss (1941-46); Earl Chudoff (1949-58); Herman Toll (1959-67); and Joshua Eilberg (1967-   ). Pennsylvania is also one of the few states to have elected a Jew as governor—Milton Shapp, elected in 1970, and reelected in 1974.

Nine Pennsylvania Jews have been United States District and Circuit Court judges. They are: Abraham L. Freedman, Max Rosenn, David Stahl, Arlin Adam, and Harry Kalodner, 3rd Circuit Court of Appeals; Herbert Fogel, Charles R. Weiner, and Louis Rosenberg, District Court. Herbert L. Teitelbaum served as United States Attorney for the Western District.

On the state-wide level, Horace Stern was chief justice of the State Supreme Court, and Herbert S. Cohen and Samuel J. Roberts were justices of the Supreme Court. The following headed various state commissions: Joseph Sharfsin, State Public Utilities Commission; Harry Shapiro, secretary of welfare; Harry Kalodner, secretary of revenue; Genevieve Blatt, secretary of internal affairs, who was the Democratic candidate for the United States Senate in 1964; Herbert S. Cohen, attorney general; Arlin Adam, secretary of welfare; Herbert Denenberg, commissioner of insurance; Joel Weisberg, director of the state bureau of consumer protection; Richard H. Lansburgh, secretary of labor and industry; Israel Packel, attorney general; and Alice F. Liveright, secretary of welfare. In 1874-75 Herbert Fineman was speaker of the State House of Representatives.

Two Jews served as president of the Philadelphia City Council, Bernard Samuel, who became acting mayor in 1941 when the mayor died, and George X. Schwartz. Samuel Dash, general counsel to the Senate Watergate Committee, was one of three Jews elected district attorney of Philadelphia County; the other two were Arlen Specter and Charles Edwin Fox. Three Jews have been president of the Philadelphia board of education—Edwin Wolf, Leon Obermayer, and William Ross. Marcus Aaron held a similar post in Pittsburgh. Aaron Hess was speaker of the State House of Representatives in 1928, and Morton Wilkin was majority and minority Republican leader of the House 1931-36. Charles W. Weiner was Democratic leader of the State Senate. Judge Sara M. Soffel of Pittsburgh was the first woman jurist in the state. Four smaller cities have had Jewish mayors: Lewis Levine, Farrell; Abraham Sass, Carbondale; Jonas Fischer, Williamsport; and Joseph Greenfield, Bradford. In 1847, Jonas A. Phillips, direct descendant of a founder of the Jewish community, was the Democratic candidate for mayor of Philadelphia. Bernard Segal, prominent member of the Philadelphia Jewish community, was the only Jew ever elected president of the American Bar Association.

* * * * *

AARONSBURG

Aaron Levy, Indian trader, land speculator, merchant, and soldier, is memorialized in this Centre County town. It is the first town in America founded by and named for a Jew. Believed to have been born in Holland in 1742, Levy came to America in 1760 and received his business training in Philadelphia and Lancaster. He settled in Northumberland about 1770 as a merchant with close business ties to the Gratzes, Simon, and Levy of Lancaster and Philadelphia, furnishing supplies to the military, dealing with farmers, and trading with Indians. In the early days of the Revolution, Levy served in the State Militia and helped finance the war by investing in treasury loans. Before the war, Levy owned large tracts of land in the frontier counties deep in Indian territory. After the war he became one of the leading land agents in Pennsylvania, buying and selling hundreds of thousands of acres.

In June, 1779, Levy bought 334½ acres located in Penn's Valley 30 miles west of Northumberland, called White Thorn Grove. With navigable waters within easy reach, and timber, quarries, and fertile soil plentiful, Levy envisaged a sizable city could develop on this strategically situated site. He called the place Aaronsburg and laid out streets 50 feet wide. He named one of the chief thoroughfares "Aaron's Square," and another "Rachel's Way," after his wife. Levy set aside several sites for future schools and houses of worship of every domination, and designated others to be used as cemeteries. In a broadside announcing his venture, on May 23, 1786, Levy informed the public that the land would be sold by lot. Purchasers received deeds signed by Levy and his wife, the latter signing in Hebrew script. On October 4, 1786, he presented his town plan at Sunbury, and it became the first town in Penn's Valley. Bypassed as a county seat, Aaronsburg never attained the size of Levy's dream. On November 16, 1789, Levy gave the trustees of the Salem Evangelical Church two lots for the construction of a church, school, and cemetery. Some seven years later he gave some ground for a Reformed Church. On October 23, 1949, nearly 30,000 people converged on Aaronsburg to celebrate the 150th anniversary of the establishment of the Salem Lutheran Church, which stands on the ground that Levy donated. The Aaronsburg Assembly, an outgrowth of the anniversary, has been set up as an interfaith event. A pewter communion service Levy gave the church is kept in a special display case. After Levy moved to Philadelphia in 1782, he joined Congregation Mikveh Israel. He died on February 23, 1815 and is buried in the congregation's cemetery. The Levys, having no children of their own, adopted Simon Gratz, one of Michael and Miriam Gratz's twelve children. Some of the property Simon Gratz inherited from his adopted father was in Dauphin County where he laid out a town called Gratz, which was incorporated in 1852.

ABINGTON

Hillel Foundation at Pennsylvania State University at Ogontz, 1600 Woodland Rd.

Old York Road Temple Beth Am, 971 Old York Rd.

ALIQUIPPA-AMBRIDGE

United Jewish Synagogue of Aliquippa-Ambridge, serving two communities on either side of the Ohio River, maintains two synagogues: Agudath Achim, Main and 21st St., Aliquippa, and Beth Samuel Synagogue and Center, 810 Kennedy Dr., Ambridge.

ALLENTOWN

Cong. Agudas Achim, 2000 Washington St.

Cong. Keneseth Israel, 2227 Chew St.

Cong. Sons of Israel, 2716 Tilghman St.

Jewish Community Center, 22nd and Tilghman Sts., has a ceramic wall tile depicting Moses receiving the Ten Commandments, and guarded by a lion of Judah and Joshua.

Jewish Federation, 22nd and Tilghman Sts.

ALTOONA

Agudas Achim Cong., 1306 17th St.

Federation of Jewish Philanthropies, 1308 17th St.

Jewish Memorial Center, 1308 17th St.

Temple Beth Israel, 3004 Union Ave.

AMBLER

Rebecca Gratz Branch of Hebrew Sunday School Society, McCann Community Bldg., Park and Lindwold Aves.

AMBRIDGE
(see Aliquippa)

ARDMORE
Main Line Reform Temple, 2233 Bryn Mawr Ave.

BALA CYNWYD
Rabbi Piotrkowski's Judaica Center, 289 Montgomery Ave.
Temple Adath Israel, 123 Old Lancaster Rd.

BANGOR
Jewish Community Center went out of existence in the 1960s when the remaining Jewish residents deeded the building to the town with the understanding that it would never be used for commercial or industrial purposes. A small plaque in the building records that it was once a Jewish institution.

BARNESBORO
Cong. B'nai Israel, 8th and Maple Sts., was closed in 1975 when the Jewish community had shrunk to five families, making a *minyan* impossible in this little coal town 20 miles north of Johnstown. The building, however, is still standing.

BARTONVILLE
Olympian Lake, at the summer camp of Philadelphia's Golden Slipper Club, is dedicated to the memory of the 11 Israeli athletes who were murdered by Arab terrorists at the 1972 Olympic Games in Munich, Germany.

BEAVER FALLS
Beaver Valley United Jewish Community Center, Route 51, Chippewa Township, houses two congregations, Agudath Achim (Conservative) and Beth Sholom (Reform).

BELLEFONTE
Old Jewish Cemetery was established by members of the Gratz family who lived here for a number of years.

BERWICK
Cong. Ohev Sholom, 503 Pine St.

BETHLEHEM
Brith Sholom Community Center, Packard and Broadhead Aves.

Cong. Agudas Achim, 1555 Linwood St.

Hillel Foundation at Lehigh University, Brith Sholom Community Center.

BLOOMSBURG

Cong. Beth Israel, 144 Fourth St.

BRADFORD

Temple Beth-El, 111 Jackson Ave.

BRISTOL

Cong. Ahavath Achim, 216 Pond St.

BROOMALL

Beth El Suburban Cong., 715 Paxon Hollow Rd., incorporated Cong. Tikvas Israel of West Philadelphia in 1973 when the latter closed.

BROWNSVILLE

Cong. O'Have Israel, 2nd St., serves a tiny community of 18 Jewish families.

BRYN MAWR

Esther and Philip Klein Hall at Harcum Junior College, Montgomery Ave., is named for a former president of the college, a well-known Jewish communal and civic leader in Philadelphia, and his wife. She was editor and publisher of the *Philadelphia Jewish Times* for many years.

Elizabeth T. Piwosky Memorial Collection of Judaica is housed in the Bryn Mawr College Library.

BUTLER

Cong. B'nai Abraham, 519 N. Main St.

CALIFORNIA

Abraham Azorsky Administration Building, campus square bordering 3rd, 4th, Park, and Hickory Sts., at California State University, is named for a former chairman of the university's board of trustees.

Sons of Jacob Cong.

CANONSBURG

Log Cabin, birthplace of higher education west of the Alleghenies. The original home of Washington and Jefferson College, it has been preserved through a campaign initiated and headed in 1942 by Harry Katz, which resulted in the long-neglected cabin being restored.

CARBONDALE
Cong. Agudath Sholom, 51½ Pike St.

CARLISLE
Hillel Counselorship at Dickinson College, Box 166, headed by a part-time director who is a member of the faculty, is the focal point of religious and cultural activities for the tiny Jewish community of Carlisle.

CARNEGIE
Cong. Ahavath Achim, Lydia and Chestnut Sts.

CHAMBERSBURG
Cong. Sons of Israel, East King and North 2nd Sts.

Israel Benevolent Society Cemetery, East Washington St., was consecrated in 1844. When the town was burned to the ground during the Civil War, most Jewish residents fled, but the cemetery remained in the care of Isaac Stine until his death in 1913. Thereafter, his descendants took on the responsibility. When his sister, the last of his family, dies, Cong. Sons of Israel will assume responsibility.

CHARLEROI
(see Monessen)

CHELTENHAM
Cong. Melrose B'nai Israel, 2nd St. and Cheltenham Ave.

CHESTER
(see Wallingford)

COATESVILLE
Cong. Beth Israel, 500 Harmony St.

Wagontown, a village about 3 miles from Coatesville, on the Old King's Highway, is the spot where, according to local legend, the name of Franks saved the lives of young people from the leading families of Lancaster in 1757. On their way to a dance of the Assembly at the State House in Philadelphia, the group was ambushed by a band of Mohawk Indians at the ford of the Brandywine River. In listing the names of the people taken captive "the magic name of Franks was uttered. . .A gleam of human kindness came into the eyes of Le Loup

Blanc, the hardened war chief. 'If this party is composed of people of the blood of the Franks and Gratzes. . .you are paroled and may return to Hickory Town,' the chief told the frightened youngsters." Hickory Town was the Indian name for Lancaster. The mention of the name of Franks and Gratz, who had dealt fairly with the Indians, prevented what might have been an Indian raid on Philadelphia and saved from capture a substantial number of the younger set of Lancaster society.

CORAOPOLIS
Temple Ahavath Sholom, 1100 Vance Ave.

CORNWALL
Sidney Hillman Recreation Hall on the 520-acre workers' playground owned by the United Textile and Clothing Workers of America, is a memorial to the man who led the union for more than 30 years until his death in 1946.

CORNWELLS HEIGHTS
Jewish Center of Neshaminy Valley, 4736 Neshaminy Blvd.

DARBY
Cong. Agudath Israel, 641 Columbia Ave.

DILLSBURG
Memorial Chapel to the Four Chaplains in Camp Tuckahoe, a 500-acre Boy Scout reservation four miles west of Dillsburg and 25 miles from York, honors the four chaplains who lost their lives on the torpedoed troop ship *Dorchester*. The land belongs to the York-Adams Council of the Boy Scouts. Rabbi Alexander D. Goode, one of the four heroic chaplains, was a charter member of Troop No. 37 at the York Jewish Community Center, and later its leader.

DONORA
Cong. Ohav Sholom, 2nd and Thompson Aves.

DOYLESTOWN
Delaware Valley College of Science and Agriculture, formerly the National Farm School, was founded in 1896 by Rabbi Joseph Krauskopf as the only agricultural college in the U.S. under Jewish auspices. Dr. Krauskopf, who was senior rabbi of Philadelphia's Reform Congregation Keneseth Israel, created the school as a free agricultural training academy for immigrant Jewish boys. He remained president of the college until his death in 1923. After World War I the institution became a junior college. The Joseph Krauskopf Memorial

Library of the College contains 15,000 volumes and thousands of periodicals and unpublished papers, as well as a replica of Krauskopf's own library as it was in his Germantown home. Besides the statuary, furniture, and pictures from his own library, a niche in the wall is covered by a plate glass window and a bronze door over which an eternal light burns. In the niche is an urn containing Krauskopf's ashes.

Dr. Krauskopf, who served as president of the Central Conference of American Rabbis from 1903-1905, was also the founder of the Society of Knowledge Seekers, which prepared the way for the launching of the Jewish Publication Society of America. During the Spanish American War, he was appointed field commissioner for the National Relief Commission, an organization whose activities resembled those of the Sanitary Commission during the Civil War and the USO during and after World War II. As field commissioner, Krauskopf was the only rabbi to tour the fighting front in Cuba. He also toured military camps in Washington, D.C., Jacksonville, Fernandia, Tampa, Chickamauga, Atlanta, and Montauk Point, L.I. His reports on the poor sanitary and medical conditions in the camps, the failings of the Red Cross, and the morale of the soldiers were an especially important contribution to the campaign for reforms in the armed forces. His special mission was devoted to the welfare of the men. He and his fellow commissioners were also charged with the task of investigating conditions among the troops, and the distribution of medical and food contributions from the American people to their sons at the front. Krauskopf, always conscious of his calling as a rabbi, sought out Jewish servicemen, conducted services for them, and took messages back home to their families. He conveyed the personal offer of Oscar S. Straus to provide a $10,000 ice plant for the American headquarters in Santiago. He distributed 1,000 Union Prayer Books as a gift from the Central Conference of American Rabbis, as well as sundry Jewish magazines, tracts, and newspapers to Jewish servicemen. In 1900, he was named special representative of the Secretary of Agriculture to study agricultural education and agricultural conditions in Europe.

David Levin Hall, a dining hall named for a college trustee, is adjacent to Krauskopf Memorial Library. ●The Mandell Science Building, housing classrooms, laboratories, and an auditorium, is named for Samuel P. Mandell.

DRESHER
Temple Sinai, Limekiln Pike and Dillon Rd.

DUBOIS
Cong. Sons of Israel, 150 W. Weber Ave.

DUNMORE
Temple Israel, 509 East Drinker St.

DUQUESNE
Beth Jacob Synagogue, 17 S. 2nd St.

EAGLEVILLE
Eagleville Hospital and Rehabilitation Center, 1332 Fitzwater St.

EASTON
B'nai Abraham Synagogue, 16th and Bushkill Sts.

Hillel Foundation at Lafayette College, care of History Dept.

Jewish Community Center, 660 Perry St.

Jewish Community Council, 660 Perry St.

Memorial to Victims of the Holocaust, on the grounds of Temple of Peace, 15th and Northampton Sts., is a 140 foot bronze abstract statuary which consists of a group of jagged limb-like forms, with a large hole cut through the center section to convey a feeling of pain. Dedicated in 1962, it has a simple inscription in front of the base: "We must not forget." Space around the memorial is filled with plantings and a couple of stone benches as a memorial to Kurt Menkel, a German refugee who was responsible for the monument. The statuary is the work of Hans D. Rawinsky, also a refugee. One of the eleven founders of Easton, which was established in 1752, was Michael Hart, the city's first shopkeeper. He provided most of the funds for the erection of Easton's first school building.

Second Baptist Church, 40 S. 6th St., built in 1842 as the first synagogue of Temple Covenant of Peace, founded in 1839, can still be recognized as a former synagogue. When it was built the structure was patterned after the Great Synagogue in Florence, Italy. Mr. and Mrs. Michael Hart were buried in a cemetery that adjoined this old building but the burial ground no longer exists.

Temple Covenant of Peace, 15th and Northampton Sts.

ELKINS PARK
Cong. Adath Jeshurun, York and Ashbourne Rds., has a design inspired by Chapter 6 of the Book of Kings, its theme being the embracing upward sweep characterized by the priestly three-fold blessing. The front of the building resembles two gently embracing wings. The same theme is carried out in the sanctuary which opens like two arms or butterfly wings to the chapel and auditorium on each side.

Cong. Beth Sholom, Old York and Foxcroft Rds., the last masterpiece of Frank Lloyd Wright, has been described as a "Mount Sinai in modern materials." Rising like a mountain of light, the synagogue is a huge triangular form of glass, aluminum, and concrete. Groups of Menorahs with seven-branched lighting face in every direction, ready to cast their glow toward the sky at night. Surmounting the dome is a symbol of the Torah, bearing in large Hebrew letters the opening words of God's revelation: "I am the Lord your God. . ." The canopy at the front entrance represents the outstretched hands of the priest blessing the people. Lighted at night, the tower symbolizes the Torah as light and Mt. Sinai as the mount of light.

Reform Congregation Keneseth Israel, York Rd. and Township Line, a wedge-shaped structure, the synagogue is noted for its series of ten stained glass windows, each 23½ feet high, whose collective theme is "The Prophetic Quest." Each window depicts an aspect of the unfolding of the Hebrew prophetic succession, based on quotations from Abraham, Elijah, Amos, Hosea, Isaiah, Jeremiah, Ezekiel, Isaiah-2, Job, and Malachi. A large museum of Judaica is located in the Tyson Foyer of the sanctuary building. A memorial plaque to President John F. Kennedy is in the religious school wing. A bust of President Franklin D. Roosevelt stands outside the spacious library. A memorial window to Rabbi Joseph Krauskopf was removed from the old building and installed in the present structure. Among the congregation's early rabbis were David Einhorn, who fled Baltimore because his outspoken opposition to slavery put his life in danger, and Samuel Hirsch, who inaugurated Sunday services in addition to Friday evening and Saturday morning services.

ELLWOOD CITY
Cong. Tree of Life, 404 Beatty Ave.

ERDENHEIM
Temple Beth Tikvah, 1001 Paper Mill Rd.

ERIE
Cong. Brith Sholom, 3207 State St.
Jewish Community Council, 32 W. 8th St.
Temple Anshe Hesed, 930 Liberty St.

FEASTERVILLE
Cong. Beth Chaim, 350 East Street Rd.
Cong. Beth David of Lower Bucks County, 350 East Street Rd.

FRACKVILLE
Cong. B'nai Israel, West Frack St.

FRANKLIN CENTER

Gallery of Great Americans, adjacent to the Franklin Mint, 17 miles southwest of Philadelphia, honors deceased Americans in 12 different fields of achievement. They are chosen annually by an election among readers of *The Reader's Digest.* Included are George Gershwin, the composer, and Nobel Prize laureate Albert Einstein. Also on display are some of the mathematical jottings Einstein made during his work on his Theory of Relativity.

GETTYSBURG

Gettysburg National Military Park has many monuments memorializing the heroes of the Battle of Gettysburg in 1863. One of these honors the 82nd Illinois Infantry, commanded by Lt. Col. Edward S. Salomon. This regiment included an all-Jewish company recruited and outfitted by B'nai B'rith's Ramah Lodge in Chicago. Salomon later served as governor of Washington Territory (see Washington). The regiment's monument has no names on it, only a brief recital of its role in the Battle of Gettysburg. It is located near the intersection of the Carlisle Road and the park's Howard Ave., north of Gettysburg.

National Civil War Wax Museum, Steinwehr Ave. at Culp St., in the town of Gettysburg, has 36 tableaux representing single incidents or famous people involved in the Civil War. Two depict Jewish involvement in the Civil War. Scene 17 shows a meeting of Confederate wartime civilian leaders, including Judah P. Benjamin, Secretary of War and later Secretary of State of the Confederate States of America (see Louisiana). Scene 20 shows John Ericson, Swedish-born inventor who built the government's ironclad warship *Monitor.* In that ship's crew was William Durst, a German-born Jew, who was a fireman. They fought the Confederate ironclad *Merrimac* to a standstill in the first naval battle of ironclads on March 9, 1862 at Hampton Roads, Va.

Park Visitors Center has on display a photograph of Dr. Simon Baruch, father of Bernard M. Baruch, who was a front line surgeon with the Confederate Army.

GLASSPORT

Sammy Weiss Library, in the Glassport Municipal Building, 5th St. and Monongahela Ave., honors Judge and former Congressman Samuel A. Weiss, a native of Glassport and a one-time national vice-president of B'nai B'rith. Established by the Glassport Lions Club, the library, which is open to the public, is supported by the Club and staffed by the Glassport Women's Club. Weiss was a football star for Duquesne University and later a football referee.

GRATZ

Hyman Gratz, son of Michael Gratz and brother of Rebecca Gratz, is memorialized in this Dauphin County town laid out in 1808 by Aaron Levy. Gratz owned several coal mines in the area.

GREENSBURG

Cong. B'nai Israel, Ludwick St. and North Hamilton Ave., is still at the same address where the congregation was originally formed in 1886.

Temple Emanu-El, 222 N. Main St., has five stained glass windows depicting the High Holy Days, Sukkot, Passover, Shavuot, and the Sabbath.

HANOVER

Hanover Hebrew Cong., 179 Second Ave. An old Jewish cemetery here was partially destroyed in the 1930s to make way for a reservoir. Some of the old tombstones were used to build a walk.

HARRISBURG

B'nai B'rith Apartments, 3rd and Chestnut Sts., a 14-story, 207-unit, nonprofit, nonsectarian housing project for elderly persons on limited incomes.

Cong. Chisuk Emuno, 5th and Division Sts.

Cong. Kesher Israel, 2500 N. 3rd St.

Cong. Ohev Sholom, 2345 N. Front St.

Jewish Community Center, 100 Vaughn St.

William Penn Memorial Museum, adjacent to the 20-story State Archives tower, honors Haym Salomon, the Revolutionary patriot, and Rebecca Gratz (see Philadelphia), educator and philanthropist. The frieze in a giant 90 by 24 foot mural above the statue of William Penn has 13 quotations of prominent Pennsylvanians. The one attributed to Salomon says: "Don't fill your mind with vain expectations and golden dreams that can never be accomplished." A statue of Rebecca Gratz is incorporated in the museum's memorial gates honoring 10 noted Pennsylvanians.

Gov. Milton Shapp's portrait is in the State Capitol. Shapp, the first Jewish governor of Pennsylvania, was elected in 1970, and reelected in 1974.

Temple Beth El, 2637 N. Front St.

United Jewish Community, 100 Vaughn St.

HAVERFORD

Jewish Student Center for Haverford and Bryn Mawr Colleges, Yarnell Hall at Haverford College.

HAVERTOWN
Suburban Jewish Center—B'nai Aaron, 560 Mill Rd.

HAZLETON
Agudath Israel Cong., N. Pine and E. Oak Sts.
Beth Israel Cong., Church and Hemlock Sts.
Jewish Community Center, Laurel and Hemlock Sts.
Jewish Community Council, Laurel and Hemlock Sts.
In 1966, Philip S. and Nathan R. Seltzer created a Greater Hazleton Foundation as a trust fund for the benefit of civic, cultural, and humanitarian activities in the area.

HOMESTEAD
Cong. Rodef Shalom, 331 E. 10th Ave.

HONESDALE
Beth Israel Synagogue, 7th and Court Sts., a white clapboard structure with a tiny steeple, is believed to be the tiniest synagogue in the U.S., seating fewer than 50 persons. It is also one of the few synagogues resembling a New England church, except for the Star of David on the tower spire. Founded in 1849, the synagogue was erected in 1856 on land donated by the Delaware and Hudson Railroad. The present building differs little from the original. In 1942, a flood that nearly wrecked the town left the synagogue in ruins. In 1964, when the building was 108 years old, a 21-foot addition was attached to the temple. A passageway connecting the two buildings was created so as not to disturb the appearance of the 26 by 40 foot building. Since 1891, the congregation has had no resident rabbi because the Jewish population has dwindled to a handful of families. However, services are held regularly with lay readers or student rabbis from Hebrew Union College-Jewish Institute of Religion officiating.

HUNTINGDON
Cong. Agudas Achim, 1009 Washington St.
Rabinowitz-Wald Room in the Beeghly Library of Juniata College memorializes Aaron Rabinowitz and Lillian Wald. Rabinowitz was a prominent New York builder who, with Herbert H. Lehman, built the Amalgamated Houses in New York, the first cooperative low rent housing project in the country. He was a great admirer of Lillian Wald, founder of New York's Henry Street Settlement, and of the public health nursing service. Lillian Wald had befriended Rabinowitz when he was a young immigrant boy on the Lower East Side. Rabinowitz had led a move to honor her by election to the Hall of Fame in New York. A well-known bibliophile, Rabinowitz obtained

thousands of books for Juniata College libraries. The seminar room dedicated to the memory of Rabinowitz and Miss Wald has photographs of them, as well as graphite portraits, hung near a Lower East Side street scene. Rabinowitz also donated to the college an Israeli terracotta jar dating from the time of King David, and a Gutenberg Bible.

INDIANA
Cong. Beth Israel, Washington and S. 5th Sts.

JENKINTOWN
Alverthorpe Gallery and Park, 511 Meeting House Rd., the rural estate of Lessing J. Rosenwald, one of the world's great bibliophiles, houses his famed collection of prints and books from the 15th century to the present. He has willed this great collection to the Library of Congress after his death. Alverthorpe Park, a 54-acre part of the Rosenwald estate, was deeded to Abington Township as a public park. The Gallery, which is the former Rosenwald house, will be converted into a cultural center.

Rabbi Piotrkowski's Judaica Center, 115 Old York Rd.

Rosenberg Hebrew Book Store, 411 Old York Rd.

JOHNSTOWN
Beth Zion Temple, 700 Indiana St.

Glosser Memorial Library Building, 248 Main St., is named for David A. Glosser, a prominent communal leader, whose estate provided the bulk of the cost of the $1 million building. There are two memorial plaques in the building citing the Glosser generosity. The Glosser family has been associated with the city for three generations.

Grandview Cemetery contains the remains of the 22 Jews who lost their lives in the famous Johnstown Flood of May 31, 1889. Some of them are buried in the so-called "Unknown Plot," next to the oldest Jewish cemetery in that area.

Jewish Community Council, meets alternately in the two synagogues of Johnstown.

Rodef Shalom Synagogue, 100 Dartmouth Ave.

Spiegel House, 616 Somerset, headquarters of the local United Cerebral Palsy Association, is the former home of Moses Spiegel, chairman of the UCPA drives for a number of years.

KING OF PRUSSIA
Temple Brith Achim-Upper Merion Community Center, 700 Moore Rd.

Wolfsohn Memorial Library of Upper Merion Township, 180

Town Center Rd., is named for the late Nathan W. Wolfsohn who provided the initial funds in 1960 for the establishment of the library.

KINGSTON
Israel Ben Zion Academy, 3rd Ave. and Institute Lane.

KITTANNING
Cong. Kneseth Israel, N. Water St.

KOPPEL
Arthur Koppel, a builder of railroad cars, is memorialized in this town of 1,200 people in Beaver County. Koppel was the founder of Arthur Koppel A.G., later renamed Orenstein & Koppel, a Berlin firm that made railway carriages and small gauge railroad equipment before World War I. It had branches in most countries of the world and its American branch grew up around what became the town of Koppel. The American branch was sold in 1916 to the Pressed Steel Car Co.

KRESGEVILLE
Joseph and Betty Harlam Camp of the Union of American Hebrew Congregations, is named for Joseph Harlam of Temple Beth Israel, Hazleton, who contributed the funds for purchase of the camp. The unique outdoor chapel is dedicated to the late Rosa B. Eisendrath, wife of the late Dr. Maurice Eisendrath, president of the U.A.H.C. A 40-foot wooden tent-like structure erected on a 30-foot triangle, the chapel's three sections, seats, and landscaping form a Star of David. On the west side of the chapel affixed to a triangular stone wall is a metal sculpture of the Burning Bush.

LAFAYETTE HILL
Cong. Or Ami, 708 Ridge Pike.

LAKE COMO
Camp Ramah in the Poconos.

LANCASTER
Cong. Shaarai Shomayim, 508 N. Duke St.
Degel Israel Synagogue, 1120 Columbia Ave.
Kaufman Hall at Franklin and Marshall College memorializes David E. Kaufmann who was U.S. Minister to Bolivia and Thailand during the Herbert Hoover and Calvin Coolidge administrations.
Old Jewish Cemetery, Liberty St., dates from the 1740s. The name "Haim" on one stone indicates the grave of an infant son of Joseph Simon, who was in business in Lancaster from the 1740s until

his death in 1804 at the age of 92. Worship services were held here as early as 1763 in Simon's house.

Mary Sachs Building of the Jewish Community Center, 2120 Oregon Pike, honors a local philanthropist and civic leader. A portrait of her hangs above a dedicatory plaque. The center houses a self-service branch of the Lancaster County Library.

LANGHORNE

Leon Obermayer Auditorium in the Woods School and Residential Treatment Center is named for the prominent Philadelphia attorney, collector of Judaica ceremonial objects, former president of the Philadelphia Board of Education, and a past president of the American Jewish Historical Society.

LANSDALE

Cong. Beth Israel, 1050 Sumneytown Pike.

LATROBE

Cong. Beth Israel, 414 Weldon St.

LEBANON

Cong. Beth Israel, 411 S. 8th St.
Temple Emanuel of South Hills (see Pittsburgh).

LEHIGHTON

Temple Israel, Bankway St.

LEVITTOWN

Cong. Beth El, 21 Penn Valley Rd.
Jewish Community Council, 4141 Woerner Ave.

Levitt and Sons, builders of the first Levittown on Long Island, are also the namesakes of this Bucks County city of 60,000 which they created.

Temple Shalom, Edgely Rd. and Mill Creek Rd.

LEWISTOWN

Cong. Ohev Sholom-Jewish Community Center, 20 East 3rd St.

LOCK HAVEN

Cong. Beth Yehuda, 320 W. Church St.

LOWER MERION

Neshamy Valley Cong., 50 Ashland Ave.

MALVERN

Haym Salomon Memorial Park has a chapel building dedicated to the memory of Max Slepin, military hero and a leader of local and state affairs from Philadelphia. Slepin served in the Army, Navy, and Marine Corps in three wars.

MCKEESPORT-WHITE OAK

Carnegie Free Library, 1507 Library Ave., has a statuette of Sophie Irene Loeb, journalist and social worker, who was born in Russia but reared in McKeesport. While writing feature articles for the *New York World* in 1910, she came into contact with the residents of New York's East Side slums and began fighting for legislative reforms to eliminate some of the deplorable conditions of these slums. She was credited with inspiring passage of the New York State widows' pension law of 1914 and also fought for national legislation to the same end. An organizer and president of the Child Welfare Committee of America, she helped create the International Children's Congress in 1926. As a member of the social service section of the League of Nations, she helped frame the international code for the care of dependent and afflicted children. She also led the fight for penny lunches for school children, for improved housing conditions, and for opening school buildings for public forums. She died in 1929. The statuette shows her holding a child in her arms and surrounded by four children. The inscription on the base of the statuette reads: "Not charity but a chance for every child." She was part of the Simons family that came to McKeesport in the 1870s from Pittsburgh, traveling by sled on a frozen river. She was a cousin of Aline MacMahon, stage and screen actress.

Cong. Gemilas Chesed, 1400 Summit St., in White Oak.
Cong. Tree of Life, Lincoln Way, in White Oak.
Temple Israel, 536 Shaw Ave.
Tree of Life-Sfard, 111 7th St.

MECHANICSBURG

Temple Beth Shalom, 913 Allandale Rd., Heritage Acres, is the first congregation on the west bank of the Susquehanna River.

MEDIA

Beth Israel of Media, Gayley Terr.
Workmen's Circle Home for the Aged, 3rd and Jackson Sts.

MERION

Akiba Academy, 223 N. Highland Ave. (Lower Merion).

Buten Museum of Wedgwood, 246 N. Borman Ave., the home of Nettie and Harry M. Buten, houses over 7,000 examples of Wedgwood china, displayed on the five first floor galleries. The second floor gallery is given over to a substantial collection of Jewish ceremonial objects.

Temple Adath Israel of the Main Line, Old Lancaster Rd. and Highland Ave., is a 12-sided structure, tent-like in design recalling the tent synagogue of the ancient Israelites. The design is carried out in 12 stained glass windows in the cupola.

MIDDLETOWN

B'nai Jacob Synagogue, cor. Water and Nisley Sts., is a small, old-fashioned Orthodox synagogue with a centrally placed bimah, that lost most of its members who have moved to Harrisburg. The synagogue is used only for the High Holy Days and on special occasions. In recent years Jewish members of the faculty of Pennsylvania State University, a new campus in Middletown, have used the synagogue as the site of Jewish forums.

MILL RUN

Kaufmann Conservation on Bear Run, halfway between Mill Run and Ohiopyle, Pa., on Route 381, is a 1,700-acre wildlife area donated to the Western Pennsylvania Conservancy, a private, nonprofit conservation organization dedicated to preservation of beauty in nature by Edgar Kaufmann, Jr., Pittsburgh department store tycoon. The most striking feature of the Kaufmann Conservation is Falling Water, a house universally considered to be one of the supreme architectural landmarks of the 20th century. It was designed by Frank Lloyd Wright in 1936 for Edgar J. Kaufmann, Sr. Built over a waterfall, the house is constructed of sandstone quarried on the property. Edgar J. Kaufmann, Jr., deeded the house and the wild acreage to the Western Pennsylvania Conservancy in 1963. Falling Water is usually open for tours from April through mid-November, from 10 a.m. to 4 p.m. Children under 12 must be left at the child care center near the entrance for which there is a slight charge.

MONESSEN

Temple Beth Am, 100 Watkins St.

MONROEVILLE

Community Office, United Jewish Fund of Greater Pittsburgh, Monroeville Mall, Office Complex 302A.

Temple David, 4415 Northern Pike.

MOUNT CARMEL
Cong. Tifereth Israel, 135 S. Maple St.

NARBERTH
Cong. Beth Am Israel, 209 Forrest Ave.

NEW CASTLE
Cong. Tifereth Israel, 403 E. Moody Ave., has a 250-year old Torah Scroll rescued from a Polish town where the synagogue was destroyed by the Nazis.
Temple Israel, Highland and Moody Aves.

NEW KENSINGTON
Cong. Beth Jacob, 1040 Kenneth Ave.

NORRISTOWN
Jewish Community Center-Tiferes Israel Cong., 1541 Powell St.

OIL CITY
Cong. Tree of Life, 316 W. 1st St.

OLD FORGE
Bikor Sholom Cong.

OLYPHANT
Cong. Bickor Cholim, 302 Lackawanna Ave.

PENN VALLEY
Har Zion Temple, Hagy's Ford and Hollow Rds.

PHILADELPHIA
Adath Tikvah Montefiore Cong. Hoffnagle St. and Summerdale Ave.

Adath Zion Cong., Pennway and Friendship Sts., has a welded, three-dimensional abstract sculpture, 12 feet high and 24 feet wide, entitled *The Heritage,* depicting the spread of Judaism.

American Philosophical Society, 104 S. 5th St., preserves among the Benjamin Franklin papers, the letters of Lt. Col. David Salisbury Franks, who helped supply American troops when they invaded Canada during the Revolutionary War and who served with Washington at Valley Forge. •Also: the letters of Dr. David Nassy, the first Jewish doctor in Philadelphia; a portrait of Dr. Cyrus Adler, a one-time vice-president of the society and also president of the Jewish Theological Seminary of America.

American Wax Museum, 5th St. bet. Market and Chestnut Sts., has among its life-size figures one of Albert Einstein.

Art Associates, 1005 Filbert St., specializes in gifts and ceremonial objects made in Israel.

Association of Jewish Children, 1301 Spenser St.

Atwater Kent Museum, 15 S. 7th St., which concentrates on Philadelphia history, displays in its banking exhibit documents and newspapers dealing with Haym Salomon's financial career during the Revolutionary War, a variety of items related to Rebecca Gratz, and 18th century artifacts from historic Mikveh Israel Synagogue.

Balch Institute, 7th and Market Sts., houses unique library and exhibition areas relating to "Ethnic, Racial, and Minority Group History and American Folklore." The library houses 500,000 books and periodicals, 20 million pages of manuscripts on microfilm and 50,000 units of microfilm publications—all dealing with the role of ethnic and racial minorities in the building of America. One of the four exhibition galleries is a multi-media orientation area that introduces the basic themes of immigration and ethnicity. Rotating exhibits focus on a wide range of subject areas related to immigrants and racial and ethnic minorities. There are collections of Yiddish and Jewish papers and also books on the history of immigration and of Jews.

Bet Arigah, 2601 Parkway, Apt. 1A, is a private studio where the art of ritual weaving, revived 20 years ago by Mrs. Sidney Quitman and Miss Evelyn Applebaum, is carried on.

Beth David Reform Cong., 5220 Wynnefield Ave.

Beth Emeth Cong., Bustleton and Unruh Aves.

Beth Israel Cong. Site, East Washington Sq., 6th St. near Walnut St., identified by a Pennsylvania Historical Museum Commission marker, notes that this was the site of the Walnut Street Prison from 1775-1838, and that part of the land was given to Beth Israel when it built a synagogue there in 1840.

Beth Tefilath Israel of Pennypack Park, 2605 Welsh Rd.

Blumberg Ritual Exhibit, 333 W. Girard Ave., displays some 100 Jewish ceremonial objects of ancient and modern design produced by Dr. Daniel Blumberg, a dentist, in his hobby workshop and exhibited in his home.

Blumhaven Library and Gallery, 4651 Leiper St., is the private library of the late Dr. Herman Blum, who assembled a major collection of early Bibles, Lincoln memorabilia, rare books, and Americana items, which is open to scholars and students.

B'nai B'rith Youth Organization Bldg., 1825 Grant Ave.

Brith Sholom Headquarters, Adelphia House, 1235 Chestnut St.

Brith Sholom House, 3939 Conshohocken Ave., is an 11-story, 313-unit apartment house for senior citizens, sponsored by Brith Sholom, the fraternal order. The building contains the Maxwell E. Verlin Library and Music Rooms, named in honor of a prominent attorney.

Chapel of Four Chaplains, within the walls of Baptist Temple (Grace Baptist Church), at the corner of Broad and Berks Sts., in the heart of the Temple University area, is a memorial to Chaplains John P. Washington (Catholic), Alexander D. Goode (Jewish), George L. Fox (Methodist), and Clark V. Poling (Baptist), who stood united in prayer as they went down with the troopship *Dorchester* when it was torpedoed in the Atlantic on Feb. 3, 1943. The four chaplains gave up their own lifejackets to servicemen who had lost theirs in the confusion. Chiseled into the deep stone are these words: "The Chapel of Four Chaplains—an Interfaith Memorial. Here is Sanctuary for Brotherhood. Never Let It Be Violated." Above the entrance burns an eternal light. On each side of the nave is an arcade of five stone arches. The center arch on the west side frames the bronze memorial tablets dedicated to all who lost their lives in the sinking of the *Dorchester*. The center arch on the east aisle faces a mural painting, a gift of Albert M. Greenfield, showing the sinking of the ship, with the four chaplains, hands clasped, in an attitude of prayer. Under the south end of the nave is a turntable on which three altars stand—Catholic, Protestant, and Jewish. At the push of a button the chapel is converted into a Catholic or Protestant church, or a synagogue. The chapel was dedicated on Feb. 3, 1951 by President Harry S. Truman. The Jewish altar was a gift of B'nai B'rith, and the Torah a gift of Brith Sholom. Behind the altar is a painting showing the cross, the Star of David, and the Tablets of the Law. Persons of every faith contributed to the 400 seat chapel.

City Hall, Broad and Market Sts., has a statue of Moses holding the Tablets of the Law adorning the south facade. •In the Mayor's reception room there is a portrait of the late Justice Horace Stern, Chief Justice of the Pennsylvania Supreme Court. •In the office of the Register of Wills are the will of Rebecca Gratz, the last testaments of the earliest Jewish settlers, and the letters of administration of Haym Salomon, describing his financial support of the American Revolution and his hopes that his widow would receive compensation. •In the Department of Records and Archives there is a record of city taxes paid by Salomon, the naturalization records of many leading Jewish citizens, and the marriage record of Julius Bien, national president of B'nai B'rith for 40 years. •The Law Library is based on the personal library of Judge Mayer Sulzberger, who served on the Court of Common Pleas from 1895-1915, having been the first Jew elected to judicial office in Philadelphia.

•In the Quarter Sessions Court there is a portrait of Joseph Simon Cohen, a prominent lawyer in the early 19th century who was secretary of the Atheneum in 1817.☐

Cong. Adath Zion, Pennway and Friendship Sts.

Cong. Beth Ahavah, 2125 Chestnut St., (First Unitarian Church), is a congregation of Jewish homosexuals.

Cong. Beth Hamedresh Hagodol-Beth Yaacov, 6018 Larchwood Ave.

Cong. Beth Tefillah of Overbrook Park, 7630 Woodbine Ave.

Cong. Beth Tikvah-B'nai Jeshurun, 1001 Paper Mill Rd.

Cong. Beth Zion-Beth Israel, 18th and Spruce Sts.

Cong. Bet Zedek-Ezrath Israel, Bustleton Ave. and Oakmont St.

Cong. B'nai Abraham, 527 Lombard St.

Cong. B'nai Israel Halberstam, 10th and Rockland Sts.

Cong. Kesher Israel, 412 Lombard St., which occupies a building that dates from the late 1700s, has been authenticated as an historic site. Originally a church, it became a synagogue in the late 1800s. An effort is being made to get community support to restore the building to prevent further deterioration. Daily and Sabbath services are still conducted there.

Cong. Ohel Jacob of Bells Corner, Bustleton Ave. and Placid St.

Cong. Ohev Zedek, Mt. Pleasant and Woolston Aves.

Cong. Rodeph Shalom, 615 N. Broad St., organized in 1795 as the second synagogue in Philadelphia, was the first to be founded by Ashkenazic Jews. The synagogue houses the Philadelphia Museum of Judaica, one of the great collections of its kind. Cantor Jacob Frankel of this congregation was the first Jewish clergyman to be commissioned an Army chaplain after President Lincoln signed the law authorizing Jewish chaplains. He was commissioned on Sept. 18, 1862. When the old Rodeph Shalom Cemetery was moved in 1973-74 to a section in the Roosevelt Memorial Park, Roosevelt Rd. at City Line, only three stones were kept in the old burial ground—those of Rabbis Henry Berkowitz, Marcus Jastrow, and Jacob Frankel.

Cong. Shaare Shamayim, 9768 Verree Rd.

Cong. Temple Judea, 6929 N. Broad St.

Consulate of Israel, 225 S. 15th St.

Samuel H. Daroff House of the American Jewish Congress, 1524 Locust St., is named for the late industrialist, philanthropist, and communal leader. The Samuel H. Daroff Elementary School, 56th and Vine, is also named for him. The Daroff (formerly Southern) Division of the Albert Einstein Medical Center, 5th and Reed Sts., is a memorial to Daroff.

Deborah Hospital headquarters, 901 Walnut St.

Declaration of Independence House and Library, 7th and

Market Sts., was occupied by Thomas Jefferson when he wrote the first draft of the Declaration of Independence. It was demolished in 1884, but has been restored to its original shape and design. Hyman and Simon Gratz acquired the building in 1798 and made it the headquarters of their wholesale grocery and export business. When plans were made for the redevelopment of Colonial Philadelphia and the creation of Independence Mall as an historic area, Samuel Cohen, a Philadelphia public relations executive, took the initiative in proposing the reconstruction of the Declaration of Independence House. The late Albert Greenfield headed a campaign for funds to erect the building after the Federal Government acquired the site for $200,000. Sol Feinstone of Washington Crossing, Pa., the leading collector of documents and letters relating to the Revolution, gave a $100,000 collection of Washington, Franklin, and Jefferson letters to the library which is part of the restored historic building .

Delaware River Bridge linking Camden, N.J., and Philadelphia, was designed by Leon S. Moisseiff, a Russian-born Jewish engineer. At the time it was completed in 1926, the span was the greatest suspension bridge in the world.

Deshler-Morris House, 5442 Germantown Ave., the oldest "White House" still standing, was owned by Col. Isaac Franks at the time George Washington moved into it on Nov. 17, 1793, and made it his temporary home. This occurred during the yellow fever epidemic in Philadelphia when the Federal Government took refuge in Germantown, now part of the city proper. Built in 1772 by David Deshler, the house was requisitioned by General Sir William Howe who made it his headquarters when he drove the Americans out of Philadelphia in 1777. Colonel Franks bought it from Deshler's heirs in 1792. Franks had taken refuge from the plague and was living in Bethlehem. He was disinclined to rent his house for less than six months, but yielded to Washington's request. Washington moved in on Nov. 17, and the next day the Cabinet, with Jefferson, Hamilton, Edmund Randolph, and Knox, met in the parlor to discuss American neutrality in the war between France and England. Washington left the house at the end of November, after arranging with Franks to rent it for six weeks in the summer of 1794. From July 30 to Sept. 20, 1974, President and Mrs. Washington lived there again. On the first occasion, Franks billed Washington for $131.56, covering rent and use of furnishings, the price of a chair broken during the President's occupancy, cost of cleaning after the President left, loss of a flatiron, a large fork, four plates, three ducks, four chickens, a bushel of potatoes, and one hundred bushels of hay. Washington balked at the bill and finally settled for $75.56. For his second stay, Franks billed the President for $201.06, which the President's cashbook shows was paid "in full" on Sept. 24,

1794. The house was acquired by Samuel Morris in 1834 (hence the name Deshler-Morris House). It became Federal property when it was deeded by one of Morris' descendants. Restored to 18th century style, the historic house is part of the Independence National Historical Park.☐

Downtown Children's Center, 366 Snyder Ave.

Downtown Jewish Home for Aged, 4001 Ford Ave.

Drexel University Hillel Foundation, 32nd and Chestnut St. Mandell Theatre at Drexel University, Chestnut St., bet. 32nd and 33rd Sts., a 484-seat playhouse, is named for Samuel P. Mandell, a university trustee and vice-president of the Food Fair Stores. A plaque honoring Mandell is in the lobby, together with an oil portrait of him.

Dropsie University

Dropsie University, Broad and York Sts., built in 1911, was designated as a national historic site in the *National Register of Historic Places* in 1975. It is the only graduate institution in America, (nonsectarian and nontheological), entirely dedicated to Hebrew, Biblical, and Middle East studies. Its students are Jews, Protestants, Catholics, Moslems, Buddhists, and non-religious—all engaged in studying the ancient languages of the Middle East. The university was founded in 1907 through a bequest of Moses Aaron Dropsie, one of Philadelphia's great citizens, who made a fortune in the law and as the builder of the city's street railway system. He left the bulk of his estate for the establishment and maintenance in Philadelphia of "a college for the promotion and instruction in the Hebrew and cognate languages and their respective literatures, and in the rabbinical learning and literature." Son of a Jewish father and Christian mother, Dropsie opted for Judaism at the age of 14, and became a devout Jew. He was president of Gratz College and one of the founders and president of the Hebrew Education Society. Dropsie University's library is world famous. Its collection of some 110,000 volumes in many languages is widely used by scholars. In its basement are three airconditioned rooms and a walk-in vault that houses hundreds of books published between 1500 and 1699, a wide variety of Bibles and books on the Bible, fragments of the Cairo Genizah, codices in ancient tongues, incunabula, manuscripts, and items of American Judaica. ●One of the greatest treasures in the manuscript center is relatively new—a unique collection on microfilm of previously inaccessible Hebraica material found in the libraries of the Soviet Union, Hungary, and Poland by Dr. Abraham A. Katsch, Dropsie's third president. The first was Dr. Cyrus Adler, who later became president of the American Jewish Committee, the American Jewish Historical Society, the Jewish Theological Seminary of America, and a founder of the National Jewish Welfare Board. His successor was the late Dr. Abraham A. Neumann. •Dropsie also owns a collection of rare *Haggadot,* including the oldest *Haggada* extent, from the Cairo Genizah, dating back to the 8th century. ❑

Albert Einstein Medical Center, Northern Division, 5455 Old York Rd., has a large bust of the great scientist in the center of the medical complex which was established in 1952 through a merger of the Jewish Hospital (founded in 1865), Mount Sinai Hospital, and Northern Liberties Hospital. The former Henry S. Frank Memorial Synagogue, modeled after 1st and 2nd century synagogues unearthed in Israel, now houses the center's personnel office.

Lewis Elkin Elementary School, D and Allegheny Sts., is named for one of the founders of the Atheneum, a famed library, who contributed his noted collection of 19th century fiction, and provided the initial funds for school teachers' pensions.

Federation Apartments, 2101 Strahle St., a 32-unit housing complex for aged citizens, is sponsored by the Federation of Jewish Agencies of Greater Philadelphia.

Federation of Jewish Agencies, 226 South 16th St., occupies part of an 18-story building it owns and from which it serves as the community planning, coordinating, and fundraising body for Greater Philadelphia Jewry.

Fels Planetarium, one of the major units of the world-famous Franklin Institute, Parkway at 20th St., was the gift of Samuel S. Fels. Opened in 1933 when the new building of the institute was erected, the planetarium was the first unit in the institute. The second planetarium in the U.S. (the first was the Adler Planetarium in Chicago, also the gift of a Jew), it has an observatory on the roof which boasts the world's largest telescope exclusively dedicated to public use. Built at a cost of $330,000, the planetarium's donor was a famous soap manufacturer and philanthropist. In 1939 Pennsylvania awarded him a medal for meritorious service. Earlier he had established the Samuel S. Fels Fund for Scientific Studies and the Fels Dynamics Institute at Temple University. The Samuel S. Fels Junior High School, Devereaux and Langdon Sts., memorializes Fels.

Fleisher Art Memorial, 715-21 Catherine St., originally known as the Graphic Sketch Club, was founded by Samuel S. Fleisher, wool manufacturer and patron of the arts, as a free art school for immigrants. The name was changed to honor Fleisher who gave the club his famed art collection. The memorial includes an art museum, gallery, and sanctuary.

Free Library of Philadelphia, Parkway at Vine and 19th Sts., houses the Fleisher Music Library, which is said to contain the most complete and largest collection of orchestral music in the world. It is an outgrowth of the Symphony Club, founded by Edwin A. Fleisher in 1909 to give talented musicians thorough orchestral training. In 1929, when the collection was deeded to the Free Library, Fleisher traveled to all of Europe's music centers to buy important orchestral music. The collection contains 15,000 works.●In the Free Library's Rare Book Department there is a Torah Scroll presented by Dropsie University; ●a collection of 800 early American children's books, a gift of Dr. A. W. Rosenbach, the famed bibliophile;   ●a number of important Hebrew manuscripts; ●a collection of *Haggadahs*; ●the Strouse collection of letters of the Presidents;   ●and a copy of the Ferrara Bible. ●The Department of Education, Philosophy, and Religion has an important collection of Hebraica and Judaica. ●In the second floor gallery are portraits of the library's presidents, including Joseph G. Rosengarten, Simon Gratz, Cyrus Adler, William Pepper, and Joseph Carson.

Germantown Jewish Center, Lincoln Dr. and Ellet St., built on a hill, has two tall pylons on one side and the Ten Commandments in stone on the other. There is also a museum of Jewish ceremonial objects, including many smuggled out of Nazi Germany by refugees.

Samuel Gompers Elementary School, 57th and Wynnefield, memorializes the principal founder and late president of the American Federation of Labor.

Rebecca Gratz Club, 532 Spruce St., is a nonsectarian, interracial Halfway House for employed young women living away from home. It is a merger of the Ezrath Nashim, founded in 1873 as a maternity hospital for poor Jewish women, and the Rebecca Gratz Club, formed in 1904 as a residence for immigrant working girls. The seventh of the 12 children of Michael and Miriam Gratz, Rebecca was born in Philadelphia in 1781. Her father was one of the leading merchants of his day. A founder of the Female Association for the Relief of Women and Children, Rebecca became the mistress of the Gratz mansion in 1811 on her father's death. The Gratz home was a famous gathering place for Philadelphia intellectuals. Among those who visited there were Washington Irving, the artists Sully and Malbone, the actress Fanny Kemble, and the aristocrats of Philadelphia society. Irving described Rebecca so movingly to Sir Walter Scott (so the story goes), that Scott was inspired to portray her as Rebecca of his immortal *Ivanhoe*. In 1818, Rebecca Gratz organized the Female Hebrew Benevolent Society, the city's first Jewish philanthropic agency outside the synagogue. Twenty years later she founded what was the first Jewish Sunday school in the U.S., which became a project of the Female Hebrew Benevolent Society. In 1858 the Sunday school was taken over by the Hebrew Sunday School Society, which Rebecca Gratz established in 1838, and is still functioning today.

Gratz College, 10th St. and Tabor Rd., is the oldest institution in the U.S. for the training of Jewish religious school teachers. It is named for Hyman Gratz, member of the historic Philadelphia family and brother of Rebecca Gratz. He provided for the establishment of the college in his will, executed in 1856, a year before his death. The college was established in 1895. •The library is named for Dr. Julian Greenstone, who served the college for more than half a century. •The Abner and Mary Schreiber Music Library, which memorializes two leaders of Har Zion Temple, is an important music research center housing the great Eric Mandell collection of Jewish music. Mandell, a cantor in Germany and later at Har Zion Temple, assembled the collection of manuscripts and printed music twice, the first having been destroyed by the Nazis.

Gratz High School, 17th St. and Luzerne, is named for Simon Gratz, brother of Hyman, who was president of the Board of Education in the 1840s.

Gratz Street, bet. 18th and 19th Sts., running north from Jefferson St. to Huntingdon St. and from Cambria St. to 68th Ave., north, is named for the entire Gratz family. Hyman and Simon Gratz were sons of Michael Gratz, Revolutionary patriot, merchant, Indian trader, and land developer. Hyman was one of the founders and president of the Pennsylvania Company for Insurance of Lives and Granting of Annuities, a pioneer insurance company, from 1837-1857. Hyman and Simon Gratz were among the founders of the Pennsylvania Academy of Fine Arts. Hyman was treasurer of Mikveh Israel Congregation and an officer of the first Jewish Publication Society.

Eleanor S. Gray Hummingbird Wing of the Bird House at the Philadelphia Zoo is a memorial to Eleanor S. Gray, erected by her husband, Maurice Gray.

Albert M. Greenfield Elementary School, 23rd and Chestnut Sts., the only public elementary school in the center city, memorializes the late realtor, philanthropist, and leader in many Jewish and civic agencies, who was in the forefront of the vast undertaking that rebuilt downtown Philadelphia.

Hebrew Sunday School Society, founded in 1838 by Rebecca Gratz, has its headquarters at 1729 Pine St. and maintains schools at 401 S. Broad St., 9230 Bustleton Ave., 6600 Bustleton Ave., Strahle and Horrocks Sts., and in the suburb of Ambler.

Sidney Hillman Medical Center, 2116 Chestnut St., memorializes the president of the Amalgamated Clothing Workers of America and one of the founders of the AFL-CIO. Adjoining the Center at 2115 Sansom St., is the Charles Winstein Geriatric Center for retired clothing workers, named for Hillman's successor as president of the ACWA.

Historical Society of Pennsylvania, 1300 Locust St., whose collection of manuscript material relating to Colonial American history is said to be second only to that in the Library of Congress. It includes 50,000 items dealing with American Jewish history in the early years of the Republic. It was a gift of Simon Gratz, merchant, ship owner, and art patron. Here, too, are the Gratz-Etting papers and family documents of the Gratzes and the families into which they married. A microfilm of the Philadelphia edition of the *Jewish Daily Forward* from 1901-1951 is also on file here.

Hospital and Home for Jewish Aged, 5301 Old York Rd.

Independence Hall, on Independence Square, south side of Chestnut St., bet. 5th and 6th Sts., is the chamber where the Continental Congress voted the final form of the Declaration of Independence on July 4, 1776. It was here on Oct. 25, 1765, that leading Philadelphia merchants pledged not to import British goods until the Stamp Act was repealed. The first signer was Mathias Bush, president of Mikveh Israel Congregation, whose son, Lewis, was fatally wounded at the Battle of Brandywine. Other Jewish merchants who signed the Non-Importation Resolutions were David Franks, Bernard and Michael Gratz, Sampson and Benjamin Levy, Moses Mordecai, and Joseph Jacobs. In the building's assembly hall, the Rev. Gershom Mendes Seixas, first spiritual leader of Mikveh Israel, protested against the adoption of a religious test for public office in Pennsylvania. In the foyer next to the chamber where the Declaration of Independence was adopted, hangs the Schuyler Regimental Flag, the banner carried by the troops of Gen. Philip Schuyler during the Revolution. The 13th star on this flag is shaped like a Magen David. When Independence Hall was restored in 1876, Frank Marx Etting, Independence Hall's chief historian, headed the restoration committee.

Israel Designs, 70 N. 2nd St., specializes in imports of religious articles, giftware, and novelties from Israel.

Maurice Jacobs Press, 1010 Arch St., is the largest Hebrew and foreign language press in the western hemisphere, capable of setting type in 200 languages and dialects using type faces in Amharic, Hebrew, Russian, Arabic, Greek, Latin, and Syriac. This firm is the successor to the Hebrew Press of the Jewish Publication Society of America.

Jefferson Hall, 1020 Locust St., of Thomas Jefferson University, has an auditorium named for D. Hays Solis-Cohen, prominent attorney and member of a family identified with Jewish communal affairs for more than 150 years. There is also a portrait of Solis-Cohen in the auditorium. The lawyer's father, Dr. Solomon Solis-Cohen, was Jefferson

University's first professor of clinical medicine. His brother, Jacob Da Silva Solis-Cohen, uncle of the lawyer, was a pioneer laryngologist. The Stein Radiation Center, 202 S. Hutchinson St., in the university's Medical College, is named for Louis Stein, president of Food Fair Stores. There is also the Louis B. and Ida K. Orlowitz Residence for medical students and interns, established by the Orlowitz family.

Jewish Community Relations Council, 260 S. 15th St.

Jewish Employment and Vocational Service, 1913 Walnut St.

Jewish Exponent, 226 S. 16th St.

Jewish Family Service, 1610 Spruce St., is the direct descendant of the Ezrath Orchin, founded in 1783, as the city's first Jewish charitable agency.

Jewish Identity League of Bnai Yiddish, 1453 Levick St.

Jewish Labor Educational Centre, 924 Walnut St.

Jewish Publication Society, 1528 Walnut St., was established in 1888 by a group of prominent men from every part of the country who came together at the invitation of Dr. Joseph Krauskopf and Dr. Solomon Solis-Cohen. Since then, virtually every major personality in American Jewish life has been identified with JPS. Its roster of authors and translators is a veritable *Who's Who* of Jewish learning and literature. JPS' publications include some of the most important works in contemporary Jewish writing as well as translations.

Jewish Times, 2417 Welsh Rd.

Jewish Ys and Centers of Greater Philadelphia, are headquartered at 401 S. Broad St. (the building was originally known as the YM-YWHA), is the second oldest Jewish community center in the country, having been founded in 1875. The main building on S. Broad St. is known as the YM & YWHA branch. Other branches are: Neighborhood Centre Branch, 6600 Bustleton Ave.; Northwest Branch, 560 E. Church Rd., Elkins Park; Senior Adult Center, Marshall and Porters Sts.; Western Branch, City Line and Haverford Rd., Merion; and Northeast Branch, Red Lion Rd. and Jamison St.

Kahn Park, 11th and Pine Sts., is named for the late Louis I. Kahn, a Philadelphia architect of international repute.

Kean Archives, 1320 Locust St., founded by Manuel Kean, is a unique pictorial repository in all media on all subjects prior to 1890, including a large file on the Old Testament, Irving Berlin, and old Jewish Philadelphia.

King David Restaurant, Tyson and Bustleton Aves., is a kosher restaurant.

Liberty Bell House, the new glass walled pavilion in Independence Mall, directly across the street from Independence Hall on Chestnut St., is the new home of the Liberty Bell, which hung in Independence Hall since 1753. The bell acquired its name from its famed inscription, "Proclaim liberty throughout the land," which is from the Book of Leviticus, 25:10. The bell was ordered from England in 1751 to mark the 50th anniversary of William Penn's Charter of Privileges of 1701. The bell arrived in Philadelphia in August, 1752, aboard the *Myrtilla,* owned by David Franks and Nathan Levy, leaders of the Jewish community. Isaac Norris, a Quaker, selected the jubilee proclamation: "And ye shall hallow the fiftieth year, and proclaim liberty throughout the land and unto all the inhabitants thereof." While the bell was being tested, it cracked, and two workmen recast it. In the recasting, the workmen transposed the lines, so that the Biblical quotation came first, followed by the line, "By the order of the Assembly, for the State House in the City of Philadelphia 1752." Another bell was sent from England to replace the cracked one, and the copy made by the Philadelphia workmen was given to St. Augustine's Church, which was burned by an anti-Catholic and anti-immigrant mob during the Native American riots of 1844. The bell was smashed, but its remains were recast into a symbolic relic and it is now at Villanova College. On July 8, 1776, the second bell pealed the joyous news of the signing of the Declaration of Independence. The crack occurred on July 8, 1835 when the bell tolled for the funeral of Chief Justice John Marshall.

Lubavitcher Chabad Center, 7622 Castor Ave.

Makom, the Jewish cultural center and coffee house for Philadelphia's Jewish college community, 2012 Walnut St.

Mann Recreation Center, 5th and Westmoreland Sts., a public recreation facility, is named for Frederick R. Mann, the city's first recreation commissioner, who was also active in many Jewish enterprises.

Martyrs Monument, 16th St. and Benjamin Franklin Pkwy., is an 18-foot bronze statue that memorializes the victims of the Nazi Holocaust. Erected in 1964, the statue is the work of Nathan Rapoport, the sculptor of the Ghetto Monument in Warsaw. A gift to the city of Philadelphia from the Association of Jewish New Americans and the Federation of Jewish Agencies, the monument portrays a dying mother, lying amid flames, a writhing child upholding the Scroll of the Torah, a patriarchal figure with arms upraised in a gesture of priestly blessing, and several arms wielding daggers. All are surrounded by a blazing Menorah and enveloped in a fiery bush.

Masonic Temple, Broad and Filbert Sts., displays a portrait of Israel Israel, a Revolutionary War patriot who was one of the earliest grandmasters of the pioneer Philadelphia lodge.

Mastbaum Elementary School, Frankford Ave. and Clementine, memorializes Jules E. Mastbaum, a pioneer in the film industry, who donated his replica of the Rodin Museum to Philadelphia.

Mikveh Israel Cemetery, Spruce St., between 8th and 9th Sts., is a national historical landmark by Act of Congress in 1956, and a local civic historical site within Independence National Park. It dates from 1740, when Thomas Penn, a descendant of Pennsylvania's founder, granted to Nathan Levy a plot of ground which John Lukens, surveyor-general of the Province of Pennsylvania, termed a burying place "for several Jews." The 127 by 30 foot burial ground is surrounded by an old brick wall and is entered by an iron gate opening into a small patio. Buried here are Rebecca Gratz, Haym Salomon, Michael Gratz, Aaron Levy, Nathan Levy, and 33 Revolutionary War soldiers. Among these are Benjamin Nones, who served as president of Mikveh Israel Congregation, which owns the cemetery; Elias Pollock; Naphtali Hart; Henry Solomon; and Philip Moses Russell, who was with Washington at Valley Forge. Special plaques set into the brick wall honor Rebecca Gratz, who is buried in the Gratz family plot, and Haym Salomon, the Revolutionary war patriot and financier. The exact location of his grave in the cemetery is unknown. On the street outside the cemetery, there is a state historical sign which reads: "Mikveh Israel Cemetery—Founded 1740. Notables buried here include Nathan Levy, whose ship brought the Liberty Bell to America; Haym Salomon, Revolutionary patriot; the Gratz family; and Aaron Levy, founder of Aaronsburg."

Lucien Moss Rehabilitation Center, 12th and Tabor, on the grounds of the Einstein Medical Center's Northern Division, is named for the noted philanthropist whose ancestor, John Moss, was a prominent merchant, art patron, and the first Jew elected to the Philadelphia Common Council in 1823.

Simon Muhr Elementary School, 12th St. and Allegheny Ave., memorializes a founder of the *Jewish Exponent* in 1887, and a former president of the Board of Education.

Museum and War Library of Military Order of Loyal Legion, 1805 Pine St., lists in its roster of Civil War officers many Philadelphia Jews, including the Rev. Jacob Frankel, spiritual leader of Congregation Rodeph Shalom, who was the first Jew commissioned as a military chaplain; Col. Max Einstein; and Dr. Jacob da Silva Solis-Cohen, a surgeon in both Army and Navy units.

Museum of American Jewish History and Mikveh Israel Cong., Independence Square East (Independence Mall), the second oldest congregation in the country, share a common roof, at 5th and Arch Sts., on Independence Mall, the urban renewal area where the synagogue was founded in 1740. The synagogue seats 200. The main Mikveh Israel Synagogue at Broad and York Sts. is up for sale. The congregation's first synagogue was in Sterling Alley, north of Cherry St., between 3rd and 4th Sts., near the new site which was acquired from the Mall Urban Renewal Area.

The new synagogue, designed by the late Louis Kahn, is adjacent to the Museum of American Jewish History and includes a library, religious school, and community hall. The museum is in a direct line between Independence Hall and the U.S. Mint. Christ Church Walkway, a greenway through Independence Mall, links historic Christ Church, a neighbor of the original Mikveh Israel Synagogue, with the new synagogue.

The synagogue design is in keeping with the 18th century architecture so as to blend with the neighboring buildings. One room in the museum displays the furniture, books, and artifacts which once graced the home of Rebecca Gratz and her brothers. On permanent exhibit is the immense collection of historic artifacts, documents, and other materials assembled by the congregation in its more than two centuries of existence. Among the items are the pen President Eisenhower used in signing the bill which declared Mikveh Israel Cemetery a national historic landmark, and the original letter President Washington wrote to Mikveh Israel and the congregations in New York, Charleston, and Richmond.

The beginnings of the congregation date from 1738 when Nathan Levy purchased what was to become the city's first burial ground two years later. Until 1776, the congregants worshipped in a small house on Sterling Alley, which ran from Cherry to Race Sts., between 3rd and 4th Sts. When large numbers of Jews from New York and Charleston came to Philadelphia during the Revolutionary War, the congregation moved to more spacious quarters in a house on Cherry Alley, between 3rd and 4th Sts. Here services were held until 1782, when the congregation consecrated its first synagogue building on Sept. 13, on Cherry St. A second Cherry Street synagogue was dedicated on Jan. 21, 1825. The Rev. Gershom Mendes Seixas of New York's Congregation Shearith Israel, who had left New York rather than stay in British occupied territory, came to Philadelphia in 1780 and was elected minister of Mikveh Israel. After the Revolutionary War, when some of the New York, Richmond, Charleston, and Savannah Jews returned to their homes, Mikveh Israel found itself in financial trouble and issued a public appeal for funds. Among the signers of the appeal were Benjamin Franklin, who contributed five pounds; David Rittenhouse, a noted astronomer; William Rush; Charles Biddle; William Bradford; and Peter Muhlenberg. Upon Washington's election as President, Mikveh Israel, together with the congregations in New York, Charleston, and Richmond, sent him a letter of congratulations. Washington's reply, one of three letters he wrote to Jewish congregations, is one of Mikveh Israel's treasured possessions. The text of Washington's letter follows:

To the Hebrew Congregations in the Cities of Philadelphia, New York, Charleston, and Richmond:

Gentlemen:
*The liberal sentiment towards each other which marks
every political and religious denomination of men in this country stands unrivalled in the history of nations—The affection of
such a people is a treasure beyond the reach of calculation; and
the repeated proofs which my fellow citizens have given of their
attachment to me, and approbation of my doings form the
purest source of my temporal felicity-The affectionate expressions of your address again excite my gratitude, and receive my
warmest acknowledgments.*
*The power and goodness of the Almighty were strongly
manifested in the events of our late glorious revolution—and
His kind interposition in our behalf has been no less visible in
the establishment of our present equal government—In war He
directed the sword—and in peace He has ruled in our
councils—my agency in both has been guided by the best inten-
tions, and a sense of the duty which I owe my country; and as
my exertions hitherto have been amply rewarded by the approbation of my fellow-citizens, I shall endeavor to deserve a con-
tinuance of it by my future conduct.*
*May the same temporal and eternal blessings which you
implore for me, rest upon your congregations.*
G. Washington

Founders and early members of Mikveh Israel were leaders of
the early American Jewish community and active in the city's political
and social life. They assisted in the colonization of Pennsylvania and
the west, and served with distinction in the Revolution. Among the
congregation's members is a long roster of patriots, military heroes,
poets, artists, scientists, and merchant princes. From 1829-1850 the
Rev. Isaac Leeser was Mikveh Israel's spiritual leader. He first won
fame with six essays he wrote for the *Richmond Whig,* in answer to an
article which originally appeared in England and was reprinted in a
New York newspaper, disparaging the Jews. Leeser published
textbooks for religious schools, formed the Jewish Publication Society
in 1845, published a monthly journal called *The Occident and Jewish
Advocate*—beginning in 1843, organized the Hebrew Sunday School
Society with Rebecca Gratz, and established Maimonides College—the
first American rabbinical school. Leeser was succeeded as *hazzan* of
Mikveh Israel by Sabato Morais, who served as professor of Bible and
Biblical Literature at Maimonides College and later became one of the
founders of the Jewish Theological Seminary of America in 1887. In
1887 he became the first Jew to receive an honorary degree from the
University of Pennsylvania. Moses Dropsie, founder of Dropsie University, and Hyman Gratz, founder of Gratz College, were members of
Mikveh Israel, as was Dr. Cyrus Adler. In 1940 the congregation
marked its 200th anniversary on which occasion it received a message

of congratulations from President Franklin D. Roosevelt. ☐

Neighborhood Centre Branch of Jewish Ys and Centers, Bustleton and Magee Aves., is a center for senior citizens.

Northeast Branch of the Jewish Ys and Centers, Jamison St. and Red Lion Rd., is housed in the Raymond and Miriam Klein Building in the Myer and Rosaline Feinstein Center. Located on a 20-acre site purchased by the Federation of Jewish Agencies, the Y branch has as its neighbors several other Federation agencies.

Northeast Walk-in Service for Older Adults, 6445-47 Castor Ave., is sponsored by the Federation's Council on the Aged.

Oxford Circle Jewish Center, Algon Ave. and Unruh St.

Samuel Paley Day Care Center, Strahle and Horrocks Sts., is named for the one-time cigarmaker whose Philadelphia radio station became the nucleus for the Columbia Broadcasting System, founded by his son William.

Pennsylvania School for the Deaf, 7500 Germantown Ave., the third oldest institution of its kind in America, was founded in 1820 as a result of the voluntary work by David G. Seixas with deaf children. A veteran of the War of 1812 and son of the Rev. Gershom Mendes Seixas, David operated a crockery store. A kindly gentleman, he befriended five boys and six girls—all deaf mutes. Seixas took these children into his home, where he clothed, fed, and taught them at his own expense. His work attracted the attention of a group of prominent citizens who, in 1820, met to consider the establishment of an institution for the instruction of the deaf and dumb. Seixas was engaged as the school's first teacher and served until 1821, when a trained teacher of the deaf was appointed.

I.L. Peretz Workmen's Circle School, 615 Bustleton Ave.

Philadelphia Academy of Fine Arts, Broad and Cherry Sts., has in its collections miniatures of Solomon and Samuel Etting, Asher and Joseph Marx, and a Gilbert Stuart painting of Col. Isaac Franks.

Philadelphia College of Textiles and Sciences, Henry Ave. and Schoolhouse Lane, has the Ingram Bergman Conference Center that memorializes a prominent alumnus and knit goods manufacturer.

Philadelphia Fellowship Commission Building, 260 S. 15th St.

Philadelphia Geriatric Center, 5301 Old York Rd. and Abram H. and Helen Weiss Institute.

Philadelphia Jewish Archives, 625 Walnut St., established by the Federation of Jewish Agencies and the Philadelphia chapter of the American Jewish Committee, houses important historical records about the Philadelphia Jewish community which are made available for scholarly research and other educational purposes. Some of the records date back to the early 18th century.

Philadelphia Museum of Art, Parkway at Fairmount Ave.,

memorializes Henry M. Phillips, one of its first members, and later chairman of the Fairmount Park Commission. The Phillips Fountain can be seen at the top of the great flight of stairs on the east side of the museum. An inscription on the parapet of the fountain reads: "Phillips Fountain—Erected with funds bequeathed for its construction and maintenance by Henry M. Phillips, who was appointed a member of the Fairmount Park Commission upon its creation in 1867, and served as its president from 1881 until his death in 1884." Phillips was an active member of Mikveh Israel and a prominent attorney who served one term in Congress from 1857-1859. ●In the museum's John G. Johnson Collection there are eleven classic paintings on Old Testament subjects: Meeting of Abraham and Melchizedek (Rubens); Adam and Eve (Fra Bartolomeo); The Prophet Samuel (Ugolino da Siena); David (Jacopo del Sellaio); Esther in the Temple (Andrea de Giusto); Moses Before the Burning Bush (Dirk Bouts); The Finding of Moses (Rembrandt): Moses Striking the Rock (Jan Steen); Susannah and the Elders (Scarsellino); Collection of Manna (Olot Master); and Adam and Eve (Bacchiacas). ●The museum also owns the $2 million collection of French impressionists, contemporary art, and ancient and modern sculptures bequeathed by Louis E. Stern. His New York apartment is recreated in four special rooms. ●A series of eight 17th century tapestries depicting Old Testament events and characters, and some 20 galleries devoted to the Arensberg Collection of modern art and pre-Columbia sculpture can also be seen. The Arensberg Collection was given to the museum by Louise and Walter Arensberg. Among the historic costumes on display in the museum are the ball gowns worn by Rebecca Machado and Rebecca Franks, daughters of wealthy Jewish merchants in early 19th century Philadelphia. ●The museum contains so many works by Jewish artists that special Jewish tours are conducted by the museum's volunteer guides.

Physic House, 321 S. 4th St., one-time home of Dr. Philip Physic, father of modern surgery, was purchased in 1965 by Walter Annenberg, then publisher of the *Philadelphia Inquirer* and later U.S. Ambassador to Great Britain, who made possible the restoration of the historic mansion.

Edgar Allen Poe House, 530 N. 7th St., where the famed author and poet lived during some of his most creative years, was acquired by Col. Richard Gimbel, member of the department store family and a noted Poe collector. He underwrote the cost of restoring the house and converting it into a Poe museum.

Powel House, 244 S. 3rd St., a city landmark, is now restored to its old grandeur. It was occupied for 40 years by Wolf Klebansky and his wife who operated a warehouse and shipping center for their bristle factory in the rear of the house. The Klebanskys carefully preserved the original woodwork, fireplaces, stairs, and ceilings. For a time the house sheltered newly-arrived Russian Jewish immigrants. The house was built in 1765 by Samuel Powel, the last Colonial mayor of the city.

Reconstructionist Rabbinical College, 2304 N. Broad St., the first new rabbinical school to be established in the U.S. in nearly half a century, was founded in 1968 by the Reconstructionist Movement in a number of vacant buildings a few blocks from Temple University and Dropsie University. The college's five-year curriculum requires students to engage in a Ph.D. studies program at Temple University while they study concurrently at the rabbinical college.

Robin Hood Dell, Fairmount Park, the summer home of the Philadelphia Orchestra and of free concerts, is a kind of monument to Frederick R. Mann, the city's former recreation commissioner and former U.S. Ambassador to Barbados. A Russian immigrant, Mann was responsible for keeping the Dell from closing in the 1940s and in 1953 established a "no box office" policy through an arrangement by which the city makes a major contribution while additional funds come from a Friends of the Dell group. When the new $8 million Dell opened in 1976, Mann was hailed as the major force back of its construction as well as the government fund-raising support.

Rodin Museum, 22nd and Benjamin Franklin Pkwy., which contains the world's largest collection of Francois Auguste Rodin's works outside of Paris, was a gift to the city of Jules Mastbaum, theatre owner and civic leader. Assembled by Mastbaum, the collection illustrates every phase of Rodin's works—drawings, watercolors, paintings, and studies in plaster. The museum is part of the Philadelphia Museum of Art. Mastbaum gave the city not only his Rodin collection, but also the building in which it is housed. A relief portrait of Mastbaum hangs in the museum's principal gallery.

Roosevelt Memorial Park, Roosevelt Blvd. at City Line, has a "Garden of Haganah," a 60-foot wide granite monument to Jewish war dead in the U.S. and Israel.

Raymond Rosen Apartments, 21st and Diamond Sts., a giant public housing project in the black community, is named in memory of a leader in the local Jewish community.

Philip H. and A.S.W. Rosenbach Museum, 2010 Delancey St., houses the collection of literary treasures of the late Dr. A.S.W. Rosenbach, world famous bibliophile, and his brother. Some of the items in the collection are a set of the first four folios of Shakespeare; a copy of the *Bay Psalm Book*—the first book printed in the U.S.; the manuscript of *Ulysses* by James Joyce; a large collection of Americana; letters and documents of many presidents of the United States and other historically important people; a collection of rare 16th and 17th century English books; and furniture and objets d'art of historical interest.

Jeanette Whitehill Rosenbaum Art Center, 1708 N. 22nd St., is a free art school established by Robert Rosenbaum as a memorial to his wife, whose hobby was liturgical art and history.

Rosenberg Hebrew Book Store, 6408 Castor Ave.

Rosen's Hebrew Books and Gifts, 6743 Castor Ave.

Ellen Phillips Samuel Memorial, on the East River drive of the Schuylkill River, below the Girard Ave. Bridge, in Fairmount Park, is an unequaled emblematic history of America in sculpture that consists of 19 statues commissioned through a 1913 bequest of $800,000 by Mrs. Samuel, a niece of Henry Phillips and member of a prominent Philadelphia Jewish family. Three major international sculpture exhibitions were held in 1930, 1940, and 1949 to select the statues to be included in this collection.

Solomon Schechter Day School, Edison and Trevise Rds.

Irving Schwartz Institute for Children and Youth, is part of the Philadelphia Psychiatric Center, Ford Rd. and Monument Ave.

Set Table, 22nd and Ranstead Sts., a kosher restaurant which took its name from the English translation of *Schulchan Aruch* (The Prepared Table), the systemized authoritative rabbinic code of Orthodox Jewry, compiled by Rabbi Joseph Caro, in Safed, Palestine, 1564-65.

Society Hill Synagogue, 418 Spruce St., now a city landmark, was originally a Baptist church built in 1829. It became the Romanian-American Synagogue in 1911. Restoration of the building began in 1972 after its establishment as a Conservative synagogue.

Solomon Solis-Cohen Elementary School, Tyson and Horrocks St., is named for the eminent physician, who was one of the two principal founders of the Jewish Publication Society of America and who served as president of the Philadelphia Board of Education.

Statue of Religious Liberty, in West Fairmount Park, opposite the east entrance to the old Horticultural Hall, is a 25-foot marble statue by Sir Moses J. Ezekiel. It was a gift of B'nai B'rith and the Union of American Hebrew Congregations to the people of the U.S. on the centennial of American independence in 1876. The statue is an allegorical group depicting Liberty protecting Religion. On the front pedestal are inscribed the words of the first Amendment to the Constitution: "Congress shall make no law respecting an establishment of religion or prohibiting the free exercise thereof." On the right side of the pedestal are the dates 1776 and 1876 and these words: "In commemoration of the centennial anniversary of American independence."

The left side bears the inscription: "Dedicated to the cause of religious liberty by the Independent Order of B'nai B'rith and Israelites of America."

Stoddard-Fleisher Elementary School, 13th and Green Sts., is named in part for Samuel Fleisher's sister, Helen, who helped establish vocational activities for young girls.

Sulzberger Junior High School, 48th and Fairmount Ave., is named for Judge Mayer Sulzberger, the first Jewish judge in Philadelphia, who was one of the outstanding 19th century leaders of the Jewish community.

Syrian Folk Shul, 8201 Castor Ave.

Talmidai Aharon, a cooperative residence for Jewish college students at the University of Pennsylvania, observes *kashruth* and *Sabbat* and is affiliated with Hillel House on the Campus.

Temple Beth Am, 9201 Old Bustleton Rd.

Temple Beth Torah, 608 Welsh Rd.

Temple Beth Zion-Beth Israel, 18th and Spruce Sts.

Temple Menorah, 4301 Tyson Ave.

Temple Sholom, Large St. and Roosevelt Blvd., has a memorial to the victims of the Holocaust in the form of two oil paintings and a six-light candelabrum that burns perpetually. Located in the foyer of the Hyman S. Driban Auditorium, are the paintings by Miriam Brown Fine, entitled *Triumph Over Tragedy* and *Eternity of Israel*.

Temple Sinai, Washington Lane and Limekiln Pike.

Temple University

Temple University has a number of places of Jewish interest: Annenberg Hall of Communications, in the Center for the Performing Arts, was a gift of Walter A. Annenberg, former Philadelphia publisher and Ambassador to Great Britain. •Charles Klein Law Building of Temple University, Broad St. and Montgomery Ave., is named for Judge Charles Klein, whose portrait hangs in the Law Library. The library in the old law school building, formerly the synagogue of Reform Congregation Keneseth Israel, was named for Judge Klein, but it was so badly damaged by a 1972 fire that it had to be torn down. •Blitman Reading Room in Annenberg Hall is named for the late William J. Blitman, city editor of the *Philadelphia News*. •Clara G. Katz House, 2014 N. Broad St., is the Hillel House at Temple. •Pearson Hall, northeast cor. Broad St. and Montgomery Ave., the university's physical education and recreation building, is named for Albert Pearson, star on the basketball team in the 1930s. •Samuel Paley Library is a memorial to the late Samuel Paley, cigar manufacturer and radio station owner. ●Chapel of the Four Chaplains (see above) is in the heart of the university campus. ☐

Temple Zion, Edison Ave. and Trevise Rd.

Union League of Philadelphia, 140 S. Broad St., a Republican party stronghold founded during the Civil War to back Lincoln and the Union cause, records in its Lincoln Memorial Hall the names of its early members who served with the Union forces, including seven prominent Jews.

United Hebrew Schools and Yeshivas, 701 Byberry Rd.

U.S. Naval Hospital, 17th and Pattison Sts., has in its chapel a stained glass window depicting scenes and symbols of Jewish history. It was a gift of the B'nai B'rith Women's Council of Philadelphia.

University of Pennsylvania

University of Pennsylvania has a number of points of Jewish interest on its campus: Annenberg School of Communications, 3623 Locust St., is named for Moses Louis Annenberg, late publisher of the *Philadelphia Inquirer*. Established in 1959, the school specializes in social communication in the mass media. ●In the Annenberg School are two theatres, the Harold Zellerbach Theatre, named for the San Francisco industrialist, and the Harold Prince Theatre, named for the Broadway producer. ●Albert M. Greenfield Human Relations Center, 3935 Locust St., established in 1951 to provide education and training, research, and community service in intergroup relations, honors the late realtor, builder, and philanthropist who built an empire in real estate, banking, retailing, hotels, and transportation. He did so much to change the face of Philadelphia that the city is sometimes called "Greenfield Acres." ●Bernard F. Gimbel Gymnasium, the university's $2.8 million athletic building, is named for the late president of Gimbel Bros. ●The Bernard F. Gimbel Marketing Center in D. Wellington Dietrich Memorial Hall, home of the Wharton School of Commerce, also honors Gimble. ●I.S. Ravdin Institute, 3400 Spruce St., a major unit of the hospital of the University of Pennsylvania, memorializes the late Dr. Isidor Ravdin, a world-renowned surgeon. A major general in the U.S. Army Medical Corps during World War II, he was a member of the team that operated on President Dwight D. Eisenhower in 1956. A plaque in the hospital testifies to his participation in 1949 in the first televised surgical operaton. ●Daroff Lecture Hall, 37th and Locust Sts., in the Wharton School of Commerce, honors Harry Daroff, founder of the Daroff clothing firm. ●Mayer Residence Hall for Graduate Students is named for Harold C. Mayer, stockbroker and philanthropist. ●Louis Marshall House, 202 S. 36th St., the Hillel

Foundation home, is named for Louis Marshall, the eminent attorney and Jewish communal leader. ●Meyer Davis Jr. Collection consists of rare books and manuscripts about Lord Byron, contributed by Meyer Davis, the orchestra leader, in memory of his son who was killed in World War II. ●University Museum, 33rd and Spruce Sts., with a large Star of David on its exterior facade, has an extensive collection of archeological finds of the Biblical period. ●David Penney Music Room in the School of Fine Arts. ●Florence and David Kaplan wing of the biology building. ●Samuel Fels Institute of Local and State Government. ●Lessing J. Rosenwald Exhibition Hall. ●A flagstone terrace, with five heroic bronze statues and 110-foot flagpole that constitute a campus memorial to university alumni who died in America's wars. It was a gift from Walter Annenberg. ●Louis I. Kahn Collection of drawings, models, and papers, housed in the School of Architecture, memorializes the man who was considered America's leading architect when he died in 1974. He had been a student and teacher at the university. The state of Pennsylvania appropriated $450,000 to buy the materials from Kahn's widow. ☐

Uptown Home for the Jewish Aged, 7900 Bustleton Ave.

Weinberg Park, 6th and Jackson Sts., is named for the late Emanuel Weinberg, a member of the Philadelphia City Council.

Weinstein Geriatric Center, 2116 Chestnut St., named for the late Charles Weinstein, manager of the Philadelphia Joint Board of the Amalgamated Clothing Workers of America for 30 years, was sponsored and financed by the Philadelphia Clothing Manufacturers Association. It is part of the Sidney Hillman Medical Center of the city's male apparel industry.

West Oak Lane Jewish Community Center, Thouron and Sedgwick Sts., a Conservative synagogue whose sanctuary and school occupy a block-long structure in the West Oak Lane section of the city, sold the property in 1976 to a Seventh Day Adventist church, preparatory to moving to the suburbs.

Willow-Crest Bamberger Home for Convalescents, 6445 Castor Ave.

Woodford Mansion, near Dauphin St., entrance at 33rd St. to Fairmount Park, was acquired in 1771 by David Franks, prominent Philadelphia synagogue leader, merchant, and shipowner, who supported the British during the Revolution. Now publicly-owned, Woodford was the center of Tory gaiety in Philadelphia during the British occupation and a time when Rebecca Franks was one of the city's leading hostesses.

Frank Yaskin Memorial Tower, which tops the Elmwood Methodist Church, 8331 Tinicum Ave., is described in a bronze tablet in the church lobby as an edifice whose bricks "were bought by Jewish friends" and "is dedicated to the glory of God in memory of Frank Yaskin." When the church's old wooden building was being rebuilt by enclosing it in a brick veneer, neighbors of various faiths pitched in with labor and materials. A group of Jews under Yaskin's leadership provided the bricks. Known as "the church which friendship built," the structure has two bricks on the sides of the tower entrance inscribed with "Shalom," and other bricks inscribed with the word for "peace" in various languages.

York House, North and South, Old York Rd. and Somerville Ave., is a pair of twin apartment buildings for the healthy Jewish aged, erected in the 1960s by the Federation of Jewish Agencies.

PHILIPSBURG

Cong. Sons of Israel, 6th and Spruce Sts.

PHOENIXVILLE

Cong. B'nai Jacob, Starr and Manavon Sts.

PITTSBURGH

Adath Israel Cong., 3257 Ward St.

Adath Jeshurun Cong., 5643 E. Liberty Blvd.

Anathan House, 1620 Murray Ave., a recreation center for older adults sponsored by the National Council of Jewish Women and the Jewish Community Center.

Beth El Cong. of South Hills, 1900 Cochran Rd., has four stained glass windows whose theme is *mitzvot* in Jewish life.

Beth Hamedrash Hagodol-Beth Jacob Cong., 1230 Colwell St., is a merger of two old congregations. Beth Hamedrash Hagodol, founded in 1873, is the oldest Orthodox congregation in western Pennsylvania. Located across from the Civic Arena, where it was built in 1964, the synagogue is open daily for morning and evening services. It is the only synagogue in the downtown area, and stands near the same neighborhood where the Jewish community was concentrated until the 1930s.

Beth Israel Center, Gill Hall Rd., Pleasant Hills suburb.

Beth Shalom Cong., 5915 Beacon St., has a collection of paintings by Israeli and American artists.

Bikur Cholim Convalescent and Nursing Home, 200 Amherst.

B'nai Emunoh Cong., 4315 Murray Ave.

B'nai Israel Cong., 327 N. Negley Ave., has a Byzantine-style domed sanctuary. The ceiling is decorated in gold leaf in a Persian Tree of Life motif. The circular architecture of the synagogue reflects the symbol of unity and eternity.

B'nai Zion Cong., 6404 Forbes St.

Bohnai Yisrael, Hebrew Institute Building, Forbes and Denniston, is a young people's congregation.

Carnegie Institute, 440 Forbes Ave., has on the third floor a panel display and exhibit of artifacts from the Carnegie Museum's dig at Tel Ashdod in Israel. The exhibit shows a chronological record of cultures in that area from 2800 B.C.E. to 600 C.E. In the Pennsylvania Room are books and journals of local Jewish interest.

Carnegie Library of Pittsburgh, 440 Forbes St., has in its Arts Division a bronze bust of J.D. Bernd, a merchant who left bequests to every charitable institution in Allegheny County on his death in 1892. To the library, Bernd left funds for books on architecture. The bust was erected through public subscription. ●The Library also has the Norma and Golda Arluck Collection of Judaica.

Carnegie Mellon University, Schenley Park, has in its Hunt Library, a notable collection of rare books bequeathed by the late Charles Rosenbloom, who had been a life trustee of the university. ●In the same library is the Dean J. Hirschfield Judaica Collection, and an 18th century Purim *Megillah* given by Rachel McMasters Miller.

Chofetz Chaim Cong., 5807 Beacon St.

City-County Building, has on the wall of the Family Division Courtroom on the sixth floor, a bronze plaque memorializing the late Samuel Goldstock, a prominent lawyer who was the founder of the Family Plan Court concept. The plaque bears a picture of the well-known Jewish and civic leader.

Civic Arena, Auditorium Place, a ten-story all-weather city and county arena with a retractable dome, was built in part with the aid of the Edgar J. Kaufmann Charitable Trust. Kaufmann headed the Kaufmann Department Store and was a leader in many civic and Jewish communal affairs.

Cneseth Israel Cong., 1112 N. Negley Ave.

Dor Hadash Cong., Hebrew Institute Bldg., Forbes and Denniston.

Duquesne University

Duquesne University, 600 Forbes Ave., has the Herman Halperin Collection consisting of 3,000 pieces of published material relating to the Bible during the Middle Ages. The collection, Rabbi Halperin's own working library, includes works in Latin, Greek, Hebrew, and German. Many of the manuscripts date back to 1330. Rabbi Halperin was spiritual leader of Tree of Life Cong. for 46 years. ●Maurice and Laura Falk Moot Court, at Duquesne University School of Law, Forbes St. and Boyd St., was a gift from the Falks in 1954. ●There are Laura Falk and Maurice Falk Lecture Halls in Duquesne University's Science Center Building. □

Edlis Building, 329 Boulevard of the Allies, is named for Adolph Edlis, who was elected to Pittsburgh's City Council in 1897, to the State Legislature in 1904, and city treasurer in 1909. He was the author of the Edlis Act against prostitution, which became the model for the Federal Mann Act.

Falk Clinic, 3601 Fifth Ave., part of the Pittsburgh Medical Center, was established by the Maurice and Laura Falk Foundation, founded in 1929 with an initial gift of $10 million from Maurice and Leon Falk, steel manufacturers and Jewish communal leaders. Since then the Falk Foundation has made grants totaling more than $33 million for economic research, political education, medicine, and culture in Pittsburgh. There is a Maurice Falk Auditorium at the Winchester-Thurston School, 555 Morewood Ave., the Laura Falk Hall of Social Studies at Chatham College, Woodland Rd., and the Maurice Falk Center for Research and Postgraduate Study in Ophthalmology at Montefiore Hospital.

Farband Educational Center, 6328 Forbes, Labor Zionist headquarters, has the Jack Arluck Memorial Library, founded by Norman and Golda Arluck in memory of their son who was killed in World War II.

Hebrew Institute of Pittsburgh, 6401 Forbes Ave., also houses the inter-ideological Jewish Community Day School, the Traditional Young Peoples Synagogue, and the Reconstructionist Dor Hadash Cong.

Hillel Academy, 5685 Beacon St.

Hillel Foundation at Carnegie-Mellon, Duquesne and Pittsburgh Universities, 315 S. Bellefield Ave.

Historical Society of Western Pennsylvania, 4338 Bigelow Blvd., has in its archives material on the Irene Kaufmann Settlement House, programs of Jewish events, and books and pamphlets about Jews in Pittsburgh and western Pennsylvania.

Jewish Chronicle, 315 S. Bellefield Ave.

Jewish Community Center, also known as the Y-IKC, 315 S. Bellefield Ave., is the present name of the well-known YM-YWHA which some years ago merged with the Irene Kaufmann Settlement. The latter was founded through a $3 million grant by Mr. and Mrs. Henry Kaufmann. The Hyman Rogal Room in the Center, dedicated to the men and women of the U.S. Armed Forces, has a 22 by 9 foot mural called the *Four Chaplains,* which depicts in symbolic form the faces and figures of the four heroic chaplains—two Protestant ministers, a Catholic priest, and Rabbi Alexander Goode—of World War II, who went down with a torpedoed military transport after giving their lifebelts to some soldiers. The mural was a gift to the Center from friends of the late Hyman Rogal in recognition of his 45 years of service to the Center. In front of the Bellefield Ave. entrance to the

Center is a piece of sculpture entitled *Infinity,* presented by the Henry Kaufmann Foundation in honor of the American Revolution Bicentennial.

Jewish Community Center, Squirrel Hill Branch, 5738 Forbes St.

Jewish Community Relations Council, 234 McKee Pl.

Jewish Family and Children's Service, 234 McKee Pl.

Jewish Home and Hospital for the Aged, 4724 Brown's Hill Rd.

Kether Torah Cong., 5706 Bartlett St.

Chester H. Lehman Memorial Scout Center and Flag Plaza, opposite Civic Center, housing the Allegheny Trails Council of the Boy Scouts of America, is part of a patriotic legacy given to the youth of the city by Vivian W. Lehman in memory of her husband, Chester H. Lehman, industrialist, philanthropist, Scout leader, and founder of one of the nation's leading steel foundries. One of the collection of historic American flags is lowered and another is raised daily by Boy Scout troops from the area. It is one of the few places in the world where the flag of the U.S.A. flies 24 hours a day. The interior of the building is decorated with the memoriabilia relating to the flags of America and is furnished with antiques and works of art from the home and office of Chester Lehman.

Lubavitcher Chabad Center, 2100 Wightman St.

Machsikei Hadas Cong., 814 N. Negley Ave.

Nehama Minsky School for Girls, 2100 Wightman St.

The Minyan, Farband Educational Center, 6328 Forbes St.

Montefiore Hospital, 3459 Fifth Ave.

Museum of Art, Carnegie Institute, 440 Forbes Ave., has in its Sarah Scaife Gallery, the Rosenbloom collection of paintings, sculpture, and prints donated by the late Charles J. Rosenbloom, philanthropist, art collector, and bibliophile, who was a trustee of the Institute. The collection consists of Chagalls, Brueghels, Cranachs, Rouaults, and 300 prints, including Durers, Rembrandts, and Whistlers. Rosenbloom, who was president of the United Jewish Federation, served on the boards of many national and international Jewish agencies.

New Light Cong., 1700 Beechwood Blvd.

North Hills Jewish Community Center, P.O. Box 11012.

Ohave Zedeck Synagogue of Oakland, 356 Craft Ave.

Parkway Jewish Center-Shaar-Ha-Shomayim, 300 Princeton Dr.

Pennsylvania Association for the Blind, 308 S. Craig St., has a plaque in its dining room-recreation area that memorializes the role of Phoebe J. Ruslander as founder of the Pittsburgh Association for the Adult Blind in 1910.

Pinsker's Book Store, 2028 Murray Ave., is the only place in the

Pittsburgh area to sell kosher wine. It also sells Hebrew books and Jewish ritual objects.

Poale Zedeck Cong., Shady and Phillips Aves.

Florence Reizenstein Middle School, adjacent to Mellon Park in East Liberty, memorializes the late Pittsburgher who was a leader in human relations work, serving on both the city and state Human Relations Commissions. Her husband, Louis J. Reizenstein, was a member of the Pittsburgh Board of Education and a former president of the United Jewish Federation.

Riverview Apartments, 52 Garetta Rd., is an independent housing complex for elderly people who are relatively healthy and independent. It is located adjacent to the Jewish Home and Hospital for the Aged.

Rodef Shalom Temple, 4905 Fifth Ave., designated as a historic landmark by the Pittsburgh Landmarks Foundation, is the oldest building in continuous use by the Jewish community. The temple operates a coffeehouse for youth and houses several large libraries, including a reference collection of 10,000 volumes, a Jewish museum of ancient and modern artifacts, a collection of modern Israeli prints, a group of bronze castings by Boris Schatz, and a collection of graphics by Lilien. The stained glass windows in the J. Leonard Levy Hall are replicas of windows in German synagogues destroyed by the Nazis. An earlier building of the Temple was the scene of the 1885 meeting of the Central Conference of American Rabbis at which the *Pittsburgh Platform* of Reform Judaism was adopted.

School for Advanced Jewish Studies, 315 S. Bellefield Ave.

Shaaray Tefillah Cong., 5741 Bartlett St.

Shaare Torah Cong., 2319 Murray Ave., has 18 double stained glass windows, 12 of which depict the Jewish holidays, fast days, and ceremonials, and six depict events in modern Jewish history. One window honors Yeshiva University, and another commemorates the establishment of the State of Israel.

Shaare Zedeck Cong., 5751 Bartlett St.

Soldiers and Sailors Memorial Building, 5th St. and Liberty Ave., has in its Legion of Valor Hall on the first floor, a memorial plaque to Lt. Col. Murray Shubin, World War II air ace, who shot down 13 Japanese planes.

Talmudical Institute and Mesivta of Pittsburgh, 5751 Bartlett St.

Temple Emanuel of South Hills, 1250 Bower Hill Rd., in suburban Lebanon, has a striking representation of the Ten Commandments in beaten gold-like metal of two-foot high Hebrew letters that flank the Ark. Also in the sanctuary are 18 dramatic floor-to-ceiling stained glass windows depicting Jewish holidays and eminent Jewish historical figures. The Menorah in brass is 8 feet high and simulates the beaten gold of the candlestick of the Temple in Jerusalem, as described in the Bible.

Temple Sinai, 5505 Forbes Ave., occupies the former Worthington estate. The new wings contain the Falk Library and the sanctuary. In the latter the walls are hung with the works of Jewish artists, many of them Israelis. One of the stained glass windows, over the Ark, depicts Jerusalem, the Eternal City. The unusual nine-branched bronze Menorahs are by Chaim Gross. The stained glass windows in the chapel review all of Jewish history. There is a fine library of Judaica and a collection of ritual objects crafted by the famous silversmith, Myer Myers.

Three Rivers Stadium, 600 Stadium Circle, home of the Pittsburgh Pirates, has in its main lobby a granite stone memorializing the late Barney Dreyfuss, who was president and owner of the team from 1900 until his death in 1932. Dreyfuss built Forbes Field in 1909, but it has since been torn down.

Torah Chaim Cong., 728 N. Negley Ave.

Tree of Life Cong., Wilkins and Shady Aves., an offshoot of Pittsburgh's original Ez Hayim Cong., founded in 1846, was organized in 1864. The chapel has four stained glass windows depicting the contribution of American Jews to the growth and development of the U.S.

United Jewish Federation of Greater Pittsburgh, 234 McKee Pl.

University of Pittsburgh

University of Pittsburgh has a number of points of Jewish interest: Archives of Industrial Society in the Hillman Library, Forbes and Bigelow Blvd., contains among its holdings on urban industrial society, records and manuscripts documenting the ethnic and immigrant experience in Pittsburgh and western Pennsylvania. ●The Gertrude and Philip Hoffman Library of Judaica in the Hillman Library, is supplemented by large gifts of books on Judaica by Jacob Rothbart, Oscar Freedel, and other members of the Jewish community. ●In the microfilm section is a complete microfilm set of the *Der Volksfreund*, a Yiddish weekly published in Pittsburgh from 1889-1922, and edited by the late Joseph Selig Glick. ●Leon Falk, Jr.'s portrait hangs in the Falk Library of the Scaife Hall of the Health Professions, DeSoto St., in recognition of contributions to the building from the Maurice Falk Medical Fund of which Leon Falk, Jr. was board chairman. ●There is also the Josephine S. Falk Research Unit of the Pittsburgh Child Guidance Center, named for the wife of Leon Falk, Jr., nephew of Maurice Falk. ●The Falk Laboratory School of the School of Education, named for Mrs. Leon Falk, Jr. ●Lou and Myra Mervis Hall, University Pl., which houses the University's Graduate School of Business, is named for Lou Mervis, a star football player at the University from 1917-1920, and his wife. He became a successful industrialist and gave the University several million dollars. ●Jonas Salk Hall, Terrace St. (formerly the Municipal Hospital), is named for the developer of the antipolio vaccine, who did much of his research in this building when it was the Municipal Hospital. □

Veterans Administration Headquarters, 1000 Liberty Ave., has an enlarged color photograph of the *Four Chaplains* mural that hangs in the Jewish Community Center, on permanent display in the reception room in the city's Federal Building.

A. Leo Weill School, Center and Soho Sts., in the old Hill District, is named for a prominent turn-of-the-century Jewish lawyer and civic reformer who helped organize the city's first Board of Education. He was president of the Civic Voters' League.

Yeshiva Achei Tmimim, 2408 Fifth Ave.

ZOA House, Forbes and Denniston, which also houses the Samuel M. Hyman Cultural Center, is the focal point for all Zionist and cultural activities in the city.

PITTSTON

Cong. Agudas Achim, 62 Broad St.
Cong. Anshe Ahavas Achim, 231 Delaware Ave., West Pittston.

PLYMOUTH

Cong. B'nai Israel, 132 W. Main St., has a plaque in its lobby dedicated to the memory of Louis Levinson "by his non-Jewish friends of Larksville." Levinson was the owner of a general store who always extended help to customers even when they were broke.

POTTSTOWN

Cong. Mercy and Truth, 575 N. Keim St.

POTTSVILLE

Oheb Zedeck Synagogue Center, 2300 Mahantongo St.
United Jewish Charities, 2300 Mahantongo St.

POYNTELLE

Alexander and Tillie Block Vacation Camp for low income senior citizens, sponsored by the Associated YM & YWHAs of Greater New York, is specially designed to meet the needs of older adults.

PUNXSUTAWNEY

Cong. Agudath Achim, Church St.

READING

B'nai B'rith House, Franklin and Maple Sts., is housing for older adults.

Cong. Beth Jacob, 955 N. 10th St.

Cong. Shomrei Habrith, 2320 Hampden Blvd.

Jewish Community Center, 1700 City Line St.

Jewish Community Council, 1700 City Line St.

Kesher Zion Synagogue Center, 1245 Perkiomen Ave.

Temple Oheb Sholom, Perkiomen Ave. and 13th St.

SCHAEFFERSTOWN

Site of Old Jewish Burial Ground is located 0.2 miles after right turn at junction of State Highway 501 and State Highway 897, according to the WPA State Guide for Pennsylvania. This reference work states that descendants of Brazilian and West Indian Jews settled here in the late 17th century. The early synagogue has vanished and the site of the cemetery has long since been covered with weeds. It was located near the summit of Tower Hill. The settlement was once called New Judea. Some historians place the date of Jews settling here at 1723, while other scholars doubt that this was a Jewish colony at all, but believe it to have been a settlement by German pietists who were strongly Old Testament-minded.

SCRANTON

Ahavath Sholom Synagogue, 1733 N. Main Ave.

Cong. Beth Shalom, Clay Ave. and Vine St.

Cong. Machzikeh Hadas, 501 Madison Ave.

Cong. Oheb Zedek, 1432 Mulberry St.

Davidow Field is the name of the playground adjacent to the Jewish Community Center. It was built by, and named for, Meyer Davidow.

Milton Eisner Yeshiva High School, 538 Monroe Ave.

Jewish Community Center, 601 Jefferson Ave.

Jewish Home of Eastern Pennsylvania, 1101 Vine St.

Madison Ave. Temple, 523 Madison Ave., dates from 1860, six years before the city was incorporated.

Penn Monroe Synagogue, 901 Olive St.

Scranton-Lackawanna Jewish Council, 601 Jefferson Ave.

Temple Hesed, Lake Scranton Rd.

Temple Israel, Gibson St. and Monroe Ave.

SHAMOKIN

Cong. B'nai Israel, 7 E. Sunbury St.

SHARON
Shenango Valley Jewish Federation, 840 Highland Rd.
Temple Beth Israel, 840 Highland Rd.

SHENANDOAH
Cong. Kehilat Israel, 35 S. Jardin St.

SHIPPINGPORT
First full-scale atomic power plant in the world, built for the Atomic Energy Commission and the Duquesne Light Co., was erected here in the late 1950s under the direction of Admiral Hyman Rickover, father of the atomic submarine.

SPRINGFIELD
Cong. Beth Tikvah, 1001 Paper Mill Rd.
Cong. Ner Tamid-Delaware County Jewish Center, 300 W. Woodland Ave.

SPRING HOUSE
Reform Congregation Beth Or, Penllyn Pike and Dager Rd.

STARLIGHT
B'nai B'rith Perlman Camp, a youth leadership training center operated by the B'nai B'rith Youth Organization, honors Mr. and Mrs. Louis L. Perlman of Chicago. Mrs. Perlman, founder of the B'nai B'rith Girls and the only woman to head the B'nai B'rith Youth Commission, also headed the B'nai B'rith Women. The camp contains the Sam Beber Leadership village, honoring the founder of BBYO. The Philip M. Klutznick Education Bldg., honoring a former B'nai B'rith president and one-time U.S. Ambassador to the U.N., has a 28 by 7 foot mural by the late A. Raymond Katz depicting incidents in Jewish history beginning with the Biblical era. The Label A. Katz Building, memorializing a late president of B'nai B'rith, includes an auditorium and facilities for religious worship.

STROUDSBURG
Temple Israel, Wallace St.

SUNBURY
Cong. Beth El, 249 Arch St.
Hillel Foundation at Bucknell University, 249 Arch St.

UNIONTOWN
Cong. Tree of Life, Pennsylvania Ave.

Jewish Community Center, 406 E. Main St.
Temple Israel, 119 E. Fayette St.

UNIVERSITY PARK

Hillel Foundation at Pennsylvania State University, 224 Locust
Lane, is known as the William M. Gerber House in memory of a prom-
inent leader of B'nai B'rith. The building has a large mural called *The
Ideals of Judaism.*

UPPER DARBY

Temple Israel, Bywood Ave. and Walnut St.

VALLEY FORGE

Freedoms Foundation Medal of Honor Grove, a permanent
memorial to the more than 3,300 heroes in uniform who have received
the Congressional Medal of Honor, includes a number of Jewish
heroes. The grove is divided into one-acre sites, one for each state,
Puerto Rico, and the District of Columbia. In the center of each state
site is a seven foot, seven inch obelisk with the names of the medal
winners listed. The General Henry Knox Building contains the cita-
tions for each Medal of Honor winner. The following are the Jewish
Medal of Honor winners: Sgt. Benjamin Kaufman, Sgt. William
Sawelson, and Sgt. Sidney Gumpertz (New York), in World War I; Sgt.
Leopold Karpeles (Massachusetts), Civil War; Benjamin B. Levy (New
York), Civil War; Abraham Cohn (New Hampshire), Civil War; Henry
Heller (Ohio), Civil War; David Obransky (Ohio), Civil War; Staff Sgt.
Isadore Jackman (Maryland), World War II; and Lt. Raymond
Zussman (Michigan), World War II.

Spirit of '76 Library at the Freedoms Foundation, was erected
by Sol and Rose Feinstone of nearby Washington Crossing. Feinstone
was a Russian-born immigrant who devoted 40 years to collecting
Americana manuscripts. The library he built collects, preserves, and
uses original manuscripts of the American Revolution—many of which
were contributed by Feinstone. There are two memorial plaques in the
library: one is the Hebrew from Genesis 1:3. The second plaque notes
that the library was built by the Feinstones and dedicated "to the
Judeo-Christian commitment of self-sacrifice for peace on earth, and
the brotherhood of free nations of free men; the spirit of '76, a struggle
of free men to remain free; the immigrants who came after the Revolution and helped build our country in freedom; the underprivileged
of all races who by uplifting themselves, will raise all mankind to a
higher humanity." □

Washington Memorial Chapel, on the site of General George
Washington's encampment from December 19, 1777 to June 19, 1778,

memorializes the heroes of Valley Forge and the religious spirit that guided them. It houses the Valley Forge Museum of American History. Among the museum's many interesting items is one of Washington's original battle flags with 13 six-pointed stars (Stars of David), carried throughout the Revolutionary War by his troops. A replica of this flag flies daily from a flagstaff at Washington's headquarters in the park, the Potts-Hewes House, situated at the junction of Valley Creek and the Schuylkill River at the intersection of River Drive and Mill Road. One of the stained glass windows in the chapel is a memorial to the Four Chaplains who lost their lives in the sinking of the troopship *Dorchester* during World War II.

According to *The Journal of Congress* (Vol. 1, pp. 248-397), the Magen David was seriously considered as the official star for the American flag. Shortly after American independence was proclaimed, Washington, Robert Morris, and Col. George Ross were named as a committee of the Continental Congress to prepare a design of an emblem for the new republic. When the committee called on a Philadelphia seamstress, (according to legend it was Betsy Ross), and asked her to "sew a dress for the newborn infant," Washington brought with him a penciled sketch of a flag consisting of five red and white stripes and a field of blue on which were 13 stars, all six-pointed. The seamstress argued that a five-pointed star was easier to sew. Had the committee not accepted her suggestion, the American flag might have had all six-pointed stars. Among those with Washington at Valley Forge was Lt. Col. David Salisbury Franks, who was on the general's staff, together with Lafayette, Alexander Hamilton, John Marshall, and two future presidents, James Madison and James Monroe. Dr. Philip Moses Russell was one of the handful of army surgeons who cared for the freezing, half-naked, and hungry men at Valley Forge all during the bitter winter. With the Rhode Island troops was Private Asher Pollock of the 2nd Rhode Island Battalion. Russell received a letter of commendation from Washington for his assiduous and faithful attention to the sick and wounded. □

WALLINGFORD
Cong. Ohev Sholom, 2 Chester Rd.

WARREN
Warren Hebrew Cong., 112 Conewango Ave.

WARRINGTON
Cong. T'feres B'nai Israel, 2478 Street Rd.

Warrington Motor Lodge, on Route 611, five miles north of Willow Grove interchange, has an interfaith chapel with a tri-faith altar.

The chapel is a remodeled barn. Beneath each of the altars is a supply of prayer books for each faith.

WASHINGTON
Beth Israel Cong., 265 North Ave.

WASHINGTON CROSSING
David Library of the American Revolution, in the Memorial Building, near the monument marking the spot where General Washington embarked for the 1776 Christmas Eve crossing of the Delaware River to catch the British at Trenton. It was founded by Sol Feinstone, a Russian-born immigrant. He is a noted collector of Revolutionary War documents and especially of George Washington's letters. The David Library, named after Feinstone's grandson and the Biblical King David, houses the largest private collection of original documents of the American Revolution period—all donated by Feinstone. He is the father of Ezra Stone, the actor and Hollywood TV producer.

Sol Feinstone Elementary School, named for the document collector, has a unique children's library. Nearby is the Feinstone Children's Forest which he created to encourage children's interest in forestry. Buckstone Farm, Feinstone's home, includes the site where Washington camped with his troops before crossing the Delaware River.

WAYNE
Cong. Har Zion, County Line and Matsonford Rds.

WEST CHESTER
Kesher Israel Cong., 206 N. Church St.

WHITE OAK
(see McKeesport)

WILKES-BARRE
B'nai B'rith Apartments, 61 East Northampton St.
Cong. Anshe Emes, 13 S. Welles St.
Cong. Anshe Sfard, 53 S. Welles St.
Cong. Ohav Zedek, 242 Franklin St.
Jewish Community Center, 50 South River St., was the focal point for the remarkable rehabilitation and reconstruction effort that enabled this community of 5,400 Jews to recover from the disastrous flood of 1972 caused by Hurricane Agnes. Almost every Jewish public building suffered heavy damage and many Jews lost homes and busi-

nesses. Through an organized program of self-help, government loans, and contributions of over $2 million from other Jewish communities, Wilkes-Barre's Jewish community was rebuilt. The community effort was so successful that by 1974 they were able to resume their own fund-raising campaigns for welfare, educational, and religious programs, and for the United Jewish Appeal.

Temple B'nai B'rith, 408 Wyoming Ave.

Temple Israel, 236 S. River St.

Wyoming Valley Jewish Committee, 60 South River St.

WILLIAMSPORT

Cong. Ohev Sholom, 1501 Cherry St.

Temple Beth Ha-Sholom, 425 Center St.

WYNNEWOOD

Main Line Reform Temple Beth Elohim, 410 Montgomery Ave., has a circular sanctuary.

Solomon Schechter Day School, 410 Montgomery Ave.

Temple Beth Hillel, 1001 Remington Rd.

Western Branch of Jewish Ys and Centers, City Line and Haverford.

YEADON

Jewish Community Center, West Cobbs Creek Pkwy. and Whitby Ave.

YORK

Cong. Adas Israel, 145 W. Market St.

Cong. Ohev Sholom, 2251 Eastern Blvd.

Alexander D. Goode Elementary School, 251 N. Broad St., memorializes Rabbi Goode, one of the four chaplains who went down with the troopship *Dorchester* when she was torpedoed during World War II. Rabbi Goode and three fellow Army chaplains—two Protestants and one Catholic—gave their lifebelts to others aboard the ship. When last seen, the four chaplains were standing and praying together with linked arms. In the school's lobby is a mural depicting all four chaplains, with a Hebrew inscription beneath the figure of Rabbi Goode. To the right of the mural is a bronze plaque with a portrait of Goode and a brief account of the heroic role of the four chaplains.

Jewish Community Center, 120 East Market St.

Temple Beth Israel, 2090 Hollywood Dr.

Wrestling Hall of Fame includes Isaac Berger, an Israeli-born athlete, who won three Olympic medals, in 1956, 1960, and 1964, and Frank Spellman who won a gold medal in the 1948 Olympic Games.

RHODE ISLAND

Rhode Island was the first of the 13 original colonies to admit Jews, thanks to its founder, Roger Williams, the nonconformist Christian clergyman.

> *I desire not that liberty to myself which I would not freely and impartially weigh out to all the consciences of the world besides; therefore I humbly conceive that it is the express and absolute duty of the civil powers to proclaim an absolute freedom of conscience in all the world.*

Williams wrote this shortly after he established a refuge in Rhode Island in 1636 for all religious nonconformists. In 1644, the first code of laws governing the colony asserted that "otherwise than thus what is herein forbidden, all men may walk as their consciences persuade them, every one in the name of his God."

Attracted by the genuine ring of religious liberty echoed in these words, Jews in the British West Indies colony of Barbados, who may already have been doing business with the merchants of Newport, shifted their base of operations to that city. The first, who may have arrived as early as 1658, were Mordecai Campanal and Moses Pacheco. They sent a favorable report to their coreligionists in the West Indies and soon the pioneers were joined by 15 families, including those of Daniel Campanal, Simon Mendes, Abraham Burgos, Jacob Tinoco, Daniel Nasy, and Saul Brown. The latter, who had been born into a Spanish family named Pardo, (which means "gray"), was the grandson, son, and brother of rabbis in Europe. Brown may well have been the first religious leader of the Newport Jews who are said to have organized Congregation Jeshuath Israel (Salvation of Israel) a few months after they settled in Newport.

The first definite evidence of a Jewish community in Rhode Island was the purchase of a Jewish burial plot by Moses Pacheco and Mordecai Campanal in 1677. This, the oldest existing Jewish cemetery in the United States, was originally 30 by 50 feet. Nearly two centuries later it became the inspiration for Henry Wadsworth Longfellow's famous poem, *The Jewish Cemetery at Newport*. Two of its founders, Mordecai and Daniel Campanal, married Christian women and their offspring scattered through New England after anglicizing their name to Campbell.

Dr. Jacob Marcus pointed out that "while full political and civil rights, universally applicable, seem implicit in Roger Williams' teaching, it is questionable if Williams himself was, in reality, willing to go that far." "Williams," says Marcus, probably felt that a combination of religious liberty and civil toleration "was all that any Jew had a right to expect." In 1663 a law was adopted which said that "no person who does not profess the Christian religion can be admitted free to this colony." The charter of 1665 had made men of all religions entitled to be freemen, but Dr. Abram V. Goodman notes in his *American Overture* that in the codification of Rhode Island's laws, published in 1719, the 1665 document was not mentioned, but a previously unrecorded statute of 1662 was cited, which read "that all men professing Christianity and of competent estates and of civil conversation. . . .(Roman Catholicks only excepted) were to be admitted as freemen." Thus Jews, Catholics, and non-believers were deprived of civil equality. In 1728 the general assembly of the colony confirmed the 1719 code, including the religious test for naturalization and the right to vote.

There was, however, no other discrimination against Jews or Catholics. Since there was no established church to which the residents had to contribute, every man in Rhode Island was free to practice his own religion. In 1685, two years after Roger Williams died, the handful of Newport Jews encountered their first serious problem. Although the British Navigation Act of 1660 (and of later years, too), excluded alien merchants from the intercolonial trade, an enterprise in which all of the first Jewish settlers in Rhode Island were engaged (unless they were naturalized and had been given the rights of free denizens), the law was largely ignored. Dr. Goodman notes, however, that the Newport Jews asked the Rhode Island Colonial Assembly in 1684 for an official declaration concerning their rights and privileges. The reply stated that the Jews might "expect as good protection as any stranger, being not of our nation residing amongst us in this his Majesty's colony, ought to have, being obedient to His Majesty's laws."

Thus the threat remained and it was first carried out in 1685. In that year, Major William Dyre, newly appointed royal surveyor-general of customs for all the American colonies, began to seize ships owned by Massachusetts merchants and to impose heavy fines on them. In Rhode Island he quarreled with the Royal governor and merchant shippers, and then sought to make an example of the Jewish traders. He charged them with violations of the Navigation Acts for selling sugar and molasses imported from the West Indies. Seven Jewish merchants and one woman (four Campanals, Saul Brown, Abraham Burgos, Aaron Verso, and the widow of Simon Mendes) had their property seized pending the outcome of the charges against them. When the case came to trial in 1685 in Newport, Major Dyre failed to appear to press his charges. The governor then ordered the charges dropped and returned the Jews' property. He levied a fine on Dyre and compelled him to pay court costs. That same year, one of the defendants, Abraham Campanal, was made a freeman, the first Jew to win this privilege in colonial Rhode Island.

Midway in the 18th century, a number of Marrano Jews from Spain and Portugal settled in Newport where they reverted to Judaism. Among these were Moses Lopez, his half-brother Aaron, and Jacob Rodriguez Rivera. Moses Lopez, who had been naturalized in New York in 1740, was for a number of years, the unpaid translator of Spanish letters and documents for the government. In 1753, the Rhode Island government granted him a ten year monopoly on the right to manufacture potash from his secret process. Aaron Lopez and members of his family, and the Riveras were among Newport's most important merchants before the Revolutionary War. Ships, shops, and warehouses were at the heart of the economic life of Newport's Jews, said Dr. Abram Goodman. Jewish vessels hailing from Newport visited the harbors up and down the Atlantic coast and frequented the West Indian islands in great numbers, Goodman observes, "exchanging New England products for sugar and molasses." Some of the vessels pursued the infamous triangular route, sailing to Africa to buy kidnapped slaves with Newport rum and exchanging the human cargoes for molasses in Jamaica and returning home with the ingredients for more rum, according to Goodman. At one time Aaron Lopez owned 30 vessels in whole or in part, and they sailed to England, Holland, Spain, Portugal, Africa, the Azores, and the Canaries. Lopez' whaling ships reached the Falkland Islands off the coast of Patagonia.

The Jewish ship owners and merchants were important factors in the whaling industry and in the manufacture of candles from sperm oil. This industry was introduced to Newport by Rivera who was one of the Jews involved in the formation of the United Company of Spermaceti Candlers in 1763. This was one of the country's first trusts. Lopez, whose second wife was Rivera's daughter Sarah, never permitted any of his ships to leave Newport on a Saturday or Sunday out of respect for the religious sentiments of Christians and Jews. Lopez and Rivera had much to do with the development of Newport as a major port before the Revolution. The diary of the Reverend Ezra Stiles, for many years minister of Newport's Congregational Church, said that no merchant in America has a more extensive trade than Lopez. He described him as "that amiable" benevolent, most hospitable, and very respectable gentleman" who was "the most universally beloved by an extensive acquaintance of any man I ever knew."

Despite this high status, Lopez encountered prejudice when he sought naturalization. Under the Act of Parliament of 1740, Jews and Protestants who had lived in a British colony for seven years were entitled to be naturalized by appearing in court with documentary evidence. The act also exempted Jews from taking the oath of loyalty on the "true faith of a Christian." James Lucena of Newport was naturalized by the Rhode Island General Assembly in 1760, but when Aaron Lopez and Isaac Elizer sought naturalization they were given a runaround and were told that Jews were not admitted "to the full freedom of this colony." Lopez was advised to ask for naturalization from the superior court which had previously turned him down. In 1762 the court again refused him, this time referring back to the law of 1663 which said that "no person who does not profess the Christian religion can be admitted free to this colony," and dismissed his petition as "wholly inconsistent with existing law." Ultimately, Lopez was naturalized in Massachusetts after he had moved his residence to Swansea, but then returned to Newport where he remained until the British occupied the town.

Despite their second class legal status, Newport's Jews took an active part in cultural enterprises. Abraham Hart, a leading merchant, and Moses Lopez, were among the charter members of the famed Redwood Library, founded in 1730. Jacob Rodriguez Rivera said it was his "great inclination to promote and forward every publick building to the utmost of my extent." By that time he had already bought 20 lottery tickets for the benefit of a new Baptist meeting house in Providence, the church originally founded in 1638 by Roger Williams. Rivera and his son-in-law, Aaron Lopez, contributed 10,000 feet of lumber for the first building of the College of Rhode Island. Moses Lindo, a merchant in Charleston, South Carolina, who dealt in indigo, was one of the first contributors to the College of Rhode Island, now Brown University, when it was founded in 1764.

Half of Newport's 18th century Jews were Germans and Poles, and thus of Ashkehazic origin, according to Rabbi Malcolm Stern, historian and genealogist. Among them were Isaac and Myer Pollok, the Harts, and Moses Michael Hays. The latter, who came from New York in 1769, became a partner of Myer Pollok in shipbuilding and freighting, but they soon went bankrupt and were thrown into debtors prison. When they were freed in 1771, Hays opened a shop and engaged in general merchandise. On the outbreak of the Revolution, Hays was falsely accused of being a Tory because he refused to take the oath of loyalty to the Americans. He regarded such an oath as an unwarranted slur on his loyalty. Only when the loyalty oath was required of all residents did Hays sign "solemnly and sincerely," and pledged his assistance "in the defense of the United Colonies."

Hays was a prominent Mason and was appointed in 1768 as deputy inspector general of the Rite of Perfection for the West Indies and North America. In 1769 he established King David's Lodge in New York, and in 1780 he reestablished it in Newport. (There is a tradition, though it is not based on evidence, that the first Masonic lodge in the colonies had been founded by Jews in Newport in 1658.)

During the last quarter of the 17th and the first half of the 18th centuries, the Jews of Newport worshipped in private homes whenever a *minyan* was available. In 1759 they decided to build a synagogue and sought and received help from New York's Congregation Shearith Israel. That same year, six cornerstones (four for the corners of the synagogue proper, and two for the adjoining school) were laid, and in 1763 the building was dedicated. Among those who laid the cornerstones were Aaron Lopez, Jacob Rodriguez Rivera, Naphtali Hart, and Isaac Elizer. Hart was the synagogue's first president. Now known as the Touro Synagogue, the sanctuary was the site of meetings of the Rhode Island General Assembly during 1781-1784, and the first sessions of the Rhode Island Supreme Court were held there. When Washington visited Newport in 1781, a town meeting was held in the synagogue. One of Washington's three letters to the Jews of the United States, written shortly after his election to the presidency, was addressed to the Newport congregation. This is the letter that contains his famous phrase that the government of the United States "gives to bigotry no sanction, to persecution no assistance." In 1947, the Touro Synagogue was dedicated as a national historic shrine by the National Park Service of the Department of the Interior.

In 1764, the Newport Jews appointed as sexton and kosher butcher one, Benjamin Myers, who had previously failed in business. He also served as steward of Newport's Jewish social club, founded in 1761 by nine merchants. The club met for cards every Wednesday night. Talk of synagogue affairs was forbidden, according to Rabbi Malcolm Stern. Stakes were limited to 20 shillings and violators were fined four bottles of good wine for the benefit of the club's wine cellar.

One of Myers' nine children, Mordecai, later moved to New York, served in the War of 1812 in which he rose to the rank of major, and at the age of 75, was elected mayor of Schenectady.

The first minister of the newly-built Newport Synagogue was Isaac Touro whose Tory inclinations led him to New York when the British left Newport in 1778. He became the acting minister of Congregation Shearith Israel while the British occupied New York. Touro, who married Moses Hays' sister and was the father of the celebrated Abraham and Judah Touro (see Massachusetts and Louisiana), was succeeded as minister by Moses Seixas, whose parents, Isaac and Rachel Seixas, had settled in Newport in 1748. Moses Seixas, brother of the Reverend Gershom Mendes Seixas of New York, was Rhode Island's first *mohel*, having learned his profession by correspondence from Abraham Abrahams, the well-known *mohel* of New York. Seixas was a founder of the Bank of Rhode Island and of the Rhode Island Grand Lodge of Masons. Acting on behalf of the Newport Jewish community, Moses Seixas presented an address of welcome and loyalty to Washington when he visited Newport on August 17, 1790. There is no evidence that Washington visited the synagogue but one pew has a marker stating that he sat there in 1790.

The eminent Reverend Ezra Stiles, who frequently attended services at the Newport Synagogue, became a close friend of the Reverend Isaac Touro with whom he often discussed the Bible and the mystical Zohar of the Kabbalists. He also developed a close intellectual and personal friendship with Rabbi Haim Isaac Carigal of Hebron, Palestine, when he came to Newport on a fundraising mission. In the 1760s and 1770s Newport's Jews played host to at least six visiting rabbis, most of whom had come as fundraisers for yeshivas in Europe and Palestine. Stiles' diary is a rich source of information about his Jewish contemporaries. The Christian clergyman frequently recorded Jewish customs as he saw them observed in the synagogue and in Jewish homes. In 1750 he noted that there were 15 Jewish households in Newport, consisting of 58 persons. Nine years later he reported that there were 25 Jewish families in the city. A provincial census in 1774 found 9,209 people in Newport of whom 121 were Jews.

At the outbreak of the Revolutionary War, when the British captured Newport, most of the Jews fled the city with the Americans. The city suffered heavy damage and commercial losses during the war, and never recovered its prewar commercial status as America's third most important port. Many of the prewar merchants were bankrupted by the war, among them Aaron Lopez who drowned accidentally while returning to Newport after the British left. By the end of the 18th century, Jewish worship in Newport came to an end since there were not enough Jews for a *minyan*. By 1818 only three Jewish families were left. The last of the pre-Revolutionary residents, Moses Lopez, left Newport in 1822 when he was 84. The synagogue was then closed, its key entrusted to members of the Gould family, who were Christians. The title to the synagogue and ownership of its religious appurtenances were vested in New York's Shearith Israel Congregation. That same year Abraham Touro, one of the sons of the synagogue's first minister, who had become a successful merchant in Boston where he had been raised by his uncle, Moses Hays, left $10,000 to the state of Rhode Island for the support and maintenance of the synagogue under the supervision of the Newport town council. In 1854, Judah Touro, Abraham's brother, having made a fortune in New Orleans, bequeathed $10,000 to pay the salary of the synagogue's reader or minister, and to maintain the old Jewish cemetery.

From 1822 until the 1880s the Newport synagogue was closed most of the time. It was opened occasionally for Rosh Hashanah services for summer visitors like Emma Lazarus, and for the funerals of descendants of the Sephardic pioneers, among them Abraham and Judah Touro. The Touro bequests explain why the synagogue, the cemetery, and the street on which they are located are all named Touro.

In 1881, some Jews from Fall River, Massachusetts, joined the newly-arrived East European Jews in Newport in a petition to the Newport City Council for permission to hold High Holy Day services in the Touro Synagogue. The request was referred to Shearith Israel in New York. They agreed, provided the Sephardic ritual was used, and sent Rabbi Henry Morais to officiate. The Ashkenazic Jews, however, were not happy with the Sephardic ritual and there was constant bickering with Shearith Israel. But since the East European Jews were not yet able to open their own synagogue, they continued to use the Touro Synagogue for the High Holidays. In 1883 the synagogue was reconsecrated and reopened, and the Reverend Abraham Pereira Mendes came from New York to act as minister. After Mendes died in 1894 the synagogue was again closed for a number of years. During that time Congregation Jeshuat Israel (the same name used by the founders of Touro Synagogue in the 17th century), was chartered and a struggle developed for control of Touro Synagogue. One year there were actually two ministers in Newport but the town council, using the Touro bequest, paid only the one recognized by Shearith Israel. On another occasion, a group of Jews actually broke into the locked Touro Synagogue to conduct Passover services and some of the worshippers were arrested. Today, Newport has three synagogues and a Jewish population of 1,200.

In the 1820s, just when the last of the Sephardic Jews were leaving Newport, Dutch Jews began settling in Providence. German

Jews followed in the 1840s. The first *minyan* was held in 1845 under the leadership of Leonard Halberstadt and Solomon Pereira, in whose home these services were conducted. Halberstadt's was one of the names on the charter granted by the Rhode Island General Assembly in 1855 to Congregation Sons of Israel. The founders were mostly single men, immigrants from Holland, Bohemia, Germany, and Austria. Providence's first Jewish cemetery was acquired in 1858 by Sons of Israel. In 1871, a second congregation, Sons of David, was organized in Providence, but the following year it was absorbed by Sons of Israel, the ancestor of the present Temple Beth El. Until 1890 the Jews of Providence worshipped in homes and rented halls. In that year the first synagogue outside of Newport was dedicated at the corner of Friendship and Fosher Streets. Other early congregations were Sons of Zion (1885), Ahavath Sholom (1891), and Mishkan Israel (1885).

By 1900 there were four cities in Rhode Island with one or more Jewish institutions, and a fifth where only High Holy Day services were held. These cities were Providence, Woonsocket, Pawtucket, Newport, and Westerly. Rhode Island had only 1,000 Jews in 1877 but with the wave of East European immigration that began in the 1880s, Providence alone reported 3,500 Jews in 1901. By 1907 there were 14 synagogues in Providence serving a Jewish population of 10,000. Ten years later Rhode Island had 20,500 Jews, 15,000 of them residing in Providence. In 1937 the Jewish population reached 27,800 and thereafter it leveled off, falling to 24,700 in 1960 and 22,000 in 1974. A 1963 population study found 6,200 Jewish households in the greater Providence area that also included Pawtucket, Cranston, Warwick, East Providence, Barrington, Bristol, Warren, West Warwick, and East Greenwich. In the 1970s much of the Jewish population had moved to the new suburban areas in Cranston, Westerly, Warwick, and Barrington and to the east side of Providence. There are also Jewish communities in Woonsocket and Kingston.

The first Jew to hold public office in Rhode Island was probably Isaac Hahn of Providence, who was elected to the lower house of the General Assembly in 1884. His son, Jerome, served on the Superior Court from 1919-1930, and sat on the State Supreme Court from 1930-1936. Philip C. Joslin of Providence, a member of the General Assembly from 1915-1926, and speaker from 1923-1926, was the father of Alfred H. Joslin, a justice of the State Supreme Court. In 1968, Rhode Island became the second New England state to elect a Jew as a governor when Frank Licht, son of East European immigrants, and a former Superior Court judge, was elected chief executive. He was reelected in 1970. In that year Richard Israel was elected state attorney general and was reelected in 1972. That was the year Roger N. Begin, a 19-year old student at Rhode Island Junior College in Woonsocket, became the first teen-ager elected to the Rhode Island Legislature, winning a seat in the State Assembly.

* * * * *

BARRINGTON

Temple Habonim-Barrington Jewish Center, 147 County Rd.

BRISTOL

United Brothers Synagogue, 205 High St., has been revived by a newly vitalized Jewish community.

BURRILLVILLE

Austin T. Levy Elementary School, Main St., Harrisville, is named for the late Austin T. Levy, a textile manufacturer, who, with his late wife, gave Burrillville many of its public buildings.

June Rockwell Levy Community Ice Rink, on the grounds of the Burrillville Junior-Senior High School, East Ave., Harrisville, is named for Mrs. Levy. On a hillside to the rear of the Assembly, in a community theatre provided by the Levys, is a memorial to them in the form of a bronze plaque in granite. Mr. and Mrs. Levy's ashes are buried at the foot of the memorial. They gave Burrillville the Assembly; the Jesse M. Smith Memorial Library, 49 Main St., Harrisville, in whose reading room there hangs a portrait of Levy; the William L. Callahan Elementary School and athletic field; the Frank H. Potter Bridgeway over the Pascoag River; the Harrisville and Pascoag post office buildings; the Northwest Community Nursing and Health Service Building; and the Burrillville Town Hall.

CRANSTON

Goldstein Chapel at the State Medical Center General Hospital, located in the Hazard Building, memorializes the late Dr. Sidney S. Goldstein, noted physician and psychiatrist, who was the first president of the Rhode Island chapter of the Academy of Religion and Mental Health, for many years superintendent of the State Hospital for Mental Disease and the State Medical Center General Hospital.

Temple Beth Torah-Cranston Jewish Center, 330 Park Ave.

Temple Sinai, 30 Hagan Ave.

KINGSTON

Hillel Foundation at University of Rhode Island, 324 Memorial Union.

NARRAGANSETT

Cong. Beth David, Kingstown Road and 5th on Narragansett Pier, is open for worship services only during the summer.

NEWPORT

August Belmont, Sr. statue, a lifesize monument, erected on Washington Square Mall, was a gift to the city of Newport by Belmont's son, Perry Belmont, a Congressman from New York and diplomat. The elder Belmont, who was born in Germany, came to the U.S. in the 1830s as a representative of the Rothschild banking family. He spent his summers in Newport where his wife's family, the Perrys, lived. Belmont, who married the daughter of Commodore Matthew C. Perry, who opened Japan to American trade in 1854, was a banker, chairman of the Democratic National Committee from 1860-1872, organizer of the first German-born regiment for the Union Army in the Civil War, and American charge d'affaires in The Hague. Although he had no ties to the Jewish community in New York, he was a constant target of anti-Semites, and during the Civil War the Southern press was particularly vicious in its attacks on him as a Jew (see New York).

Cong. Ahavas Achim, 136 Kay St.

Newport Historical Society, 82 Touro St., preserves many of the letters and business records of the city's 18th century Jewish merchants and shippers.

Old Jewish Cemetery, 2 Bellevue Ave., dates back to 1677 and is the oldest recorded Jewish burial ground in the U.S. Most of the inscriptions are in Hebrew and English, but one is in Latin, two are in Spanish, and one in Portuguese. Among the distinguished Jews buried here are Jacob Rodriguez Rivera, Moses Seixas, and Abraham and Judah Touro. The latter, who died January 18, 1854 in New Orleans, was first buried in New Orleans and then reinterred in the Newport cemetery in June of that year. His funeral in Newport was proclaimed a day of public mourning, with the city hall bell tolling and the old synagogue opened for a service for the first time in many years. Also buried here are members of the Lopez family and the mother of the Touro brothers. In the cemetery there is a monument to the Reverend Isaac Touro who is buried in Kingston, Jamaica. For many years the street on which the cemetery is located was known as Jew Street. After Judah Touro's death it was renamed South Touro Street but it became Bellevue Street in the 1860's. When Henry Wadsworth Longfellow visited Newport, there were virtually no Jews left in the city. The Hebrew burial ground so inspired the poet that he composed his famous poem, *The Jewish Cemetery at Newport*. The following are a few stanzas which reflect his deep feeling and interest:

"How strange it seems! These Hebrews in their graves
Close by the street of this fair seaport town,
Silent beside the never-silent waves,
At rest in all this moving up and down!

And these sepulchral stones, so old and brown,
That pave with level flags their burial-place,
Seem like the tablets of the Law, thrown down
And broken by Moses at the mountain's base.

The very names recorded here are strange,
Of foreign accent, and of different clime;
Alvares and Rivera interchange
With Abraham and Jacob of old times.

How came they here? What burst of Christian hate
What persecution, merciless and blind,
Drove o'er the sea–that desert desolate–
These Ishmaels and Hagars of mankind?

Pride and humiliation hand in hand
Walked with them through the world where'er they went,
Trampled and beaten were they as the sand,
And yet unshaken as the continent."

Oliver Hazard Perry House, 29 Touro St., is sometimes also referred to as the Seixas House. In 1795, Moses Seixas established the Bank of Rhode Island in this building, using it until 1818 when it was purchased by Commodore Oliver Hazard Perry, who lived in it only briefly. In recent years it was occupied by the Salvation Army.

Redwood Library and Athenaeum, 50 Bellevue Ave., founded as a philosophical society in 1730 and incorporated in 1747, numbered among its first supporters Jacob Rodriguez Rivera, Aaron and Moses Lopez, Abraham Hart, and Joseph Jacobs. Judah Touro bequeathed to the library $3,000 for the purchase of books, and another $1,000 to pay for repairs. In the library are Gilbert Stuart's portrait of Rivera, and a painting of Judah Touro. The library houses the Bailey Gitelson Library of American Jewish History, donated to the Society of the Friends of Touro Synagogue in memory of his mother.

Abram Rivera House, 8 Washington Sq., home of the Newport National Bank, was built in 1793 by a member of the distinguished Jewish family of merchants and shipowners.

Touro Street is off Washington Sq.

Touro Park, on Mill St., memorializes Judah Touro who gave

the city $10,000 to buy and improve the grounds and land around the Old Stone Mill. Touro bequeathed $350,000 in 1854 to various Jewish and non-Jewish institutions throughout the country.

Touro Street is on Washington Sq.

Touro Synagogue, (Cong. Jeshuat Israel), 85 Touro St., the oldest existing synagogue building in North America, was the first Jewish house of worship to be designated a national historic shrine. On August 31, 1947, the National Park Service of the U.S. Department of the Interior, erected a bronze tablet of designation on the synagogue grounds. The inscription gives a few highlights of the sanctuary's history:

National Historic Site
TOURO SYNAGOGUE
of
Jeshuat Israel Congregation
Founded 1658

This oldest synagogue building in the United States was designed by Peter Harrison. Ground was broken August 1, 1759. It was dedicated on December 2, 1763. Here 1781-84 the Rhode Island General Assembly met, and during Washington's visit to Newport in 1781 a town meeting was held here. The State Supreme Court held sessions here at that period. The building was reopened for religious services on August 2, 1850. In 1790 George Washington wrote to this congregation that ...."Happily the government of the United States....Gives to bigotry no sanction, to persecution no assistance."

National
Park Service
United States
Department of the Interior

In a message to the congregation in 1947, President Harry Truman said:

The setting apart of this historic shrine as a national monument is symbolic of our tradition of freedom, which has inspired men and women of every creed, race, and ancestry to contribute their highest gifts to the development of our national culture. I trust that through long centuries to come the spirit of good will and tolerance will ever dominate the hearts and minds of the American people.

The site of the synagogue, a lot 40 by 35 feet, was bought from Ebenezer Allen of Sandwich, Mass., for $187.50. Peter Harrison, the architect, who had never seen a synagogue, created Touro Synagogue which has been called "one of the most perfect works of Colonial architecture," from a study of the plans and pictures of synagogues abroad. He did it as a labor of love because there is no record that he ever received a fee. It took four years to build what the residents of Newport called "the Jews' church." Every one of the 196,715 bricks used in the construction was imported from England. No nails were used, only wooden pegs. In design, seating arrangements, and columns, the structure created by Harrison was similar to the famed Sephardic synagogue in Amsterdam, Holland, erected in 1675. The seats do not face the Ark but run along the north and south walls. At right angles to the Ark is wainscotted paneling, leaving clear the area between the bimah in the center and the Ark at the east end. The whole building stands at an acute angle to the street so that the Ark faces toward Jerusalem. Supporting the roof and the women's gallery are 12 pillars, six to a side, each carved out of the trunk of a New England tree and representing one of the 12 tribes of Israel. A 12-branched candelabra suspended from the ceiling was brought from Europe where it had been part of a Spanish monastery converted from a synagogue. Four smaller candelabras were the work of American craftsmen and the gifts of congregants, Jacob and Abraham Rivera, Naphtali Hart Myers, and Aaron Lopez. Tall brass candlesticks are affixed to the railing in front of the Ark, a gift in 1766 of Enoch Lyon. The Ner Tamid that swings from the ceiling was a gift in 1765 of Samuel Judah. The clock on the balcony is inscribed "Judah Jacobs, London, Anno Mundi 5529" (1769). The congregation's first Torah was said to have been 200 years old when it was brought from Amsterdam. The silver ornaments decorating the Torah Scrolls include two sets of *rimmonim* fabricated by Myer Myers, the celebrated pre-Revolutionary Jewish silversmith, who made church bells, silver plates, and buckles for the aristocracy. One of the three breastplates that hang on the Torah Scrolls was made in Poland in the 18th century and a second dates from the same time in Gemany.

The most unique feature of the synagogue is an underground tunnel, entered through a trap door in the center of the reading desk from which the *hazzan* leads the congregation in prayer. Why the tunnel was built into the synagogue is still a mystery. Some unromantic historians believe it was merely a storage area, while others claim it was a symbol to remind children of the persecution their ancestors suffered at the hands of the Inquisition, a time when Jews worshipped in secret in underground areas at the risk of their lives. In fact, the tunnel may have been nothing but a precaution—an unfinished channel of escape (it does not have an exit), provided by men whose past was still haunted by terror and persecution and may have felt safer with an escape route that might be useful in the event sudden flight became necessary. The tunnel has long been closed off. In the tiny schoolroom adjoining the north gallery is a link with London's historic Sephardic synagogue in the form of a painting done in 1675 by Aaron de Chavez. It depicts the initial Hebrew words of the Ten Commandments with Spanish translations interlined, and Moses and Aaron flanking the twin Tablets of Law. Over the Ark hangs another painting depicting the Decalogue, surmounted by the crowns of the Torah, the ancient Israelite priesthood, and the royal house of David. This picture was once believed to be the work of Gilbert Stuart, but during restoration work preceding the Synagogue's 200th anniversary, a cleaning of the canvas revealed the name "Benjamin Howland, 1828" on the back of the frame. Howland was Newport's city clerk for many years.

A facsimile of Washington's letter to the congregation is affixed to an interior wall. The text of the letter follows:

> *To the Hebrew Congregation in Newport, Rhode Island. Gentlemen: While I receive with much satisfaction, your address replete with expressions of affection and esteem; I rejoice in the opportunity of assuring you that I shall always retain a grateful remembrance of the cordial welcome I experienced in my visit to Newport from all classes of citizens. The reflection on the days of difficulty and danger which are past is rendered the more sweet, from a consciousness that they are succeded by days of uncommon prosperity and security. If we have wisdom to make the best use of the advantages with which we are now favored, we cannot fail, under the just administration of a good Government, to become a great and happy people.*
>
> *The Citizens of the United States of America have a right to applaud themselves for having given to mankind examples of an enlarged and liberal policy worthy of imitation. All possess alike liberty of conscience and immunities of citizenship. It is now no more that toleration is spoken of, as if it was by the indulgence of one class of people, that another enjoyed the exercise of their inherent natural rights. For happily the Government of the United States, which gives to bigotry no sanction, to persecution no assistance, requires only that they who live under its protection should demean themselves as good citizens, in giving it on all occasions their effectual support.*
>
> *It would be inconsistent with the frankness of my character not to avow that I am pleased with your favorable opinion of my administration, and fervent wishes for my felicity. May the Children of the Stock of Abraham, who dwell in this land, continue to merit and enjoy the good will of the other inhabitants; while everyone shall sit in safety under his own vine and*

fig tree, and there shall be none to make him afraid. May the father of all mercies scatter light and not darkness in our paths, and make us all in our several vocations useful here, and in his own due time and way everlastingly happy.

G. Washington

When the Jews of Newport, then numbering some 80 families, decided to build the synagogue in 1759, they appealed for help to Shearith Israel Congregation in New York and to the Jewish communities in London, Jamaica, Curacao, and Surinam. New York contributed £140.0.6, about a tenth of the total cost. Smaller sums came from England and the West Indies. New York also sent 100 pounds of wax for making candles, and individuals contributed various appurtenances. When the Touro Synagogue was dedicated in 1763, (5524 according to the Hebrew calendar) it was the second synagogue erected in the American colonies, Shearith Israel having dedicated its synagogue in New York in 1730. After being closed for more than half a century, the synagogue was reopened for summer visitors to Newport in 1850.

Thereafter, services were held in the synagogue for funerals, occasionally for the High Holy Days, and for private worship by such men as Judge Philip J. Joachimsen of New York in the 1850s, in the next decade, by Lawrence Blumenthal and his son, Dr. Mark Blumenthal. In 1881, the Rev. Henry S. Morais, as a young man, came to Newport and conducted services on both days of Rosh Hashanah. It was not until 1883, when the Rev. Abraham Pereira Mendes arrived in Newport, that the community was revived and the synagogue reopened for regular services. (It is still used for services today.) Until then the Torah Scrolls and other ritual objects had to be brought from New York whenever the synagogue was opened and then they were returned to Shearith Israel which owns the objects and title to the synagogue. In 1926, when Newport had 125 Jewish families, the old one-room school attached to the historic synagogue could no longer accommodate all the children, and the synagogue itself was too small to house all in the community. At that time the old Sheffield House was purchased and moved to Touro Street opposite the synagogue and rebuilt as a school and social center. During World Wars I and II the old synagogue was also used by Jewish personnel on duty at Fort Adams, and later at the U.S. Naval Training Station. A room on the second floor of the synagogue has been restored and furnished as a museum of Touro Synagogue memorabilia. Over the gate in front of the synagogue are inscribed these words: "Erected 5603 (1843) from a bequest made by Abraham Touro, Esq." The visitor's book has Emma Lazarus' poem, *In the Jewish Synagogue at Newport,* pasted in it. The following is a stanza from the poem, written in July, 1867 while she was summering in Newport:

The weary ones, the sad, the suffering,
All found their comfort in the holy place
And children's gladness and men's gratitude,
Took voice and mingled in the chant of praise.

In 1939, on Newport's tercentennial, the Jews of the city erected a simple memorial to religious and civil liberty on the grounds of the synagogue. Inside the stone and iron fence that surrounds the synagogue, the memorial has a bronze plaque on which are inscribed these words from the Rhode Island charter of 1663:

Dedicated to the principle that all and everye person and per-
sons may from tyme to tyme and at all times hereafter freelye
and dullye have and enjoye his and their owne judgments and
consciences in matters of religious concernments.

A full-time guide is on duty to show visitors around. The synagogue is maintained by membership dues and supplementary funds raised by the Society of the Friends of Touro Synagogue, a private organization which hopes eventually to erect a museum on the synagogue grounds.

PAWTUCKET

Cong. Chave Shalom, 305 High St.
Rhode Island Jewish Herald, 99 Webster St.

PROVIDENCE

Brown University

Brown University, Prospect St., has a number of points of Jewish interest: The Little Chapel has a stained glass window dedicated to the brotherhood of all creeds, which was installed in 1946. ●J.C. Brown Library owns many documents and records of the United Company of Spermaceti Chandlers, a Colonial industrial trust, whose agreement of incorporation includes three Jewish signatures: Aaron Lopez, Naphtali Hart, and Jacob Rodriguez Rivera. The library also has hundreds of letters documenting the business activities of Rhode Island Jews in the 18th century. ●Samuel Rappaporte, Jr., House of Hillel, on Brown University campus, 80 Brown St. In the garden is a massive sculpture entitled *Imperishable,* by Martin Newman, which conveys in abstract style the indomitable spirit of faith and courage which has sustained the Jewish people over the centuries. ●Albert and Vera List Art Museum was a gift of a well-known New York Jewish couple who have also contributed generously to Jewish causes. ●John D. Rockefeller, Jr. Library, houses a collection of general

Judaica materials. ●John Hay Library, 20 Prospect St., houses three Jewish collections—the unique Menasseh Vaxer Yiddish Collection of almost 1,700 volumes of Yiddish poetry, drama, and fiction contributed by Vaxer in 1967; the Albert and Selma F. Pilavin Collection of Judaica and Hebraica, once the personal library of Rabbi Edward J. Kiev, for many years librarian of the New York campus of Hebrew Union College-Jewish Institute of Religion; and the Jacob Shartenberg Collection contributed in 1896 by Jacob Shartenberg. The John Hay Library also has a collection of over 1,500 volumes devoted to the legend of the Wandering Jew.

Jews supported Brown University from its earliest days when it was known as Rhode Island College. Jacob Rodriguez Rivera, one of Newport's leading 18th century merchants, contributed to the college's first building through the purchase of lottery tickets. His son-in-law, Aaron Lopez, an even more important merchant, contributed 10,000 feet of lumber for the first building. In 1770, the college trustees who had solicited funds from the Jews of Rhode Island, voted that "the children of Jews may be admitted into this institution and entirely enjoy the freedom of their own religion without any constraint or imposition whatever." In 1774, the trustees ruled that every student must attend public worship on Sundays, "except such as regularly & statedly keep the Seventh Day as a Sabbath." At that time there were no Jewish students in the college. □

Community Voice, Jewish Federation of Rhode Island, 130 Sessions St.

Cong. Mishkon Tfiloh, 203 Summit Ave.

Cong. Shaare Zedek, 688 Broad St.

Cong. Sons of Jacob, 24 Douglas Ave.

Cong. Tifereth Israel, Broad and Graham Sts.

David Friedman Center, the culinary arts facility of Johnson and Wales College of Culinary Arts, Abbott Park Pl., named after the Providence industrialist and philanthropist.

Jewish Community Center, 401 Elmgrove Ave., has in its lobby marble busts of the Center's first two presidents, Max L. Grant and Milton Sapinsley, both the work of Chaim Gross. In front of the building is a huge Chanukah Menorah.

Jewish Education Bureau of Greater Rhode Island, 130 Sessions St., houses the Harry Elkin Memorial Library of Judaica.

Jewish Family and Children's Service, 229 Wayland Ave.

Jewish Federation of Rhode Island, 130 Sessions St., is housed in the Mr. and Mrs. Max Alperin Building.

Jewish Home for the Aged of Rhode Island, 99 Hillside Ave.

The Miriam Hospital, 164 Summit Ave.

New England Academy of Torah, 450 Elmgrove Ave.

Providence Hebrew Day School, 450 Elmgrove Ave.

Rhode Island Historical Society, 52 Power St., possesses many colonial letters dealing with Jews, some letters of Judah Touro, and log books owned by Jewish shippers of the 18th century.

Rhode Island Jewish Historical Association, 130 Sessions St., founded in 1951, preserves books, records, pamphlets, letters, manuscripts, prints, photographs, paintings, and other historical material relating to the history of the Jews of Rhode Island. It publishes the *Rhode Island Jewish Historical Notes,* a scholarly historical journal.

Rhode Island School of Design, 224 Benefit St., has in its Museum of Art, the Albert Pilavin Collection of 20th Century Art, established by the widow of Albert Pilavin.

Samuels Dental Clinic, Rhode Island State Hospital, 593 Eddy St., was a gift of Joseph Samuels in 1929.

Silver Square, corner of Arms St. and Douglas Ave., memorializes Alfred Silver, the first Jewish soldier from Rhode Island killed in the Korean War.

State House, Smith St., has a plaque just inside the entrance to the executive chambers erected by the American Jewish Tercentenary Committee of Rhode Island in 1954, which records Rhode Island Jewry's expression of gratitude to Roger Williams and its appreciation of the role of the Jewish pioneers in the early days of the state. In the Governor's office hangs a portrait of Frank Licht, who served as governor of Rhode Island from 1969-1973.

Temple Beth David-Anshei Kovno, 145 Oakland Ave.

Temple Beth El, 70 Orchard Ave., has a Biblical garden that includes plants, trees, shrubs, and herbs which have special Old Testament significance. In the garden is the Ten Commandments tablet which once adorned Providence's first synagogue, Cong. Sons of Israel and David, which was erected in 1890 and torn down to make way for a freeway. The Temple building has been described as an 80 by 93 foot barrel vault turned sideways. The ceiling of the sanctuary has wooden beams.

Temple Beth Israel, 155 Niagara St.

Temple Beth Sholom, 275 Camp St.

Temple Emanu-El, 99 Taft Ave.

Touro St. is a small thoroughfare in the northern part of the city, named for Judah Touro.

Roger Williams Spring, 242 Main St. at Alamo Lane, is the site where Roger Williams and his followers landed in 1636, and was purchased in 1930 by Judge J. Jerome Hahn of the State Supreme Court. He donated it to the city as a park in memory of his father, Isaac

Hahn, who, in 1884, was elected to the State General Assembly, the first Jew in the state to win elective office.

WARWICK

Temple Beth Am, 40 Gardiner St.

Temple Judea, 50 Lackena Ave.

WESTERLY

Cong. Sharah Zedek, Bunion St.

WOONSOCKET

Cong. B'nai Israel, 224 Prospect St., has eight 22-foot high stained glass windows which form the structural support of the front of the building erected in 1962, although the congregation dates back to 1866. Both the exterior facade and the interior form of the synagogue recall the lines of the tent sanctuaries of the ancient Israelites. As worshippers come up the front steps, on either side they catch a glimpse of a sweeping concrete canopy, elliptical in form, which symbolizes the omnipotent eye of God looking down upon his people.

VERMONT

The first state to enter the Union after the original 13, Vermont was one of the last to have a permanent Jewish community. When Vermont became the 14th state in 1791, there were no known Jewish residents within its borders. Jewish merchants and fur traders who were in business in New York's upper Hudson Valley and the area around Lake George and Lake Champlain, between 1750 and 1786, may on occasion have crossed into Vermont, but they never lived there.

Old records mention a Benjamin Jacobs as having obtained permission, in 1782, from the authorities of the then independent Republic of Vermont to pass through Windsor en route to Quebec to negotiate an exchange of prisoners. If this man was a Jew, he may have been the same Benjamin Jacobs who in 1781 was a New England agent of Aaron Lopez of Leicester, Massachusetts, and Newport, Rhode Island, (see also Massachusetts and Rhode Island). He could also have been a kinsman of Samuel Jacobs of Montreal, who had extensive commercial interests at Crown Point, just across Lake Champlain. At least one Jew owned land in Vermont prior to 1791, although there is no evidence that he ever lived there or even visited there. He was Benjamin Judah, a New York merchant and an officer of Congregation Shearith Israel, whose Vermont property was part of the so-called New Hampshire Grants. These grants, made indiscriminately by British kings and royal governors, provoked bitter disputes between New York, which claimed the area, and actual settlers, who ultimately fought the rule of New York as strenuously as that of George III. In

1789, Alexander Hamilton petitioned the New York State Legislature to relinquish its claims to the New Hampshire Grants, and to consent to statehood for Vermont. Among the 60 signatories to the petition, all of whom owned property in the contested region, were John Jay and Benjamin Judah.

Perhaps the first known Jewish resident of Vermont was the bearer of one of the most distinguished names in Jewish history. He was Joshua Montefiore, an uncle of the celebrated Sir Moses Montefiore, who was 73 when he settled down at St. Albans in 1835, with a second wife—a Christian. Although he raised a family of eight children in Vermont, Montefiore established no Jewish community, since all his offspring were brought up as Christians.

Vermont's first Jewish community sprang up at Poultney soon after the Civil War. Families named Stern, Scheff, Heineberg, and Seligman were living there before the war, and a Colonel H.A. Seligson served in a Vermont regiment. Jewish peddlers from northern New York, western Massachusetts, and nearby Canada who hawked their wares through the Vermont countryside probably tired of the long journey home for the Sabbath and the holidays, decided to live in Poultney. A congregation was founded there in the early 1870s. Old settlers even recalled that there was a small synagogue in Poultney. In the state's first Jewish cemetery, established at nearby East Poultney, the oldest grave is dated 1876. The commercial decline of Poultney at the turn of the century caused the disintegration of the Jewish community. Most of its members moved to Burlington and Rutland.

The oldest existing Jewish community, and also the largest, is in Burlington. M.S. Wolk, who arrived in 1878, is credited with being Burlington's first Jewish resident. Two years later, Morris Levin moved to Winooski, and Abram Marcus joined Wolk at Burlington. Marcus brought along Nathan Lamport, with whom he had spent the High Holy Days at Franklin Falls, New York. David, Isaac, Harris, and Zorach Rosenberg, Joseph Frank, Henry London, and Isaac Perelman were other early Jewish settlers. These settlers prevailed upon A. Moscovitz, a *shohet,* to join them.

Sabbath services were held in Burlington as early as 1880, in the home of Isaac Perelman. Pack peddlers who traveled all the towns of the state wended their way back to Burlington every Friday for a prearranged Sabbath rendezvous. Out of these services developed the Ohavi Zedeck Society, organized by 18 young men. This society was the beginning of Ohavi Zedeck Synagogue. In 1882 a synagogue was opened in rented quarters on Champlain Street and then moved to the corner of Cherry and Church Streets where a small synagogue was erected. Congregation Chai Odom, founded in 1888, built a synagogue in 1889 on Hyde Street. A third congregation, Ahavath Gerim, was established in 1906.

Rutland has the second oldest Jewish community. What is now the Rutland Jewish Center was founded in the early 1900s as Congregation Adath Israel in West Rutland. In 1907, a small synagogue was built in West Rutland to serve the needs of the 18 Jewish families living there and in Rutland. As the Jewish population shifted to Rutland, periodic services were held there until Adath Israel moved from West Rutland. Until 1919, the congregation met in homes and halls. In that year it rented quarters at West and Elm Streets.

The first generation of Jewish settlers in Vermont consisted mostly of small storekeepers and peddlers catering to the needs of the workers in the textile factories and to the farmers. As late as 1910 there was only one Jewish farm family in the state. The Jewish Agricultural Society made but four loans to Jewish farmers in Vermont between 1900 and 1933. Only a tiny fraction of the Russian and Romanian immigrants of the early 1900s found their way to Vermont. Between 1901 and 1917, the Industrial Removal Office settled 95 Jewish immigrants in 17 Vermont towns and cities.

Vermont has always had fewer Jews than any of the New England states. Its remoteness from Boston and New York, and from major ports of debarkation for Jewish immigrants, made it too difficult for many Jews to get to Vermont. In 1877 there were only 120 Jews in the state. By 1905 there had been an almost ten-fold increase to 1,000. Of this number, 700 resided in Burlington. Smaller numbers lived in Barre (26), Newport (15), West Rutland (15), St. Albans (8), Bristol (3), St. Johnsbury (3), and solitary families in Middlebury, Richford, and Vergennes.

By 1917, the Jewish population had more than doubled to 2,221. There was not much change by 1927 (2,036) and 1937 (2,000), but the distribution was altered. Burlington remained the largest community with 1,000 Jews, followed by Rutland (250), Bennington (102), St. Albans (92), Montpelier (75), St. Johnsbury (78), Springfield (24), Winooski (14), Swanton (15), and 21 other places each with ten or less Jews. In the years between World War I and World War II, the Jewish population did not increase. It was just above 2,000 in 1940 and about the same in 1950. It grew to 2,330 in 1973 but declined to 1,855 in 1975. Burlington has remained the largest Jewish community (1,225 in 1974), and Rutland continued to be the second largest Jewish community (280). Bennington, home of Bennington College, grew to 120, due to a number of Jewish faculty families. There were also 100 Jews in St. Albans and the same number in St. Johnsbury. In the 1970s there were some 22 other places with Jewish residents.

The two most prominent Jews in the state in the 1960s and

1970s were Dr. Edward Bloustein, president of Bennington College, and Jerry Diamond, who was elected attorney general of Vermont in 1974. Bloustein has since moved on to the presidency of Rutgers University in New Jersey. Jerry Diamond, a transplanted Tennesseean, moved to Brattleboro in 1969 as clerk to a Federal judge. After practicing law for four years, he was appointed to fill a vacancy as state's attorney for Windom County. In 1970 he was elected to the same office for a two-year term and was reelected in 1972. In 1974 he was elected president of the Vermont States Attorneys. Diamond was one of the founders and a former president of the Brattleboro Jewish Community. Jay H. Gordon, a native of Vermont (residing in Bellows Falls), created a stir in 1965 when he became the first Democrat elected state auditor of accounts. He had previously served on the Vermont Board of Accountancy.

N. Henry Press of St. Albans, a former state commander of the American Legion, was chairman of the State Public Service Commission in the 1950s. George L. Agel was city prosecutor of Burlington 1922-23, and police commissioner from 1931-34. Abraham Feen was city prosecutor of Burlington 1934-35. Simon Godfrey of St. Albans, was elected to the State Legislature in 1948. Bernard Lisman (Burlington), a former president of the Vermont Junior Bar Conference, Samuel W. Fishman (Vergennes), Myron Samuelson (Burlington), and Arthur Dick (Rutland), have all served as municipal court judges.

* * * * *

BARRE
Cong. Thiphereth Moshe, 18 N. Main St.

BENNINGTON
Temple Beth El, 225 North St.

BRATTLEBORO
Brattleboro Jewish Community, Box 261, RFD #2, Putney, 05346.

BURLINGTON
Cong. Ahavath Gerim, 191 College St.
Hillel Foundation at University of Vermont, 389 College St.
Ohavi Zedeck Synagogue, 188 N. Prospect St., is the oldest congregation in the state.
Temple Sinai, 195 Summit St.

EAST POULTNEY
Old Jewish Cemetery, a fenced-in plot, 100 feet square, is the

only vestige of the first Jewish community in the state, established in Poultney in the 1870s. The burial ground contains graves of Jewish veterans of World Wars I and II. The property is now owned by the Rutland Jewish community.

GILMAN

Isaac Gilman, a Russian-born Jew who made this village the site of one of the leading paper mills in the country, is memorialized in the name of this Essex County village on the banks of the Connecticut River. Gilman was a modestly successful paper jobber in New York when he became interested in a small paper mill at Fitzdale, Vermont. Gradually, his investment in the company required him to spend more time in Vermont, where he ultimately made his home. Pioneering in the manufacture of kraft paper in the U.S., Gilman built the plant into the largest paper mill in the state. He gave the village of Fitzdale a new railroad station, a hotel, a hospital, a waterworks, a recreation hall, a fire department, an athletic field, a skating rink, and a town band. Gilman financed new homes for the village's workers and new stores for the merchants. He even paid for a music instructor for the village's children. Fitzdale's Catholic and Protestant churches were built by this Orthodox Jew who was the only Jewish resident in the village. In 1914, the citizens voted to change the village's name from Fitzdale to Gilman. The Gilman Paper Co. is the main economic support of Gilman and most of the township of Lunenberg.

MARLBORO

Marlboro Music Festival, on campus of Marlboro College, founded in 1950 by Rudolf Serkin, the noted pianist, with his father-in-law Adolf Busch, the violinist, and the latter's brother, Herman Busch, cellist, is an annual summer music commune where 100 musicians of all ages, but all top professionals, come to study and perform with Serkin and other famed artists.

MONTPELIER

Cong. Beth Jacob, 10 Harrison Ave.

Vermont State Library, 2nd floor of the Supreme Court Building, State St., has a copy of a bibliographical rarity known as the First Vermont Bible, printed in 1812, on the press of Stephen Daye, and employs characters with Hebrew features.

RUTLAND

Jewish Center, 96 Grove St., is the state's second oldest Jewish congregation. It occupies a well-known landmark, the former Baxter Memorial Library, whose entire exterior is Vermont marble.

ST. ALBANS

Grave of Joshua Montefiore, 3 miles from St. Albans on Route 7, on the left side of the highway on the way to Swanton. The grave is on the old Montefiore property, several hundred yards west of the highway. Situated in a densely wooded area, the grave is not visible from the road. It is marked by a plain stone slab on which the following words can be made out with difficulty: "Joshua Montefiore. Born in the City of London, England August 10, 1762. Died the 26th June 1843 in the 81st year of his age." The grave is situated on a farm owned by the family of Montefiore's grandson, Dr. H.N. Montefiore, who was a Christian. Mrs. Fred M. Taber, a granddaughter, who lived in Swanton, was pleased that her ancestor was to be included in this book. Mrs. Taber, also a Christian, said her grandfather was "the first Jew to settle in Vermont." Joshua Montefiore was the son of Moses Vita Montefiore, the first member of the family to settle in England, where he arrived in 1758. Joshua was one of 17 children. One of his brothers, Joseph Elias, was the father of the renowned Sir Moses Montefiore. Soldier, lawyer, editor, and adventurer, Joshua Montefiore came to America in 1803 at the age of 41. He settled in Philadelphia where an American edition of his *Commercial Dictionary* was published. When he was 73, Montefiore moved to St. Albans with his second wife, a Christian. There, on a farm, Montefiore raised eight children while engaged in agriculture and the practice of law. When he knew he was dying, Montefiore instructed his family not to inter him in a Christian cemetery. From memory he is said to have written out an English translation of the Jewish burial service to be used when he was laid to rest. In keeping with his wishes, he was buried in a grave on his own farm.

ST. JOHNSBURY

Cong. Beth El, 76 Railroad St.

WEST VIRGINIA

In the one hundred years between 1773 and 1873 West Virginia twice missed playing an important role in American Jewish history. Had West Virginia's bid in 1873 to become the site of the soon-to-be-established Hebrew Union College been accepted, the center of Reform Judaism would have been Charleston, West Virginia, rather than Cincinnati, Ohio. A century earlier, the failure of pre-Revolutionary efforts to establish the 14th colony in what is now West Virginia prevented large areas of the state from becoming the property of Jews.

In the wake of the Anglo-French struggle for control of the Ohio and Mississippi River Valleys, efforts were made to colonize the western area. English traders and their associates lost heavily until the French were driven out. Their suffering continued when the Indian allies of the French, under the leadership of Chief Pontiac, attacked every western outpost in 1763. As compensation for these losses, the Indians of the Six Nations ceded to the British a large stretch east and south of the Ohio River, including a substantial area of what is now West Virginia. Among the 22 "suff'ring traders" who were to be repaid through the Treaty of Fort Stanwix, negotiated on behalf of all the traders in 1768, were David Franks, Joseph Simon, and Levy Andrew Levy. Anticipating this cession, the traders and their backers had created the Indiana Company to sell the land and persuade colonists to settle there.

Jewish traders had also participated in the plans of the Grand Ohio Company, which was mapping the Vandalia Colony in and around West Virginia. This company, incidentally, had a charter that limited rights to Christians. Gradually, the land interests of all the

Jewish entrepreneurs engaged in these ventures were merged into a grand alliance of the speculative companies while their London agent, Benjamin Franklin, sought the approval of the British government for the colonization schemes. The opposition of Virginia, which claimed most of these lands, British hesitation in London, and the outbreak of the Revolutionary War prevented the establishment in what is now West Virginia as the 14th colony. As late as 1779, the Gratzes were pressing the Virginia legislature to validate the West Virginia claims.

After the Revolution, Michael Gratz was allied with James Wilson, a signer of the Declaration of Independence, Levi Hollingsworth, Charles Willing, and Dorsey Pentecost, all of Pennsylvania, in the ownership of 321,000 acres in what is now Fayette County, West Virginia, on which they planned a colony. A survey of the area in 1784 described it as being on the Guyundott, Little and Big Sandy Rivers "near the tract owned by His Excellency George Washington." In analyzing the letters and papers of Barnard and Michael Gratz from 1754 to 1774, historian William Vincent Byars in his book, *B. and M. Gratz, Merchants of Philadelphia, 1754-1798,* concluded that these documents were essential data in determining the historical beginnings of West Virginia, as well as of Ohio, Indiana, Kentucky, and Missouri, because the Gratzes were among the leading commercial pioneers and promoters in those areas.

Although their West Virginia colonizing ventures never materialized, the 18th century Jewish entrepreneurs were factors in the early history of the region. As a leading purveyor to British troops, David Franks helped equip George Washington's expedition through western Virginia in 1758, when he reconquered Fort Duquesne. The forts that sprang up along the northwestern Virginia frontier in the 1750s and 1760s were undoubtedly outfitted in part by Jewish traders from Lancaster, Philadelphia, and Fort Pitt. Gratz (through Gratz & Gibson), and Simon (through Simon and Campbell), both firms operating out of Fort Pitt, furnished supplies for settlers and troops heading down the Ohio past West Virginia. Simon was an agent for Virginia during Lord Dunsmore's War with the Indians in 1774, advancing the funds and supplies for the building of Fort Fincastle on the present site of Wheeling.

Because of their business interests in Virginia, it is also possible that the Gratzes had agents in that portion of the state that is now West Virginia. Isaiah Isaacs, one of the earliest Jewish settlers in Virginia, speculated in West Virginia lands. Some of the tracts which he and his partner, Jacob I. Cohen, hired Daniel Boone to locate in 1781, may have been within the present borders of West Virginia. Notwithstanding this extensive 18th century preoccupation with West Virginia, there is no indication that any Jews settled there until well

into the 19th century. Certainly there were no religious or civil in-
equalities to bar them. All of what is now West Virginia was part of
Virginia until 1863, and the Virginia bill of rights set an' example for
the rest of the states.

Settlers who began moving west after 1800 found little to attract them in the mountainous terrain of western Virginia as they
headed over the National Road to Ohio and beyond. Westward-bound
Jews, too, bypassed this region in favor of Pittsburgh, Cleveland, Cincinnati, Louisville, and St. Louis. Only after Wheeling and Charleston
became important trading towns in the 1830s and 1840s, did Jews
begin settling there, probably coming as pack peddlers from Baltimore
and Pittsburgh.

The oldest Jewish community of West Virginia is in Wheeling,
where the first Jewish organization in the state—a cemetery
association—was organized in 1849 and a burial ground was acquired.
This would indicate a Jewish settlement before 1849. Informal worship
services were probably held in Wheeling as early as 1846. An Alexander Heyman of Wheeling was one of the first subscribers to *The Occident,* the Philadelphia Jewish paper, in 1843. The Reverend Meyer
Mannheim, who had led the informal worship services before 1849,
was the first to be buried in the cemetery. Congregation Leshem
Shomayim, later known as the Eoff Street Temple, then Woodsdale
Temple, and now called Temple Shalom, was founded in 1849, making
it the oldest in the state. A Ladies Hebrew Benevolent Society, organized in 1865, raised a large part of the funds that made possible
the building of the first synagogue in 1892.

Charleston's earliest congregation, B'nai Israel, traces its beginnings to the Hebrew Educational Council, organized in 1873, three
years before the congregation was formally established. There were
quite a few Jews living in Charleston before and during the Civil War.
Meyer H. May was living in the city in 1854. Mayer Hirsch was there
about 1860. Moses and Philip Franberger, who had opened a clothing
store in the city in the early 1860s, were arrested by raiding Confederate forces as Union sympathizers and imprisoned in the notorious
Libby Prison in Richmond. Dr. Daniel Mayer, the first doctor in
Kanawha County, arrived in 1862 together with Seymour Hess.
Mayer, one of the eight Jews from West Virginia who served in the
Civil War, was a captain in the 5th Infantry. He had family connec-
tions in Cincinnati and during the war he went there to obtain medi-
cal supplies and to arrange for hospitalization for his men. While in
Cincinnati, Captain Mayer called on Rabbis Isaac Mayer Wise and
Max Lilienthal who promised to collect comfort items for Mayer's men.

On May 30, 1866, Mayer received a letter from the adjutant
general of West Virginia saying:

*I am directed by His Excellency, the Governor, to present you
the enclosed medal in accordance with a joint resolution of the
Legislature of the State of West Virginia, adopted February 1,
1866, as a slight testimonial of the high appreciation by the
State of your devotion, patriotism and services in suppression
of the late rebellion.*

Solomon Lowenstein, who served in the 23rd Ohio Volunteers under
Major William McKinley, the future president, settled in Charleston
after the war as a harness maker. From this he expanded into
wholesale and retail hardware, leather goods, and banking.

There were fewer than 500 Jews in West Virginia after the
Civil War, but one of them made a good try at getting Hebrew Union
College to locate within its borders. J.D. Walker, a delegate from
Charleston to the first convention of the Union of American Hebrew
Congregations in Cincinnati in 1873, offered the Union ten acres of
land in Charleston as the site of the college. Simultaneously, Captain
Mayer, by then a man of considerable means, donated 100 acres of
timber and mineral land in Boone County, just south of Charleston.
Although Charleston was not designated as the home of Hebrew
Union College, part of its assets before it opened in 1875 were coal
lands in West Virginia. Among the prominent officials in the new
state after the war were two Jews. Captain Daniel Mayer was the
state's second commissioner of immigration and Joseph Shields, also of
Charleston, collector of internal revenue.

Parkersburg's first Jewish settlers arrived in the 1850s. A
YMHA, organized in 1869, was the first Jewish organization. Samuel
Newberger served on Parkersburg's City Council before the Civil War.
Samuel Gideon, who settled in Huntington in 1872, a year after the
city was founded, was an early president of the board of education.
The first synagogue, established in 1886, was an outgrowth of the Al-
lemania Social Club, formed in 1880. Morgantown had four Jewish
families in 1898. One of these was headed by the late Louis Solomon
who opened a small glass works in 1889 which expanded into the
largest glass importing business in the country. Solomon sold glass to
the Marconi Wireless Telegraph Company and became a major supplier
of glass to the automobile industry. The Tree of Life Synagogue was
organized in 1921 when the city had 120 Jews. The first synagogue
dates from 1943.

Jews settled in Bluefield in the 1880s and in Beckley around
1910. In the Fayette County towns of Mount Hope, Oak Hill, Scarboro,
and Thurman, Jewish storekeepers were in business as early as 1895.
Jews settled in Fairmount and Clarksburg in 1899 and 1903, respectively. Martinsburg had perhaps a dozen Jewish families when a new

synagogue was dedicated with a parade from an older building. During the ceremony the Volunteer Fire Company band played *Onward Christian Soldiers!* The town's Purim ball was once a major social event for the whole community, with both Jewish and Christian girls vying for the title of Miss Queen Esther.

By 1900, the *American Jewish Year Book* reported that there were 1,500 Jews in the state where they were factors in developing the tobacco, pottery, and milling industries in the wholesale trades, and in the business life of the factory and coal towns. The Jews who arrived in West Virginia in the last decades of the 19th century included many from East Europe who had first settled in western Pennsylvania and eastern Ohio. Among these were the parents of the late Benjamin Rosenbloom, who served in Congress from 1921-1925. He had previously been a member of the State Senate where he led the losing fight against Prohibition. In Congress, he was a pioneer in the early efforts to rid the nation's streams of pollution. Another son of East European immigrants was Sam Solins of the town of Welch. President of the McDowell County Public Library and instrumental in promoting the country's first World War I memorial building, Solins was one of the founders of the American Legion in 1919.

Between 1901 and 1905, the Industrial Removal Office placed 124 Jews in 23 West Virginia communities. An effort to establish Jewish farm settlements in the early 1900s failed. A study of Jewish farmers in America, published in 1910, reported only one family of Jews on the land in West Virginia. Industrial growth between World War I and II encouraged further Jewish settlement in most of the cities and large towns. Jewish merchants, scientists, technicians, plant managers, chain store executives, and professionals took up residence there. Because so much of West Virginia's economy was based on coal, some of the towns and cities lost population, including Jews, when oil gradually replaced coal as the country's major fuel. In the 1960s and 1970s, however, when coal regained its former popularity, and when the natural gas, plastics, paper and pottery industries expanded, the state gained new residents, but not many Jews.

The Jewish population of the state hit its peak in 1937, when it totaled 7,980, compared with 7,500 in 1927, 5,440 in 1920, and 5,130 in 1917. Charleston is now, as it has been for a century, the largest Jewish community of West Virginia. It grew from 92 in 1877 to 1,000 in 1916, 1,500 in 1936, 1,625 in 1960, and fell back to 1,125 in 1974. Huntington, once the second largest Jewish community, grew from 71 in 1905; to 150 in 1912; to 600 in 1943; to 750 in 1955; and then dropped to 350 in 1974. Wheeling with 775 Jews is now the second largest community. There are also communities in Beckley, Bluefield, Clarksburg, Fairmont, Morgantown, Parkersburg, Weirton, Logan,

Welch, and Williamson. The decline of the Jewish population was dramatized in figures published during the observance of the 75th anniversary of Charleston's oldest synagogue in 1972. The Jewish population was then 1,178, down from 2,150 in 1950. Between 1950 and 1972, 603 Jews moved to Charleston, 971 moved away. During the same time there were 219 deaths and 149 births in the Jewish community.

As part of the back-to-the-land movement that gained headway in the 1970s because of a growing concern over the environment, at least one Jewish couple settled in rural West Virginia. Naomi and Harvey Cohen, former New Yorkers who met at the New York University Law School, settled at Cow Creek in 1970 on an 119-acre farm they bought. They had originally come to West Virginia as lawyers to assist the underprivileged residents of the rural areas.

The shrinking Jewish population has led to synagogue mergers in Huntington and Wheeling. In the latter city, the older Woodsdale Temple (Cong. Leshem Shomayim), combined with the Synagogue of Israel. The latter's building is maintained by the merged congregation but services are held at Temple Shalom. In Huntington, Oheb Sholom Temple and B'nai Israel Synagogue were consolidated under the name of B'nai Sholom Congregation. A single rabbi serves the combined congregation. Prayer booklets containing a combination of material from the *Reform Union Prayer Book* and the *Silverman Prayer Book* of the Conservatives are used for Friday night services. Wearing of the hat is optional. Worshippers who wish a service on the second day of holidays are accommodated. Both buildings are used on an alternative basis until 1978 when a decision will be made as to their future. Each congregation had about 200 family members when the merger took place in 1974.

The first two Jews elected to the State Legislature were David Mayer and Jacob Fisher, who were both elected in 1889. Fisher later served for 10 years in the State Senate, and for 16 years as a judge of the Braxton County Court (1911-1927). Leo Loeb was president pro tem of the Charleston City Council in 1911. Ivar Boyarsky, who died in 1970, was a member of the State House of Delegates for more than 20 years and served as speaker in 1947. Samuel Gideon of Huntington was president of the Cabell County Court. Fred H. Clark, who was a member of the State Public Service Commission, served on the State Supreme Court of Appeals in the 1960s. Howard Caplan of Clarksburg was United States Attorney for Northern West Virginia. Jews who have been mayors were: Charles Nass, Glenville; Aaron Catzen, Clark; David Shear, Romney; Ruby Rubenstein, Thomas; Leo Schaffer, Thurmond; Harold L. Frankel, Huntington; and Benjamin Rosenbloom, vice-mayor, Wheeling. Frankel was chairman of the Tri-

State Airport Authority, and Stanely Loewenstein of Charleston, was chairman of the Greater Kanawha Valley Foundation. Jesse A. Bloch, for many years president of the Bloch Bros. Tobacco Co., was a member of the State Senate. In 1920 he cast the tie-breaking vote for West Virginia's adoption of the 19th Amendment giving women the right to vote.

* * * * *

BECKLEY
Nathan Street is named for Nathan Pickus, who was among the first Jewish settlers in the city in 1910.
Temple Beth El, 107 Queen St.

BLUEFIELD
Cong. Ahavath Sholom, 632 Albemarle St.

CHARLESTON
Cong. B'nai Jacob, Elizabeth and Virginia Sts.
Federation of Jewish Charities, 1576 Virginia St., E.
Joe Loewenstein Memorial Fountain, in front of the Kanawha County Public Library, 123 Capitol St., depicting the mountains of West Virginia, honors a native son of Charleston, whose father, Solomon, settled here in the late 1860s. The Loewensteins were originally in the hardware business and then became associated with the Charleston National Bank. Joseph and his brother Isaac were both presidents of the bank, and Joseph's son, Stanley, was also an officer of the bank.
Temple Israel, Kanawha Blvd. and Chesapeake Ave.

CLARKSBURG
Cong. Tree of Life, 425 W. Pike St.

FAIRMONT
Temple Beth El, 405 Fourth St.

HUNTINGTON
B'nai Israel Synagogue, 900 9th St., and Ohev Sholom Synagogue, 949 10th Ave., have consolidated as Cong. B'nai Sholom, but both buildings are used alternatively on Friday evenings.
Federation of Jewish Charities, P.O. Box 947.
Dr. Isadore H. Hirschman, former president of the Huntington Chamber of Commerce, 522 9th St., is honored in the chamber building where his portrait hangs. President at one time or another of

every major Jewish organization in the city, Dr. Hirschman was a member of a family that settled in Huntington in the 1850s.

LOGAN
Cong. B'nai El, 651 Stratton St.

MARTINSBURG
Cong. Beth Jacob, 124 W. Martin St.

MORGANTOWN
Cong. Tree of Life, 242 S. High St.
Hillel Foundation at University of West Virginia, 1420 E. University Ave.
University of West Virginia Library, across Prospect St., has among its manuscripts a rare Hebrew manuscript of the Book of Ruth.

NEWELL
Louis L. Aaron, of Pittsburgh, and his associates founded this pottery manufacturing town just across the Ohio River from East Liverpool, Ohio, in the 1880s, when they organized the Homer Laughlin China Co., one of the world's largest pottery makers. The town is built around the pottery works. Aaron, who settled in Pittsburgh in 1861 and became one of its leading industrialists, was one of the builders of Pittsburgh's Jewish community. His son, Marcus Aaron, devoted most of his adult life to civic welfare and education, serving as president of the Pittsburgh Board of Education, the State Board of Education, and a leader in many Jewish religious and communal affairs.

PARKERSBURG
B'nai Israel Temple, 1703 20th St.

SALEM
United Israel Altar, one of the five regional branches of the United Israel World Union, an organization of ex-Christians who have embraced Judaism, is located on George Washington Highway.

WEIRTON
Cong. Beth Israel, 500 Brookline Dr.

WELCH
Temple Emanuel, Riverside Dr.

WHEELING
Bloch Brothers Tobacco Plant, a two-block long factory on the

river front, 39th and 41st Sts. and Water St., is the place where Mail Pouch chewing tobacco, whose ads on barns and fences were familiar to several generations of tourists, is manufactured. Founded in 1879 by S.S. and Aaron Bloch, the company originated the ribbon-cut type of tobacco and was the first to use tobacco leaf for making cut chewing tobacco. Because of Mail Pouch's widespread use among the early oil and gas drillers in West Virginia, a package of this chewing tobacco in a man's overalls was as good as a letter of introduction for West Virginians who first went to the Kansas and Oklahoma oil fields.

Fort Henry Site, marked by a bronze plaque imbedded in a small stone on Main St., between 11th and Ohio Sts., is a reminder that Fort Fincastle in 1774 was erected here with the aid of supplies and funds advanced by the Jewish merchant, Joseph Simon. The name of the fort was later changed to Fort Henry in honor of Patrick Henry. Wheeling grew up around this fort.

Good Lake, in Wheeling Park, was given to the city in memory of L.S. Good, late Wheeling merchant, by his sons, Sam and Sidney Good.

Good North America Zoo, in Oglebay Park, was established by Mr. and Mrs. Laurence Good in memory of their son, Philip. This is the only zoo in the country that houses only wildlife native to the American continent.

Temple Sholom, Bethany Pike and Walnut Ave., which has a circular dome over its sanctuary, is the former Woodsdale Temple and the oldest existing congregation in the state, having been founded in 1849. The new name was adopted when the Woodsdale Temple merged with the Synagogue of Israel, 115½ Edginton Lane. The consolidated congregation uses the Bethany Pike building and will maintain the other building until 1978.

Trades and Labor Monument, in Kossuth Park, adjacent to the Fort Henry Bridge entrance on I-70, was erected by the employees of the Pollack Tobacco Company in honor of August Pollack, one of the city's first tobacco manufacturers and a friend of organized labor. The Pollacks were pioneers in developing the stogie. August Pollack was the first president of the Woodsdale Temple when it was known as Congregation Leshem Shomayim in 1849.

WILBUR

United Israel Altar of the United Israel World Union is located near West Union, between Clarksburg and Parkersburg.

WILLIAMSON

Temple B'nai Israel, College Hill.

AROUND THE
JEWISH CALENDAR

SEPTEMBER-OCTOBER

Annually, there is a ceremony at the flagpole at State and Whitehall Sts. in lower Manhattan, commemorating the landing of the first group of 23 Jewish settlers in America. The ceremony is co-sponsored by the Jewish Historical Society of New York and the American Jewish Historical Society.

Tashlich, the custom of the first day of *Rosh Hashanah* of casting bread crumbs into a body of water and reciting prayers, may be observed at various spots along the Hudson River, and in Brooklyn, at the Williamsburg Bridge, Botanic Gardens, Prospect Park, Brighton Beach, and Coney Island. The custom symbolizes the casting off of sins.

On *Yom Kippur,* most Orthodox and Hasidic Jews wear a *kittle*—a long white robe-like garment, to symbolize purity (and the purification) of our sins.

Prior to *Sukkot,* it is interesting to go to the Lower East Side to see the brisk business in *s'chach,* the greenery for the *Sukkah* and *lulovim* and *esrogim* on Canal Street between Essex or Orchard Streets. A number of restaurants build *Sukkahs* for the holiday where people can eat their meals. The Jewish Theological Seminary of America, 3080 Broadway, builds a very large and beautiful *Sukkah* decorated with pines. Congregation Shearith Israel and Yeshiva University also erect *Sukkot.* On the roof of the 50-story Monsanto Building, 43 W. 42nd St., a *Sukkah* is erected. Called the "*Sukkah* in the Sky," the custom was started by Jack Weiler, realtor and philanthropist.

On *Simhas Torah* night, thousands of people from all parts of the city are attracted to the Satmar Rebbe's synagogue on Rodney St. (between Bedford and Lee Aves.), in Williamsburg. Police are often on hand to control

646

the curious visitors waiting for the early morning *hakafos* (procession), to parade, swaying, clapping, and chanting right into the middle of the street, which has been cordoned off for the occasion. Other colorful *Simhas Torah* celebrations include the ones at Lubavitcher Yeshivoth, 770 Eastern Parkway (Crown Heights section of Brooklyn); Bobover Yeshiva, in Borough Park, Brooklyn; the Mesivta Rabbi Chaim Berlin Yeshiva, Ave. N. (Flatbush section of Brooklyn); the Machzike Talmud Torah School of Borough Park, 4622 14th Ave. (Brooklyn); and the Mirrer Yeshiva Central Institute, 1791 Ocean Parkway (Flatbush section of Brooklyn). (See also: section on Brooklyn.)

NOVEMBER

Services for Thanksgiving Day have been a custom at Congregation Shearith Israel (Spanish and Portuguese Synagogue), Central Park West at 70th St., since 1871. The Metropolitan Synagogue, 10 Park Ave., conducts a joint Thanksgiving service with the Community Church.

DECEMBER

Chanukah celebrations consist of the kindling of lights on Menorahs (candelabra) for eight consecutive days. The celebration begins with the first day with one candle and thereafter increased one each day for the remainder of the Chanukah period. Synagogues and Jewish Community Centers throughout New York City and its suburbs conduct programs to mark the Maccabean festival. The largest of these celebrations is at the 92nd St. YM-YWHA and Brooklyn College.

FEBRUARY

February is the special month for brotherhood, and a number of synagogues and churches in New York sponsor joint programs to mark the occasion. One of the most notable is the *Brotherhood Service* conducted by the Metropolitan Synagogue Choir and the Choir of the Church of the Master.

MARCH

As *Purim* usually falls during this month (occasionally the last week in February), there is a Jewish Music Festival, held from *Purim* to Passover under the national auspices of the Jewish Music Council of the National Jewish Welfare Board (JWB), and a number of events in New York, as well as throughout the country, to mark this occasion. The Sephardic Cultural Program of Yeshiva University and the Workmen's Circle sponsor music festivals also. The Israeli Dance Festival is also held in New York in March. It is during this month (also part of February and of April), that many groups tour the Streit Matzoth factory in lower Manhattan and the Horowitz Margareten Kosher Foods Co., in Queens, to see how matzo is made.

During the *Purim* celebration in Williamsburg, Brooklyn, the visitor will see small boys with *payot* masquerading in the streets as grown-up Hasidim, with beards made from absorbent cotton, or little girls pretending that they are Queen Esther. Purim in Williamsburg is a joyous time for young and old alike. In the evening at the Satmar Rebbe's (Rodney St.), the singing is ecstatic and wild. At the Lubavitcher Rebbe's synagogue, 770 Eastern Parkway (Crown Heights, Brooklyn), the singing is somewhat more subdued. Later, the Rebbe talks on a subject related to *Purim*, then lifts up his cup of wine—a signal for his followers to lift theirs, and they all drink, and the singing and swaying begin again, lasting far into the night.

For the *megillah*-reading, the visitor should go to Congregation Shearith Israel, Central Park West and 70th St. The National Council of Young Israel, 3 West 16th St., conducts an annual *Purim* program for children. The 92nd Street YM & YWHA conducts a *Purim* carnival, as do many Jewish Community Centers, synagogues, and Jewish schools.

A number of synagogues and Centers mark the Jewish Music Festival, including the Metropolitan Synagogue, 10 Park Ave.; the 92nd Street Y; and Temple Emanu-El.

APRIL

This is usually the month of Passover, and the services at Congregation Shearith Israel are among those especially worth attending. Particularly beautiful are the portions of the service when both congregation and choir join with the Reader in the chanting of prayers set in poetic form.

The making of *shmura* matzoh in Williamsburg may be seen by arranging in advance with a matzoh bakery. Jewish schools can take their students on this kind of tour to see how this strictly guarded handmade matzoh is made. The Satmar Matzoh Bakery, 427 Broadway, Brooklyn, will conduct tours of groups. The Streit Matzoth Co., 150 Rivington St. and the Horowitz-Margareten Kosher Foods Co., 29-00 Review Ave., Long Island City, Queens, will also conduct tours of groups. These, however, are not *shmura* matzos.

MAY

Festivities, parades, and picnics mark *Lag B'Omer* at Lubavitcher world headquarters in Brooklyn. Thousands of yeshiva, Hebrew, and public school children march side by side along Eastern Parkway in Crown Heights, to the beat of drums and gay music. The Parkway, lined with thousands of spectators, is cordoned off by the police for the occasion.

Shavuot, during May or June, is the feast of the first fruits. The entire synagogue of Congregation Shearith Israel is bedecked with greens. The steps leading to the holy Ark are covered with many beautiful and colorful flowers that symbolize the fruits that were brought as offerings in Temple days. An additional service takes place during the afternoon of *Shavuot* preceding *Mincha*. The *Azharoth* are chanted, and this is followed by the reading of the Book of Ruth. On the first day, the traditional 248 positive commandments of the Torah, in the poem composed by Solomon ibn Gabirol, are read, and then the first half of the Book of Ruth is cantillated. On the second day, the 365 negative commandments are read, after which the second half of the Book of Ruth is read. Both the *Azharoth* and the Bible are read by all the congregants present, each consecutively reading a single verse.

Every year on Memorial Day, Congregation Shearith Israel marks the graves of soldiers and other patriots of the American Revolution in its historic cemetery on St. James Place below Chatham Square, in its cemetery on West 21st St., and in its graveyard on West 11th St. (see HISTORIC CEMETERIES).

JUNE

Israel Independence Day, observed on the 5th of Iyar in the Hebrew calendar, is usually marked by the Salute to Israel Parade early in June, under the auspices of the American Zionist Youth Foundation.

JULY

On the black fast day of *Tisha B'Av*, which falls in July or August, Congregation Shearith Israel is draped in black and the services are not read from the *tebah*, the reading desk from which every service is read during the entire year, but, as a sign of sadness and mourning, from a table set low in front of the *tebah*. This table is also draped in black and has chairs for the *hazzanim* and the presiding officer. The 12 white tapers that surround the reading desk are covered in black, and the Ark also has a black covering. Everything is shrouded in darkness to commemorate one of the most tragic events in Jewish history—the destruction of the Temple in Jerusalem.

The *hazzan* begins the service with the chant of Psalm 137, "By the rivers of Babylon there we sat, yea, we also wept. . ." The sorrowful melody sets the mood for the entire service. The chant is solemn and mournful and permeated with the sound of lamentation. Following the *Amidah*, the service continues with a *kinah*, a dirge. Then the Book of Lamentations is read. The first chapter is read by the *hazzan*, and after that each chapter is read either by another *hazzan* or a member of the congregation. After the Book of Lamentations is finished, other dirges are sung, each of which has a melancholy and touching melody of its own. One of the unusual and interesting aspects of this part of the service is that often the accentuation in the reading is purposely incorrect. This is to emphasize the unusually sorrowful occasion and the fact that everything is changed for the worse on this sad day. Before the closing *kinah* is read, the Reader announces the number of years that have passed since the destruction of the Temple. The final chapter in the evening liturgy is then read, beginning with the words, "For the sake of my Temple and for the glory of Zion, the renowned city, will I weep day and night." The words, "May our prayer be accepted with loving favor," are omitted. On the following day, even the Torah Scroll is covered in black, and the beautiful silver bells that usually adorn the scroll are replaced with two black coverings.

AUGUST

Though there is little activity during this month of specific Jewish interest (unless *Tisha B'Av* occurs during August, see above), the *shofar* is blown at the end of morning devotions during daily services. This custom is performed during the month of *Elul* preceding Rosh Hashanah.

There are other activities of Jewish interest held throughout the year. For a more comprehensive listing, consult *The Jewish Week*, which also includes radio and TV programs of special interest to Jews.

Index

Index

A Abrams, Abraham I., 285, 297, 523, 617
Adams, President John, 92
Adams, President John Quincy, 59, 151
Adelph Zadick Aleph, 35
Adler, Dr. Cyrus, 115, 177, 347, 512, 557-578, 582, 584, 591
Adler, Felix, 390, 402-403, 487
Aguilar, Grace, 445
Aleichem, Sholom, 401, 409, 415-416, 442, 445, 450, 487, 503
Alliance Israelite Universelle, 196, 201
Altman, Benjamin, 193, 375, 416, 445
American Assoc. of Jewish Education, 177
American Friends of the Hebrew Univ., 202
American Hebrew, 414
American Israel Public Affairs Committee, 71, 73
American Jewish Archives, 29, 56, 550
American Jewish Committee, 67, 89, 94-95, 120, 154, 313, 350, 367, 456-457, 484, 529, 582, 592
American Jewish Congress, 177, 277-278, 303-304, 312-313, 349, 351, 367, 419, 456-457, 471, 522, 557, 580
American Jewish Historical Society, 93, 113, 147, 152, 177, 180, 191, 550, 557, 574, 582, 647
American Jewish Year Book, 100, 128, 455, 457, 641
American Jews in World War II, 404
American Jewish Joint Distribution Committee, 59, 350-352, 457, 503
American Mizrachi Women, 448, 457
American Museum of Immigration, 414
American Organization Directory, 455
American ORT Federation, 136, 315, 317, 336, 464, 470
American Overture, 50, 613
Annenberg, Walter H., 98, 210, 593, 596, 598
Anti-Defamation League, 184, 262, 304, 310, 367, 456-457
Arthur, President Chester, 86, 95
Auerbach, Beatrice Fox, 32, 39, 47

B Bacharach Family, 197, 200-202, 214
Balaban, Barney, 81, 84
Bamberger, Louis, 193, 217-218, 223-224
Barnert, Nathan, 211
Baruch, Bernard M., 73, 90, 96, 274, 323, 387, 390, 456, 470, 482, 569
Baruch, Simon, 274, 390, 470, 482, 569
Beame, Mayor Abraham, 386, 390, 496
Behrend, Bernhard, 65, 67, 241
Belkin, Dr. Samuel, 348
Belmont, August, 274, 298, 307, 311, 365, 621